Camelot 3000

mike w. barr & brian bolland
WRITER/CO-CREATORS/ARTISTS

bruce d. patterson & terry austin
EMBELLISHERS

john constanza
LETTERER

tatjana wood
COLORIST

CONTINUING LEGENDS CHRONICLED BY
sir thomas mallory

JENETTE KAHN
President and Publisher

DICK GIORDANO
V.P.–Executive editor

LEN WEIN
Editor–Original Series

RICHARD BRUNING
Editor–Collected Edition

MARK WAID
Assistant Editor

TERRI CUNNINGHAM
Mgr.–Editorial Admin.

PAT BASTIENNE
Mgr.–Editorial Coord.

BOB ROZAKIS
Production Director

PAUL LEVITZ
Executive V.P.

JOE ORLANDO
V.P.–Creative Director

BRUCE BRISTOW
Marketing Director

MATT RAGONE
Circulation Director

PAT CALDON
Controller

CAMELOT 3000

Published by DC Comics Inc., 666 Fifth Ave., New York, NY 10103

Copyright © 1988, All Rights Reserved.

All characters featured in this publication and the distinctive likenesses and related indicia thereof are trademarks of DC Comics Inc.

Originally published in 12 issues in magazine form, 1982–1985.

First Printing. Printed in Canada

acknowledgments

Dr. Sally Slocum
University of Akron; Arthurian consultant

Len Wein
Editor; for assembling the knights

Rick Magyar
A friend in deed

—**Mike W. Barr**

Thanks to Dick Giordano for his inking assistance on Chapter Six

Cover illustration by Brian Bolland and Bill Wray

Book design by Janice Walker

Art direction by Richard Bruning

Epic Beginnings

by Don and Maggie Thompson, Co-editors, *Comics Buyer's Guide*

There are many reasons for giving this story the added permanence of book publication—besides the obvious reason that it is an excellent story with outstanding art.

It is also something of a milestone.

The original publication of *Camelot 3000* helped change the face of comic book publishing in many ways, all of them important.

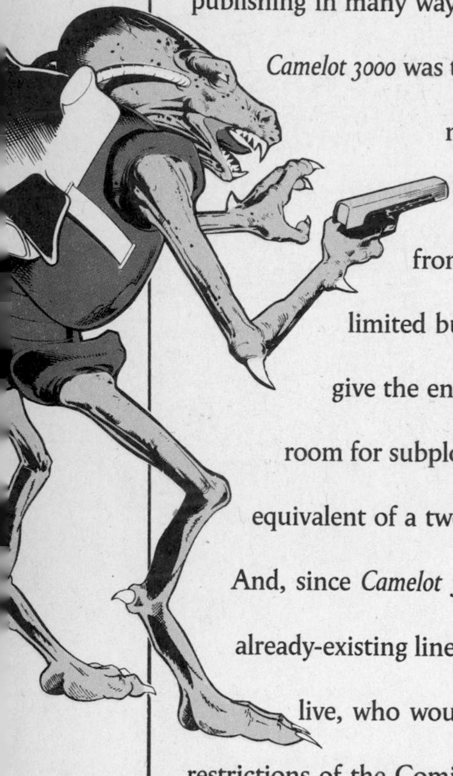

Camelot 3000 was the first comic book maxi-series. Like television programming, comic books have mini-series (two to six issues) and maxi-series (generally twelve issues, though anything from eight to sixteen could qualify). Twelve issues was a limited but sizeable number, allowing the writer room enough to give the entire series form: a beginning, a middle, and an end, with room for subplots and character development. In other words, it was the equivalent of a twelve-chapter novel.

And, since *Camelot 3000* did not involve any continuing characters from an already-existing line of comic books, there were no guarantees of who would live, who would die, or who would triumph. (It was also outside the restrictions of the Comics Code Authority, the industry's self-censorship board. This gave *Camelot* the freedom the printed word has in magazines and books, allowing an honest look at adult themes—including, but not limited to, sex.)

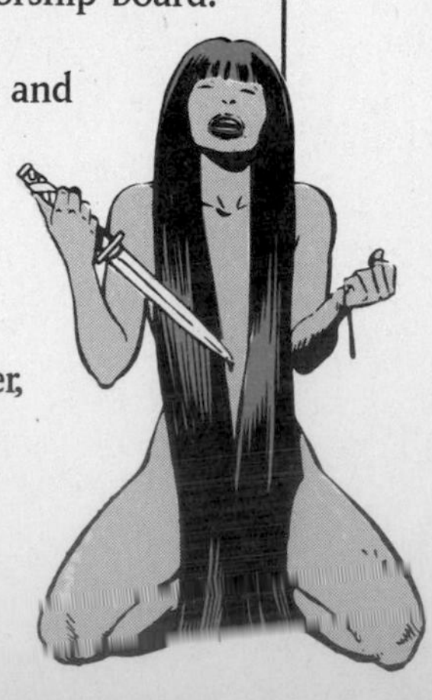

It was DC's first comic book to be printed on high-quality paper, with reproduction previously undreamed of for comic books, which traditionally had been printed on the cheapest paper by

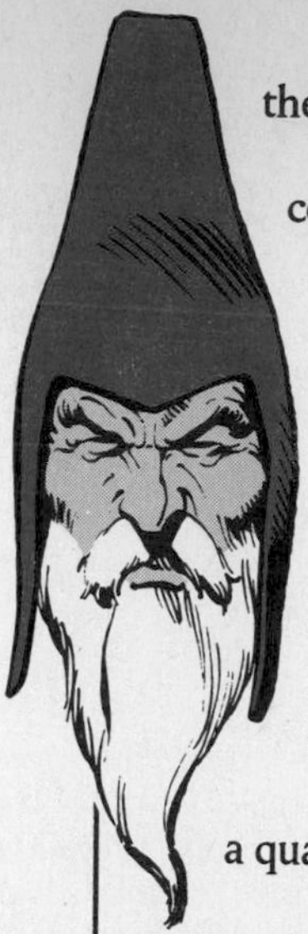

the cheapest methods. *Camelot 3000* was, within its realm, a "coffee table" comic book.

It was one of the first DC comic books to be distributed solely through the nation's comics shops; it was not available on newsstands. Publishing comic books for newsstand distribution has always meant publishing about twice as many copies as one hopes to sell and accepting returns on the unsold books; that works for items cheaply produced, but not for such a quality product as *Camelot 3000.* With this book, store owners placed advance orders based on their expert opinions of how many copies they could sell. DC, in turn, knew from the orders exactly how many copies to print; there would be no "wasted" copies. This system made the entire project possible, since it guaranteed the series the audience which made such a risky and expensive project a viable publishing option.

Camelot 3000 was DC Comics' first comic book for mature readers. This may have been the most important "first" of all. Because the American mindset long ago branded comics "for kids only," the new genre of comics—those reaching for an older audience—was nearly impossible to position in the marketplace. By using the system of selling comic books directly to specialty stores which knew their audiences and could steer readers with an adult taste towards an adult product, DC could successfully target its new audience.

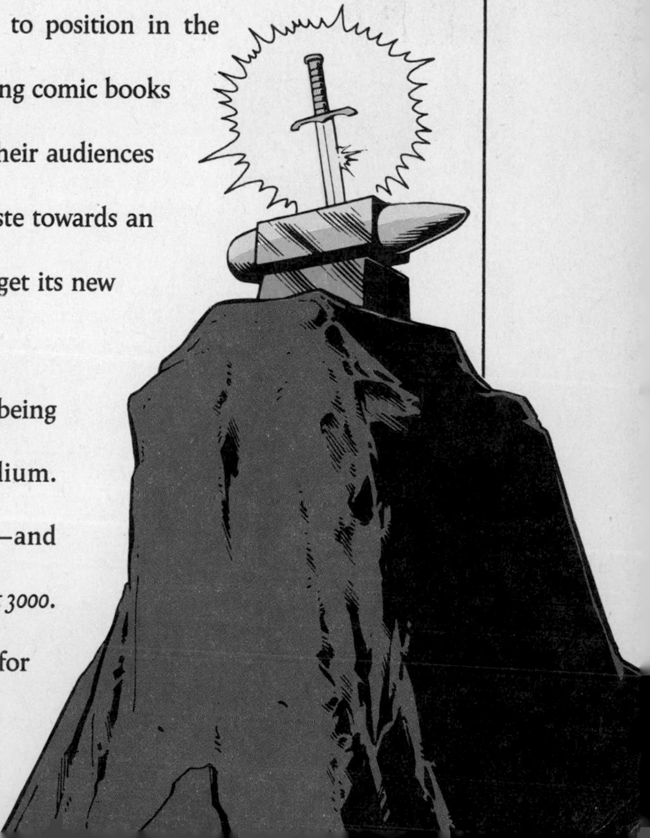

Comic books have been accused of being an old-fashioned, slow-to-change medium. We are all lucky that DC strove for—and achieved—a number of firsts with *Camelot 3000.*

Just how lucky, you are about to read for yourself.

opening knight

by Mike W. Barr

I *have made no attempt to conform strictly to the lines of the accepted Arthurian legend, largely because I do not think it bears much relation to truth. What the truth was, nobody knows. That there was a truth—although there are no incontrovertible facts recorded in history about Arthur—is beyond dispute: otherwise, his legend would not have survived to become known worldwide and to be recognized as an imperishable part of Britain's heritage.*

—Victor Canning, in his foreword to *The Crimson Chalice*

Since my writing of the comic book series known as *Camelot 3000*, I have come to be regarded as something of an expert on the Arthurian mythos, that body of legend and precious little fact regarding the time, personality, and surroundings of the hero known for generations simply as King Arthur.

For better or worse (probably worse, regarding my standing amongst the academics), I must confess this is not true. My knowledge of the Arthurian mythos comes entirely from one course, taken in college, and a great deal of diverse reading from more sources that can readily be documented, many of which have been lost to time. Rather than looking upon this as a flaw, I chose to regard it as the continuation of a great tradition. After all, the legends of King Arthur did not spring from one carefully-organized and uniformly-coordinated source. Over the centuries, chroniclers added to and subtracted from the mythos as they chose, keeping what they liked and reducing in importance—or even eliminating—what they did not. One charming anecdote derived from my college course was the story that Winston Churchill, during the dark days of World War II, likened the struggle of the English people against the forces of Hitler to that of King Arthur's struggle to bring justice to the world.

Therefore, in the writing of *Camelot 3000*, I took from the legends precisely what I could use in writing the comic and ignored or ruthlessly discarded that which I could not. My understanding of the Arthurian mythos, then, is that of a perhaps more-than-usually well-informed layman, but no more. What I can cull from my notes on the origins and history of the Arthurian mythos can roughly be boiled down to the following:

That there was an historical British hero who served as the basis for the King Arthur Pendragon of legend has now been proved beyond any reasonable doubt. What *is* subject to doubt is his actual name and his rank in the military organization in which he served. The roots of the legend begin in the fifth century after the birth of Christ, when the Roman-occupied province of Britain was threatened by invading Saxons. The Roman troops were abruptly withdrawn, leaving the natives to defend themselves against the invaders. After an alliance between the Britons and Saxons collapsed, the Britons joined forces under a military leader whose name was *Ambrosius Aurelianus*, who is said to have slain the leader of the Saxons. Most authorities maintain that it was Ambrosius who is the "true" King Arthur, though some claim it was his second-in-command who served as Arthur's basis.

The first reference to a warrior named Arthur occurs in the chronicle *Gododdin* around the year 600, using Arthur as a standard by which other warriors should be judged. In the year 800, the historian Nennius, in his *Historia Brittonum*, calls Arthur the *dux bellorum*—the leader in battle—and described many of his conquests over the Saxons. Later well-documented sources such as the *Easter Annals*, a part of the British Museum's *Historical Miscellany*, tell of the battle of Camlann (Camelot?), in which both Arthur and his foe Medraut—Modred—perished.

It has also been suggested that Arthur is in some way connected to an ancient Gallic bear-goddess called *Artio*. To further confuse the issue, some authorities maintain the historical Arthur may have been a descendant of a community of Sarmatian troops who were posted to Britain in A.D. 225, and who encouraged his fellows to battle the Saxon invaders, leading by heroic example. Weight is given to this theory by the idea that the name Arthur—which poses problems from the standpoint of Celtic derivation— was in fact a *title* derived from the name of the initial commander of the Sarmatians, Lucius *Artorius* Castus.

Even less is known about the historical Arthur's death, with one source claiming Arthur died in a civil war which broke out among the restless Britons after the defeat of the Saxons.

The quest for the real Camelot is as fascinating, and as frustrating. In the late 1960s, historians began looking for the site from which Arthur would have conducted his campaigns and, perhaps, found it, in a site called Cadbury Castle, in southern England, where fortifications were discovered and dated back to some time after A.D. 470, the period of Arthur.

Despite this dearth of facts—or perhaps because of them—the character of King Arthur readily seized the popular imagination and was quickly embellished with friends, foes, and all manner of spectacular deeds, as have been all popular heroes from Paul Bunyan to George Washington.

One of the earliest written records of the Arthurian mythos was an ancient French manuscript divided into three or four volumes, containing tales called *Merlin*, *Lancelot*, *Gareth*, *Tristan*, *Queste del Saint Grail*, and *Le Mort Artu*. It was probably this manuscript, and perhaps others, that inspired the man who is most responsible for perpetuating the Arthurian mythos, *Sir Thomas Malory*.

Malory was born around 1395 and eventually succeeded his father as squire of Newbold Revel, the family's ancestral estate. He served in the military during the time that the presence of Joan of Arc had turned the French tide against the English, and it is probable that Malory was present when she was burned at the stake.

Malory's later life was equally eventful. He was often in trouble with the authorities, and he was imprisoned for fighting with the Lancastrian rebels in 1462 and served his sentence in the infamous Newgate Prison. It was there that Malory researched and wrote his *Le Morte D'Arthur*. Malory died on either March 12 or 14, 1471, and did not see his work published.

Malory truly believed in the spirit of chivalry, justice, and adventure exemplified by King Arthur and the Knights of the Round Table, a belief that is clear to anyone who reads *Le Morte D'Arthur*, the work that consolidated and popularized the Arthurian mythos for his generation and all since. It was *Le Morte D'Arthur*—or an adaptation thereof—that has served as the basis for every version of the Arthurian mythos to this day, including T.H. White's *The Once and Future King*, which itself inspired Alan Jay Lerner and Frederick Loewe's musical *Camelot*. *Camelot 3000* has broken some ground in that it is the first Arthurian exploit to tell of Arthur's oft-prophesized *return*, rather than retell exploits already told, but *Camelot 3000* would not exist had not Sir Thomas Malory written *Le Morte D'Arthur*. It is said that Malory saw himself as Sir Lancelot, the knight who received double punishment for his sins, and, like Lancelot, he will be forever remembered as one of King Arthur's most faithful knights.

On September 24, 1986, I stood with Brian Bolland at Stonehenge in England. The weather was, to strict recall, neither misty nor gloomy, yet an eerie mood seemed to pervade the day, and I felt rather odd, somehow at once both sombre and elated. I gazed at the site often connected with the wizard Merlin, and it seemed quite credible that not only was the magician out there, but so was his ruler and former apprentice, Arthur, impatiently awaiting the day when king and mage would both return.

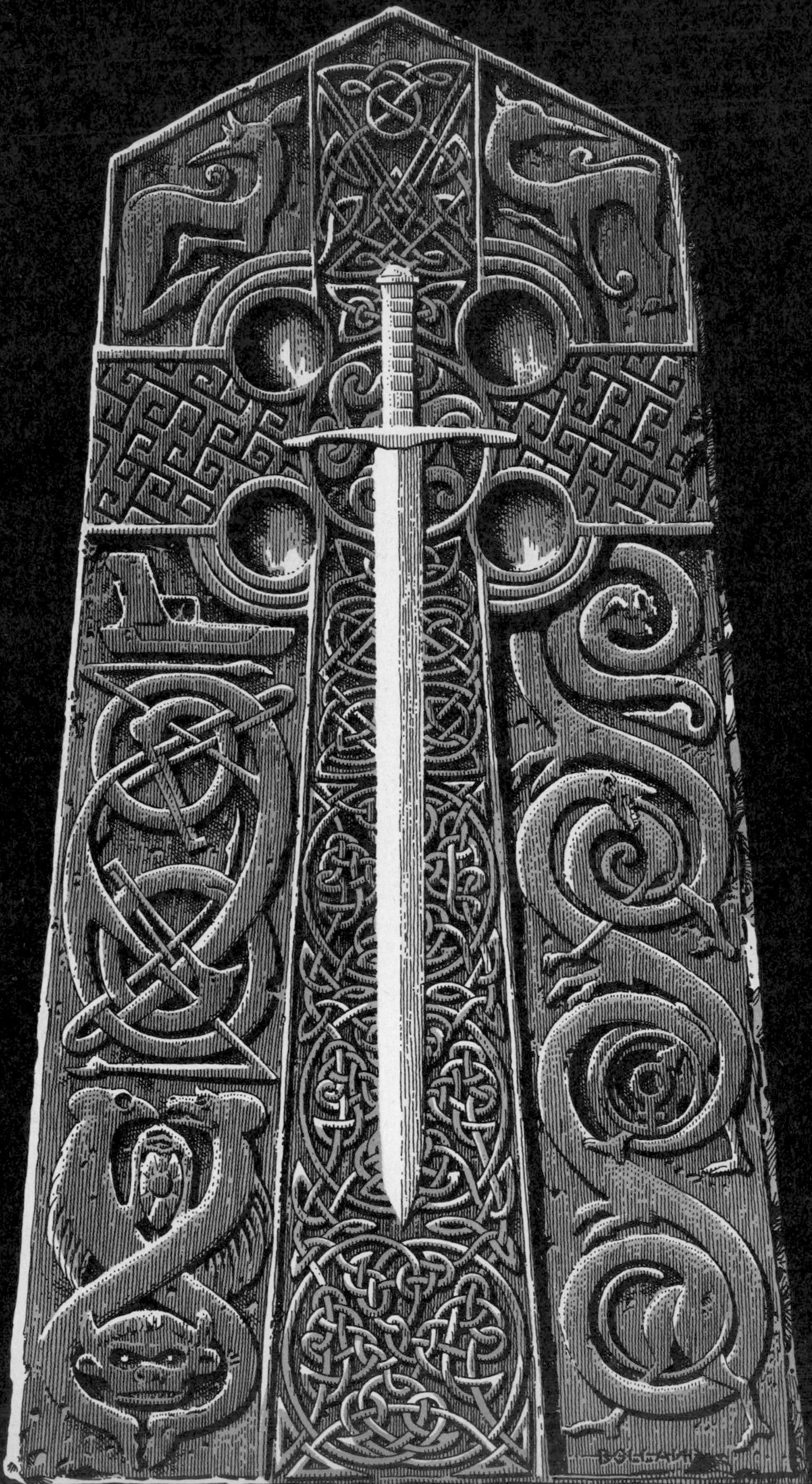

CHAPTER 1

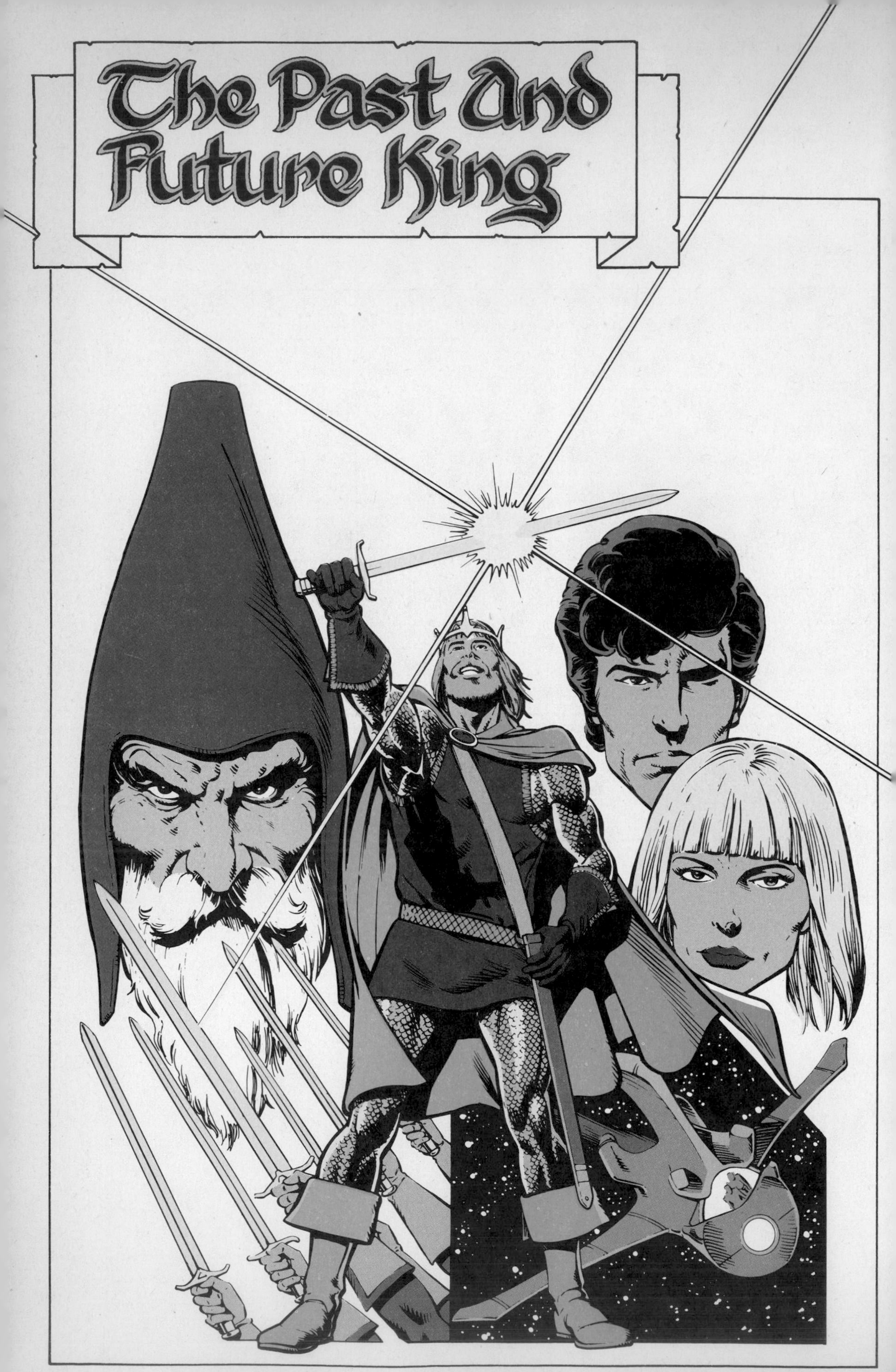
The Past And Future King

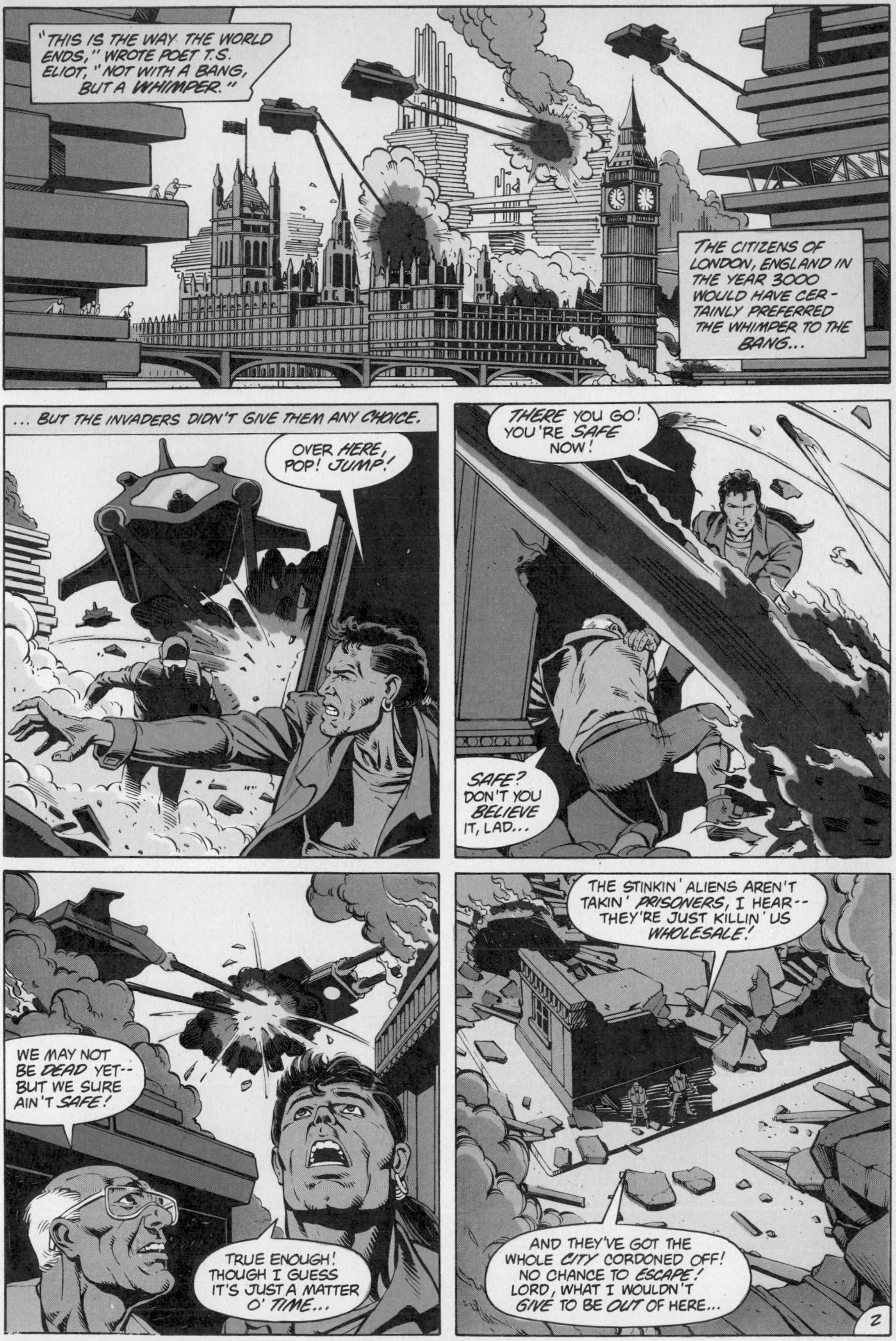
"THIS IS THE WAY THE WORLD ENDS," WROTE POET T.S. ELIOT, "NOT WITH A BANG, BUT A WHIMPER."
THE CITIZENS OF LONDON, ENGLAND IN THE YEAR 3000 WOULD HAVE CERTAINLY PREFERRED THE WHIMPER TO THE BANG...
... BUT THE INVADERS DIDN'T GIVE THEM ANY CHOICE.
OVER HERE, POP! JUMP!
THERE YOU GO! YOU'RE SAFE NOW!
SAFE? DON'T YOU BELIEVE IT, LAD...
WE MAY NOT BE DEAD YET-- BUT WE SURE AIN'T SAFE!
TRUE ENOUGH! THOUGH I GUESS IT'S JUST A MATTER O' TIME...
THE STINKIN' ALIENS AREN'T TAKIN' PRISONERS, I HEAR-- THEY'RE JUST KILLIN' US WHOLESALE!
AND THEY'VE GOT THE WHOLE CITY CORDONED OFF! NO CHANCE TO ESCAPE! LORD, WHAT I WOULDN'T GIVE TO BE OUT OF HERE...

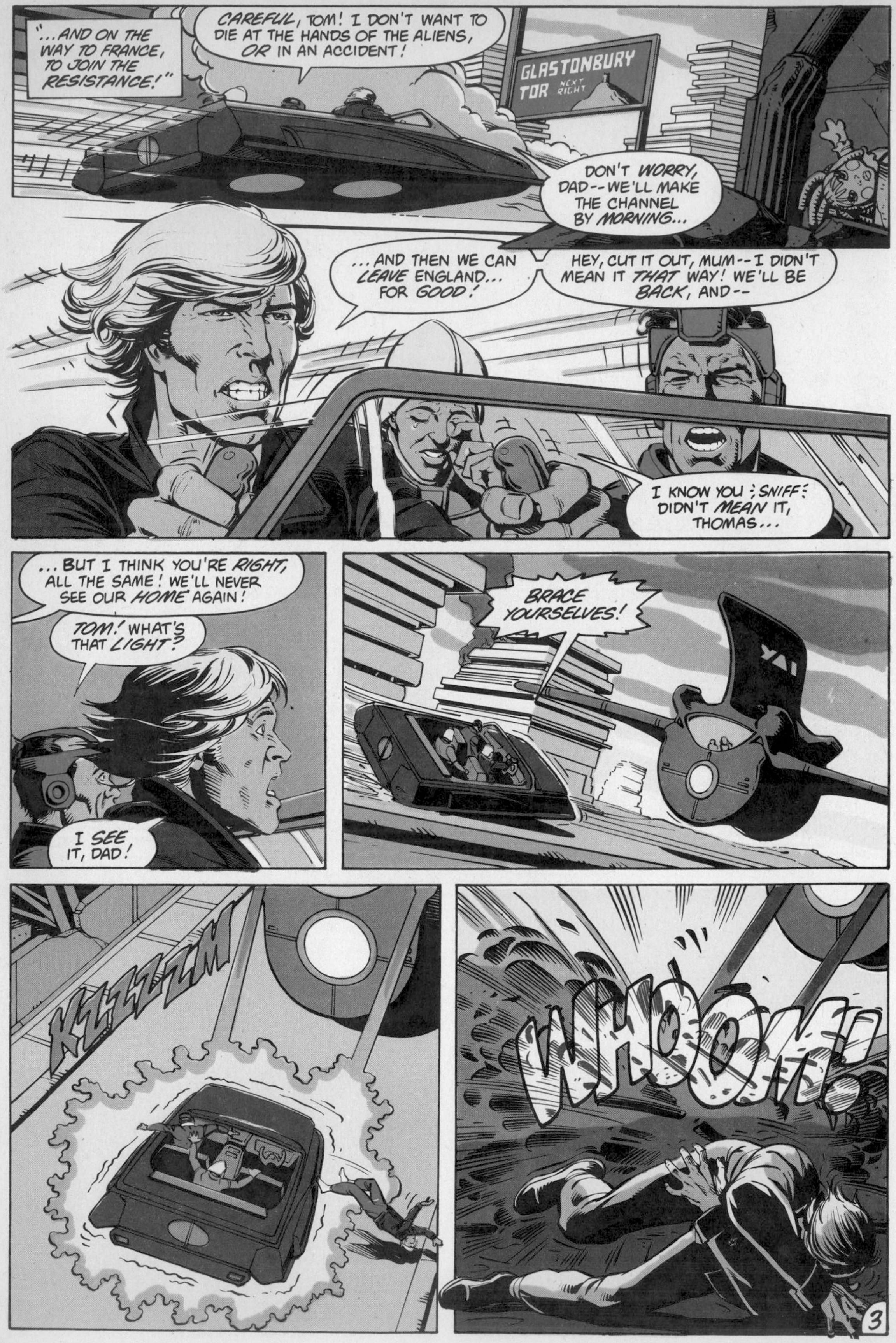
"...AND ON THE WAY TO FRANCE, TO JOIN THE RESISTANCE!"
CAREFUL, TOM! I DON'T WANT TO DIE AT THE HANDS OF THE ALIENS, OR IN AN ACCIDENT!
GLASTONBURY TOR NEXT RIGHT
DON'T WORRY, DAD--WE'LL MAKE THE CHANNEL BY MORNING...
...AND THEN WE CAN LEAVE ENGLAND... FOR GOOD!
HEY, CUT IT OUT, MUM--I DIDN'T MEAN IT THAT WAY! WE'LL BE BACK, AND--
I KNOW YOU :SNIFF: DIDN'T MEAN IT, THOMAS...
...BUT I THINK YOU'RE RIGHT, ALL THE SAME! WE'LL NEVER SEE OUR HOME AGAIN!
TOM! WHAT'S THAT LIGHT?
I SEE IT, DAD!
BRACE YOURSELVES!
KZZZZM
WHOOOM!
3

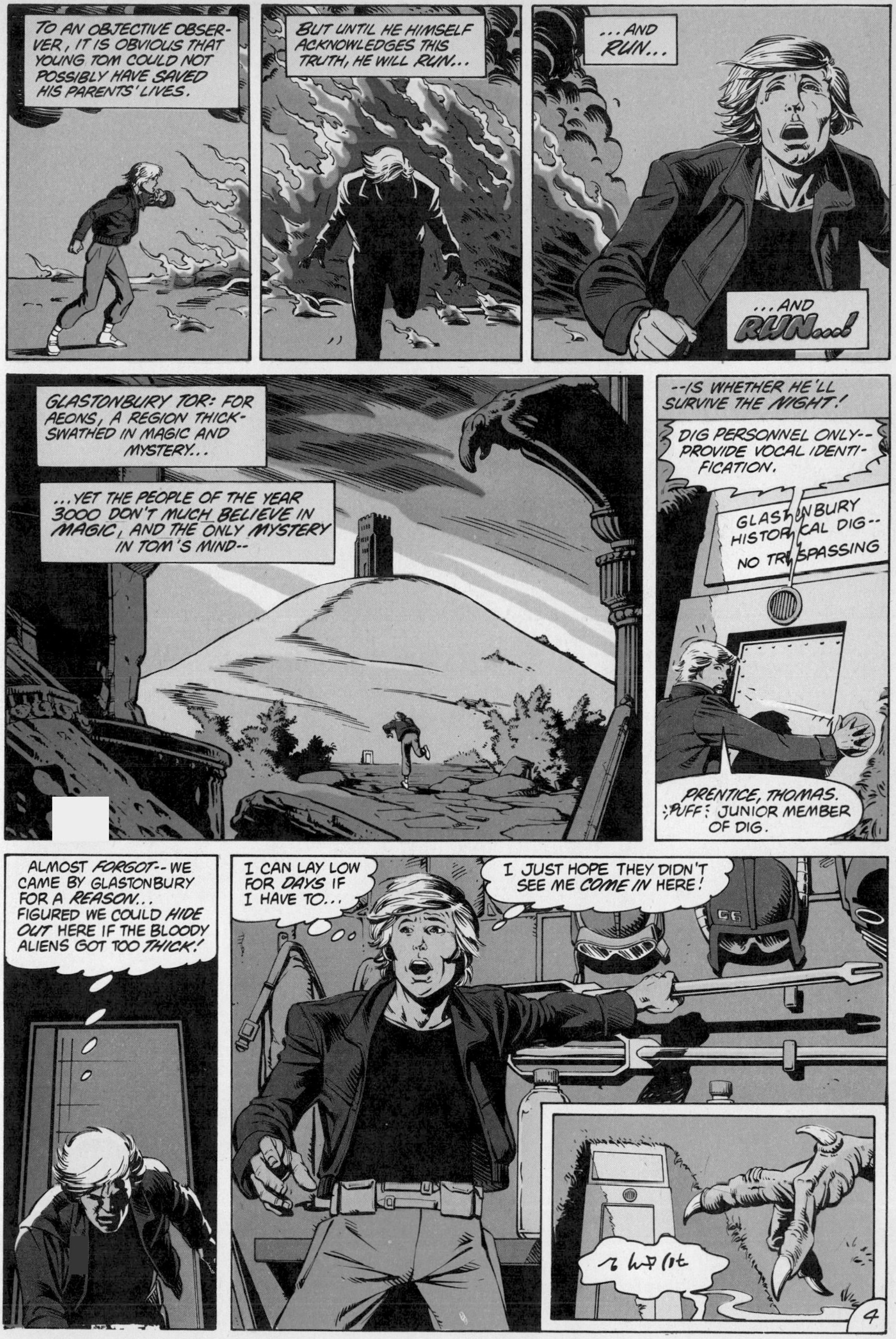

TO AN OBJECTIVE OBSERVER, IT IS OBVIOUS THAT YOUNG TOM COULD NOT POSSIBLY HAVE SAVED HIS PARENTS' LIVES.
BUT UNTIL HE HIMSELF ACKNOWLEDGES THIS TRUTH, HE WILL RUN...
...AND RUN...
...AND RUN...!
GLASTONBURY TOR: FOR AEONS, A REGION THICK-SWATHED IN MAGIC AND MYSTERY...
...YET THE PEOPLE OF THE YEAR 3000 DON'T MUCH BELIEVE IN MAGIC, AND THE ONLY MYSTERY IN TOM'S MIND--
--IS WHETHER HE'LL SURVIVE THE NIGHT!
DIG PERSONNEL ONLY--PROVIDE VOCAL IDENTIFICATION.
GLASTONBURY HISTORICAL DIG-- NO TRESPASSING
PRENTICE, THOMAS. *PUFF* JUNIOR MEMBER OF DIG.
ALMOST FORGOT--WE CAME BY GLASTONBURY FOR A REASON... FIGURED WE COULD HIDE OUT HERE IF THE BLOODY ALIENS GOT TOO THICK!
I CAN LAY LOW FOR DAYS IF I HAVE TO...
I JUST HOPE THEY DIDN'T SEE ME COME IN HERE!
GG

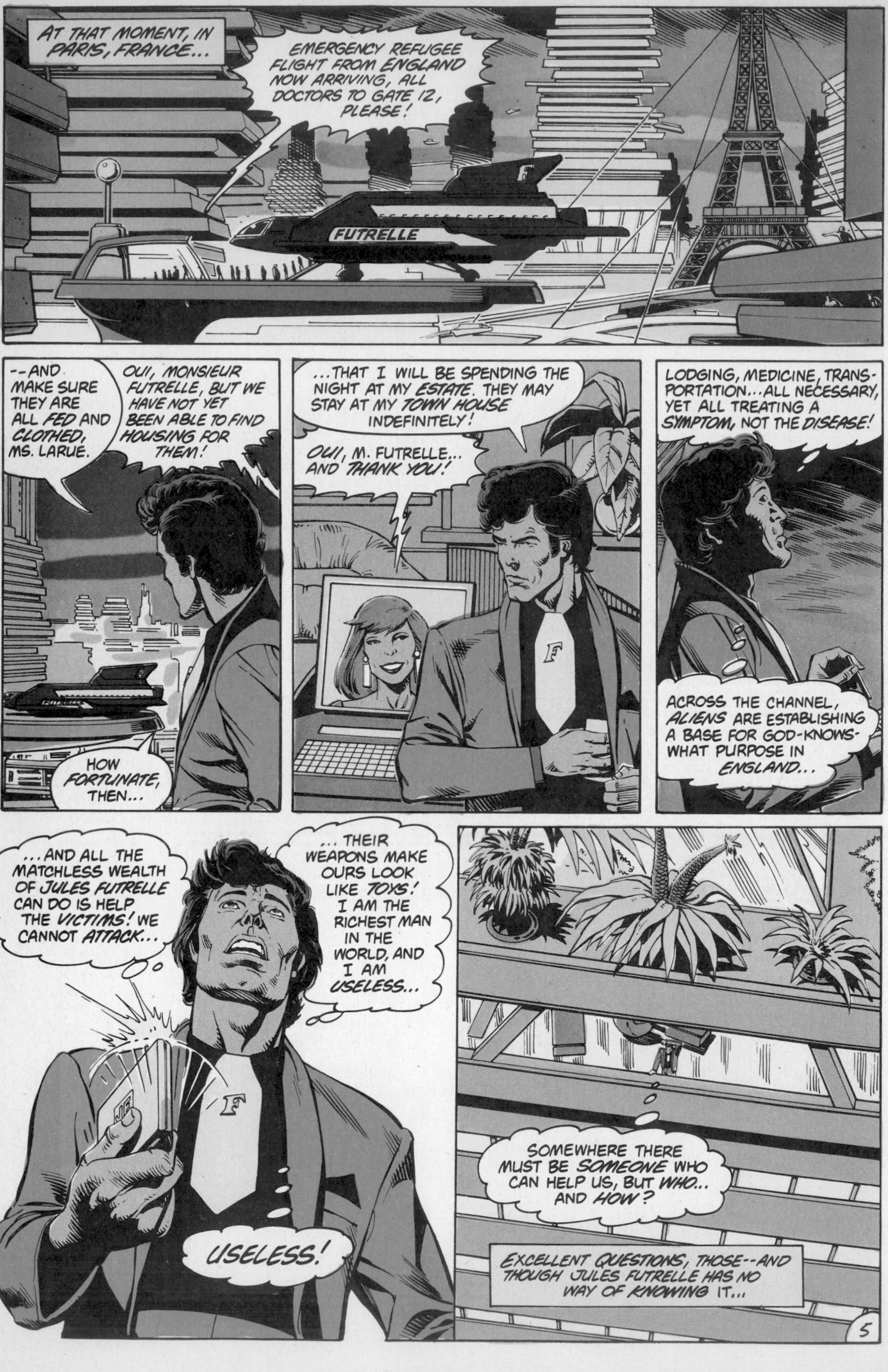
AT THAT MOMENT, IN PARIS, FRANCE...
EMERGENCY REFUGEE FLIGHT FROM ENGLAND NOW ARRIVING, ALL DOCTORS TO GATE 12, PLEASE!
FUTRELLE
--AND MAKE SURE THEY ARE ALL FED AND CLOTHED, MS. LARUE.
OUI, MONSIEUR FUTRELLE, BUT WE HAVE NOT YET BEEN ABLE TO FIND HOUSING FOR THEM!
HOW FORTUNATE, THEN...
...THAT I WILL BE SPENDING THE NIGHT AT MY ESTATE. THEY MAY STAY AT MY TOWN HOUSE INDEFINITELY!
OUI, M. FUTRELLE... AND THANK YOU!
LODGING, MEDICINE, TRANSPORTATION... ALL NECESSARY, YET ALL TREATING A SYMPTOM, NOT THE DISEASE!
ACROSS THE CHANNEL, ALIENS ARE ESTABLISHING A BASE FOR GOD-KNOWS-WHAT PURPOSE IN ENGLAND...
...AND ALL THE MATCHLESS WEALTH OF JULES FUTRELLE CAN DO IS HELP THE VICTIMS! WE CANNOT ATTACK...
...THEIR WEAPONS MAKE OURS LOOK LIKE TOYS! I AM THE RICHEST MAN IN THE WORLD, AND I AM USELESS...
USELESS!
SOMEWHERE THERE MUST BE SOMEONE WHO CAN HELP US, BUT WHO... AND HOW?
EXCELLENT QUESTIONS, THOSE--AND THOUGH JULES FUTRELLE HAS NO WAY OF KNOWING IT...
5

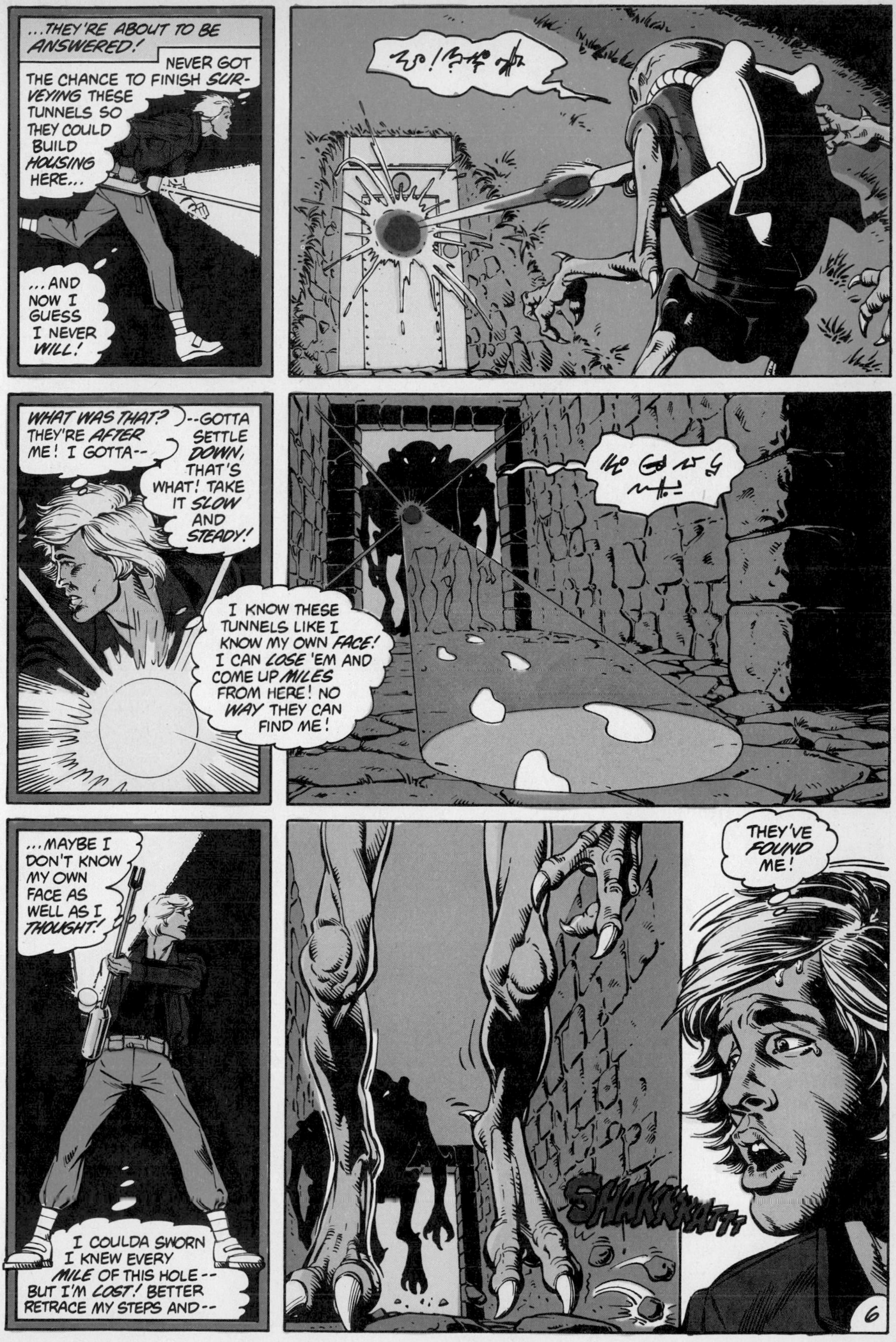
...THEY'RE ABOUT TO BE ANSWERED!
NEVER GOT THE CHANCE TO FINISH SURVEYING THESE TUNNELS SO THEY COULD BUILD HOUSING HERE...
...AND NOW I GUESS I NEVER WILL!
WHAT WAS THAT? THEY'RE AFTER ME! I GOTTA--
--GOTTA SETTLE DOWN, THAT'S WHAT! TAKE IT SLOW AND STEADY!
I KNOW THESE TUNNELS LIKE I KNOW MY OWN FACE! I CAN LOSE 'EM AND COME UP MILES FROM HERE! NO WAY THEY CAN FIND ME!
...MAYBE I DON'T KNOW MY OWN FACE AS WELL AS I THOUGHT!
I COULDA SWORN I KNEW EVERY MILE OF THIS HOLE--BUT I'M LOST! BETTER RETRACE MY STEPS AND--
THEY'VE FOUND ME!
SHAKKKHATT
6

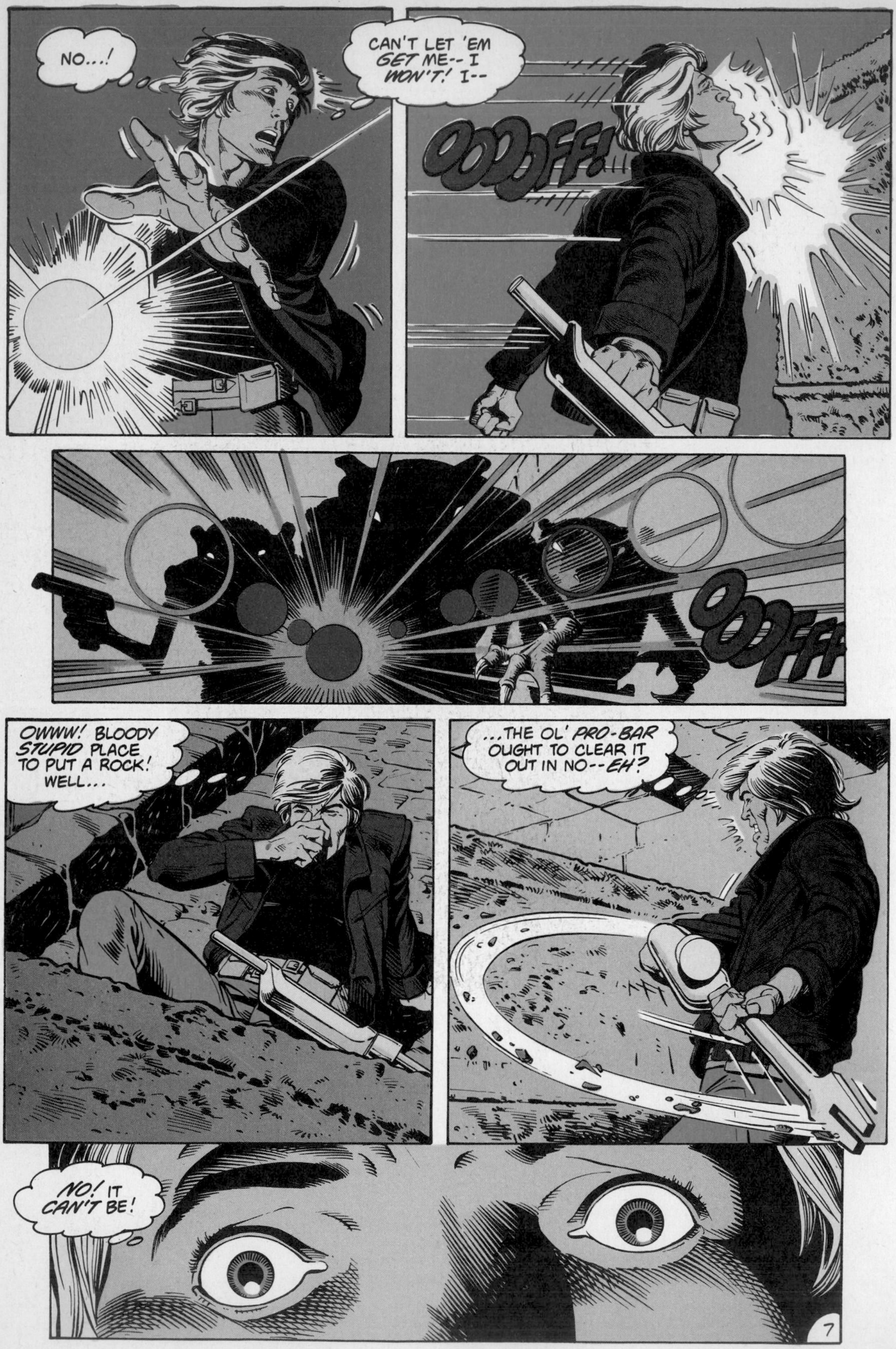
NO...!
CAN'T LET 'EM GET ME-- I WON'T! I--
OOOOFF!
OOOFFF
OWWW! BLOODY STUPID PLACE TO PUT A ROCK! WELL...
...THE OL' PRO-BAR OUGHT TO CLEAR IT OUT IN NO--EH?
NO! IT CAN'T BE!

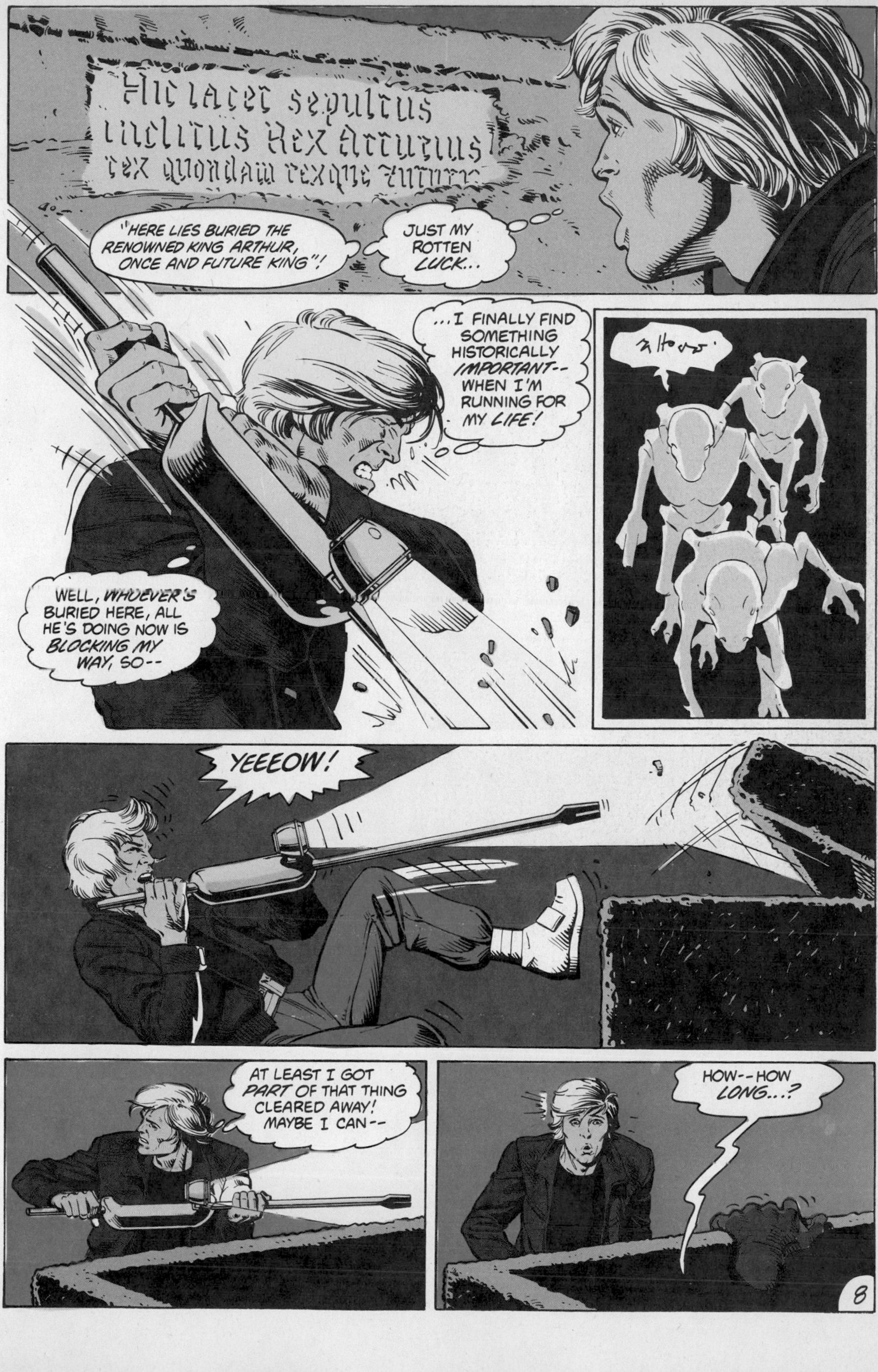
Hic iacet sepultus
inclitus Rex Arturius
rex quondam rexque futurus
"HERE LIES BURIED THE RENOWNED KING ARTHUR, ONCE AND FUTURE KING"!
JUST MY ROTTEN LUCK...
...I FINALLY FIND SOMETHING HISTORICALLY IMPORTANT-- WHEN I'M RUNNING FOR MY LIFE!
WELL, WHOEVER'S BURIED HERE, ALL HE'S DOING NOW IS BLOCKING MY WAY, SO--
YEEEOW!
AT LEAST I GOT PART OF THAT THING CLEARED AWAY! MAYBE I CAN--
HOW--HOW LONG...?

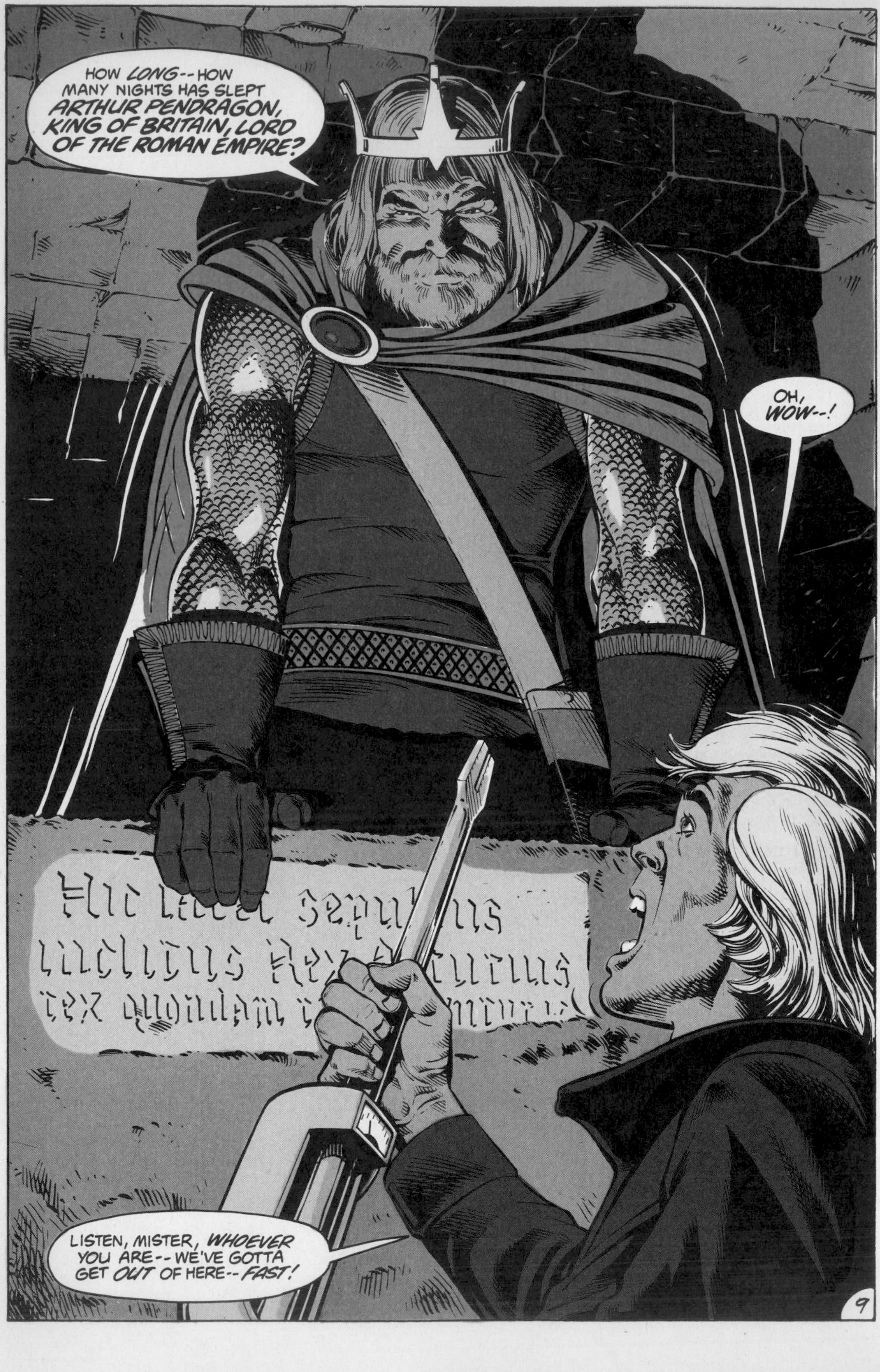
HOW LONG--HOW MANY NIGHTS HAS SLEPT ARTHUR PENDRAGON, KING OF BRITAIN, LORD OF THE ROMAN EMPIRE?
OH, WOW--!
LISTEN, MISTER, WHOEVER YOU ARE--WE'VE GOTTA GET OUT OF HERE--FAST!

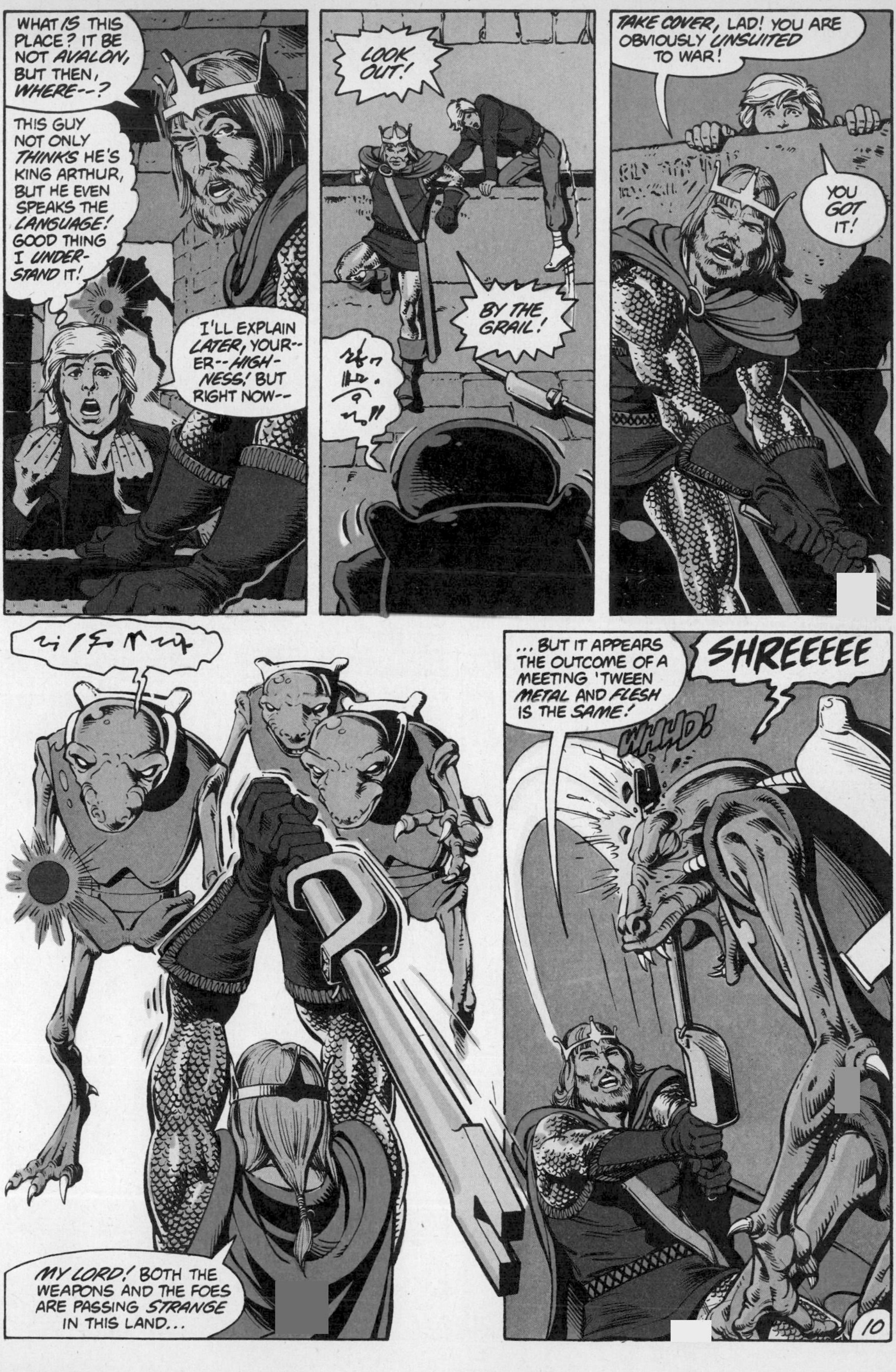
WHAT *IS* THIS PLACE? IT BE NOT *AVALON*, BUT THEN, *WHERE--?*
THIS GUY NOT ONLY *THINKS* HE'S KING ARTHUR, BUT HE EVEN SPEAKS THE *LANGUAGE!* GOOD THING I *UNDERSTAND* IT!
I'LL EXPLAIN *LATER*, YOUR--ER--*HIGHNESS!* BUT RIGHT NOW--
LOOK OUT!
BY THE GRAIL!
TAKE COVER, LAD! YOU ARE OBVIOUSLY *UNSUITED* TO WAR!
YOU *GOT* IT!
MY LORD! BOTH THE WEAPONS AND THE FOES ARE PASSING *STRANGE* IN THIS LAND...
... BUT IT APPEARS THE OUTCOME OF A MEETING 'TWEEN *METAL* AND *FLESH* IS THE *SAME!*
SHREEEEE
WHUD!

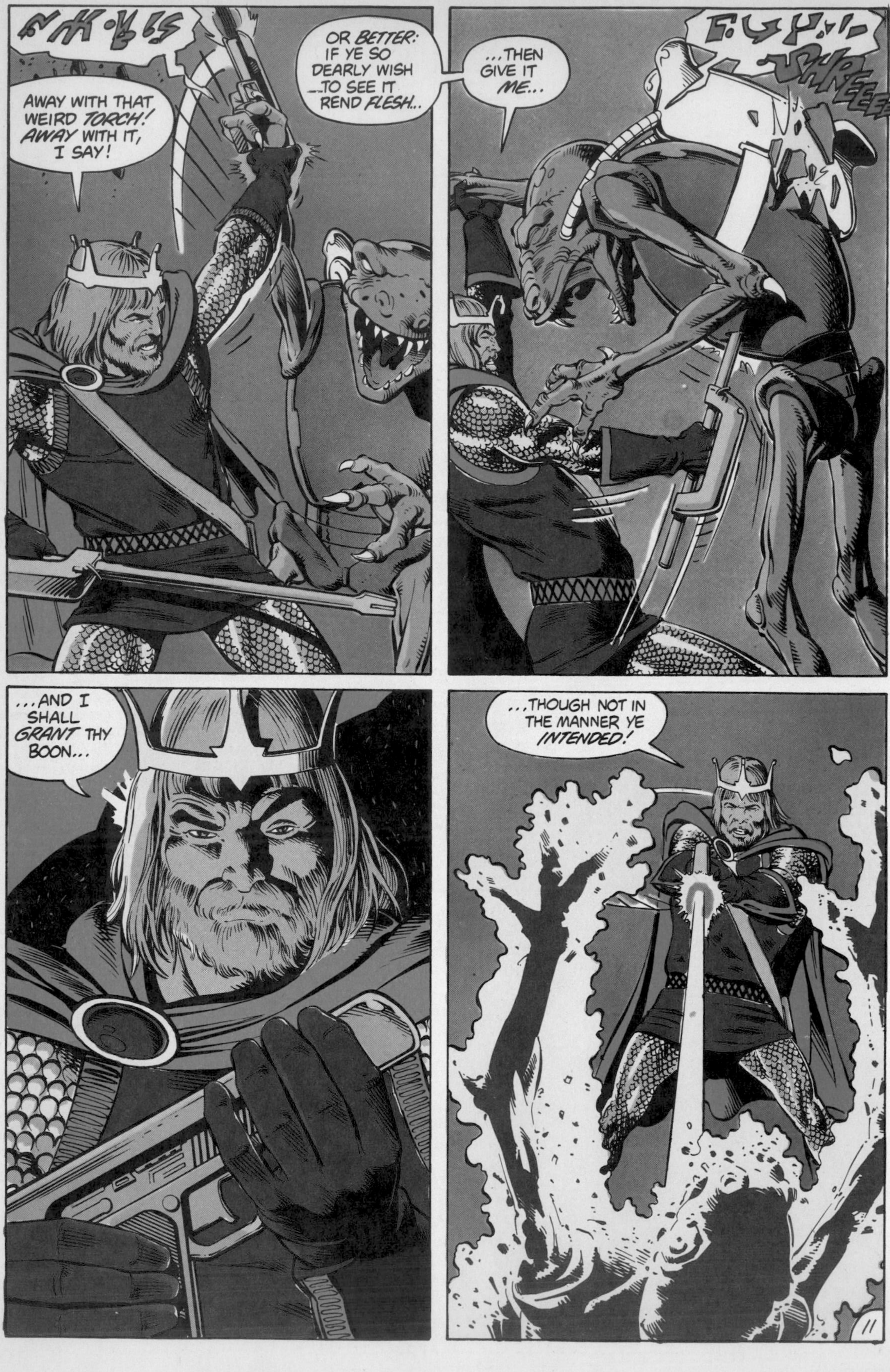

AWAY WITH THAT WEIRD TORCH! AWAY WITH IT, I SAY!
OR BETTER: IF YE SO DEARLY WISH -- TO SEE IT REND FLESH...
...THEN GIVE IT ME...
SHREEEE
...AND I SHALL GRANT THY BOON...
...THOUGH NOT IN THE MANNER YE INTENDED!
11

I AM SORE TEMPTED TO KEEP THIS WEAPON-- AND *WHY NOT?*

ITS *OWNER* HAS NO FURTHER USE FOR IT!

TH--THAT WAS *AMAZING!*

AMAZING? NO, LAD, THE DIMMEST SQUIRE OF THE *TABLE ROUND* COULD EASILY VANQUISH SUCH FOES AS *THESE!*

BUT TELL ME NOW... WHAT *PLACE* AND *TIME* IS THIS?

WELL, WE'RE UNDER *GLASTONBURY TOR,* AND--AND IT'S THE YEAR *3000!*

THE YEAR *3000,* YE SAY? BY JESU, I SLEPT FOR SOMEWHAT LONGER THAN I *THOUGHT...*

...BUT IT SEEMS TO HAVE SERVED ITS PURPOSE, FOR THE WOUND GIVEN ME BY THE EVIL *MODRED* IS *HEALED!*

...IN THE BATTLE... AT *SALISBURY DOWN?*

WHAT? THEN MY MENTOR DID NOT *FAIL* ME! HE *SAID* THE WORLD WOULD KNOW OF *KING ARTHUR AND THE TABLE ROUND!*

I MUST *FIND* HIM, LAD! WOULD YOU *COME* WITH ME? I'LL *NEED* A SQUIRE IN THIS STRANGE ERA!

I--I'M *SORRY,* YOUR...ER...MAJESTY, I *CAN'T!*

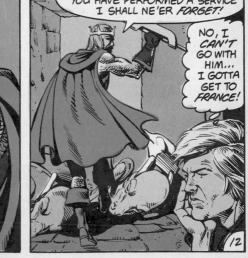

AS YE WILL THEN, LAD! BUT KNOW YOU HAVE PERFORMED A SERVICE I SHALL NE'ER *FORGET!*

NO, I *CAN'T* GO WITH HIM... I GOTTA GET TO *FRANCE!*

12.

BUT *WHY?* MUM AND DAD ARE DEAD NOW; AND I ESPECIALLY WANTED TO SEE THEM *SAFE!*

I'VE GOT NO FRIENDS OR RELATIVES IN FRANCE!

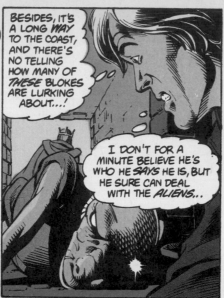

BESIDES, IT'S A LONG *WAY* TO THE COAST, AND THERE'S NO TELLING HOW MANY OF *THESE* BLOKES ARE LURKING ABOUT...!

I DON'T FOR A MINUTE BELIEVE HE'S WHO HE *SAYS* HE IS, BUT HE SURE CAN DEAL WITH THE *ALIENS...*

WAIT A MINUTE, YOUR MAJESTY! I'M COMING *WITH* YOU!

SPLENDID, LAD! BUT NO NEED TO STAND ON *CEREMONY.* YOU MAY CALL ME *KING ARTHUR!*

I FORGOT THEY MIGHT HAVE *GUARDS* OUT HERE! HOW WE GONNA GET *AROUND* 'EM, KING ARTHUR?

SIMPLY *PUT,* LAD...

...WE'RE NOT!

SHREEEEE

COME *ON,* KING ARTHUR! WE'D BETTER GET OUTTA HERE BEFORE A LOT *MORE* OF THEM SHOW UP!

YOU ECHO MY THOUGHTS TO THE *LETTER,* LAD, BUT--

BUT *WHAT?*

13

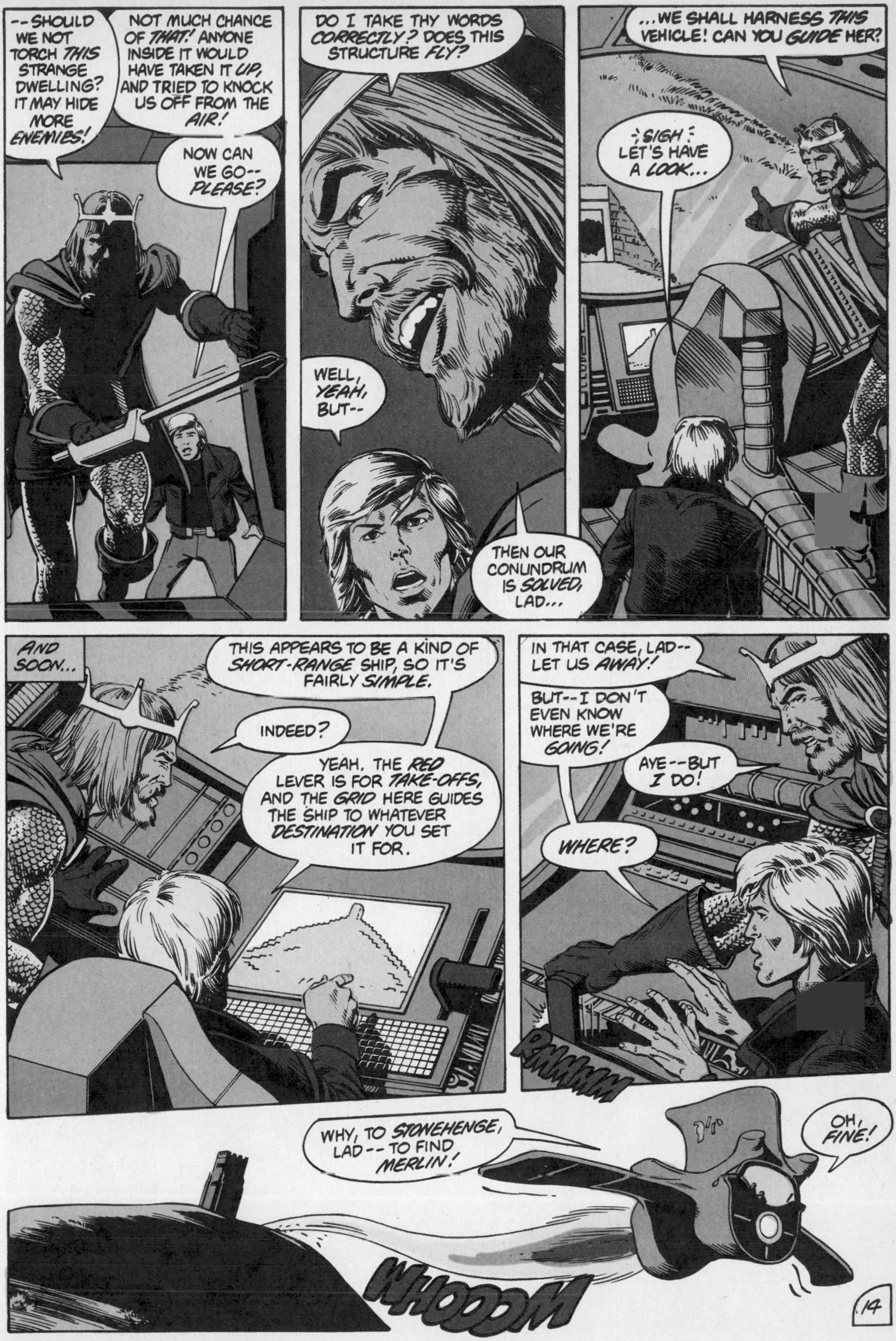

--SHOULD WE NOT TORCH THIS STRANGE DWELLING? IT MAY HIDE MORE ENEMIES!
NOT MUCH CHANCE OF THAT! ANYONE INSIDE IT WOULD HAVE TAKEN IT UP, AND TRIED TO KNOCK US OFF FROM THE AIR!
NOW CAN WE GO--PLEASE?
DO I TAKE THY WORDS CORRECTLY? DOES THIS STRUCTURE FLY?
WELL, YEAH, BUT--
THEN OUR CONUNDRUM IS SOLVED, LAD...
...WE SHALL HARNESS THIS VEHICLE! CAN YOU GUIDE HER?
SIGH LET'S HAVE A LOOK...
AND SOON...
THIS APPEARS TO BE A KIND OF SHORT-RANGE SHIP, SO IT'S FAIRLY SIMPLE.
INDEED?
YEAH, THE RED LEVER IS FOR TAKE-OFFS, AND THE GRID HERE GUIDES THE SHIP TO WHATEVER DESTINATION YOU SET IT FOR.
IN THAT CASE, LAD--LET US AWAY!
BUT--I DON'T EVEN KNOW WHERE WE'RE GOING!
AYE--BUT I DO!
WHERE?
RMMMM
WHY, TO STONEHENGE, LAD--TO FIND MERLIN!
OH, FINE!
WHOOOM

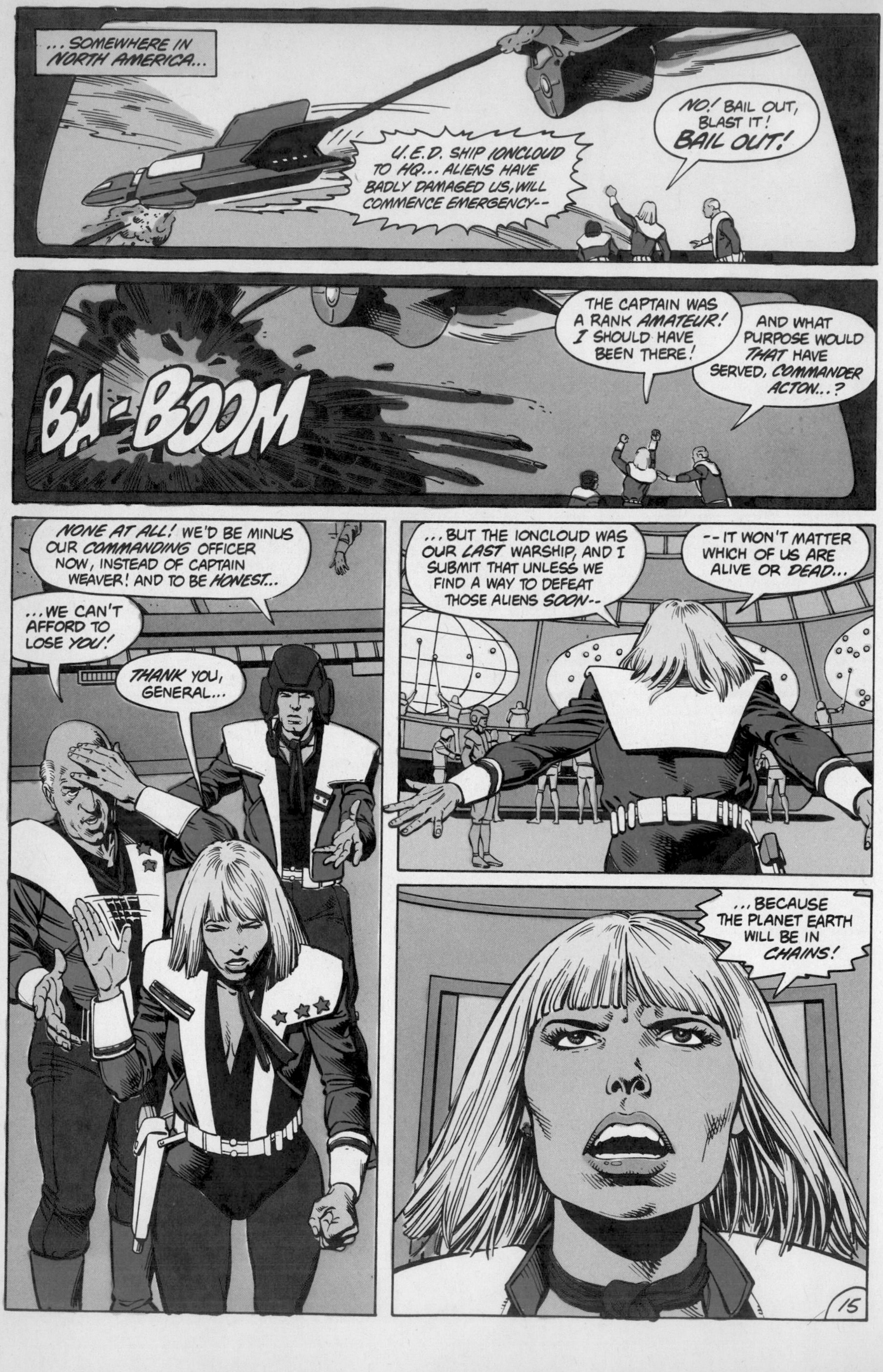
...SOMEWHERE IN NORTH AMERICA...
U.E.D. SHIP IONCLOUD TO HQ... ALIENS HAVE BADLY DAMAGED US, WILL COMMENCE EMERGENCY--
NO! BAIL OUT, BLAST IT! BAIL OUT!
BA-BOOM
THE CAPTAIN WAS A RANK AMATEUR! I SHOULD HAVE BEEN THERE!
AND WHAT PURPOSE WOULD THAT HAVE SERVED, COMMANDER ACTON...?
NONE AT ALL! WE'D BE MINUS OUR COMMANDING OFFICER NOW, INSTEAD OF CAPTAIN WEAVER! AND TO BE HONEST...
...WE CAN'T AFFORD TO LOSE YOU!
THANK YOU, GENERAL...
...BUT THE IONCLOUD WAS OUR LAST WARSHIP, AND I SUBMIT THAT UNLESS WE FIND A WAY TO DEFEAT THOSE ALIENS SOON--
--IT WON'T MATTER WHICH OF US ARE ALIVE OR DEAD...
...BECAUSE THE PLANET EARTH WILL BE IN CHAINS!
15

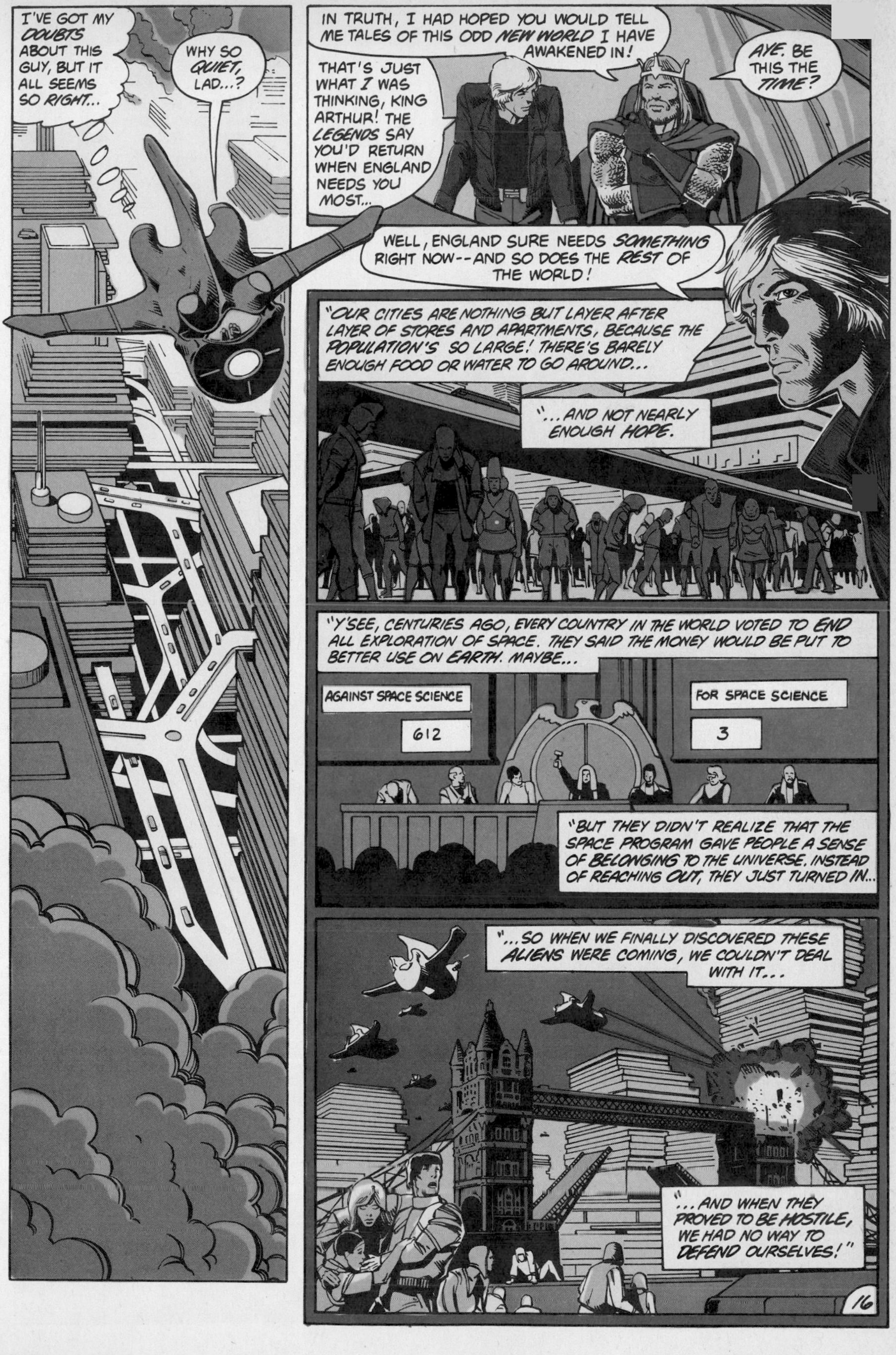
I'VE GOT MY DOUBTS ABOUT THIS GUY, BUT IT ALL SEEMS SO RIGHT...
WHY SO QUIET, LAD...?
IN TRUTH, I HAD HOPED YOU WOULD TELL ME TALES OF THIS ODD NEW WORLD I HAVE AWAKENED IN!
THAT'S JUST WHAT I WAS THINKING, KING ARTHUR! THE LEGENDS SAY YOU'D RETURN WHEN ENGLAND NEEDS YOU MOST...
AYE. BE THIS THE TIME?
WELL, ENGLAND SURE NEEDS SOMETHING RIGHT NOW--AND SO DOES THE REST OF THE WORLD!
"OUR CITIES ARE NOTHING BUT LAYER AFTER LAYER OF STORES AND APARTMENTS, BECAUSE THE POPULATION'S SO LARGE! THERE'S BARELY ENOUGH FOOD OR WATER TO GO AROUND...
"...AND NOT NEARLY ENOUGH HOPE.
"Y'SEE, CENTURIES AGO, EVERY COUNTRY IN THE WORLD VOTED TO END ALL EXPLORATION OF SPACE. THEY SAID THE MONEY WOULD BE PUT TO BETTER USE ON EARTH. MAYBE...
AGAINST SPACE SCIENCE
612
FOR SPACE SCIENCE
3
"BUT THEY DIDN'T REALIZE THAT THE SPACE PROGRAM GAVE PEOPLE A SENSE OF BELONGING TO THE UNIVERSE. INSTEAD OF REACHING OUT, THEY JUST TURNED IN...
"...SO WHEN WE FINALLY DISCOVERED THESE ALIENS WERE COMING, WE COULDN'T DEAL WITH IT...
"...AND WHEN THEY PROVED TO BE HOSTILE, WE HAD NO WAY TO DEFEND OURSELVES!"
16

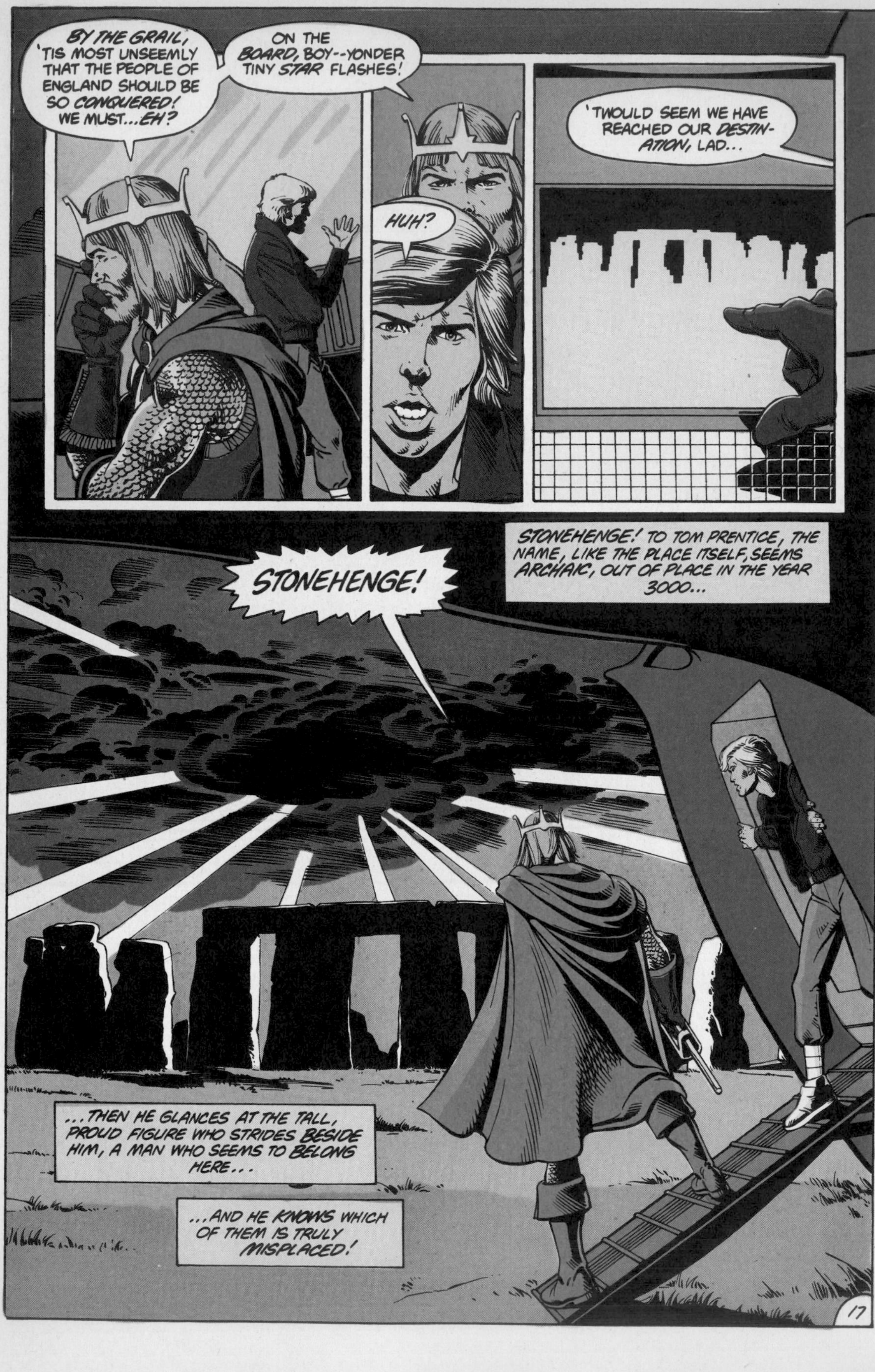
BY THE GRAIL, 'TIS MOST UNSEEMLY THAT THE PEOPLE OF ENGLAND SHOULD BE SO CONQUERED! WE MUST...EH?
ON THE BOARD, BOY--YONDER TINY STAR FLASHES!
HUH?
'TWOULD SEEM WE HAVE REACHED OUR DESTINATION, LAD...
STONEHENGE!
STONEHENGE! TO TOM PRENTICE, THE NAME, LIKE THE PLACE ITSELF, SEEMS ARCHAIC, OUT OF PLACE IN THE YEAR 3000...
...THEN HE GLANCES AT THE TALL, PROUD FIGURE WHO STRIDES BESIDE HIM, A MAN WHO SEEMS TO BELONG HERE...
...AND HE KNOWS WHICH OF THEM IS TRULY MISPLACED!
17

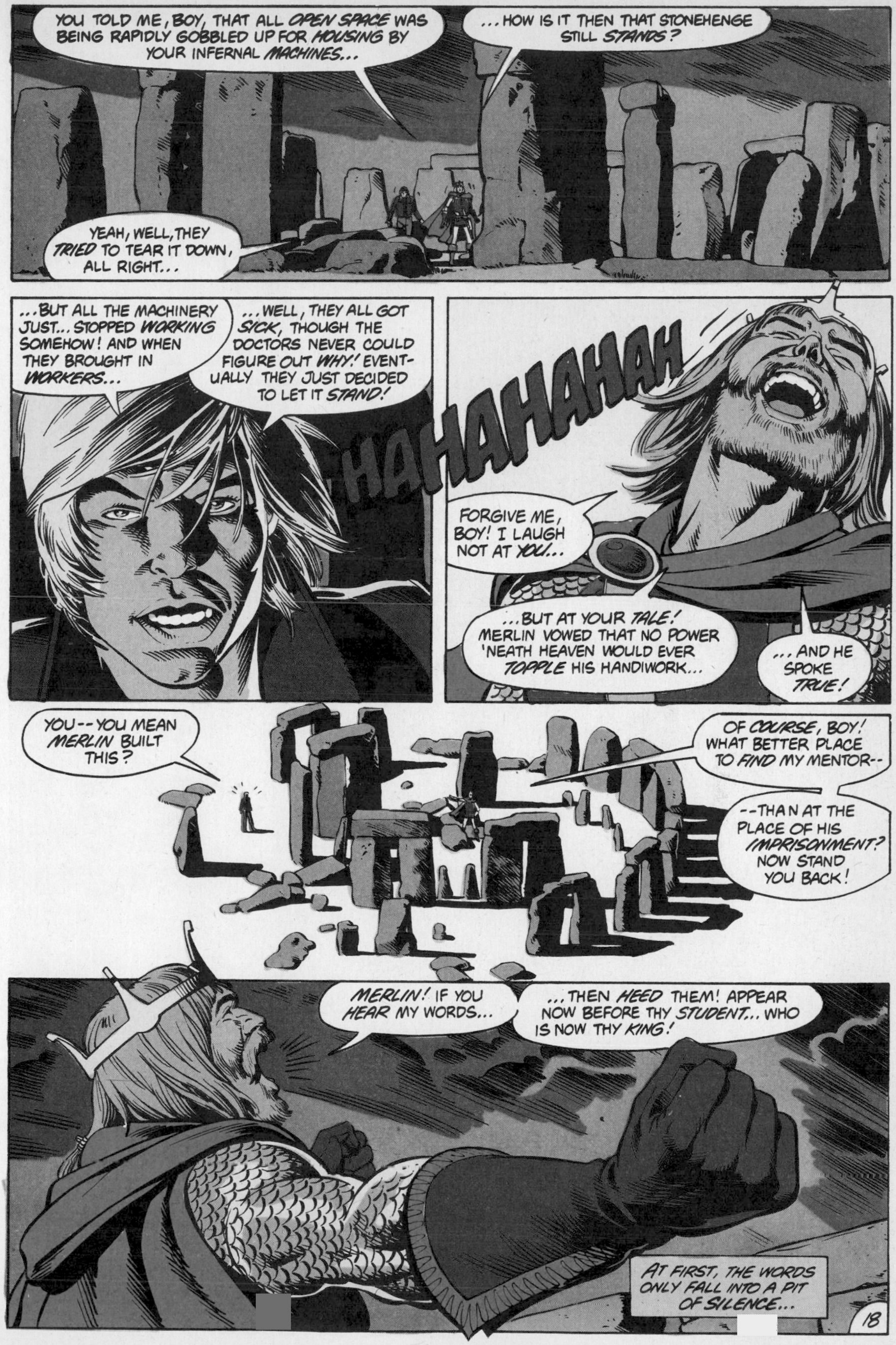
YOU TOLD ME, BOY, THAT ALL OPEN SPACE WAS BEING RAPIDLY GOBBLED UP FOR HOUSING BY YOUR INFERNAL MACHINES...
...HOW IS IT THEN THAT STONEHENGE STILL STANDS?
YEAH, WELL, THEY TRIED TO TEAR IT DOWN, ALL RIGHT...
...BUT ALL THE MACHINERY JUST... STOPPED WORKING SOMEHOW! AND WHEN THEY BROUGHT IN WORKERS...
...WELL, THEY ALL GOT SICK, THOUGH THE DOCTORS NEVER COULD FIGURE OUT WHY! EVENTUALLY THEY JUST DECIDED TO LET IT STAND!
HAHAHAHAH
FORGIVE ME, BOY! I LAUGH NOT AT YOU...
...BUT AT YOUR TALE! MERLIN VOWED THAT NO POWER 'NEATH HEAVEN WOULD EVER TOPPLE HIS HANDIWORK...
...AND HE SPOKE TRUE!
YOU--YOU MEAN MERLIN BUILT THIS?
OF COURSE, BOY! WHAT BETTER PLACE TO FIND MY MENTOR--
--THAN AT THE PLACE OF HIS IMPRISONMENT? NOW STAND YOU BACK!
MERLIN! IF YOU HEAR MY WORDS...
...THEN HEED THEM! APPEAR NOW BEFORE THY STUDENT... WHO IS NOW THY KING!
AT FIRST, THE WORDS ONLY FALL INTO A PIT OF SILENCE...

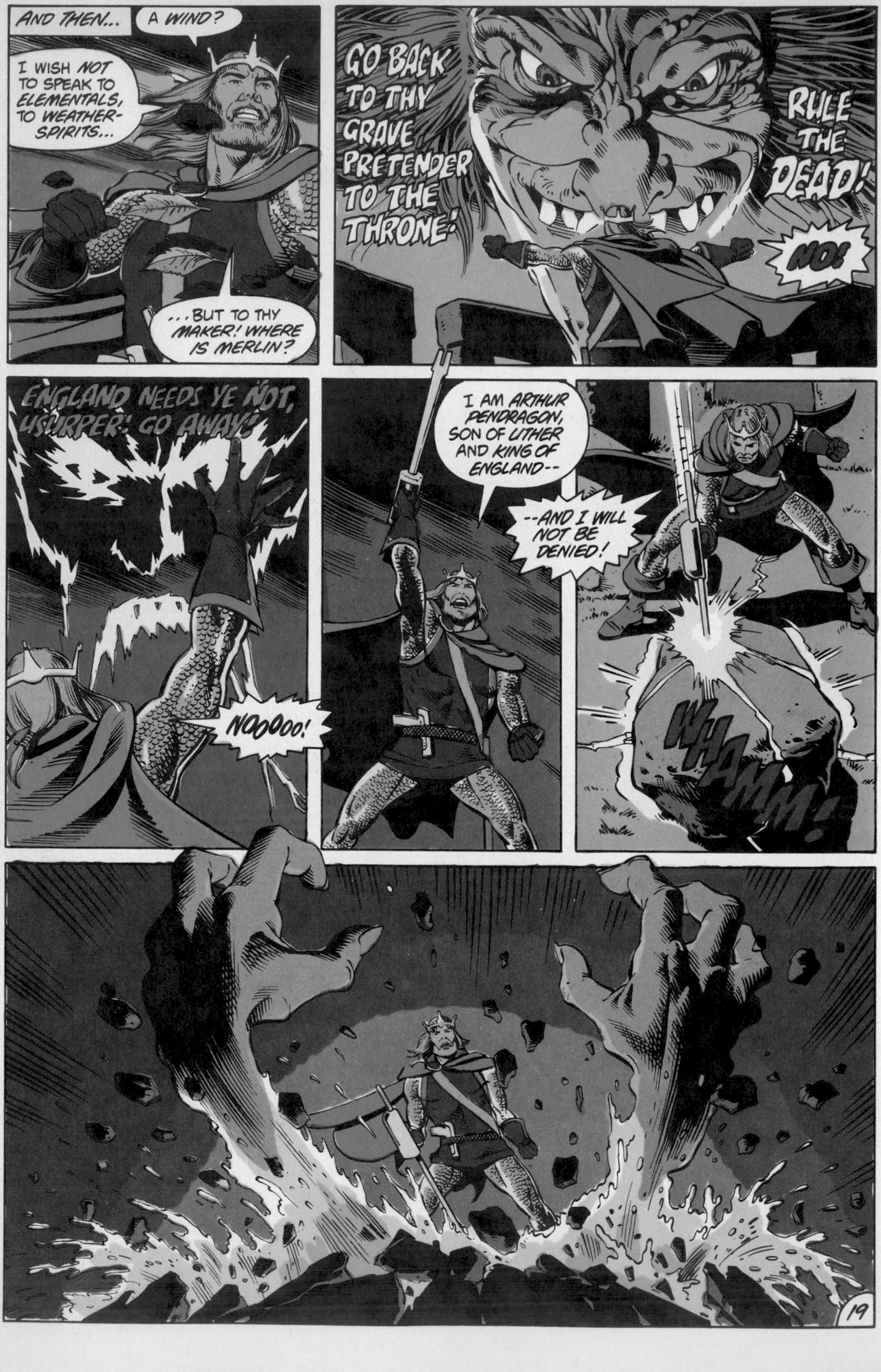
AND THEN...
A WIND?
I WISH NOT TO SPEAK TO ELEMENTALS, TO WEATHER-SPIRITS...
...BUT TO THY MAKER! WHERE IS MERLIN?
GO BACK TO THY GRAVE PRETENDER TO THE THRONE!
RULE THE DEAD!
NO!
ENGLAND NEEDS YE NOT, USURPER! GO AWAY!
NOOOOO!
I AM ARTHUR PENDRAGON, SON OF UTHER AND KING OF ENGLAND--
--AND I WILL NOT BE DENIED!
WHAMM!
19

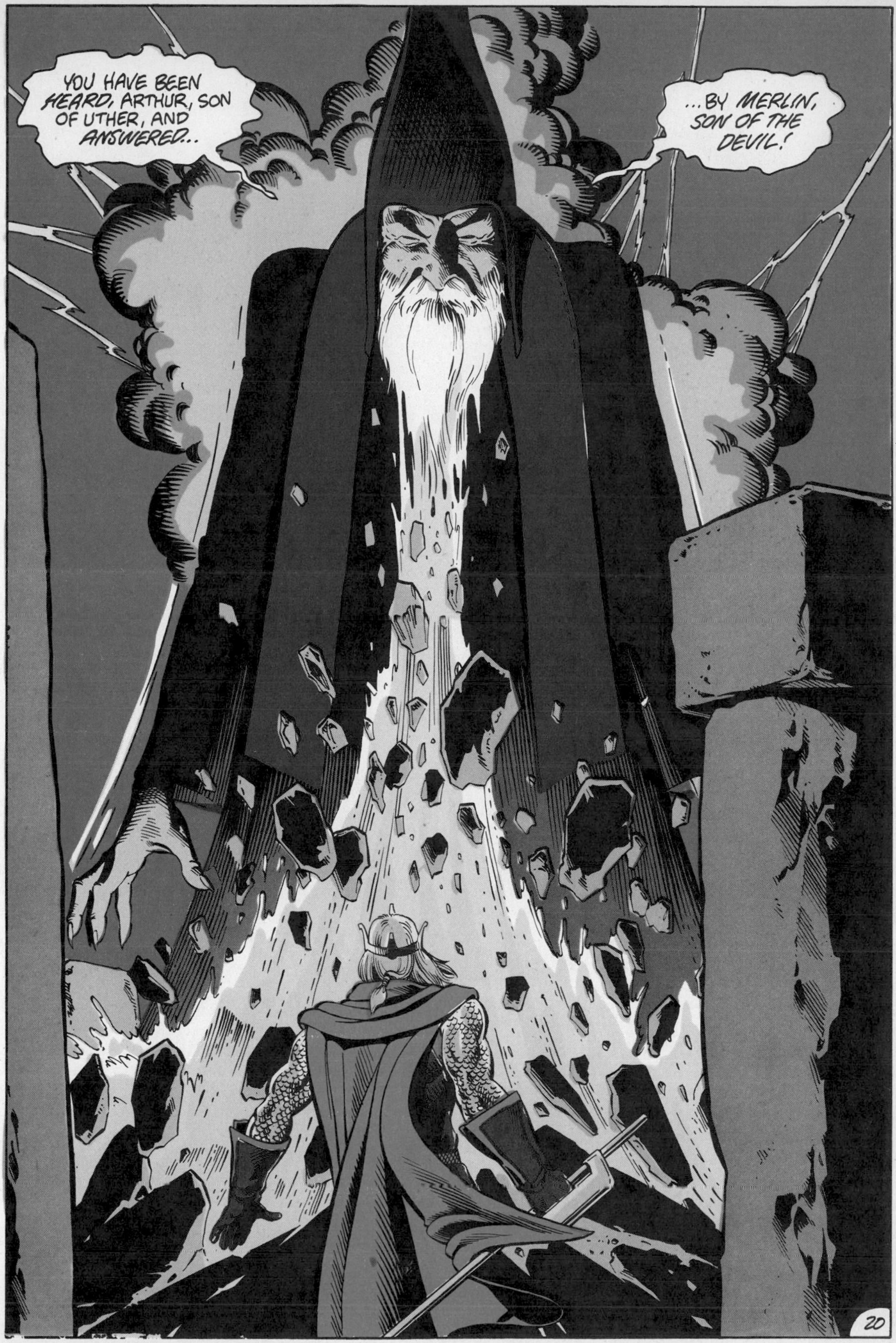
YOU HAVE BEEN HEARD, ARTHUR, SON OF UTHER, AND ANSWERED...
...BY MERLIN, SON OF THE DEVIL!

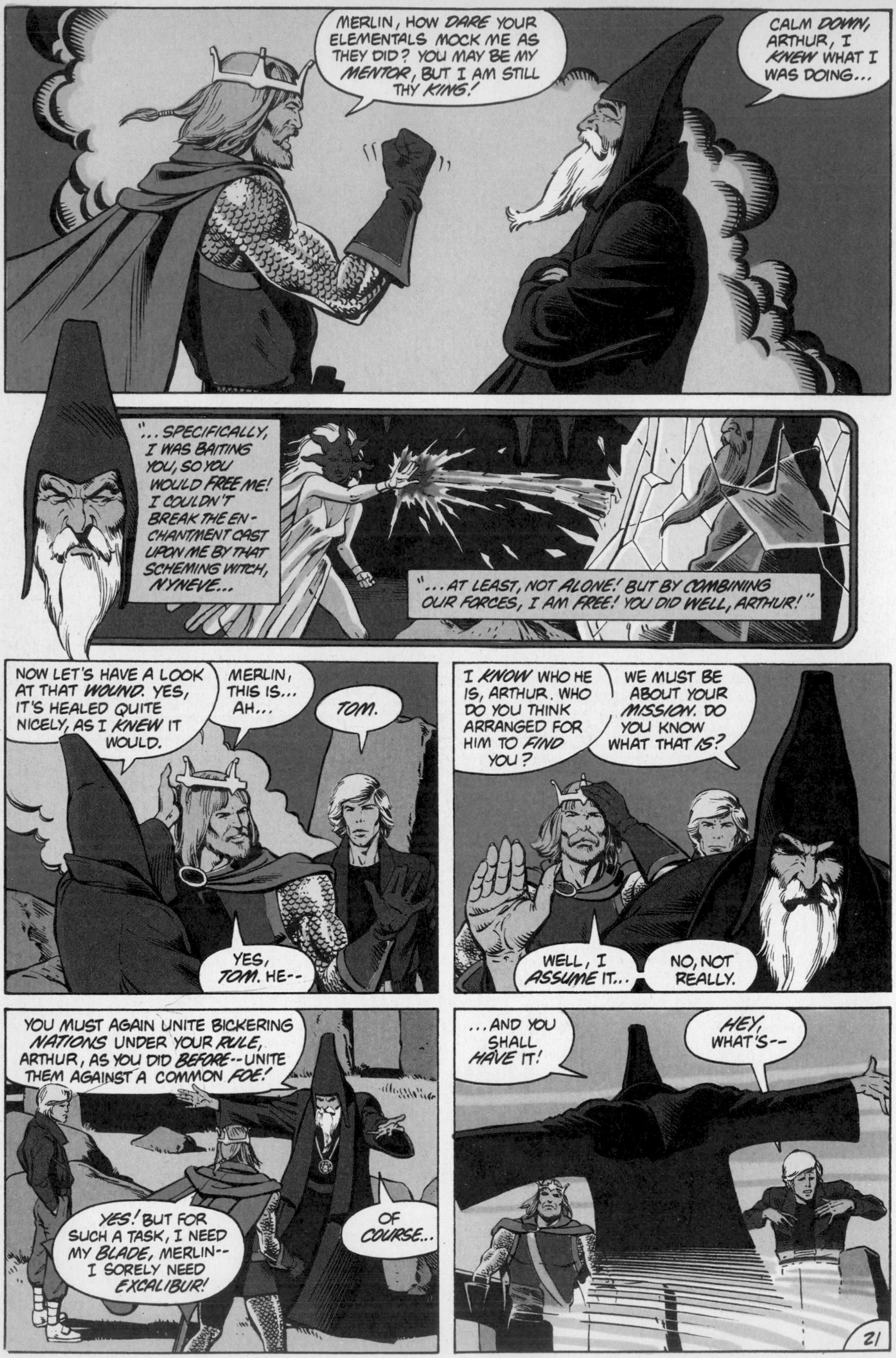
MERLIN, HOW DARE YOUR ELEMENTALS MOCK ME AS THEY DID? YOU MAY BE MY MENTOR, BUT I AM STILL THY KING!
CALM DOWN, ARTHUR, I KNEW WHAT I WAS DOING...
"...SPECIFICALLY, I WAS BAITING YOU, SO YOU WOULD FREE ME! I COULDN'T BREAK THE EN-CHANTMENT CAST UPON ME BY THAT SCHEMING WITCH, NYNEVE...
"...AT LEAST, NOT ALONE! BUT BY COMBINING OUR FORCES, I AM FREE! YOU DID WELL, ARTHUR!"
NOW LET'S HAVE A LOOK AT THAT WOUND. YES, IT'S HEALED QUITE NICELY, AS I KNEW IT WOULD.
MERLIN, THIS IS... AH...
TOM.
YES, TOM. HE--
I KNOW WHO HE IS, ARTHUR. WHO DO YOU THINK ARRANGED FOR HIM TO FIND YOU?
WE MUST BE ABOUT YOUR MISSION. DO YOU KNOW WHAT THAT IS?
WELL, I ASSUME IT...
NO, NOT REALLY.
YOU MUST AGAIN UNITE BICKERING NATIONS UNDER YOUR RULE, ARTHUR, AS YOU DID BEFORE--UNITE THEM AGAINST A COMMON FOE!
YES! BUT FOR SUCH A TASK, I NEED MY BLADE, MERLIN-- I SORELY NEED EXCALIBUR!
OF COURSE...
...AND YOU SHALL HAVE IT!
HEY, WHAT'S--

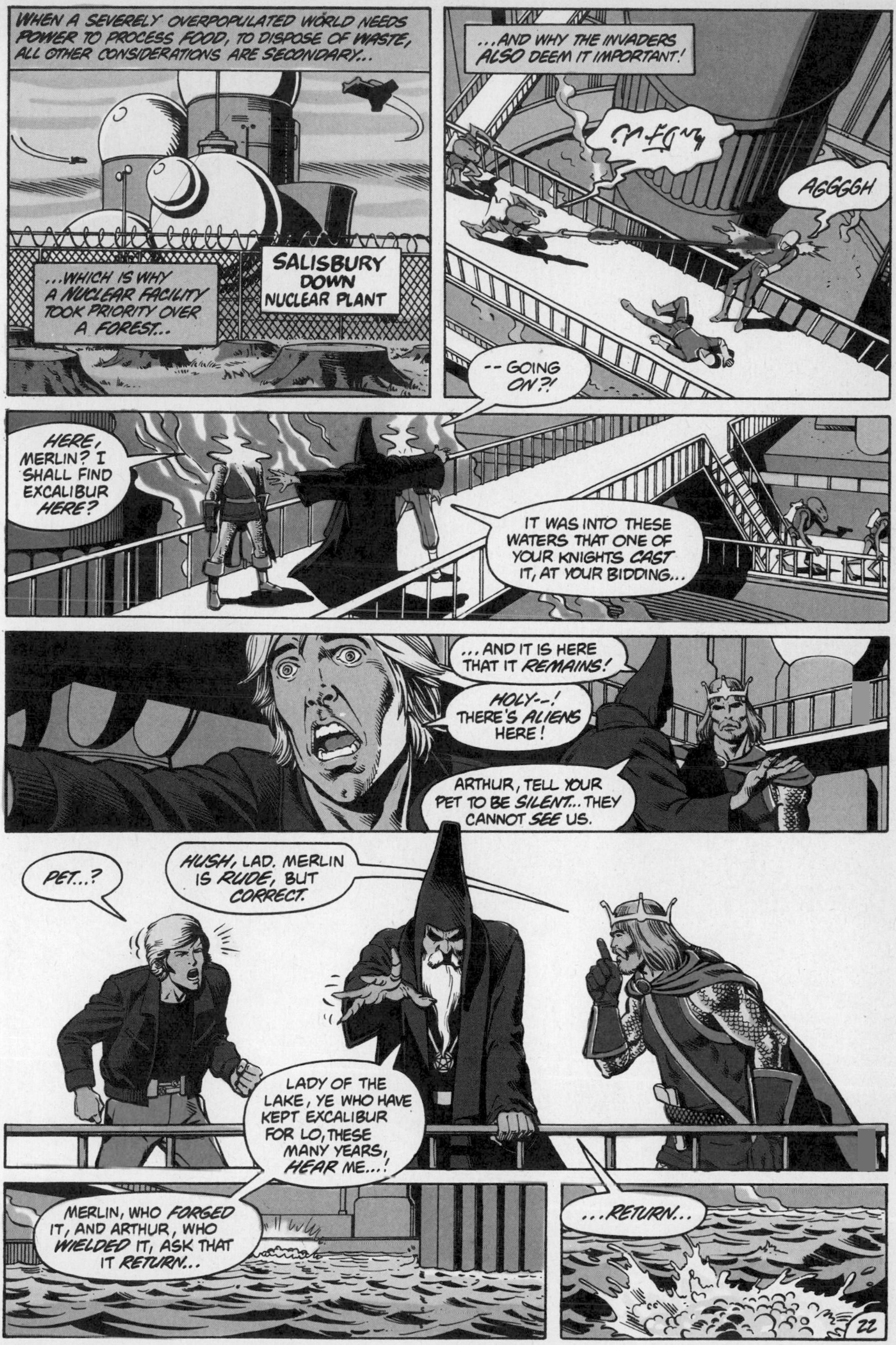

WHEN A SEVERELY OVERPOPULATED WORLD NEEDS POWER TO PROCESS FOOD, TO DISPOSE OF WASTE, ALL OTHER CONSIDERATIONS ARE SECONDARY...
...WHICH IS WHY A NUCLEAR FACILITY TOOK PRIORITY OVER A FOREST...
SALISBURY DOWN NUCLEAR PLANT
...AND WHY THE INVADERS ALSO DEEM IT IMPORTANT!
AGGGGH
--GOING ON?!
HERE, MERLIN? I SHALL FIND EXCALIBUR HERE?
IT WAS INTO THESE WATERS THAT ONE OF YOUR KNIGHTS CAST IT, AT YOUR BIDDING...
...AND IT IS HERE THAT IT REMAINS!
HOLY--! THERE'S ALIENS HERE!
ARTHUR, TELL YOUR PET TO BE SILENT... THEY CANNOT SEE US.
PET...?
HUSH, LAD. MERLIN IS RUDE, BUT CORRECT.
LADY OF THE LAKE, YE WHO HAVE KEPT EXCALIBUR FOR LO, THESE MANY YEARS, HEAR ME...!
MERLIN, WHO FORGED IT, AND ARTHUR, WHO WIELDED IT, ASK THAT IT RETURN...
...RETURN...

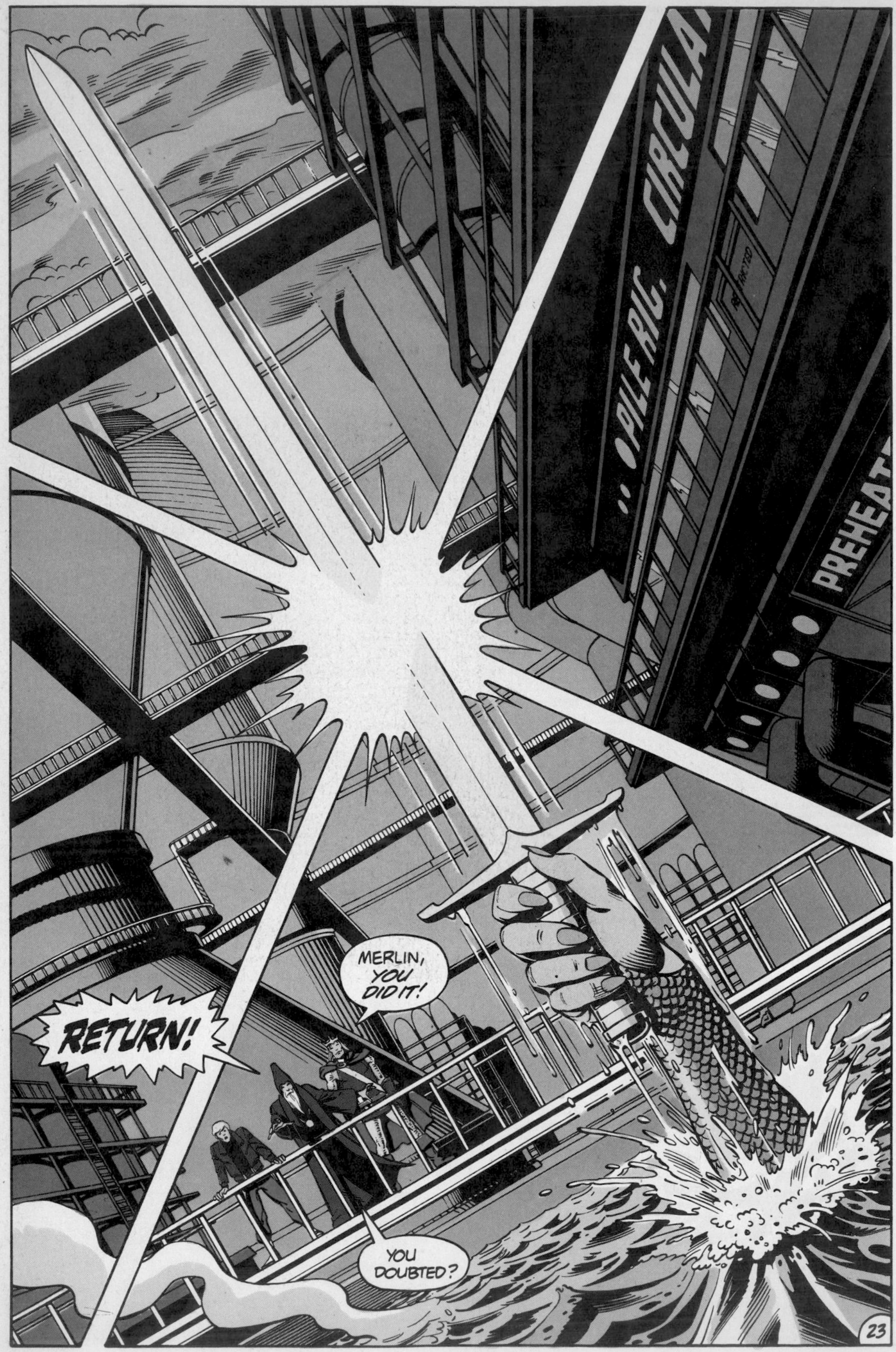
RETURN!
MERLIN, YOU DID IT!
YOU DOUBTED?

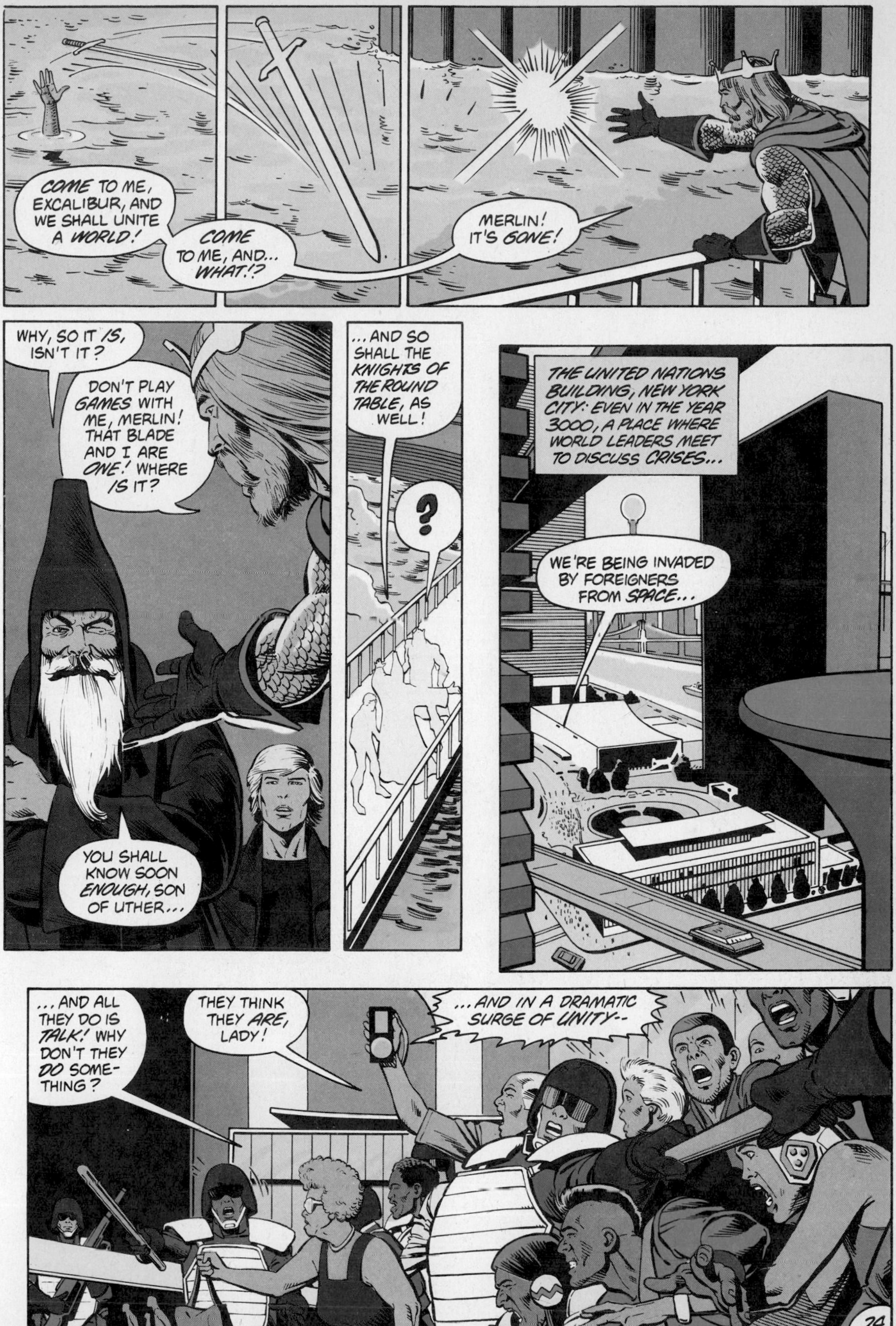
COME TO ME, EXCALIBUR, AND WE SHALL UNITE A WORLD!
COME TO ME, AND... WHAT!?
MERLIN! IT'S GONE!
WHY, SO IT IS, ISN'T IT?
DON'T PLAY GAMES WITH ME, MERLIN! THAT BLADE AND I ARE ONE! WHERE IS IT?
YOU SHALL KNOW SOON ENOUGH, SON OF UTHER...
...AND SO SHALL THE KNIGHTS OF THE ROUND TABLE, AS WELL!
?
THE UNITED NATIONS BUILDING, NEW YORK CITY: EVEN IN THE YEAR 3000, A PLACE WHERE WORLD LEADERS MEET TO DISCUSS CRISES...
WE'RE BEING INVADED BY FOREIGNERS FROM SPACE...
...AND ALL THEY DO IS TALK! WHY DON'T THEY DO SOMETHING?
THEY THINK THEY ARE, LADY!
...AND IN A DRAMATIC SURGE OF UNITY--
24

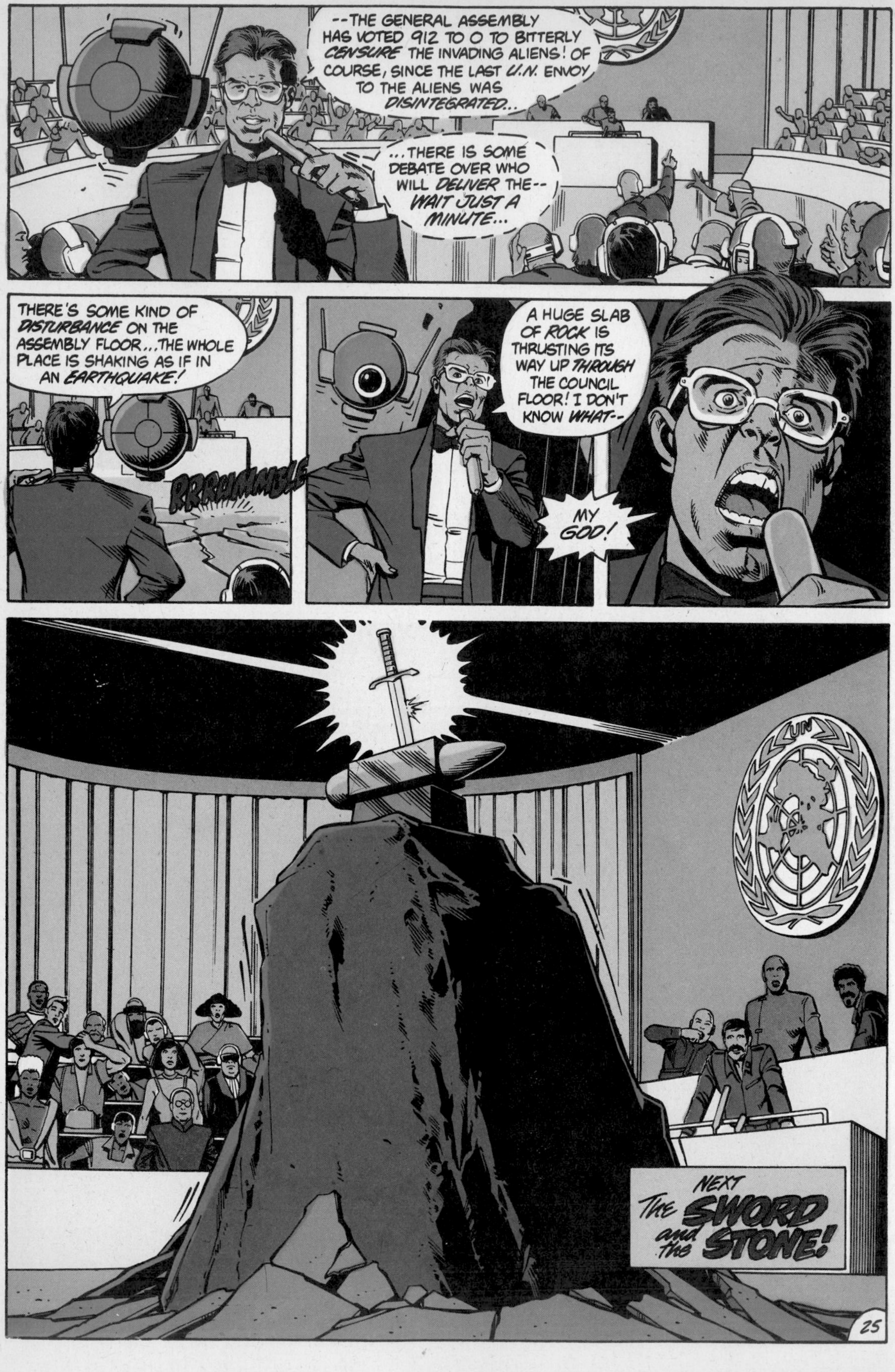
--THE GENERAL ASSEMBLY HAS VOTED 912 TO 0 TO BITTERLY CENSURE THE INVADING ALIENS! OF COURSE, SINCE THE LAST U.N. ENVOY TO THE ALIENS WAS DISINTEGRATED...
...THERE IS SOME DEBATE OVER WHO WILL DELIVER THE-- WAIT JUST A MINUTE...
THERE'S SOME KIND OF DISTURBANCE ON THE ASSEMBLY FLOOR...THE WHOLE PLACE IS SHAKING AS IF IN AN EARTHQUAKE!
RRRUMMBLE
A HUGE SLAB OF ROCK IS THRUSTING ITS WAY UP THROUGH THE COUNCIL FLOOR! I DON'T KNOW WHAT--
MY GOD!
UN
NEXT
The SWORD and the STONE!

chapter 2

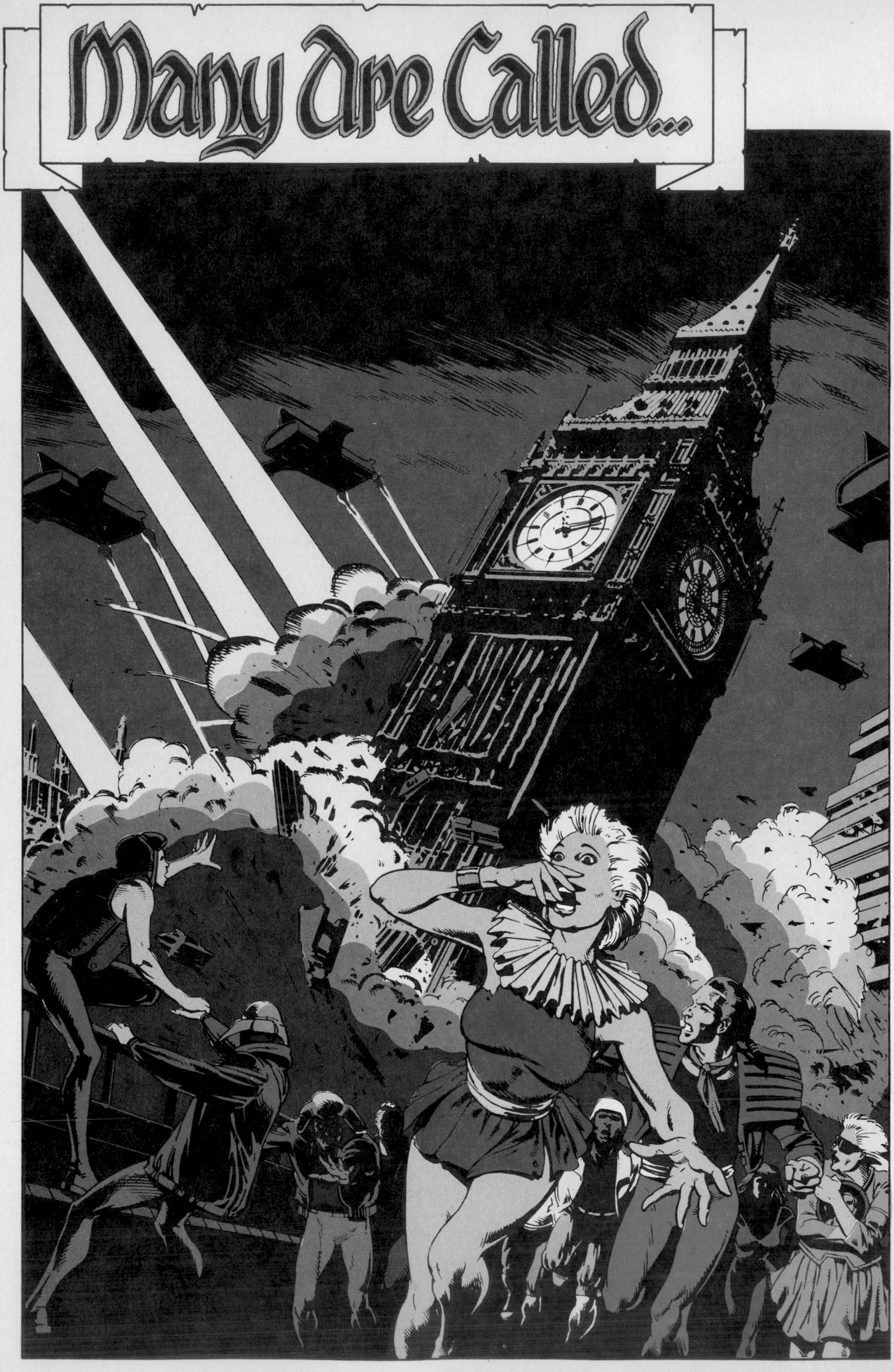
Many Are Called...

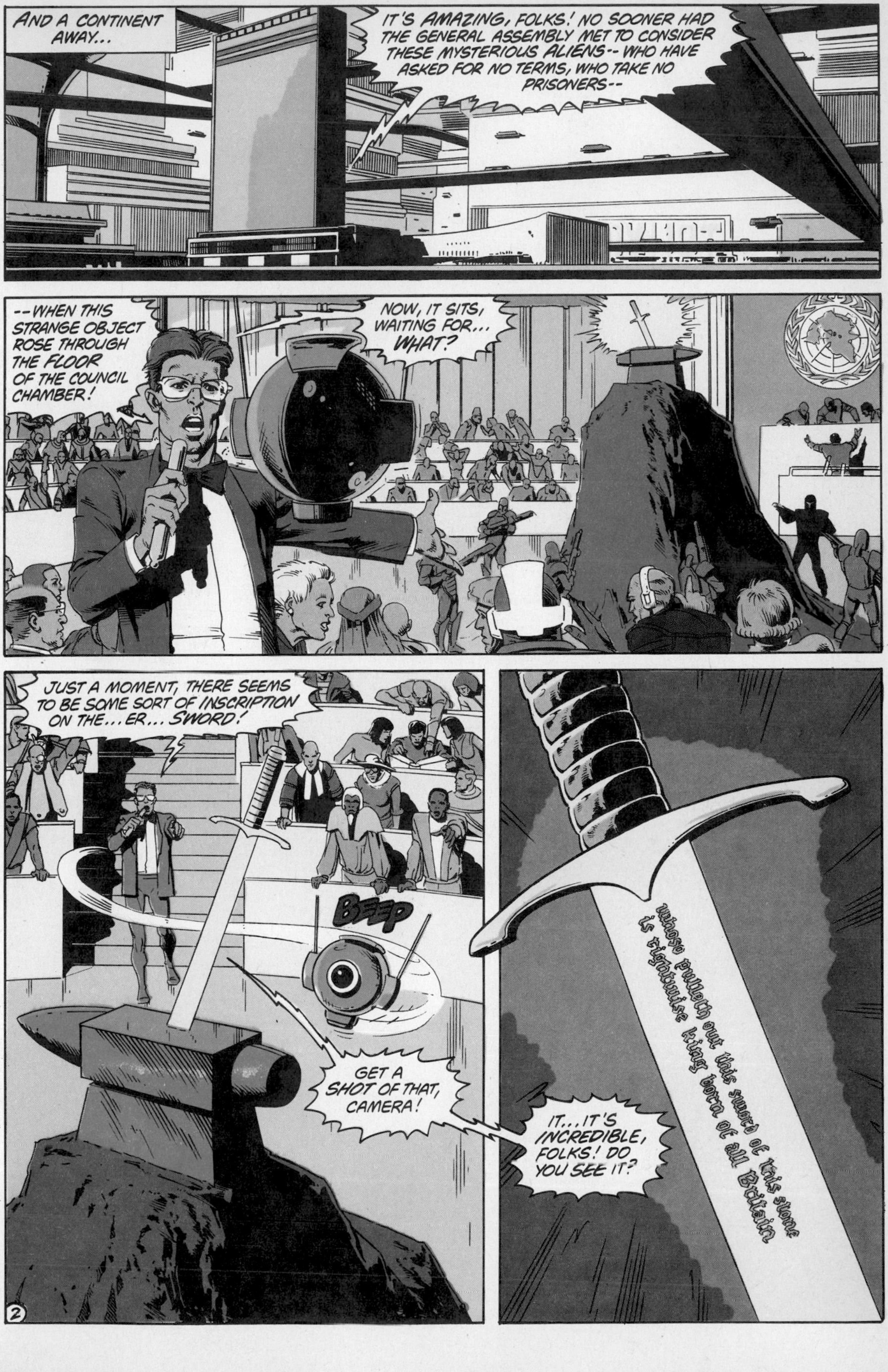
AND A CONTINENT AWAY...
IT'S AMAZING, FOLKS! NO SOONER HAD THE GENERAL ASSEMBLY MET TO CONSIDER THESE MYSTERIOUS ALIENS-- WHO HAVE ASKED FOR NO TERMS, WHO TAKE NO PRISONERS--
--WHEN THIS STRANGE OBJECT ROSE THROUGH THE FLOOR OF THE COUNCIL CHAMBER!
NOW, IT SITS, WAITING FOR... WHAT?
JUST A MOMENT, THERE SEEMS TO BE SOME SORT OF INSCRIPTION ON THE... ER... SWORD!
BEEP
GET A SHOT OF THAT, CAMERA!
IT... IT'S INCREDIBLE, FOLKS! DO YOU SEE IT?
Whoso pulleth out this sword of this stone
is rightwise king born of all Britain

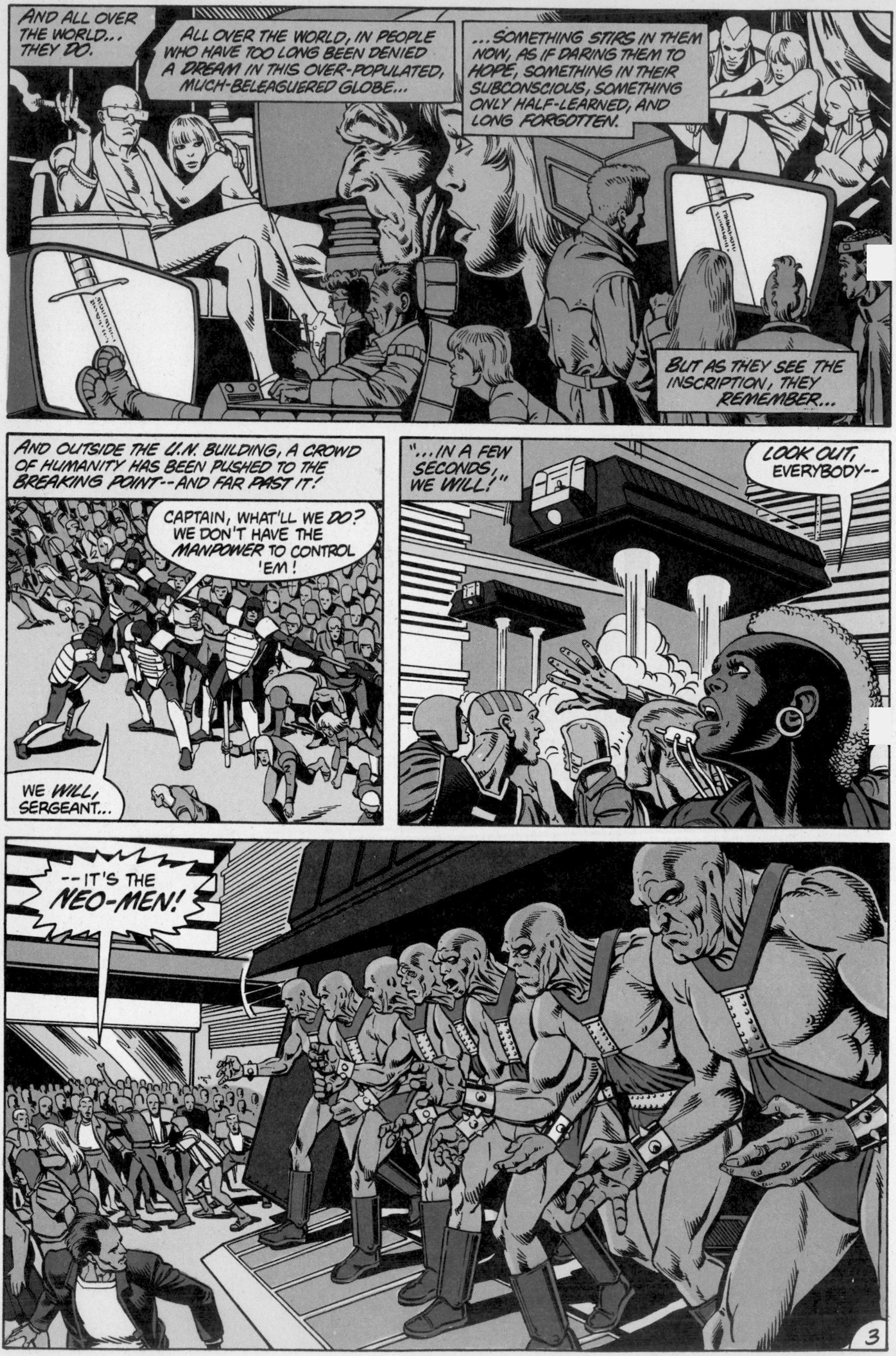

AND ALL OVER THE WORLD... THEY DO.
ALL OVER THE WORLD, IN PEOPLE WHO HAVE TOO LONG BEEN DENIED A DREAM IN THIS OVER-POPULATED, MUCH-BELEAGUERED GLOBE...
...SOMETHING STIRS IN THEM NOW, AS IF DARING THEM TO HOPE, SOMETHING IN THEIR SUBCONSCIOUS, SOMETHING ONLY HALF-LEARNED, AND LONG FORGOTTEN.
BUT AS THEY SEE THE INSCRIPTION, THEY REMEMBER...
AND OUTSIDE THE U.N. BUILDING, A CROWD OF HUMANITY HAS BEEN PUSHED TO THE BREAKING POINT--AND FAR PAST IT!
CAPTAIN, WHAT'LL WE DO? WE DON'T HAVE THE MANPOWER TO CONTROL 'EM!
WE WILL, SERGEANT...
"...IN A FEW SECONDS, WE WILL!"
LOOK OUT, EVERYBODY--
--IT'S THE NEO-MEN!

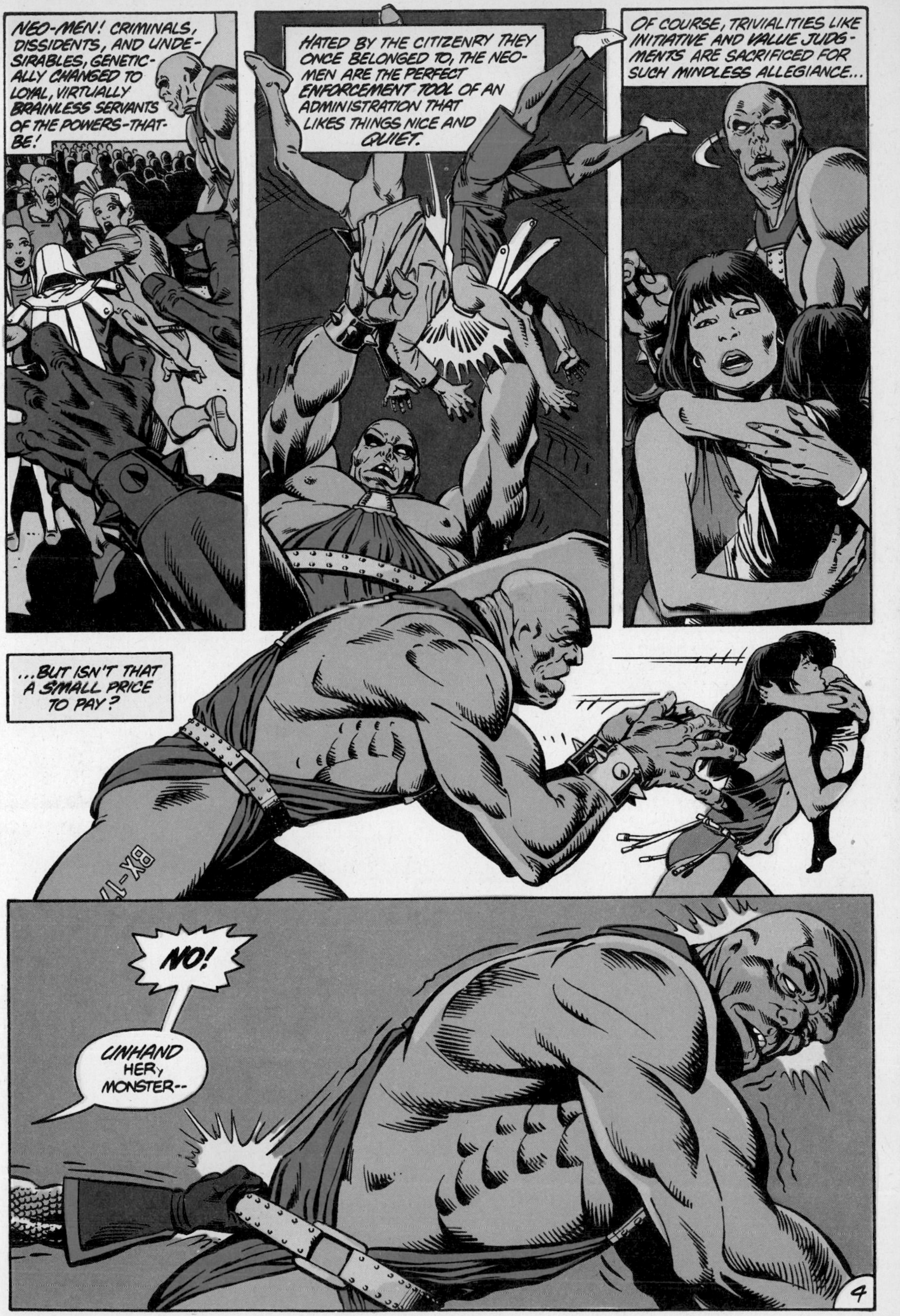
NEO-MEN! CRIMINALS, DISSIDENTS, AND UNDESIRABLES, GENETICALLY CHANGED TO LOYAL, VIRTUALLY BRAINLESS SERVANTS OF THE POWERS-THAT-BE!
HATED BY THE CITIZENRY THEY ONCE BELONGED TO, THE NEO-MEN ARE THE PERFECT ENFORCEMENT TOOL OF AN ADMINISTRATION THAT LIKES THINGS NICE AND QUIET.
OF COURSE, TRIVIALITIES LIKE INITIATIVE AND VALUE JUDGMENTS ARE SACRIFICED FOR SUCH MINDLESS ALLEGIANCE...
...BUT ISN'T THAT A SMALL PRICE TO PAY?
BX-17
NO!
UNHAND HER, MONSTER--

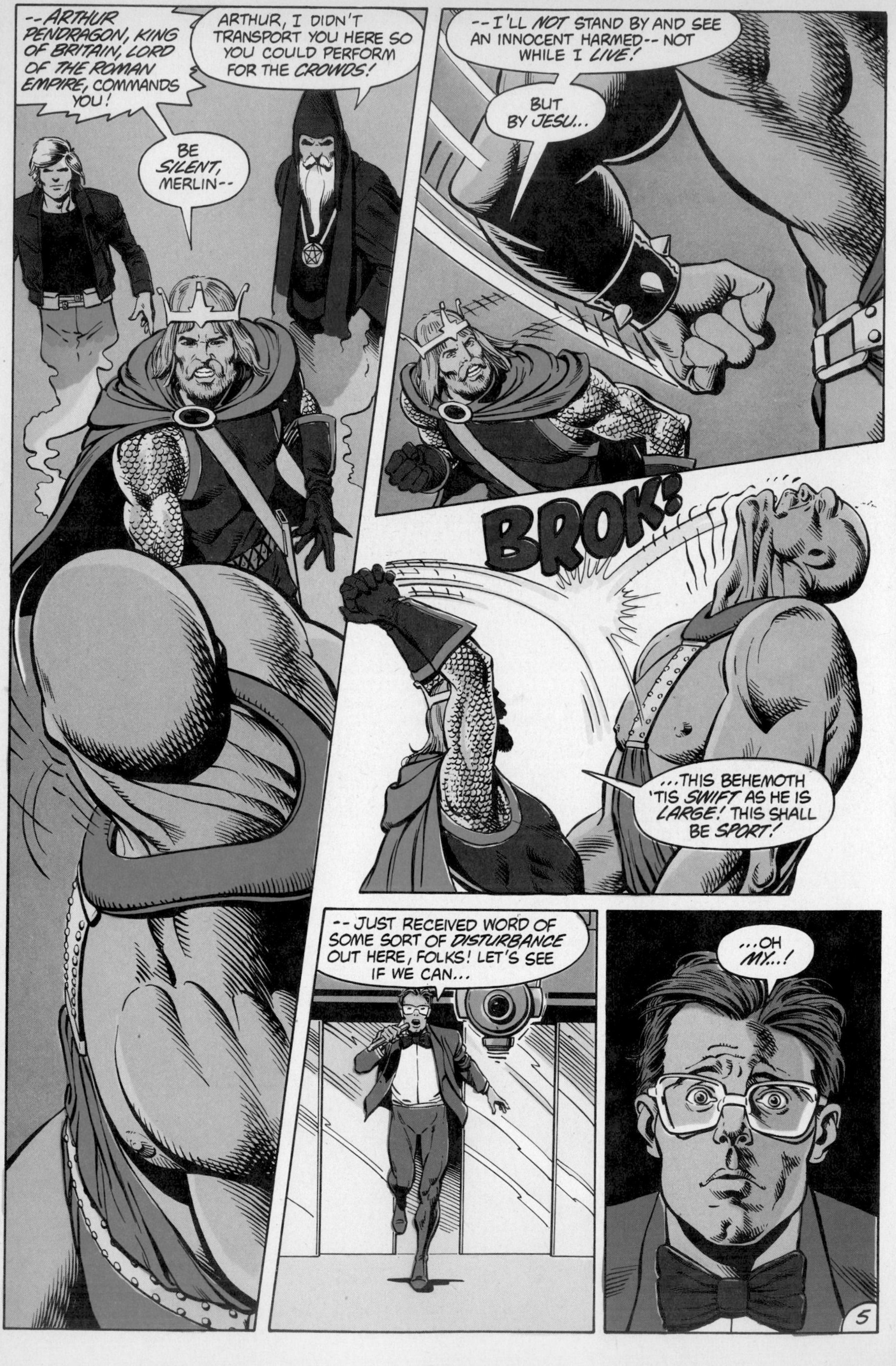
--ARTHUR PENDRAGON, KING OF BRITAIN, LORD OF THE ROMAN EMPIRE, COMMANDS YOU!
ARTHUR, I DIDN'T TRANSPORT YOU HERE SO YOU COULD PERFORM FOR THE CROWDS!
BE SILENT, MERLIN--
--I'LL NOT STAND BY AND SEE AN INNOCENT HARMED-- NOT WHILE I LIVE!
BUT BY JESU...
BROK!
...THIS BEHEMOTH 'TIS SWIFT AS HE IS LARGE! THIS SHALL BE SPORT!
--JUST RECEIVED WORD OF SOME SORT OF DISTURBANCE OUT HERE, FOLKS! LET'S SEE IF WE CAN...
...OH MY...!
5

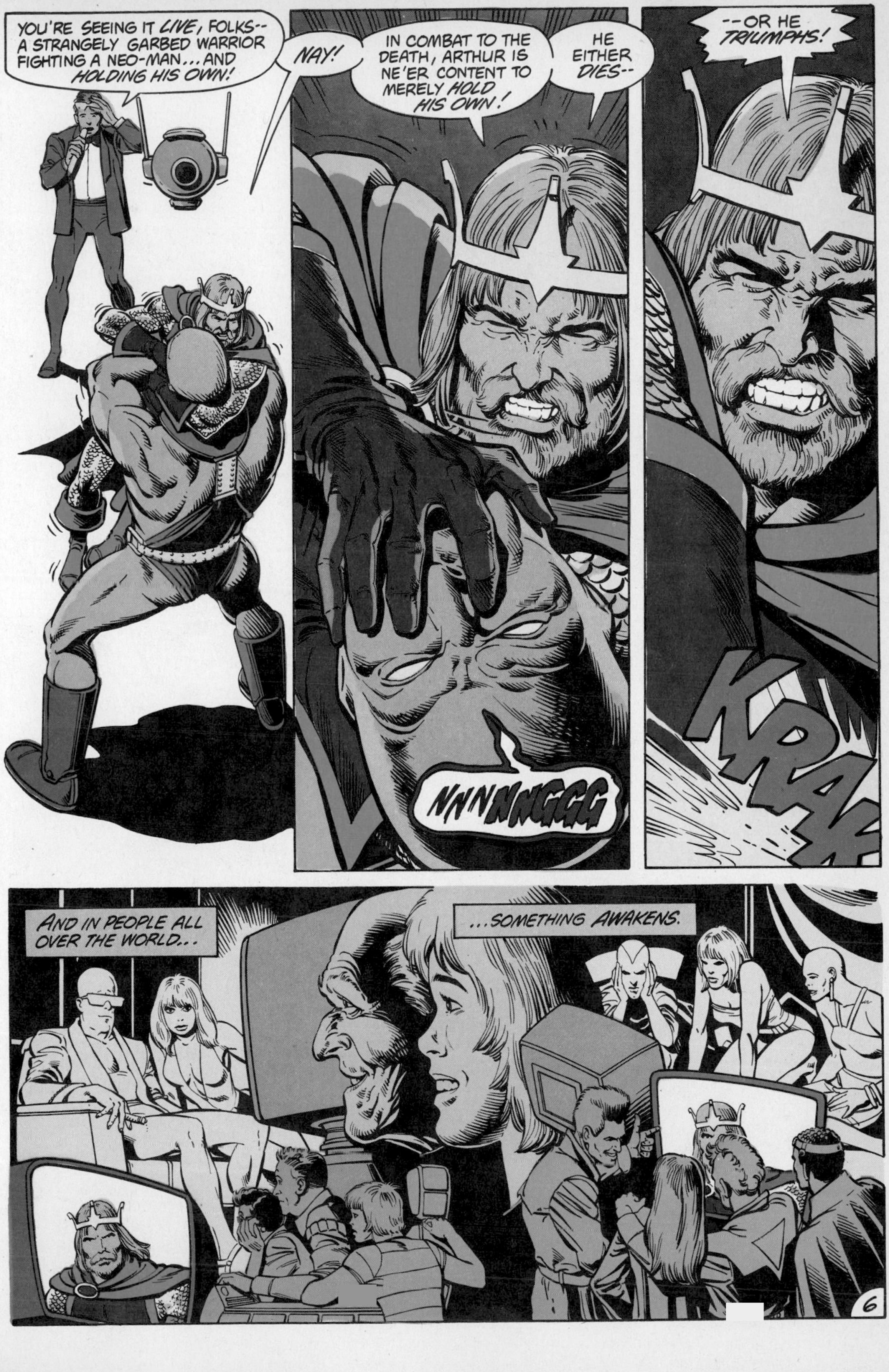

YOU'RE SEEING IT LIVE, FOLKS-- A STRANGELY GARBED WARRIOR FIGHTING A NEO-MAN... AND HOLDING HIS OWN!
NAY!
IN COMBAT TO THE DEATH, ARTHUR IS NE'ER CONTENT TO MERELY HOLD HIS OWN!
HE EITHER DIES--
--OR HE TRIUMPHS!
NNNNNGGG
KRAK
AND IN PEOPLE ALL OVER THE WORLD...
...SOMETHING AWAKENS.
6

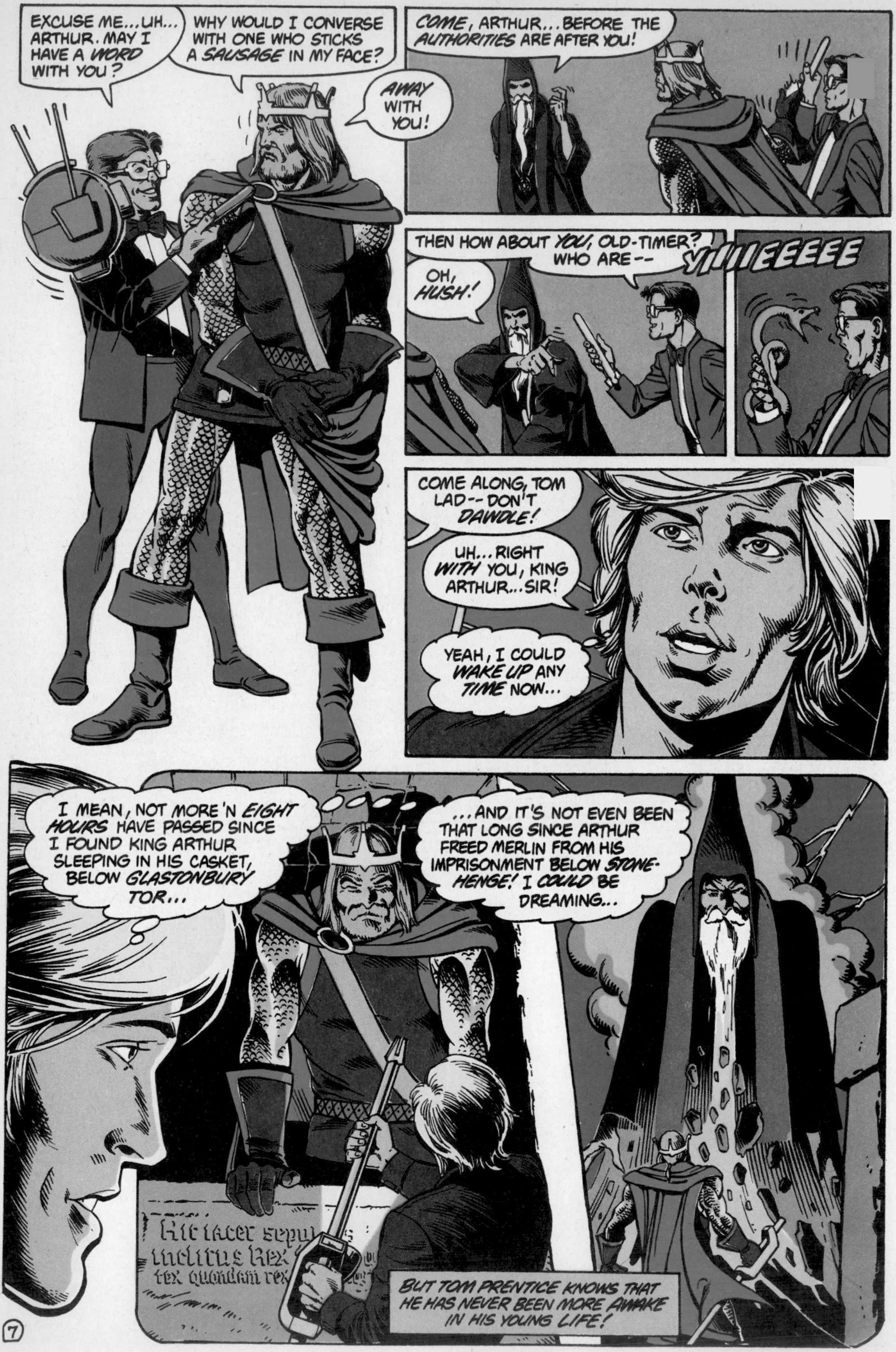
EXCUSE ME...UH... ARTHUR. MAY I HAVE A WORD WITH YOU?
WHY WOULD I CONVERSE WITH ONE WHO STICKS A SAUSAGE IN MY FACE?
AWAY WITH YOU!
COME, ARTHUR...BEFORE THE AUTHORITIES ARE AFTER YOU!
THEN HOW ABOUT YOU, OLD-TIMER? WHO ARE--
OH, HUSH!
YIIIIEEEEE
COME ALONG, TOM LAD--DON'T DAWDLE!
UH...RIGHT WITH YOU, KING ARTHUR...SIR!
YEAH, I COULD WAKE UP ANY TIME NOW...
I MEAN, NOT MORE'N EIGHT HOURS HAVE PASSED SINCE I FOUND KING ARTHUR SLEEPING IN HIS CASKET, BELOW GLASTONBURY TOR...
...AND IT'S NOT EVEN BEEN THAT LONG SINCE ARTHUR FREED MERLIN FROM HIS IMPRISONMENT BELOW STONE-HENGE! I COULD BE DREAMING...
Hic iacet sepu
inclitus Rex
rex quondam rex
BUT TOM PRENTICE KNOWS THAT HE HAS NEVER BEEN MORE AWAKE IN HIS YOUNG LIFE!

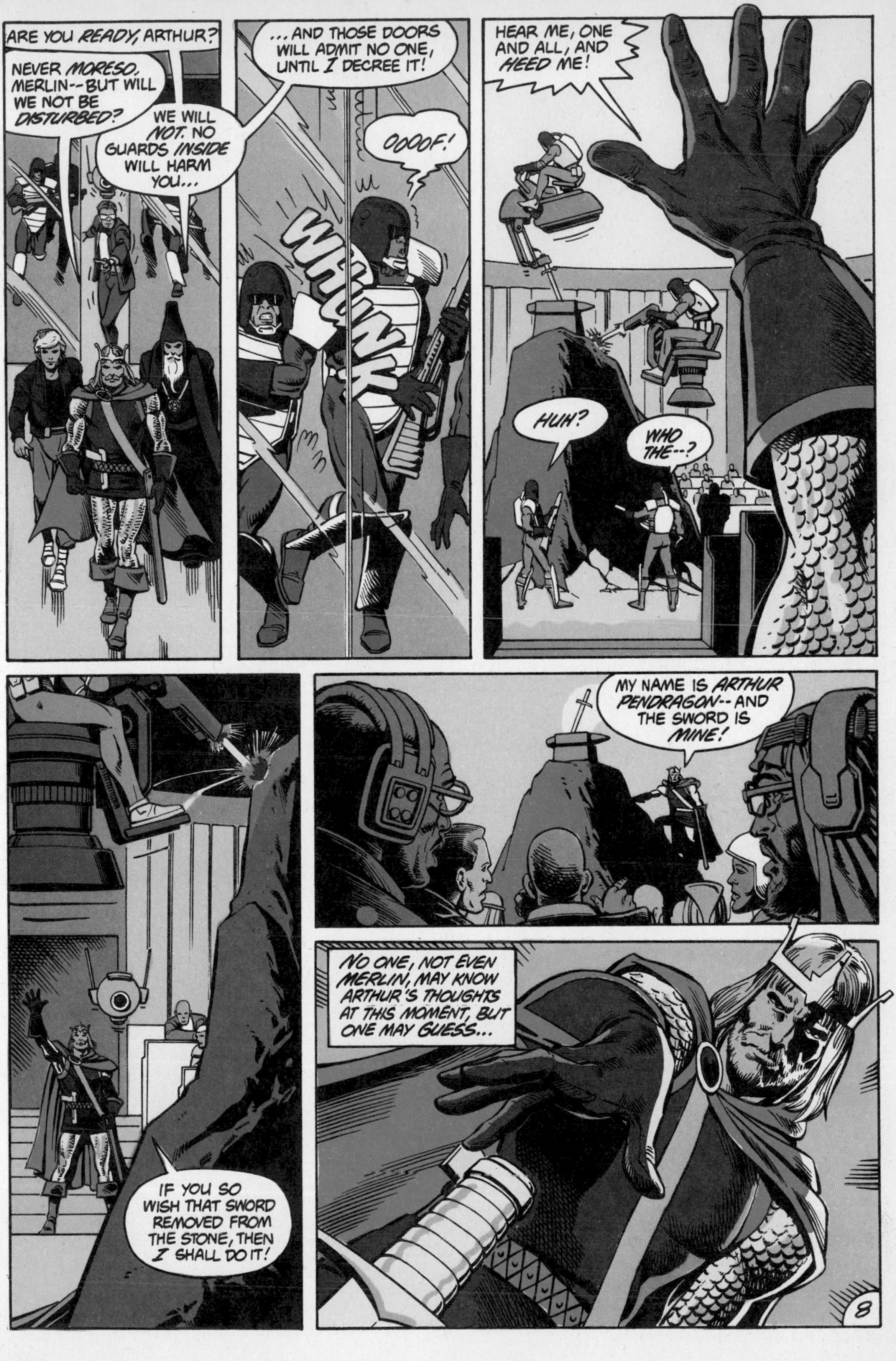
ARE YOU *READY*, ARTHUR?
NEVER *MORESO*, MERLIN--BUT WILL WE NOT BE *DISTURBED*?
WE WILL *NOT*. NO GUARDS *INSIDE* WILL HARM YOU...
...AND THOSE DOORS WILL ADMIT NO ONE, UNTIL *I* DECREE IT!
OOOOF!
WHUNK
HEAR ME, ONE AND ALL, AND *HEED* ME!
HUH?
WHO THE--?
IF YOU SO WISH THAT SWORD REMOVED FROM THE STONE, THEN *I* SHALL DO IT!
MY NAME IS *ARTHUR PENDRAGON*--AND THE SWORD IS *MINE!*
NO ONE, NOT EVEN MERLIN, MAY KNOW ARTHUR'S THOUGHTS AT THIS MOMENT, BUT ONE MAY GUESS...

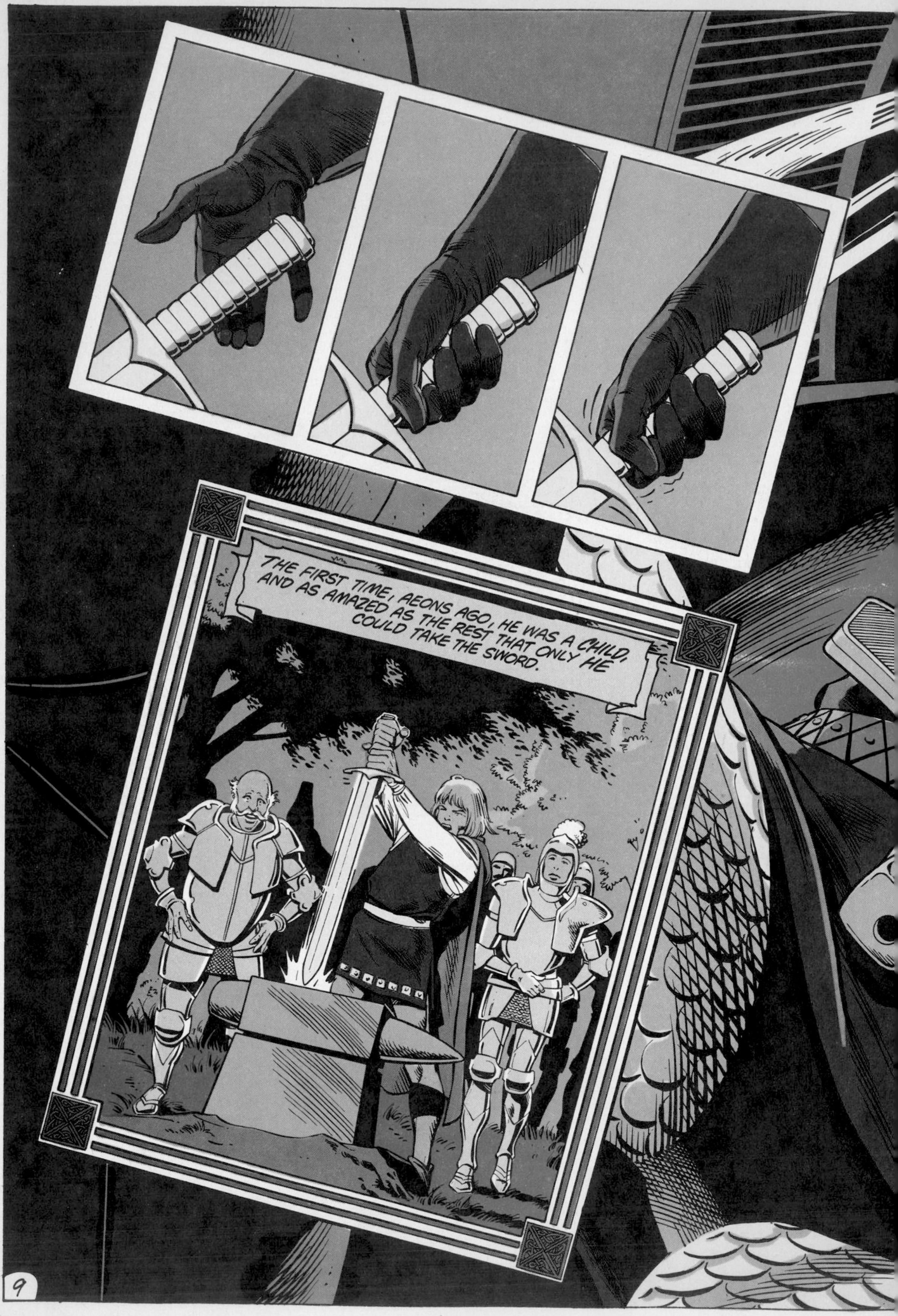
THE FIRST TIME, AEONS AGO, HE WAS A CHILD, AND AS AMAZED AS THE REST THAT ONLY HE COULD TAKE THE SWORD.

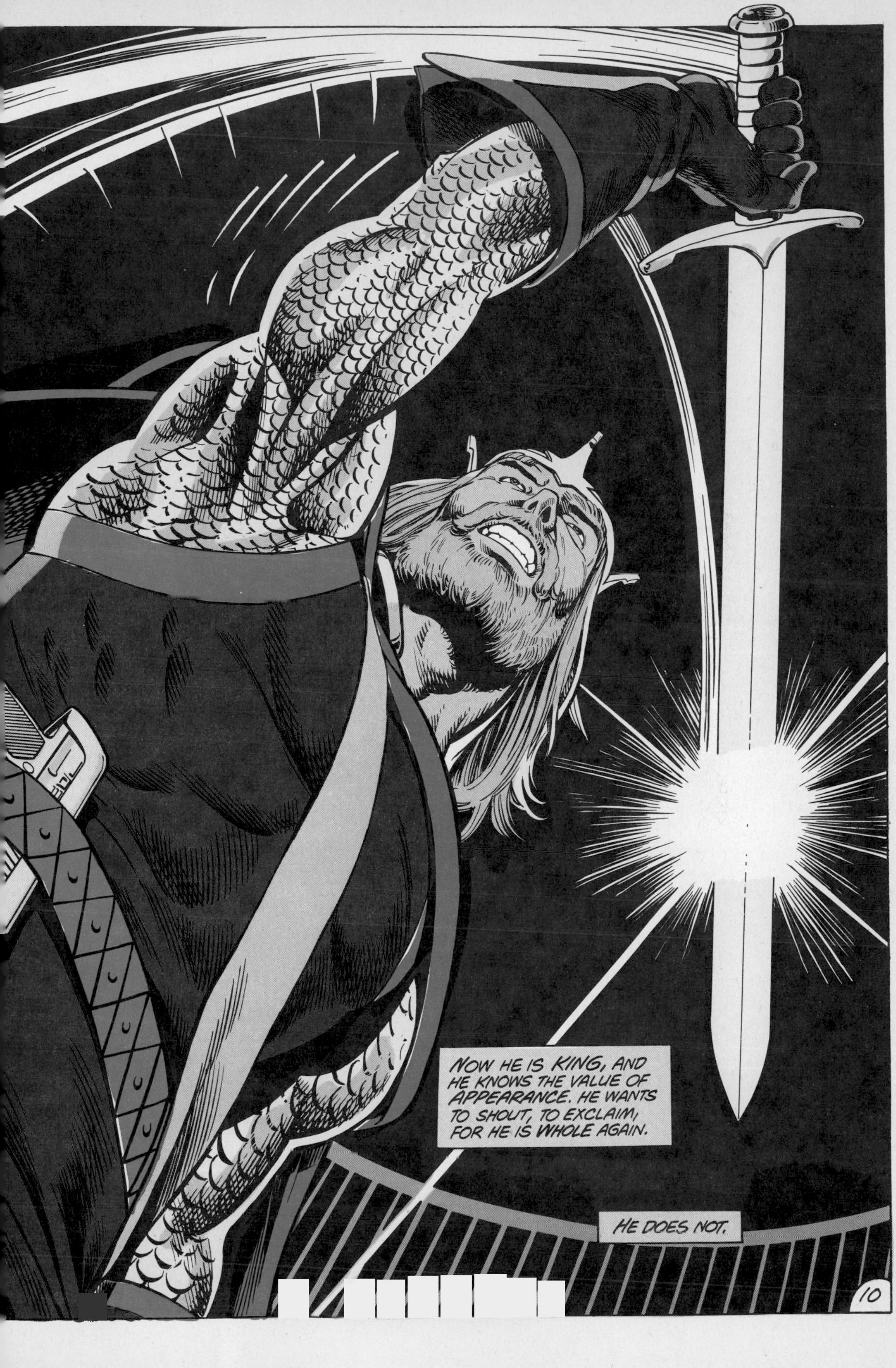
NOW HE IS KING, AND HE KNOWS THE VALUE OF APPEARANCE. HE WANTS TO SHOUT, TO EXCLAIM, FOR HE IS WHOLE AGAIN.
HE DOES NOT.

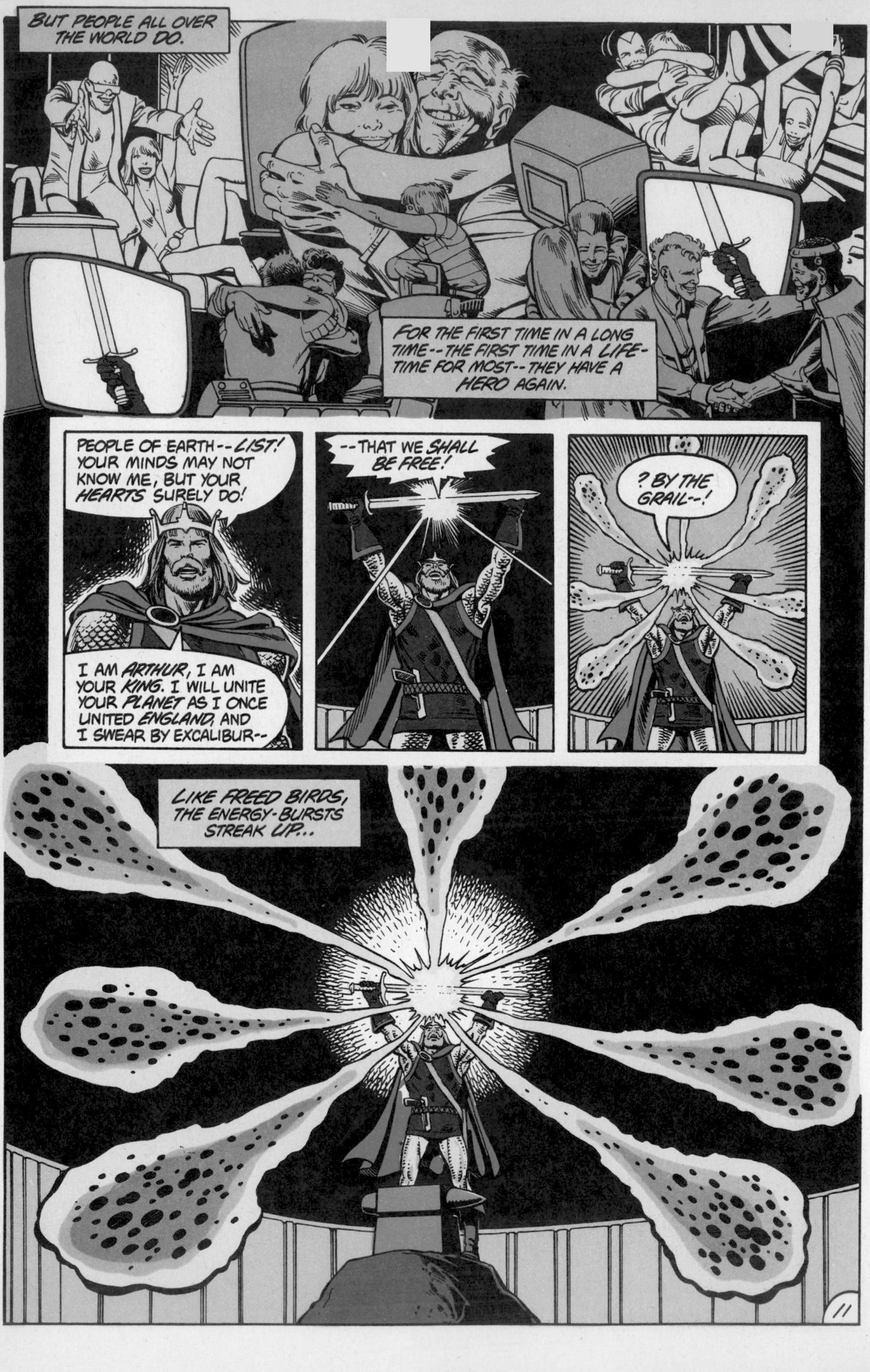
BUT PEOPLE ALL OVER THE WORLD DO.
FOR THE FIRST TIME IN A LONG TIME--THE FIRST TIME IN A LIFE-TIME FOR MOST--THEY HAVE A HERO AGAIN.
PEOPLE OF EARTH--LIST! YOUR MINDS MAY NOT KNOW ME, BUT YOUR HEARTS SURELY DO!
I AM ARTHUR, I AM YOUR KING. I WILL UNITE YOUR PLANET AS I ONCE UNITED ENGLAND, AND I SWEAR BY EXCALIBUR--
--THAT WE SHALL BE FREE!
? BY THE GRAIL--!
LIKE FREED BIRDS, THE ENERGY-BURSTS STREAK UP...
11

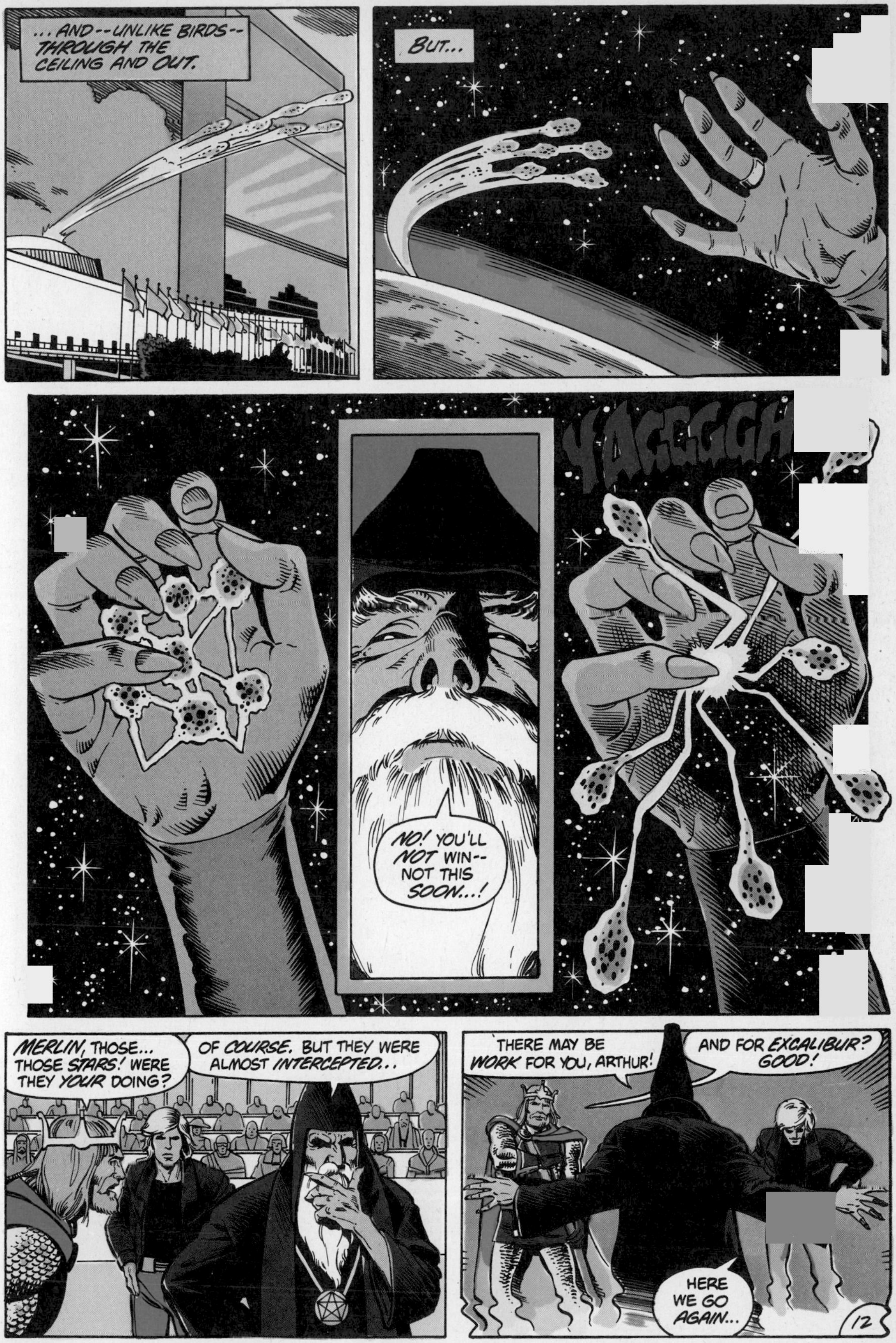
...AND--UNLIKE BIRDS--THROUGH THE CEILING AND OUT.
BUT...
YAGGGGH
NO! YOU'LL NOT WIN--NOT THIS SOON...!
MERLIN, THOSE... THOSE STARS! WERE THEY YOUR DOING?
OF COURSE. BUT THEY WERE ALMOST INTERCEPTED...
THERE MAY BE WORK FOR YOU, ARTHUR!
AND FOR EXCALIBUR? GOOD!
HERE WE GO AGAIN...
12

UNITED EARTH DEFENSE
SUPREME HEADQUARTERS

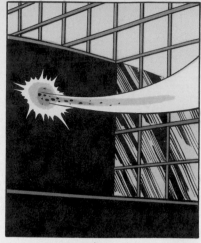

GOOD EVENING, COMMANDER ACTON. WILL YOU BE *NEEDING* ANYTHING, MA'AM?

NO...NO, I *WON'T*, SERGEANT, THANK YOU.

VERY GOOD, MA'AM.

NOT UNLESS YOU KNOW OF A WAY TO REPEL THE ALIEN INVADERS, SERGEANT...*THAT* WE NEED RIGHT *NOW.*
;SIGH;

COMMANDER JOAN ACTON ORDERS HER MIND TO SLEEP, AND SHE MIGHT *SUCCEED*...

...BUT...

;GASP;

SUDDENLY, SLEEP IS *BANISHED.* FOR THE FIRST TIME IN HER CURRENT LIFE, JOAN ACTON REMEMBERS...

13

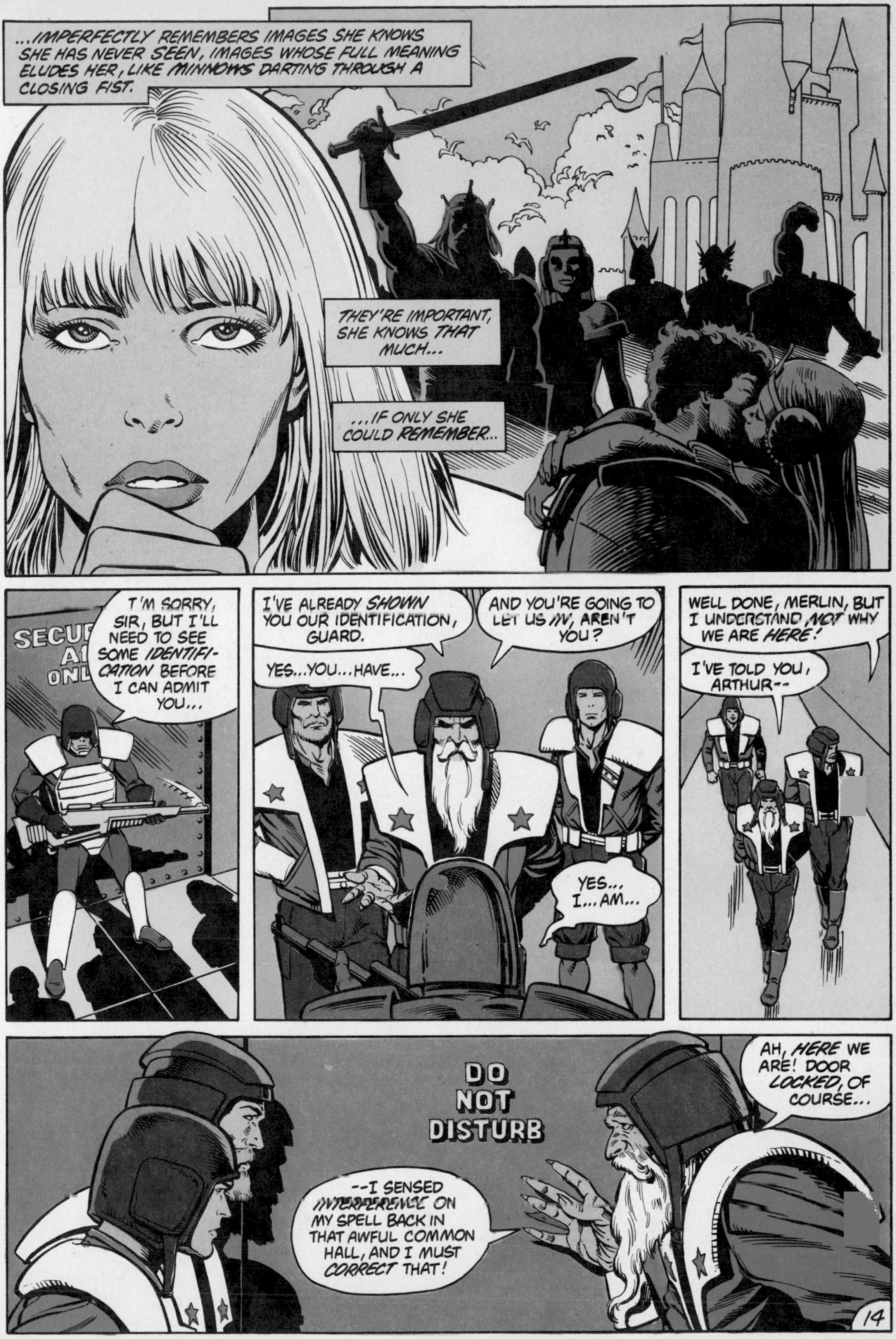
...IMPERFECTLY REMEMBERS IMAGES SHE KNOWS SHE HAS NEVER SEEN, IMAGES WHOSE FULL MEANING ELUDES HER, LIKE MINNOWS DARTING THROUGH A CLOSING FIST.
THEY'RE IMPORTANT, SHE KNOWS THAT MUCH...
...IF ONLY SHE COULD REMEMBER...
I'M SORRY, SIR, BUT I'LL NEED TO SEE SOME IDENTIFICATION BEFORE I CAN ADMIT YOU...
I'VE ALREADY SHOWN YOU OUR IDENTIFICATION, GUARD.
YES...YOU...HAVE...
AND YOU'RE GOING TO LET US IN, AREN'T YOU?
YES... I...AM...
WELL DONE, MERLIN, BUT I UNDERSTAND NOT WHY WE ARE HERE!
I'VE TOLD YOU, ARTHUR--
DO NOT DISTURB
AH, HERE WE ARE! DOOR LOCKED, OF COURSE...
--I SENSED INTERFERENCE ON MY SPELL BACK IN THAT AWFUL COMMON HALL, AND I MUST CORRECT THAT!

...BUT THAT'S LESS TROUBLE THAN THESE BOTHERSOME *COSTUMES!* THERE.

WHO ARE--? NO, DON'T *BOTHER* ME WITH DETAILS...

PRAISE GOD, IT CANNOT BE... BUT IT *IS*...!

GUINEVERE! YOU *TOO* HAVE SURVIVED! FAITH, THIS IS--

ALL RIGHT, THAT DOES IT, I'M CALLING *SECURITY!*

NOT WHEN I'VE PARALYZED YOUR *VOCAL CORDS,* COMMANDER ACTON!

MERLIN, DID SHE SLEEP THESE MANY YEARS, AS *I?* WHY DOES SHE NOT *RECOGNIZE* ME?

...JUST GET OUT OF HERE-- *NOW!*

SHE DID NOT "SLEEP" ALL THIS TIME, *ARTHUR,* SHE IS A *REINCARNATE*-- HER *SOUL* HAS BEEN REBORN IN ANOTHER *BODY!*

AYE. LIKE *RESOLING* A PAIR OF *BOOTS?*

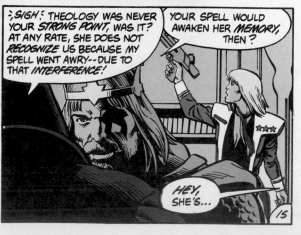

∴SIGH∴ THEOLOGY WAS NEVER YOUR *STRONG POINT,* WAS IT? AT ANY RATE, SHE DOES NOT *RECOGNIZE* US BECAUSE MY SPELL WENT AWRY--DUE TO THAT *INTERFERENCE!*

YOUR SPELL WOULD AWAKEN HER *MEMORY,* THEN?

HEY, SHE'S...

15

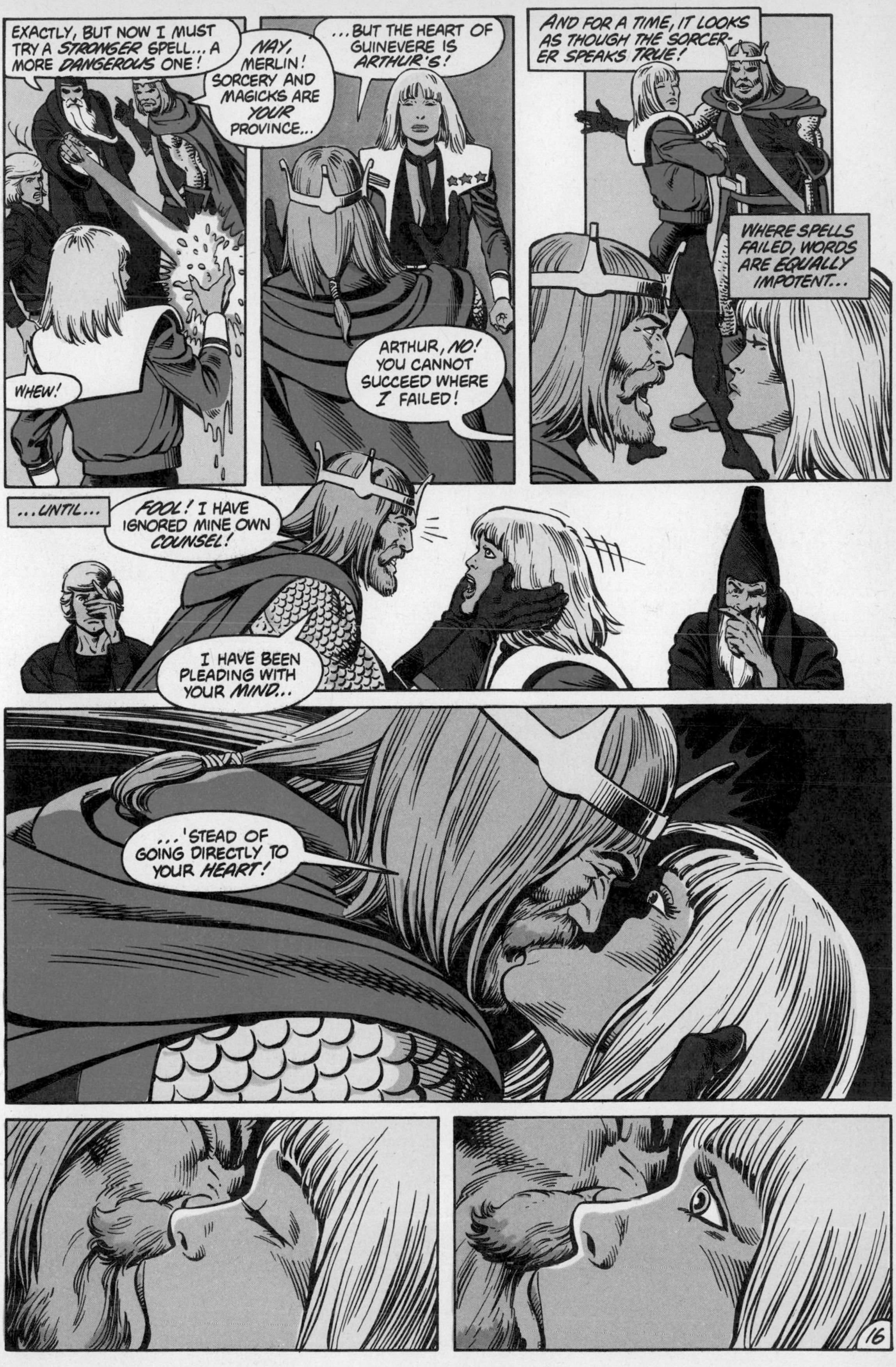
EXACTLY, BUT NOW I MUST TRY A STRONGER SPELL... A MORE DANGEROUS ONE!
NAY, MERLIN! SORCERY AND MAGICKS ARE YOUR PROVINCE...
...BUT THE HEART OF GUINEVERE IS ARTHUR'S!
WHEW!
ARTHUR, NO! YOU CANNOT SUCCEED WHERE I FAILED!
AND FOR A TIME, IT LOOKS AS THOUGH THE SORCERER SPEAKS TRUE!
WHERE SPELLS FAILED, WORDS ARE EQUALLY IMPOTENT...
...UNTIL...
FOOL! I HAVE IGNORED MINE OWN COUNSEL!
I HAVE BEEN PLEADING WITH YOUR MIND...
...'STEAD OF GOING DIRECTLY TO YOUR HEART!
16

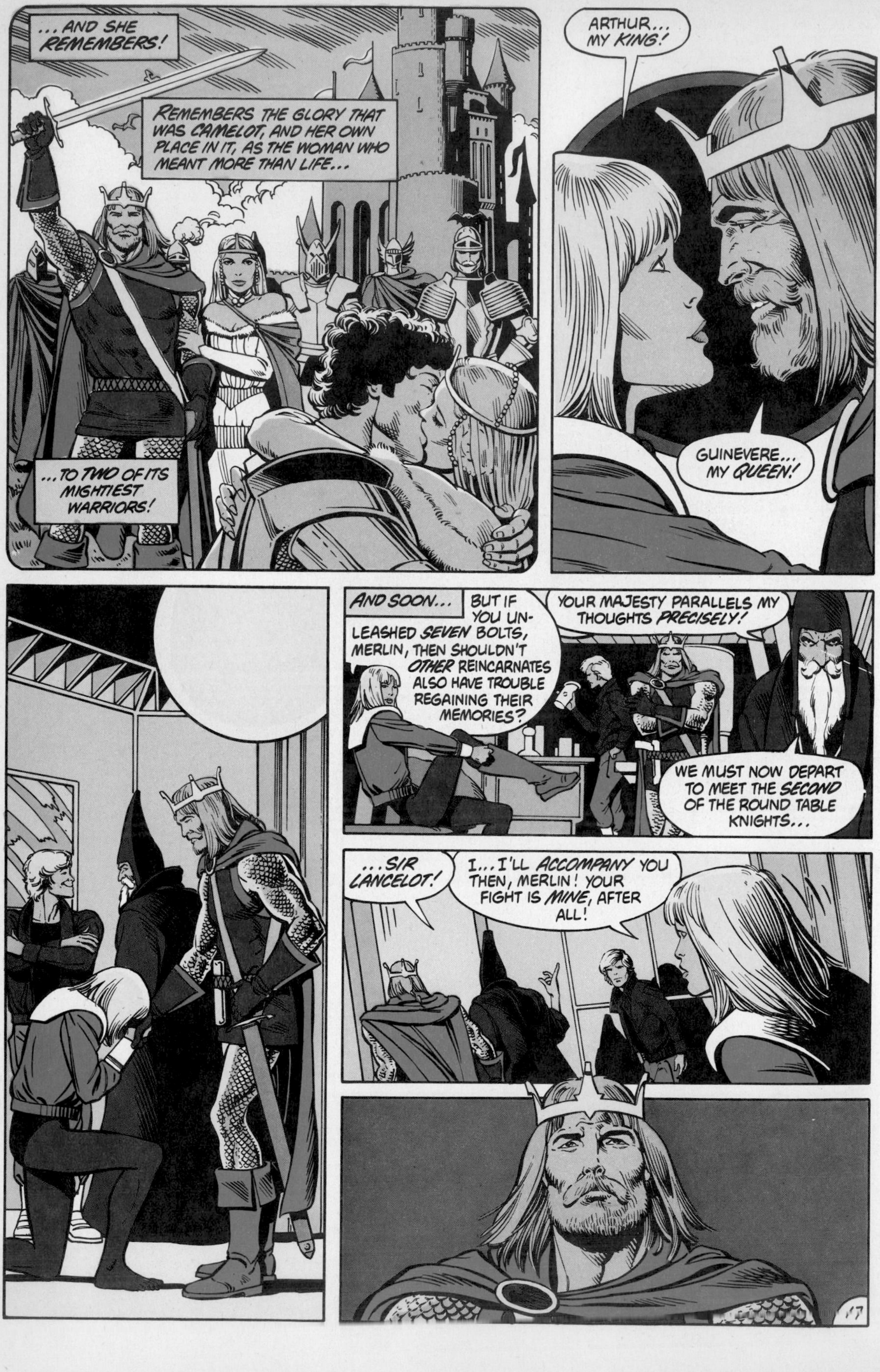
...AND SHE REMEMBERS!
REMEMBERS THE GLORY THAT WAS CAMELOT, AND HER OWN PLACE IN IT, AS THE WOMAN WHO MEANT MORE THAN LIFE...
...TO TWO OF ITS MIGHTIEST WARRIORS!
ARTHUR... MY KING!
GUINEVERE... MY QUEEN!
AND SOON...
BUT IF YOU UNLEASHED SEVEN BOLTS, MERLIN, THEN SHOULDN'T OTHER REINCARNATES ALSO HAVE TROUBLE REGAINING THEIR MEMORIES?
YOUR MAJESTY PARALLELS MY THOUGHTS PRECISELY!
WE MUST NOW DEPART TO MEET THE SECOND OF THE ROUND TABLE KNIGHTS...
...SIR LANCELOT!
I... I'LL ACCOMPANY YOU THEN, MERLIN! YOUR FIGHT IS MINE, AFTER ALL!
17

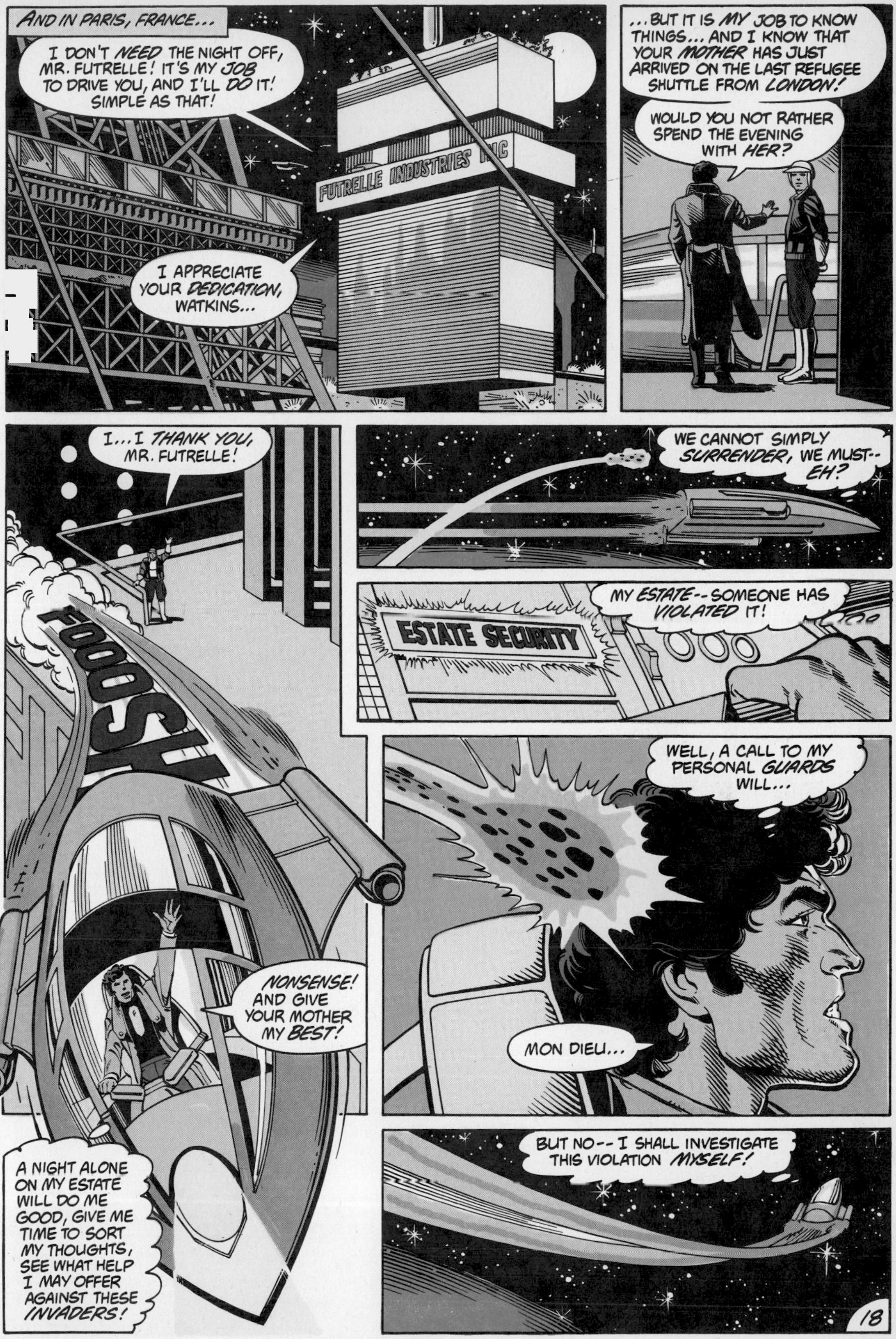
AND IN PARIS, FRANCE...
I DON'T NEED THE NIGHT OFF, MR. FUTRELLE! IT'S MY JOB TO DRIVE YOU, AND I'LL DO IT! SIMPLE AS THAT!
FUTRELLE INDUSTRIES INC
I APPRECIATE YOUR DEDICATION, WATKINS...
...BUT IT IS MY JOB TO KNOW THINGS... AND I KNOW THAT YOUR MOTHER HAS JUST ARRIVED ON THE LAST REFUGEE SHUTTLE FROM LONDON!
WOULD YOU NOT RATHER SPEND THE EVENING WITH HER?
I...I THANK YOU, MR. FUTRELLE!
FOOOSH
NONSENSE! AND GIVE YOUR MOTHER MY BEST!
A NIGHT ALONE ON MY ESTATE WILL DO ME GOOD, GIVE ME TIME TO SORT MY THOUGHTS, SEE WHAT HELP I MAY OFFER AGAINST THESE INVADERS!
WE CANNOT SIMPLY SURRENDER, WE MUST-- EH?
ESTATE SECURITY
MY ESTATE--SOMEONE HAS VIOLATED IT!
WELL, A CALL TO MY PERSONAL GUARDS WILL...
MON DIEU...
BUT NO-- I SHALL INVESTIGATE THIS VIOLATION MYSELF!
18

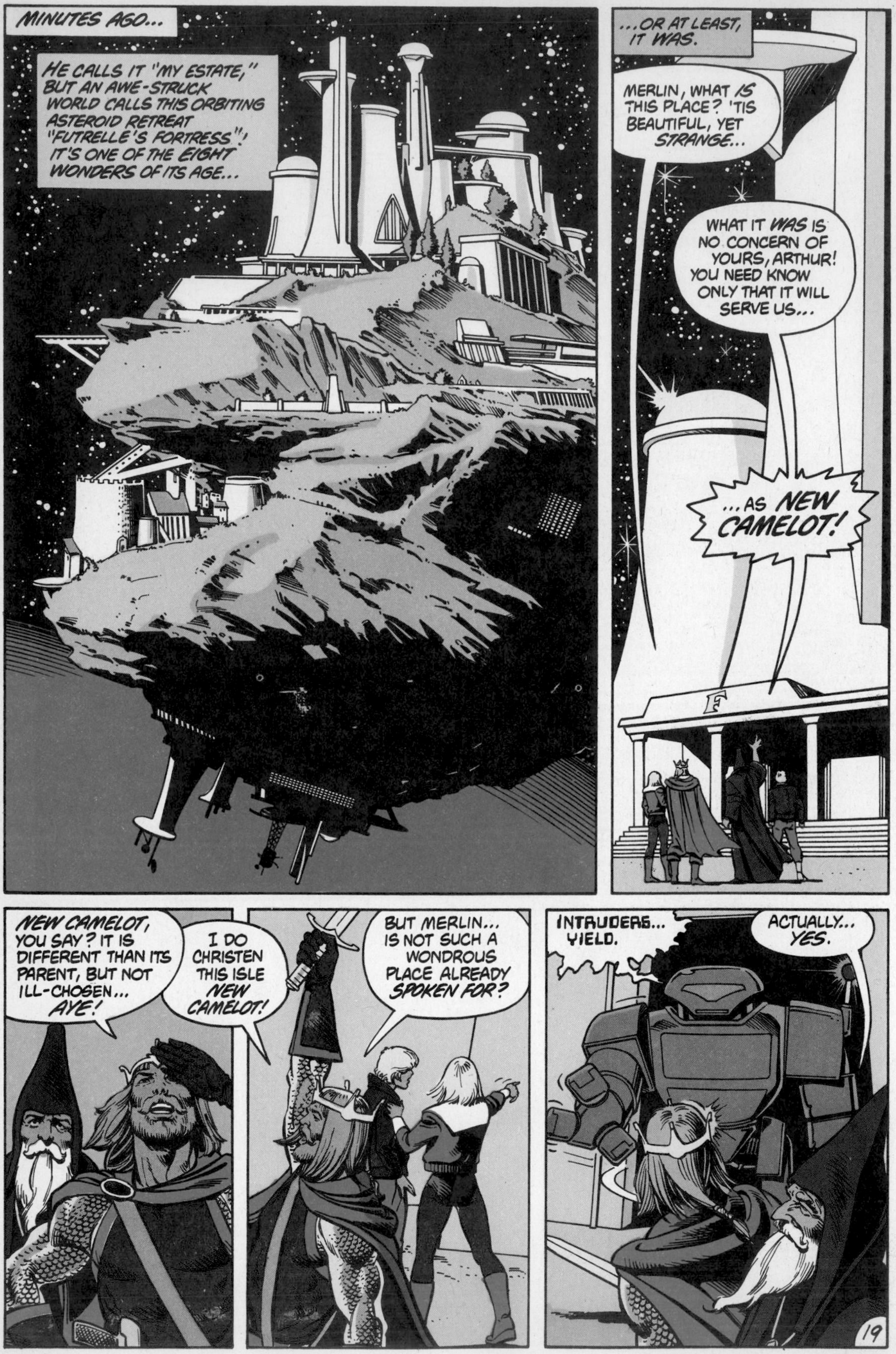
MINUTES AGO...
HE CALLS IT "MY ESTATE," BUT AN AWE-STRUCK WORLD CALLS THIS ORBITING ASTEROID RETREAT "FUTRELLE'S FORTRESS"! IT'S ONE OF THE EIGHT WONDERS OF ITS AGE...
...OR AT LEAST, IT WAS.
MERLIN, WHAT IS THIS PLACE? 'TIS BEAUTIFUL, YET STRANGE...
WHAT IT WAS IS NO CONCERN OF YOURS, ARTHUR! YOU NEED KNOW ONLY THAT IT WILL SERVE US...
...AS NEW CAMELOT!
F
NEW CAMELOT, YOU SAY? IT IS DIFFERENT THAN ITS PARENT, BUT NOT ILL-CHOSEN... AYE!
I DO CHRISTEN THIS ISLE NEW CAMELOT!
BUT MERLIN... IS NOT SUCH A WONDROUS PLACE ALREADY SPOKEN FOR?
INTRUDERS... YIELD.
ACTUALLY... YES.
19

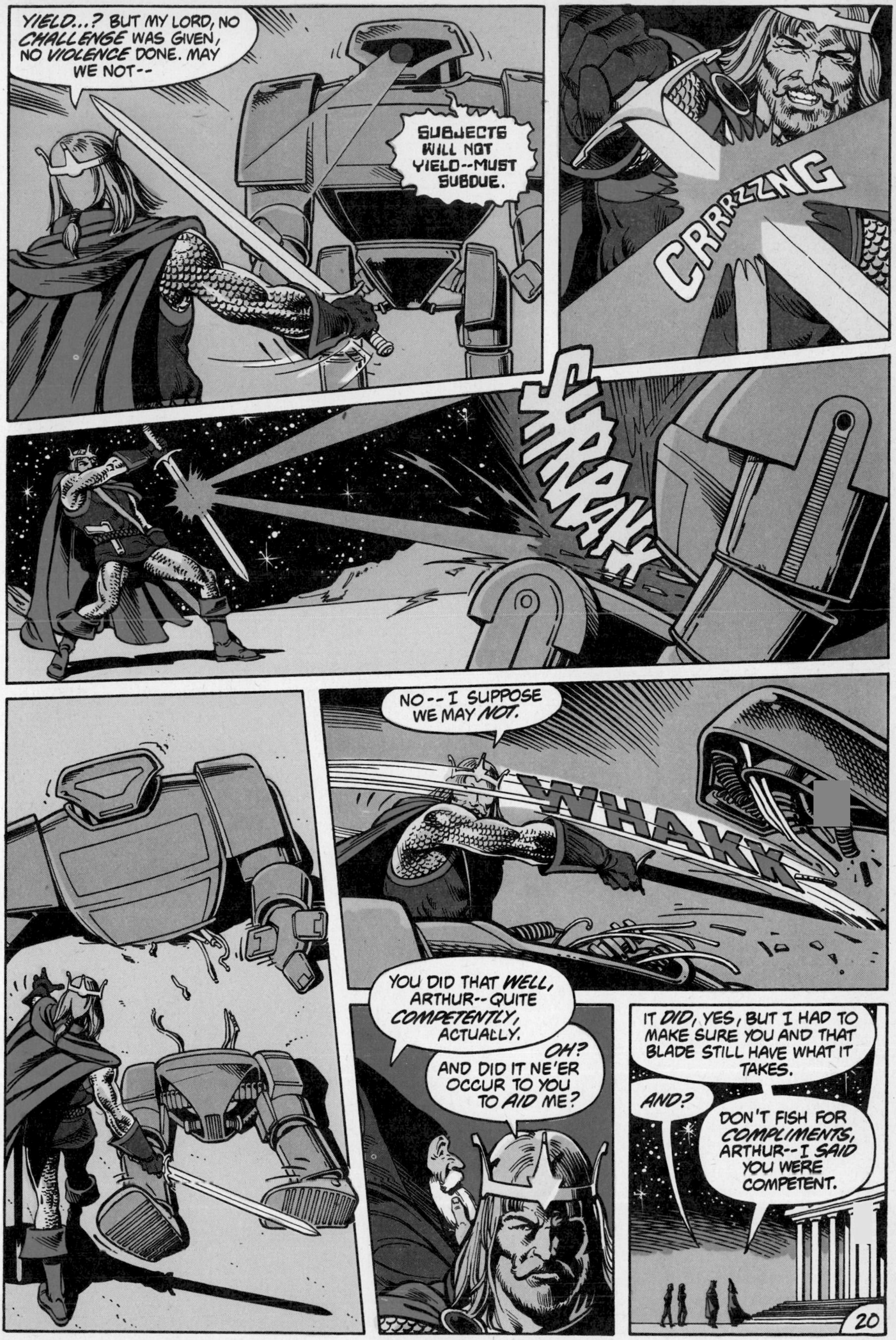
YIELD...? BUT MY LORD, NO CHALLENGE WAS GIVEN, NO VIOLENCE DONE. MAY WE NOT--
SUBJECTS WILL NOT YIELD--MUST SUBDUE.
CRRRZZNG
SHRRAKK
NO--I SUPPOSE WE MAY NOT.
WHAKK
YOU DID THAT WELL, ARTHUR--QUITE COMPETENTLY, ACTUALLY.
OH? AND DID IT NE'ER OCCUR TO YOU TO AID ME?
IT DID, YES, BUT I HAD TO MAKE SURE YOU AND THAT BLADE STILL HAVE WHAT IT TAKES.
AND?
DON'T FISH FOR COMPLIMENTS, ARTHUR--I SAID YOU WERE COMPETENT.
20

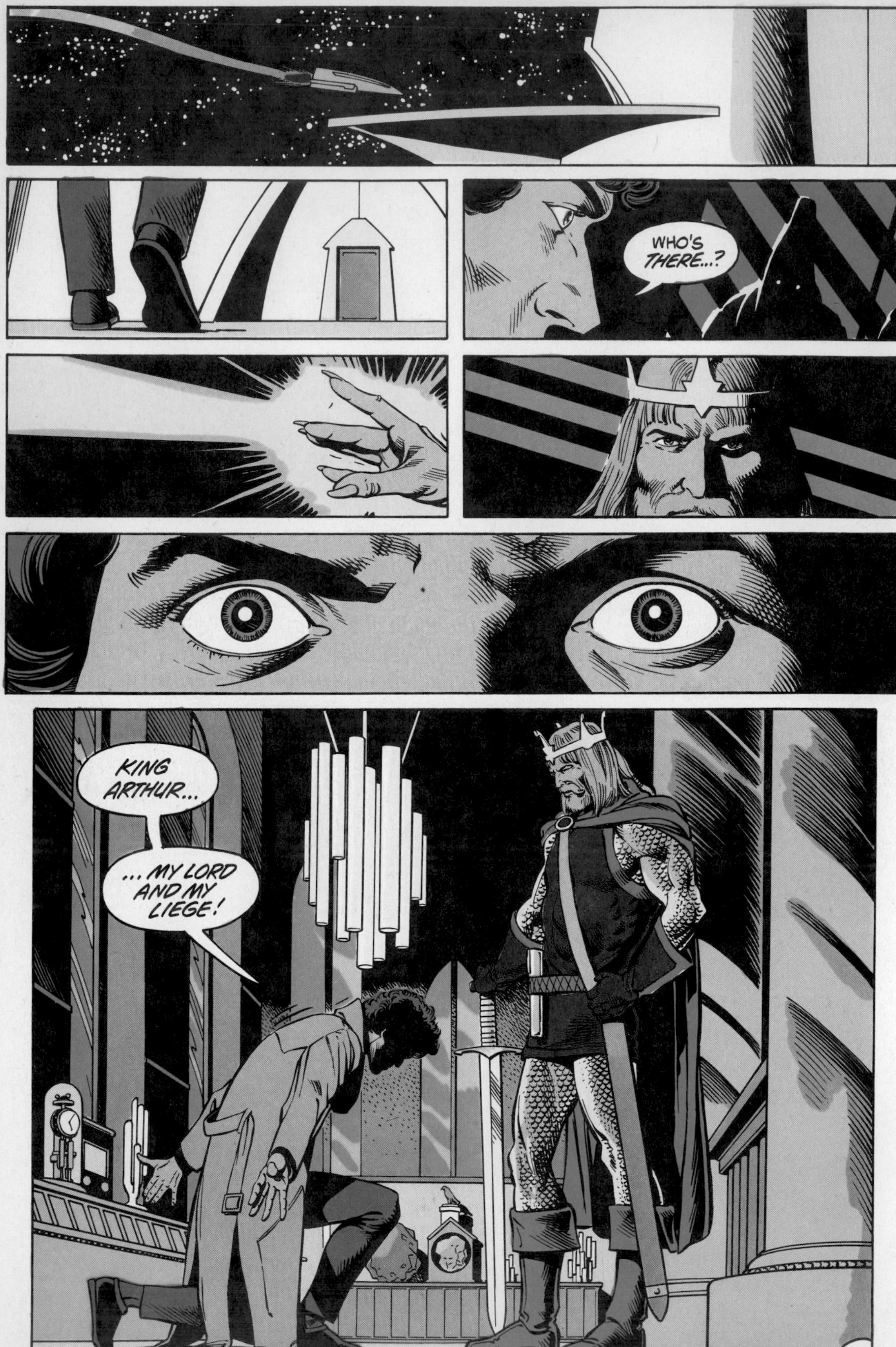
WHO'S THERE...?
KING ARTHUR...
...MY LORD AND MY LIEGE!

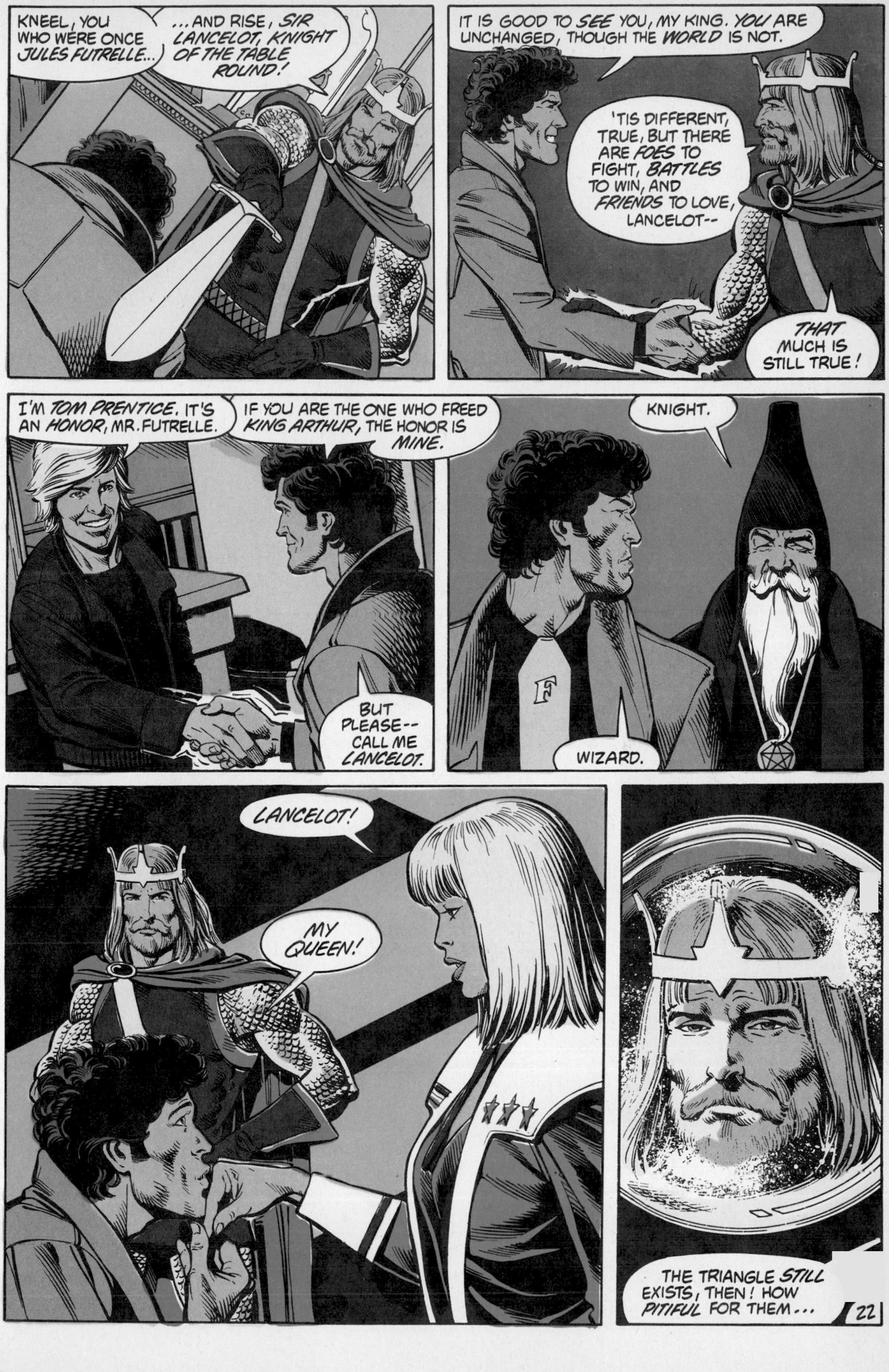
KNEEL, YOU WHO WERE ONCE JULES FUTRELLE...
...AND RISE, SIR LANCELOT, KNIGHT OF THE TABLE ROUND!
IT IS GOOD TO SEE YOU, MY KING. YOU ARE UNCHANGED, THOUGH THE WORLD IS NOT.
'TIS DIFFERENT, TRUE, BUT THERE ARE FOES TO FIGHT, BATTLES TO WIN, AND FRIENDS TO LOVE, LANCELOT--
THAT MUCH IS STILL TRUE!
I'M TOM PRENTICE. IT'S AN HONOR, MR. FUTRELLE.
IF YOU ARE THE ONE WHO FREED KING ARTHUR, THE HONOR IS MINE.
BUT PLEASE-- CALL ME LANCELOT.
KNIGHT.
WIZARD.
LANCELOT!
MY QUEEN!
THE TRIANGLE STILL EXISTS, THEN! HOW PITIFUL FOR THEM...

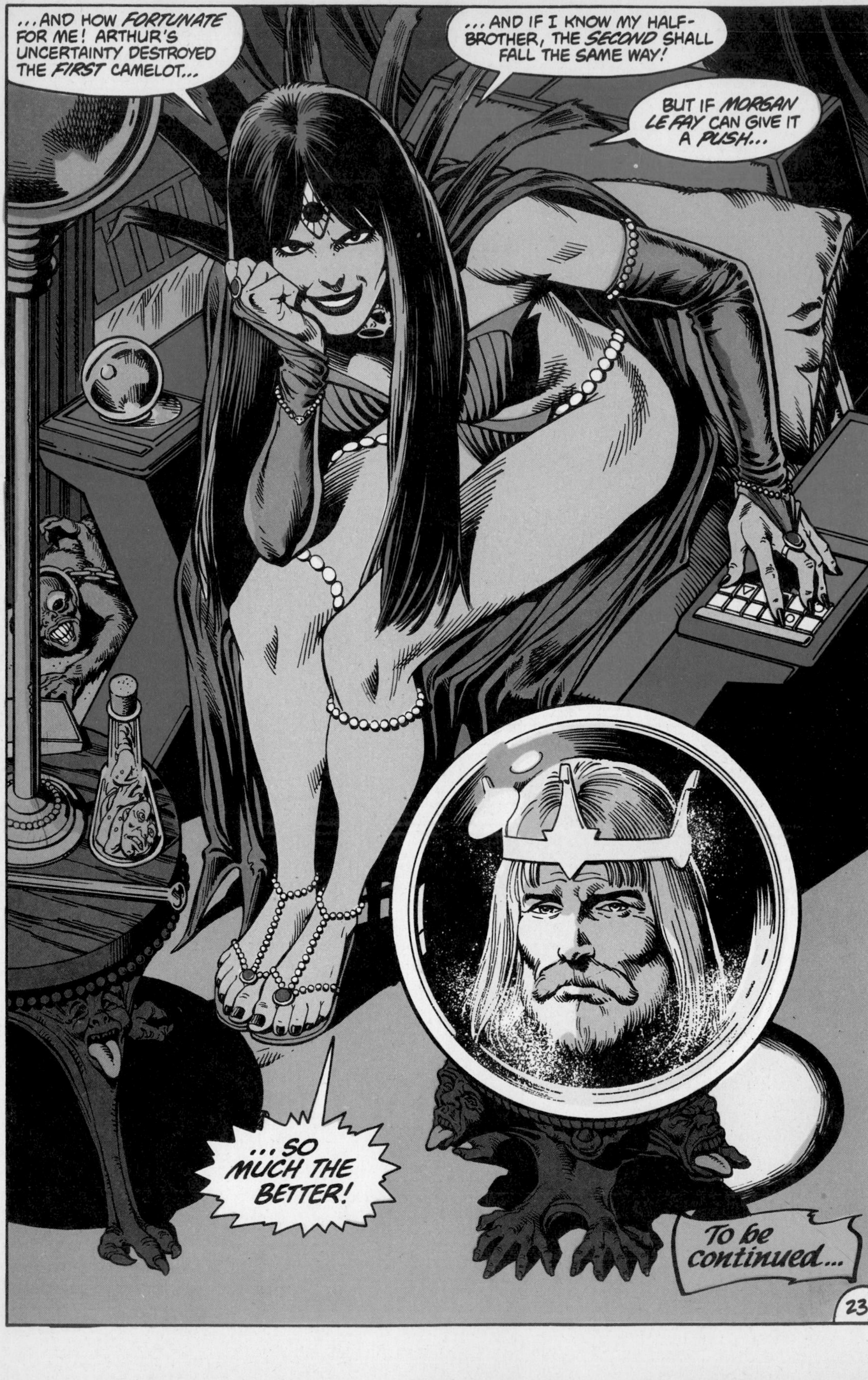
...AND HOW FORTUNATE FOR ME! ARTHUR'S UNCERTAINTY DESTROYED THE FIRST CAMELOT...
...AND IF I KNOW MY HALF-BROTHER, THE SECOND SHALL FALL THE SAME WAY!
BUT IF MORGAN LE FAY CAN GIVE IT A PUSH...
...SO MUCH THE BETTER!
To be continued...

chapter
3

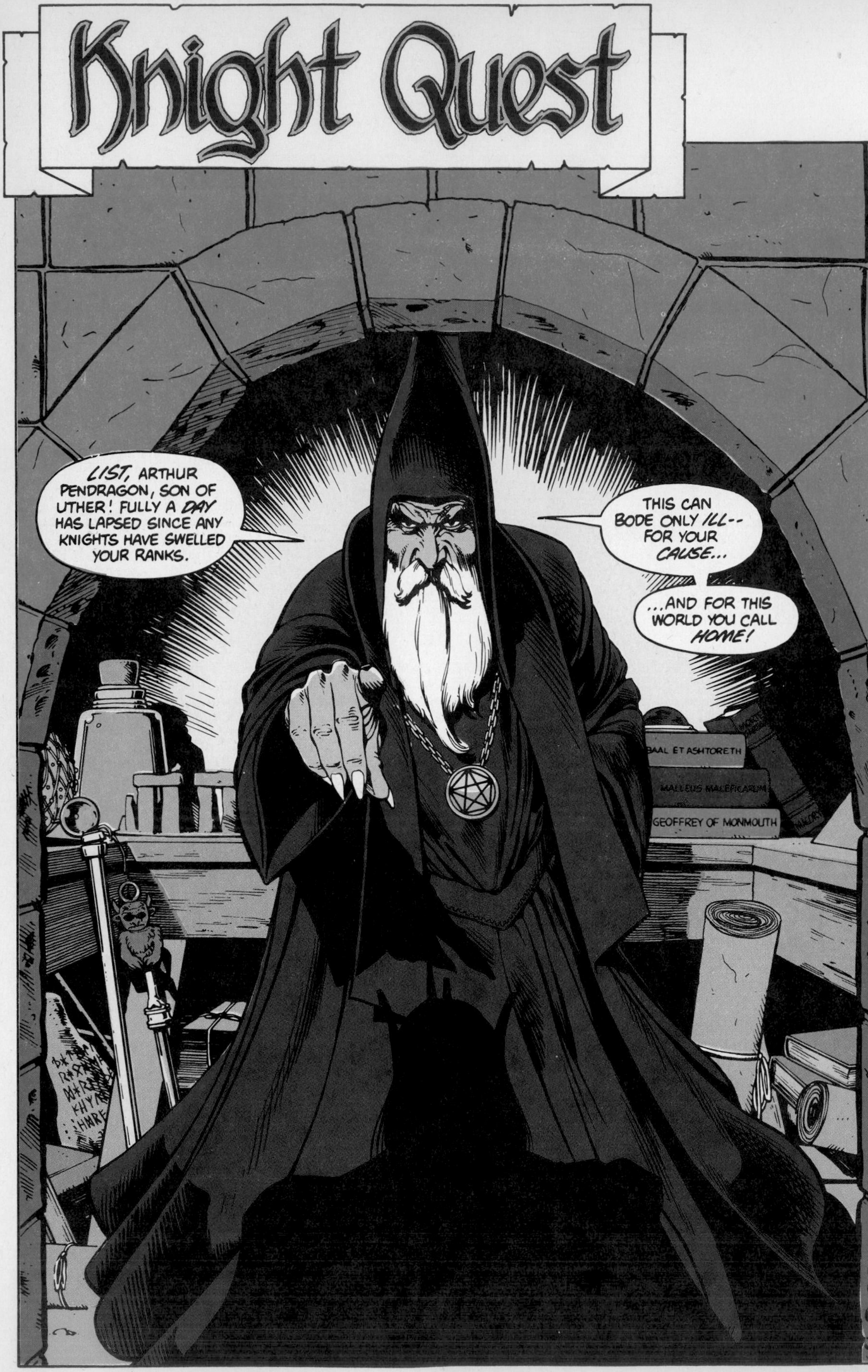
Knight Quest
LIST, ARTHUR PENDRAGON, SON OF UTHER! FULLY A DAY HAS LAPSED SINCE ANY KNIGHTS HAVE SWELLED YOUR RANKS.
THIS CAN BODE ONLY ILL-- FOR YOUR CAUSE...
...AND FOR THIS WORLD YOU CALL HOME!
BAAL ET ASHTORETH
MALLEUS MALEFICARUM
GEOFFREY OF MONMOUTH

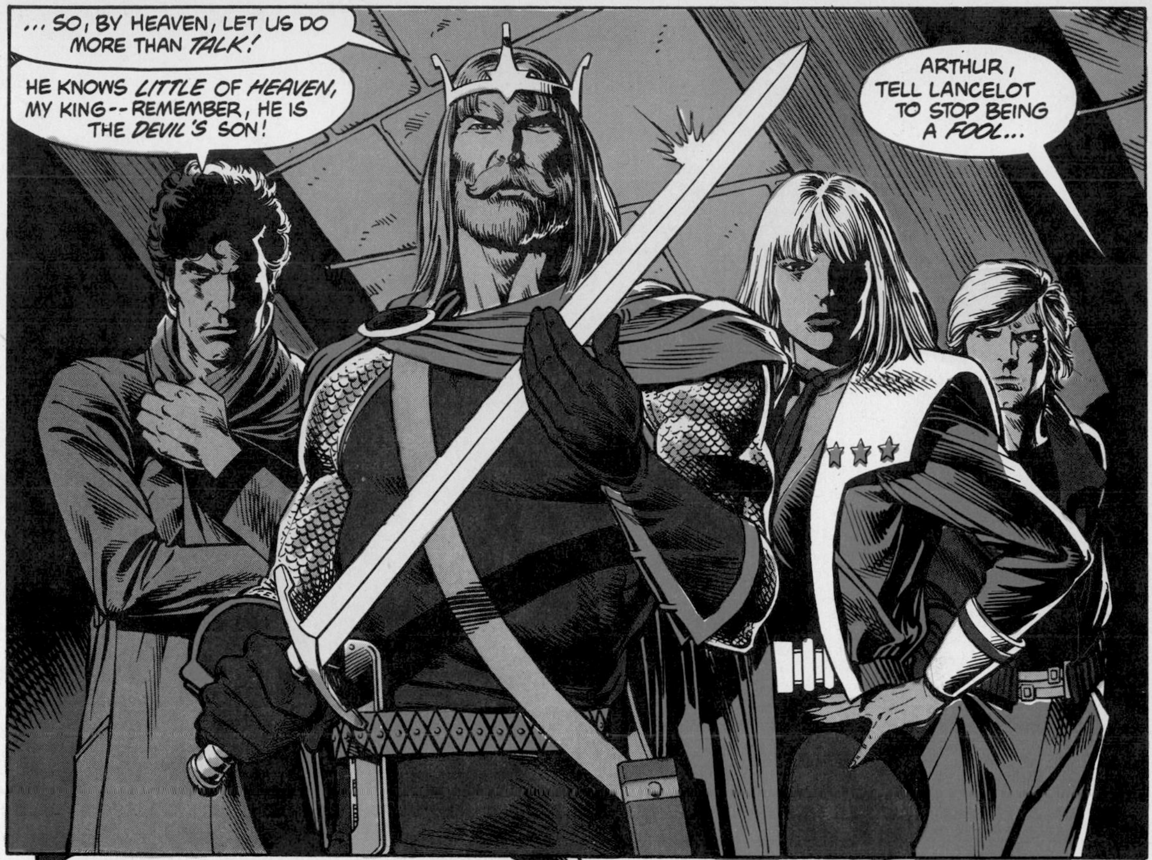
...SO, BY HEAVEN, LET US DO MORE THAN TALK!
HE KNOWS LITTLE OF HEAVEN, MY KING--REMEMBER, HE IS THE DEVIL'S SON!
ARTHUR, TELL LANCELOT TO STOP BEING A FOOL...

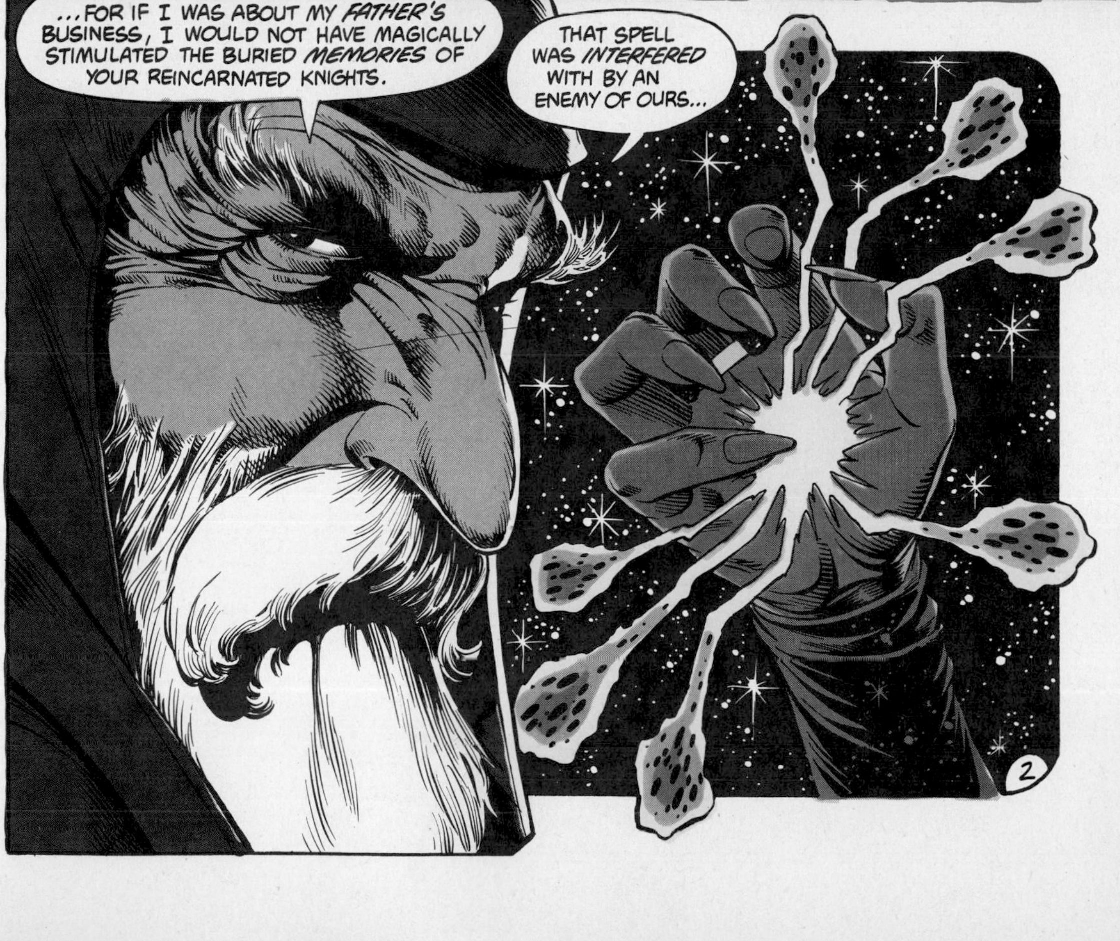
...FOR IF I WAS ABOUT MY FATHER'S BUSINESS, I WOULD NOT HAVE MAGICALLY STIMULATED THE BURIED MEMORIES OF YOUR REINCARNATED KNIGHTS.
THAT SPELL WAS INTERFERED WITH BY AN ENEMY OF OURS...
2

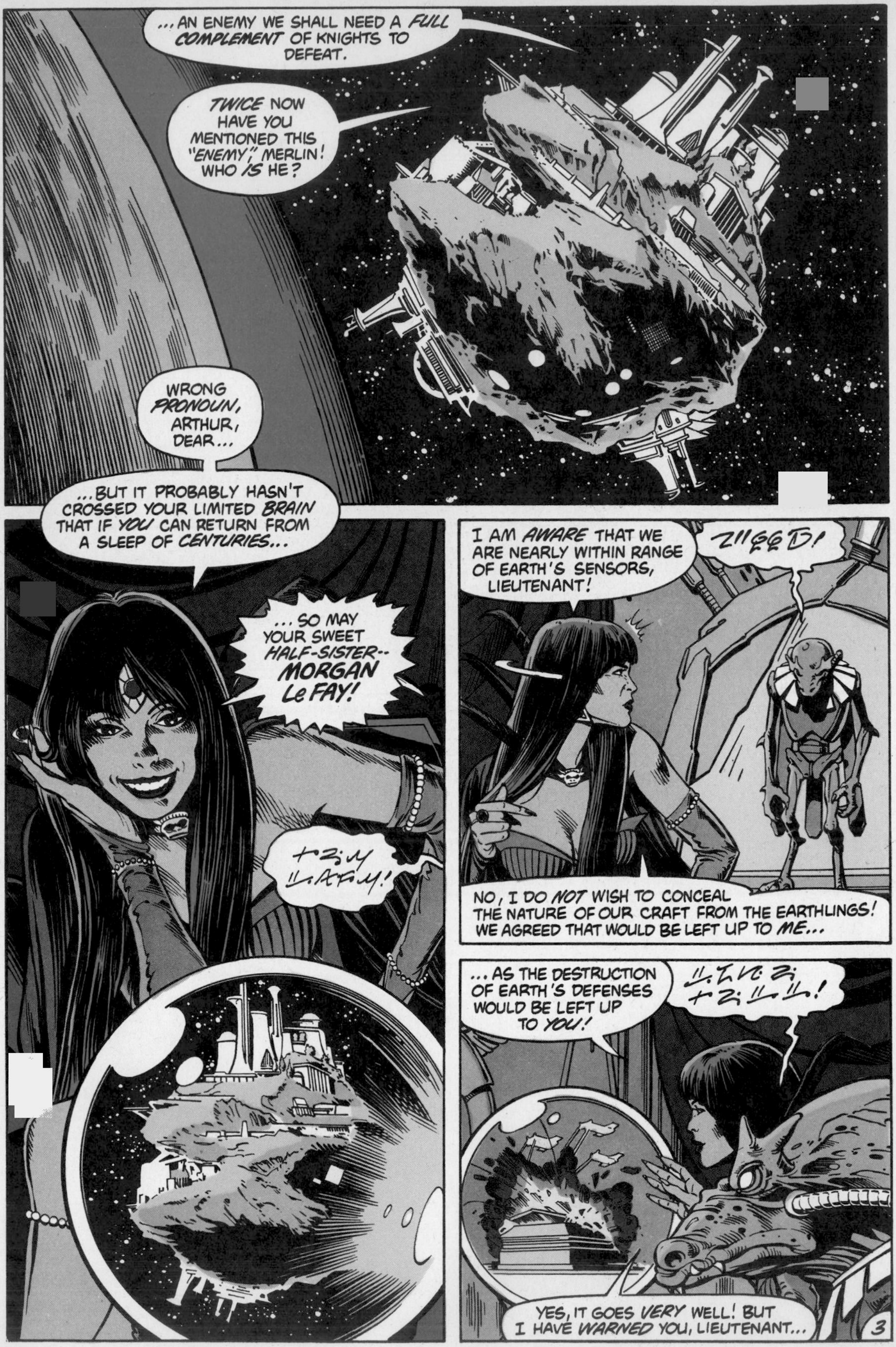
...AN ENEMY WE SHALL NEED A FULL COMPLEMENT OF KNIGHTS TO DEFEAT.
TWICE NOW HAVE YOU MENTIONED THIS "ENEMY," MERLIN! WHO IS HE?
WRONG PRONOUN, ARTHUR, DEAR...
...BUT IT PROBABLY HASN'T CROSSED YOUR LIMITED BRAIN THAT IF YOU CAN RETURN FROM A SLEEP OF CENTURIES...
...SO MAY YOUR SWEET HALF-SISTER-- MORGAN Le FAY!
I AM AWARE THAT WE ARE NEARLY WITHIN RANGE OF EARTH'S SENSORS, LIEUTENANT!
NO, I DO NOT WISH TO CONCEAL THE NATURE OF OUR CRAFT FROM THE EARTHLINGS! WE AGREED THAT WOULD BE LEFT UP TO ME...
...AS THE DESTRUCTION OF EARTH'S DEFENSES WOULD BE LEFT UP TO YOU!
YES, IT GOES VERY WELL! BUT I HAVE WARNED YOU, LIEUTENANT...

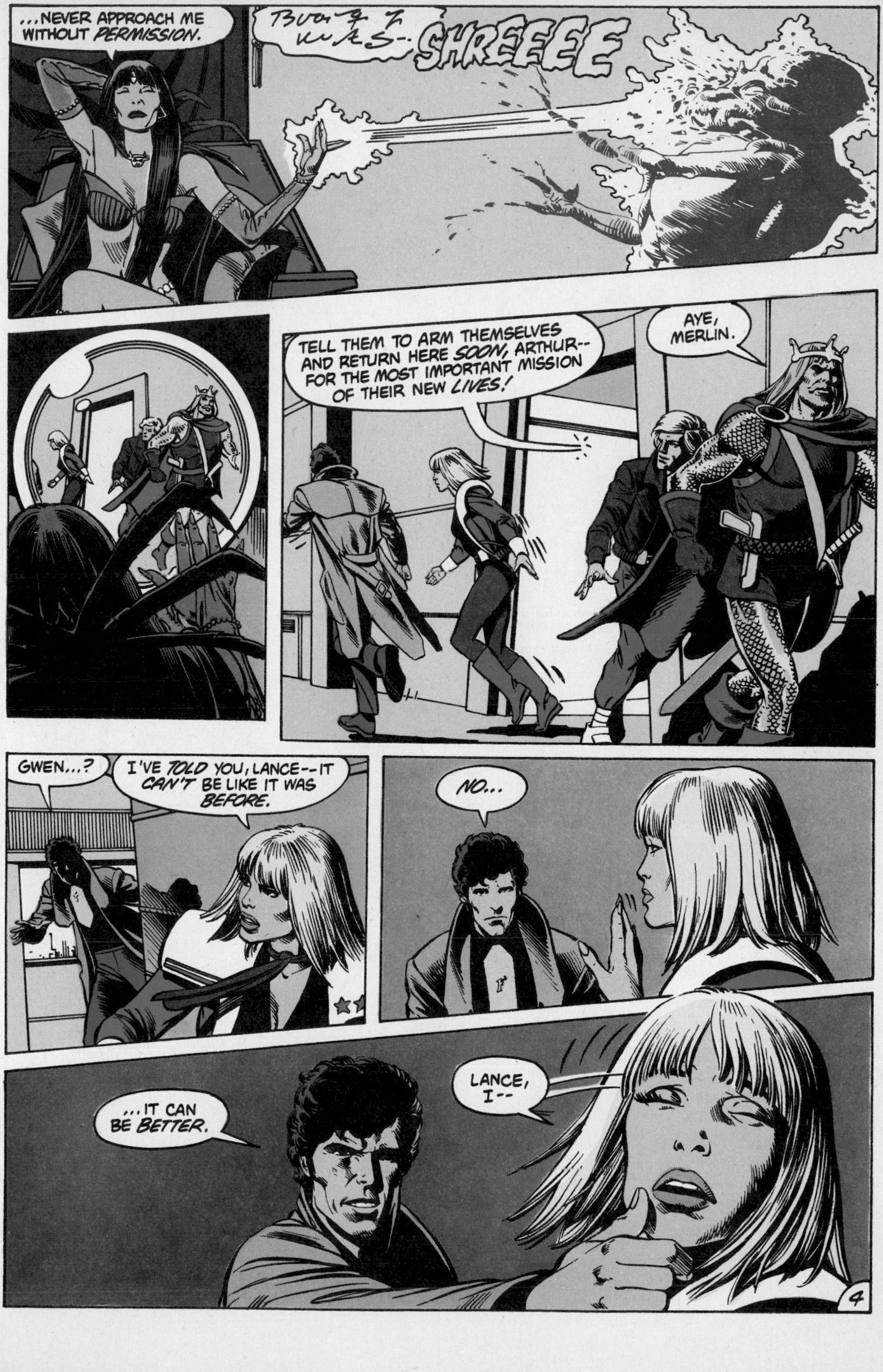
...NEVER APPROACH ME WITHOUT PERMISSION.
SHREEEE
TELL THEM TO ARM THEMSELVES AND RETURN HERE SOON, ARTHUR-- FOR THE MOST IMPORTANT MISSION OF THEIR NEW LIVES!
AYE, MERLIN.
GWEN...?
I'VE TOLD YOU, LANCE--IT CAN'T BE LIKE IT WAS BEFORE.
NO...
...IT CAN BE BETTER.
LANCE, I--

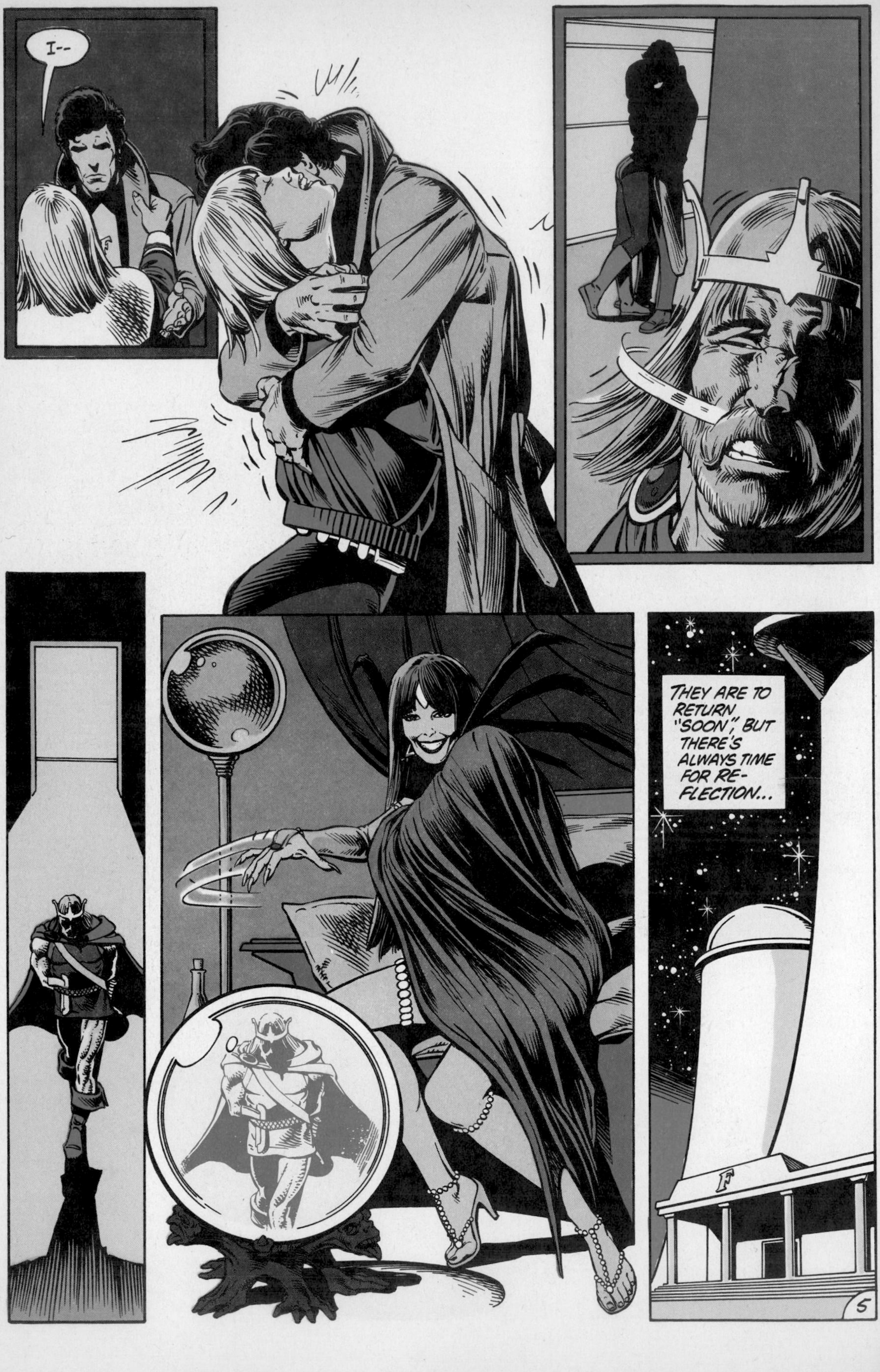
I--
THEY ARE TO RETURN "SOON," BUT THERE'S ALWAYS TIME FOR RE-FLECTION...
5

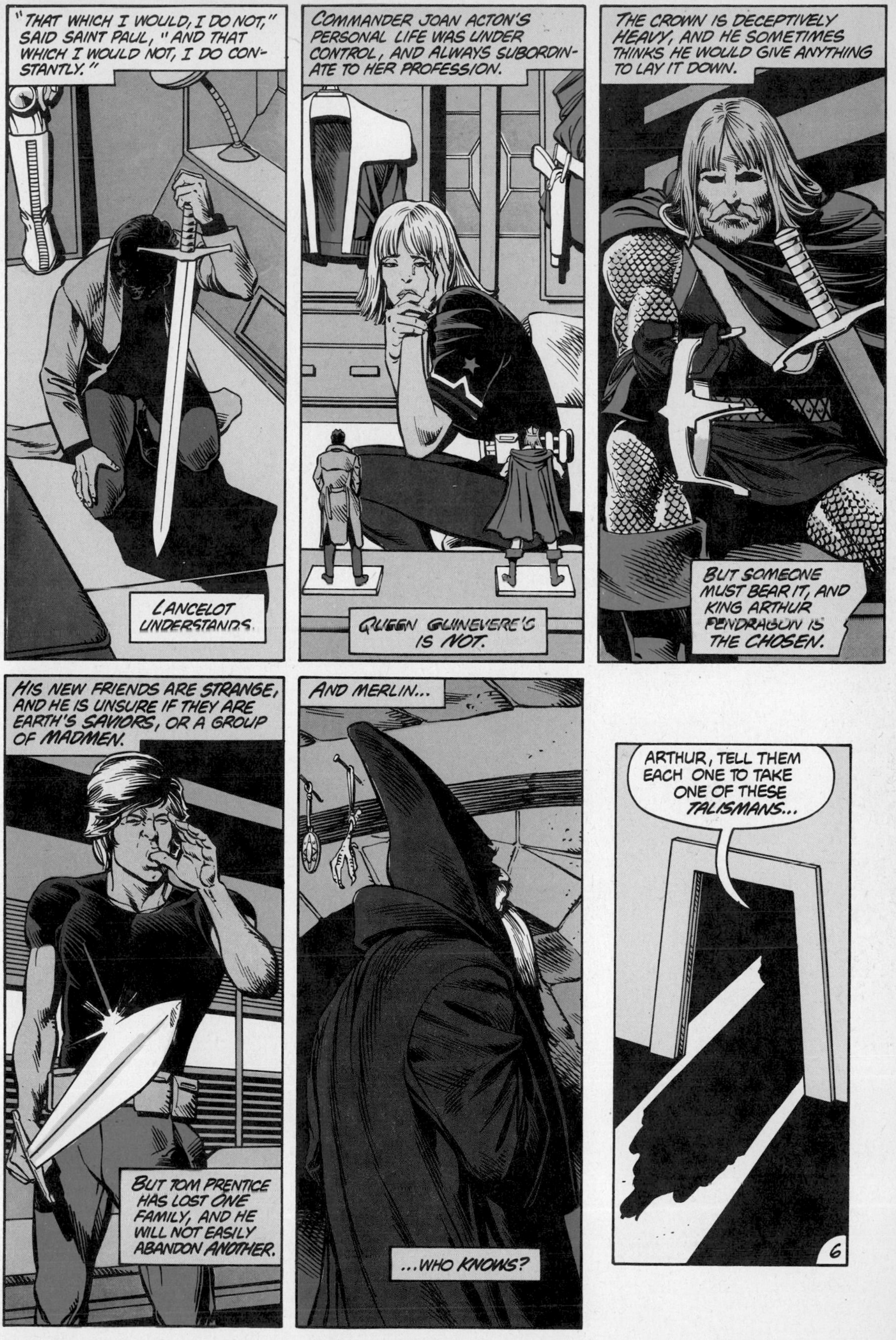
"THAT WHICH I WOULD, I DO NOT," SAID SAINT PAUL, "AND THAT WHICH I WOULD NOT, I DO CONSTANTLY."
LANCELOT UNDERSTANDS.
COMMANDER JOAN ACTON'S PERSONAL LIFE WAS UNDER CONTROL, AND ALWAYS SUBORDINATE TO HER PROFESSION.
QUEEN GUINEVERE'S IS NOT.
THE CROWN IS DECEPTIVELY HEAVY, AND HE SOMETIMES THINKS HE WOULD GIVE ANYTHING TO LAY IT DOWN.
BUT SOMEONE MUST BEAR IT, AND KING ARTHUR PENDRAGON IS THE CHOSEN.
HIS NEW FRIENDS ARE STRANGE, AND HE IS UNSURE IF THEY ARE EARTH'S SAVIORS, OR A GROUP OF MADMEN.
BUT TOM PRENTICE HAS LOST ONE FAMILY, AND HE WILL NOT EASILY ABANDON ANOTHER.
AND MERLIN...
...WHO KNOWS?
ARTHUR, TELL THEM EACH ONE TO TAKE ONE OF THESE TALISMANS...
6

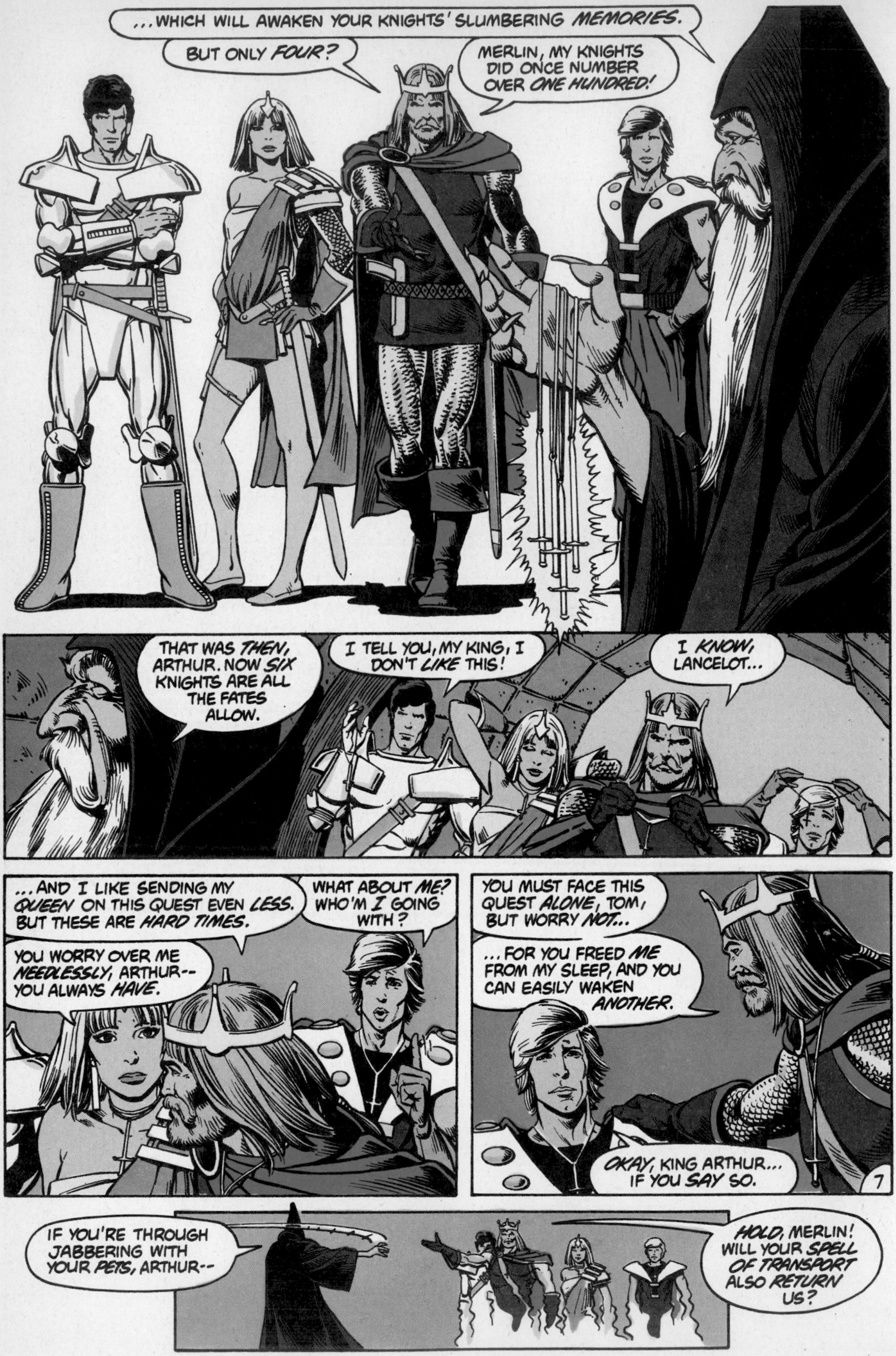
...WHICH WILL AWAKEN YOUR KNIGHTS' SLUMBERING MEMORIES.
BUT ONLY FOUR?
MERLIN, MY KNIGHTS DID ONCE NUMBER OVER ONE HUNDRED!
THAT WAS THEN, ARTHUR. NOW SIX KNIGHTS ARE ALL THE FATES ALLOW.
I TELL YOU, MY KING, I DON'T LIKE THIS!
I KNOW, LANCELOT...
...AND I LIKE SENDING MY QUEEN ON THIS QUEST EVEN LESS. BUT THESE ARE HARD TIMES.
WHAT ABOUT ME? WHO'M I GOING WITH?
YOU WORRY OVER ME NEEDLESSLY, ARTHUR-- YOU ALWAYS HAVE.
YOU MUST FACE THIS QUEST ALONE, TOM, BUT WORRY NOT...
...FOR YOU FREED ME FROM MY SLEEP, AND YOU CAN EASILY WAKEN ANOTHER.
OKAY, KING ARTHUR... IF YOU SAY SO.
7
IF YOU'RE THROUGH JABBERING WITH YOUR PETS, ARTHUR--
HOLD, MERLIN! WILL YOUR SPELL OF TRANSPORT ALSO RETURN US?

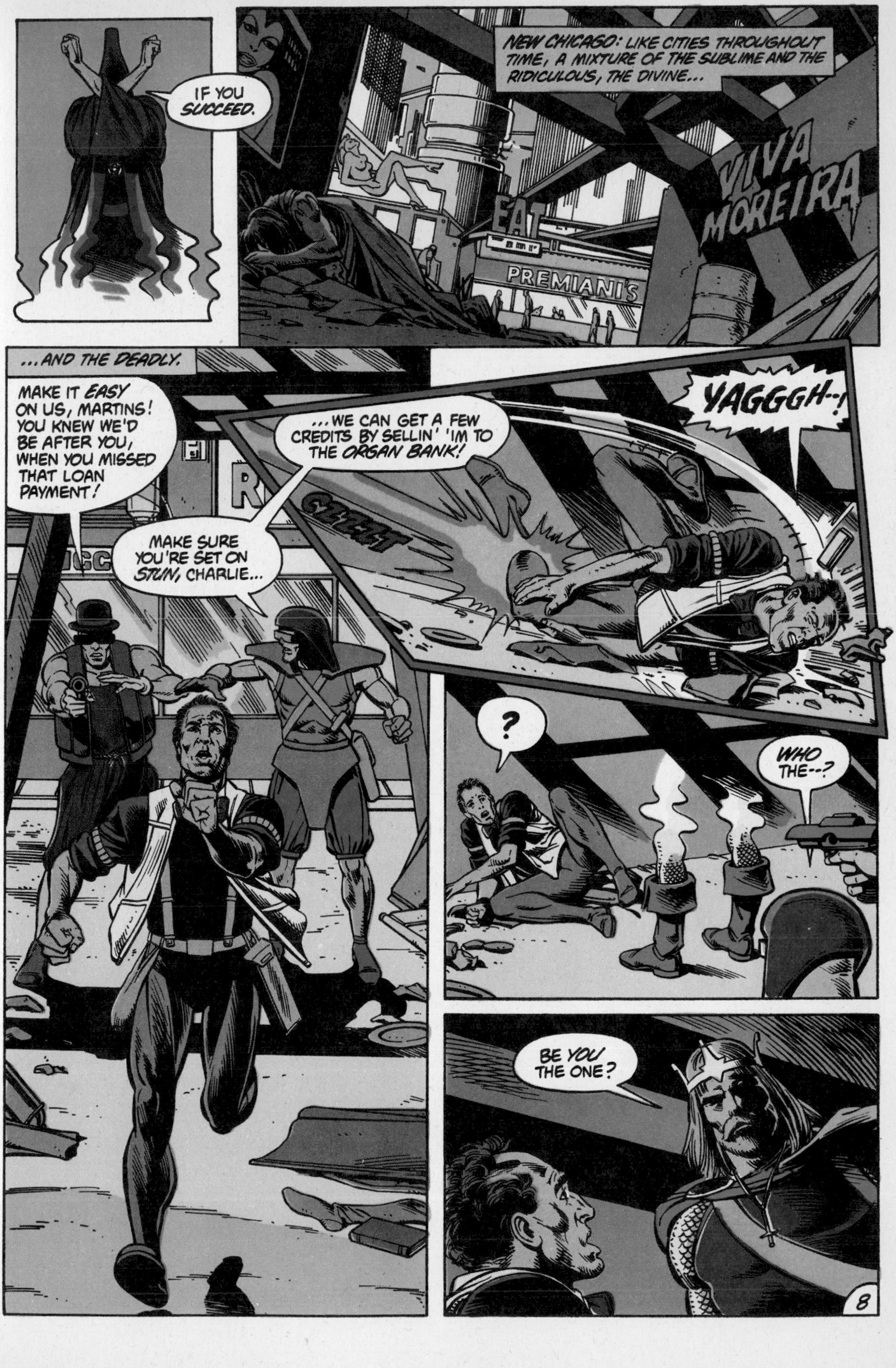
IF YOU SUCCEED.
NEW CHICAGO: LIKE CITIES THROUGHOUT TIME, A MIXTURE OF THE SUBLIME AND THE RIDICULOUS, THE DIVINE...
VIVA MOREIRA
EAT
PREMIANI'S
...AND THE DEADLY.
MAKE IT EASY ON US, MARTINS! YOU KNEW WE'D BE AFTER YOU, WHEN YOU MISSED THAT LOAN PAYMENT!
MAKE SURE YOU'RE SET ON STUN, CHARLIE...
...WE CAN GET A FEW CREDITS BY SELLIN' 'IM TO THE ORGAN BANK!
YAGGGH--!
?
WHO THE--?
BE YOU THE ONE?
8

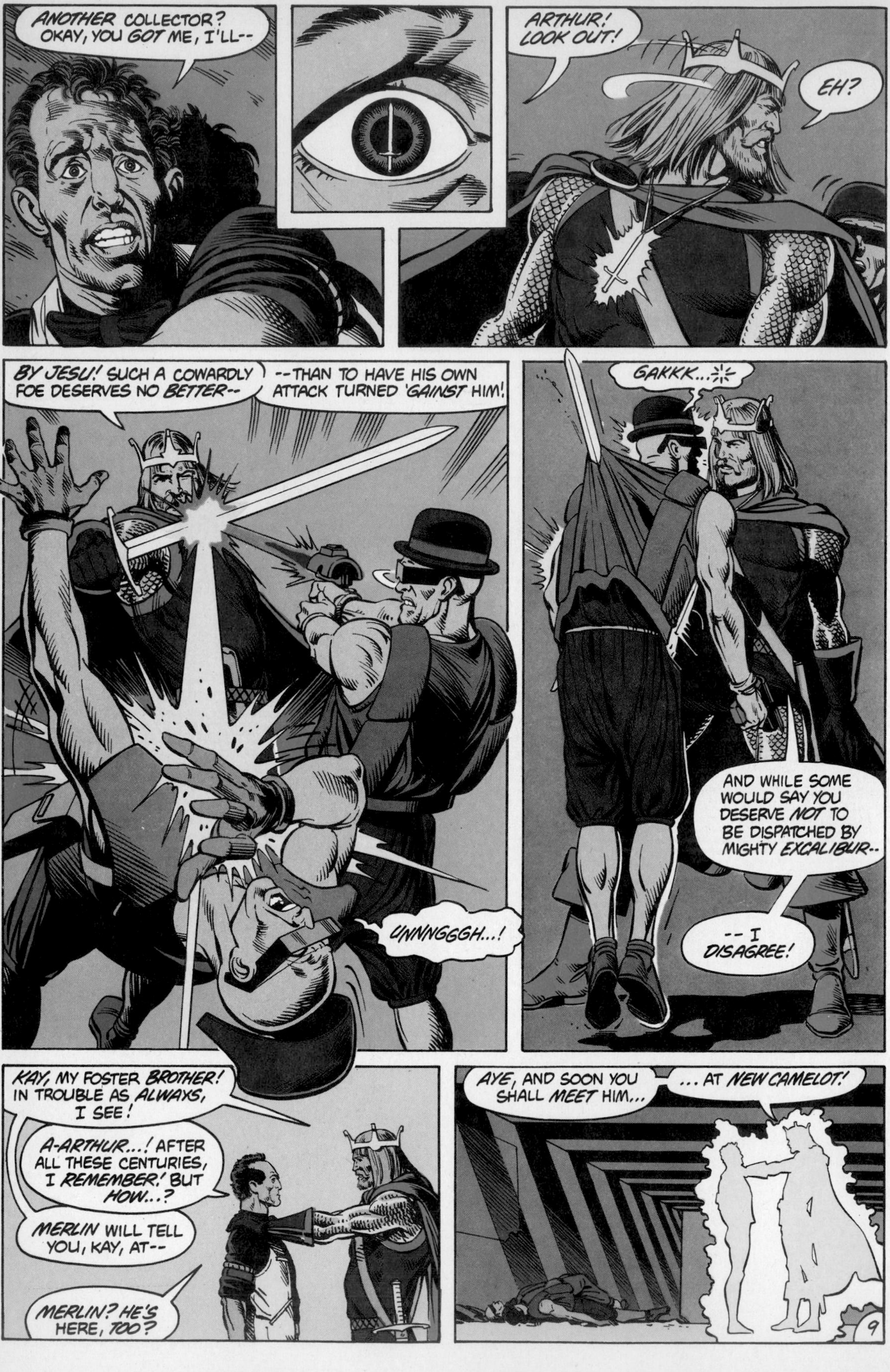

ANOTHER COLLECTOR? OKAY, YOU GOT ME, I'LL--
ARTHUR! LOOK OUT!
EH?
BY JESU! SUCH A COWARDLY FOE DESERVES NO BETTER--
--THAN TO HAVE HIS OWN ATTACK TURNED 'GAINST HIM!
UNNNGGGH...!
GAKKK...
AND WHILE SOME WOULD SAY YOU DESERVE NOT TO BE DISPATCHED BY MIGHTY EXCALIBUR--
-- I DISAGREE!
KAY, MY FOSTER BROTHER! IN TROUBLE AS ALWAYS, I SEE!
A-ARTHUR...! AFTER ALL THESE CENTURIES, I REMEMBER! BUT HOW...?
MERLIN WILL TELL YOU, KAY, AT--
MERLIN? HE'S HERE, TOO?
AYE, AND SOON YOU SHALL MEET HIM...
...AT NEW CAMELOT!

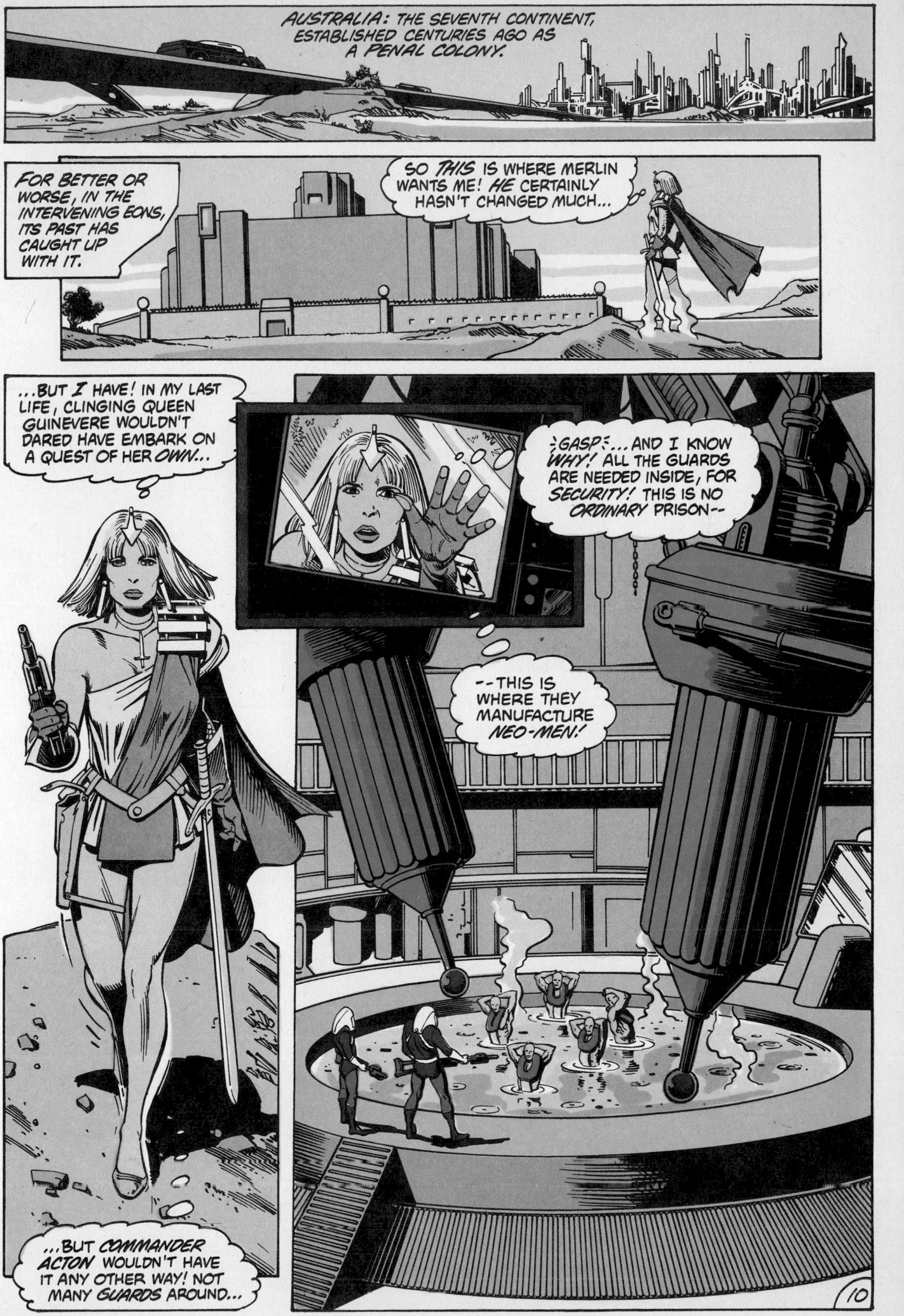
AUSTRALIA: THE SEVENTH CONTINENT, ESTABLISHED CENTURIES AGO AS A PENAL COLONY.
FOR BETTER OR WORSE, IN THE INTERVENING EONS, ITS PAST HAS CAUGHT UP WITH IT.
SO THIS IS WHERE MERLIN WANTS ME! HE CERTAINLY HASN'T CHANGED MUCH...
...BUT I HAVE! IN MY LAST LIFE, CLINGING QUEEN GUINEVERE WOULDN'T DARED HAVE EMBARK ON A QUEST OF HER OWN...
...BUT COMMANDER ACTON WOULDN'T HAVE IT ANY OTHER WAY! NOT MANY GUARDS AROUND...
:GASP:...AND I KNOW WHY! ALL THE GUARDS ARE NEEDED INSIDE, FOR SECURITY! THIS IS NO ORDINARY PRISON--
--THIS IS WHERE THEY MANUFACTURE NEO-MEN!
10

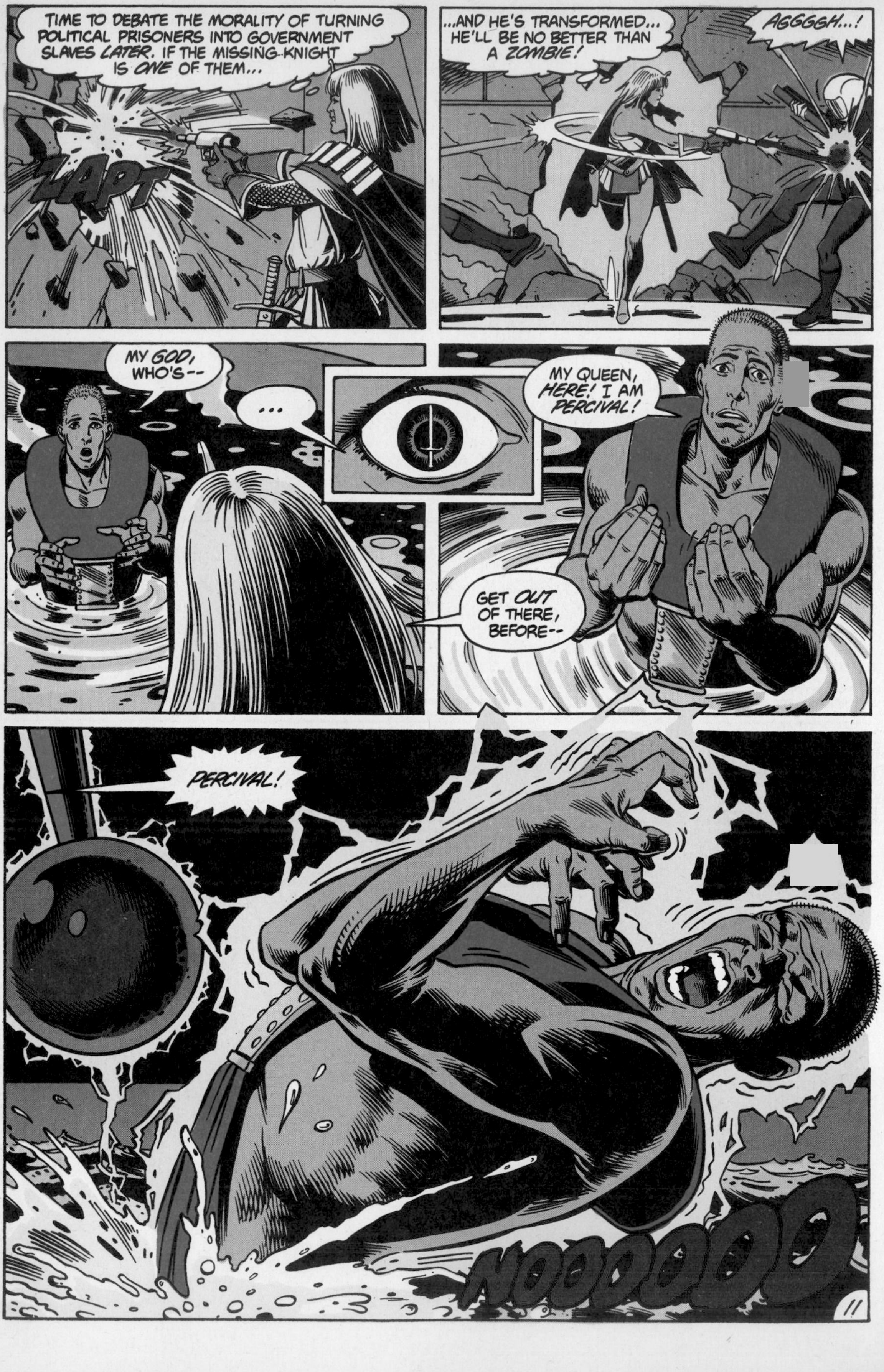
TIME TO DEBATE THE MORALITY OF TURNING POLITICAL PRISONERS INTO GOVERNMENT SLAVES LATER. IF THE MISSING KNIGHT IS ONE OF THEM...
ZAPT
...AND HE'S TRANSFORMED... HE'LL BE NO BETTER THAN A ZOMBIE!
AGGGGH...!
MY GOD, WHO'S--
...
MY QUEEN, HERE! I AM PERCIVAL!
GET OUT OF THERE, BEFORE--
PERCIVAL!
NOOOOOOO

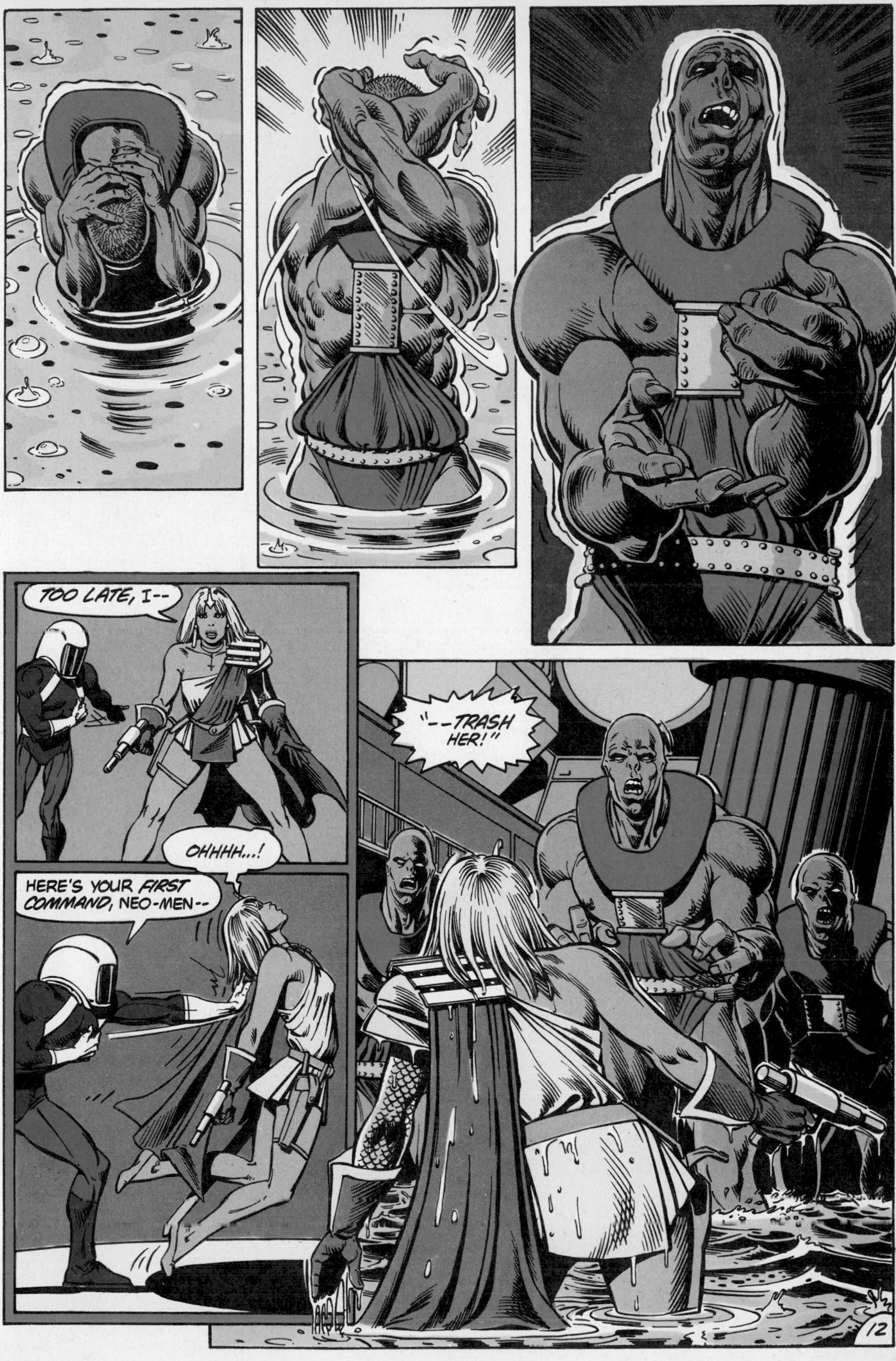
TOO LATE, I--
OHHHH...!
HERE'S YOUR FIRST COMMAND, NEO-MEN--
"--TRASH HER!"
12

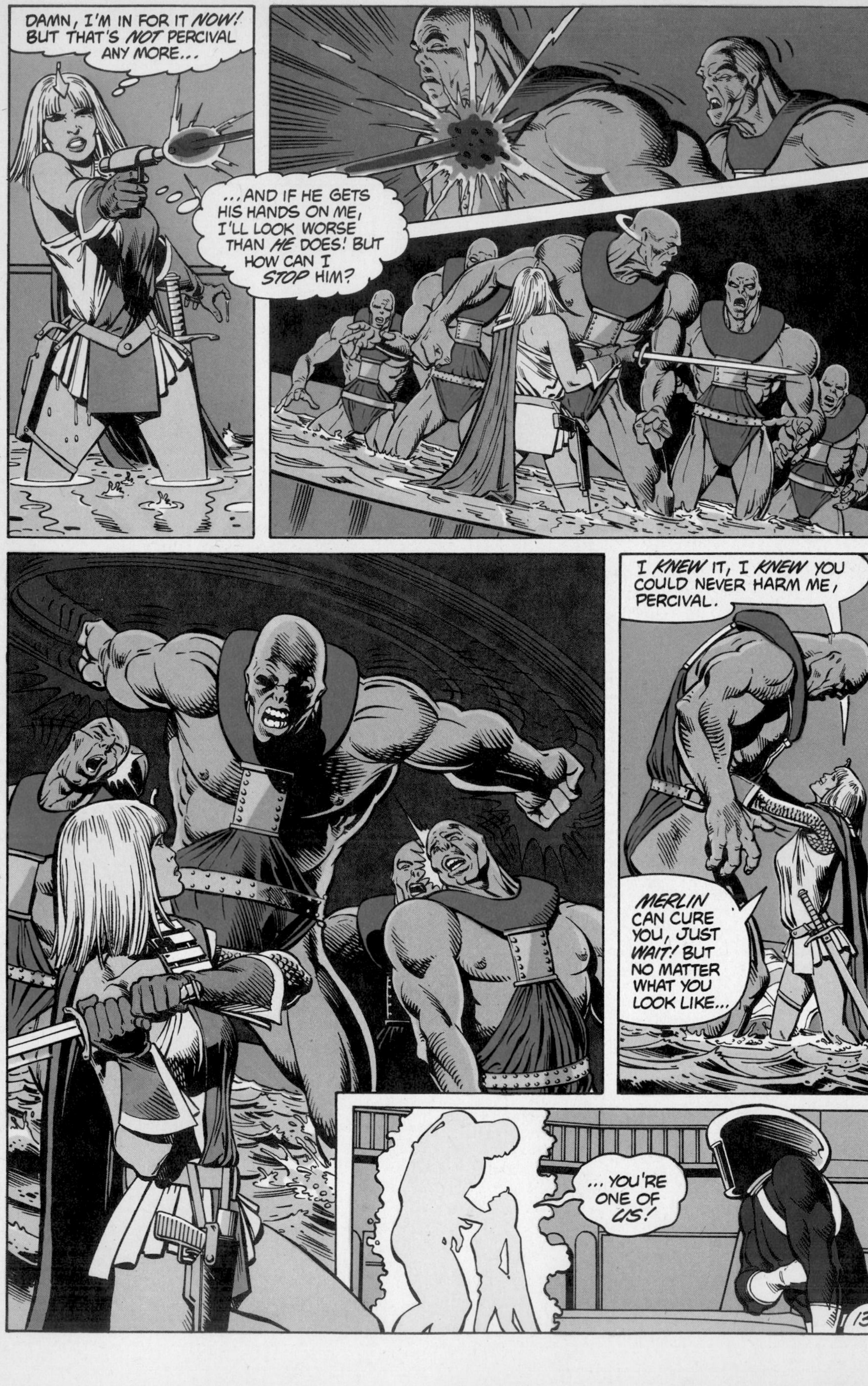
DAMN, I'M IN FOR IT NOW! BUT THAT'S NOT PERCIVAL ANY MORE...
...AND IF HE GETS HIS HANDS ON ME, I'LL LOOK WORSE THAN HE DOES! BUT HOW CAN I STOP HIM?
I KNEW IT, I KNEW YOU COULD NEVER HARM ME, PERCIVAL.
MERLIN CAN CURE YOU, JUST WAIT! BUT NO MATTER WHAT YOU LOOK LIKE...
...YOU'RE ONE OF US!
13

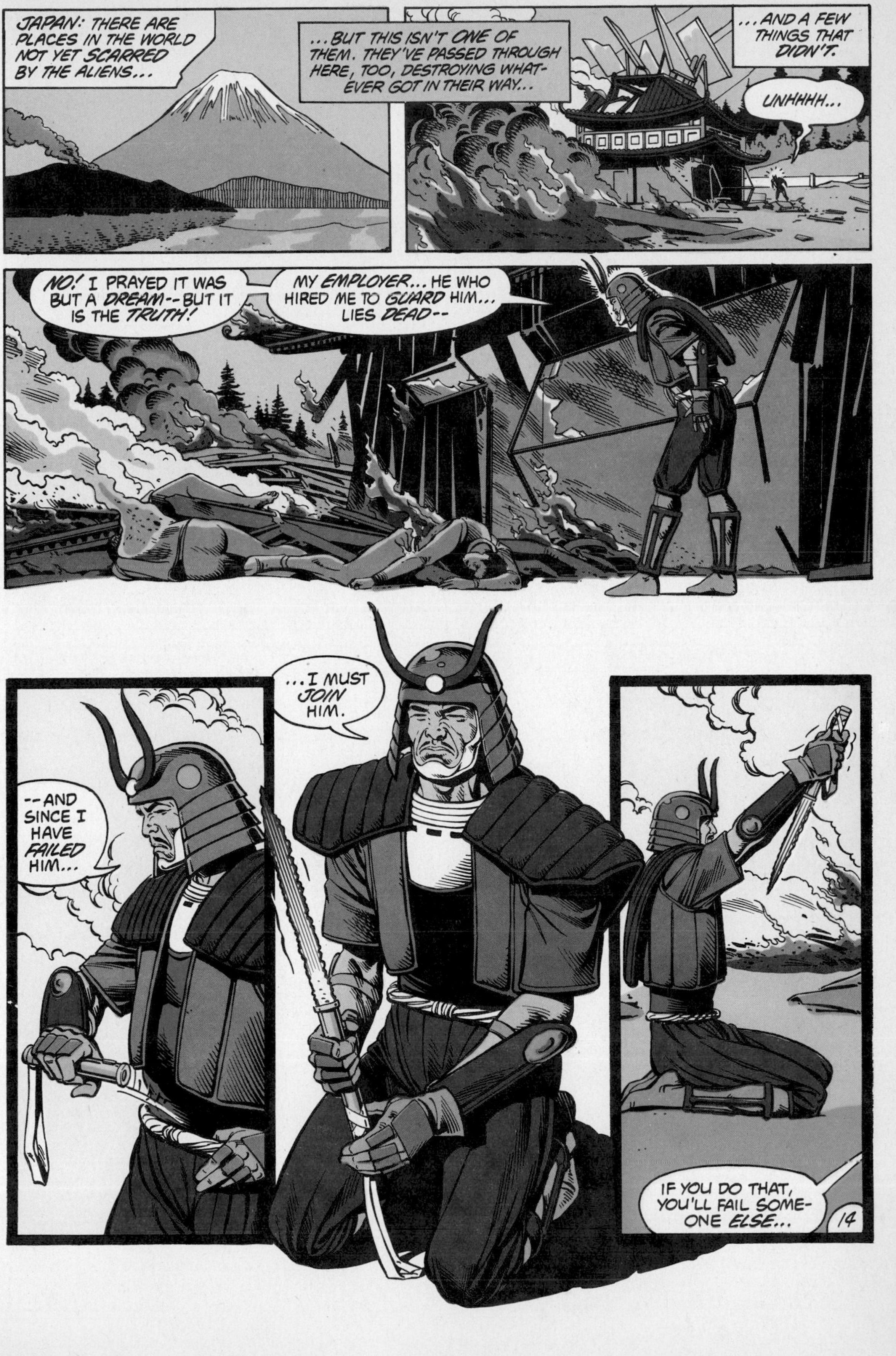
JAPAN: THERE ARE PLACES IN THE WORLD NOT YET SCARRED BY THE ALIENS...
...BUT THIS ISN'T ONE OF THEM. THEY'VE PASSED THROUGH HERE, TOO, DESTROYING WHATEVER GOT IN THEIR WAY...
...AND A FEW THINGS THAT DIDN'T.
UNHHHH...
NO! I PRAYED IT WAS BUT A DREAM--BUT IT IS THE TRUTH!
MY EMPLOYER... HE WHO HIRED ME TO GUARD HIM... LIES DEAD--
--AND SINCE I HAVE FAILED HIM...
...I MUST JOIN HIM.
IF YOU DO THAT, YOU'LL FAIL SOMEONE ELSE...
14

...THE FINEST MAN WHO EVER *LIVED--ARTHUR PENDRAGON!*

THAT *CHARM,* IT--

--IT...

FATHER?

GALAHAD...?

MY *SON?*

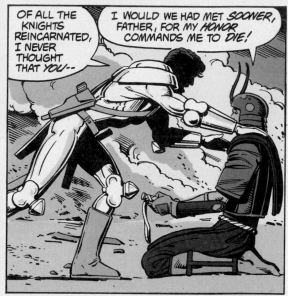

OF ALL THE KNIGHTS REINCARNATED, I NEVER THOUGHT THAT *YOU*--

I WOULD WE HAD MET *SOONER,* FATHER, FOR MY *HONOR* COMMANDS ME TO *DIE!*

MY *GOD* COMMANDS YOU TO *LIVE,* GALAHAD, AND *FIGHT* AS A *KNIGHT* OF THE *ROUND TABLE!*

WHY ELSE WOULD YOU BE *HERE,* NOW?

I--

I WILL *JOIN* YOU, FATHER-- FOR *NOW.*

AND FOR ALL OF OUR *QUEST,* GALAHAD!

PERHAPS.

15

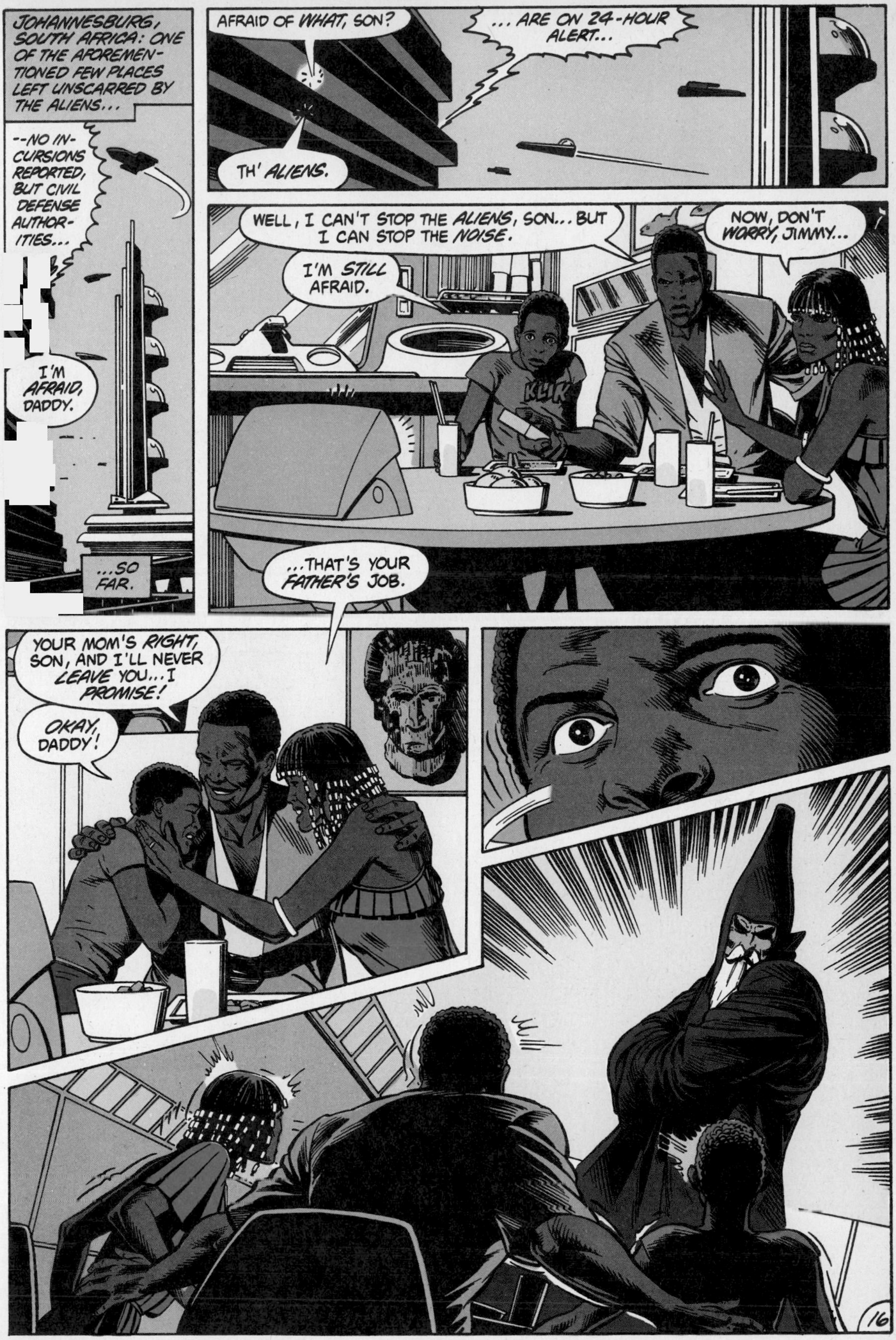
JOHANNESBURG, SOUTH AFRICA: ONE OF THE AFOREMENTIONED FEW PLACES LEFT UNSCARRED BY THE ALIENS...
--NO INCURSIONS REPORTED, BUT CIVIL DEFENSE AUTHORITIES...
I'M AFRAID, DADDY.
...SO FAR.
AFRAID OF WHAT, SON?
... ARE ON 24-HOUR ALERT...
TH' ALIENS.
WELL, I CAN'T STOP THE ALIENS, SON... BUT I CAN STOP THE NOISE.
I'M STILL AFRAID.
NOW, DON'T WORRY, JIMMY...
...THAT'S YOUR FATHER'S JOB.
YOUR MOM'S RIGHT, SON, AND I'LL NEVER LEAVE YOU... I PROMISE!
OKAY, DADDY!
KLIK

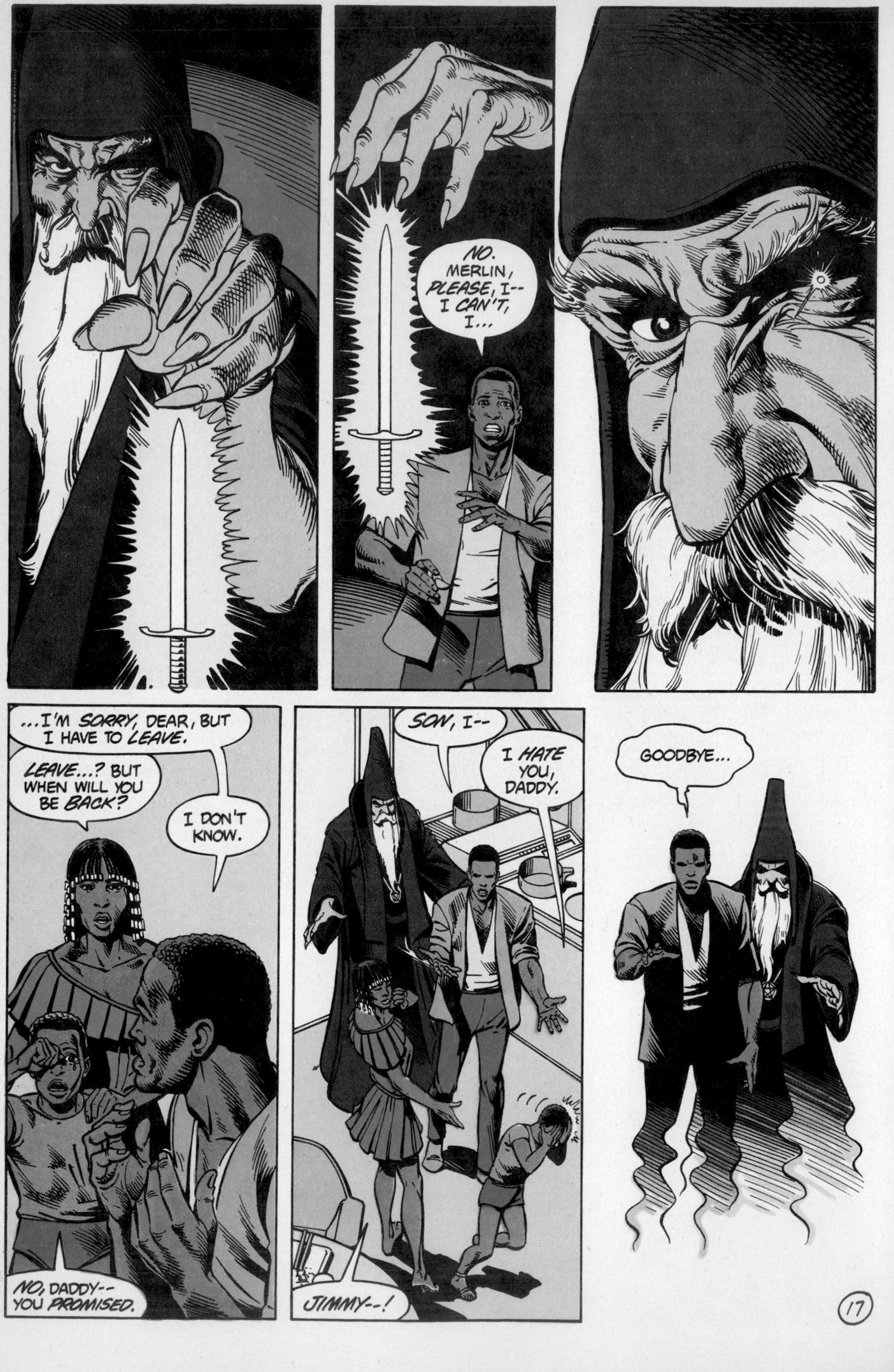
NO. MERLIN, PLEASE, I-- I CAN'T, I...
...I'M SORRY, DEAR, BUT I HAVE TO LEAVE.
LEAVE...? BUT WHEN WILL YOU BE BACK?
I DON'T KNOW.
NO, DADDY-- YOU PROMISED.
SON, I--
I HATE YOU, DADDY.
JIMMY--!
GOODBYE...

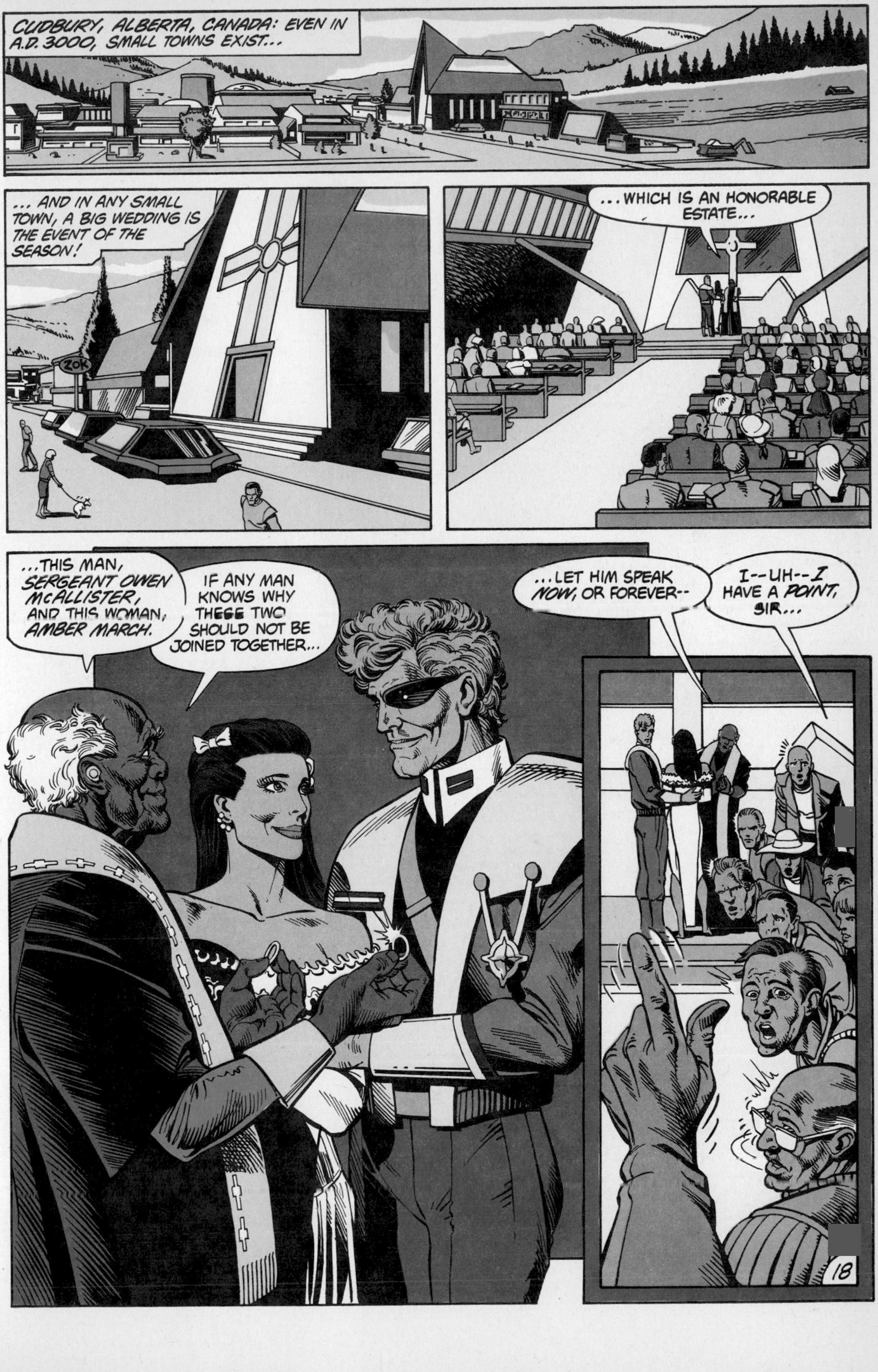
CUDBURY, ALBERTA, CANADA: EVEN IN A.D. 3000, SMALL TOWNS EXIST...
... AND IN ANY SMALL TOWN, A BIG WEDDING IS THE EVENT OF THE SEASON!
ZOK
... WHICH IS AN HONORABLE ESTATE...
...THIS MAN, SERGEANT OWEN McALLISTER, AND THIS WOMAN, AMBER MARCH.
IF ANY MAN KNOWS WHY THESE TWO SHOULD NOT BE JOINED TOGETHER...
...LET HIM SPEAK NOW, OR FOREVER--
I--UH--I HAVE A POINT, SIR...

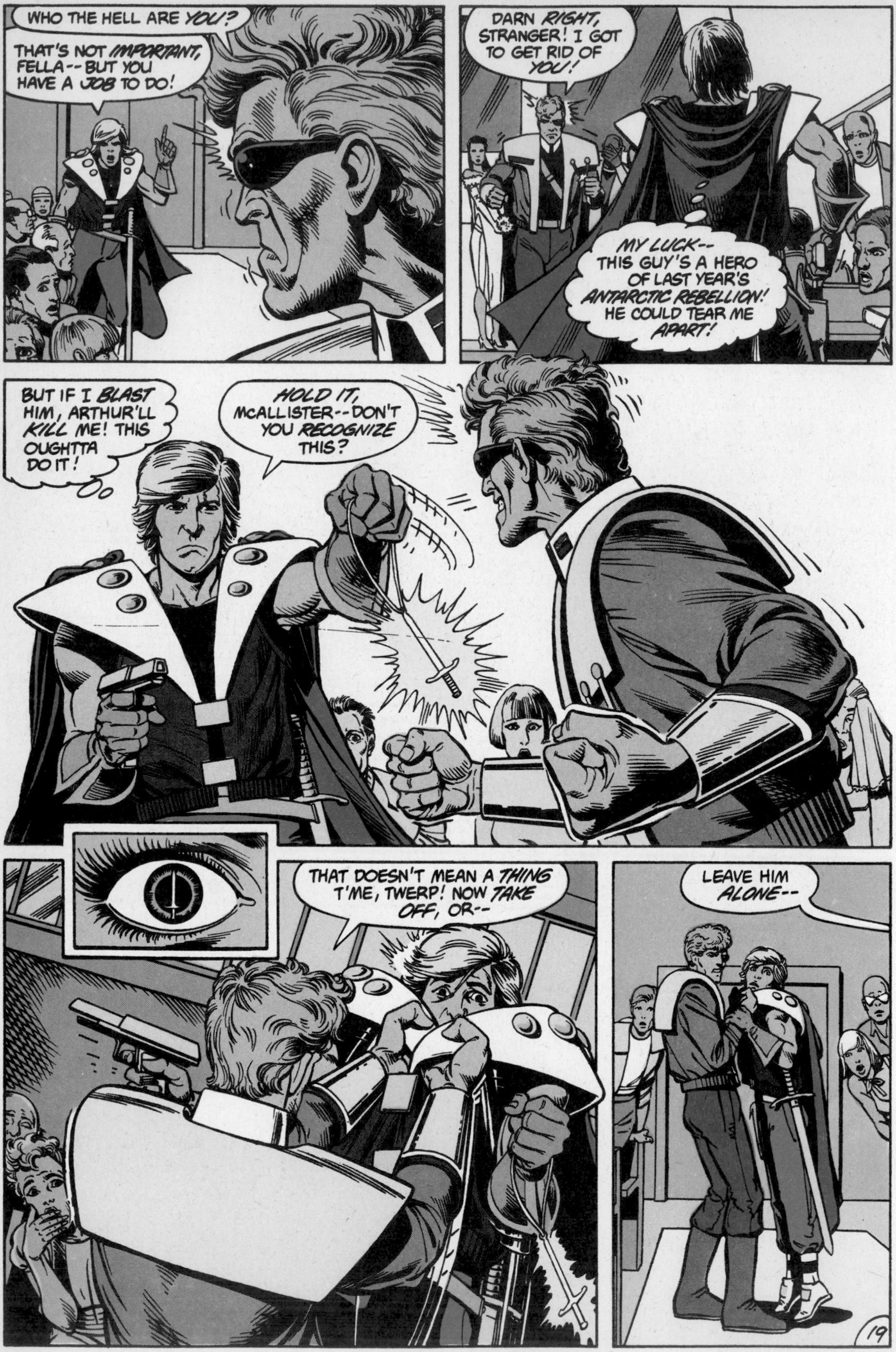
WHO THE HELL ARE YOU?
THAT'S NOT IMPORTANT, FELLA--BUT YOU HAVE A JOB TO DO!
DARN RIGHT, STRANGER! I GOT TO GET RID OF YOU!
MY LUCK-- THIS GUY'S A HERO OF LAST YEAR'S ANTARCTIC REBELLION! HE COULD TEAR ME APART!
BUT IF I BLAST HIM, ARTHUR'LL KILL ME! THIS OUGHTTA DO IT!
HOLD IT, McALLISTER--DON'T YOU RECOGNIZE THIS?
THAT DOESN'T MEAN A THING T'ME, TWERP! NOW TAKE OFF, OR--
LEAVE HIM ALONE--
19

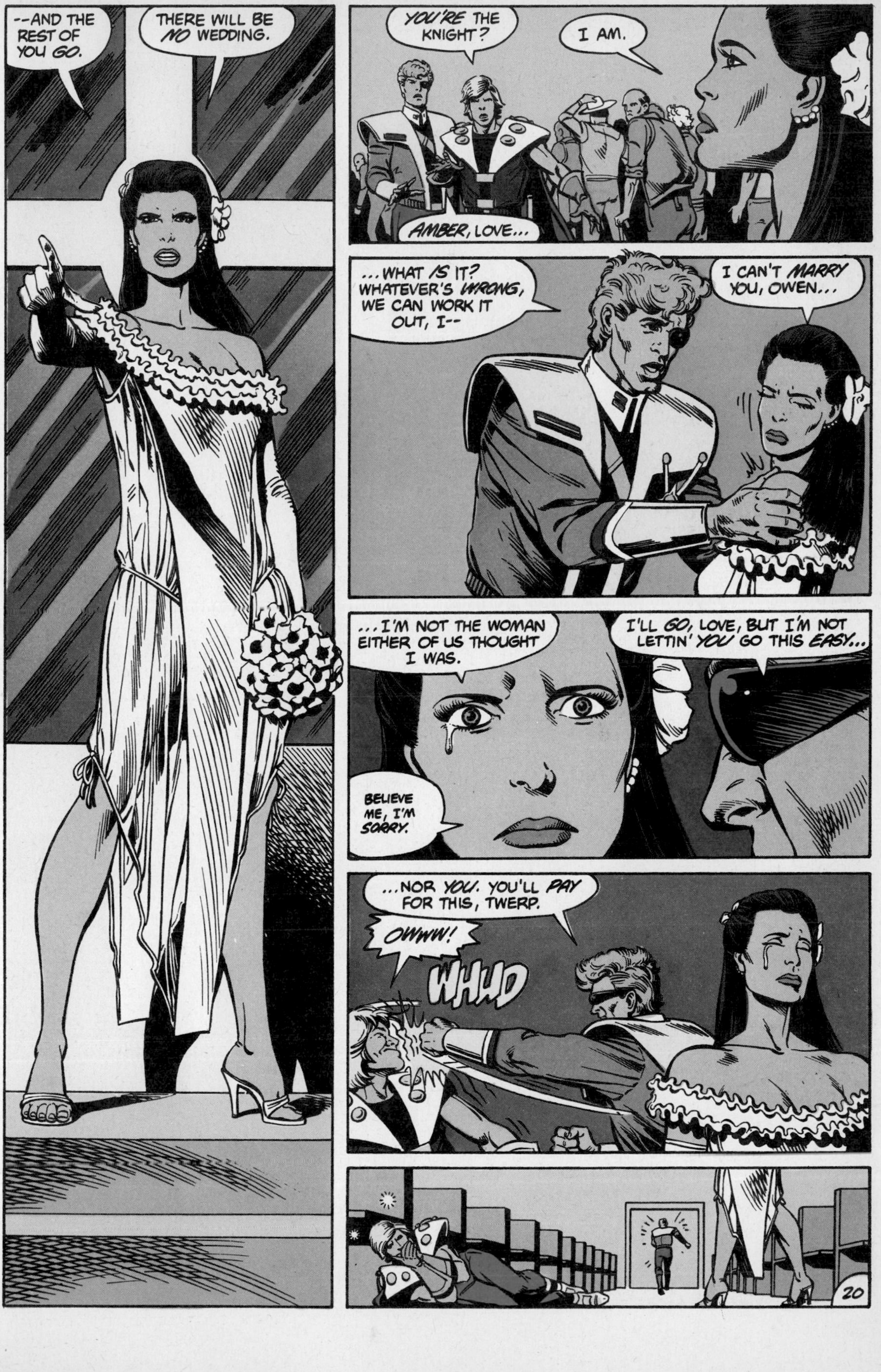
--AND THE REST OF YOU GO.
THERE WILL BE NO WEDDING.
YOU'RE THE KNIGHT?
I AM.
AMBER, LOVE...
...WHAT IS IT? WHATEVER'S WRONG, WE CAN WORK IT OUT, I--
I CAN'T MARRY YOU, OWEN...
...I'M NOT THE WOMAN EITHER OF US THOUGHT I WAS.
BELIEVE ME, I'M SORRY.
I'LL GO, LOVE, BUT I'M NOT LETTIN' YOU GO THIS EASY...
...NOR YOU. YOU'LL PAY FOR THIS, TWERP.
OWWW!
WHUD
20

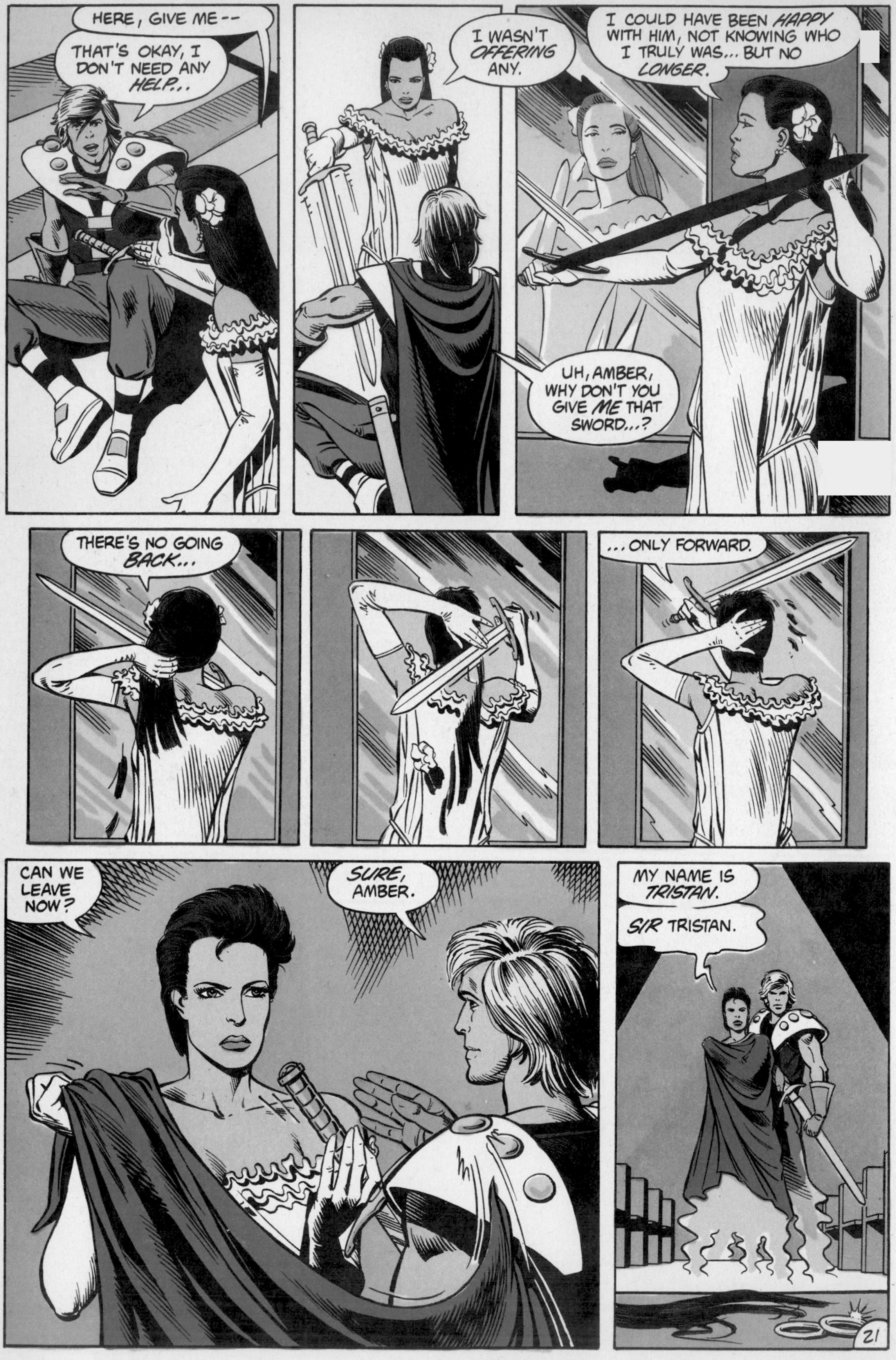
HERE, GIVE ME--
THAT'S OKAY, I DON'T NEED ANY HELP...
I WASN'T OFFERING ANY.
I COULD HAVE BEEN HAPPY WITH HIM, NOT KNOWING WHO I TRULY WAS... BUT NO LONGER.
UH, AMBER, WHY DON'T YOU GIVE ME THAT SWORD...?
THERE'S NO GOING BACK...
...ONLY FORWARD.
CAN WE LEAVE NOW?
SURE, AMBER.
MY NAME IS TRISTAN.
SIR TRISTAN.

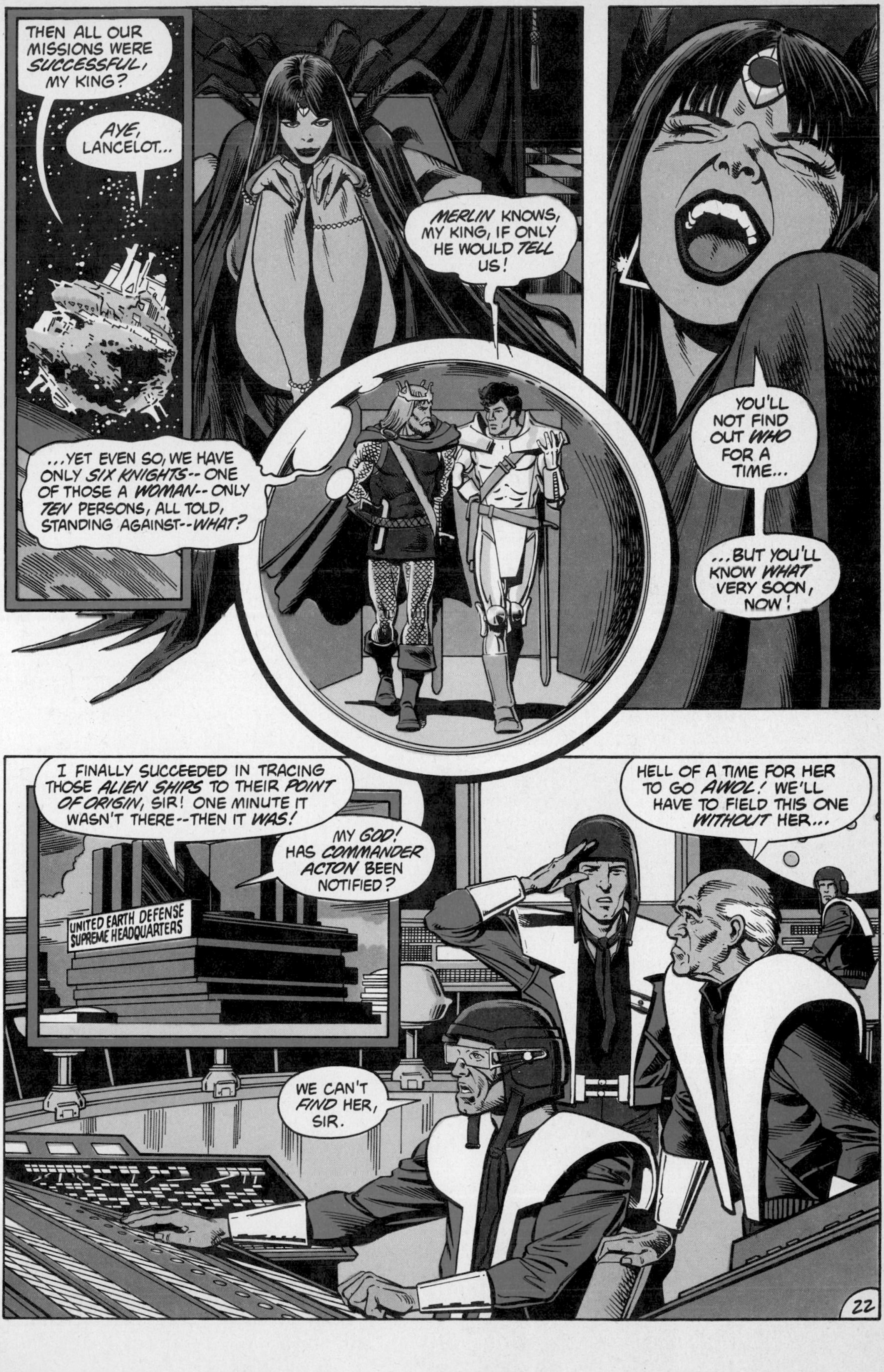

THEN ALL OUR MISSIONS WERE SUCCESSFUL, MY KING?
AYE, LANCELOT...
...YET EVEN SO, WE HAVE ONLY SIX KNIGHTS-- ONE OF THOSE A WOMAN-- ONLY TEN PERSONS, ALL TOLD, STANDING AGAINST--WHAT?
MERLIN KNOWS, MY KING, IF ONLY HE WOULD TELL US!
YOU'LL NOT FIND OUT WHO FOR A TIME...
...BUT YOU'LL KNOW WHAT VERY SOON, NOW!
I FINALLY SUCCEEDED IN TRACING THOSE ALIEN SHIPS TO THEIR POINT OF ORIGIN, SIR! ONE MINUTE IT WASN'T THERE--THEN IT WAS!
MY GOD! HAS COMMANDER ACTON BEEN NOTIFIED?
UNITED EARTH DEFENSE SUPREME HEADQUARTERS
WE CAN'T FIND HER, SIR.
HELL OF A TIME FOR HER TO GO AWOL! WE'LL HAVE TO FIELD THIS ONE WITHOUT HER...

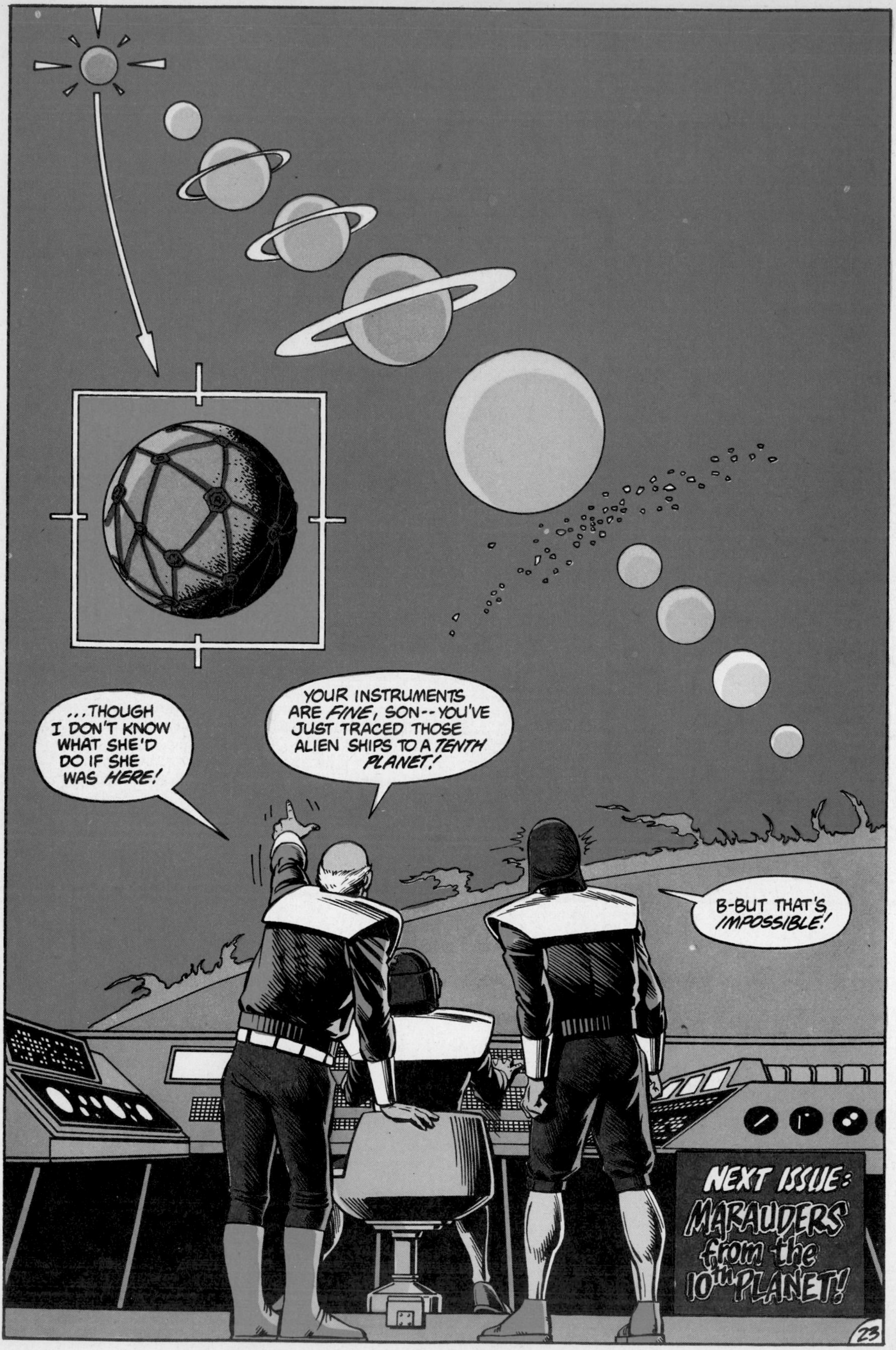
...THOUGH I DON'T KNOW WHAT SHE'D DO IF SHE WAS HERE!
YOUR INSTRUMENTS ARE FINE, SON--YOU'VE JUST TRACED THOSE ALIEN SHIPS TO A TENTH PLANET!
B-BUT THAT'S IMPOSSIBLE!
NEXT ISSUE: MARAUDERS from the 10th PLANET!
23

CHAPTER
4

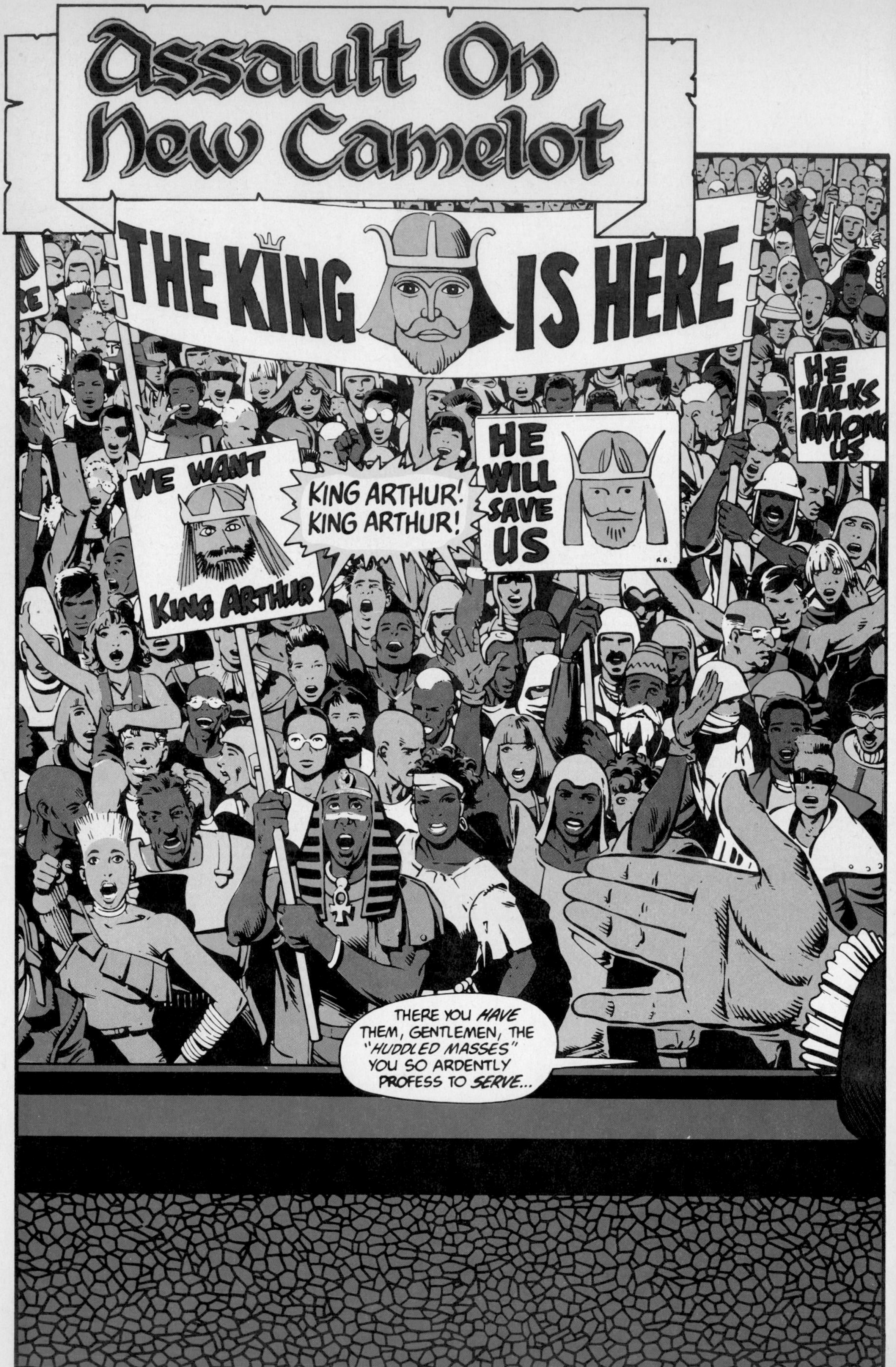
Assault On New Camelot
THE KING IS HERE
HE WALKS AMONG US
WE WANT KING ARTHUR
KING ARTHUR! KING ARTHUR!
HE WILL SAVE US
THERE YOU *HAVE* THEM, GENTLEMEN, THE "*HUDDLED MASSES*" YOU SO ARDENTLY PROFESS TO *SERVE*...

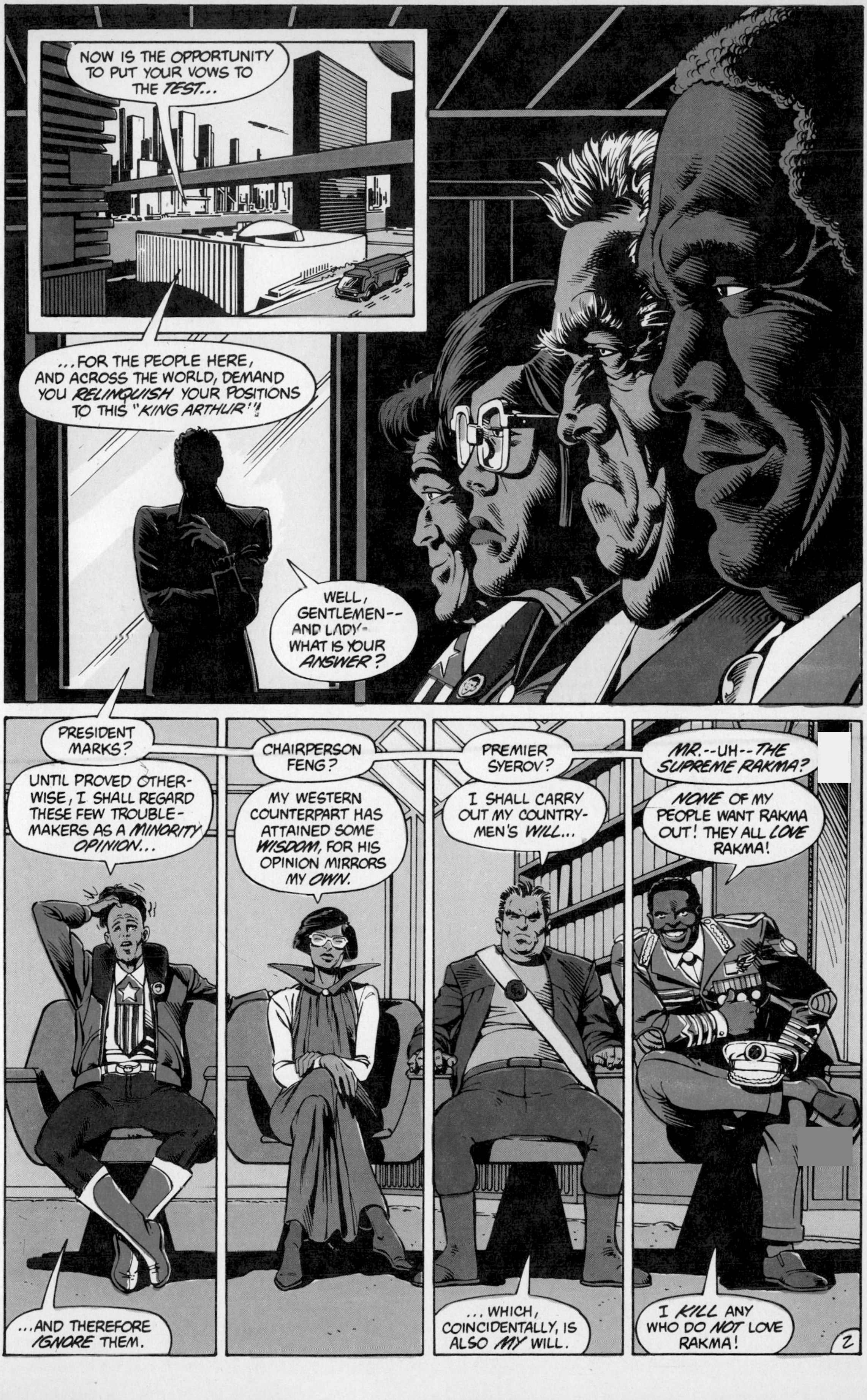
NOW IS THE OPPORTUNITY TO PUT YOUR VOWS TO THE *TEST*...
...FOR THE PEOPLE HERE, AND ACROSS THE WORLD, DEMAND YOU *RELINQUISH* YOUR POSITIONS TO THIS "*KING ARTHUR*"!
WELL, GENTLEMEN-- AND LADY-- WHAT IS YOUR *ANSWER*?
PRESIDENT MARKS?
UNTIL PROVED OTHERWISE, I SHALL REGARD THESE FEW TROUBLEMAKERS AS A *MINORITY OPINION*...
...AND THEREFORE *IGNORE* THEM.
CHAIRPERSON FENG?
MY WESTERN COUNTERPART HAS ATTAINED SOME *WISDOM*, FOR HIS OPINION MIRRORS MY *OWN*.
PREMIER SYEROV?
I SHALL CARRY OUT MY COUNTRYMEN'S *WILL*...
...WHICH, COINCIDENTALLY, IS ALSO *MY* WILL.
MR.--UH--THE SUPREME RAKMA?
NONE OF MY PEOPLE WANT RAKMA OUT! THEY ALL *LOVE* RAKMA!
I *KILL* ANY WHO DO *NOT* LOVE RAKMA!
2

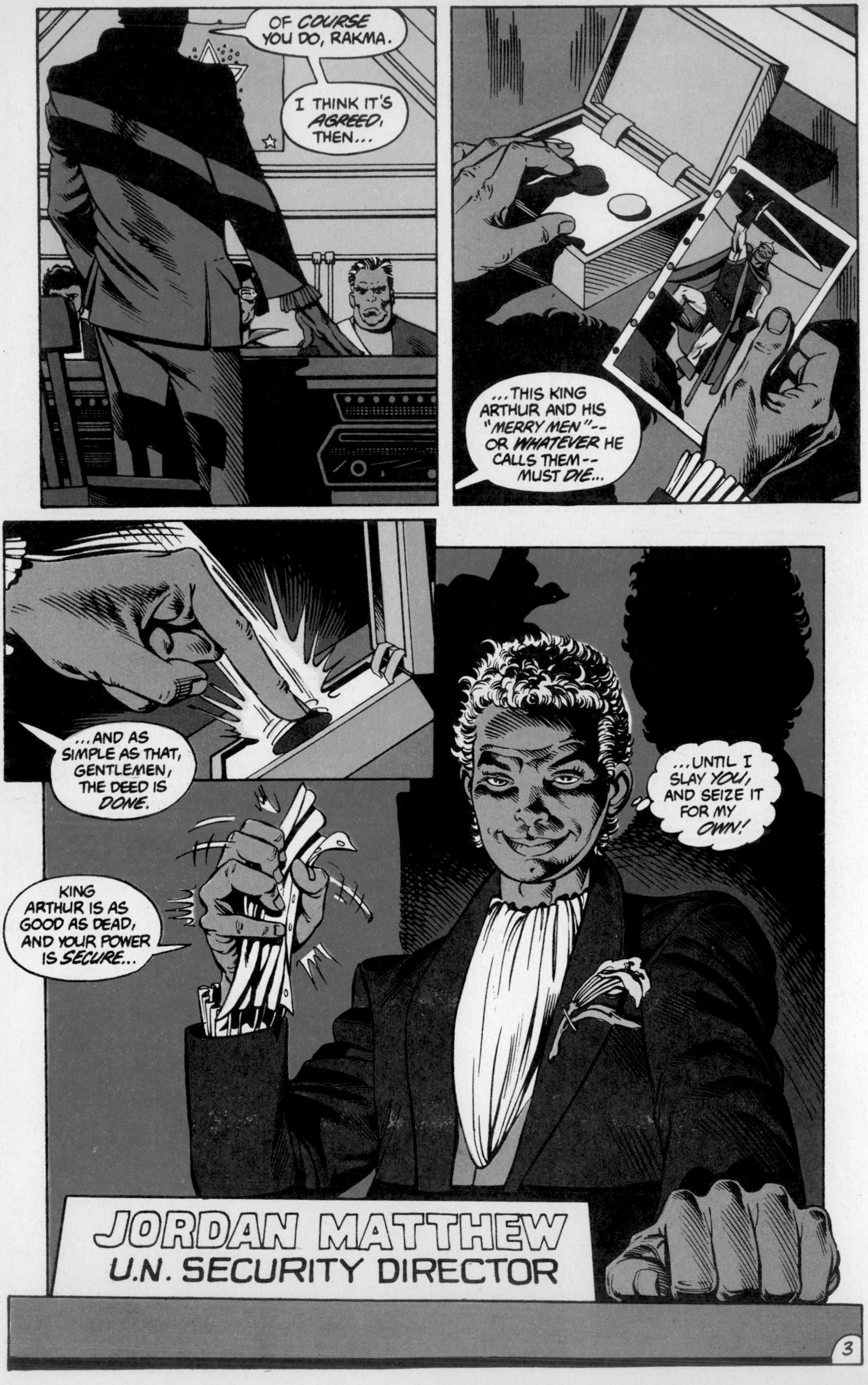
OF COURSE YOU DO, RAKMA.
I THINK IT'S AGREED, THEN...
...THIS KING ARTHUR AND HIS "MERRY MEN"-- OR WHATEVER HE CALLS THEM-- MUST DIE...
...AND AS SIMPLE AS THAT, GENTLEMEN, THE DEED IS DONE.
KING ARTHUR IS AS GOOD AS DEAD, AND YOUR POWER IS SECURE...
...UNTIL I SLAY YOU, AND SEIZE IT FOR MY OWN!
JORDAN MATTHEW
U.N. SECURITY DIRECTOR

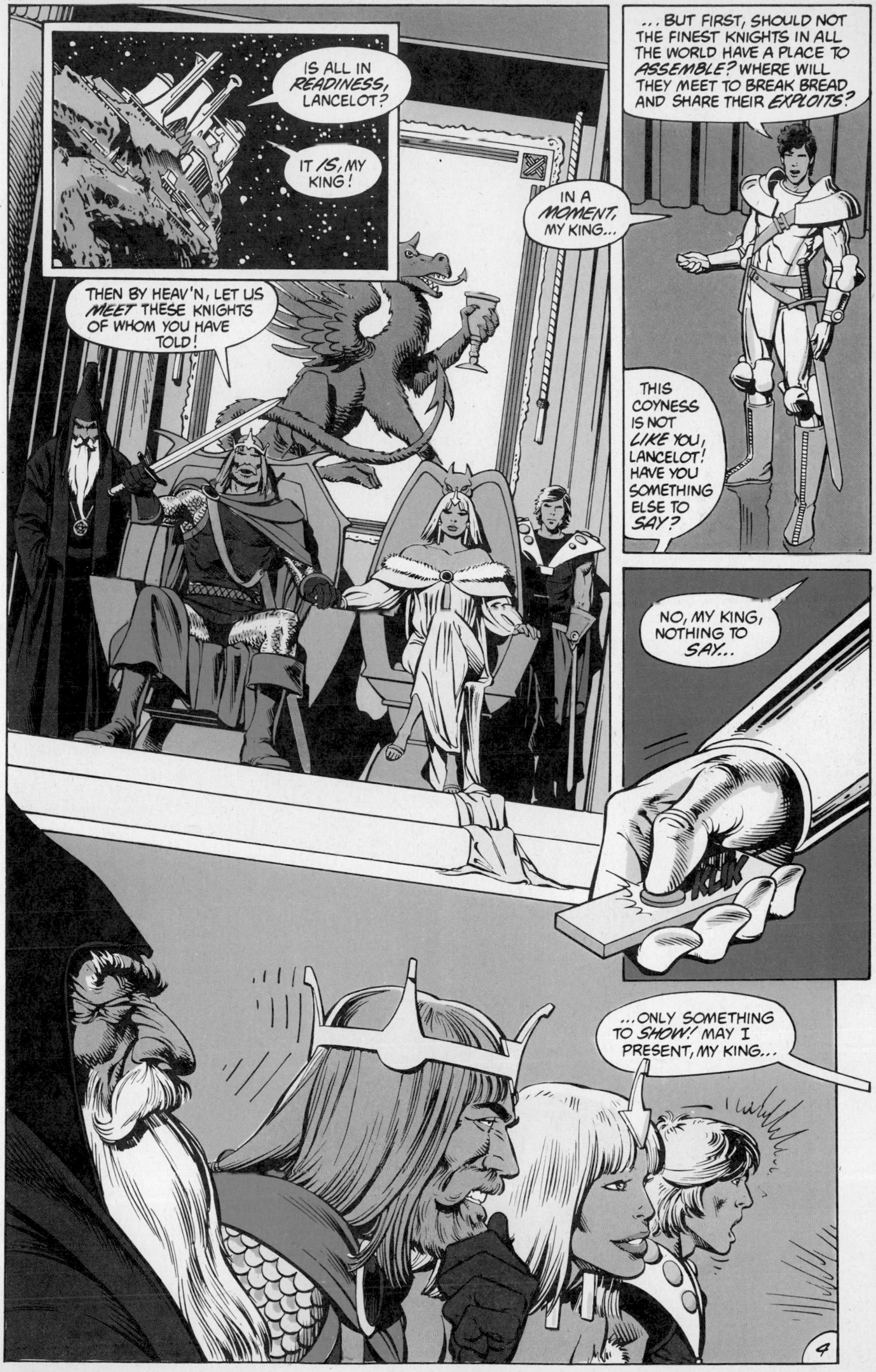
IS ALL IN READINESS, LANCELOT?
IT IS, MY KING!
THEN BY HEAV'N, LET US MEET THESE KNIGHTS OF WHOM YOU HAVE TOLD!
IN A MOMENT, MY KING...
...BUT FIRST, SHOULD NOT THE FINEST KNIGHTS IN ALL THE WORLD HAVE A PLACE TO ASSEMBLE? WHERE WILL THEY MEET TO BREAK BREAD AND SHARE THEIR EXPLOITS?
THIS COYNESS IS NOT LIKE YOU, LANCELOT! HAVE YOU SOMETHING ELSE TO SAY?
NO, MY KING, NOTHING TO SAY...
KLIK
...ONLY SOMETHING TO SHOW! MAY I PRESENT, MY KING...

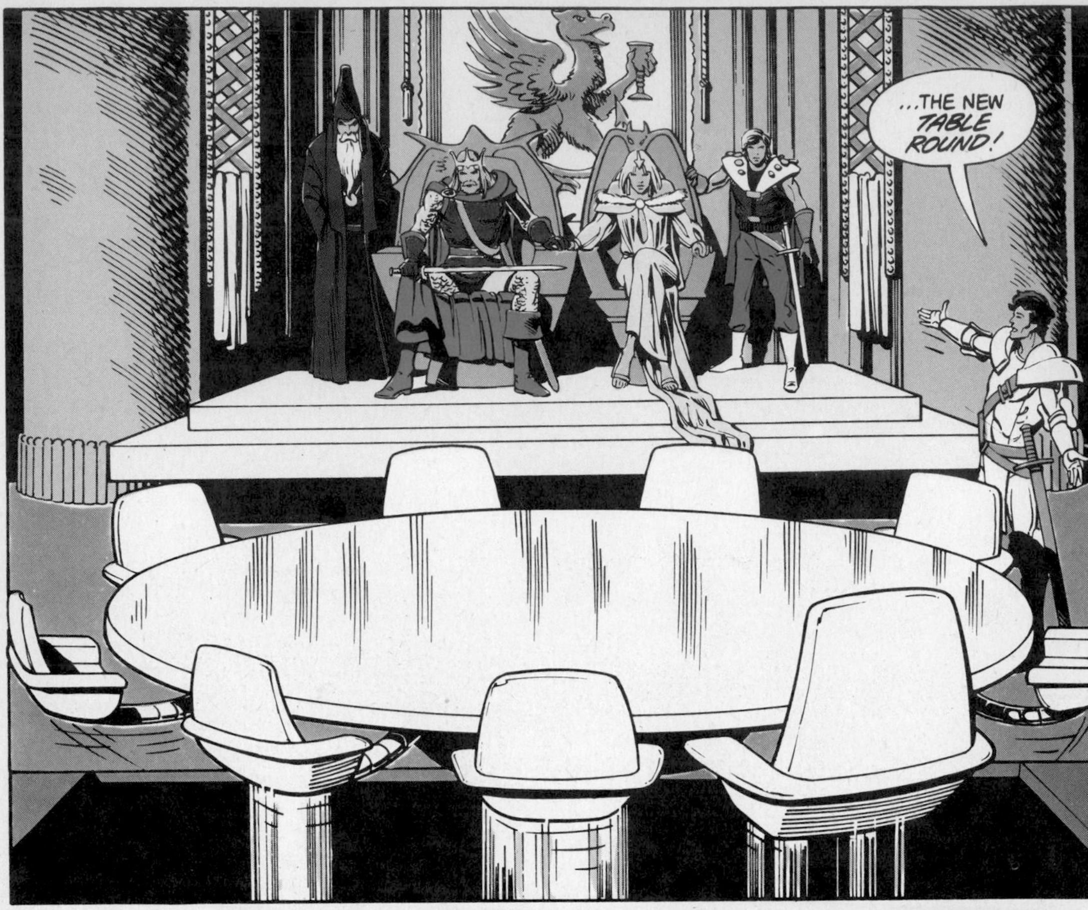
...THE NEW TABLE ROUND!

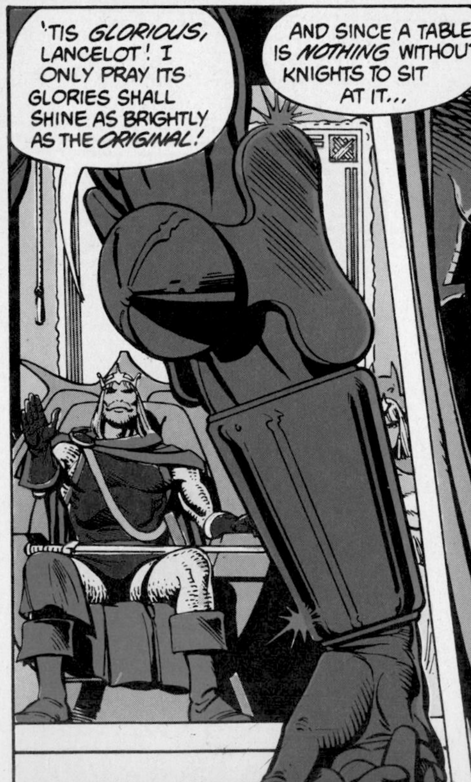
'TIS GLORIOUS, LANCELOT! I ONLY PRAY ITS GLORIES SHALL SHINE AS BRIGHTLY AS THE ORIGINAL!
AND SINCE A TABLE IS NOTHING WITHOUT KNIGHTS TO SIT AT IT...
...MY KING, YOUR KNIGHTS OF THE TABLE ROUND!

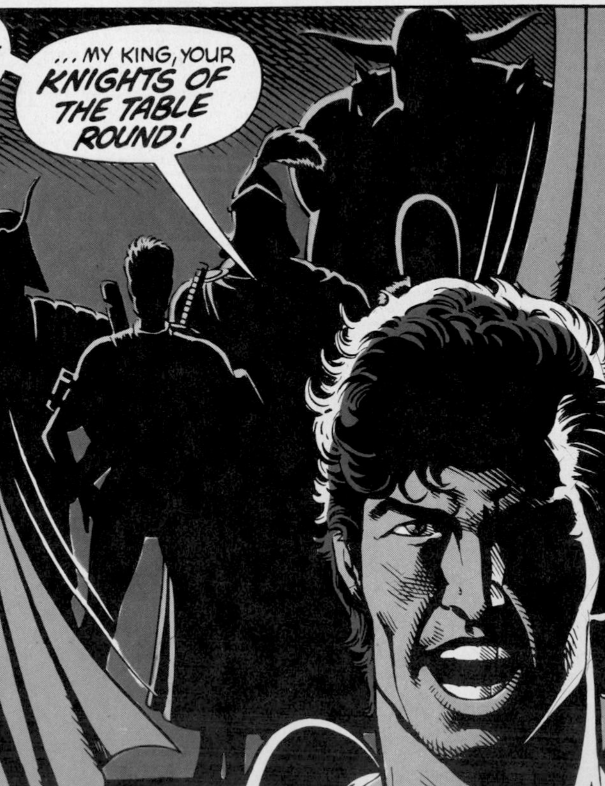

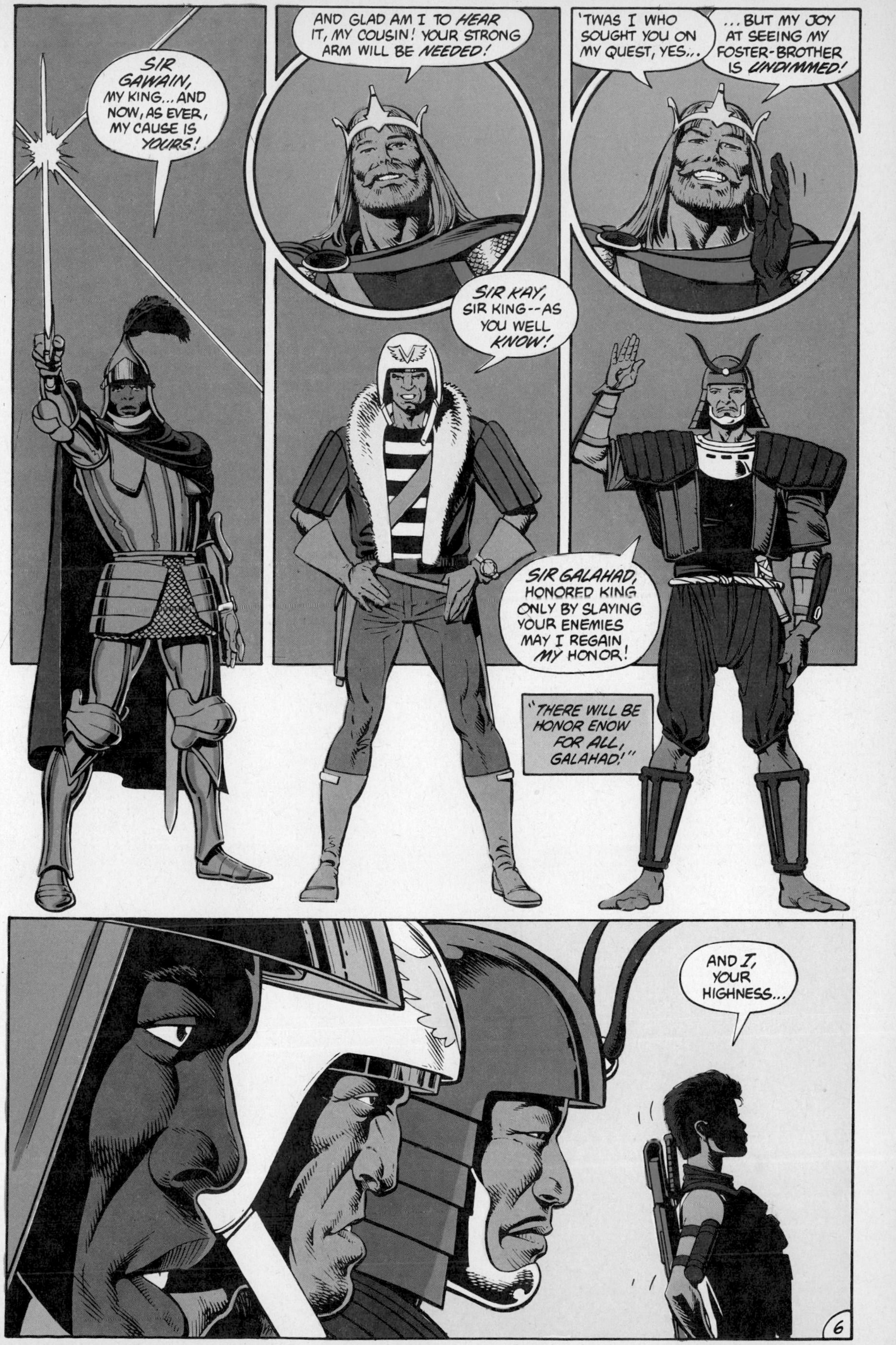
SIR GAWAIN, MY KING... AND NOW, AS EVER, MY CAUSE IS YOURS!
AND GLAD AM I TO HEAR IT, MY COUSIN! YOUR STRONG ARM WILL BE NEEDED!
SIR KAY, SIR KING--AS YOU WELL KNOW!
'TWAS I WHO SOUGHT YOU ON MY QUEST, YES...
...BUT MY JOY AT SEEING MY FOSTER-BROTHER IS UNDIMMED!
SIR GALAHAD, HONORED KING ONLY BY SLAYING YOUR ENEMIES MAY I REGAIN MY HONOR!
"THERE WILL BE HONOR ENOW FOR ALL, GALAHAD!"
AND I, YOUR HIGHNESS...
6

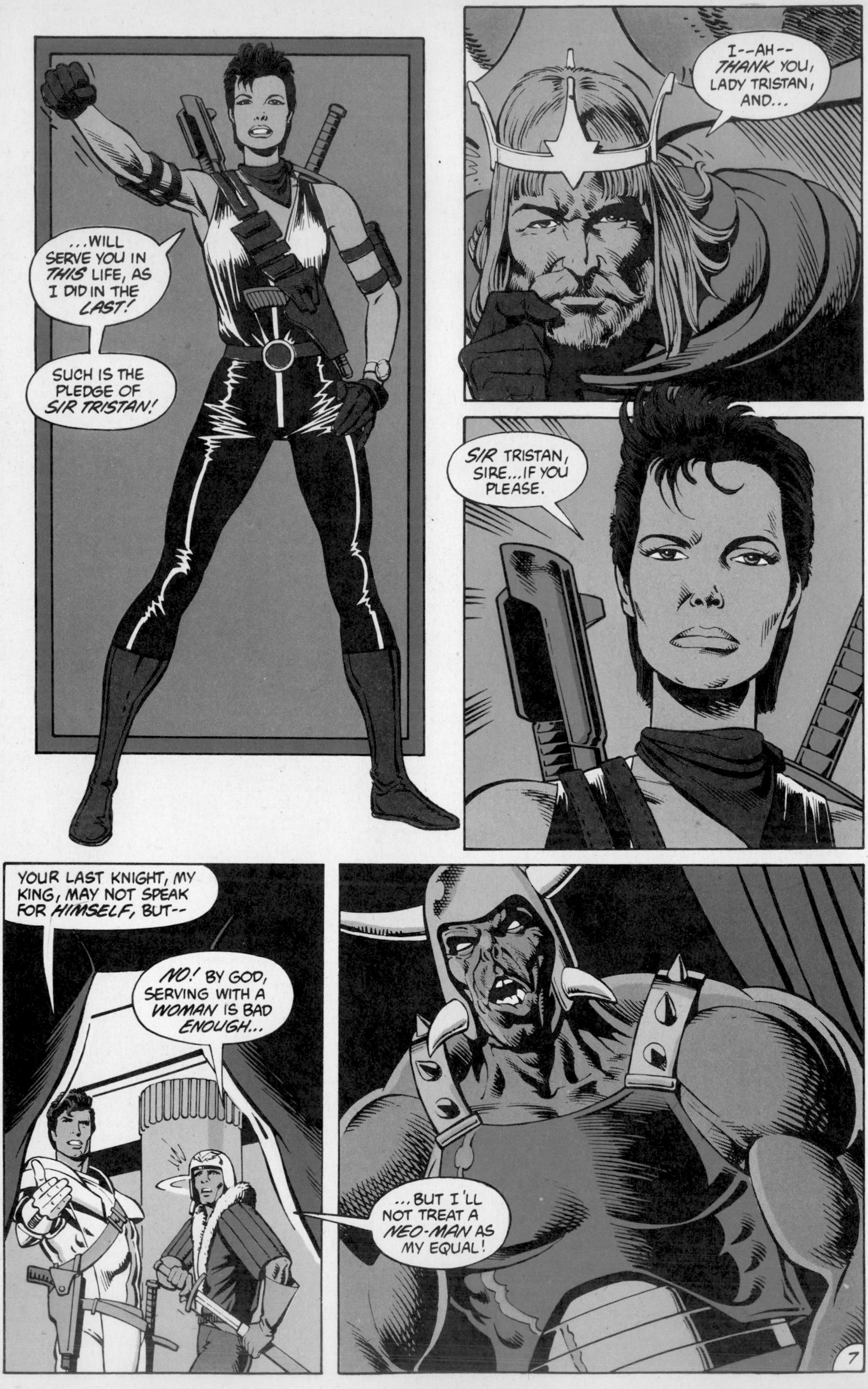
...WILL SERVE YOU IN THIS LIFE, AS I DID IN THE LAST!
SUCH IS THE PLEDGE OF SIR TRISTAN!
I--AH-- THANK YOU, LADY TRISTAN, AND...
SIR TRISTAN, SIRE...IF YOU PLEASE.
YOUR LAST KNIGHT, MY KING, MAY NOT SPEAK FOR HIMSELF, BUT--
NO! BY GOD, SERVING WITH A WOMAN IS BAD ENOUGH...
...BUT I'LL NOT TREAT A NEO-MAN AS MY EQUAL!
7

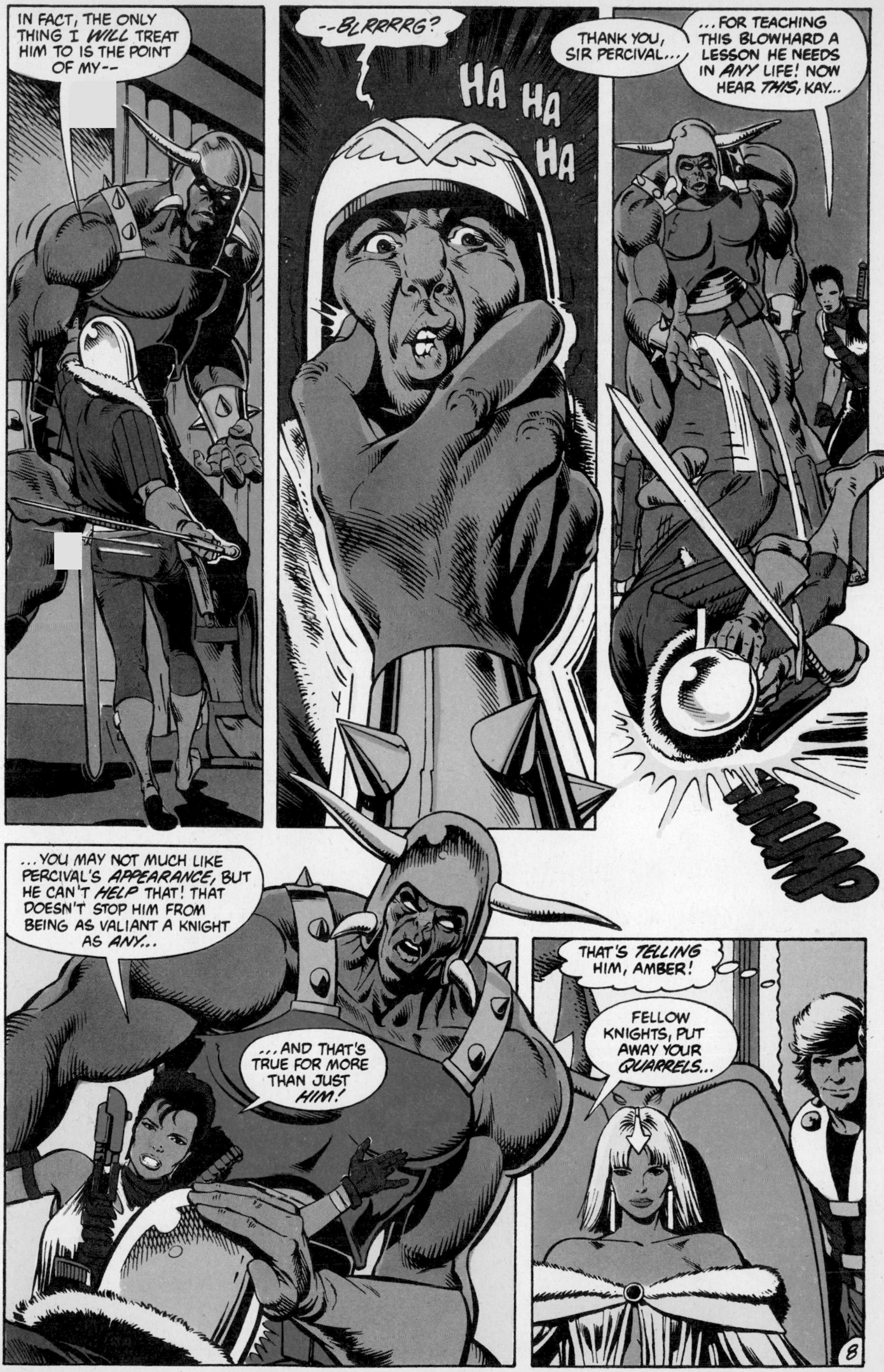
IN FACT, THE ONLY THING I *WILL* TREAT HIM TO IS THE POINT OF MY--
--BLRRRRG?
HA HA HA
THANK YOU, SIR PERCIVAL...
...FOR TEACHING THIS BLOWHARD A LESSON HE NEEDS IN *ANY* LIFE! NOW HEAR *THIS*, KAY...
THUMP
...YOU MAY NOT MUCH LIKE PERCIVAL'S *APPEARANCE*, BUT HE CAN'T *HELP* THAT! THAT DOESN'T STOP HIM FROM BEING AS VALIANT A KNIGHT AS *ANY*...
...AND THAT'S TRUE FOR MORE THAN JUST *HIM*!
THAT'S *TELLING* HIM, AMBER!
FELLOW KNIGHTS, PUT AWAY YOUR *QUARRELS*...

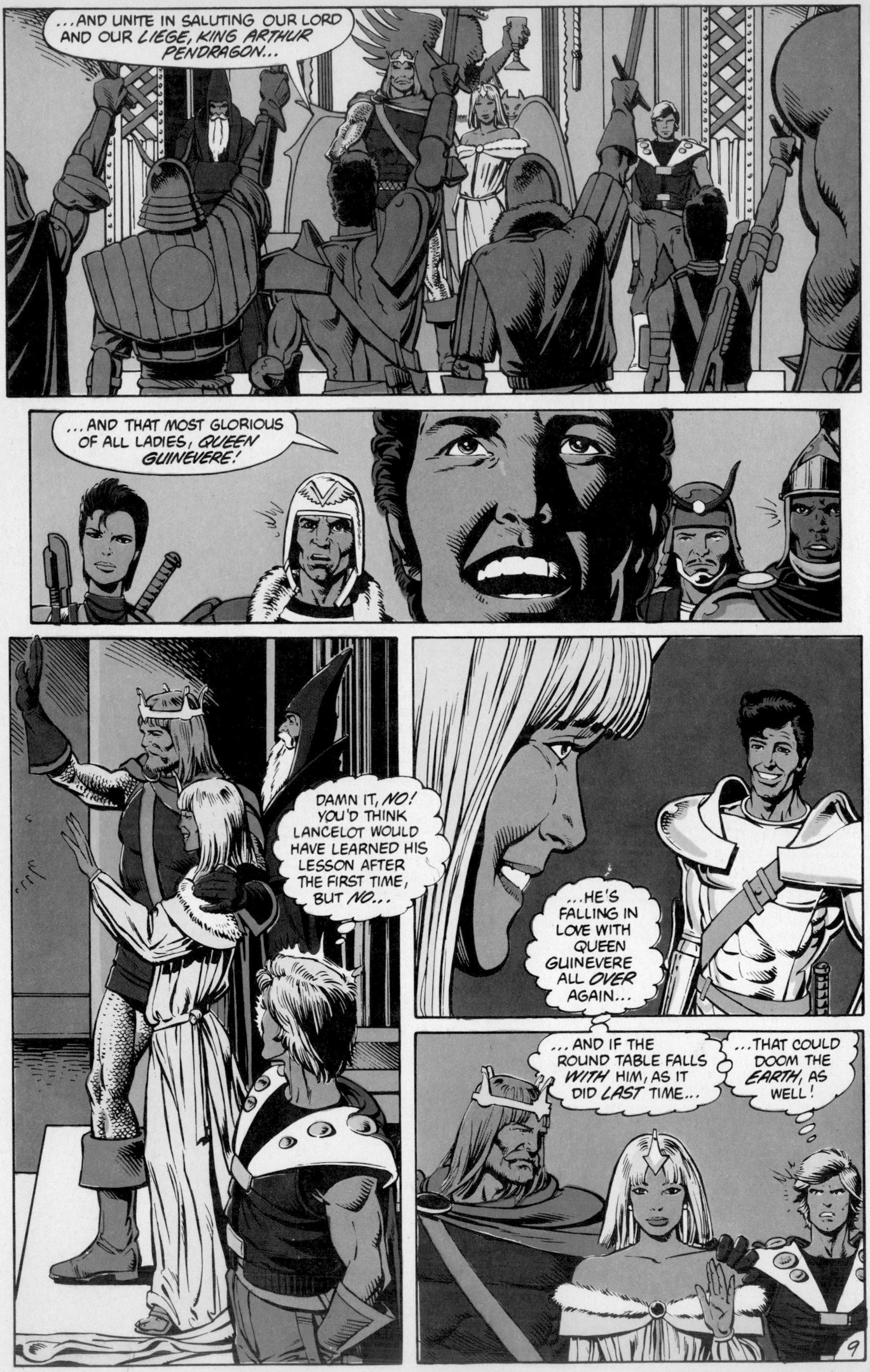
...AND UNITE IN SALUTING OUR LORD AND OUR LIEGE, KING ARTHUR PENDRAGON...
...AND THAT MOST GLORIOUS OF ALL LADIES, QUEEN GUINEVERE!
DAMN IT, NO! YOU'D THINK LANCELOT WOULD HAVE LEARNED HIS LESSON AFTER THE FIRST TIME, BUT NO...
...HE'S FALLING IN LOVE WITH QUEEN GUINEVERE ALL OVER AGAIN...
...AND IF THE ROUND TABLE FALLS WITH HIM, AS IT DID LAST TIME...
...THAT COULD DOOM THE EARTH, AS WELL!
9

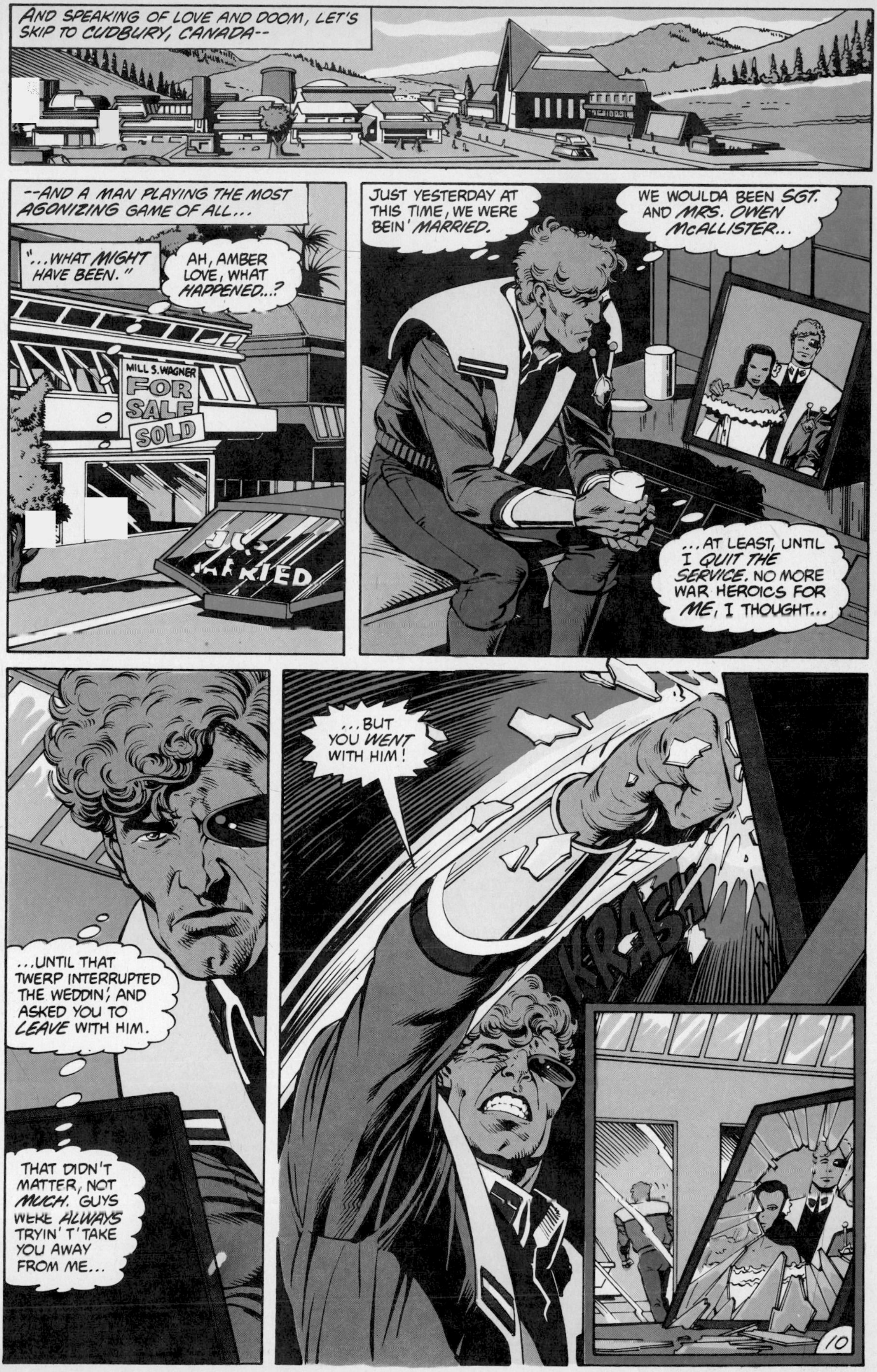
AND SPEAKING OF LOVE AND DOOM, LET'S SKIP TO CUDBURY, CANADA--
--AND A MAN PLAYING THE MOST AGONIZING GAME OF ALL...
"...WHAT MIGHT HAVE BEEN."
AH, AMBER LOVE, WHAT HAPPENED...?
MILL S. WAGNER
FOR SALE
SOLD
JUST YESTERDAY AT THIS TIME, WE WERE BEIN' MARRIED.
WE WOULDA BEEN SGT. AND MRS. OWEN McALLISTER...
...AT LEAST, UNTIL I QUIT THE SERVICE. NO MORE WAR HEROICS FOR ME, I THOUGHT...
...UNTIL THAT TWERP INTERRUPTED THE WEDDIN', AND ASKED YOU TO LEAVE WITH HIM.
THAT DIDN'T MATTER, NOT MUCH. GUYS WERE ALWAYS TRYIN' T'TAKE YOU AWAY FROM ME...
...BUT YOU WENT WITH HIM!
KRASH
10

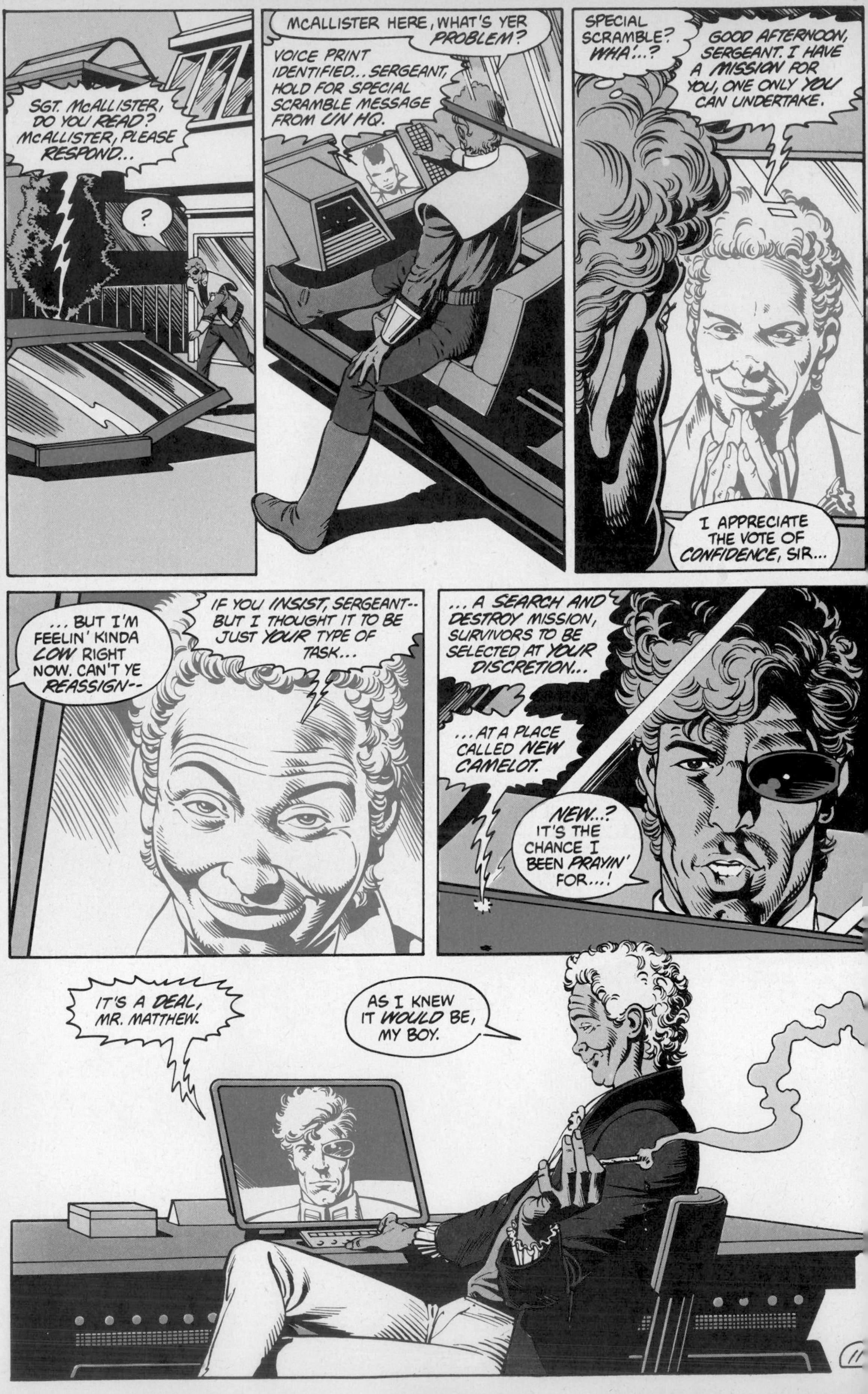
SGT. McALLISTER, DO YOU READ? McALLISTER, PLEASE RESPOND...
?
McALLISTER HERE, WHAT'S YER PROBLEM?
VOICE PRINT IDENTIFIED... SERGEANT, HOLD FOR SPECIAL SCRAMBLE MESSAGE FROM UN HQ.
SPECIAL SCRAMBLE? WHA'...?
GOOD AFTERNOON, SERGEANT. I HAVE A MISSION FOR YOU, ONE ONLY YOU CAN UNDERTAKE.
I APPRECIATE THE VOTE OF CONFIDENCE, SIR...
... BUT I'M FEELIN' KINDA LOW RIGHT NOW. CAN'T YE REASSIGN--
IF YOU INSIST, SERGEANT-- BUT I THOUGHT IT TO BE JUST YOUR TYPE OF TASK...
... A SEARCH AND DESTROY MISSION, SURVIVORS TO BE SELECTED AT YOUR DISCRETION...
... AT A PLACE CALLED NEW CAMELOT.
NEW...? IT'S THE CHANCE I BEEN PRAYIN' FOR...!
IT'S A DEAL, MR. MATTHEW.
AS I KNEW IT WOULD BE, MY BOY.

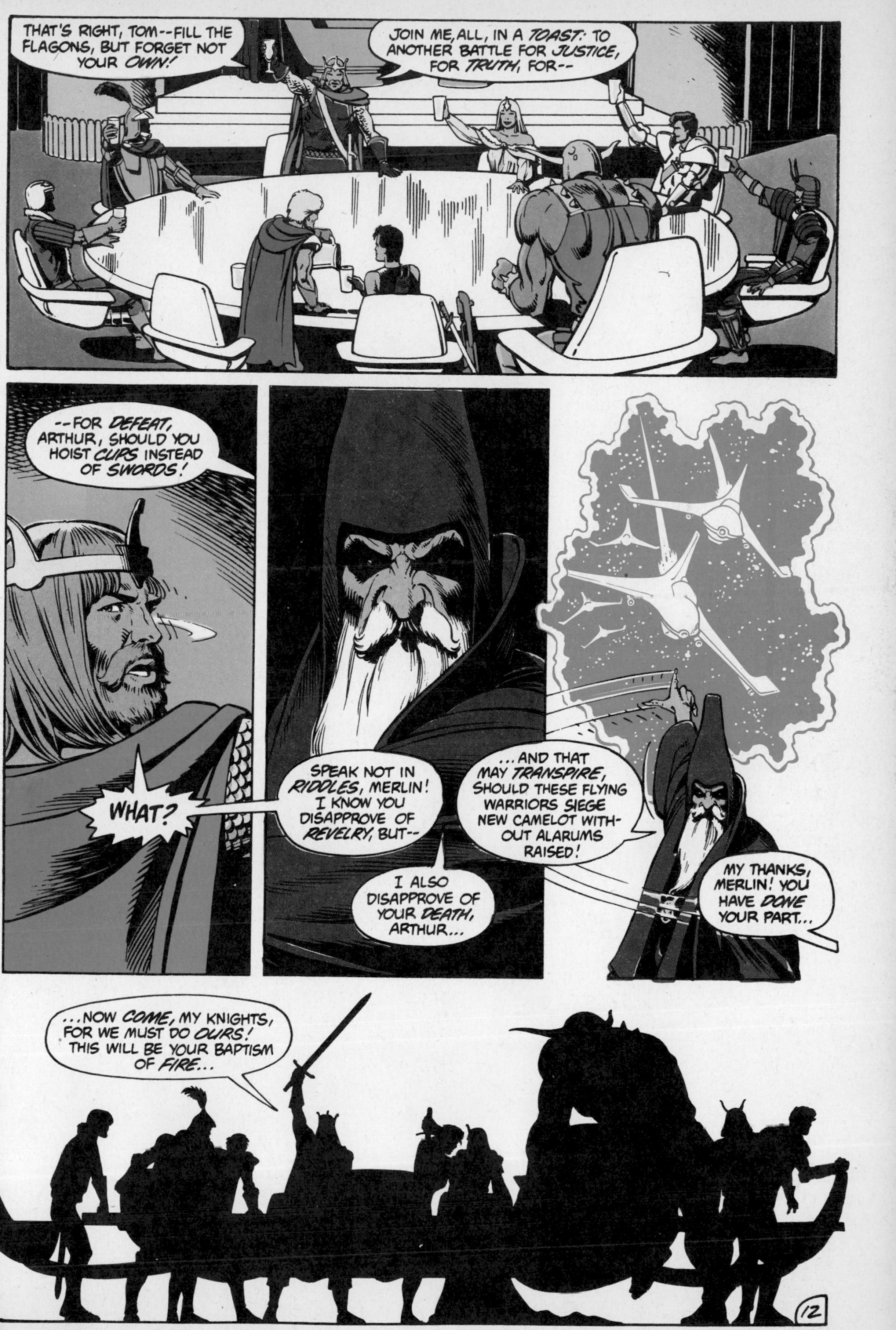
THAT'S RIGHT, TOM--FILL THE FLAGONS, BUT FORGET NOT YOUR OWN!
JOIN ME, ALL, IN A TOAST: TO ANOTHER BATTLE FOR JUSTICE, FOR TRUTH, FOR--
--FOR DEFEAT, ARTHUR, SHOULD YOU HOIST CUPS INSTEAD OF SWORDS!
WHAT?
SPEAK NOT IN RIDDLES, MERLIN! I KNOW YOU DISAPPROVE OF REVELRY, BUT--
I ALSO DISAPPROVE OF YOUR DEATH, ARTHUR...
...AND THAT MAY TRANSPIRE, SHOULD THESE FLYING WARRIORS SIEGE NEW CAMELOT WITHOUT ALARUMS RAISED!
MY THANKS, MERLIN! YOU HAVE DONE YOUR PART...
...NOW COME, MY KNIGHTS, FOR WE MUST DO OURS! THIS WILL BE YOUR BAPTISM OF FIRE...

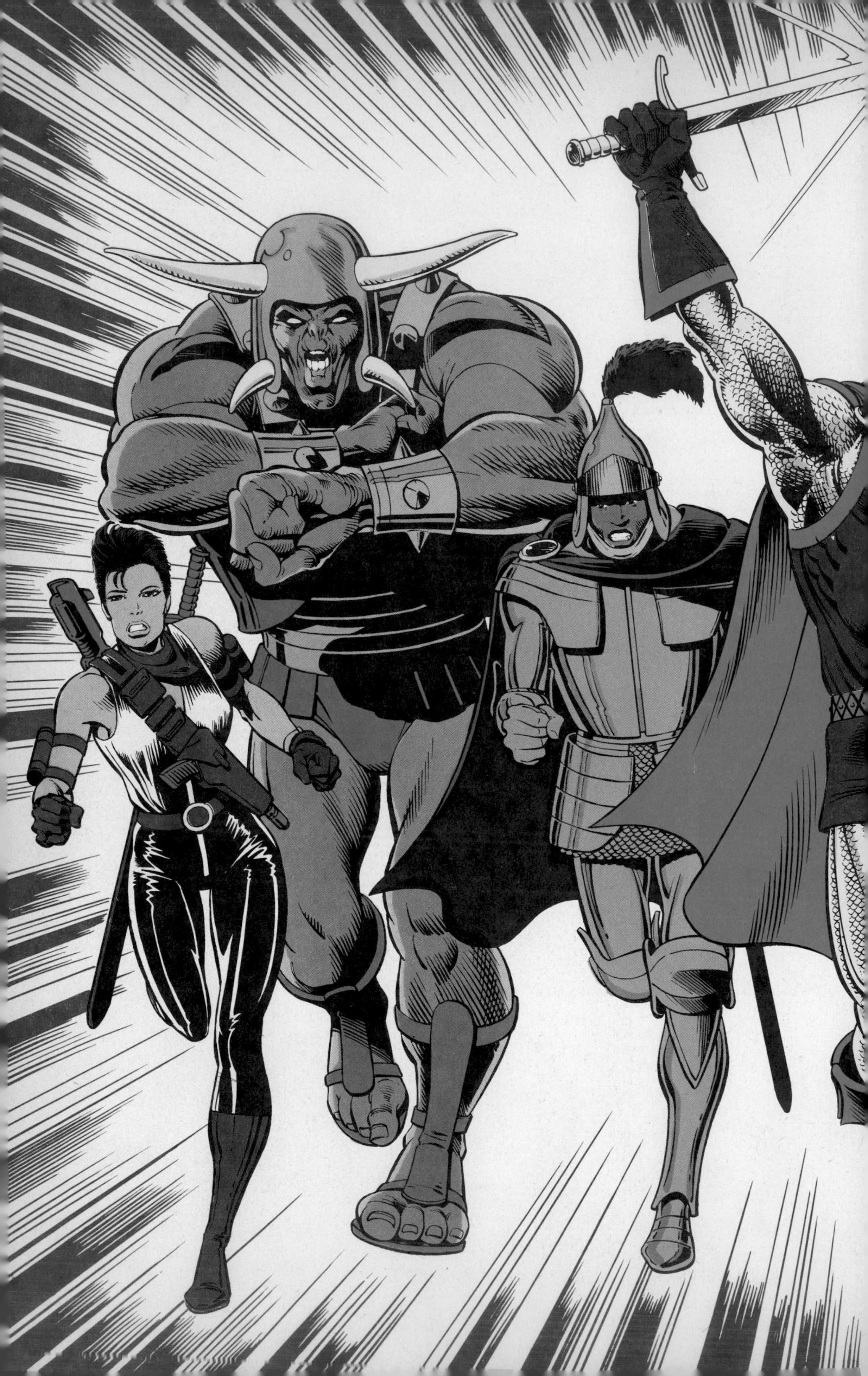

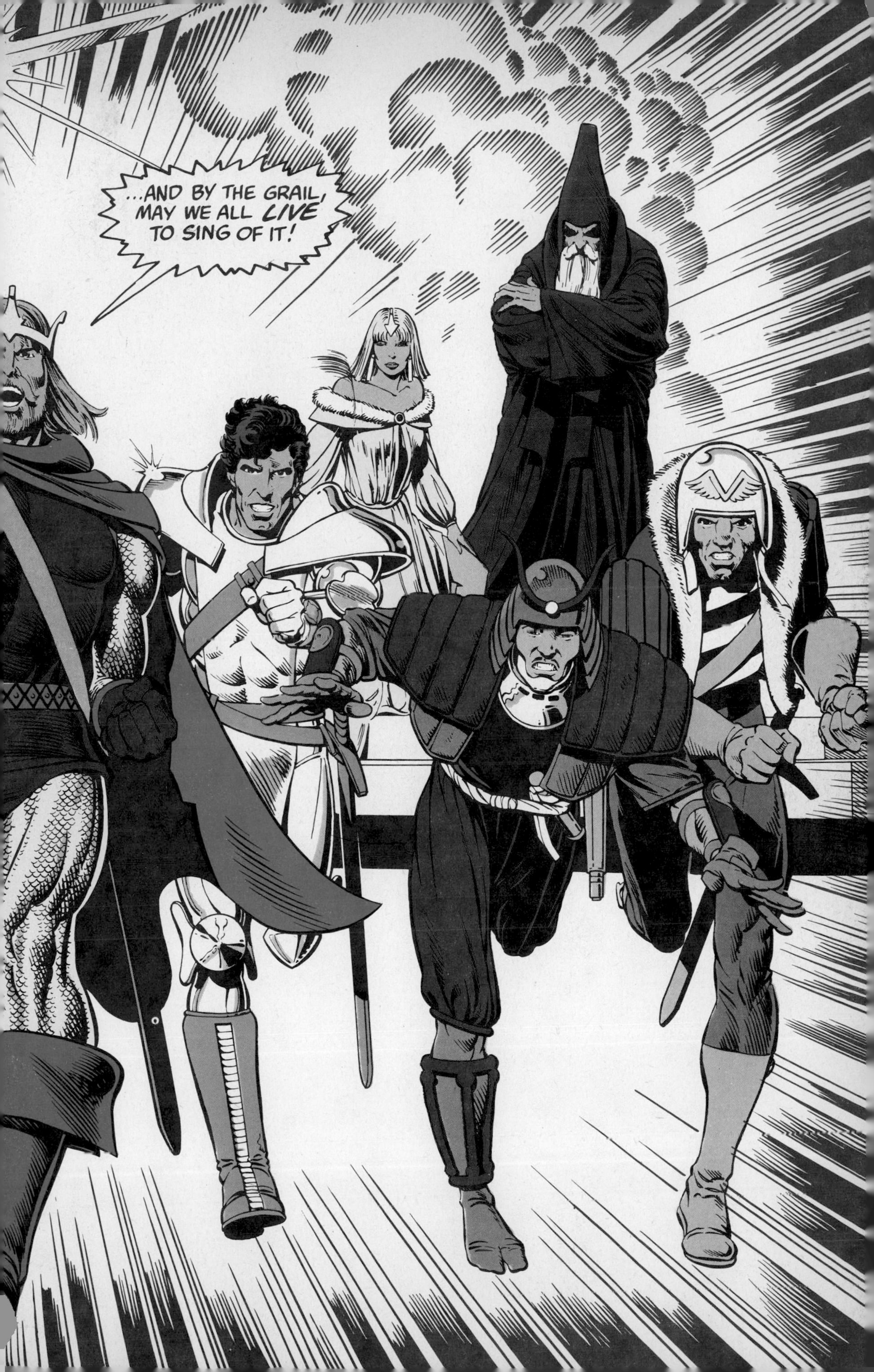
...AND BY THE GRAIL, MAY WE ALL LIVE TO SING OF IT!

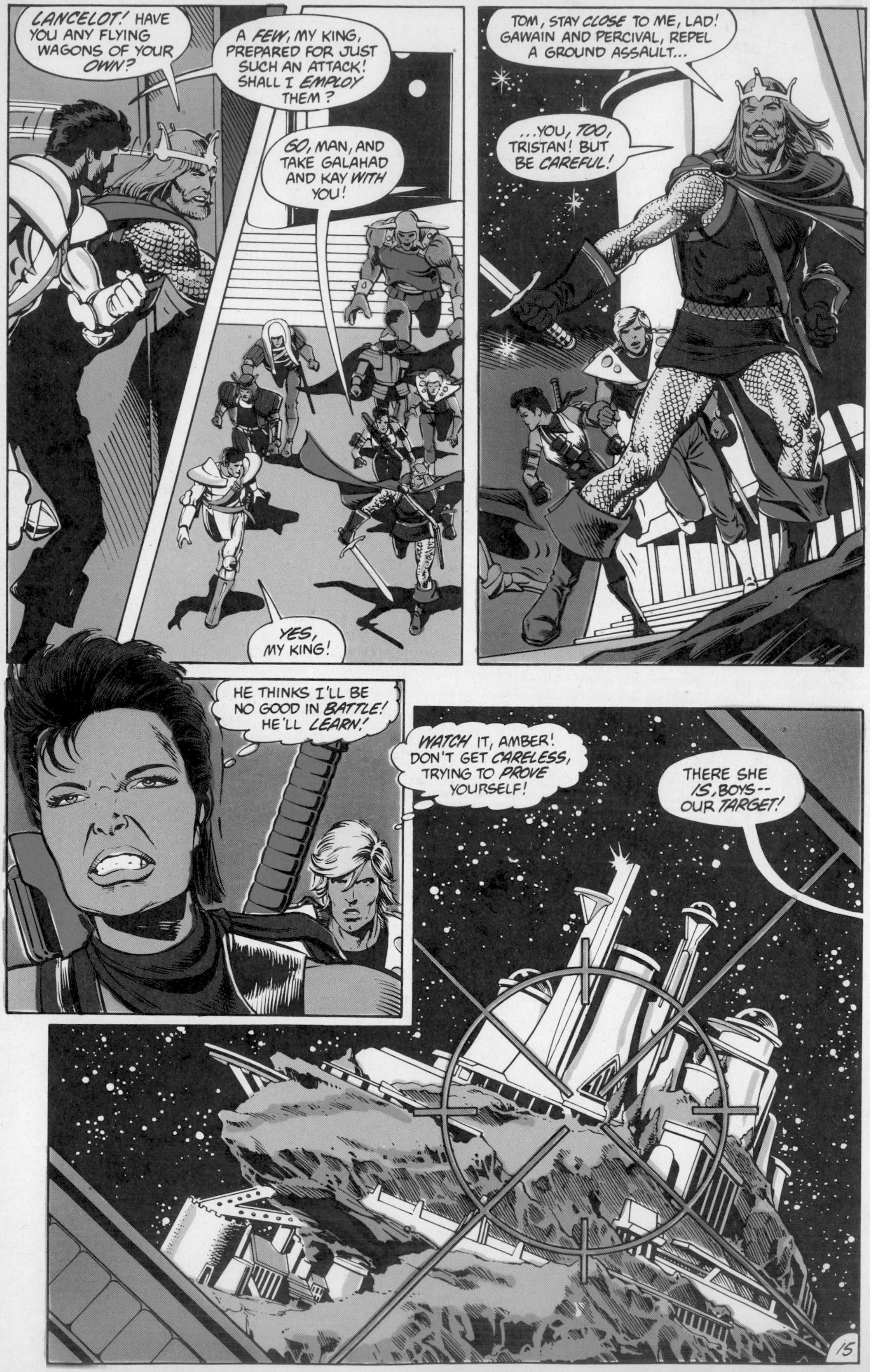
LANCELOT! HAVE YOU ANY FLYING WAGONS OF YOUR OWN?
A FEW, MY KING, PREPARED FOR JUST SUCH AN ATTACK! SHALL I EMPLOY THEM?
GO, MAN, AND TAKE GALAHAD AND KAY WITH YOU!
YES, MY KING!
TOM, STAY CLOSE TO ME, LAD! GAWAIN AND PERCIVAL, REPEL A GROUND ASSAULT...
...YOU, TOO, TRISTAN! BUT BE CAREFUL!
HE THINKS I'LL BE NO GOOD IN BATTLE! HE'LL LEARN!
WATCH IT, AMBER! DON'T GET CARELESS, TRYING TO PROVE YOURSELF!
THERE SHE IS, BOYS-- OUR TARGET!
15

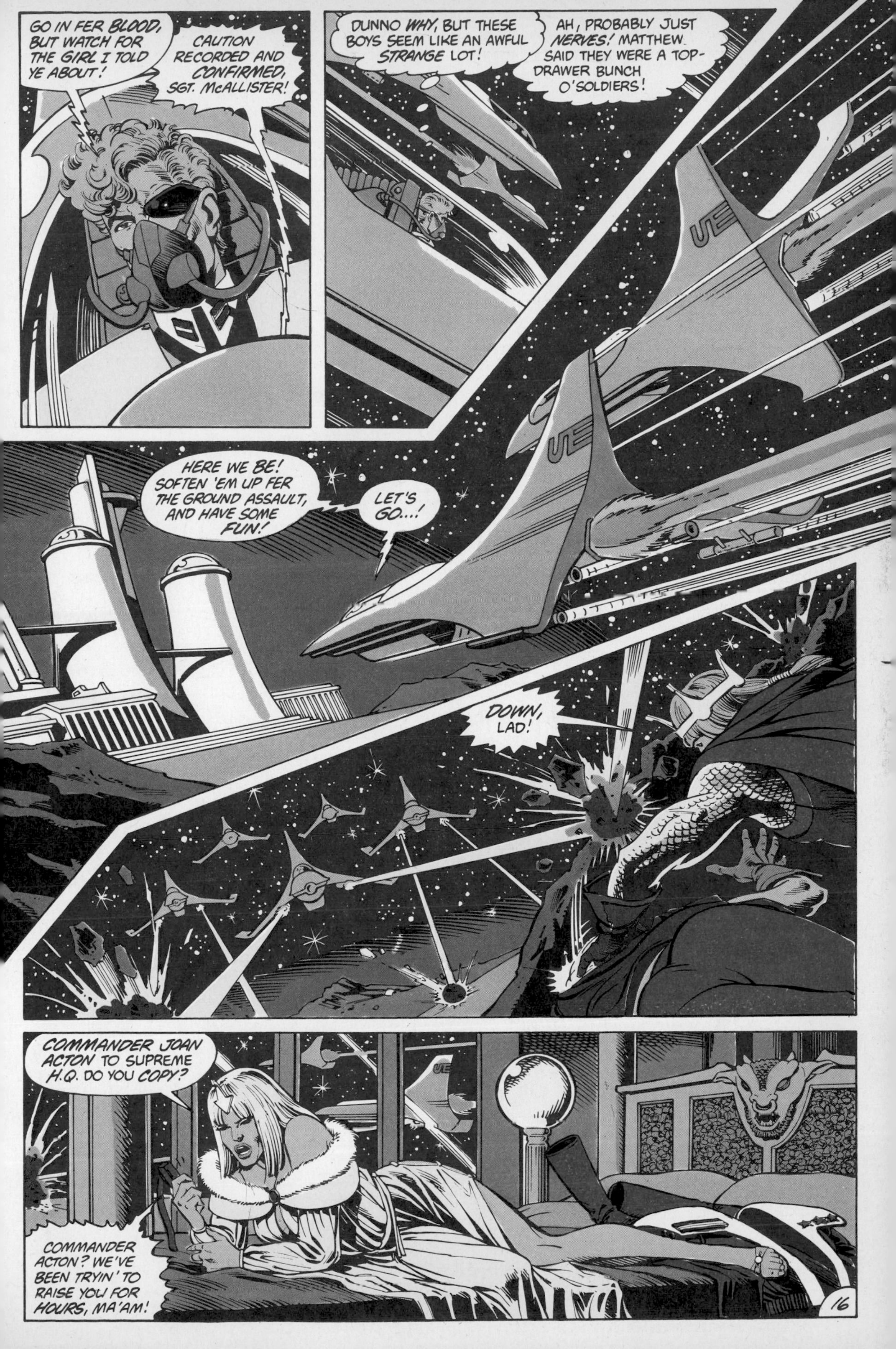
GO IN FER BLOOD, BUT WATCH FOR THE GIRL I TOLD YE ABOUT!
CAUTION RECORDED AND CONFIRMED, SGT. McALLISTER!
DUNNO WHY, BUT THESE BOYS SEEM LIKE AN AWFUL STRANGE LOT!
AH, PROBABLY JUST NERVES! MATTHEW SAID THEY WERE A TOP-DRAWER BUNCH O'SOLDIERS!
HERE WE BE! SOFTEN 'EM UP FER THE GROUND ASSAULT, AND HAVE SOME FUN!
LET'S GO...!
DOWN, LAD!
COMMANDER JOAN ACTON TO SUPREME H.Q. DO YOU COPY?
COMMANDER ACTON? WE'VE BEEN TRYIN' TO RAISE YOU FOR HOURS, MA'AM!

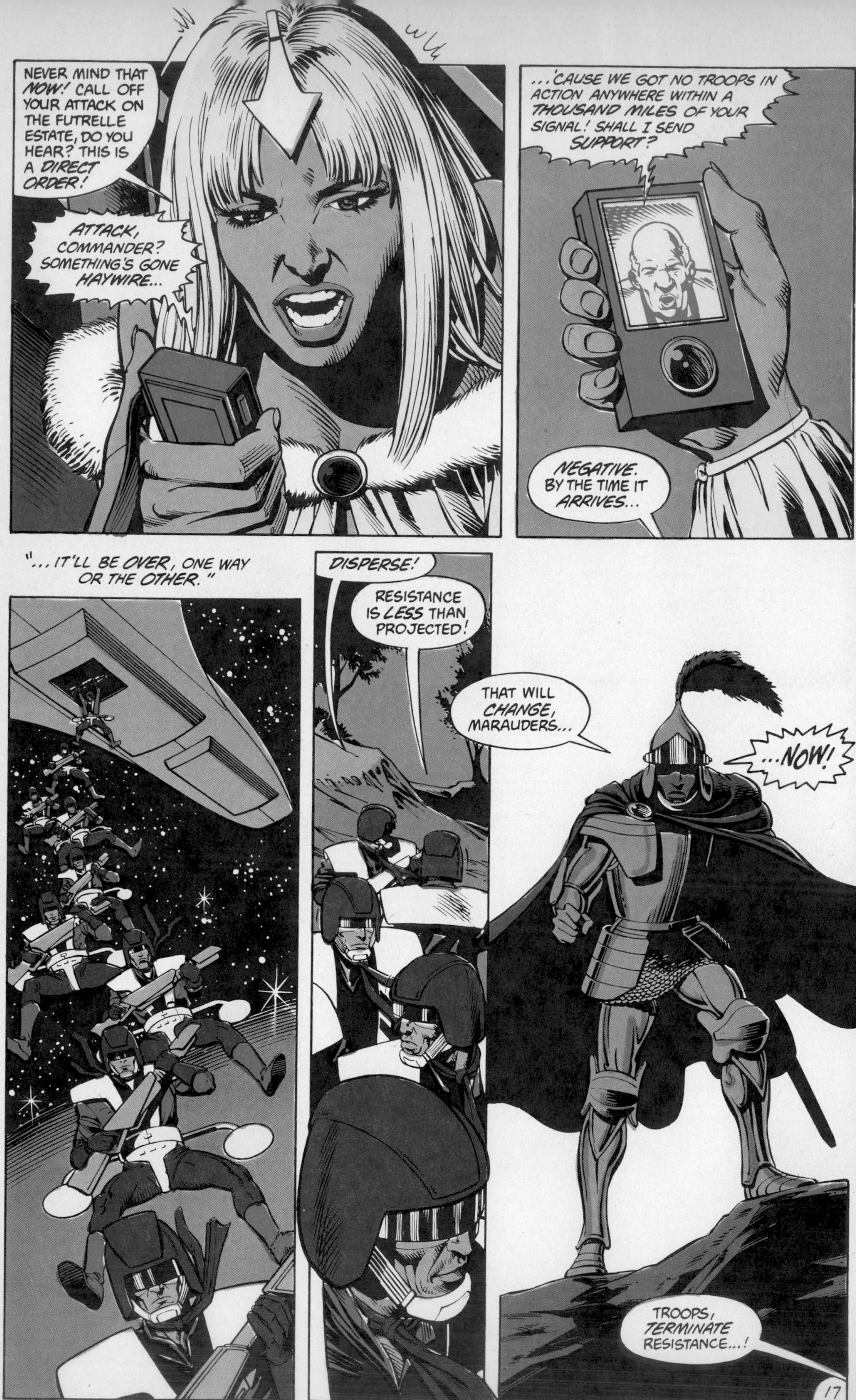
NEVER MIND THAT NOW! CALL OFF YOUR ATTACK ON THE FUTRELLE ESTATE, DO YOU HEAR? THIS IS A DIRECT ORDER!
ATTACK, COMMANDER? SOMETHING'S GONE HAYWIRE...
...'CAUSE WE GOT NO TROOPS IN ACTION ANYWHERE WITHIN A THOUSAND MILES OF YOUR SIGNAL! SHALL I SEND SUPPORT?
NEGATIVE. BY THE TIME IT ARRIVES...
"...IT'LL BE OVER, ONE WAY OR THE OTHER."
DISPERSE!
RESISTANCE IS LESS THAN PROJECTED!
THAT WILL CHANGE, MARAUDERS...
...NOW!
TROOPS, TERMINATE RESISTANCE...!
17

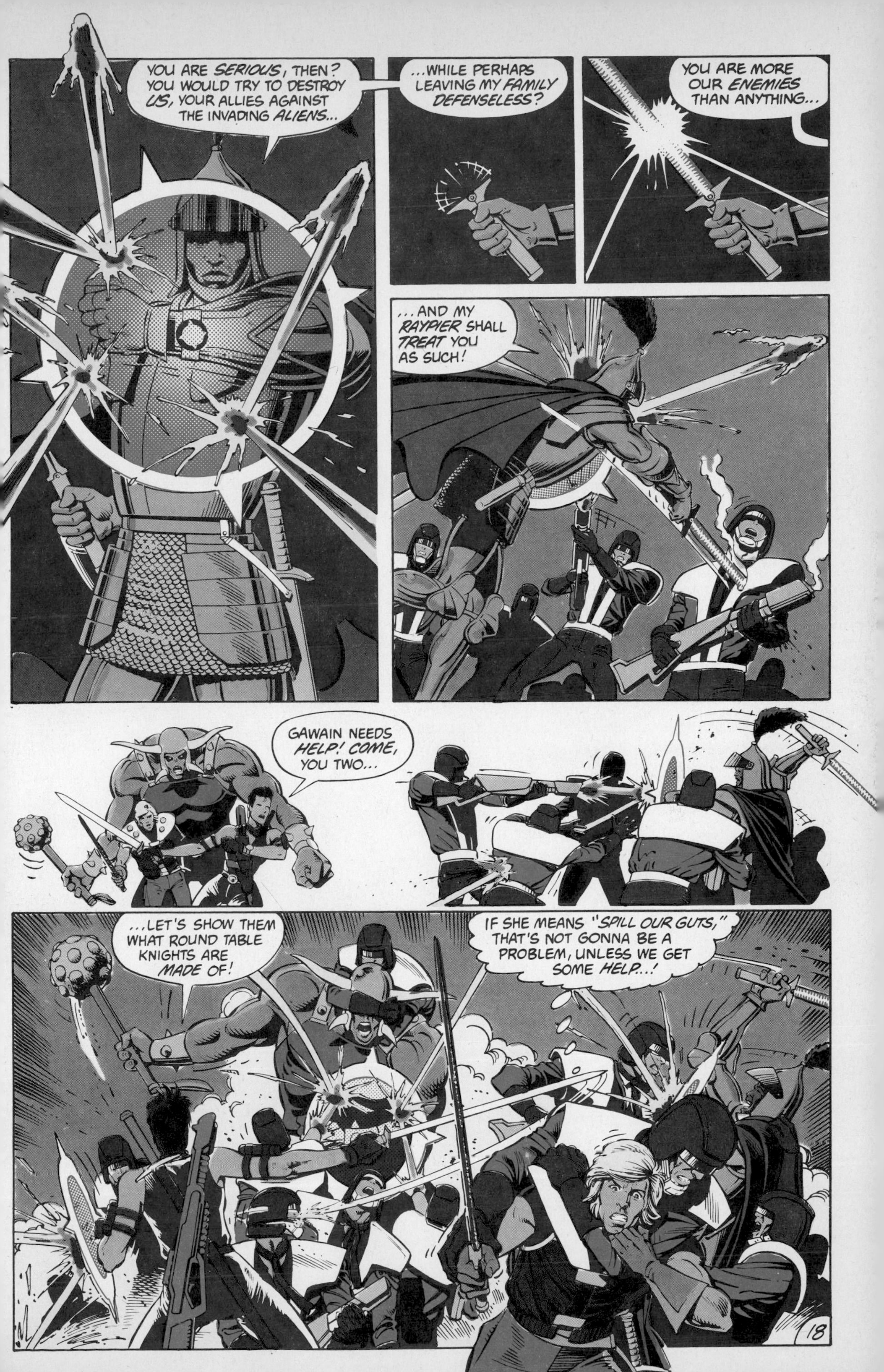
YOU ARE SERIOUS, THEN? YOU WOULD TRY TO DESTROY US, YOUR ALLIES AGAINST THE INVADING ALIENS...
...WHILE PERHAPS LEAVING MY FAMILY DEFENSELESS?
YOU ARE MORE OUR ENEMIES THAN ANYTHING...
...AND MY RAYPIER SHALL TREAT YOU AS SUCH!
GAWAIN NEEDS HELP! COME, YOU TWO...
...LET'S SHOW THEM WHAT ROUND TABLE KNIGHTS ARE MADE OF!
IF SHE MEANS "SPILL OUR GUTS," THAT'S NOT GONNA BE A PROBLEM, UNLESS WE GET SOME HELP...!
18

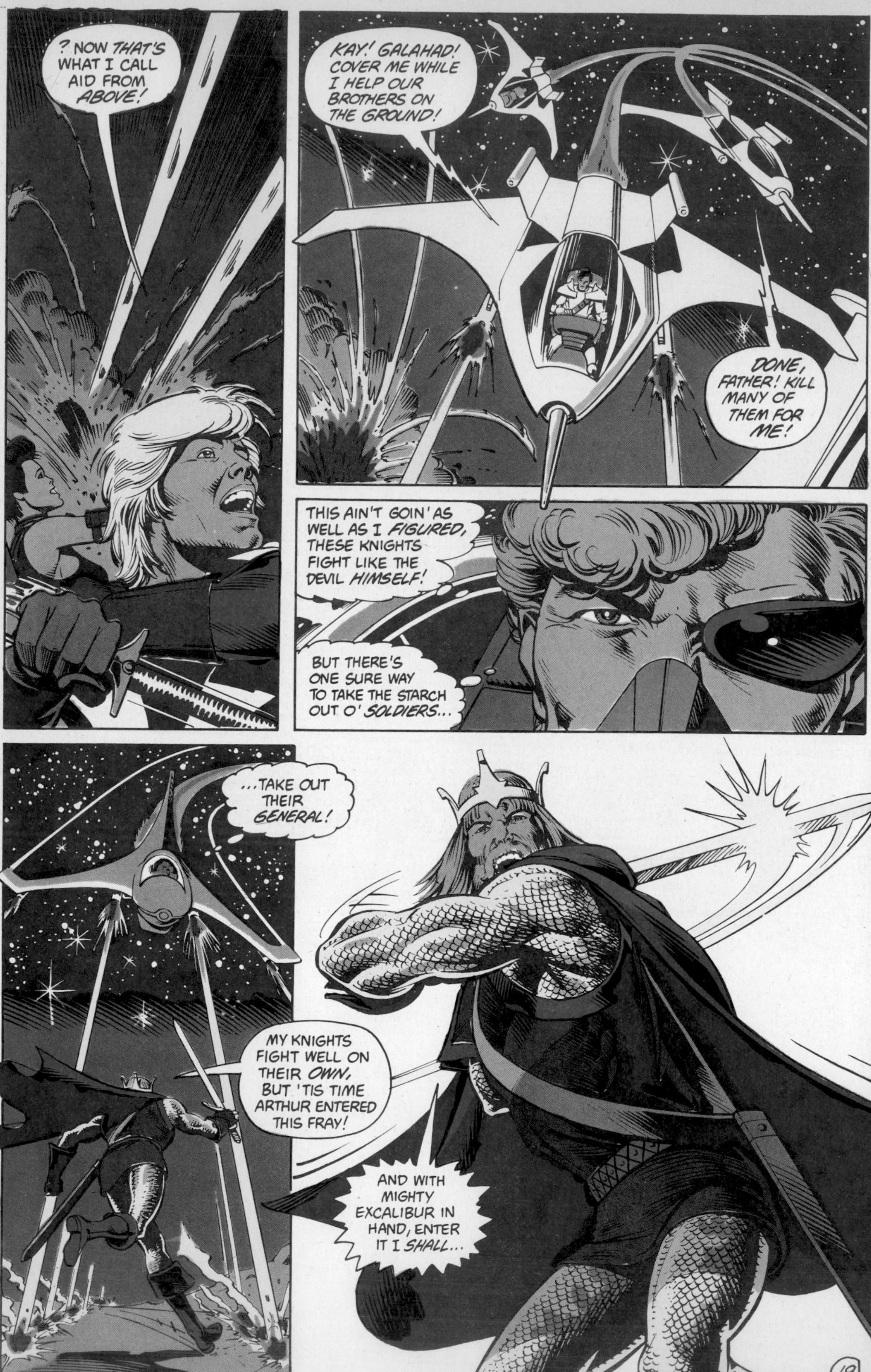

? NOW THAT'S WHAT I CALL AID FROM ABOVE!
KAY! GALAHAD! COVER ME WHILE I HELP OUR BROTHERS ON THE GROUND!
DONE, FATHER! KILL MANY OF THEM FOR ME!
THIS AIN'T GOIN' AS WELL AS I FIGURED, THESE KNIGHTS FIGHT LIKE THE DEVIL HIMSELF!
BUT THERE'S ONE SURE WAY TO TAKE THE STARCH OUT O' SOLDIERS...
...TAKE OUT THEIR GENERAL!
MY KNIGHTS FIGHT WELL ON THEIR OWN, BUT 'TIS TIME ARTHUR ENTERED THIS FRAY!
AND WITH MIGHTY EXCALIBUR IN HAND, ENTER IT I SHALL...

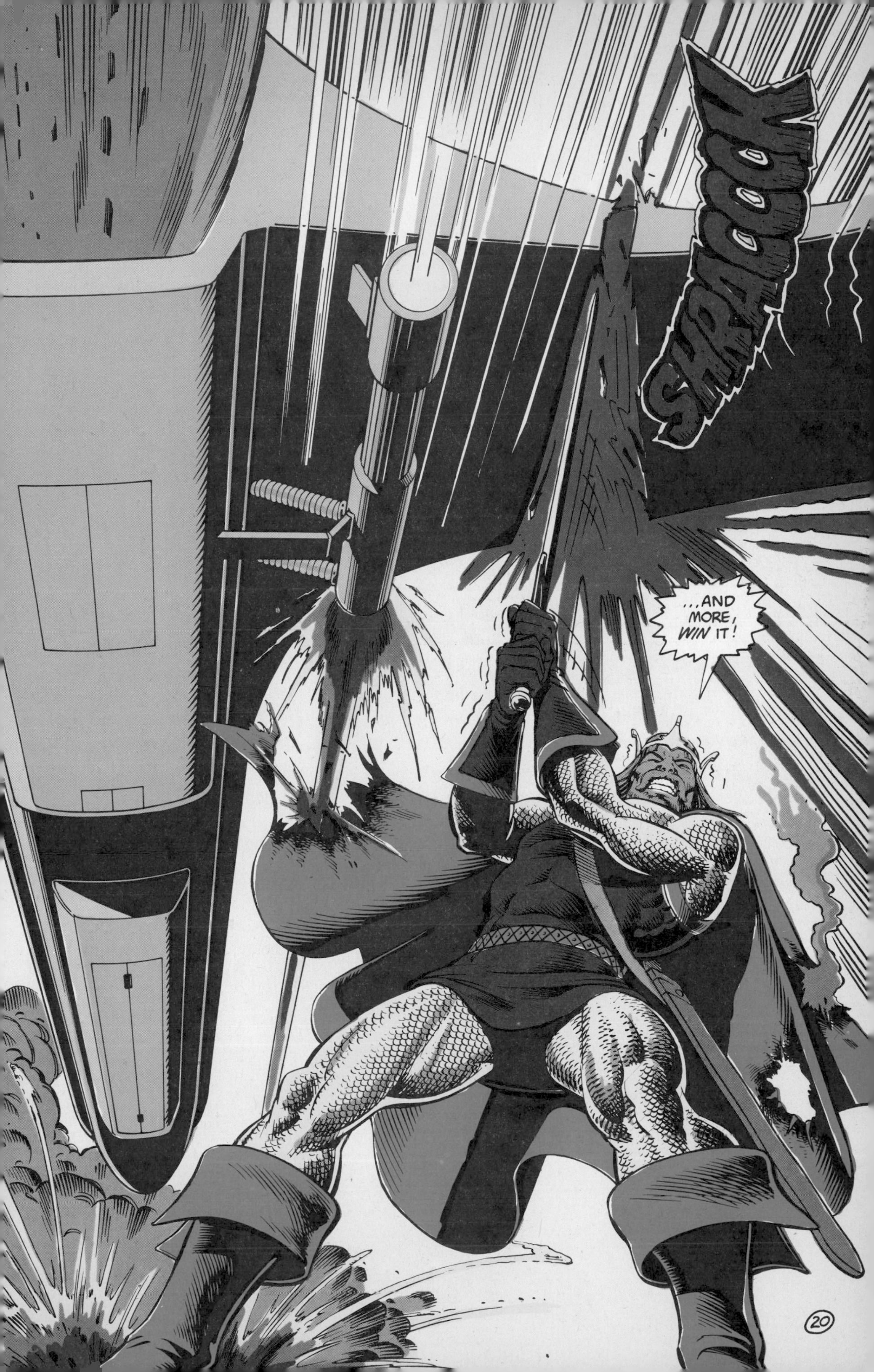
SHRAKK
...AND MORE, WIN IT!

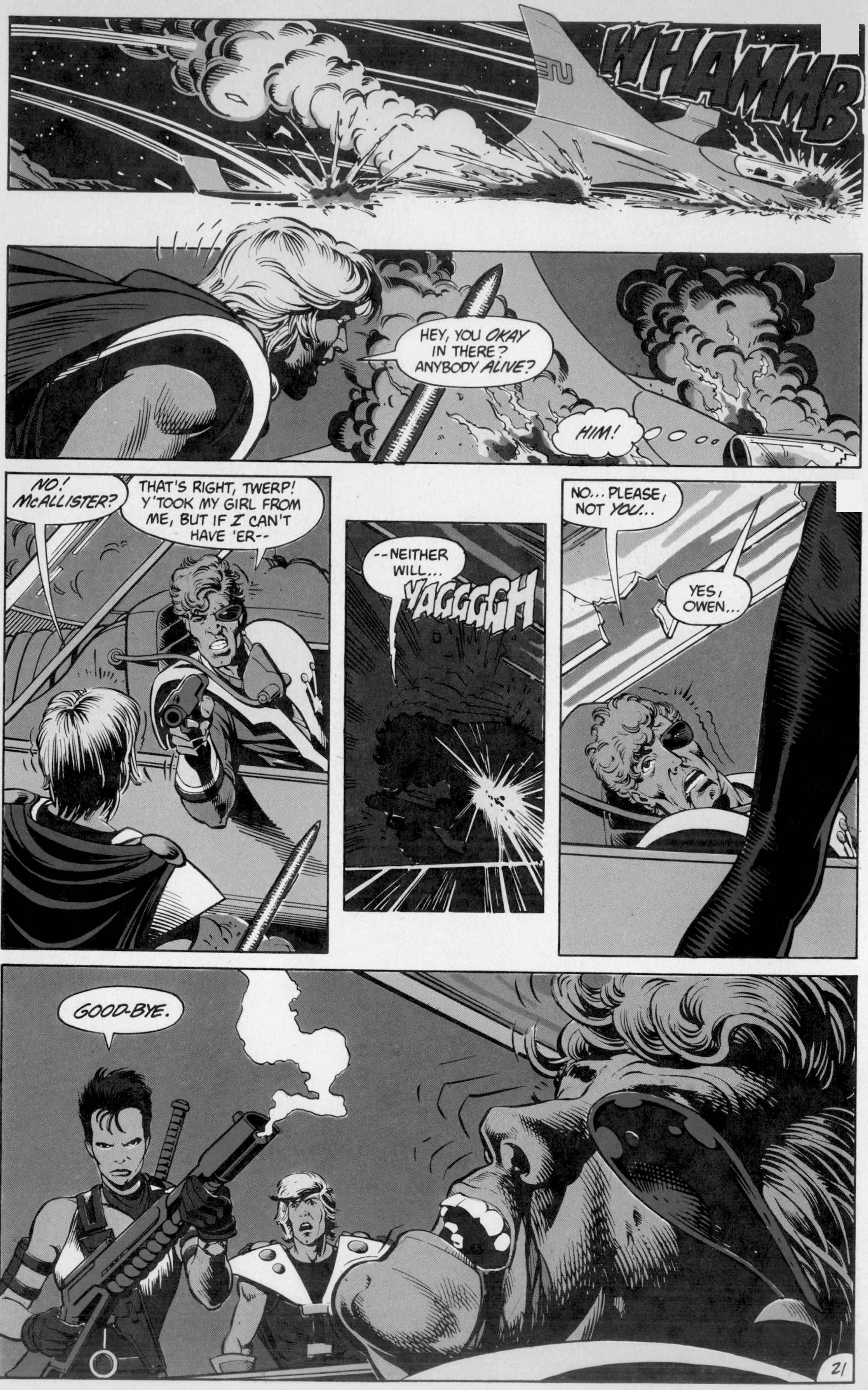
WHAMMB
HEY, YOU OKAY IN THERE? ANYBODY ALIVE?
HIM!
NO! McALLISTER?
THAT'S RIGHT, TWERP! Y'TOOK MY GIRL FROM ME, BUT IF I CAN'T HAVE 'ER--
--NEITHER WILL...
YAGGGGH
NO... PLEASE, NOT YOU...
YES, OWEN...
GOOD-BYE.

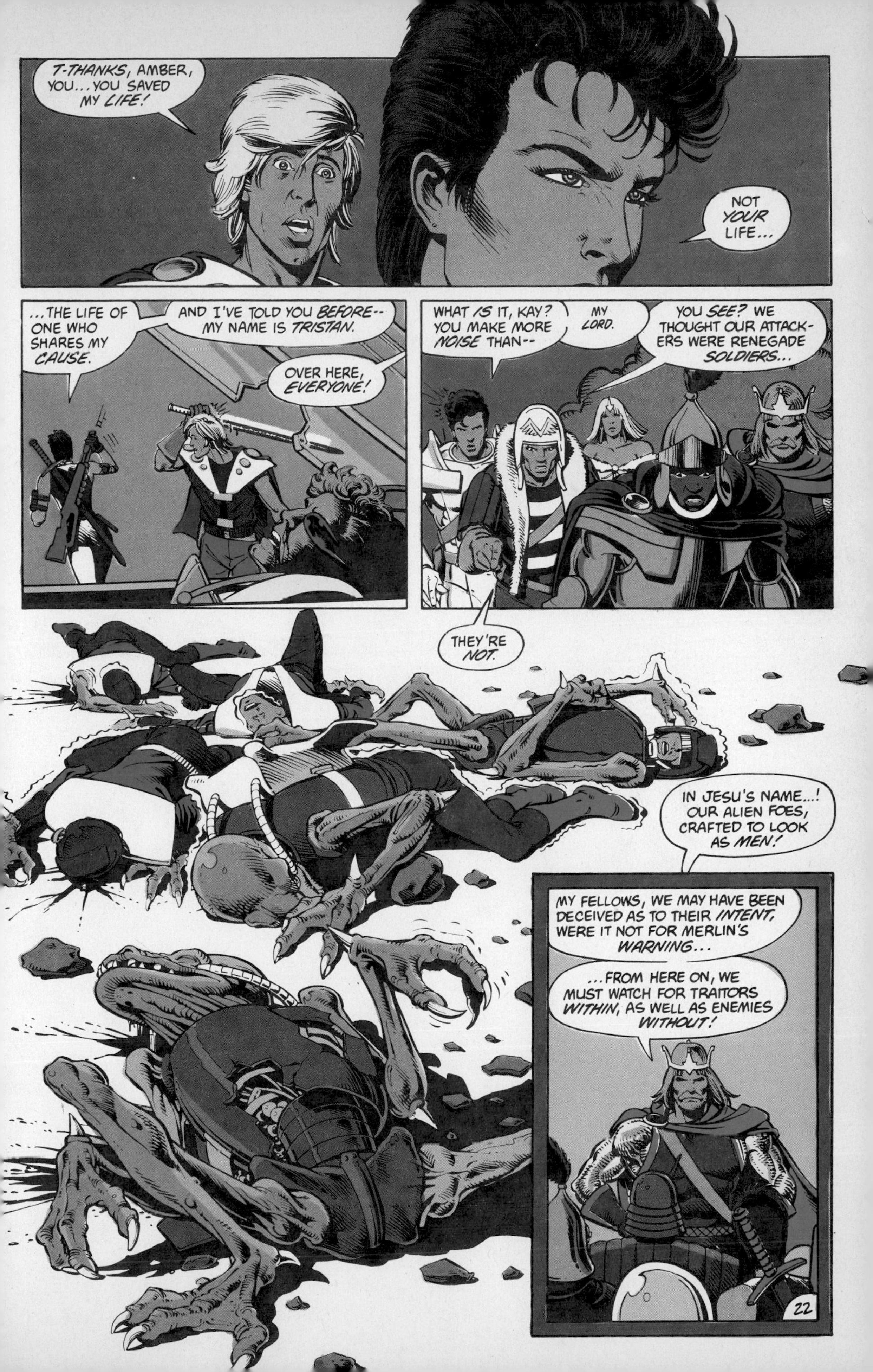
T-THANKS, AMBER, YOU... YOU SAVED MY LIFE!
NOT YOUR LIFE...
...THE LIFE OF ONE WHO SHARES MY CAUSE.
AND I'VE TOLD YOU BEFORE-- MY NAME IS TRISTAN.
OVER HERE, EVERYONE!
WHAT IS IT, KAY? YOU MAKE MORE NOISE THAN--
MY LORD.
YOU SEE? WE THOUGHT OUR ATTACKERS WERE RENEGADE SOLDIERS...
THEY'RE NOT.
IN JESU'S NAME...! OUR ALIEN FOES, CRAFTED TO LOOK AS MEN!
MY FELLOWS, WE MAY HAVE BEEN DECEIVED AS TO THEIR INTENT, WERE IT NOT FOR MERLIN'S WARNING...
...FROM HERE ON, WE MUST WATCH FOR TRAITORS WITHIN, AS WELL AS ENEMIES WITHOUT!
22

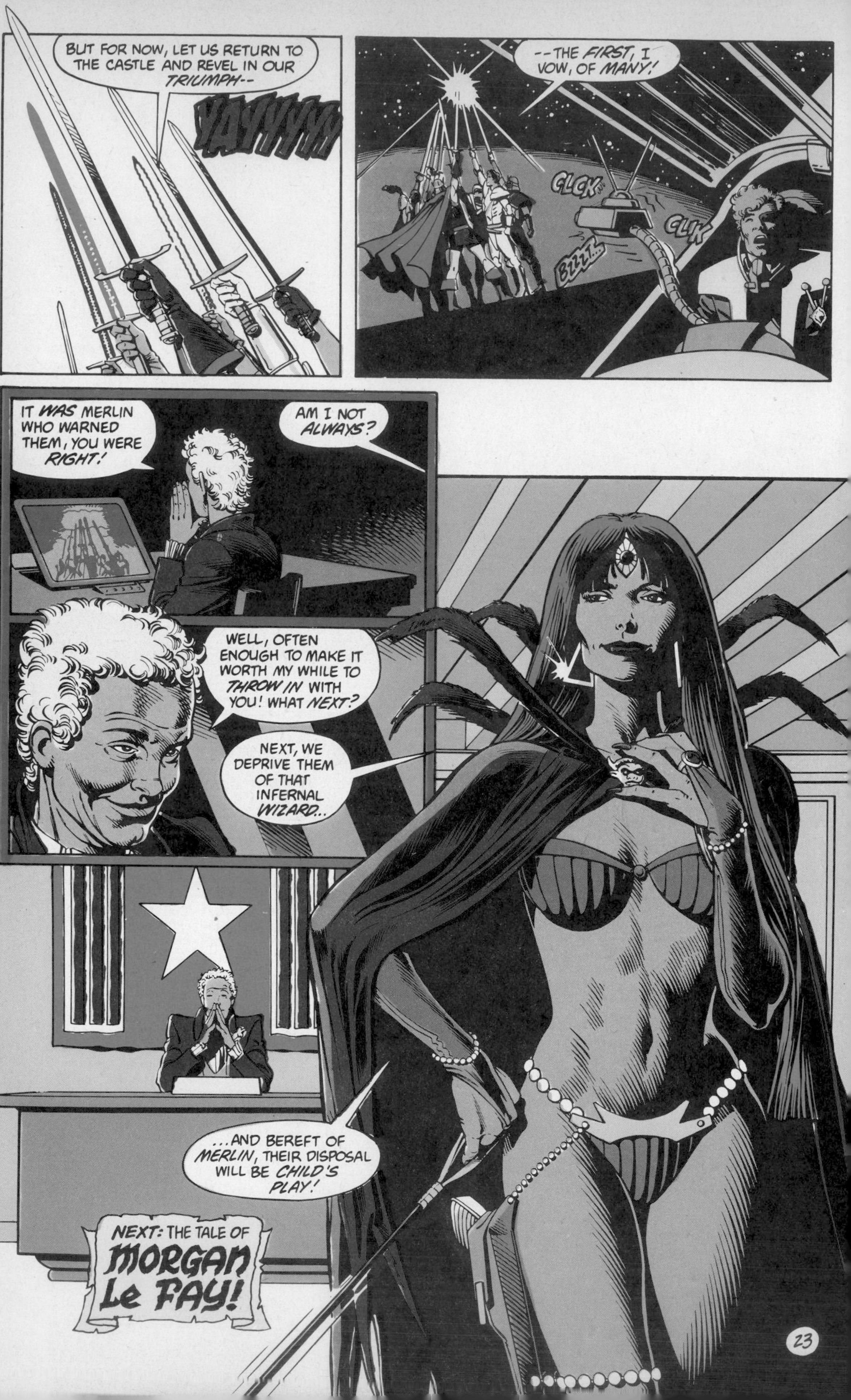

BUT FOR NOW, LET US RETURN TO THE CASTLE AND REVEL IN OUR TRIUMPH--
YAYYYY
--THE FIRST, I VOW, OF MANY!
CLCK
CLIK
BZZT...
IT WAS MERLIN WHO WARNED THEM, YOU WERE RIGHT!
AM I NOT ALWAYS?
WELL, OFTEN ENOUGH TO MAKE IT WORTH MY WHILE TO THROW IN WITH YOU! WHAT NEXT?
NEXT, WE DEPRIVE THEM OF THAT INFERNAL WIZARD...
...AND BEREFT OF MERLIN, THEIR DISPOSAL WILL BE CHILD'S PLAY!
NEXT: THE TALE OF MORGAN Le FAY!

CHAPTER
5

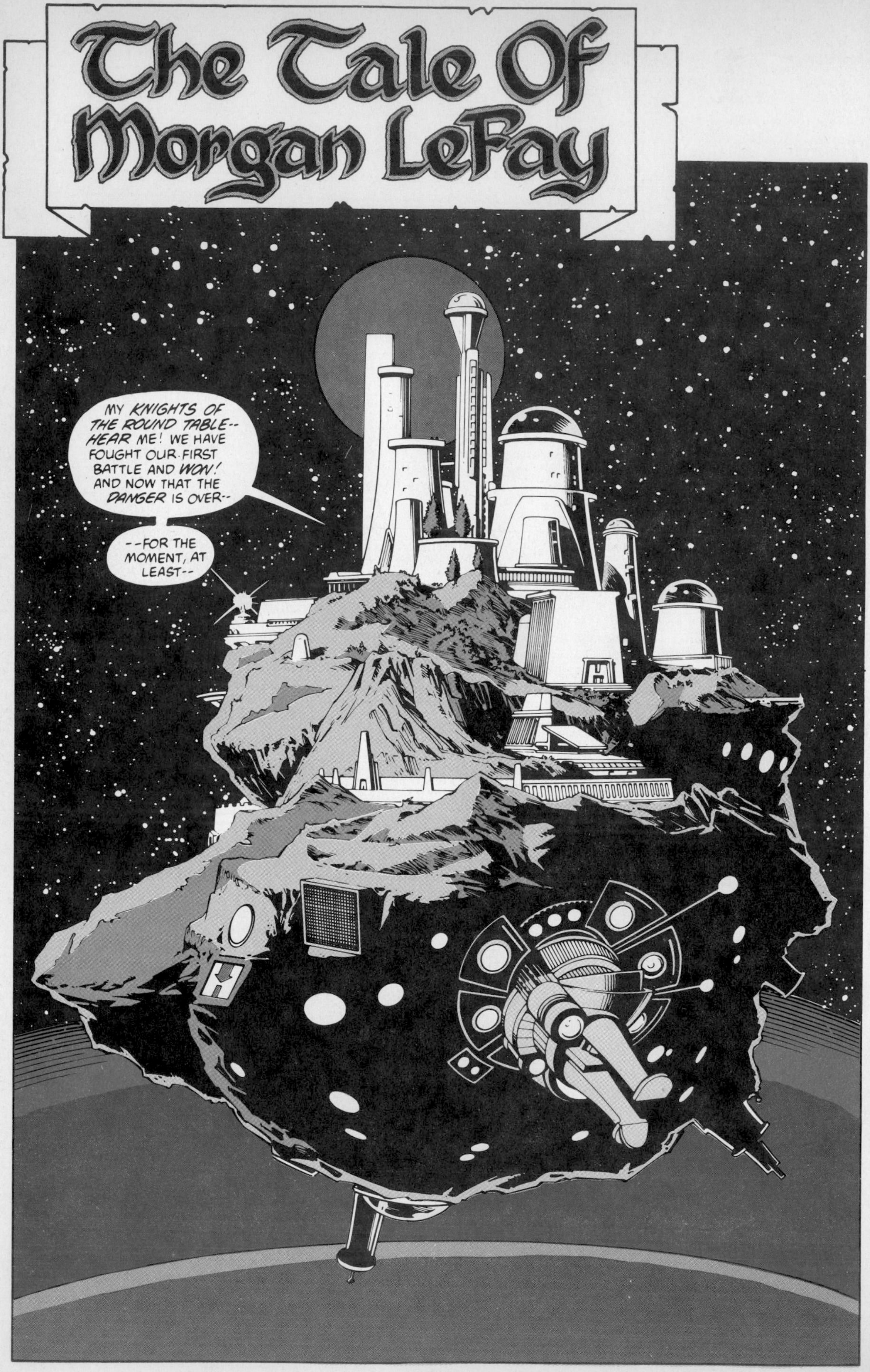
The Tale Of Morgan LeFay
MY KNIGHTS OF THE ROUND TABLE-- HEAR ME! WE HAVE FOUGHT OUR FIRST BATTLE AND WON! AND NOW THAT THE DANGER IS OVER--
--FOR THE MOMENT, AT LEAST--

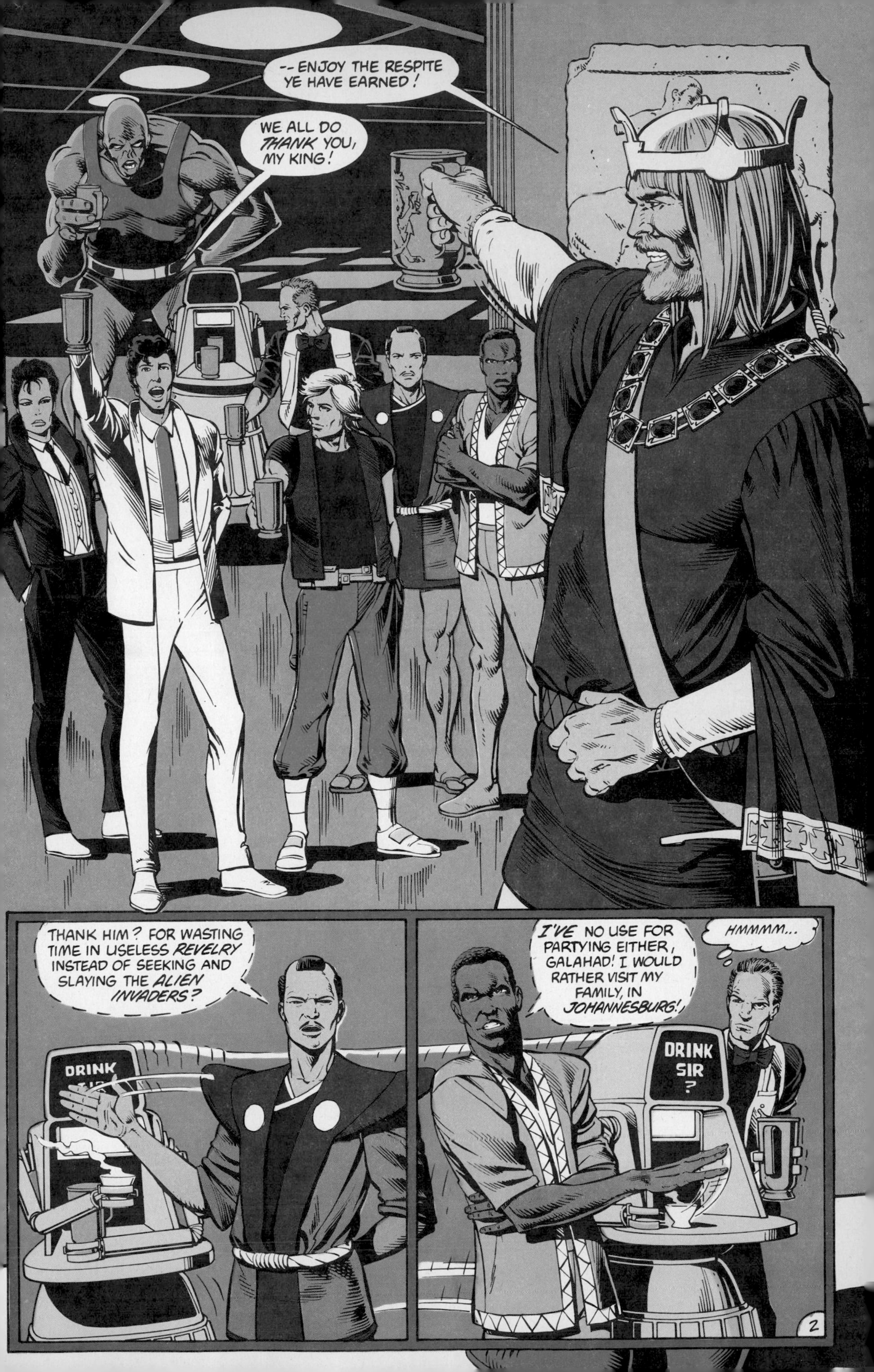

-- ENJOY THE RESPITE YE HAVE EARNED!
WE ALL DO THANK YOU, MY KING!
THANK HIM? FOR WASTING TIME IN USELESS REVELRY INSTEAD OF SEEKING AND SLAYING THE ALIEN INVADERS?
DRINK
I'VE NO USE FOR PARTYING EITHER, GALAHAD! I WOULD RATHER VISIT MY FAMILY, IN JOHANNESBURG!
HMMMM...
DRINK SIR ?
2

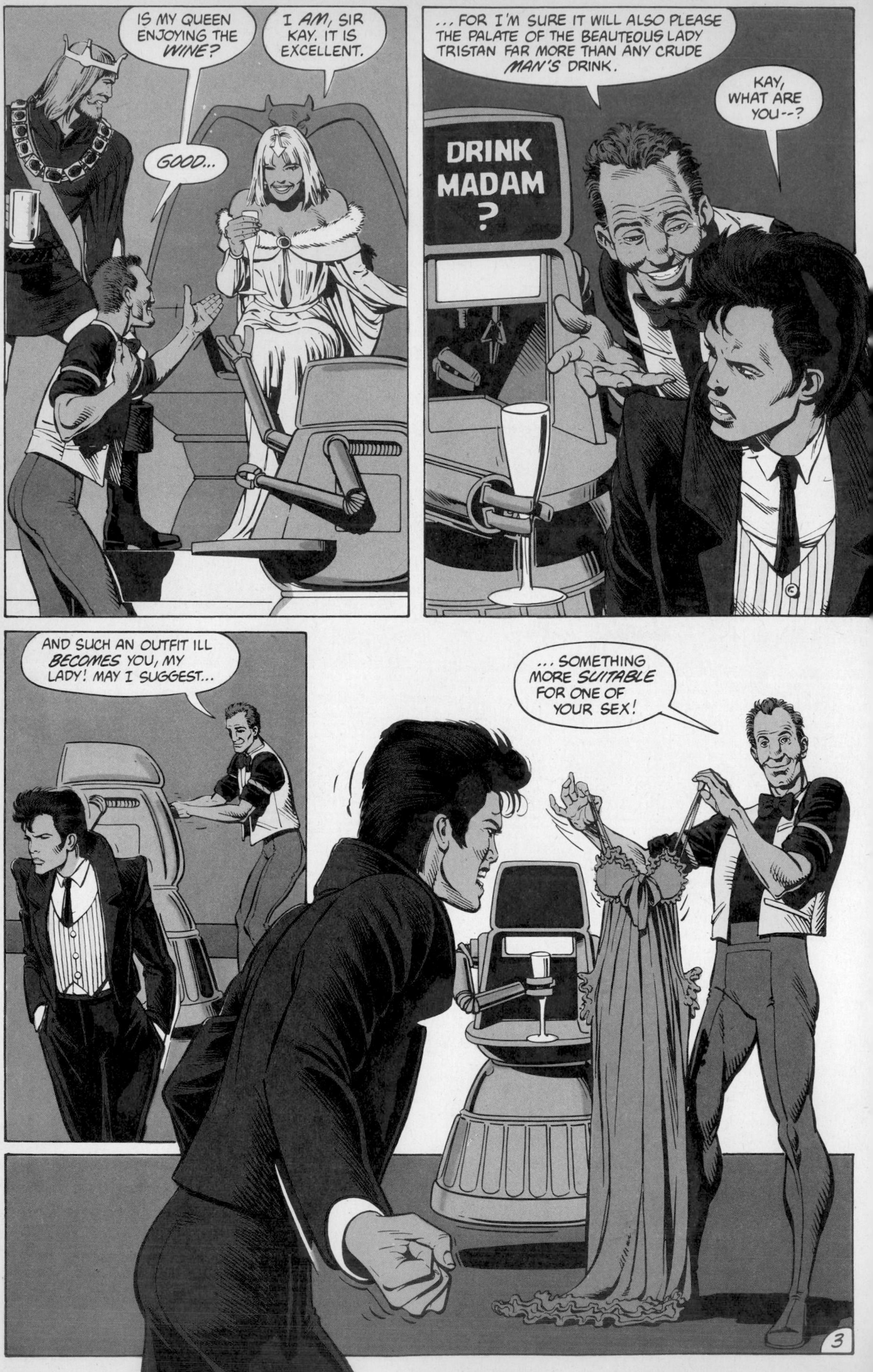
IS MY QUEEN ENJOYING THE WINE?
I AM, SIR KAY. IT IS EXCELLENT.
GOOD...
...FOR I'M SURE IT WILL ALSO PLEASE THE PALATE OF THE BEAUTEOUS LADY TRISTAN FAR MORE THAN ANY CRUDE MAN'S DRINK.
DRINK MADAM ?
KAY, WHAT ARE YOU--?
AND SUCH AN OUTFIT ILL BECOMES YOU, MY LADY! MAY I SUGGEST...
...SOMETHING MORE SUITABLE FOR ONE OF YOUR SEX!
3

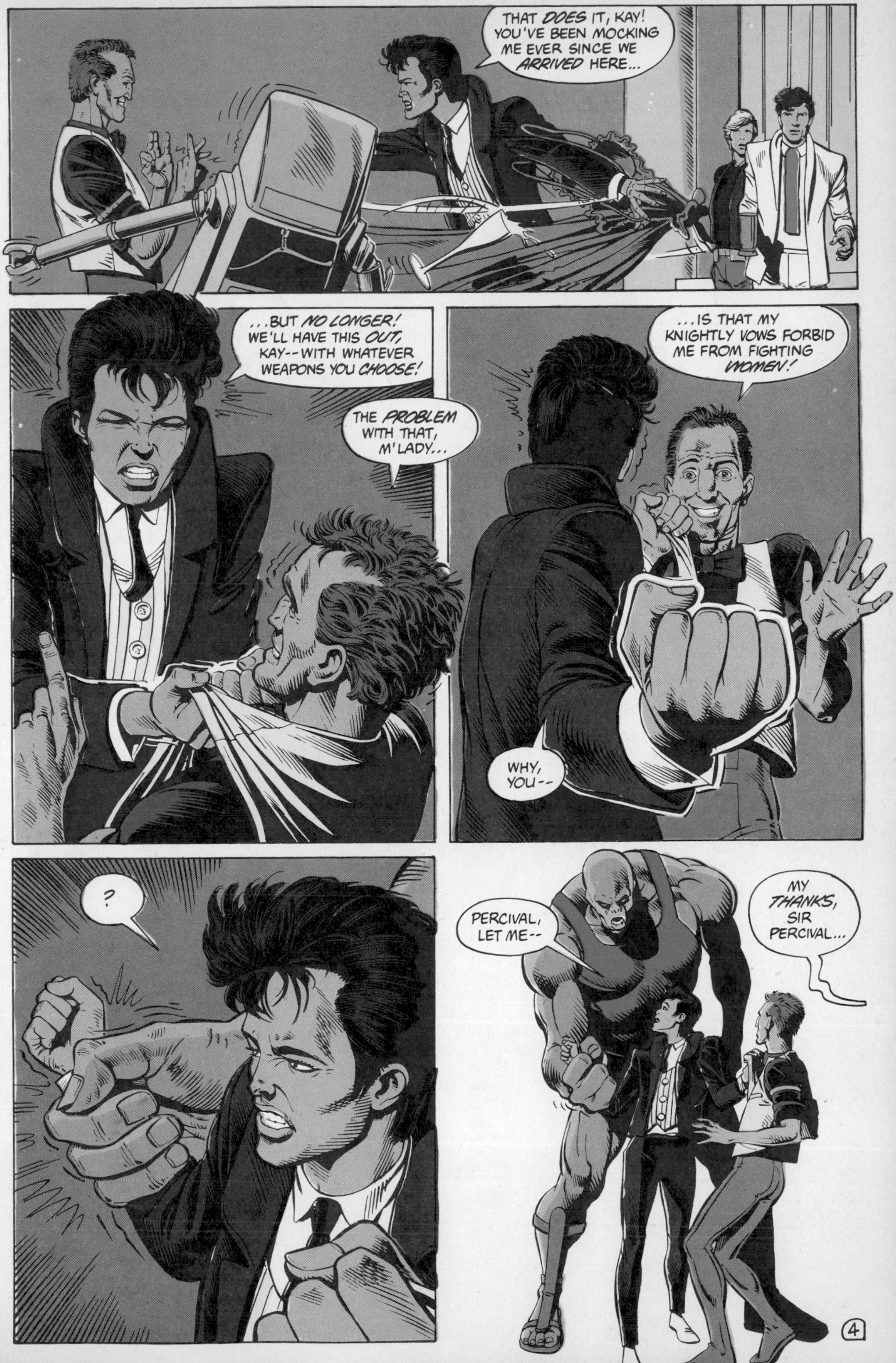

THAT DOES IT, KAY! YOU'VE BEEN MOCKING ME EVER SINCE WE ARRIVED HERE...
...BUT NO LONGER! WE'LL HAVE THIS OUT, KAY--WITH WHATEVER WEAPONS YOU CHOOSE!
THE PROBLEM WITH THAT, M'LADY...
...IS THAT MY KNIGHTLY VOWS FORBID ME FROM FIGHTING WOMEN!
WHY, YOU--
?
PERCIVAL, LET ME--
MY THANKS, SIR PERCIVAL...

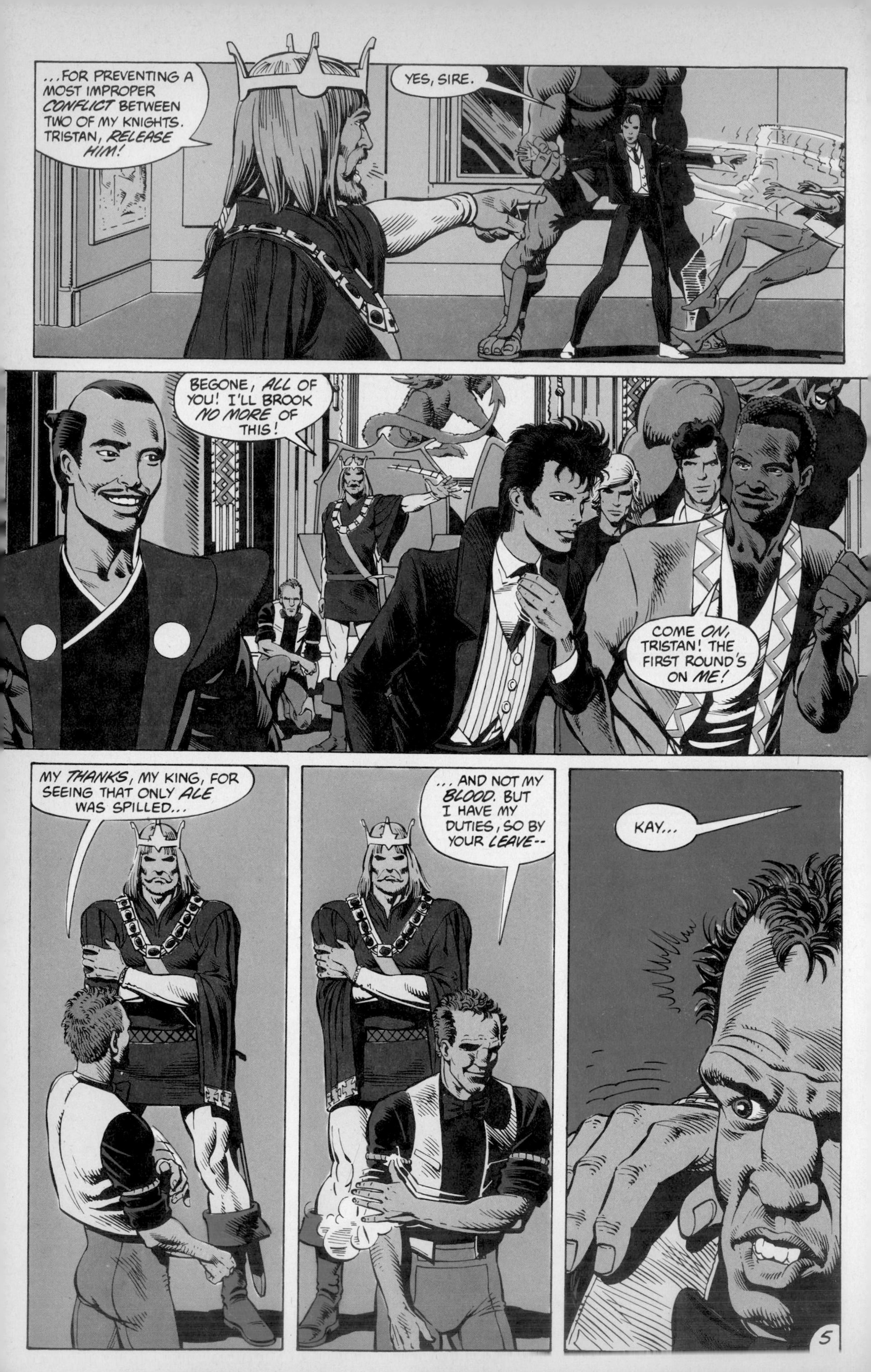
...FOR PREVENTING A MOST IMPROPER CONFLICT BETWEEN TWO OF MY KNIGHTS. TRISTAN, RELEASE HIM!
YES, SIRE.
BEGONE, ALL OF YOU! I'LL BROOK NO MORE OF THIS!
COME ON, TRISTAN! THE FIRST ROUND'S ON ME!
MY THANKS, MY KING, FOR SEEING THAT ONLY ALE WAS SPILLED...
...AND NOT MY BLOOD. BUT I HAVE MY DUTIES, SO BY YOUR LEAVE--
KAY...

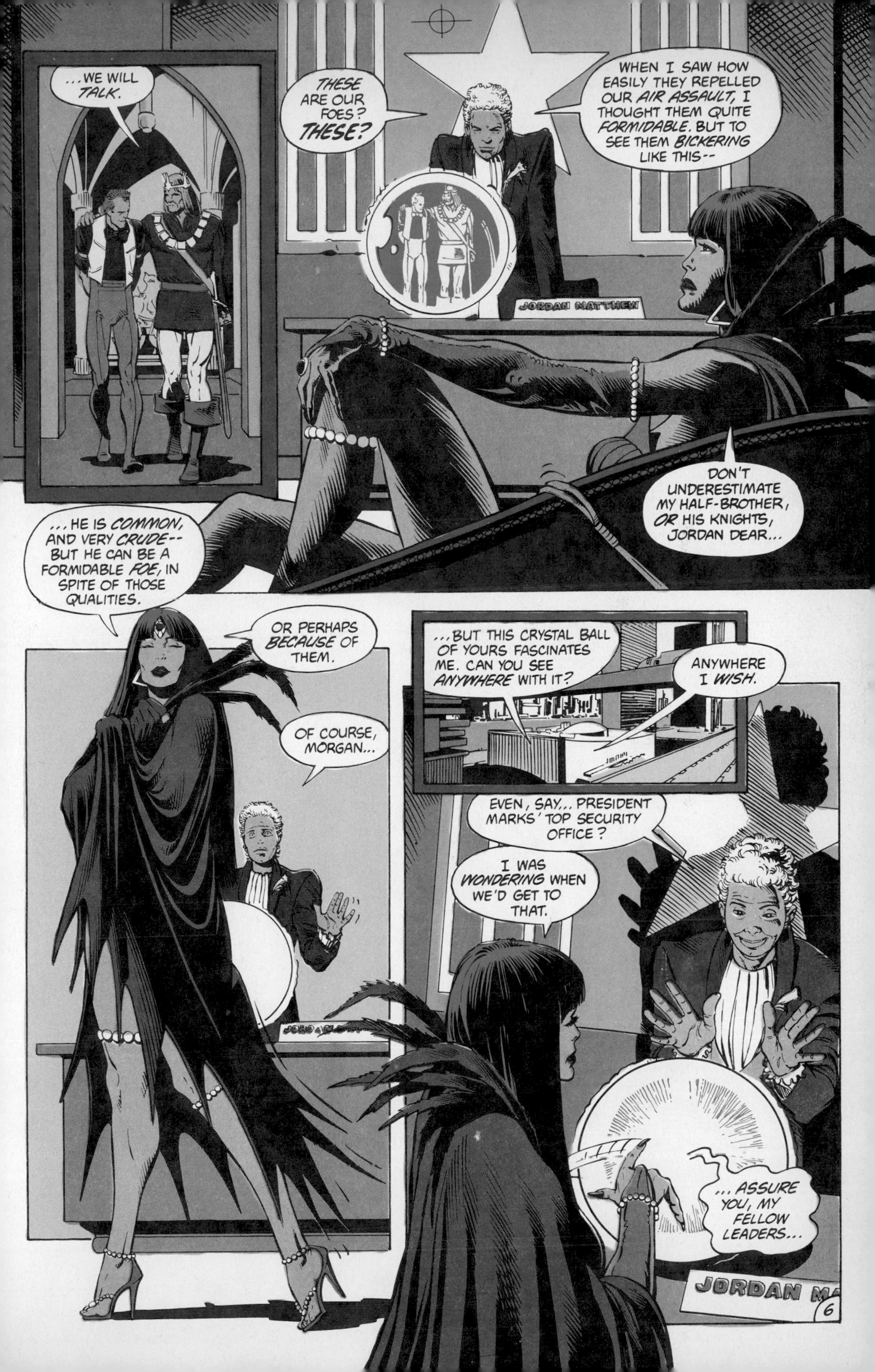
...WE WILL TALK.
THESE ARE OUR FOES? THESE?
WHEN I SAW HOW EASILY THEY REPELLED OUR AIR ASSAULT, I THOUGHT THEM QUITE FORMIDABLE. BUT TO SEE THEM BICKERING LIKE THIS--
JORDAN MATTHEW
DON'T UNDERESTIMATE MY HALF-BROTHER, OR HIS KNIGHTS, JORDAN DEAR...
...HE IS COMMON, AND VERY CRUDE-- BUT HE CAN BE A FORMIDABLE FOE, IN SPITE OF THOSE QUALITIES.
OR PERHAPS BECAUSE OF THEM.
OF COURSE, MORGAN...
...BUT THIS CRYSTAL BALL OF YOURS FASCINATES ME. CAN YOU SEE ANYWHERE WITH IT?
ANYWHERE I WISH.
EVEN, SAY... PRESIDENT MARKS' TOP SECURITY OFFICE?
I WAS WONDERING WHEN WE'D GET TO THAT.
...ASSURE YOU, MY FELLOW LEADERS...
JORDAN MA
6

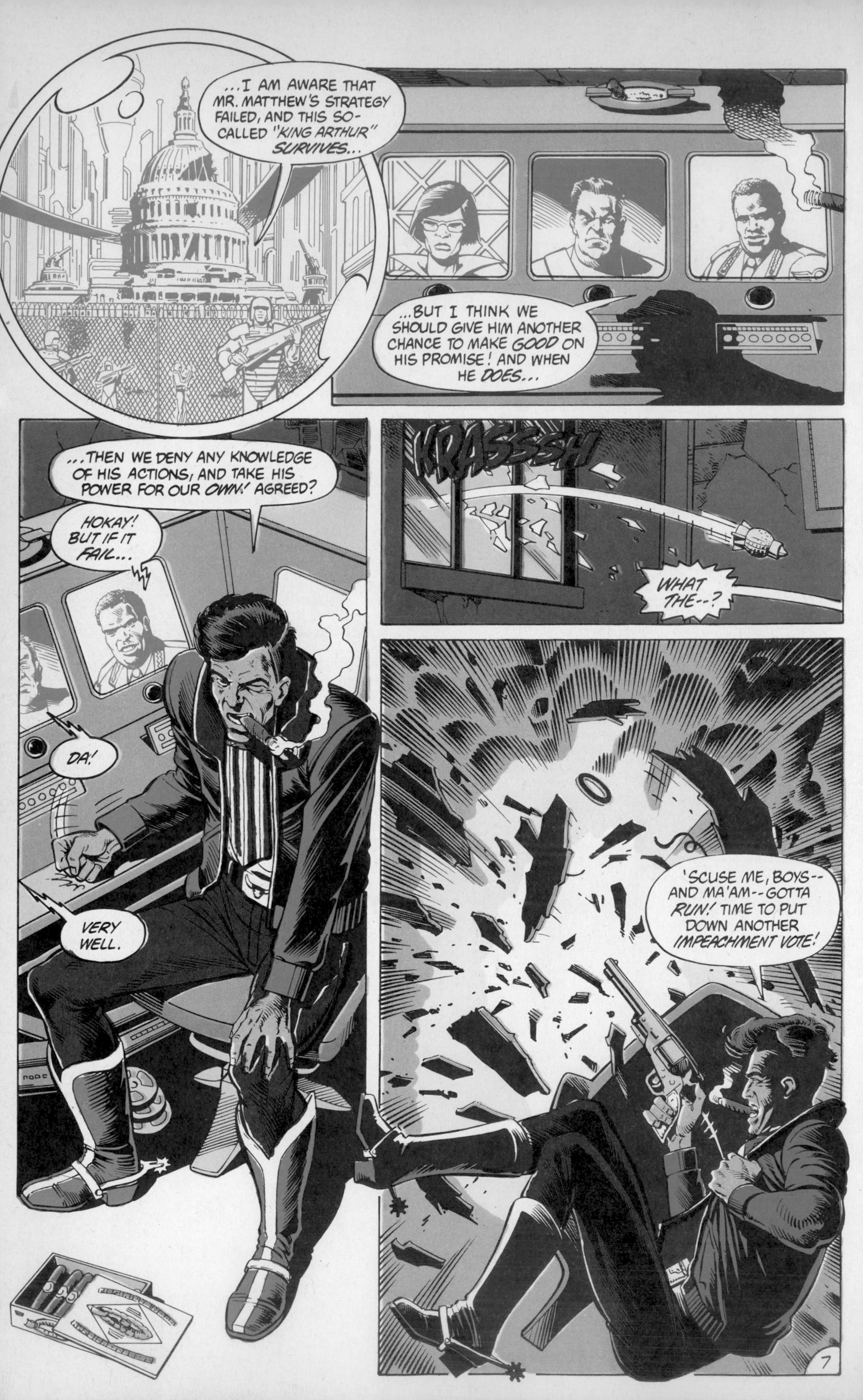
...I AM AWARE THAT MR. MATTHEW'S STRATEGY FAILED, AND THIS SO-CALLED "KING ARTHUR" SURVIVES...
...BUT I THINK WE SHOULD GIVE HIM ANOTHER CHANCE TO MAKE GOOD ON HIS PROMISE! AND WHEN HE DOES...
...THEN WE DENY ANY KNOWLEDGE OF HIS ACTIONS, AND TAKE HIS POWER FOR OUR OWN! AGREED?
HOKAY! BUT IF IT FAIL...
DA!
VERY WELL.
KRASSSSH
WHAT THE--?
'SCUSE ME, BOYS-- AND MA'AM--GOTTA RUN! TIME TO PUT DOWN ANOTHER IMPEACHMENT VOTE!
7

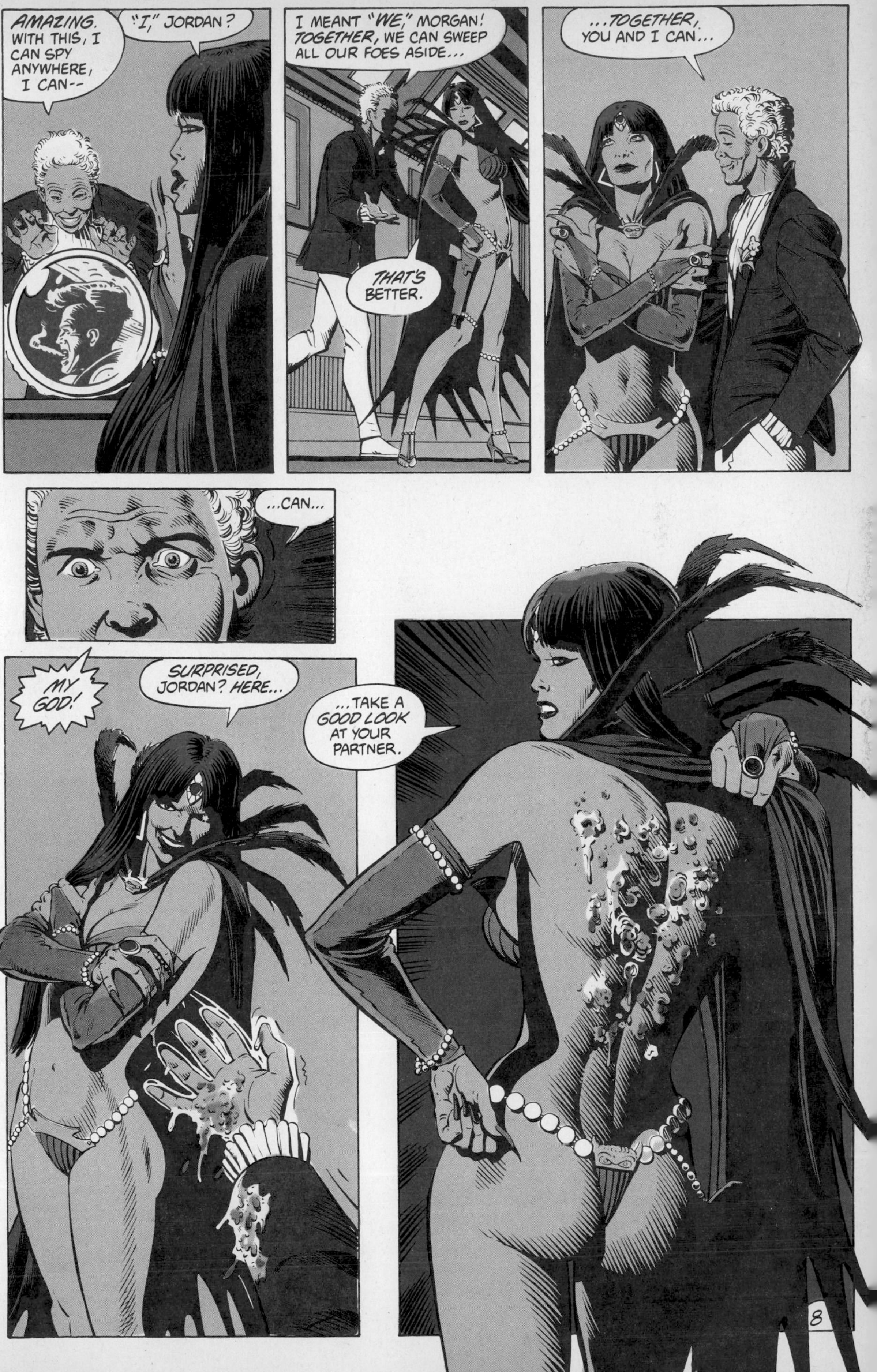
AMAZING. WITH THIS, I CAN SPY ANYWHERE, I CAN--
"I," JORDAN?
I MEANT "WE," MORGAN! TOGETHER, WE CAN SWEEP ALL OUR FOES ASIDE...
THAT'S BETTER.
...TOGETHER, YOU AND I CAN...
...CAN...
MY GOD!
SURPRISED, JORDAN? HERE...
...TAKE A GOOD LOOK AT YOUR PARTNER.

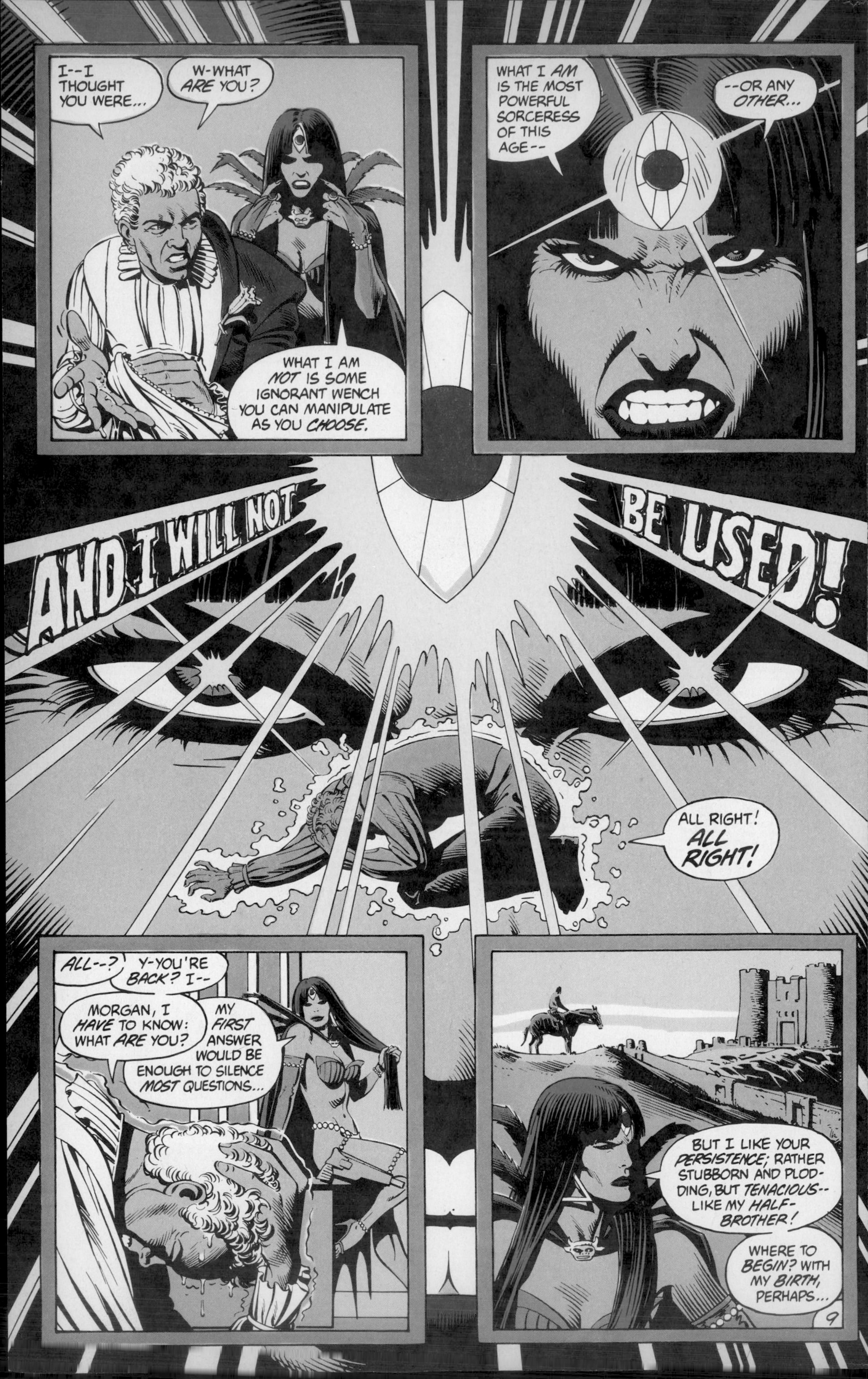
I--I THOUGHT YOU WERE...
W-WHAT ARE YOU?
WHAT I AM NOT IS SOME IGNORANT WENCH YOU CAN MANIPULATE AS YOU CHOOSE.
WHAT I AM IS THE MOST POWERFUL SORCERESS OF THIS AGE--
--OR ANY OTHER...
AND I WILL NOT BE USED!
ALL RIGHT! ALL RIGHT!
ALL--? Y-YOU'RE BACK? I--
MORGAN, I HAVE TO KNOW: WHAT ARE YOU?
MY FIRST ANSWER WOULD BE ENOUGH TO SILENCE MOST QUESTIONS...
BUT I LIKE YOUR PERSISTENCE; RATHER STUBBORN AND PLOD-DING, BUT TENACIOUS-- LIKE MY HALF-BROTHER!
WHERE TO BEGIN? WITH MY BIRTH, PERHAPS...
9

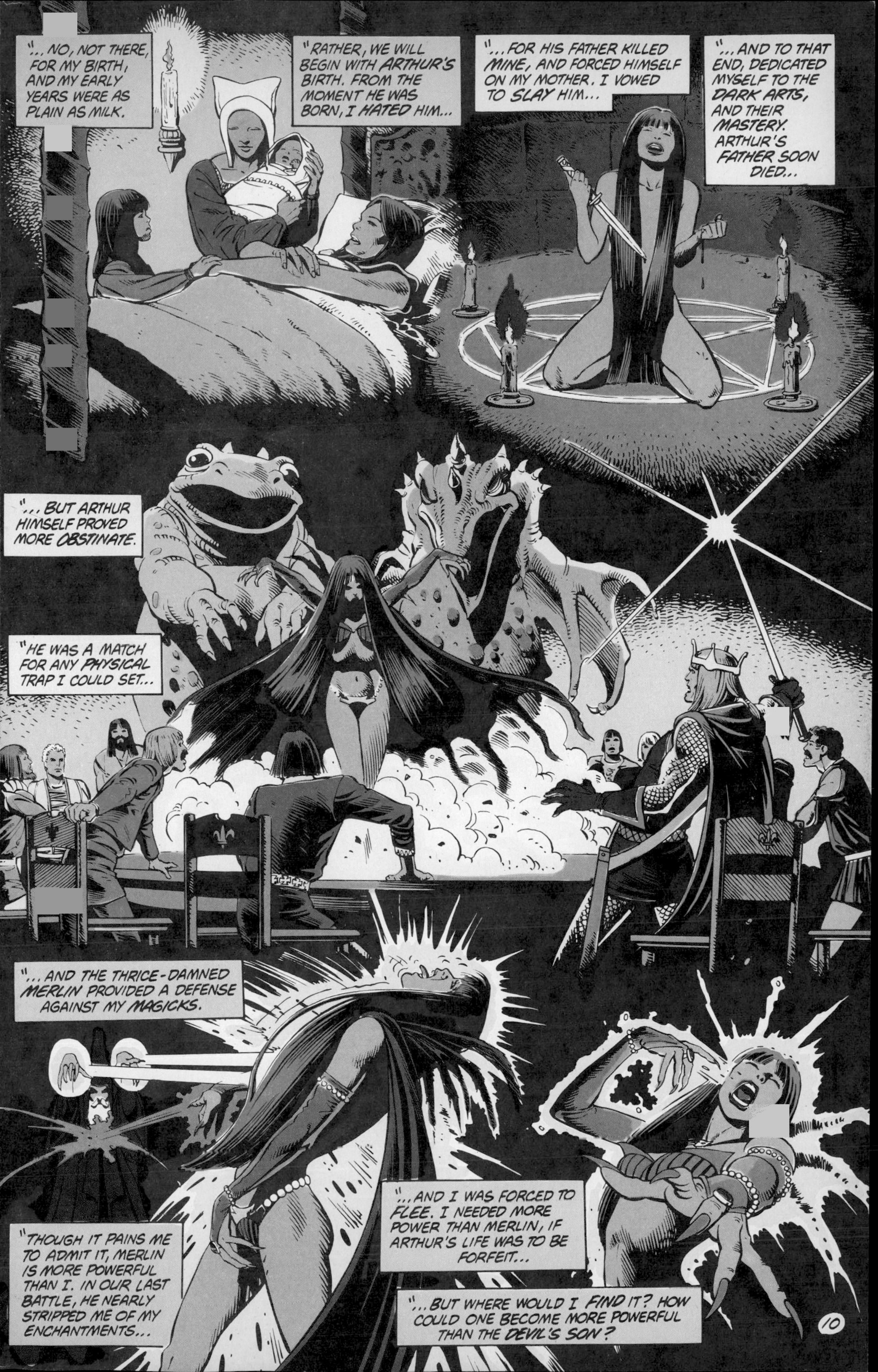
"...NO, NOT THERE, FOR MY BIRTH, AND MY EARLY YEARS WERE AS PLAIN AS MILK.
"RATHER, WE WILL BEGIN WITH ARTHUR'S BIRTH. FROM THE MOMENT HE WAS BORN, I HATED HIM...
"...FOR HIS FATHER KILLED MINE, AND FORCED HIMSELF ON MY MOTHER. I VOWED TO SLAY HIM...
"...AND TO THAT END, DEDICATED MYSELF TO THE DARK ARTS, AND THEIR MASTERY. ARTHUR'S FATHER SOON DIED...
"...BUT ARTHUR HIMSELF PROVED MORE OBSTINATE.
"HE WAS A MATCH FOR ANY PHYSICAL TRAP I COULD SET...
"...AND THE THRICE-DAMNED MERLIN PROVIDED A DEFENSE AGAINST MY MAGICKS.
"THOUGH IT PAINS ME TO ADMIT IT, MERLIN IS MORE POWERFUL THAN I. IN OUR LAST BATTLE, HE NEARLY STRIPPED ME OF MY ENCHANTMENTS...
"...AND I WAS FORCED TO FLEE. I NEEDED MORE POWER THAN MERLIN, IF ARTHUR'S LIFE WAS TO BE FORFEIT...
"...BUT WHERE WOULD I FIND IT? HOW COULD ONE BECOME MORE POWERFUL THAN THE DEVIL'S SON?

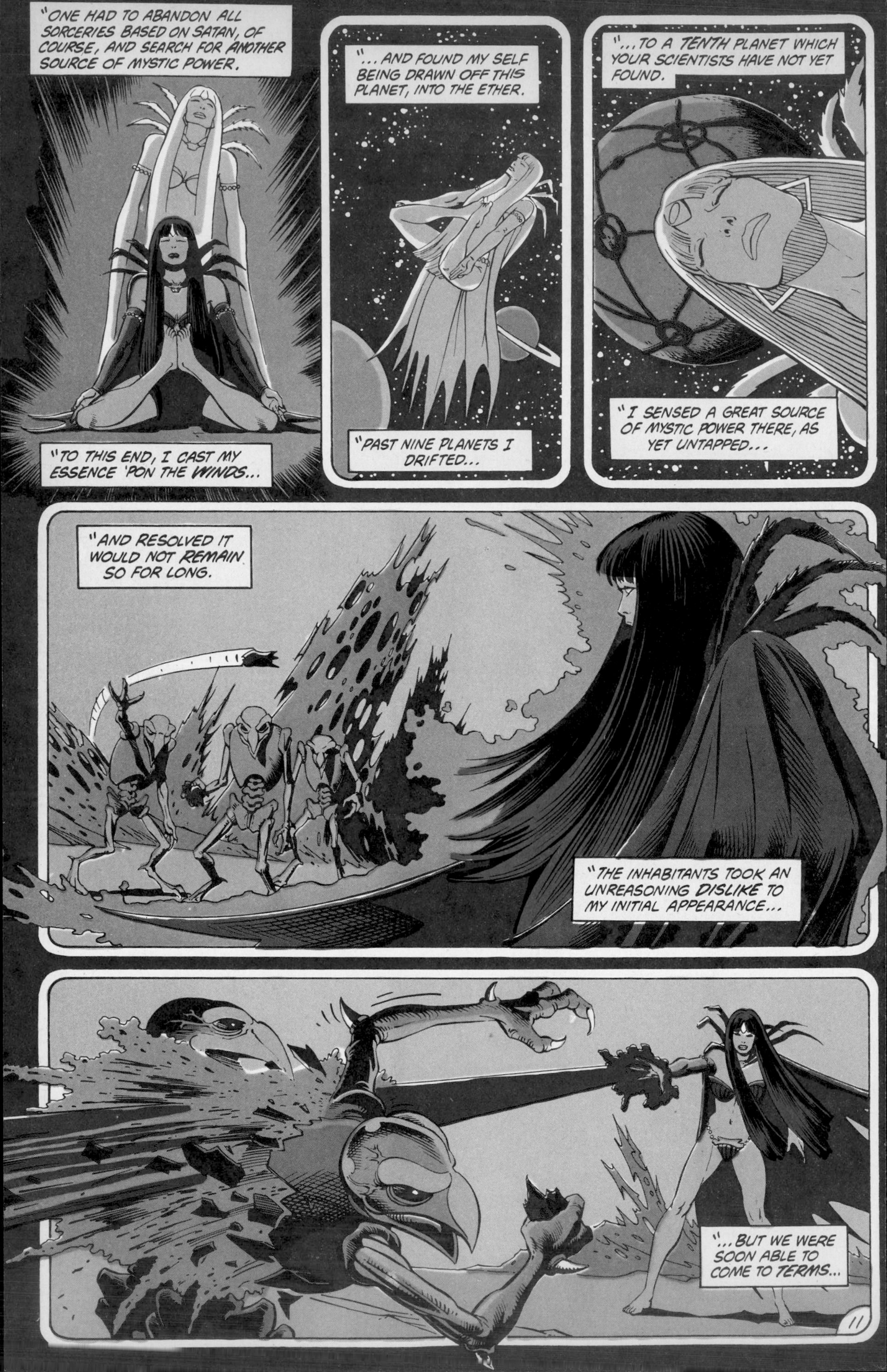
"ONE HAD TO ABANDON ALL SORCERIES BASED ON SATAN, OF COURSE, AND SEARCH FOR ANOTHER SOURCE OF MYSTIC POWER.
"TO THIS END, I CAST MY ESSENCE 'PON THE WINDS...
"... AND FOUND MY SELF BEING DRAWN OFF THIS PLANET, INTO THE ETHER.
"PAST NINE PLANETS I DRIFTED...
"...TO A TENTH PLANET WHICH YOUR SCIENTISTS HAVE NOT YET FOUND.
"I SENSED A GREAT SOURCE OF MYSTIC POWER THERE, AS YET UNTAPPED...
"AND RESOLVED IT WOULD NOT REMAIN SO FOR LONG.
"THE INHABITANTS TOOK AN UNREASONING DISLIKE TO MY INITIAL APPEARANCE...
"...BUT WE WERE SOON ABLE TO COME TO TERMS...

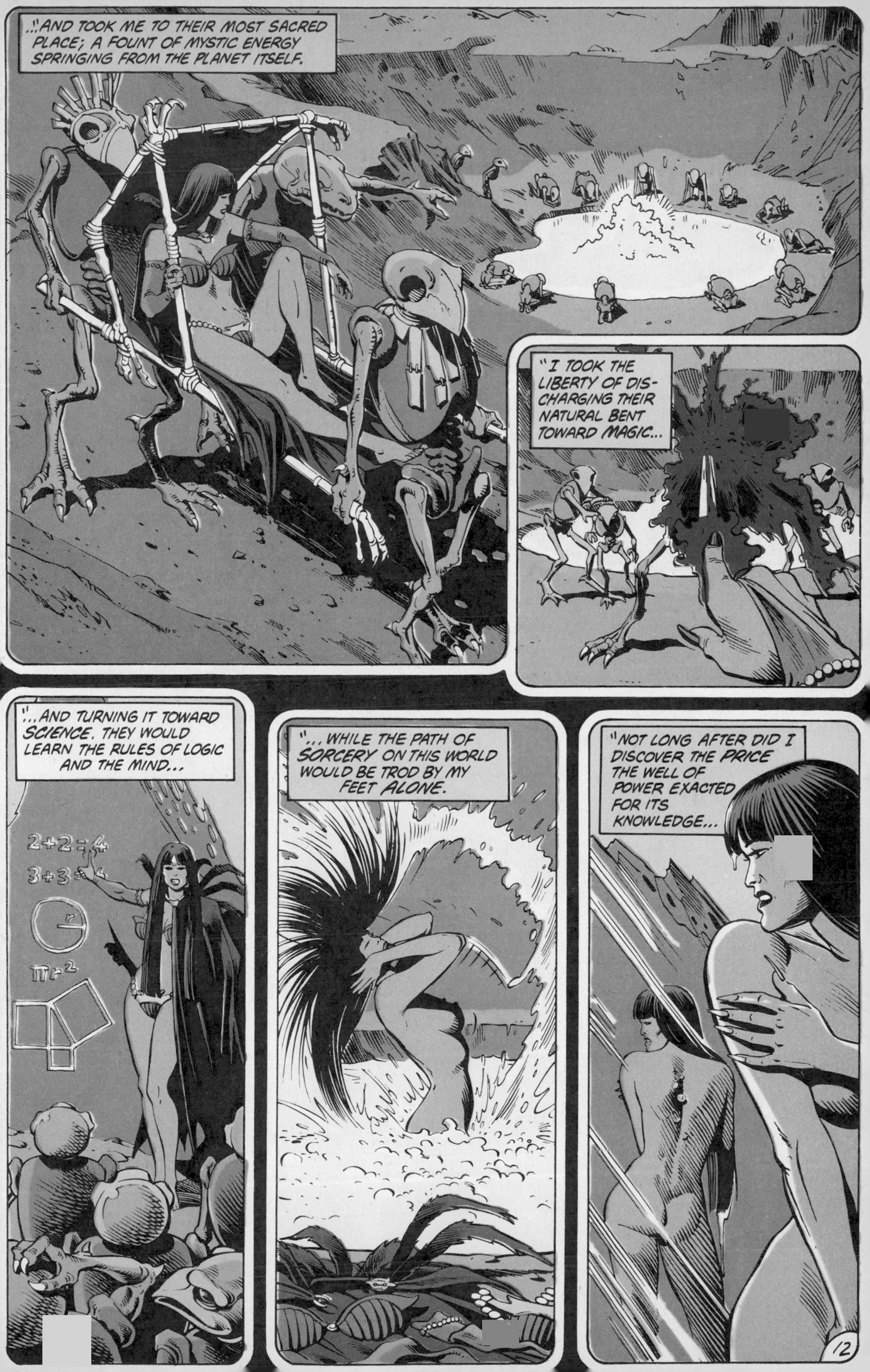

..."AND TOOK ME TO THEIR MOST SACRED PLACE; A FOUNT OF MYSTIC ENERGY SPRINGING FROM THE PLANET ITSELF.
"I TOOK THE LIBERTY OF DIS-CHARGING THEIR NATURAL BENT TOWARD MAGIC...
"...AND TURNING IT TOWARD SCIENCE. THEY WOULD LEARN THE RULES OF LOGIC AND THE MIND...
"...WHILE THE PATH OF SORCERY ON THIS WORLD WOULD BE TROD BY MY FEET ALONE.
"NOT LONG AFTER DID I DISCOVER THE PRICE THE WELL OF POWER EXACTED FOR ITS KNOWLEDGE...

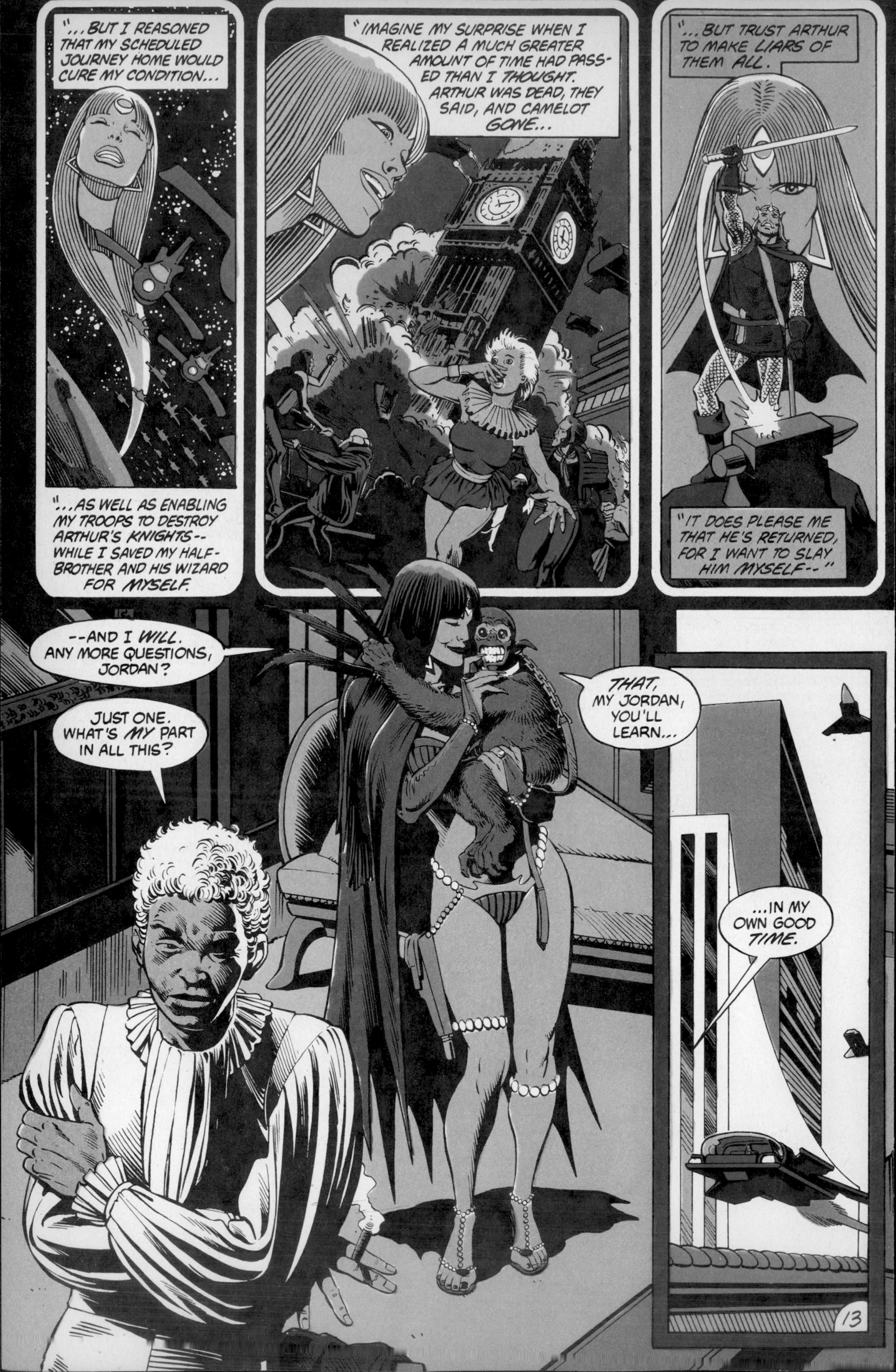

"...BUT I REASONED THAT MY SCHEDULED JOURNEY HOME WOULD CURE MY CONDITION...
"...AS WELL AS ENABLING MY TROOPS TO DESTROY ARTHUR'S KNIGHTS-- WHILE I SAVED MY HALF-BROTHER AND HIS WIZARD FOR MYSELF.
"IMAGINE MY SURPRISE WHEN I REALIZED A MUCH GREATER AMOUNT OF TIME HAD PASSED THAN I THOUGHT. ARTHUR WAS DEAD, THEY SAID, AND CAMELOT GONE...
"...BUT TRUST ARTHUR TO MAKE LIARS OF THEM ALL.
"IT DOES PLEASE ME THAT HE'S RETURNED, FOR I WANT TO SLAY HIM MYSELF--"
--AND I WILL. ANY MORE QUESTIONS, JORDAN?
JUST ONE. WHAT'S MY PART IN ALL THIS?
THAT, MY JORDAN, YOU'LL LEARN...
...IN MY OWN GOOD TIME.
13

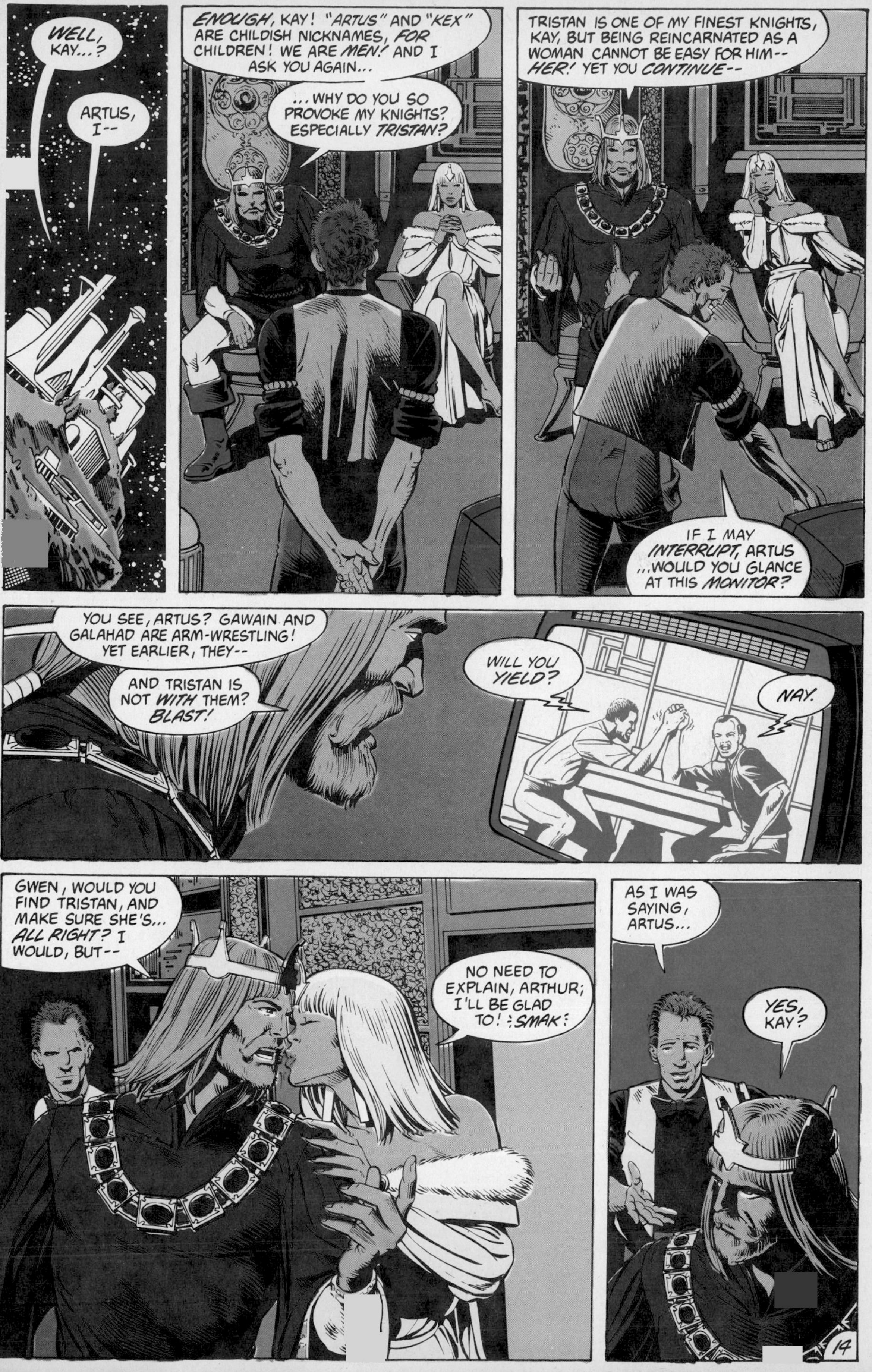
WELL, KAY...?
ARTUS, I--
ENOUGH, KAY! "ARTUS" AND "KEX" ARE CHILDISH NICKNAMES, FOR CHILDREN! WE ARE MEN! AND I ASK YOU AGAIN...
...WHY DO YOU SO PROVOKE MY KNIGHTS? ESPECIALLY TRISTAN?
TRISTAN IS ONE OF MY FINEST KNIGHTS, KAY, BUT BEING REINCARNATED AS A WOMAN CANNOT BE EASY FOR HIM-- HER! YET YOU CONTINUE--
IF I MAY INTERRUPT, ARTUS ...WOULD YOU GLANCE AT THIS MONITOR?
YOU SEE, ARTUS? GAWAIN AND GALAHAD ARE ARM-WRESTLING! YET EARLIER, THEY--
AND TRISTAN IS NOT WITH THEM? BLAST!
WILL YOU YIELD?
NAY.
GWEN, WOULD YOU FIND TRISTAN, AND MAKE SURE SHE'S... ALL RIGHT? I WOULD, BUT--
NO NEED TO EXPLAIN, ARTHUR; I'LL BE GLAD TO! :SMAK:
AS I WAS SAYING, ARTUS...
YES, KAY?

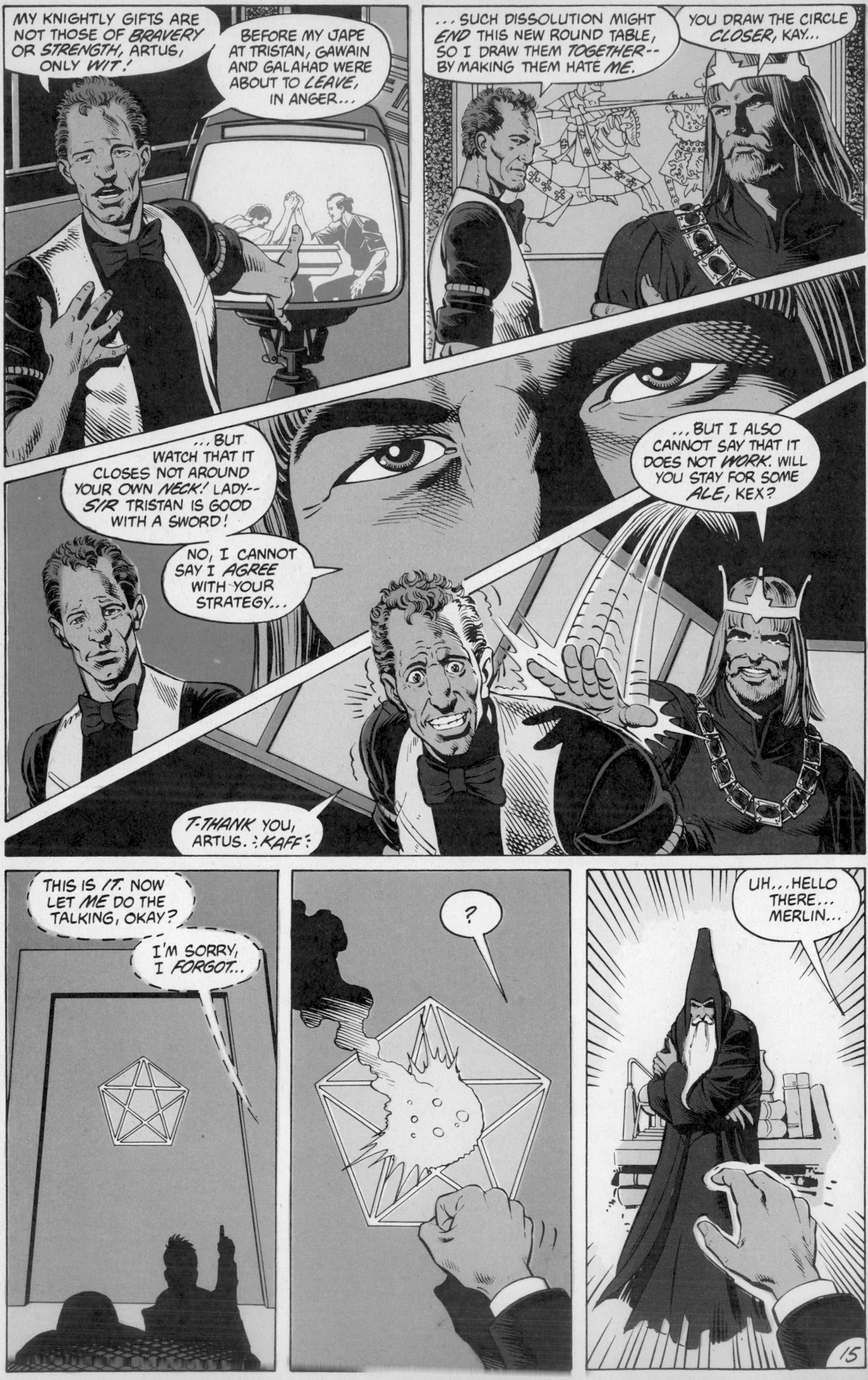
MY KNIGHTLY GIFTS ARE NOT THOSE OF BRAVERY OR STRENGTH, ARTUS, ONLY WIT!
BEFORE MY JAPE AT TRISTAN, GAWAIN AND GALAHAD WERE ABOUT TO LEAVE, IN ANGER...
...SUCH DISSOLUTION MIGHT END THIS NEW ROUND TABLE, SO I DRAW THEM TOGETHER-- BY MAKING THEM HATE ME.
YOU DRAW THE CIRCLE CLOSER, KAY...
...BUT WATCH THAT IT CLOSES NOT AROUND YOUR OWN NECK! LADY-- SIR TRISTAN IS GOOD WITH A SWORD!
NO, I CANNOT SAY I AGREE WITH YOUR STRATEGY...
...BUT I ALSO CANNOT SAY THAT IT DOES NOT WORK. WILL YOU STAY FOR SOME ALE, KEX?
T-THANK YOU, ARTUS. KAFF
THIS IS IT. NOW LET ME DO THE TALKING, OKAY?
I'M SORRY, I FORGOT...
?
UH...HELLO THERE... MERLIN...

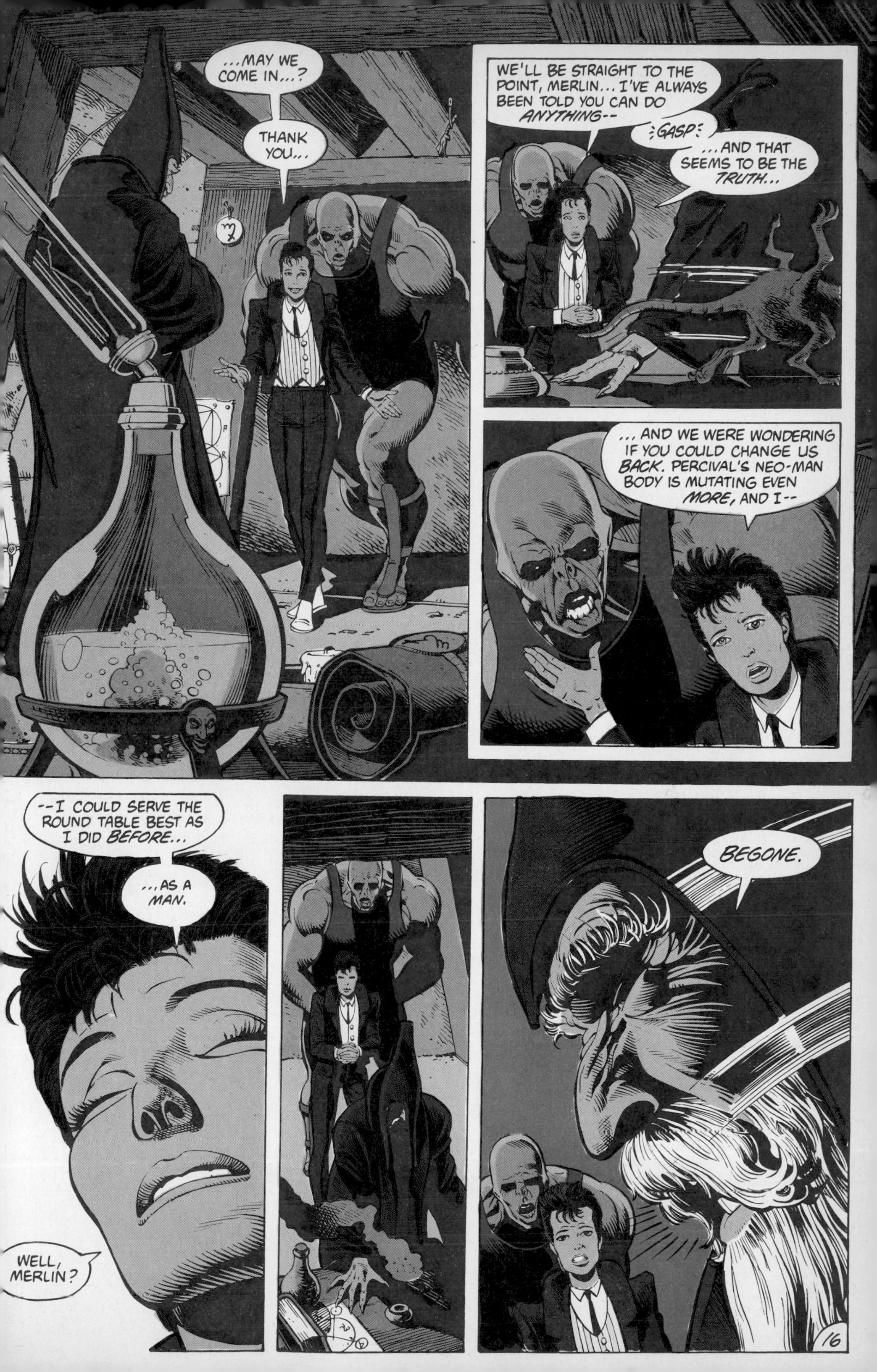
...MAY WE COME IN...?
THANK YOU...
WE'LL BE STRAIGHT TO THE POINT, MERLIN... I'VE ALWAYS BEEN TOLD YOU CAN DO *ANYTHING*--
GASP
...AND THAT SEEMS TO BE THE *TRUTH*...
...AND WE WERE WONDERING IF YOU COULD CHANGE US *BACK*. PERCIVAL'S NEO-MAN BODY IS MUTATING EVEN *MORE*, AND I--
--I COULD SERVE THE ROUND TABLE BEST AS I DID *BEFORE*...
...AS A MAN.
WELL, MERLIN?
BEGONE.
16

BUT...YOU CAN'T JUST--

BEGONE.

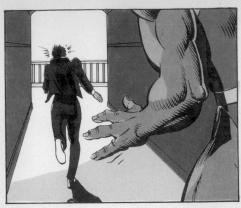

HELLO, TRISTAN! I DIDN'T THINK YOU'D MIND IF I--

YOU!

THEY SENT YOU TO *TALK* TO ME, DIDN'T THEY? "TRISTAN DOESN'T KNOW HER *PLACE*, SHE ISN'T BEING A GOOD GIRL!"

"SHE'LL LISTEN TO *YOU*," THEY SAID, "YOU'RE BOTH *WOMEN*!"

TRISTAN, I --

WHEN WILL YOU LEARN I'M NOT LIKE *ANY* OF YOU? NOW PLEASE-- GET OUT!

VERY WELL, TRISTAN! :SIGH:

TRISTANNNNNN

17

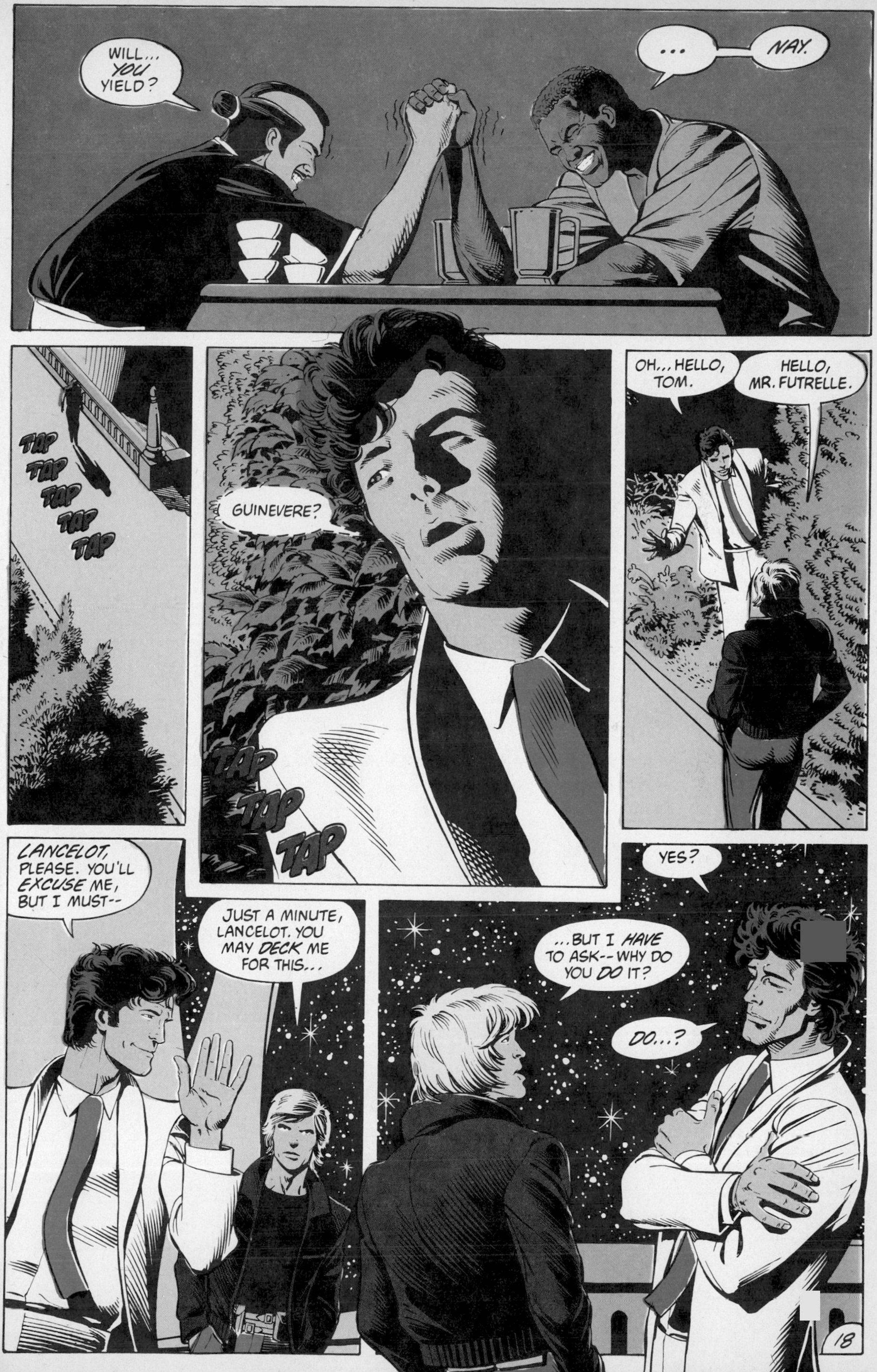
WILL... YOU YIELD?
... NAY.
TAP TAP TAP TAP TAP
GUINEVERE?
TAP TAP TAP
OH... HELLO, TOM.
HELLO, MR. FUTRELLE.
LANCELOT, PLEASE. YOU'LL EXCUSE ME, BUT I MUST--
JUST A MINUTE, LANCELOT. YOU MAY DECK ME FOR THIS...
YES?
...BUT I HAVE TO ASK--WHY DO YOU DO IT?
DO...?

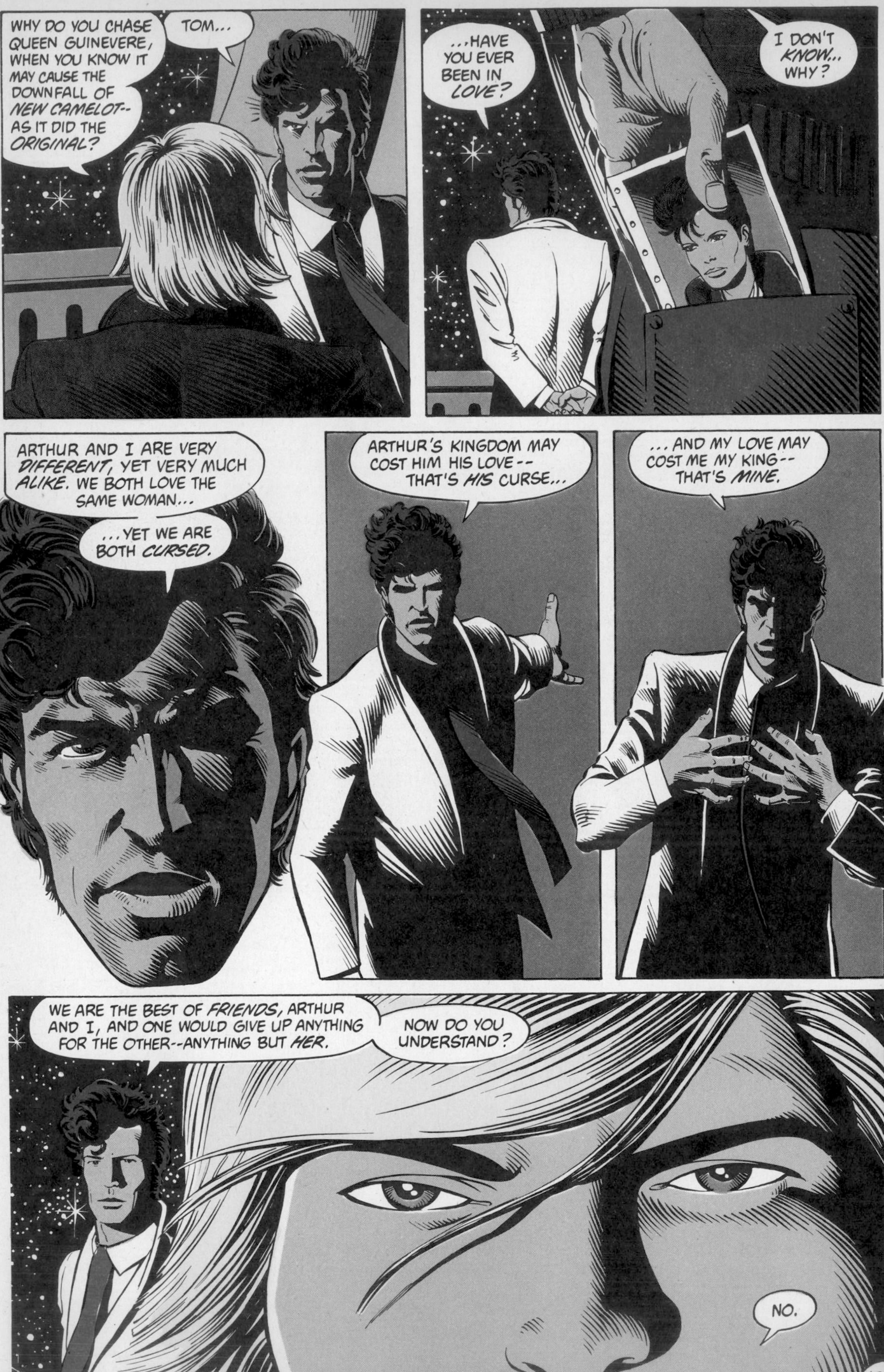

WHY DO YOU CHASE QUEEN GUINEVERE, WHEN YOU KNOW IT MAY CAUSE THE DOWNFALL OF NEW CAMELOT-- AS IT DID THE ORIGINAL?
TOM...
...HAVE YOU EVER BEEN IN LOVE?
I DON'T KNOW... WHY?
ARTHUR AND I ARE VERY DIFFERENT, YET VERY MUCH ALIKE. WE BOTH LOVE THE SAME WOMAN...
...YET WE ARE BOTH CURSED.
ARTHUR'S KINGDOM MAY COST HIM HIS LOVE-- THAT'S HIS CURSE...
...AND MY LOVE MAY COST ME MY KING-- THAT'S MINE.
WE ARE THE BEST OF FRIENDS, ARTHUR AND I, AND ONE WOULD GIVE UP ANYTHING FOR THE OTHER--ANYTHING BUT HER.
NOW DO YOU UNDERSTAND?
NO.

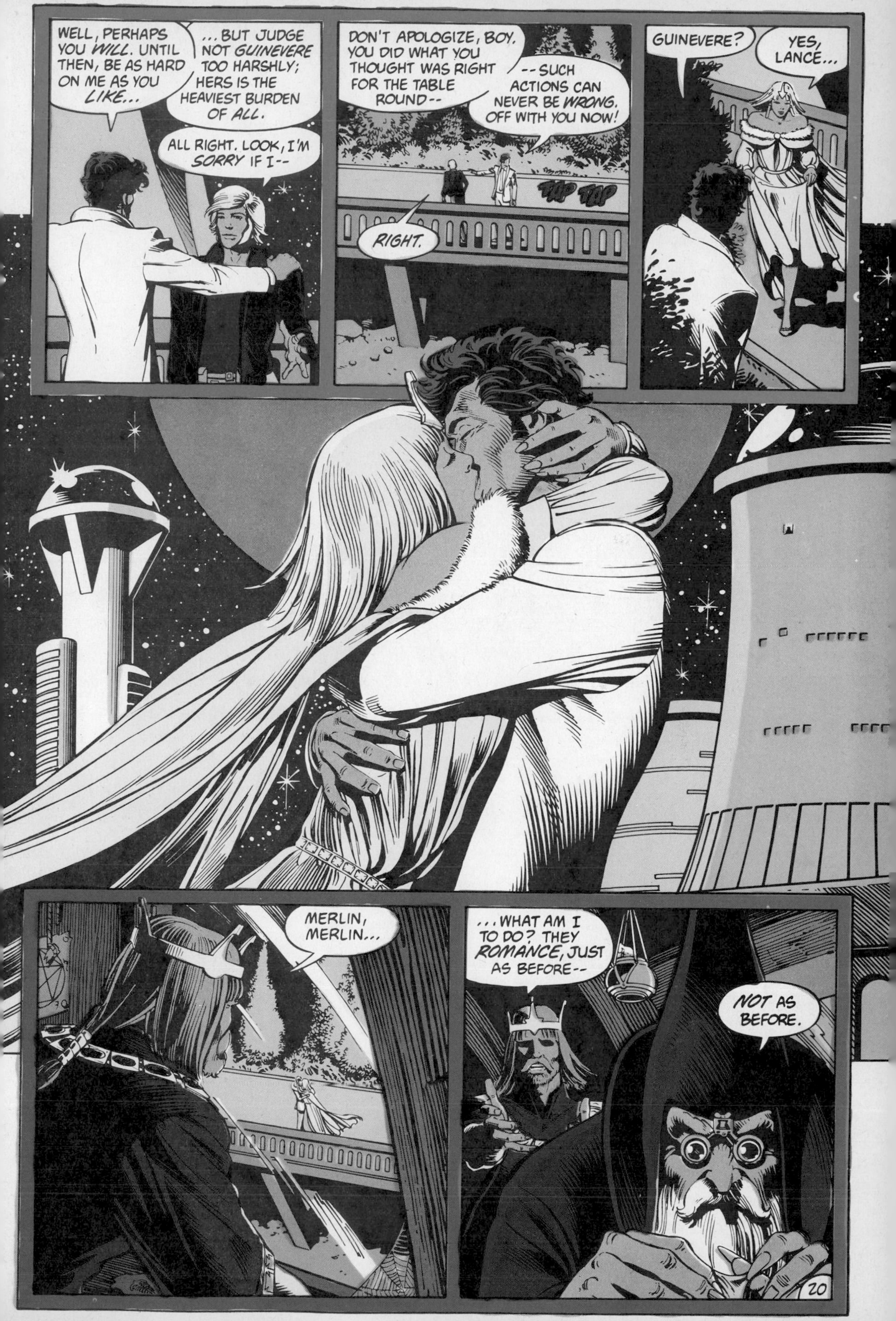

WELL, PERHAPS YOU WILL. UNTIL THEN, BE AS HARD ON ME AS YOU LIKE...
...BUT JUDGE NOT GUINEVERE TOO HARSHLY; HERS IS THE HEAVIEST BURDEN OF ALL.
ALL RIGHT. LOOK, I'M SORRY IF I--
DON'T APOLOGIZE, BOY. YOU DID WHAT YOU THOUGHT WAS RIGHT FOR THE TABLE ROUND--
--SUCH ACTIONS CAN NEVER BE WRONG. OFF WITH YOU NOW!
RIGHT.
TAP TAP
GUINEVERE?
YES, LANCE...
MERLIN, MERLIN...
...WHAT AM I TO DO? THEY ROMANCE, JUST AS BEFORE--
NOT AS BEFORE.

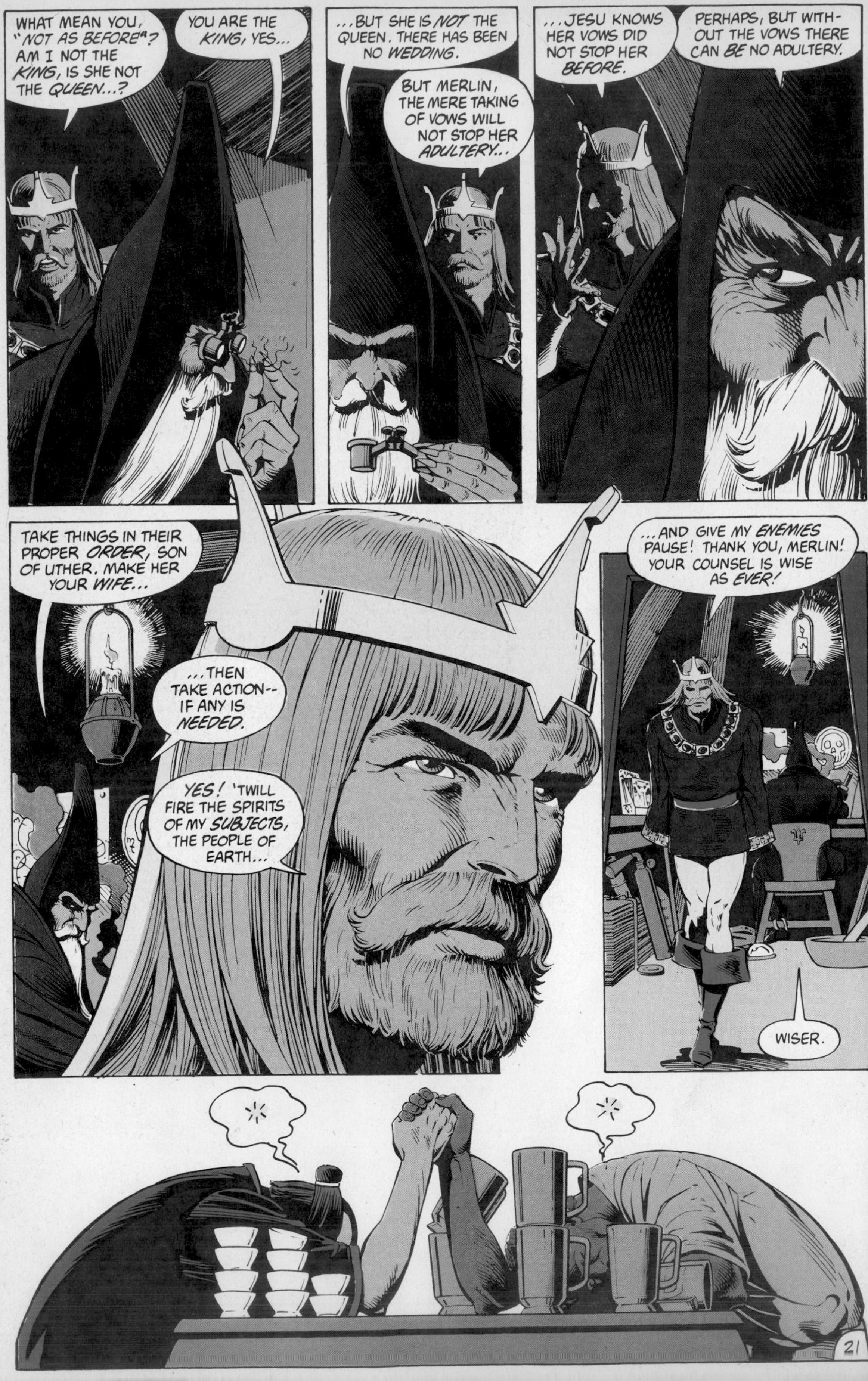

WHAT MEAN YOU, "NOT AS BEFORE"? AM I NOT THE KING, IS SHE NOT THE QUEEN...?
YOU ARE THE KING, YES...
...BUT SHE IS NOT THE QUEEN. THERE HAS BEEN NO WEDDING.
BUT MERLIN, THE MERE TAKING OF VOWS WILL NOT STOP HER ADULTERY...
...JESU KNOWS HER VOWS DID NOT STOP HER BEFORE.
PERHAPS, BUT WITH-OUT THE VOWS THERE CAN BE NO ADULTERY.
TAKE THINGS IN THEIR PROPER ORDER, SON OF UTHER. MAKE HER YOUR WIFE...
...THEN TAKE ACTION-- IF ANY IS NEEDED.
YES! 'TWILL FIRE THE SPIRITS OF MY SUBJECTS, THE PEOPLE OF EARTH...
...AND GIVE MY ENEMIES PAUSE! THANK YOU, MERLIN! YOUR COUNSEL IS WISE AS EVER!
WISER.

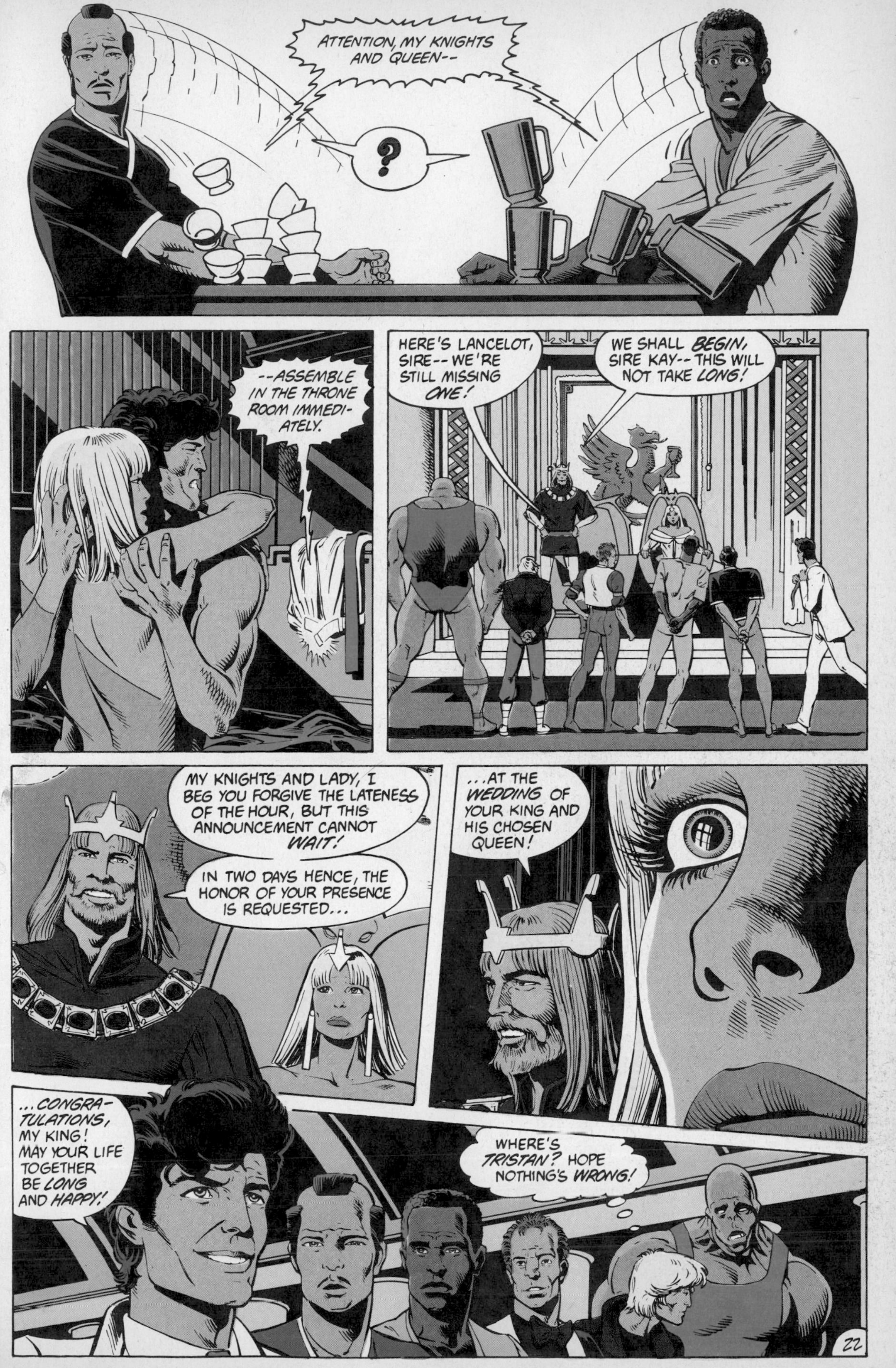
ATTENTION, MY KNIGHTS AND QUEEN--
?
--ASSEMBLE IN THE THRONE ROOM IMMEDI-ATELY.
HERE'S LANCELOT, SIRE-- WE'RE STILL MISSING ONE!
WE SHALL BEGIN, SIRE KAY-- THIS WILL NOT TAKE LONG!
MY KNIGHTS AND LADY, I BEG YOU FORGIVE THE LATENESS OF THE HOUR, BUT THIS ANNOUNCEMENT CANNOT WAIT!
IN TWO DAYS HENCE, THE HONOR OF YOUR PRESENCE IS REQUESTED...
...AT THE WEDDING OF YOUR KING AND HIS CHOSEN QUEEN!
...CONGRA-TULATIONS, MY KING! MAY YOUR LIFE TOGETHER BE LONG AND HAPPY!
WHERE'S TRISTAN? HOPE NOTHING'S WRONG!

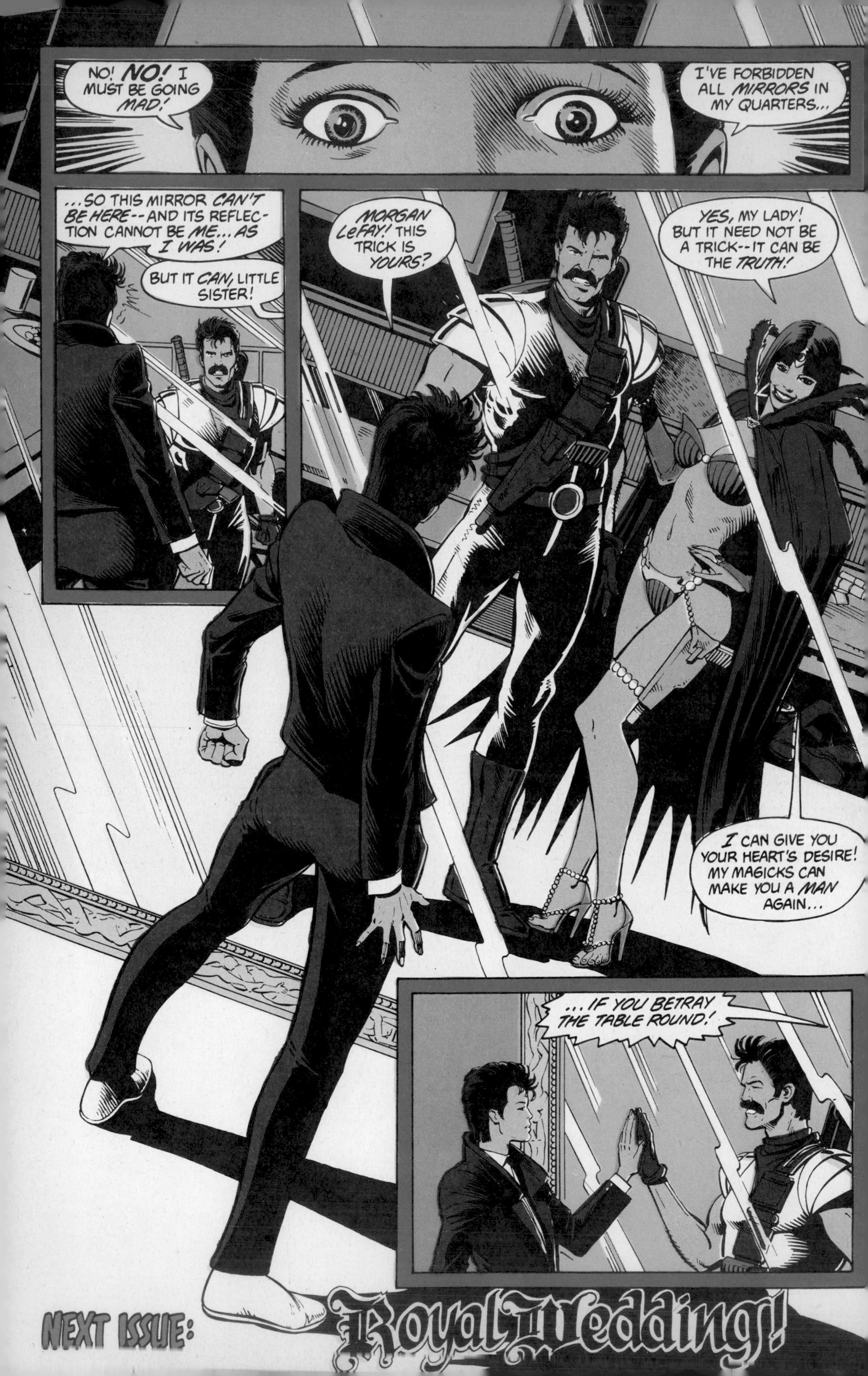
NO! NO! I MUST BE GOING MAD!
I'VE FORBIDDEN ALL MIRRORS IN MY QUARTERS...
...SO THIS MIRROR CAN'T BE HERE--AND ITS REFLECTION CANNOT BE ME... AS I WAS!
BUT IT CAN, LITTLE SISTER!
MORGAN LeFAY! THIS TRICK IS YOURS?
YES, MY LADY! BUT IT NEED NOT BE A TRICK--IT CAN BE THE TRUTH!
I CAN GIVE YOU YOUR HEART'S DESIRE! MY MAGICKS CAN MAKE YOU A MAN AGAIN...
...IF YOU BETRAY THE TABLE ROUND!
NEXT ISSUE: Royal Wedding!

Chapter
6

Royal ~~Wedding~~ Funeral

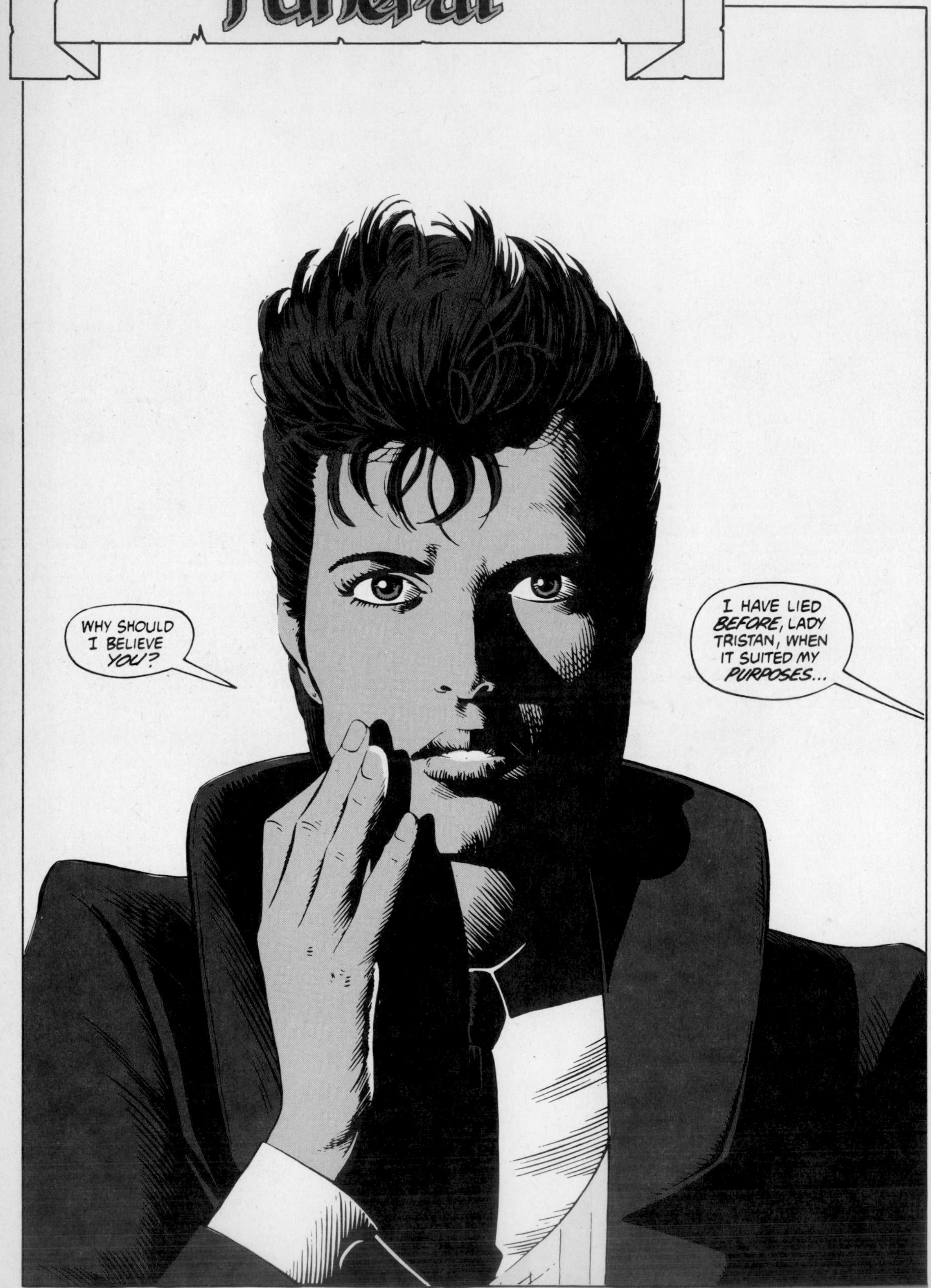
WHY SHOULD I BELIEVE *YOU*?
I HAVE LIED *BEFORE*, LADY TRISTAN, WHEN IT SUITED MY *PURPOSES*...

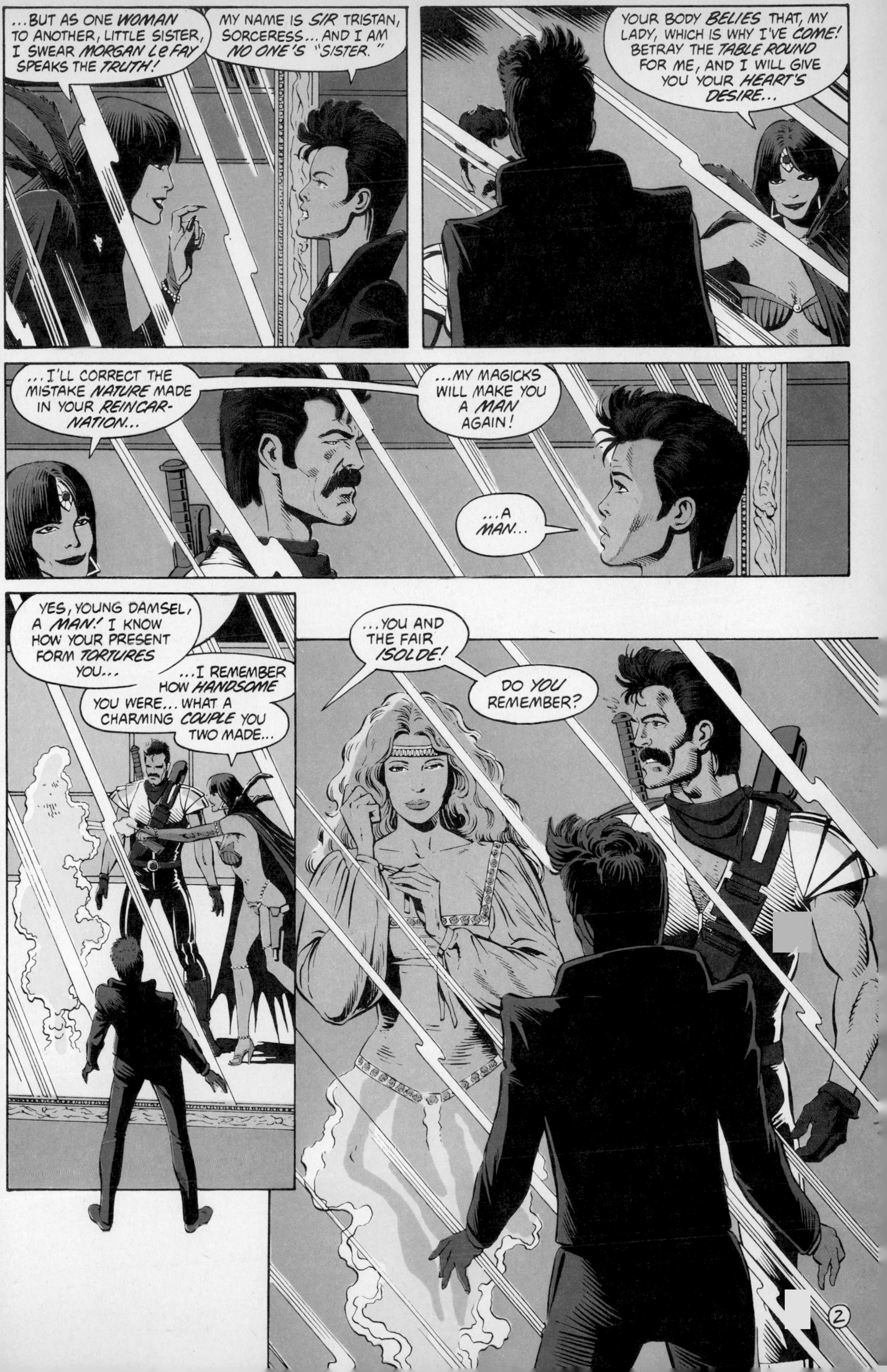
...BUT AS ONE WOMAN TO ANOTHER, LITTLE SISTER, I SWEAR MORGAN LE FAY SPEAKS THE TRUTH!
MY NAME IS SIR TRISTAN, SORCERESS... AND I AM NO ONE'S "SISTER."
YOUR BODY BELIES THAT, MY LADY, WHICH IS WHY I'VE COME! BETRAY THE TABLE ROUND FOR ME, AND I WILL GIVE YOU YOUR HEART'S DESIRE...
...I'LL CORRECT THE MISTAKE NATURE MADE IN YOUR REINCAR-NATION...
...MY MAGICKS WILL MAKE YOU A MAN AGAIN!
...A MAN...
YES, YOUNG DAMSEL, A MAN! I KNOW HOW YOUR PRESENT FORM TORTURES YOU...
...I REMEMBER HOW HANDSOME YOU WERE... WHAT A CHARMING COUPLE YOU TWO MADE...
...YOU AND THE FAIR ISOLDE!
DO YOU REMEMBER?

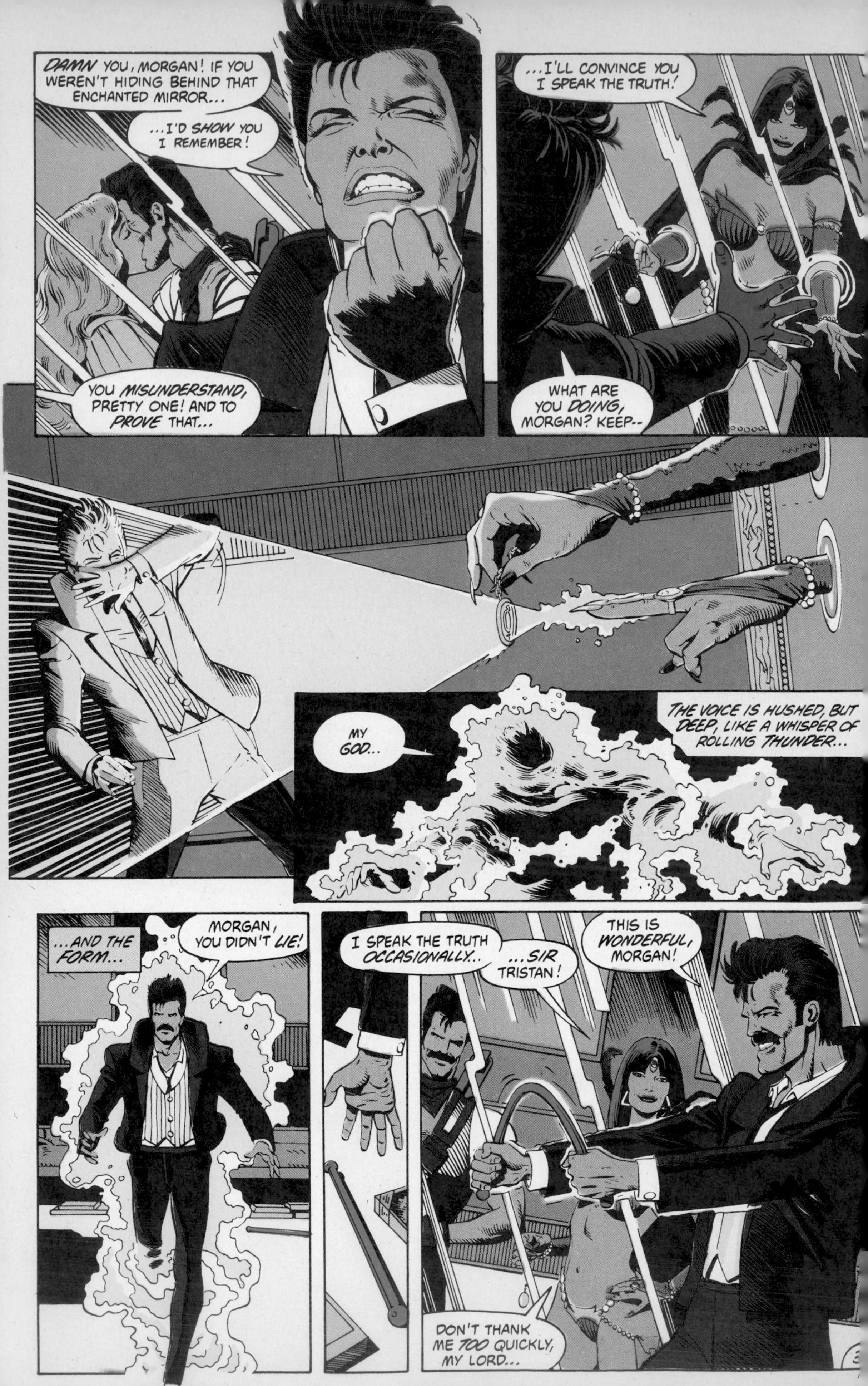
DAMN YOU, MORGAN! IF YOU WEREN'T HIDING BEHIND THAT ENCHANTED MIRROR...
...I'D SHOW YOU I REMEMBER!
YOU MISUNDERSTAND, PRETTY ONE! AND TO PROVE THAT...
...I'LL CONVINCE YOU I SPEAK THE TRUTH!
WHAT ARE YOU DOING, MORGAN? KEEP--
MY GOD...
THE VOICE IS HUSHED, BUT DEEP, LIKE A WHISPER OF ROLLING THUNDER...
...AND THE FORM...
MORGAN, YOU DIDN'T LIE!
I SPEAK THE TRUTH OCCASIONALLY...
...SIR TRISTAN!
THIS IS WONDERFUL, MORGAN!
DON'T THANK ME TOO QUICKLY, MY LORD...

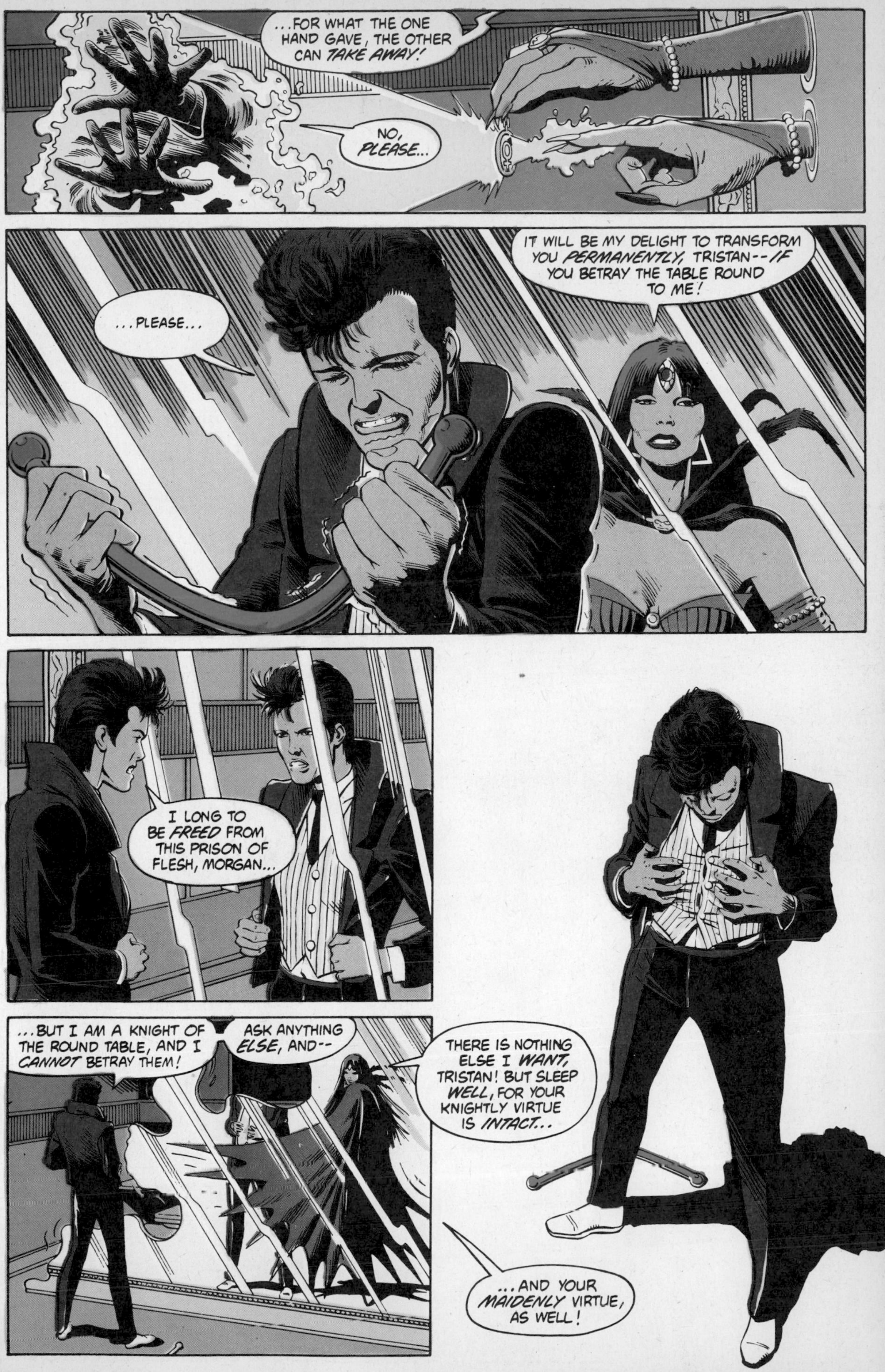

...FOR WHAT THE ONE HAND GAVE, THE OTHER CAN *TAKE AWAY!*
NO, *PLEASE*...
IT WILL BE MY DELIGHT TO TRANSFORM YOU *PERMANENTLY,* TRISTAN--*IF* YOU BETRAY THE TABLE ROUND TO ME!
...PLEASE...
I LONG TO BE *FREED* FROM THIS PRISON OF FLESH, MORGAN...
...BUT I AM A KNIGHT OF THE ROUND TABLE, AND I *CANNOT* BETRAY THEM!
ASK ANYTHING *ELSE,* AND--
THERE IS NOTHING ELSE I *WANT,* TRISTAN! BUT SLEEP *WELL,* FOR YOUR KNIGHTLY VIRTUE IS *INTACT*...
...AND YOUR *MAIDENLY* VIRTUE, AS WELL!

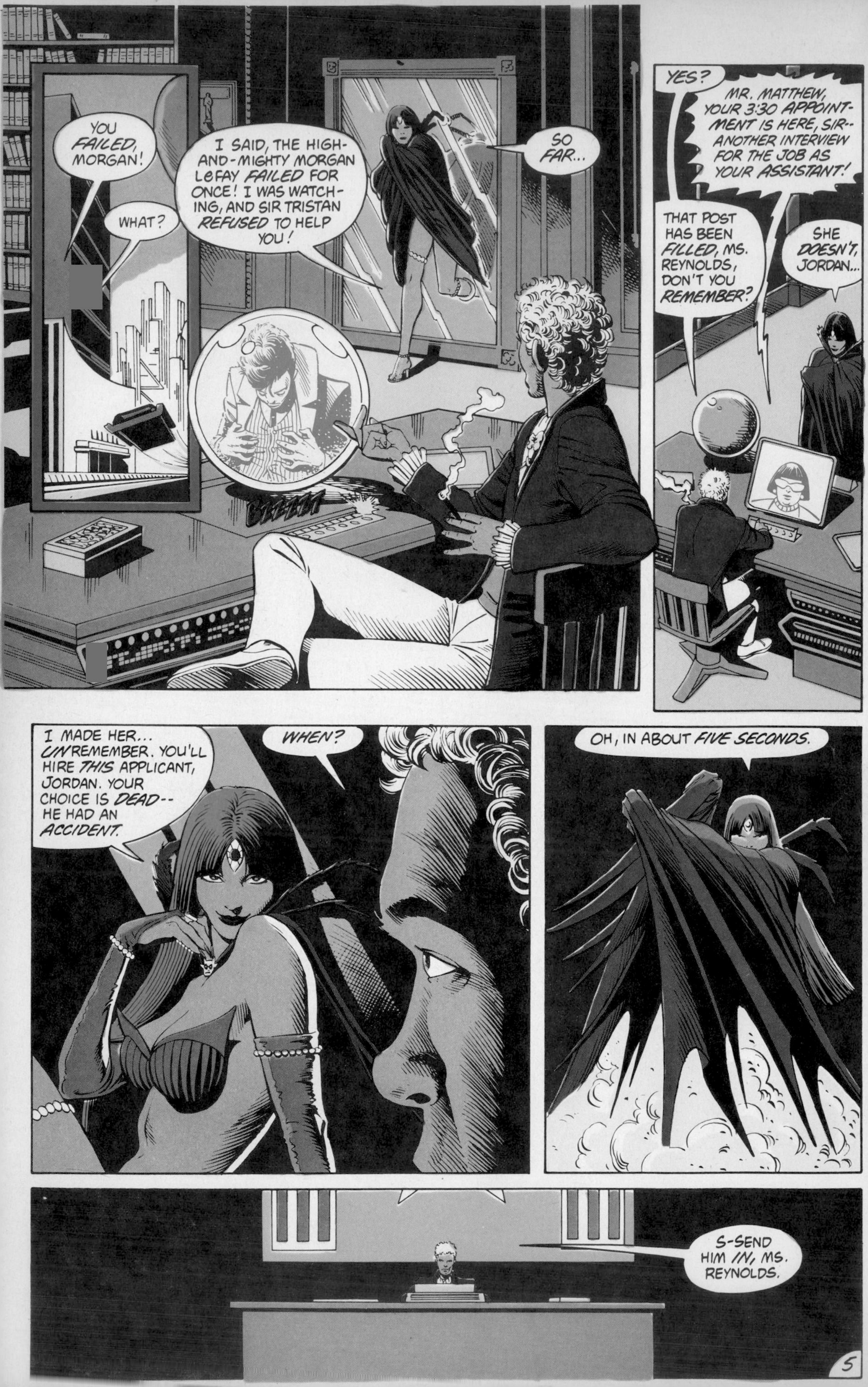
YOU FAILED, MORGAN!
WHAT?
I SAID, THE HIGH-AND-MIGHTY MORGAN LeFAY FAILED FOR ONCE! I WAS WATCHING, AND SIR TRISTAN REFUSED TO HELP YOU!
SO FAR...
YES?
MR. MATTHEW, YOUR 3:30 APPOINTMENT IS HERE, SIR-- ANOTHER INTERVIEW FOR THE JOB AS YOUR ASSISTANT!
THAT POST HAS BEEN FILLED, MS. REYNOLDS, DON'T YOU REMEMBER?
SHE DOESN'T, JORDAN...
I MADE HER... UNREMEMBER. YOU'LL HIRE THIS APPLICANT, JORDAN. YOUR CHOICE IS DEAD-- HE HAD AN ACCIDENT.
WHEN?
OH, IN ABOUT FIVE SECONDS.
S-SEND HIM IN, MS. REYNOLDS.

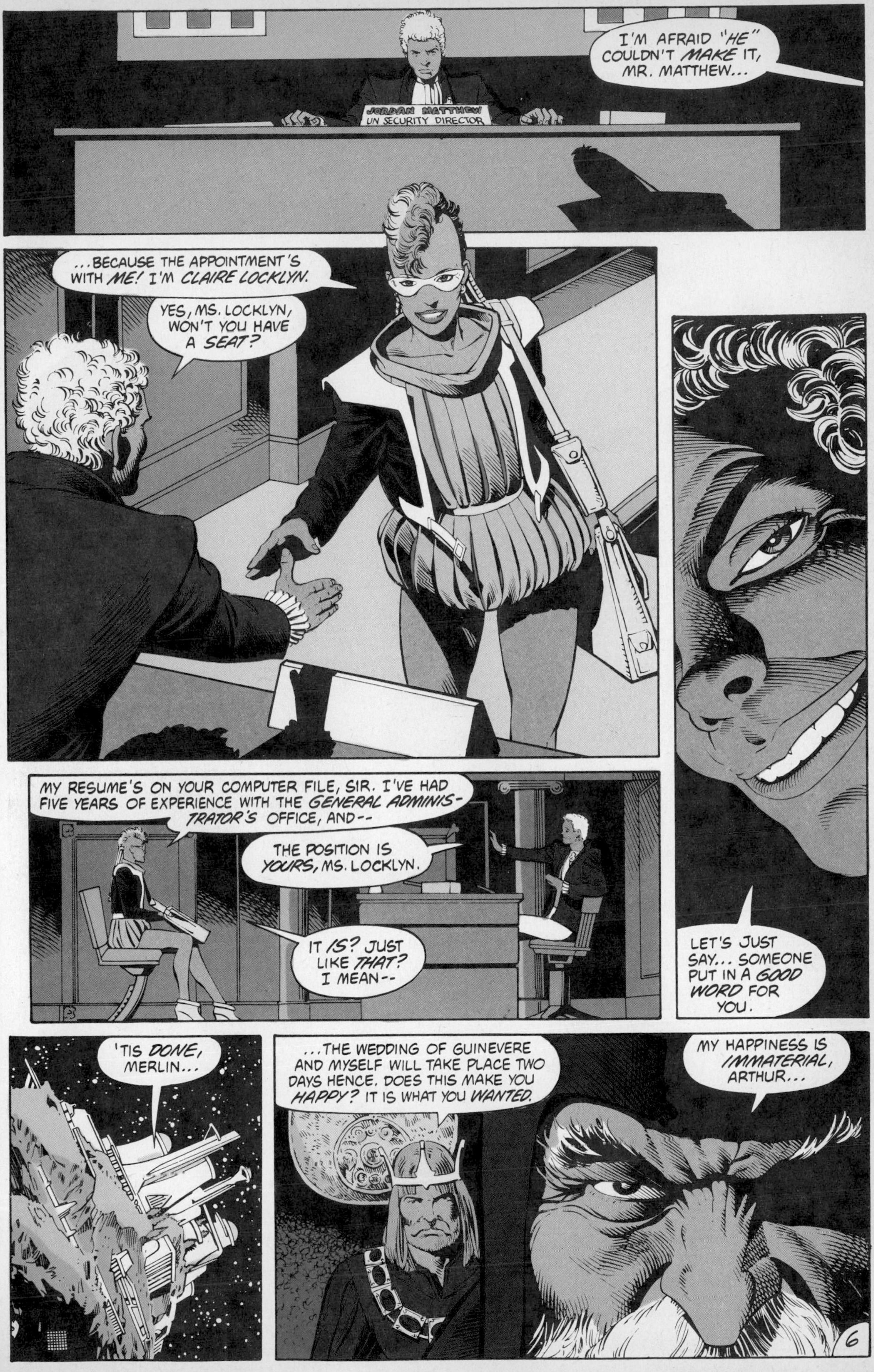
JORDAN MATTHEW
UN SECURITY DIRECTOR
I'M AFRAID "HE" COULDN'T MAKE IT, MR. MATTHEW...
...BECAUSE THE APPOINTMENT'S WITH ME! I'M CLAIRE LOCKLYN.
YES, MS. LOCKLYN, WON'T YOU HAVE A SEAT?
MY RESUME'S ON YOUR COMPUTER FILE, SIR. I'VE HAD FIVE YEARS OF EXPERIENCE WITH THE GENERAL ADMINISTRATOR'S OFFICE, AND--
THE POSITION IS YOURS, MS. LOCKLYN.
IT IS? JUST LIKE THAT? I MEAN--
LET'S JUST SAY... SOMEONE PUT IN A GOOD WORD FOR YOU.
'TIS DONE, MERLIN...
...THE WEDDING OF GUINEVERE AND MYSELF WILL TAKE PLACE TWO DAYS HENCE. DOES THIS MAKE YOU HAPPY? IT IS WHAT YOU WANTED.
MY HAPPINESS IS IMMATERIAL, ARTHUR...
6

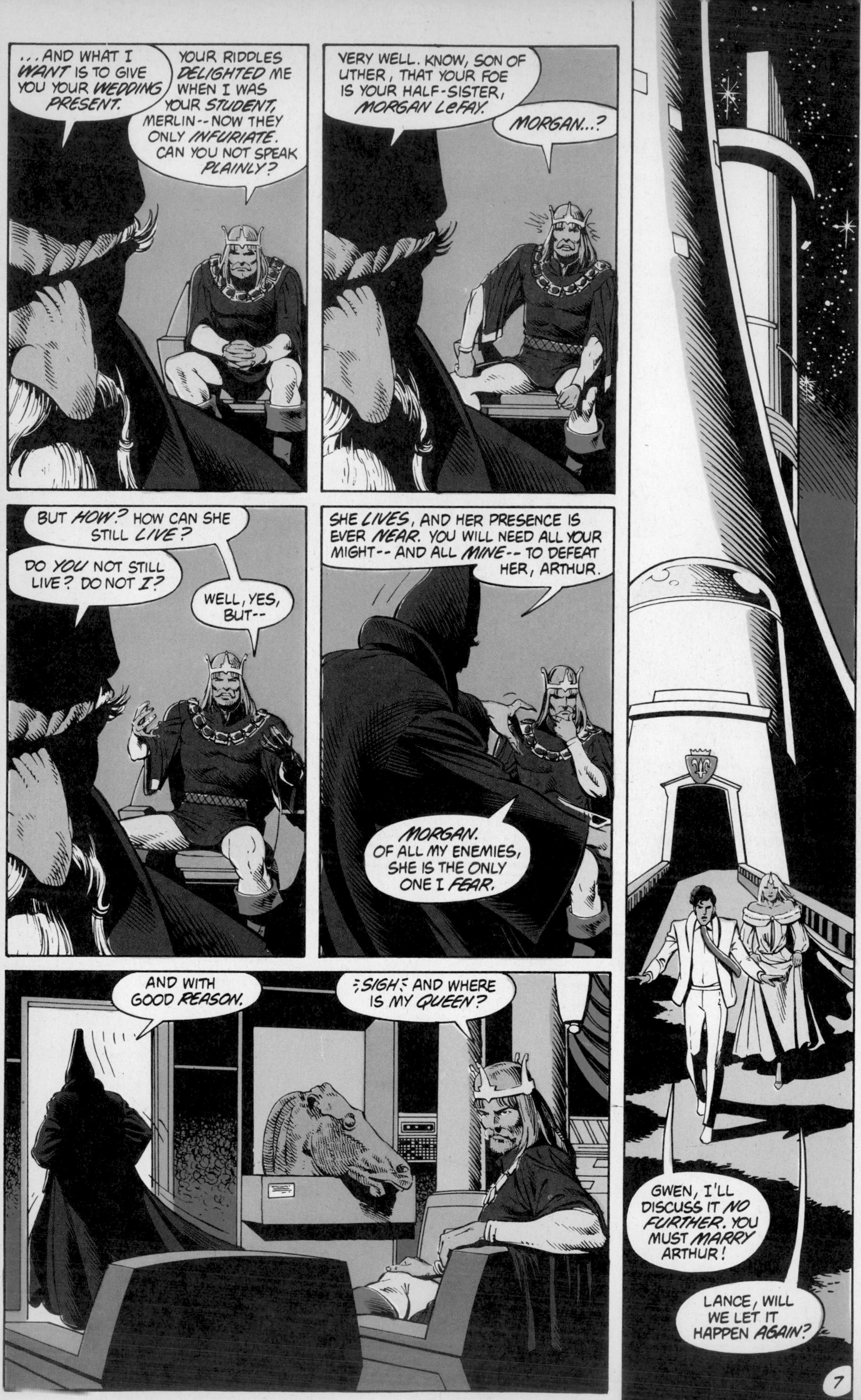
...AND WHAT I WANT IS TO GIVE YOU YOUR WEDDING PRESENT.
YOUR RIDDLES DELIGHTED ME WHEN I WAS YOUR STUDENT, MERLIN--NOW THEY ONLY INFURIATE. CAN YOU NOT SPEAK PLAINLY?
VERY WELL. KNOW, SON OF UTHER, THAT YOUR FOE IS YOUR HALF-SISTER, MORGAN LeFAY.
MORGAN...?
BUT HOW? HOW CAN SHE STILL LIVE?
DO YOU NOT STILL LIVE? DO NOT I?
WELL, YES, BUT--
SHE LIVES, AND HER PRESENCE IS EVER NEAR. YOU WILL NEED ALL YOUR MIGHT--AND ALL MINE--TO DEFEAT HER, ARTHUR.
MORGAN. OF ALL MY ENEMIES, SHE IS THE ONLY ONE I FEAR.
AND WITH GOOD REASON.
SIGH AND WHERE IS MY QUEEN?
GWEN, I'LL DISCUSS IT NO FURTHER. YOU MUST MARRY ARTHUR!
LANCE, WILL WE LET IT HAPPEN AGAIN?

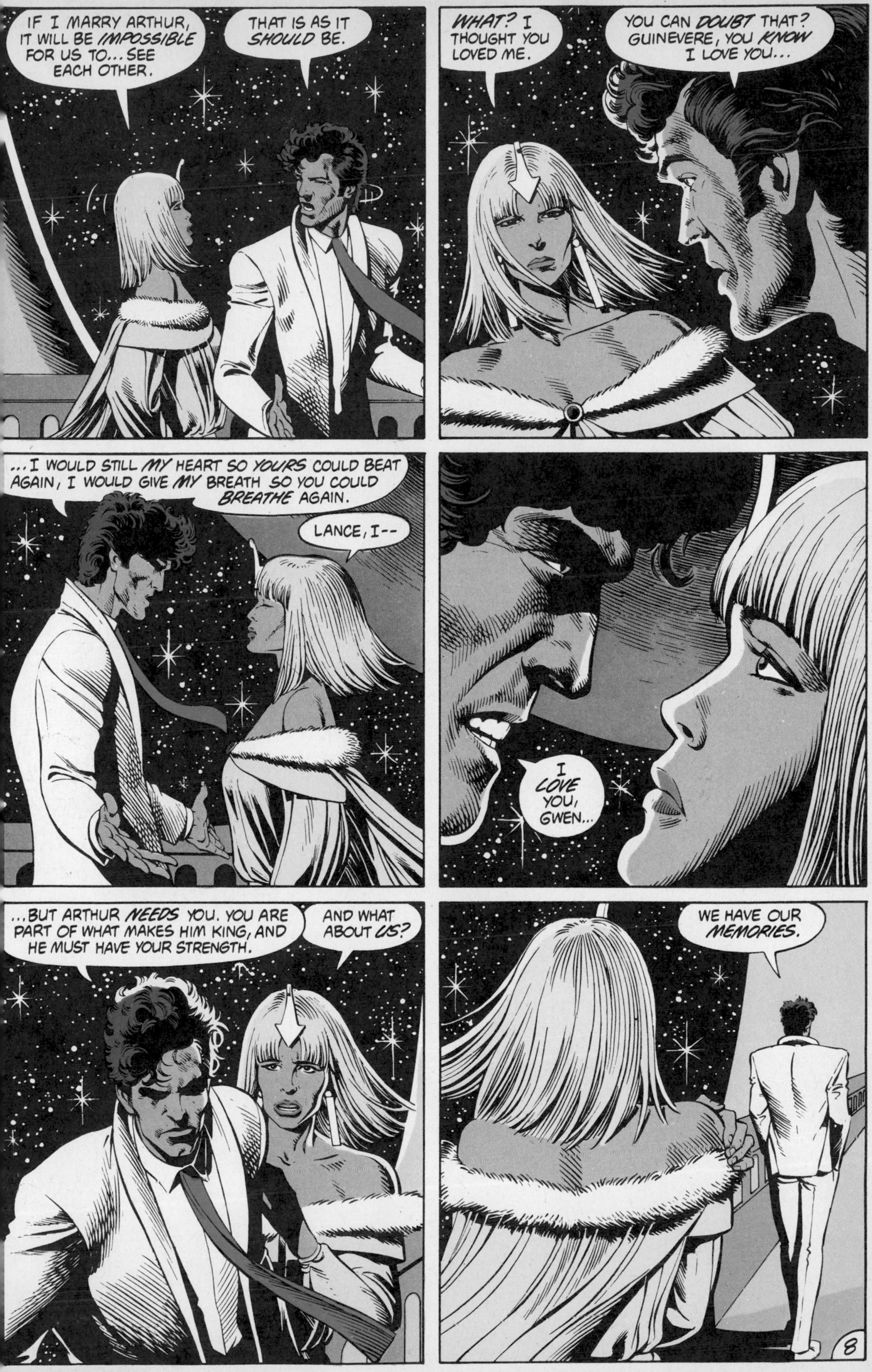
IF I MARRY ARTHUR, IT WILL BE *IMPOSSIBLE* FOR US TO... SEE EACH OTHER.
THAT IS AS IT *SHOULD* BE.
WHAT? I THOUGHT YOU LOVED ME.
YOU CAN *DOUBT* THAT? GUINEVERE, YOU *KNOW* I LOVE YOU...
...I WOULD STILL *MY* HEART SO *YOURS* COULD BEAT AGAIN, I WOULD GIVE *MY* BREATH SO YOU COULD *BREATHE* AGAIN.
LANCE, I--
I *LOVE* YOU, GWEN...
...BUT ARTHUR *NEEDS* YOU. YOU ARE PART OF WHAT MAKES HIM KING, AND HE MUST HAVE YOUR STRENGTH.
AND WHAT ABOUT *US?*
WE HAVE OUR *MEMORIES*.

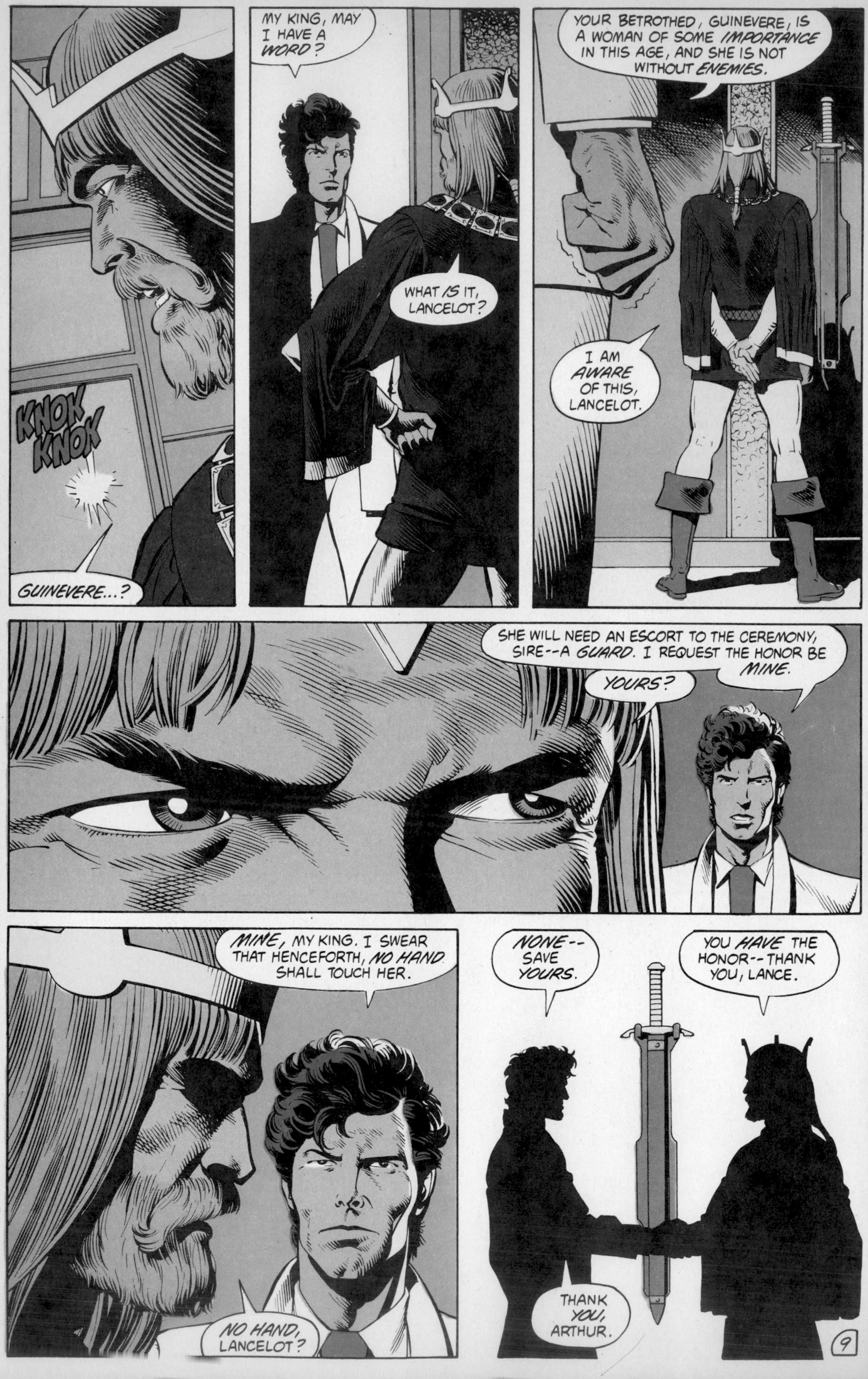
KNOK KNOK
GUINEVERE...?
MY KING, MAY I HAVE A WORD?
WHAT IS IT, LANCELOT?
YOUR BETROTHED, GUINEVERE, IS A WOMAN OF SOME IMPORTANCE IN THIS AGE, AND SHE IS NOT WITHOUT ENEMIES.
I AM AWARE OF THIS, LANCELOT.
SHE WILL NEED AN ESCORT TO THE CEREMONY, SIRE--A GUARD. I REQUEST THE HONOR BE MINE.
YOURS?
MINE, MY KING. I SWEAR THAT HENCEFORTH, NO HAND SHALL TOUCH HER.
NO HAND, LANCELOT?
NONE-- SAVE YOURS.
YOU HAVE THE HONOR--THANK YOU, LANCE.
THANK YOU, ARTHUR.

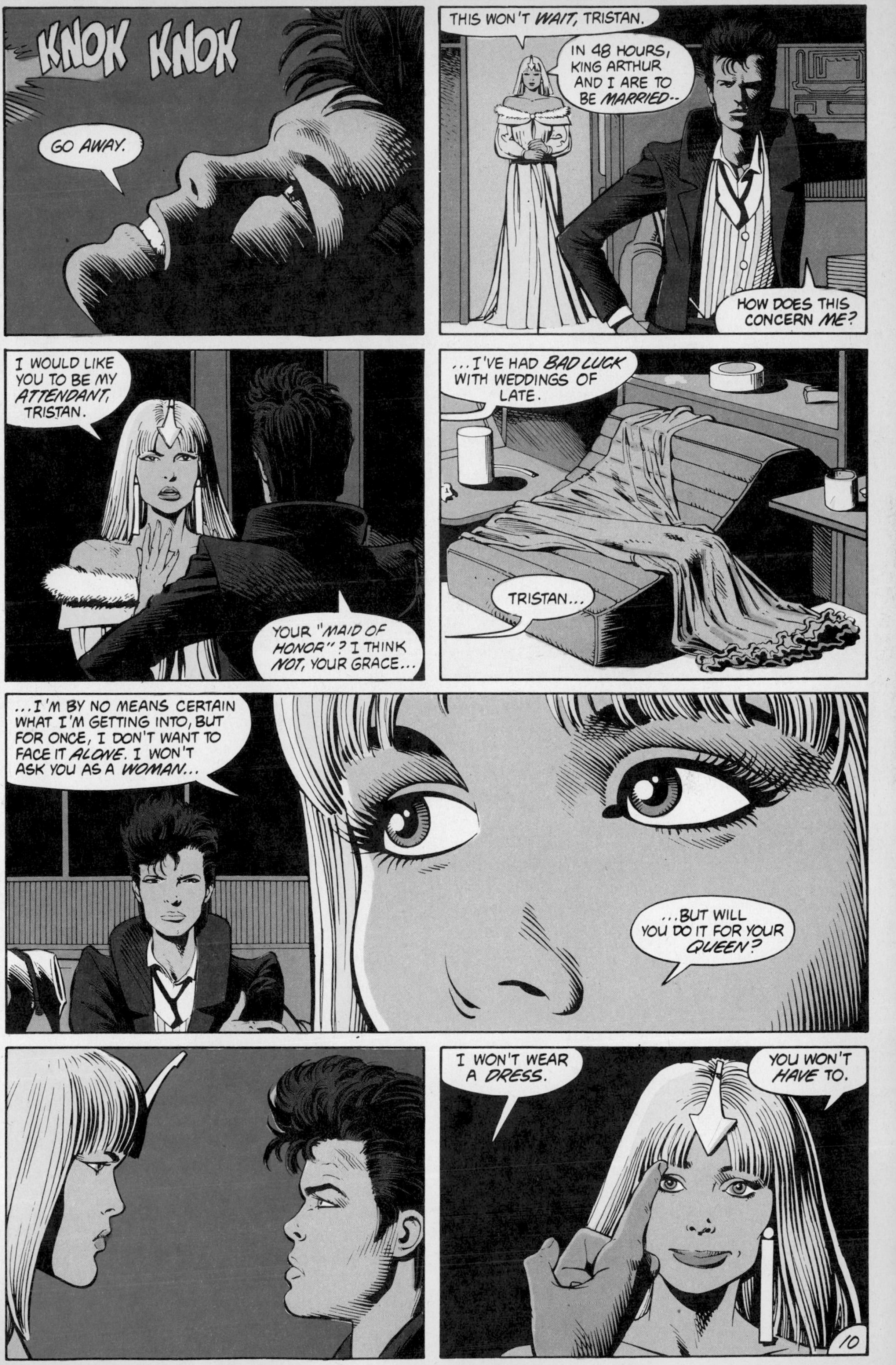
KNOK KNOK
GO AWAY.
THIS WON'T WAIT, TRISTAN.
IN 48 HOURS, KING ARTHUR AND I ARE TO BE MARRIED--
HOW DOES THIS CONCERN ME?
I WOULD LIKE YOU TO BE MY ATTENDANT, TRISTAN.
YOUR "MAID OF HONOR"? I THINK NOT, YOUR GRACE...
...I'VE HAD BAD LUCK WITH WEDDINGS OF LATE.
TRISTAN...
...I'M BY NO MEANS CERTAIN WHAT I'M GETTING INTO, BUT FOR ONCE, I DON'T WANT TO FACE IT ALONE. I WON'T ASK YOU AS A WOMAN...
...BUT WILL YOU DO IT FOR YOUR QUEEN?
I WON'T WEAR A DRESS.
YOU WON'T HAVE TO.
10

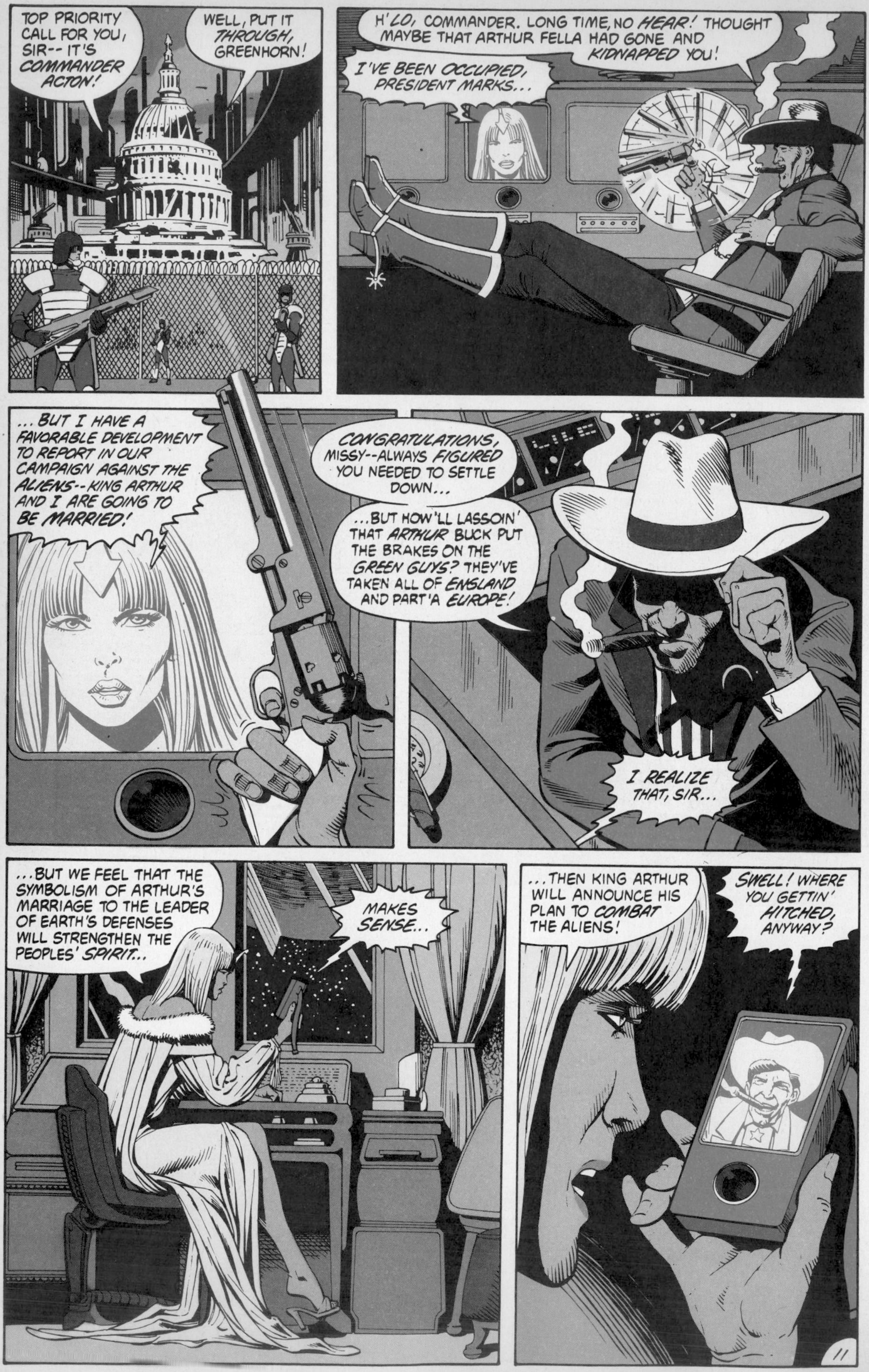

TOP PRIORITY CALL FOR YOU, SIR-- IT'S COMMANDER ACTON!
WELL, PUT IT THROUGH, GREENHORN!
H'LO, COMMANDER. LONG TIME, NO HEAR! THOUGHT MAYBE THAT ARTHUR FELLA HAD GONE AND KIDNAPPED YOU!
I'VE BEEN OCCUPIED, PRESIDENT MARKS...
...BUT I HAVE A FAVORABLE DEVELOPMENT TO REPORT IN OUR CAMPAIGN AGAINST THE ALIENS--KING ARTHUR AND I ARE GOING TO BE MARRIED!
CONGRATULATIONS, MISSY--ALWAYS FIGURED YOU NEEDED TO SETTLE DOWN...
...BUT HOW'LL LASSOIN' THAT ARTHUR BUCK PUT THE BRAKES ON THE GREEN GUYS? THEY'VE TAKEN ALL OF ENGLAND AND PART'A EUROPE!
I REALIZE THAT, SIR...
...BUT WE FEEL THAT THE SYMBOLISM OF ARTHUR'S MARRIAGE TO THE LEADER OF EARTH'S DEFENSES WILL STRENGTHEN THE PEOPLES' SPIRIT...
MAKES SENSE...
...THEN KING ARTHUR WILL ANNOUNCE HIS PLAN TO COMBAT THE ALIENS!
SWELL! WHERE YOU GETTIN' HITCHED, ANYWAY?

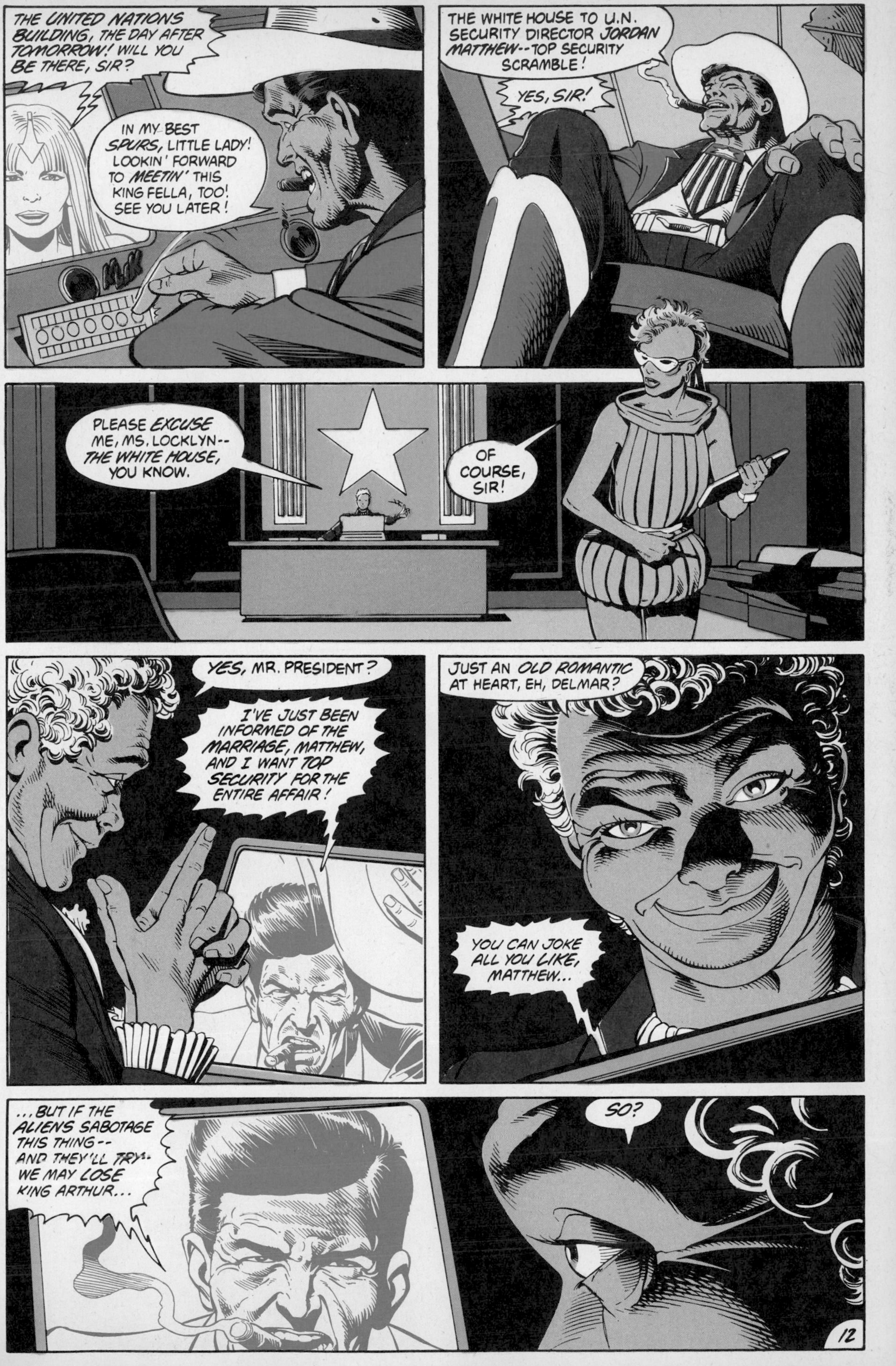
THE UNITED NATIONS BUILDING, THE DAY AFTER TOMORROW! WILL YOU BE THERE, SIR?
IN MY BEST SPURS, LITTLE LADY! LOOKIN' FORWARD TO MEETIN' THIS KING FELLA, TOO! SEE YOU LATER!
THE WHITE HOUSE TO U.N. SECURITY DIRECTOR JORDAN MATTHEW--TOP SECURITY SCRAMBLE!
YES, SIR!
PLEASE EXCUSE ME, MS. LOCKLYN-- THE WHITE HOUSE, YOU KNOW.
OF COURSE, SIR!
YES, MR. PRESIDENT?
I'VE JUST BEEN INFORMED OF THE MARRIAGE, MATTHEW, AND I WANT TOP SECURITY FOR THE ENTIRE AFFAIR!
JUST AN OLD ROMANTIC AT HEART, EH, DELMAR?
YOU CAN JOKE ALL YOU LIKE, MATTHEW...
...BUT IF THE ALIENS SABOTAGE THIS THING-- AND THEY'LL TRY-- WE MAY LOSE KING ARTHUR...
SO?
12

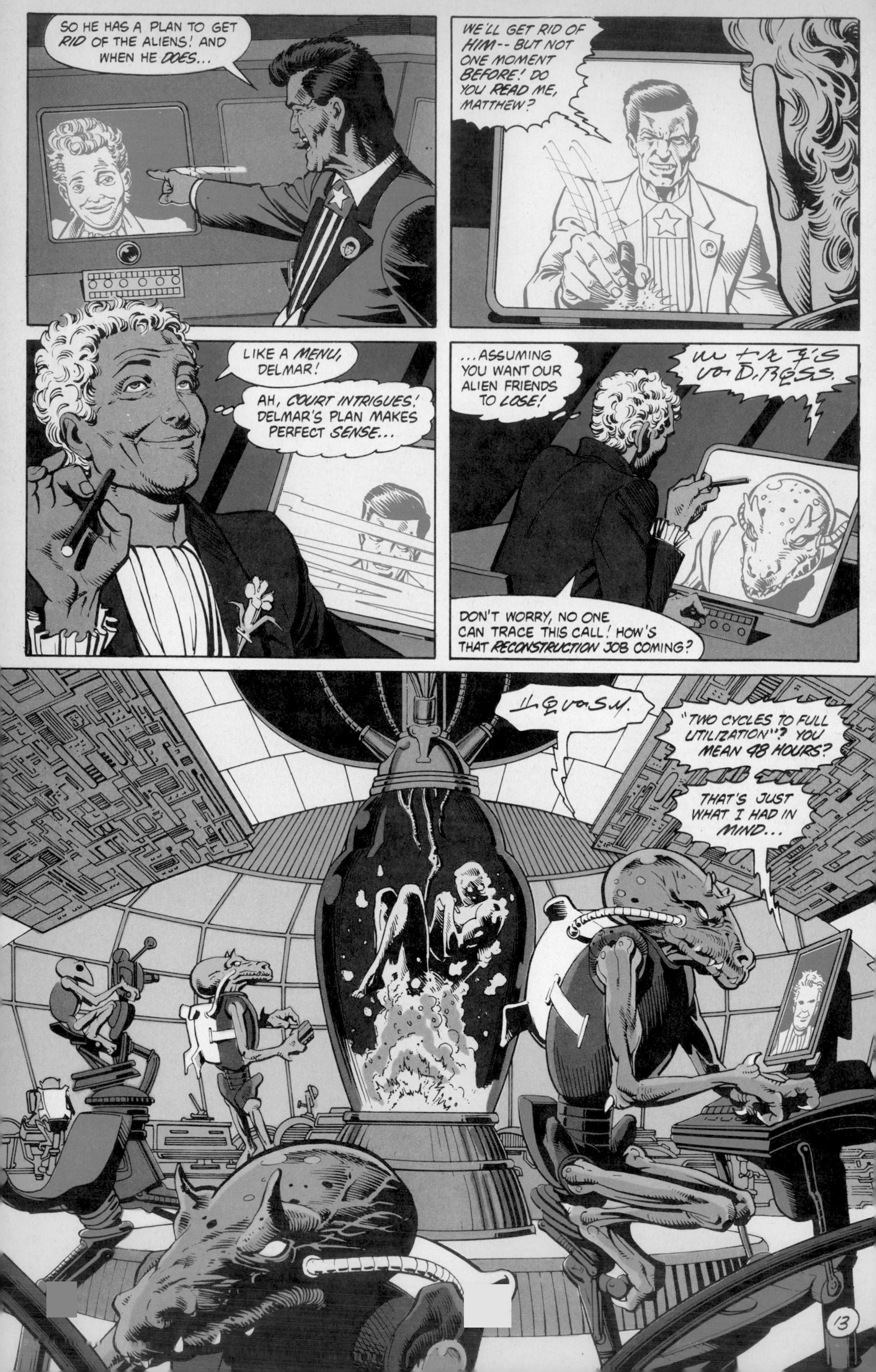
SO HE HAS A PLAN TO GET RID OF THE ALIENS! AND WHEN HE DOES...
WE'LL GET RID OF HIM-- BUT NOT ONE MOMENT BEFORE! DO YOU READ ME, MATTHEW?
LIKE A MENU, DELMAR!
AH, COURT INTRIGUES! DELMAR'S PLAN MAKES PERFECT SENSE...
...ASSUMING YOU WANT OUR ALIEN FRIENDS TO LOSE!
DON'T WORRY, NO ONE CAN TRACE THIS CALL! HOW'S THAT RECONSTRUCTION JOB COMING?
"TWO CYCLES TO FULL UTILIZATION"? YOU MEAN 48 HOURS?
THAT'S JUST WHAT I HAD IN MIND...

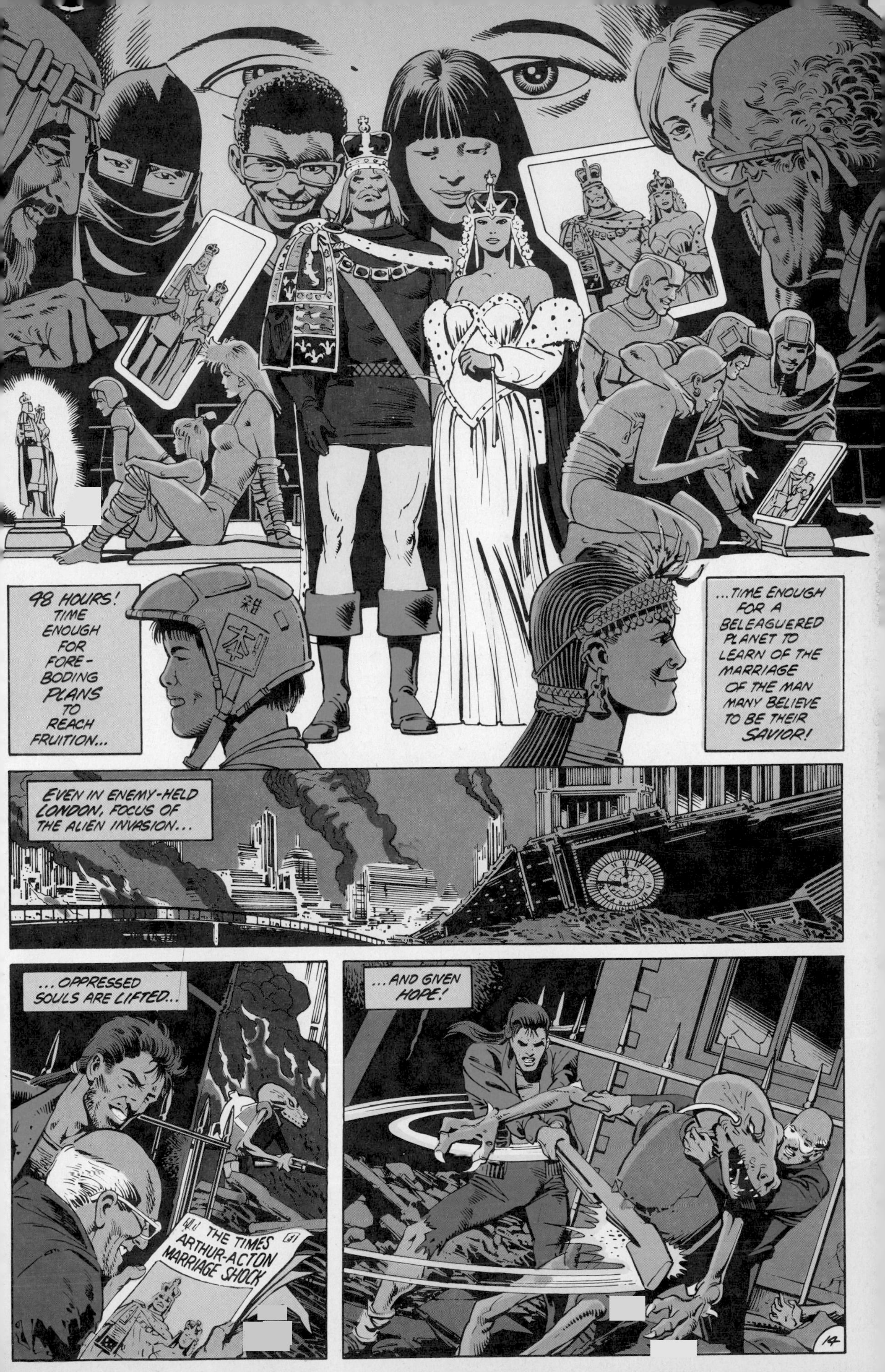

98 HOURS! TIME ENOUGH FOR FORE-BODING PLANS TO REACH FRUITION...
...TIME ENOUGH FOR A BELEAGUERED PLANET TO LEARN OF THE MARRIAGE OF THE MAN MANY BELIEVE TO BE THEIR SAVIOR!
EVEN IN ENEMY-HELD LONDON, FOCUS OF THE ALIEN INVASION...
...OPPRESSED SOULS ARE LIFTED...
THE TIMES
ARTHUR-ACTON MARRIAGE SHOCK
...AND GIVEN HOPE!
14

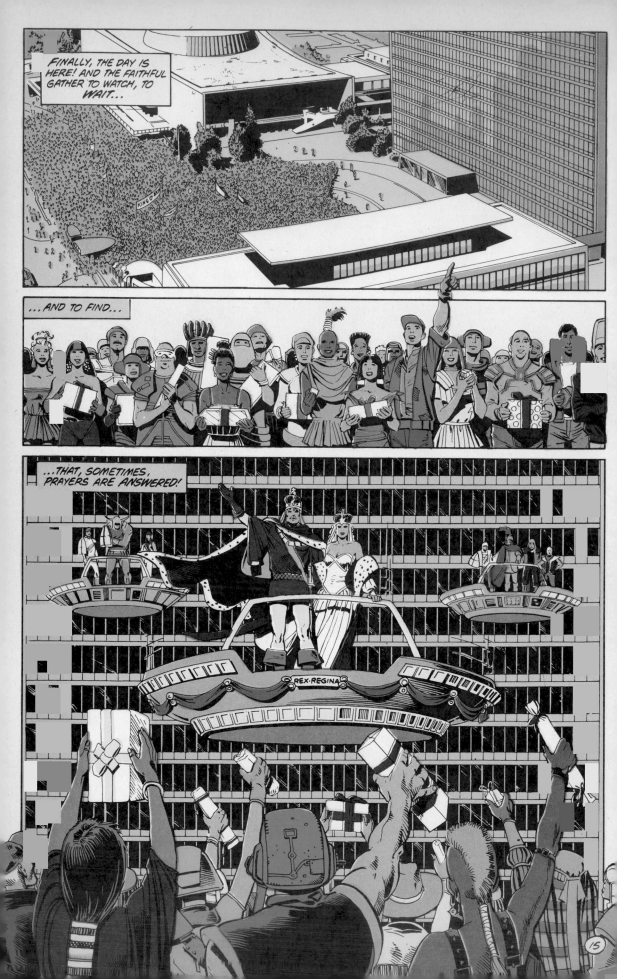

FINALLY, THE DAY IS HERE! AND THE FAITHFUL GATHER TO WATCH, TO WAIT...

...AND TO FIND...

...THAT, SOMETIMES, PRAYERS ARE ANSWERED!

REX·REGINA

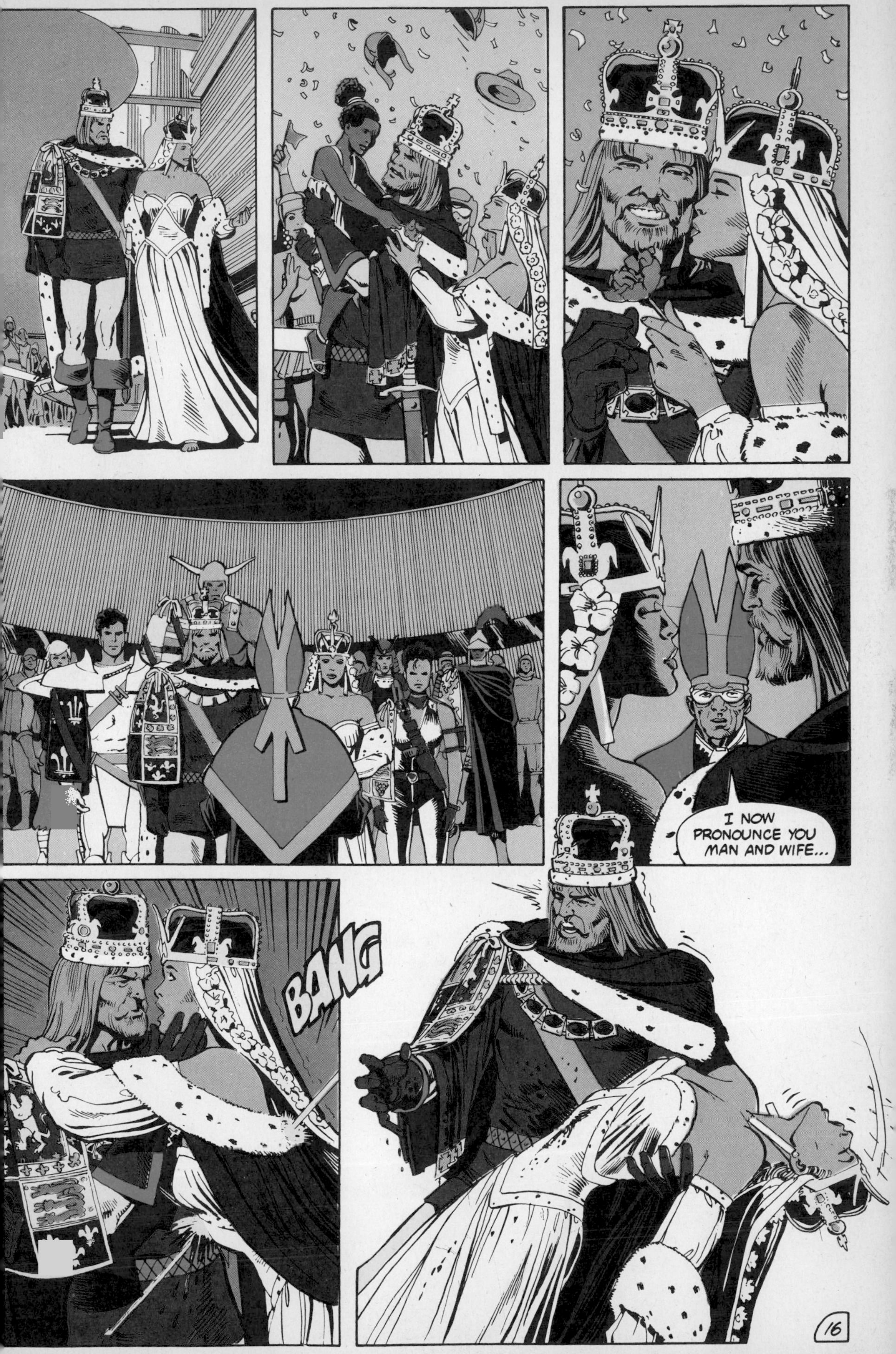
I NOW PRONOUNCE YOU MAN AND WIFE...
BANG

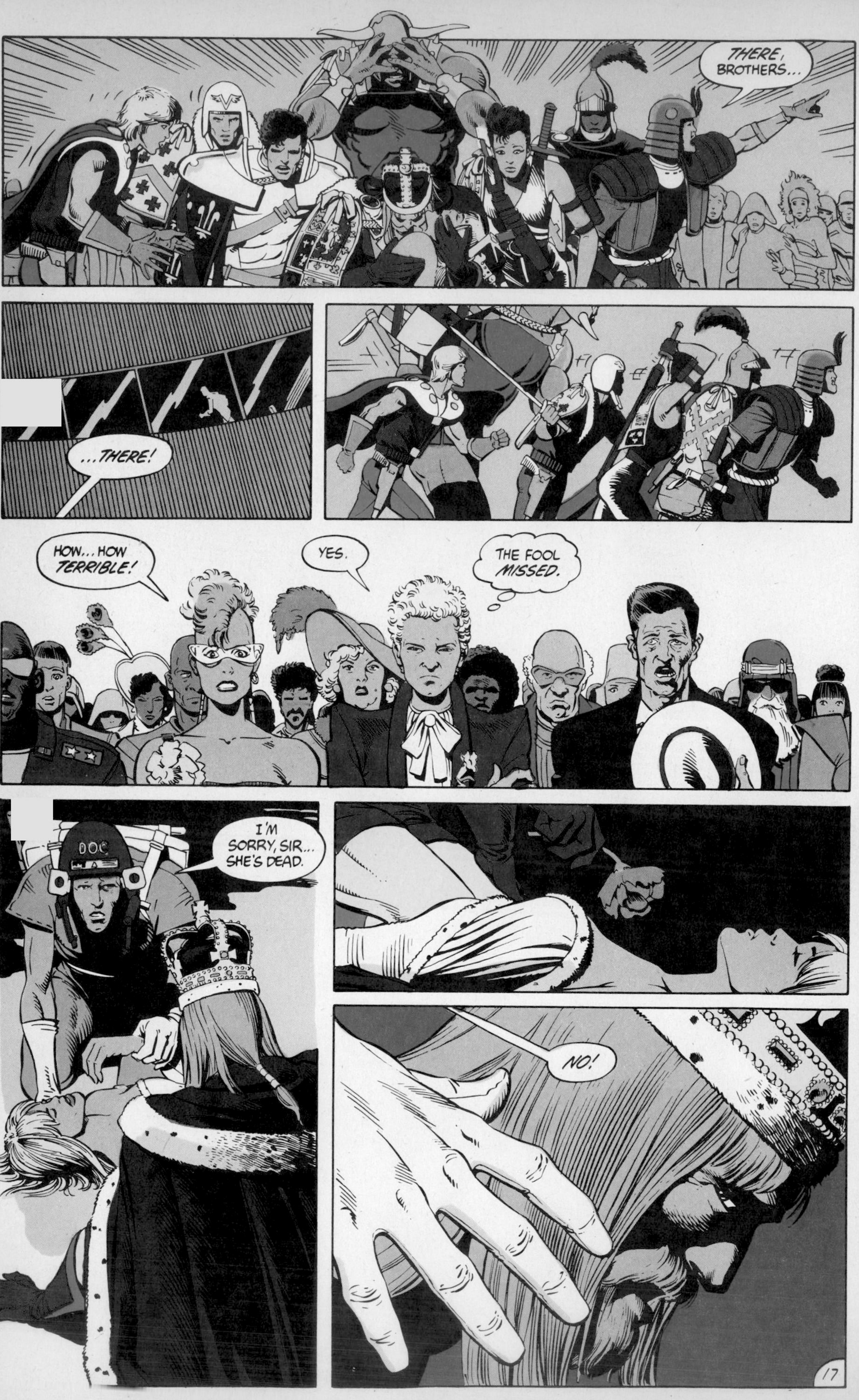
THERE, BROTHERS...
...THERE!
HOW... HOW TERRIBLE!
YES.
THE FOOL MISSED.
DOC
I'M SORRY, SIR... SHE'S DEAD.
NO!
17

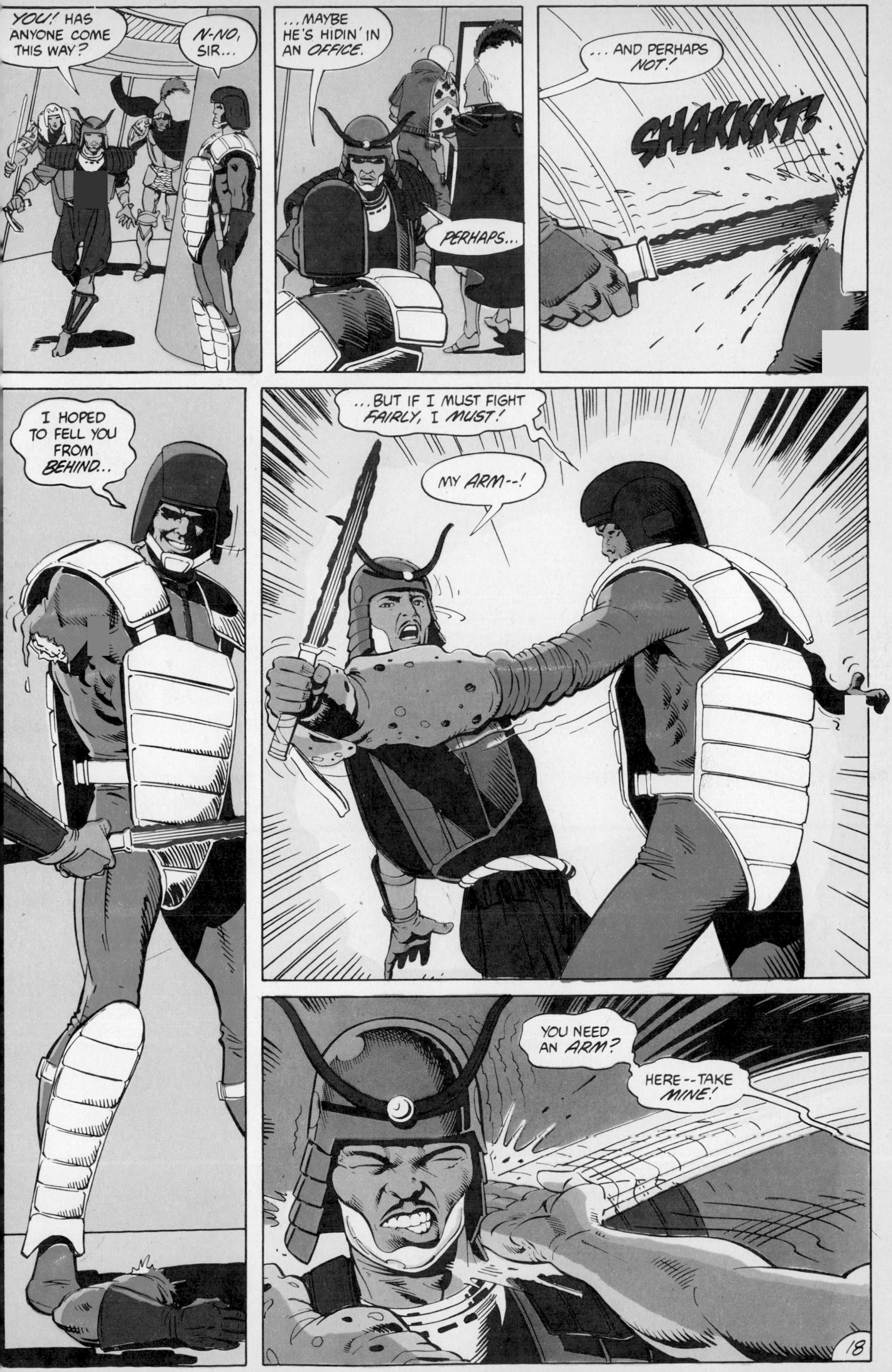
YOU! HAS ANYONE COME THIS WAY?
N-NO, SIR...
...MAYBE HE'S HIDIN' IN AN OFFICE.
PERHAPS...
...AND PERHAPS NOT!
SHAKKKT!
I HOPED TO FELL YOU FROM BEHIND...
...BUT IF I MUST FIGHT FAIRLY, I MUST!
MY ARM--!
YOU NEED AN ARM?
HERE--TAKE MINE!

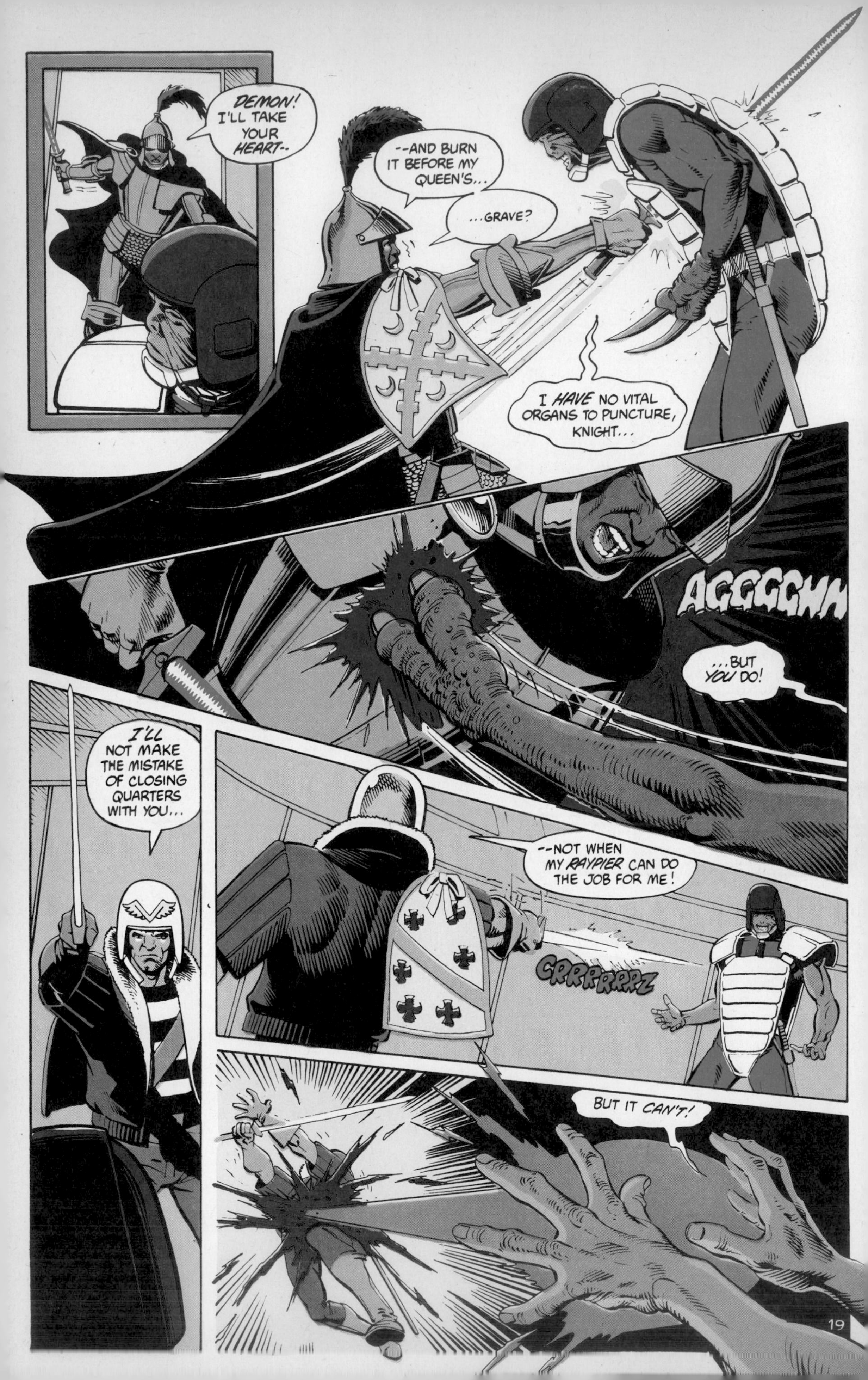

DEMON! I'LL TAKE YOUR HEART-.
--AND BURN IT BEFORE MY QUEEN'S...
...GRAVE?
I HAVE NO VITAL ORGANS TO PUNCTURE, KNIGHT...
AGGGGHH
...BUT YOU DO!
I'LL NOT MAKE THE MISTAKE OF CLOSING QUARTERS WITH YOU...
--NOT WHEN MY RAYPIER CAN DO THE JOB FOR ME!
CRRRRRRZ
BUT IT CAN'T!

LANCELOT, 'TIS *USELESS!*

NO, MY KING!

THIS DAY WAS MEANT FOR *LIFE,* NOT *DEATH!* THIS *SHOULD NOT* BE...

...I PRAY IT *WILL* NOT BE!

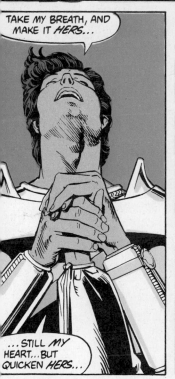

TAKE MY BREATH, AND MAKE IT *HERS...*

...STILL *MY* HEART...BUT QUICKEN *HERS...*

TAKE MY *LIFE...* BUT LET *HER*--

LANCE!

RETURN? ALL RIGHT, BUT I...

...I...

...THANK YOU...

20

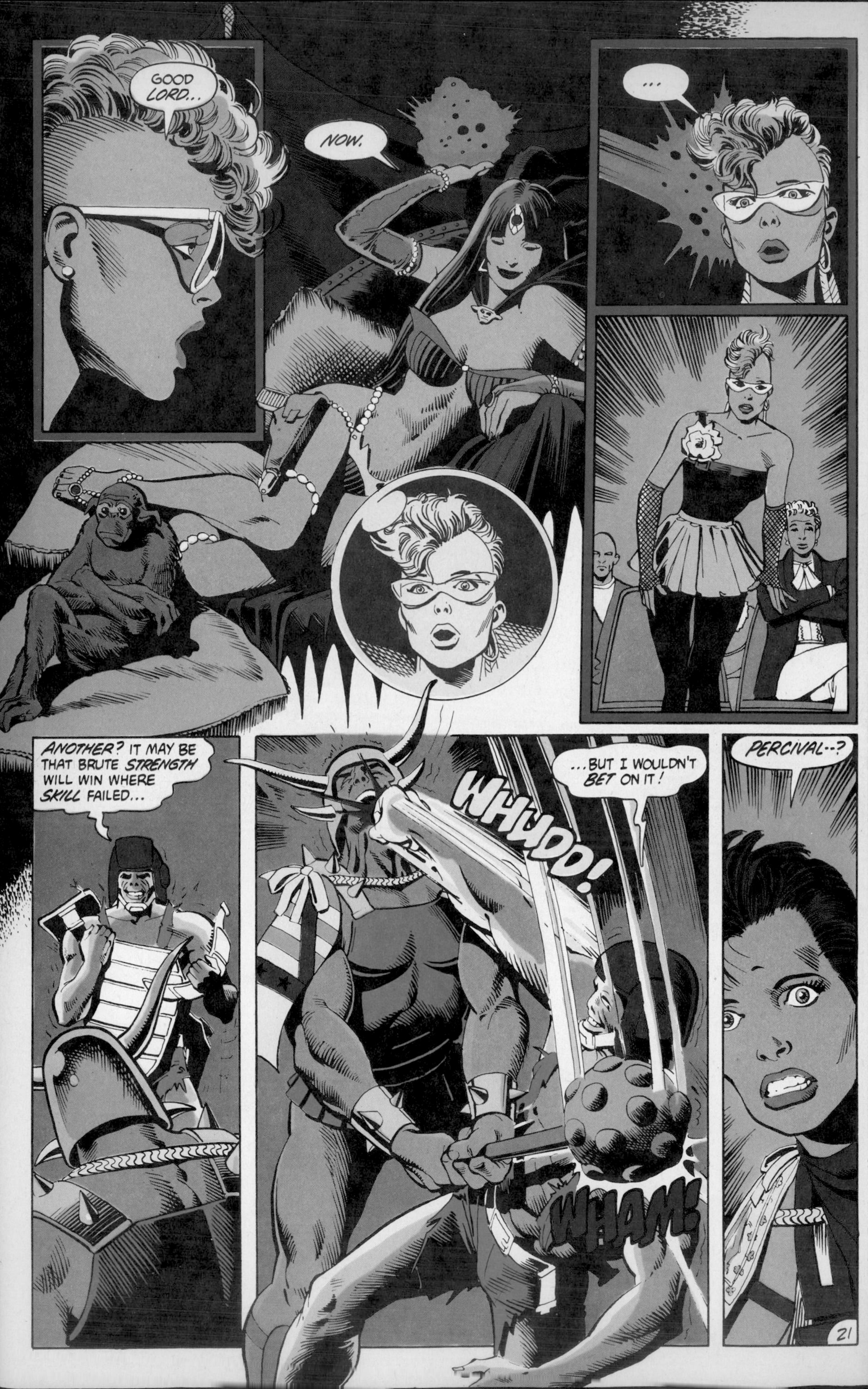

GOOD LORD...
NOW.
...
ANOTHER? IT MAY BE THAT BRUTE STRENGTH WILL WIN WHERE SKILL FAILED...
...BUT I WOULDN'T BET ON IT!
WHUDD!
WHAM!
PERCIVAL--?

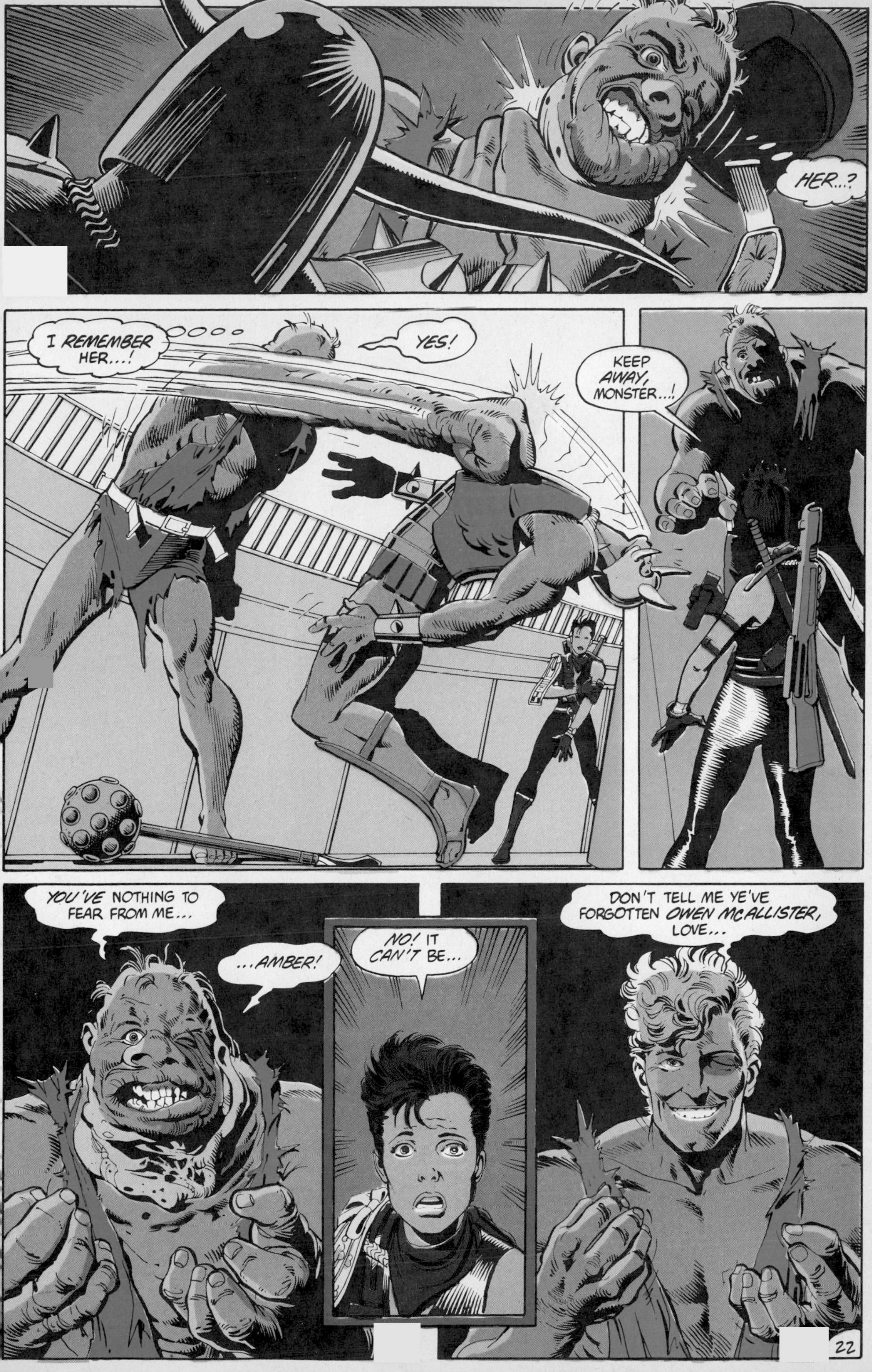
HER...?
I REMEMBER HER...!
YES!
KEEP AWAY, MONSTER...!
YOU'VE NOTHING TO FEAR FROM ME...
...AMBER!
NO! IT CAN'T BE...
DON'T TELL ME YE'VE FORGOTTEN OWEN MCALLISTER, LOVE...
22

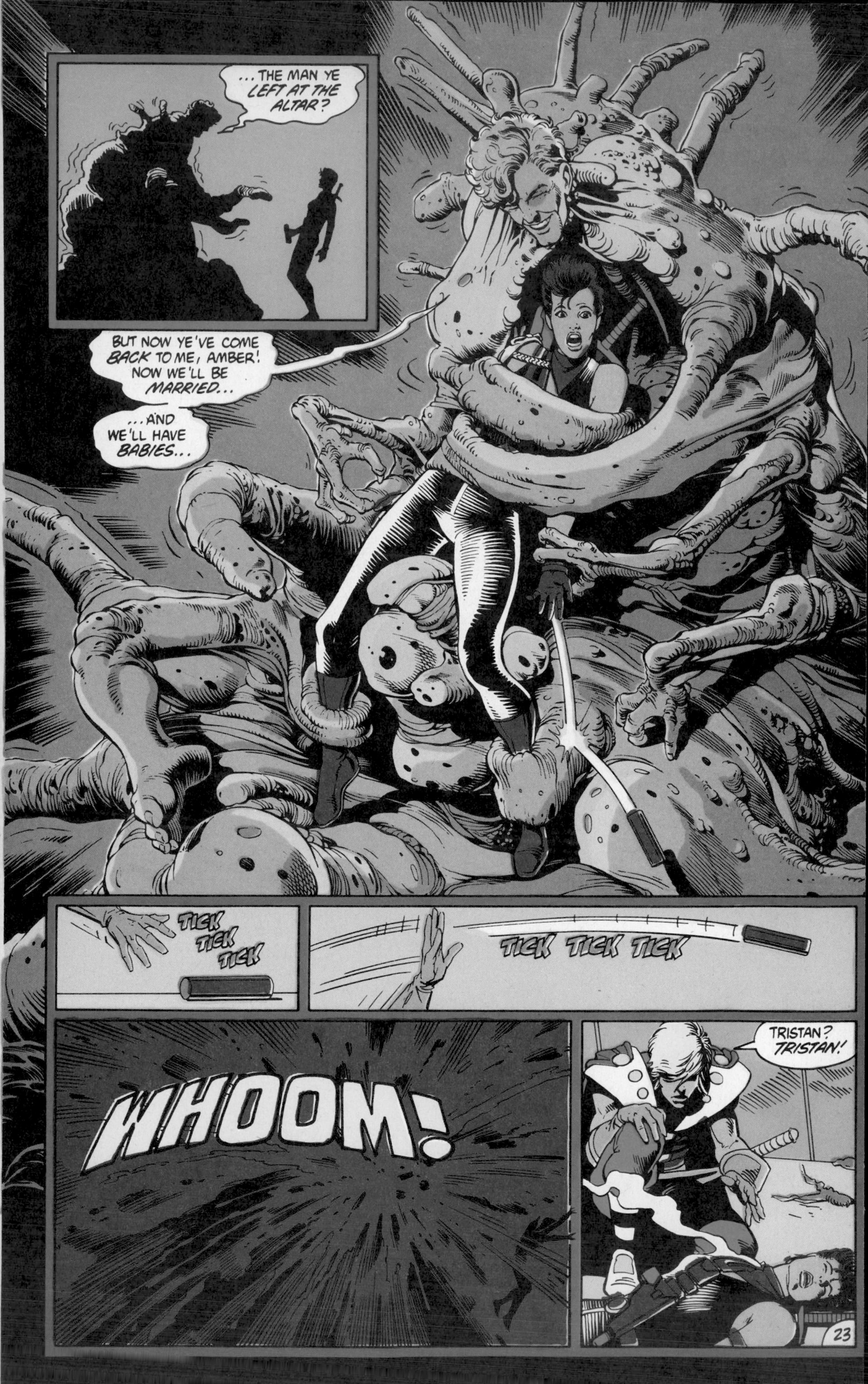

... THE MAN YE LEFT AT THE ALTAR?
BUT NOW YE'VE COME BACK TO ME, AMBER! NOW WE'LL BE MARRIED...
...AND WE'LL HAVE BABIES...
TICK TICK TICK
TICK TICK TICK
WHOOM!
TRISTAN? TRISTAN!

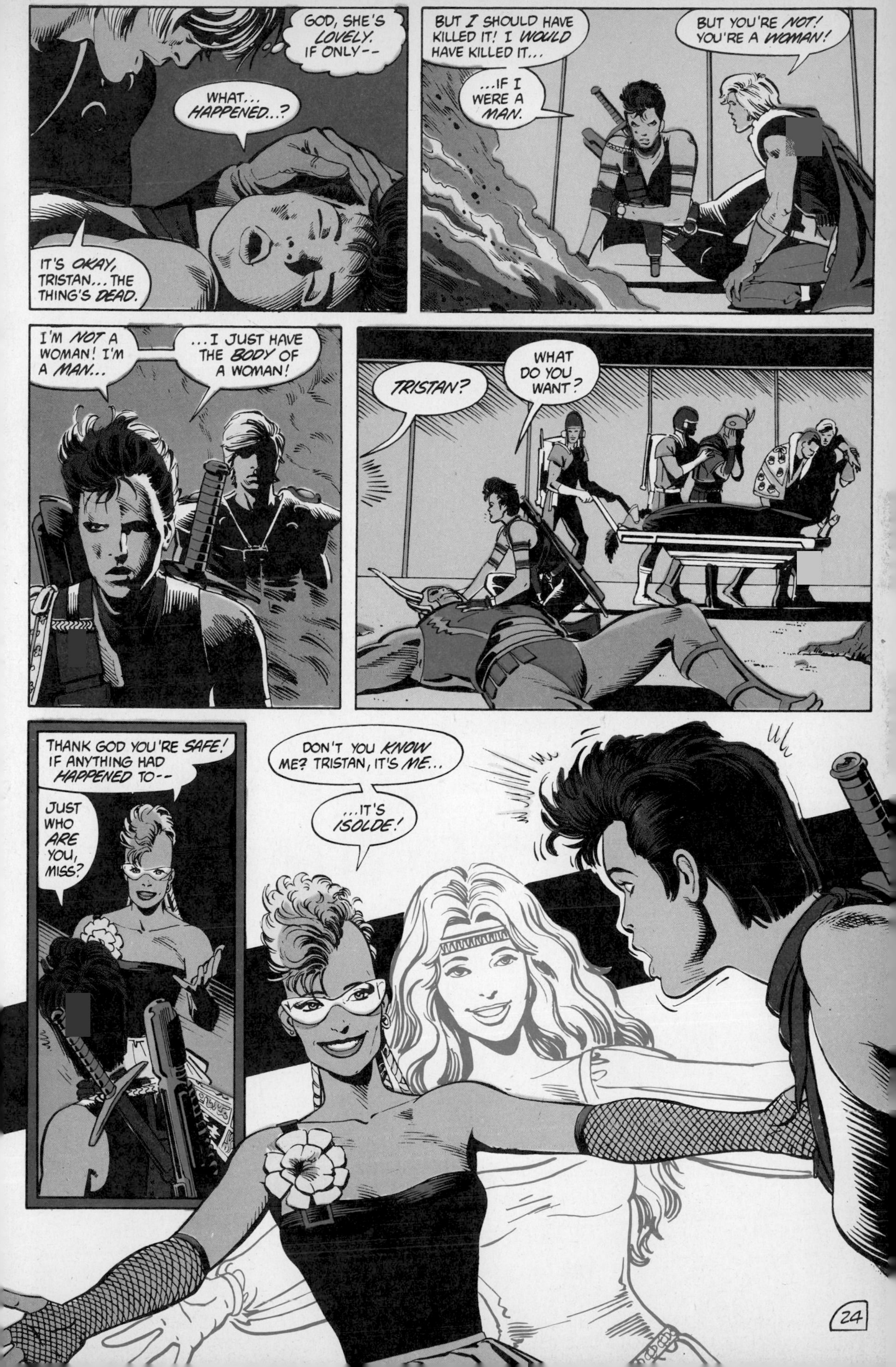
GOD, SHE'S LOVELY. IF ONLY--
WHAT... HAPPENED...?
IT'S OKAY, TRISTAN... THE THING'S DEAD.
BUT I SHOULD HAVE KILLED IT! I WOULD HAVE KILLED IT...
...IF I WERE A MAN.
BUT YOU'RE NOT! YOU'RE A WOMAN!
I'M NOT A WOMAN! I'M A MAN...
...I JUST HAVE THE BODY OF A WOMAN!
TRISTAN?
WHAT DO YOU WANT?
THANK GOD YOU'RE SAFE! IF ANYTHING HAD HAPPENED TO--
JUST WHO ARE YOU, MISS?
DON'T YOU KNOW ME? TRISTAN, IT'S ME...
...IT'S ISOLDE!

CHAPTER 7

Betrayal

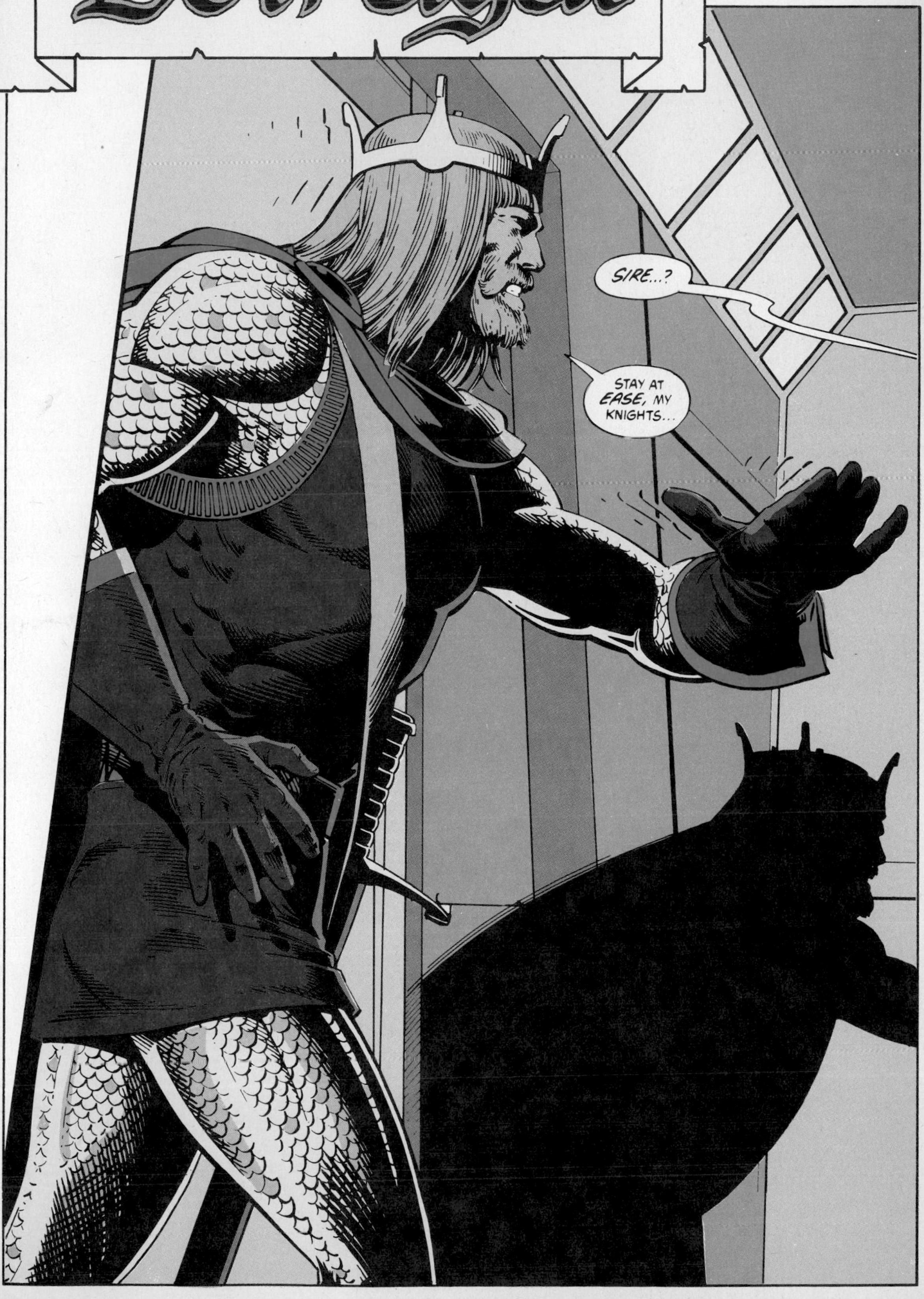
SIRE...?
STAY AT EASE, MY KNIGHTS...

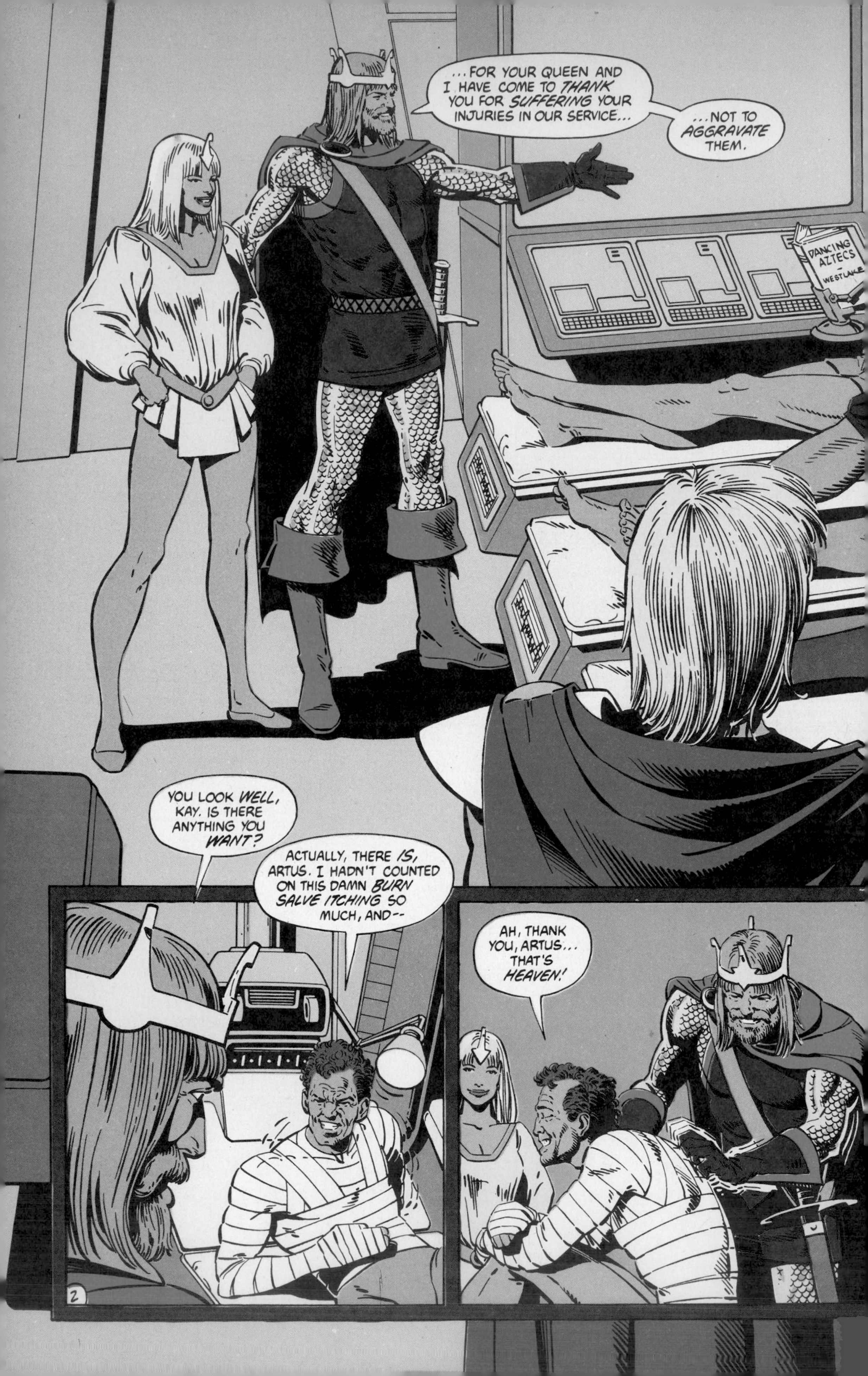
...FOR YOUR QUEEN AND I HAVE COME TO THANK YOU FOR SUFFERING YOUR INJURIES IN OUR SERVICE...
...NOT TO AGGRAVATE THEM.
DANCING AZTECS
WESTLAKE
YOU LOOK WELL, KAY. IS THERE ANYTHING YOU WANT?
ACTUALLY, THERE IS, ARTUS. I HADN'T COUNTED ON THIS DAMN BURN SALVE ITCHING SO MUCH, AND--
AH, THANK YOU, ARTUS... THAT'S HEAVEN!
2

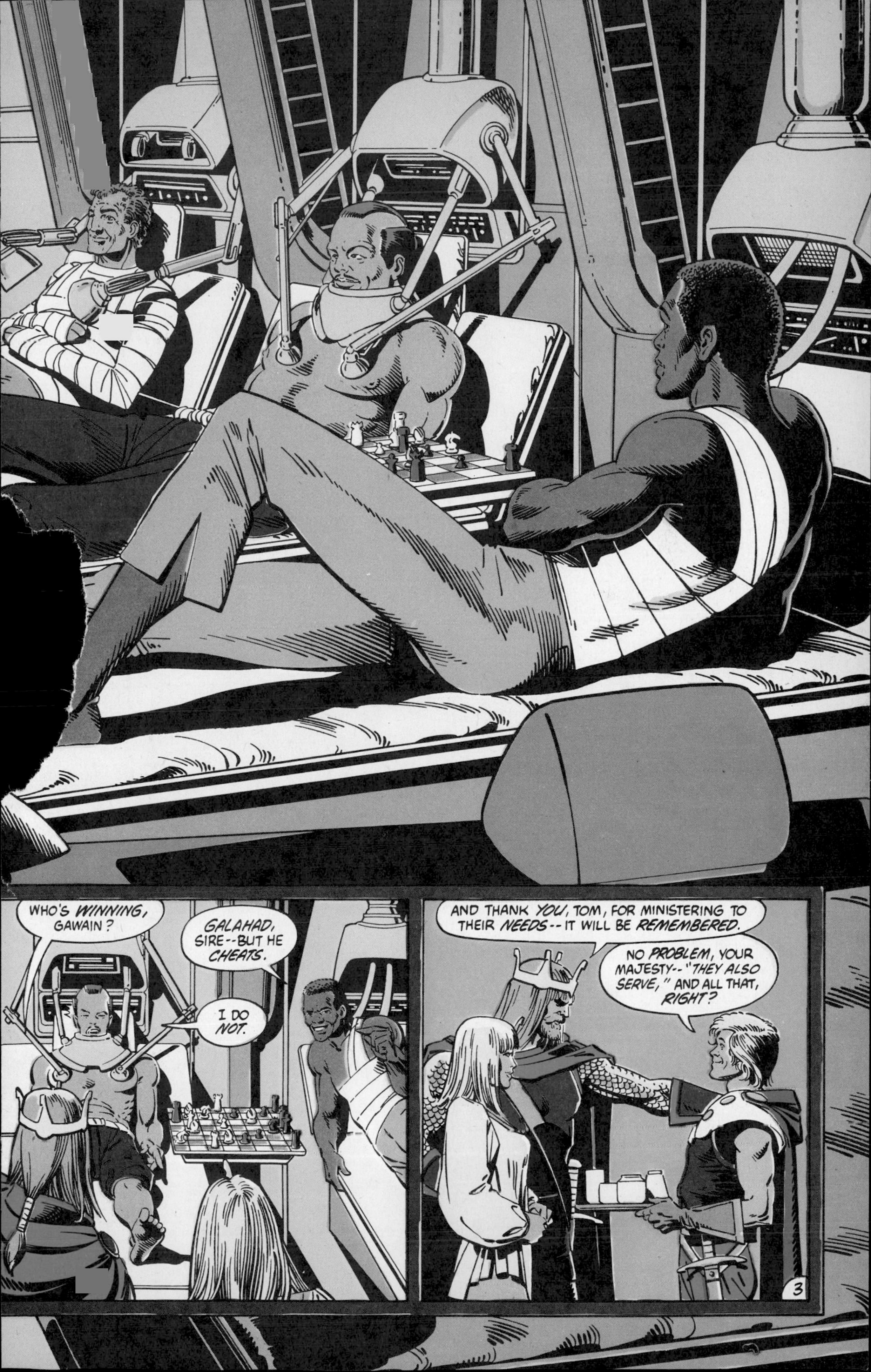

WHO'S WINNING, GAWAIN?
GALAHAD, SIRE--BUT HE CHEATS.
I DO NOT.
AND THANK YOU, TOM, FOR MINISTERING TO THEIR NEEDS--IT WILL BE REMEMBERED.
NO PROBLEM, YOUR MAJESTY--"THEY ALSO SERVE," AND ALL THAT, RIGHT?
3

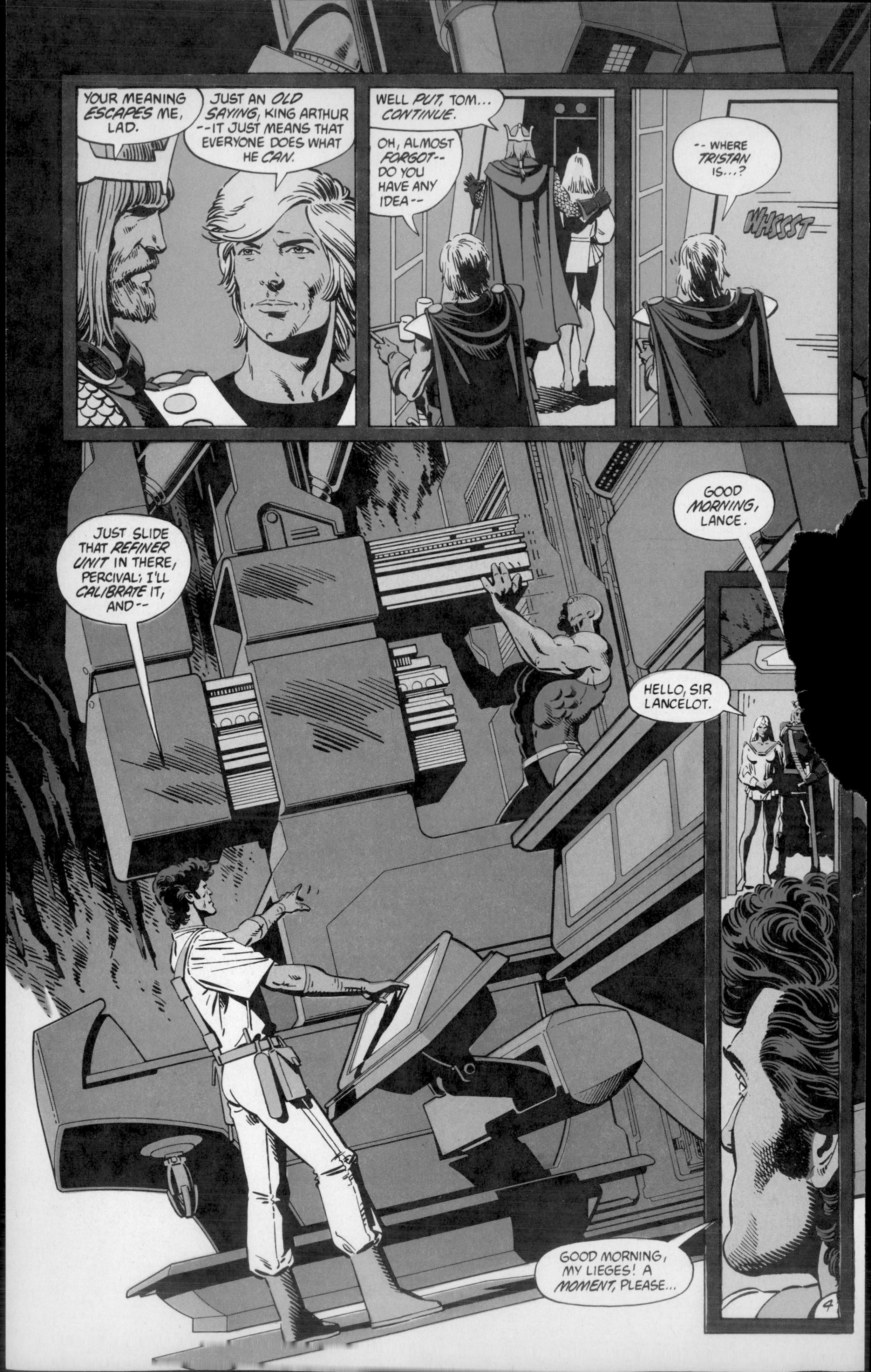
YOUR MEANING ESCAPES ME, LAD.
JUST AN OLD SAYING, KING ARTHUR --IT JUST MEANS THAT EVERYONE DOES WHAT HE CAN.
WELL PUT, TOM... CONTINUE.
OH, ALMOST FORGOT-- DO YOU HAVE ANY IDEA --
-- WHERE TRISTAN IS...?
WHSSST
JUST SLIDE THAT REFINER UNIT IN THERE, PERCIVAL; I'LL CALIBRATE IT, AND --
GOOD MORNING, LANCE.
HELLO, SIR LANCELOT.
GOOD MORNING, MY LIEGES! A MOMENT, PLEASE...
4

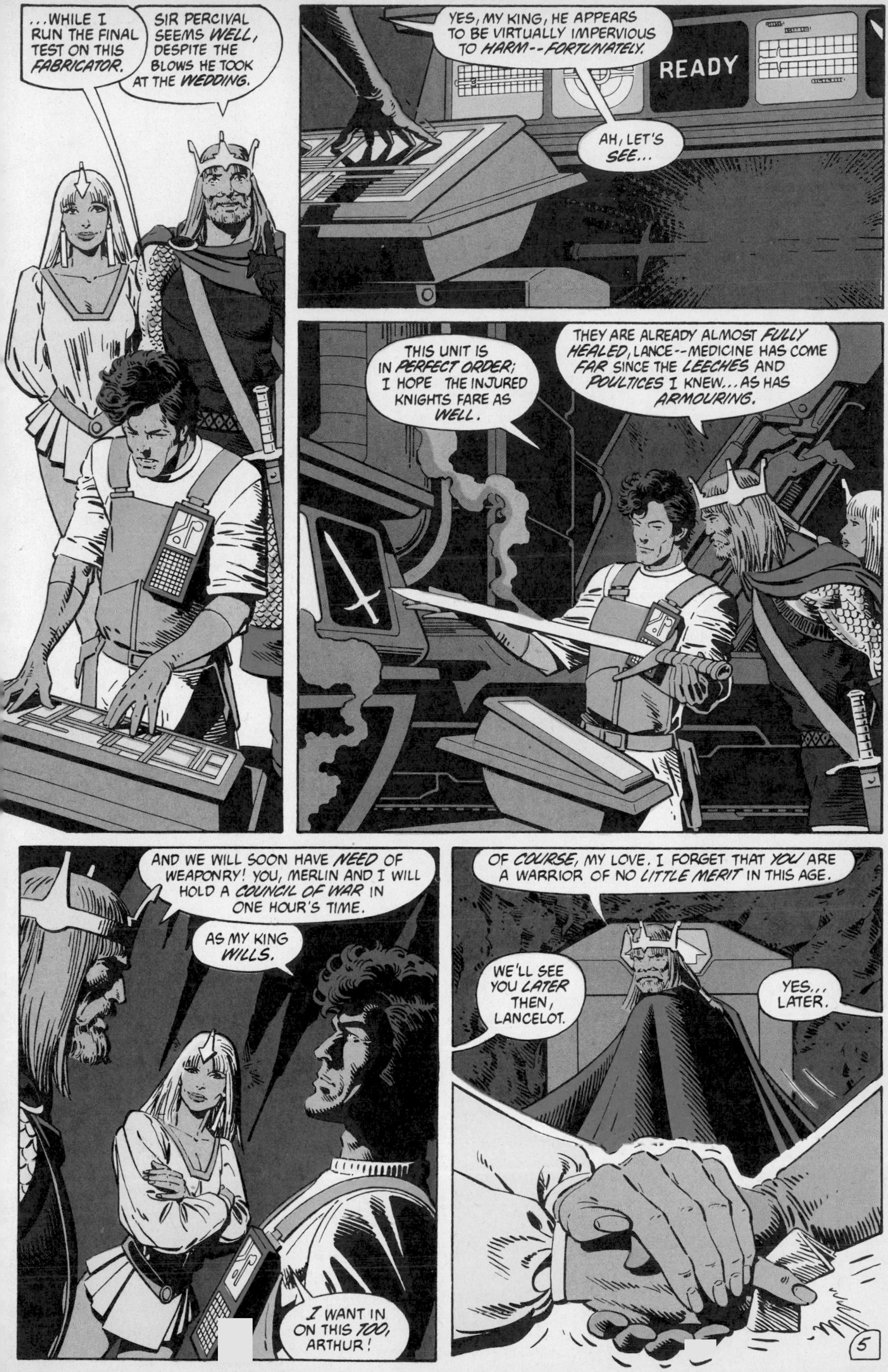
...WHILE I RUN THE FINAL TEST ON THIS FABRICATOR.
SIR PERCIVAL SEEMS WELL, DESPITE THE BLOWS HE TOOK AT THE WEDDING.
YES, MY KING, HE APPEARS TO BE VIRTUALLY IMPERVIOUS TO HARM--FORTUNATELY.
READY
AH, LET'S SEE...
THIS UNIT IS IN PERFECT ORDER; I HOPE THE INJURED KNIGHTS FARE AS WELL.
THEY ARE ALREADY ALMOST FULLY HEALED, LANCE--MEDICINE HAS COME FAR SINCE THE LEECHES AND POULTICES I KNEW... AS HAS ARMOURING.
AND WE WILL SOON HAVE NEED OF WEAPONRY! YOU, MERLIN AND I WILL HOLD A COUNCIL OF WAR IN ONE HOUR'S TIME.
AS MY KING WILLS.
I WANT IN ON THIS TOO, ARTHUR!
OF COURSE, MY LOVE. I FORGET THAT YOU ARE A WARRIOR OF NO LITTLE MERIT IN THIS AGE.
WE'LL SEE YOU LATER THEN, LANCELOT.
YES... LATER.
5

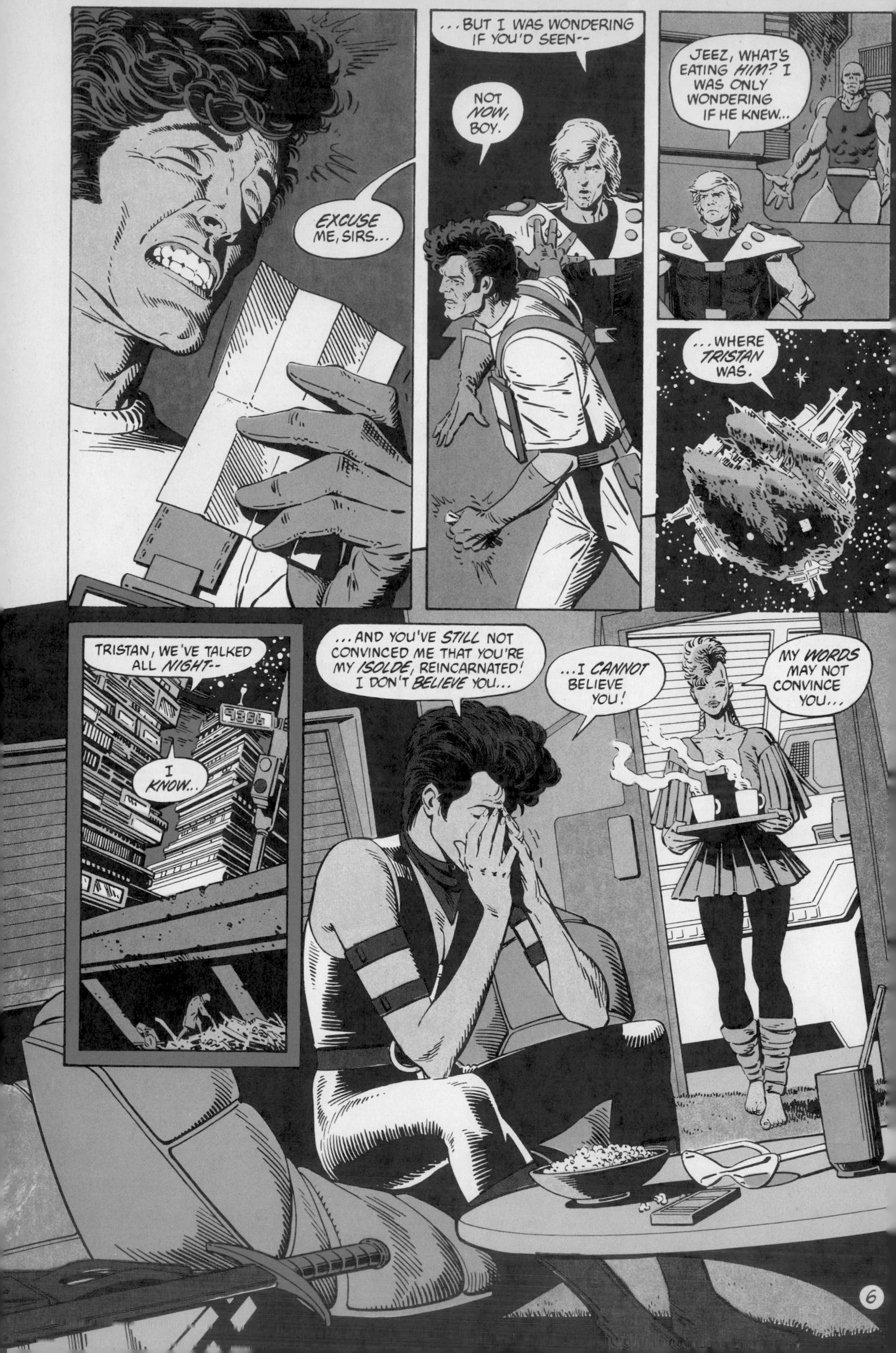
EXCUSE ME, SIRS...
...BUT I WAS WONDERING IF YOU'D SEEN--
NOT NOW, BOY.
JEEZ, WHAT'S EATING HIM? I WAS ONLY WONDERING IF HE KNEW...
...WHERE TRISTAN WAS.
TRISTAN, WE'VE TALKED ALL NIGHT--
I KNOW...
...AND YOU'VE STILL NOT CONVINCED ME THAT YOU'RE MY ISOLDE, REINCARNATED! I DON'T BELIEVE YOU...
...I CANNOT BELIEVE YOU!
MY WORDS MAY NOT CONVINCE YOU...

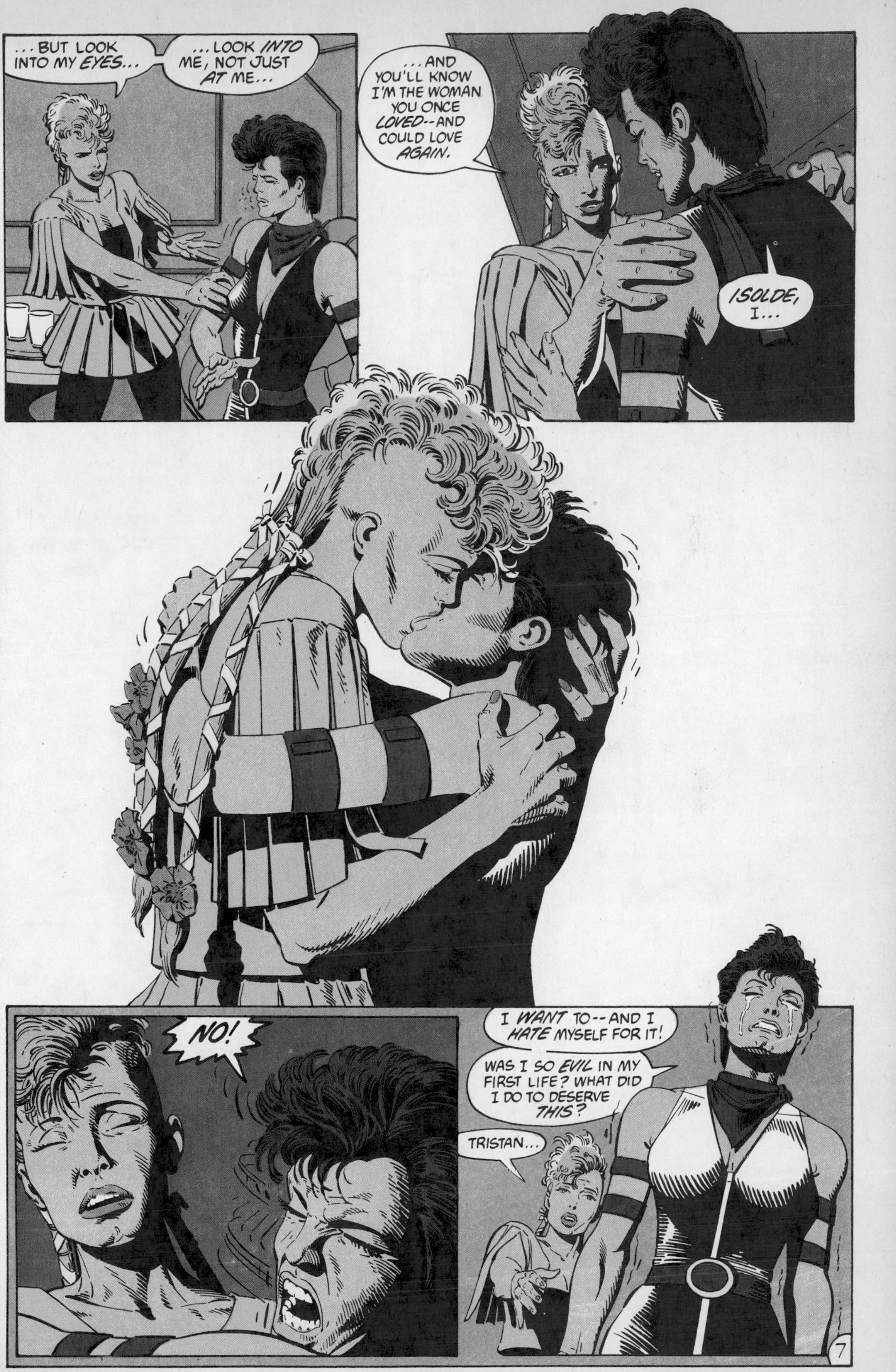
...BUT LOOK INTO MY *EYES*...
...LOOK *INTO* ME, NOT JUST *AT* ME...
...AND YOU'LL KNOW I'M THE WOMAN YOU ONCE *LOVED*--AND COULD LOVE *AGAIN*.
ISOLDE, I...
NO!
I *WANT* TO--AND I *HATE* MYSELF FOR IT!
WAS I SO *EVIL* IN MY FIRST LIFE? WHAT DID I DO TO DESERVE *THIS*?
TRISTAN...

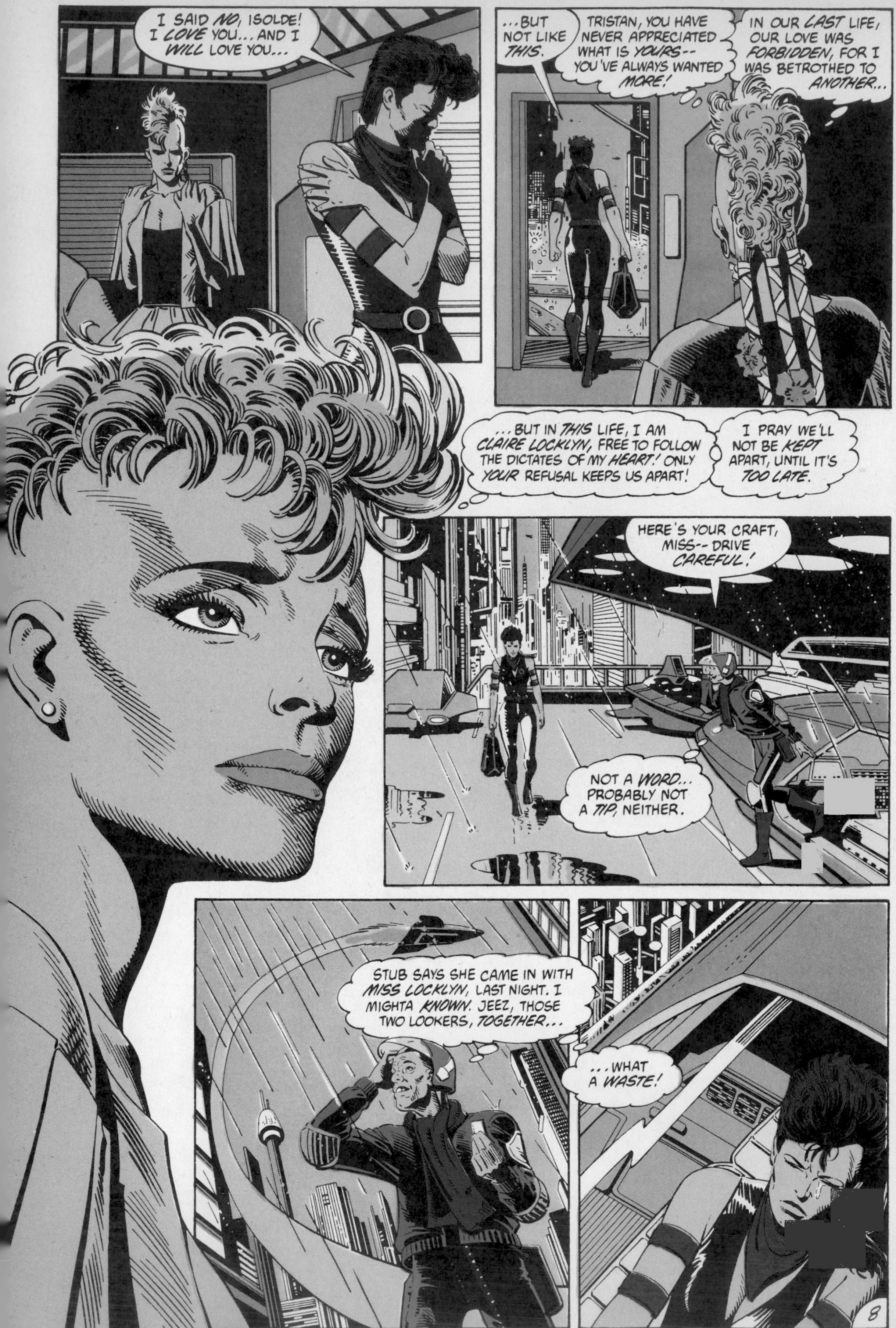

I SAID NO, ISOLDE! I LOVE YOU... AND I WILL LOVE YOU...
...BUT NOT LIKE THIS.
TRISTAN, YOU HAVE NEVER APPRECIATED WHAT IS YOURS-- YOU'VE ALWAYS WANTED MORE!
IN OUR LAST LIFE, OUR LOVE WAS FORBIDDEN, FOR I WAS BETROTHED TO ANOTHER...
...BUT IN THIS LIFE, I AM CLAIRE LOCKLYN, FREE TO FOLLOW THE DICTATES OF MY HEART! ONLY YOUR REFUSAL KEEPS US APART!
I PRAY WE'LL NOT BE KEPT APART, UNTIL IT'S TOO LATE.
HERE'S YOUR CRAFT, MISS-- DRIVE CAREFUL!
NOT A WORD... PROBABLY NOT A TIP, NEITHER.
STUB SAYS SHE CAME IN WITH MISS LOCKLYN, LAST NIGHT. I MIGHTA KNOWN. JEEZ, THOSE TWO LOOKERS, TOGETHER...
...WHAT A WASTE!

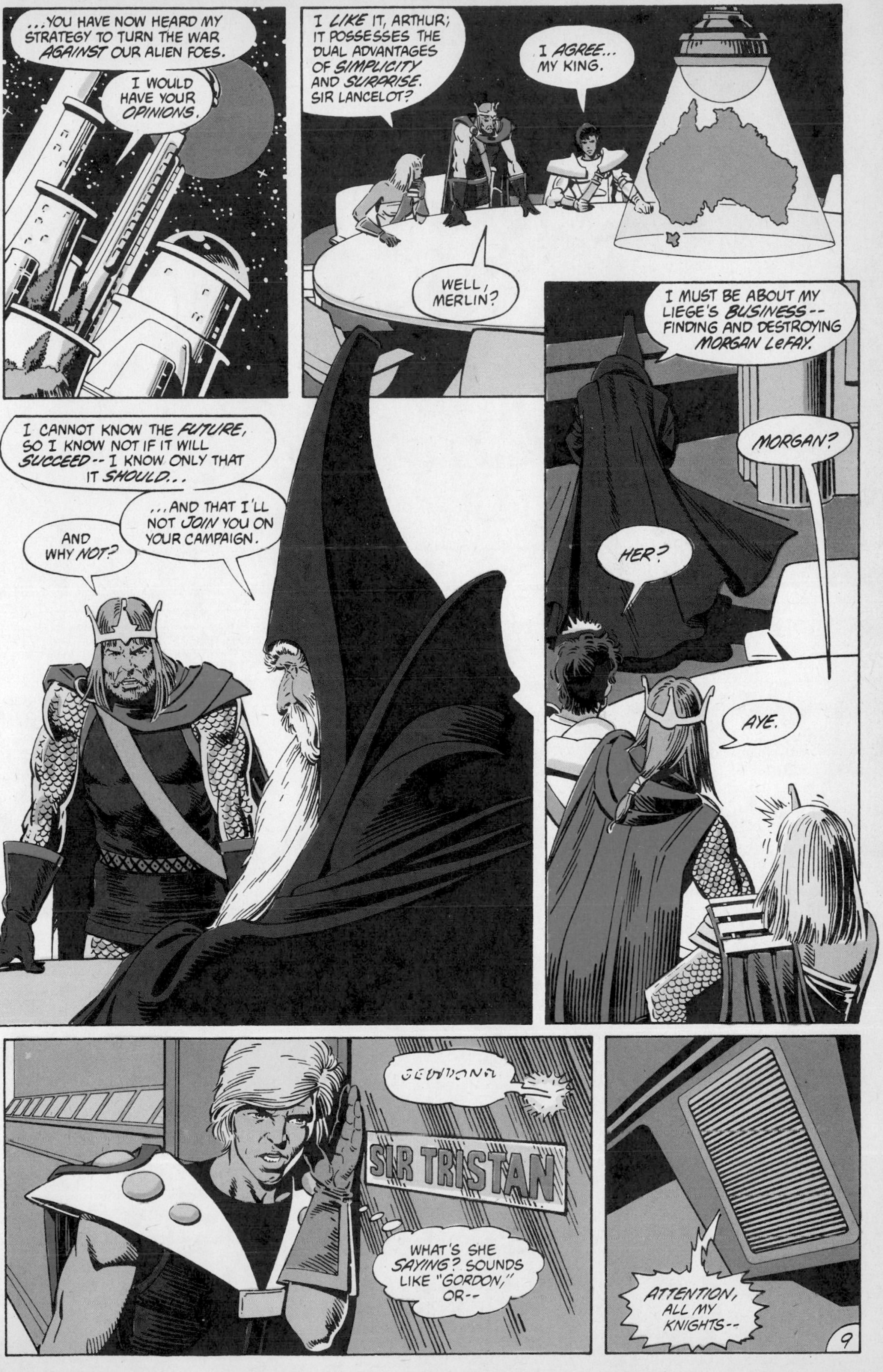
...YOU HAVE NOW HEARD MY STRATEGY TO TURN THE WAR AGAINST OUR ALIEN FOES.
I WOULD HAVE YOUR OPINIONS.
I LIKE IT, ARTHUR; IT POSSESSES THE DUAL ADVANTAGES OF SIMPLICITY AND SURPRISE. SIR LANCELOT?
I AGREE... MY KING.
WELL, MERLIN?
I CANNOT KNOW THE FUTURE, SO I KNOW NOT IF IT WILL SUCCEED-- I KNOW ONLY THAT IT SHOULD...
...AND THAT I'LL NOT JOIN YOU ON YOUR CAMPAIGN.
AND WHY NOT?
I MUST BE ABOUT MY LIEGE'S BUSINESS-- FINDING AND DESTROYING MORGAN LeFAY.
MORGAN?
HER?
AYE.
SIR TRISTAN
WHAT'S SHE SAYING? SOUNDS LIKE "GORDON," OR--
ATTENTION, ALL MY KNIGHTS--
9

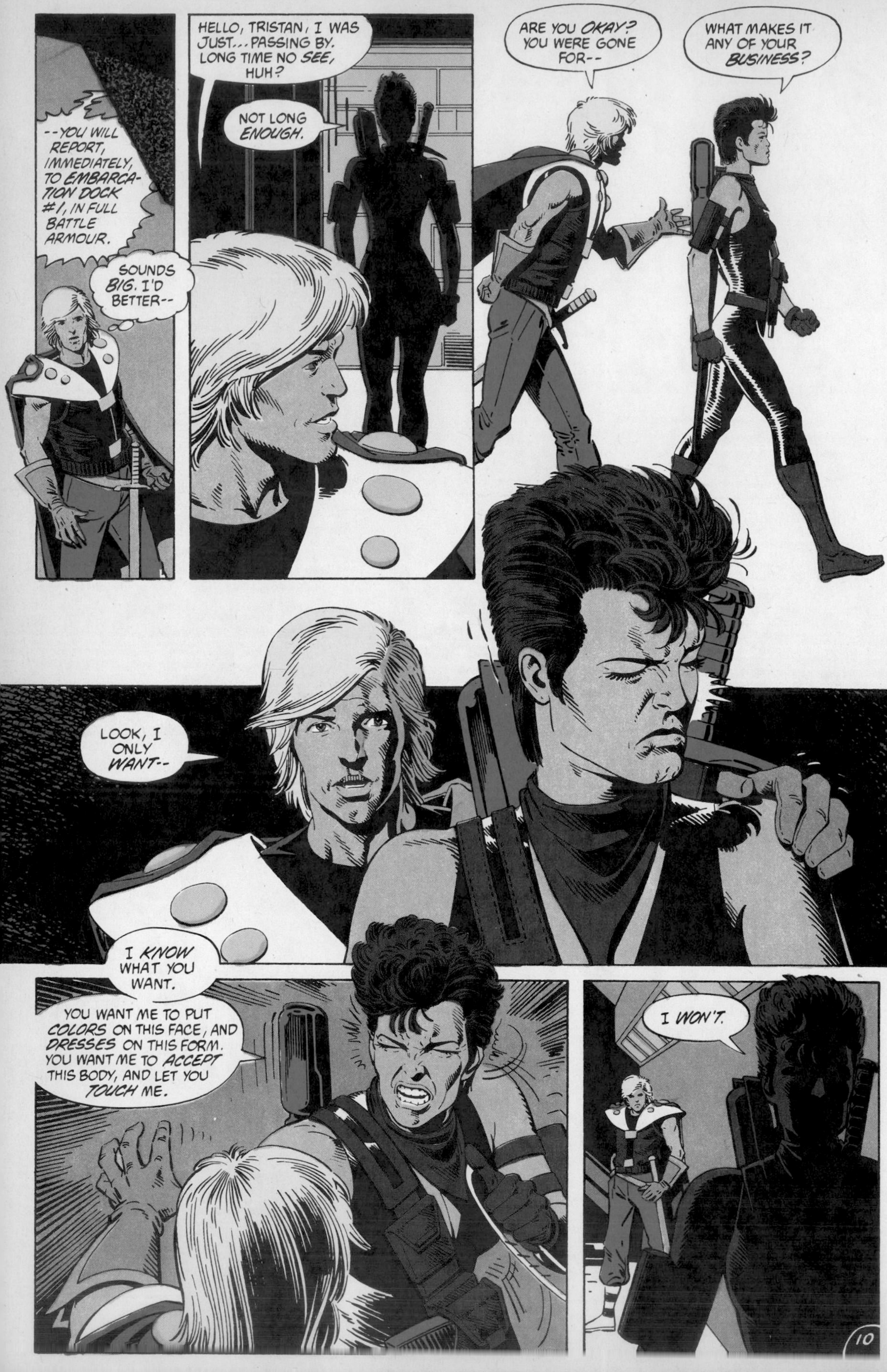
--YOU WILL REPORT, IMMEDIATELY, TO EMBARCATION DOCK #1, IN FULL BATTLE ARMOUR.
SOUNDS BIG. I'D BETTER--
HELLO, TRISTAN, I WAS JUST... PASSING BY. LONG TIME NO SEE, HUH?
NOT LONG ENOUGH.
ARE YOU OKAY? YOU WERE GONE FOR--
WHAT MAKES IT ANY OF YOUR BUSINESS?
LOOK, I ONLY WANT--
I KNOW WHAT YOU WANT.
YOU WANT ME TO PUT COLORS ON THIS FACE, AND DRESSES ON THIS FORM. YOU WANT ME TO ACCEPT THIS BODY, AND LET YOU TOUCH ME.
I WON'T.
10

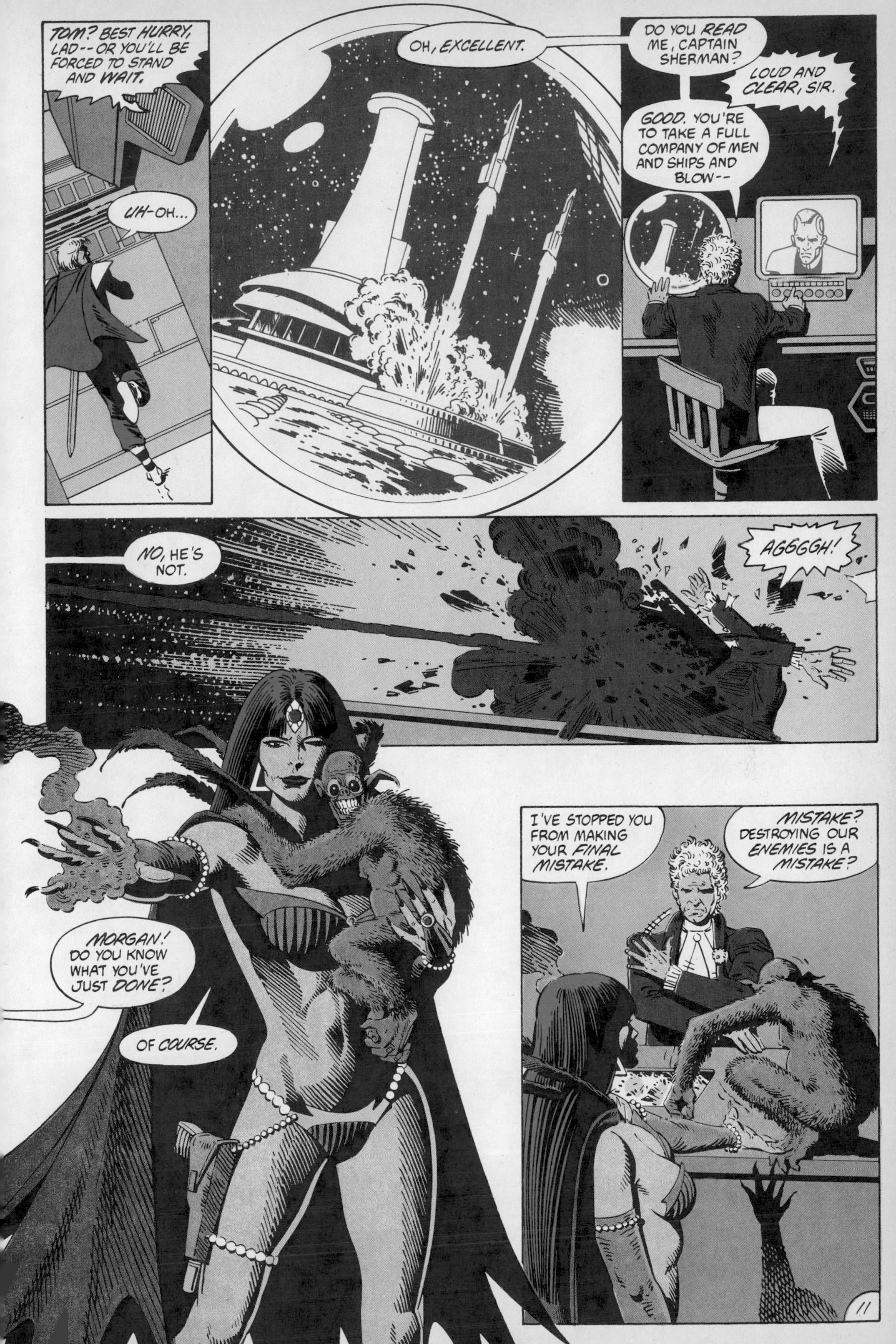

TOM? BEST HURRY, LAD--OR YOU'LL BE FORCED TO STAND AND WAIT.
UH-OH...
OH, EXCELLENT.
DO YOU READ ME, CAPTAIN SHERMAN?
LOUD AND CLEAR, SIR.
GOOD. YOU'RE TO TAKE A FULL COMPANY OF MEN AND SHIPS AND BLOW--
NO, HE'S NOT.
AGGGGH!
MORGAN! DO YOU KNOW WHAT YOU'VE JUST DONE?
OF COURSE.
I'VE STOPPED YOU FROM MAKING YOUR FINAL MISTAKE.
MISTAKE? DESTROYING OUR ENEMIES IS A MISTAKE?

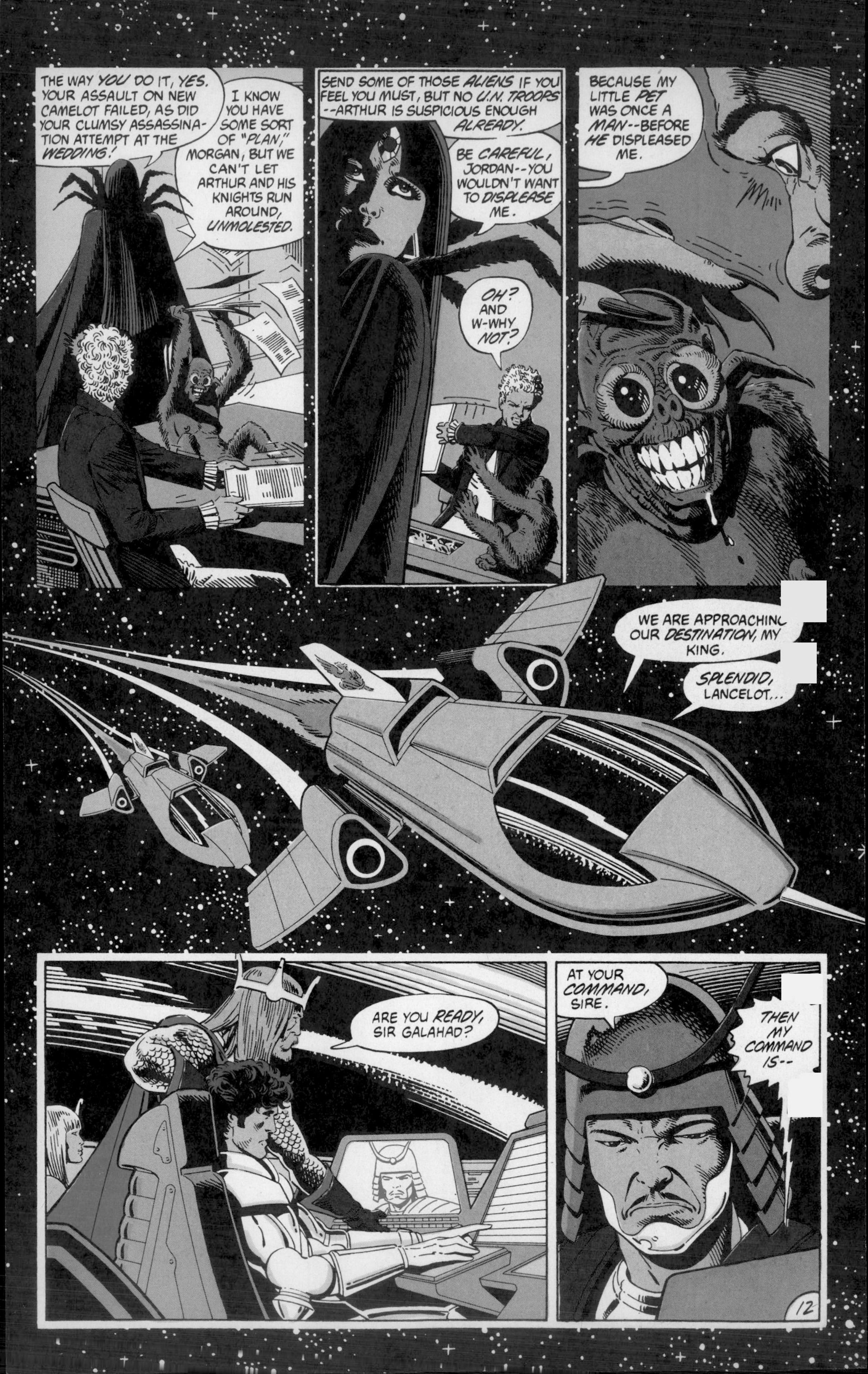
THE WAY YOU DO IT, YES. YOUR ASSAULT ON NEW CAMELOT FAILED, AS DID YOUR CLUMSY ASSASSINATION ATTEMPT AT THE WEDDING!
I KNOW YOU HAVE SOME SORT OF "PLAN," MORGAN, BUT WE CAN'T LET ARTHUR AND HIS KNIGHTS RUN AROUND, UNMOLESTED.
SEND SOME OF THOSE ALIENS IF YOU FEEL YOU MUST, BUT NO U.N. TROOPS --ARTHUR IS SUSPICIOUS ENOUGH ALREADY.
BE CAREFUL, JORDAN--YOU WOULDN'T WANT TO DISPLEASE ME.
OH? AND W-WHY NOT?
BECAUSE MY LITTLE PET WAS ONCE A MAN--BEFORE HE DISPLEASED ME.
WE ARE APPROACHING OUR DESTINATION, MY KING.
SPLENDID, LANCELOT...
ARE YOU READY, SIR GALAHAD?
AT YOUR COMMAND, SIRE.
THEN MY COMMAND IS--
12

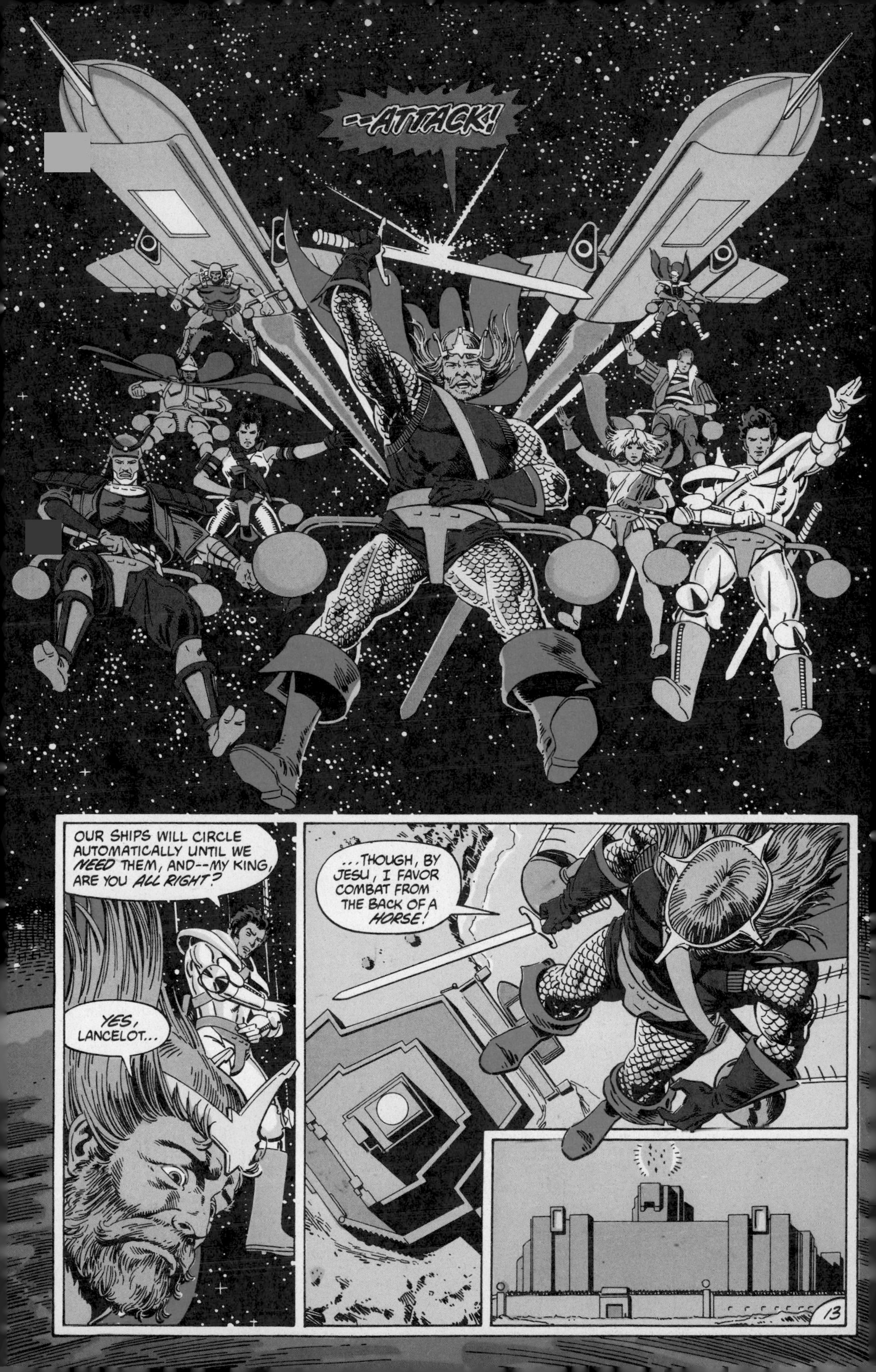
--ATTACK!
OUR SHIPS WILL CIRCLE AUTOMATICALLY UNTIL WE NEED THEM, AND--MY KING, ARE YOU ALL RIGHT?
YES, LANCELOT...
...THOUGH, BY JESU, I FAVOR COMBAT FROM THE BACK OF A HORSE!
13

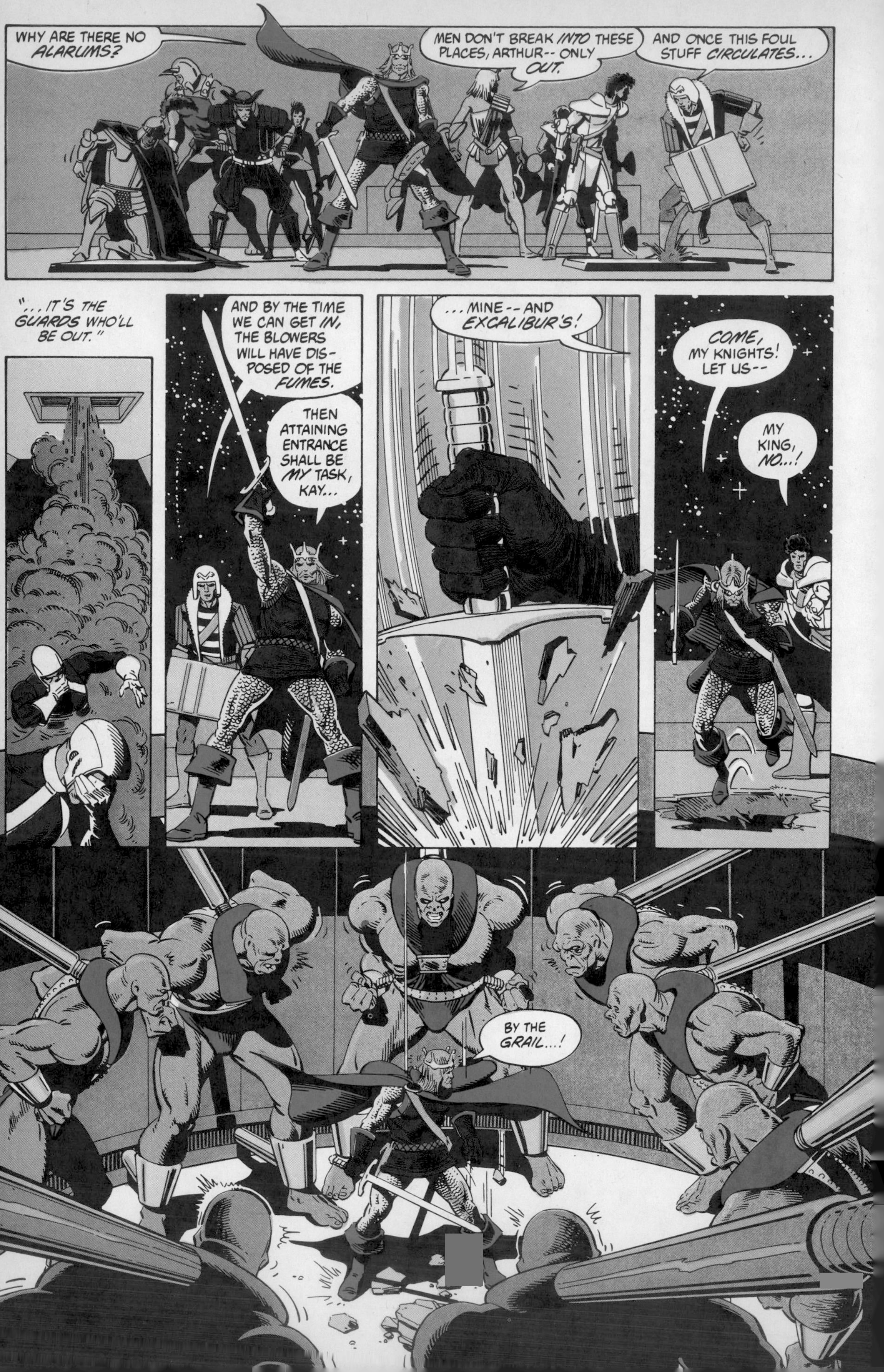
WHY ARE THERE NO ALARUMS?
MEN DON'T BREAK INTO THESE PLACES, ARTHUR-- ONLY OUT.
AND ONCE THIS FOUL STUFF CIRCULATES...
"...IT'S THE GUARDS WHO'LL BE OUT."
AND BY THE TIME WE CAN GET IN, THE BLOWERS WILL HAVE DISPOSED OF THE FUMES.
THEN ATTAINING ENTRANCE SHALL BE MY TASK, KAY...
...MINE--AND EXCALIBUR'S!
COME, MY KNIGHTS! LET US--
MY KING, NO...!
BY THE GRAIL...!

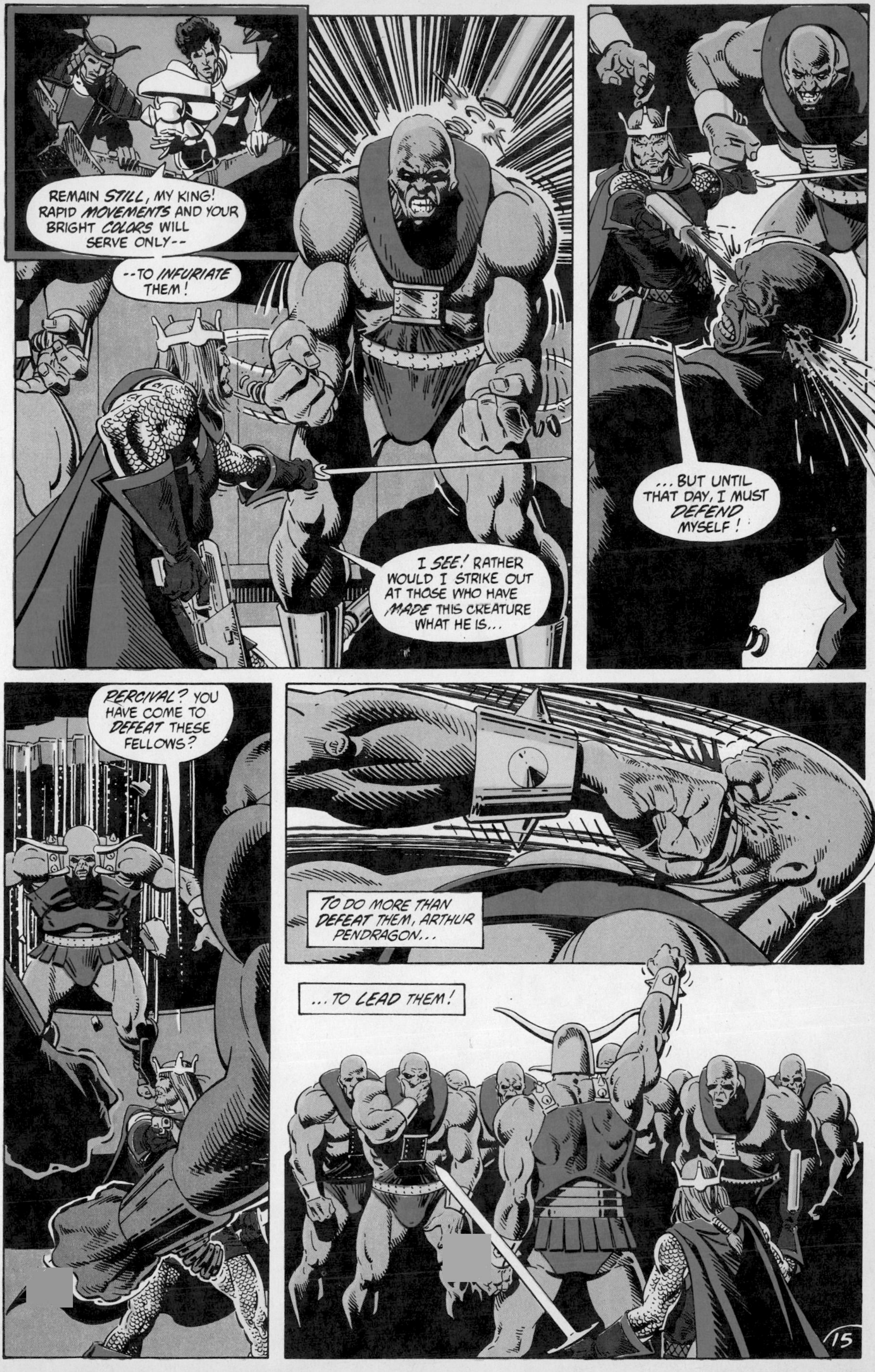

REMAIN STILL, MY KING! RAPID MOVEMENTS AND YOUR BRIGHT COLORS WILL SERVE ONLY--
--TO INFURIATE THEM!
I SEE! RATHER WOULD I STRIKE OUT AT THOSE WHO HAVE MADE THIS CREATURE WHAT HE IS...
...BUT UNTIL THAT DAY, I MUST DEFEND MYSELF!
PERCIVAL? YOU HAVE COME TO DEFEAT THESE FELLOWS?
TO DO MORE THAN DEFEAT THEM, ARTHUR PENDRAGON...
...TO LEAD THEM!
15

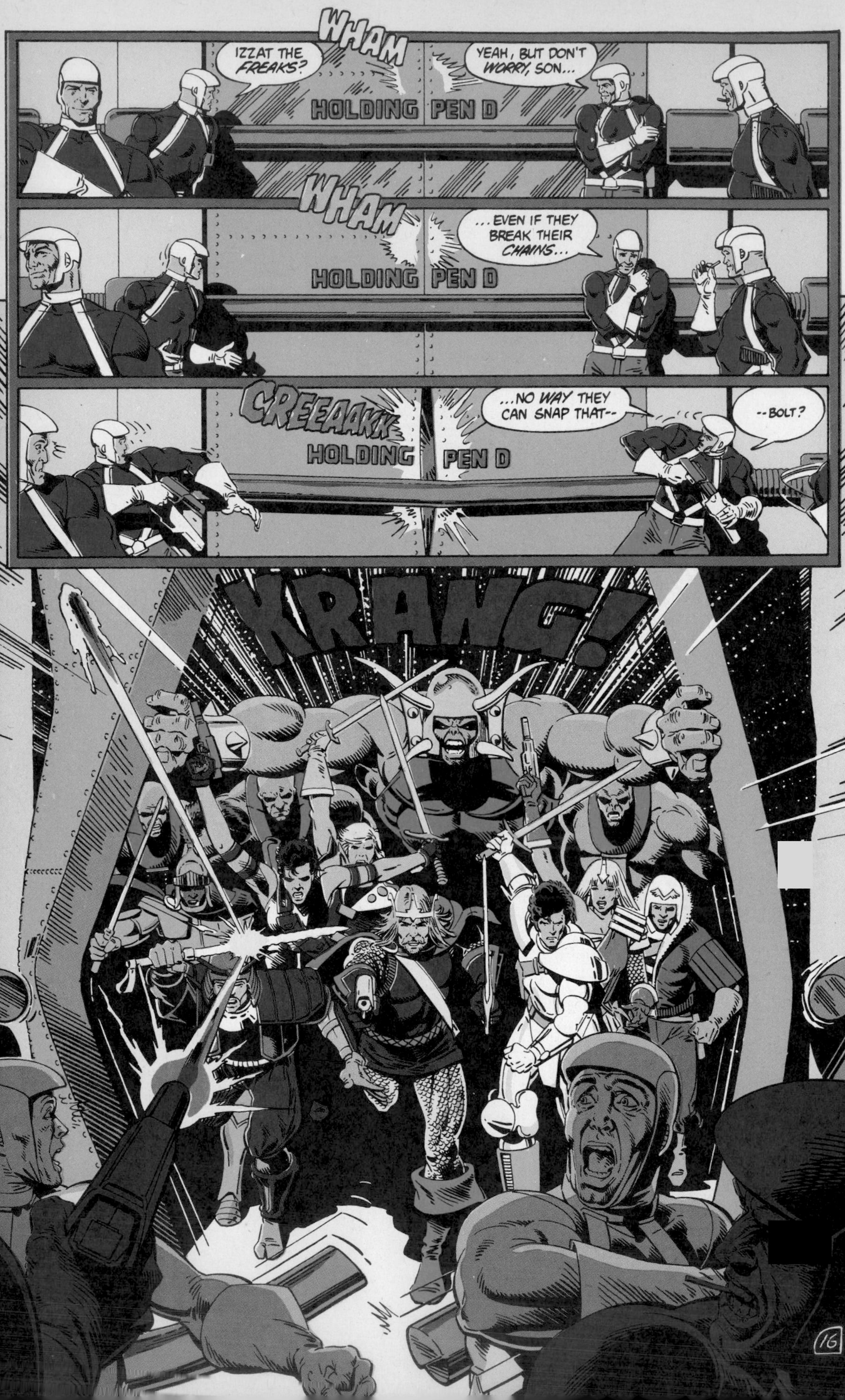
WHAM
IZZAT THE FREAKS?
YEAH, BUT DON'T WORRY, SON...
HOLDING PEN D
WHAM
...EVEN IF THEY BREAK THEIR CHAINS...
HOLDING PEN D
CREEAAKK
...NO WAY THEY CAN SNAP THAT--
--BOLT?
HOLDING PEN D
KRANG!

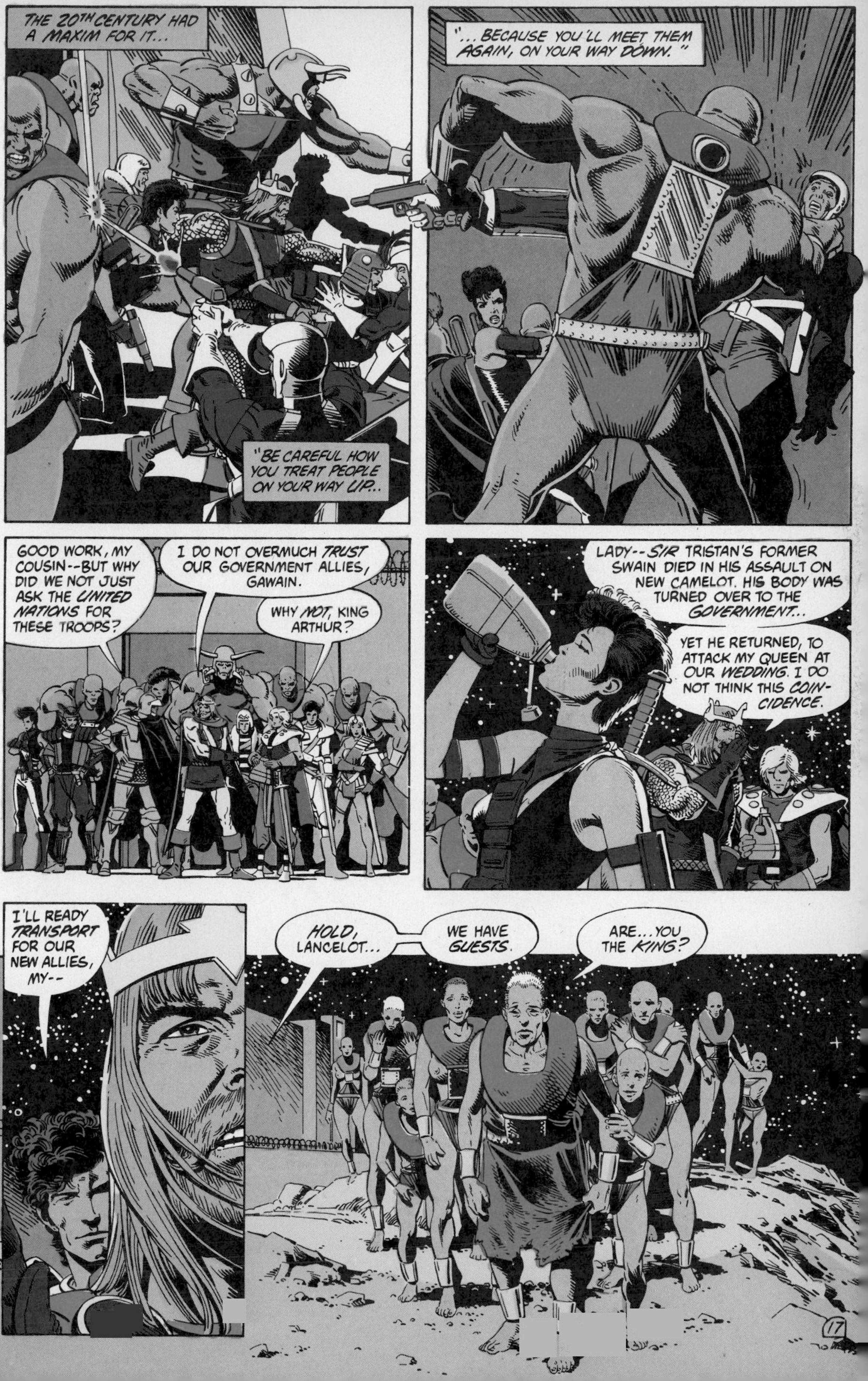
THE 20TH CENTURY HAD A MAXIM FOR IT...
"BE CAREFUL HOW YOU TREAT PEOPLE ON YOUR WAY UP...
"... BECAUSE YOU'LL MEET THEM AGAIN, ON YOUR WAY DOWN."
GOOD WORK, MY COUSIN--BUT WHY DID WE NOT JUST ASK THE UNITED NATIONS FOR THESE TROOPS?
I DO NOT OVERMUCH TRUST OUR GOVERNMENT ALLIES, GAWAIN.
WHY NOT, KING ARTHUR?
LADY--SIR TRISTAN'S FORMER SWAIN DIED IN HIS ASSAULT ON NEW CAMELOT. HIS BODY WAS TURNED OVER TO THE GOVERNMENT...
YET HE RETURNED, TO ATTACK MY QUEEN AT OUR WEDDING. I DO NOT THINK THIS COINCIDENCE.
I'LL READY TRANSPORT FOR OUR NEW ALLIES, MY--
HOLD, LANCELOT...
WE HAVE GUESTS.
ARE... YOU THE KING?
17

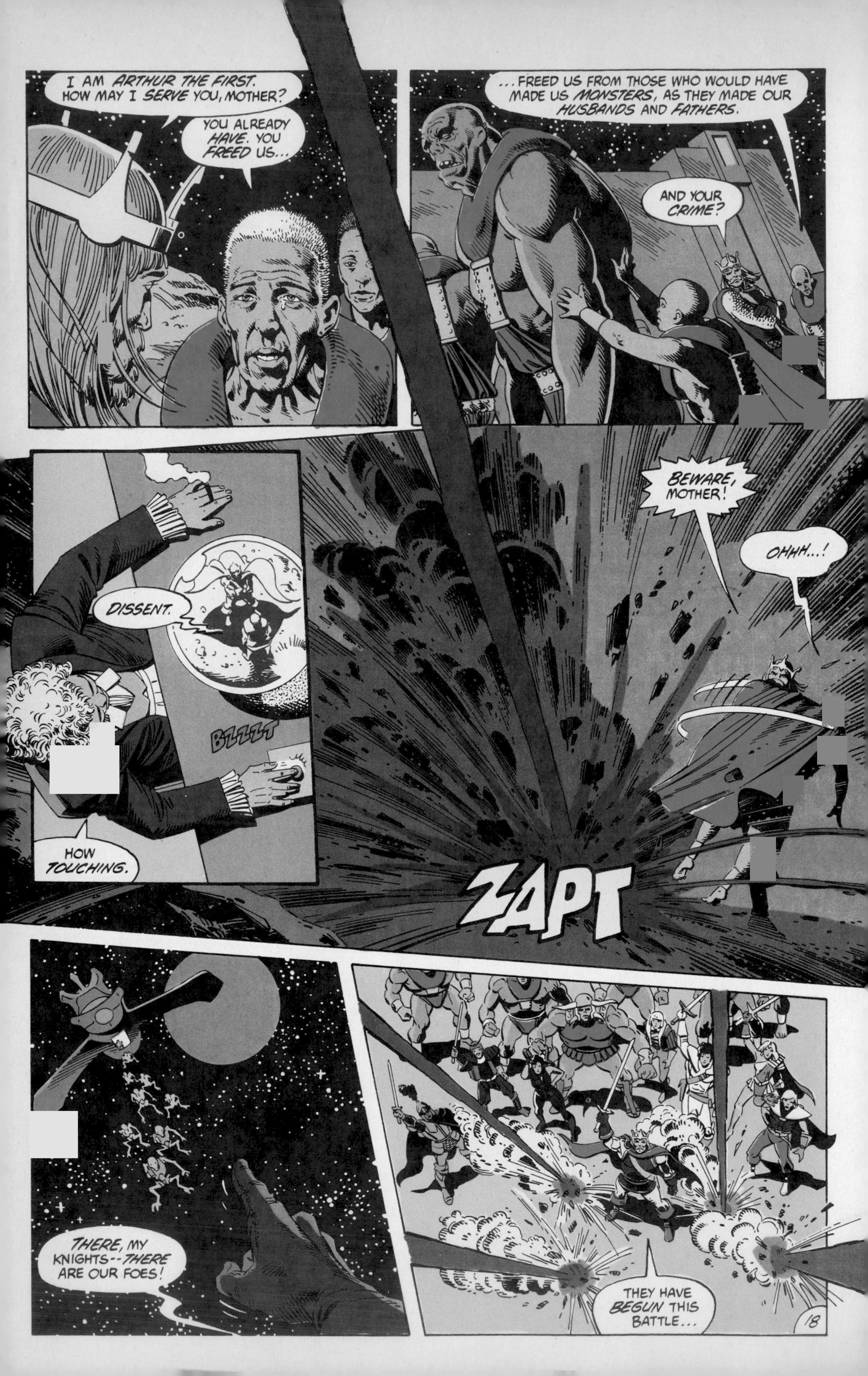
I AM *ARTHUR THE FIRST.* HOW MAY I *SERVE* YOU, MOTHER?
YOU ALREADY *HAVE.* YOU *FREED* US...
...FREED US FROM THOSE WHO WOULD HAVE MADE US *MONSTERS,* AS THEY MADE OUR *HUSBANDS* AND *FATHERS.*
AND YOUR *CRIME?*
DISSENT.
BLZZZT
HOW *TOUCHING.*
BEWARE, MOTHER!
OHHH...!
ZAPT
THERE, MY KNIGHTS--*THERE* ARE OUR FOES!
THEY HAVE *BEGUN* THIS BATTLE...
18

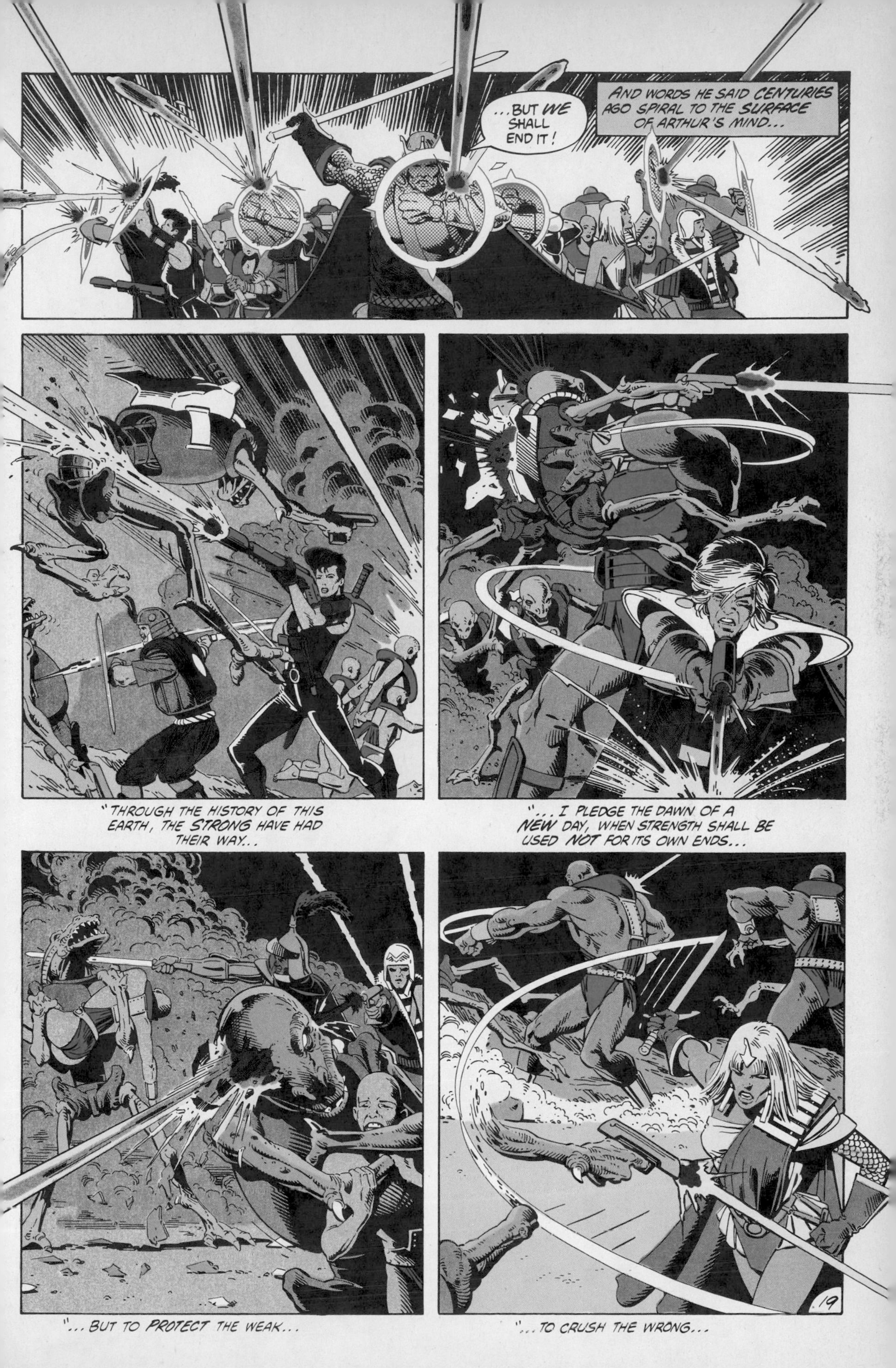
...BUT WE SHALL END IT!
AND WORDS HE SAID CENTURIES AGO SPIRAL TO THE SURFACE OF ARTHUR'S MIND...
"THROUGH THE HISTORY OF THIS EARTH, THE STRONG HAVE HAD THEIR WAY...
"... I PLEDGE THE DAWN OF A NEW DAY, WHEN STRENGTH SHALL BE USED NOT FOR ITS OWN ENDS...
"... BUT TO PROTECT THE WEAK...
"...TO CRUSH THE WRONG...

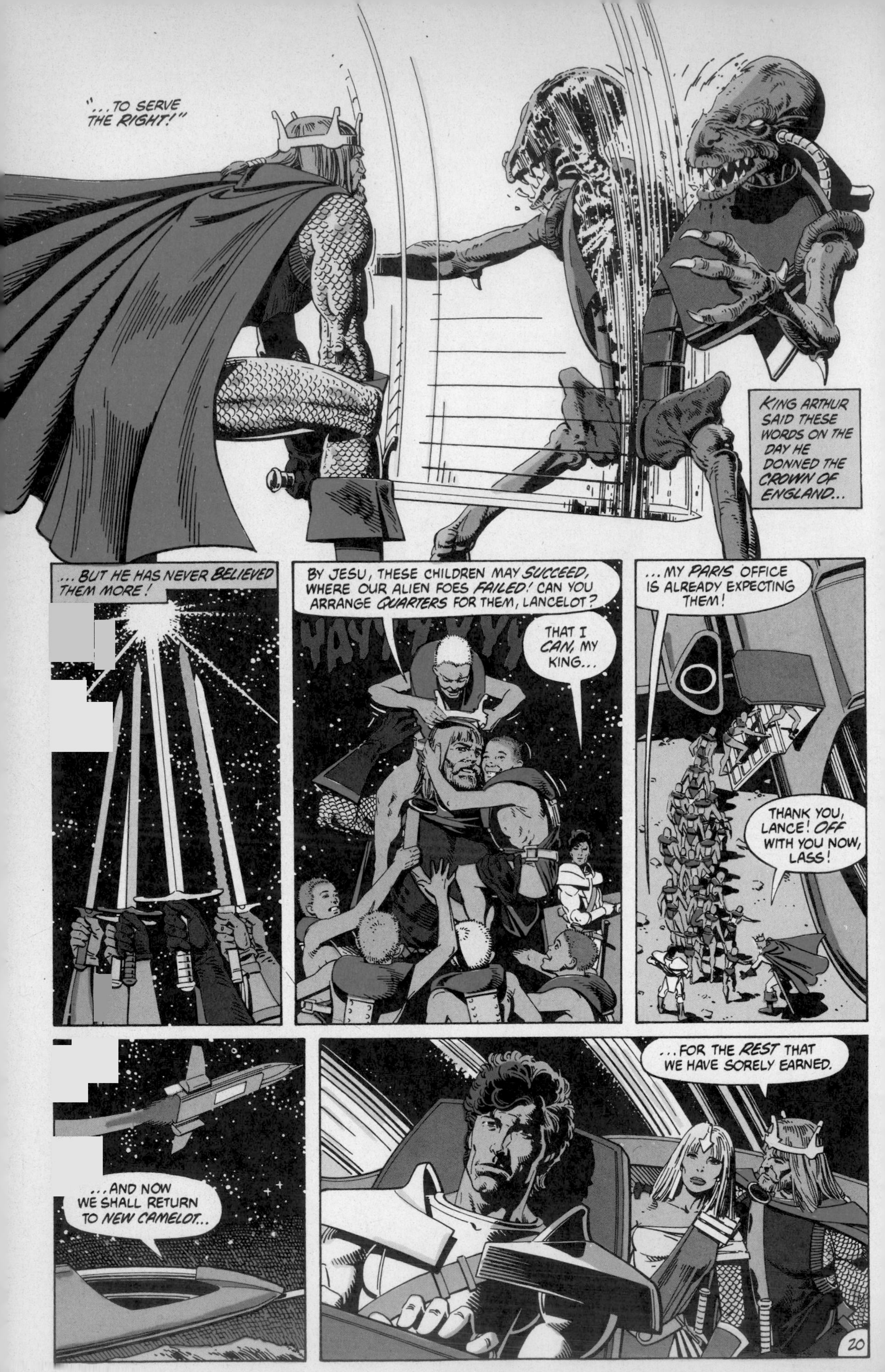
"...TO SERVE THE RIGHT!"
KING ARTHUR SAID THESE WORDS ON THE DAY HE DONNED THE CROWN OF ENGLAND...
...BUT HE HAS NEVER BELIEVED THEM MORE!
BY JESU, THESE CHILDREN MAY SUCCEED, WHERE OUR ALIEN FOES FAILED! CAN YOU ARRANGE QUARTERS FOR THEM, LANCELOT?
THAT I CAN, MY KING...
...MY PARIS OFFICE IS ALREADY EXPECTING THEM!
THANK YOU, LANCE! OFF WITH YOU NOW, LASS!
...AND NOW WE SHALL RETURN TO NEW CAMELOT...
...FOR THE REST THAT WE HAVE SORELY EARNED.
20

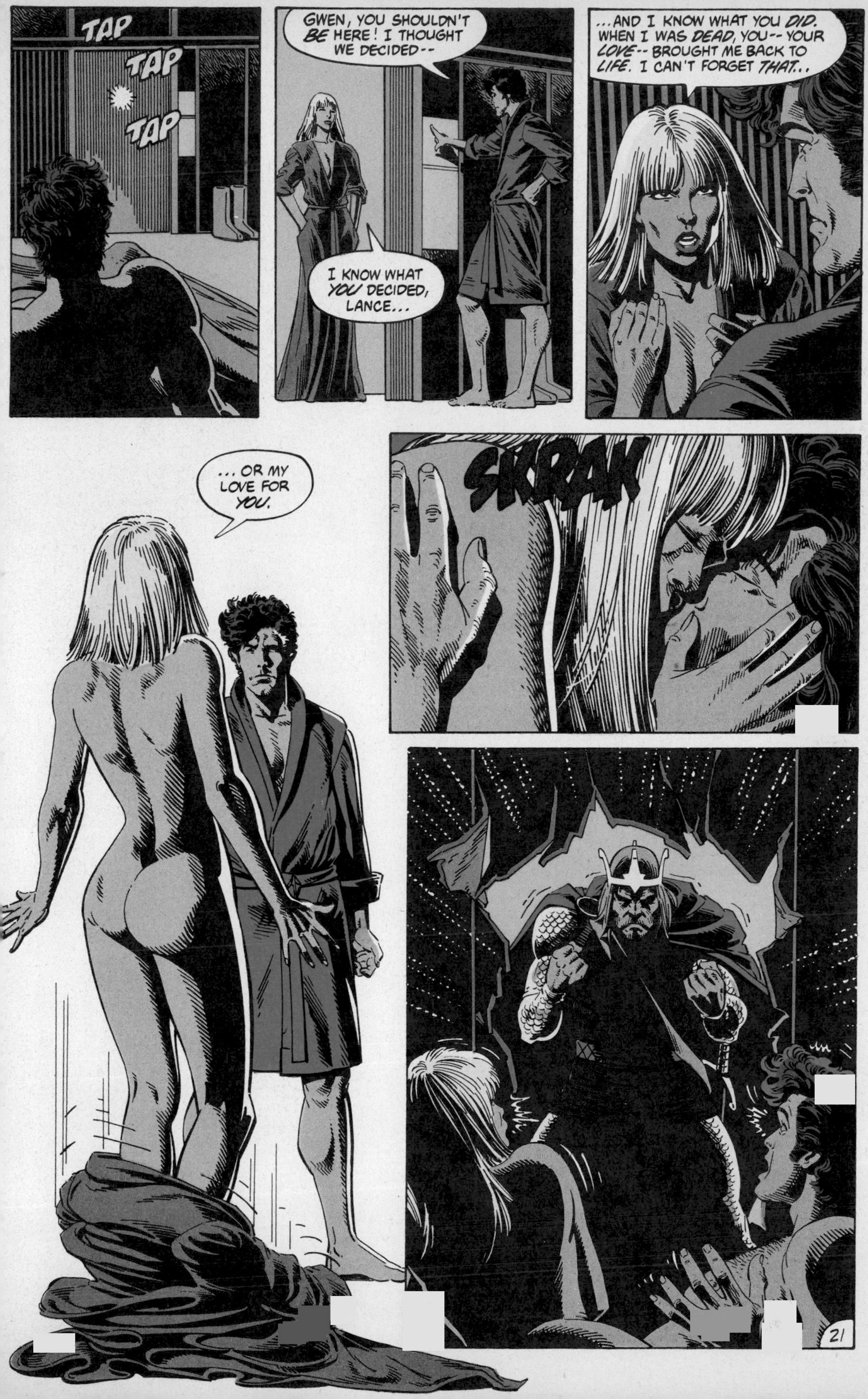
TAP
TAP
TAP
GWEN, YOU SHOULDN'T BE HERE! I THOUGHT WE DECIDED--
I KNOW WHAT YOU DECIDED, LANCE...
...AND I KNOW WHAT YOU DID. WHEN I WAS DEAD, YOU--YOUR LOVE--BROUGHT ME BACK TO LIFE. I CAN'T FORGET THAT...
...OR MY LOVE FOR YOU.
SKRAK

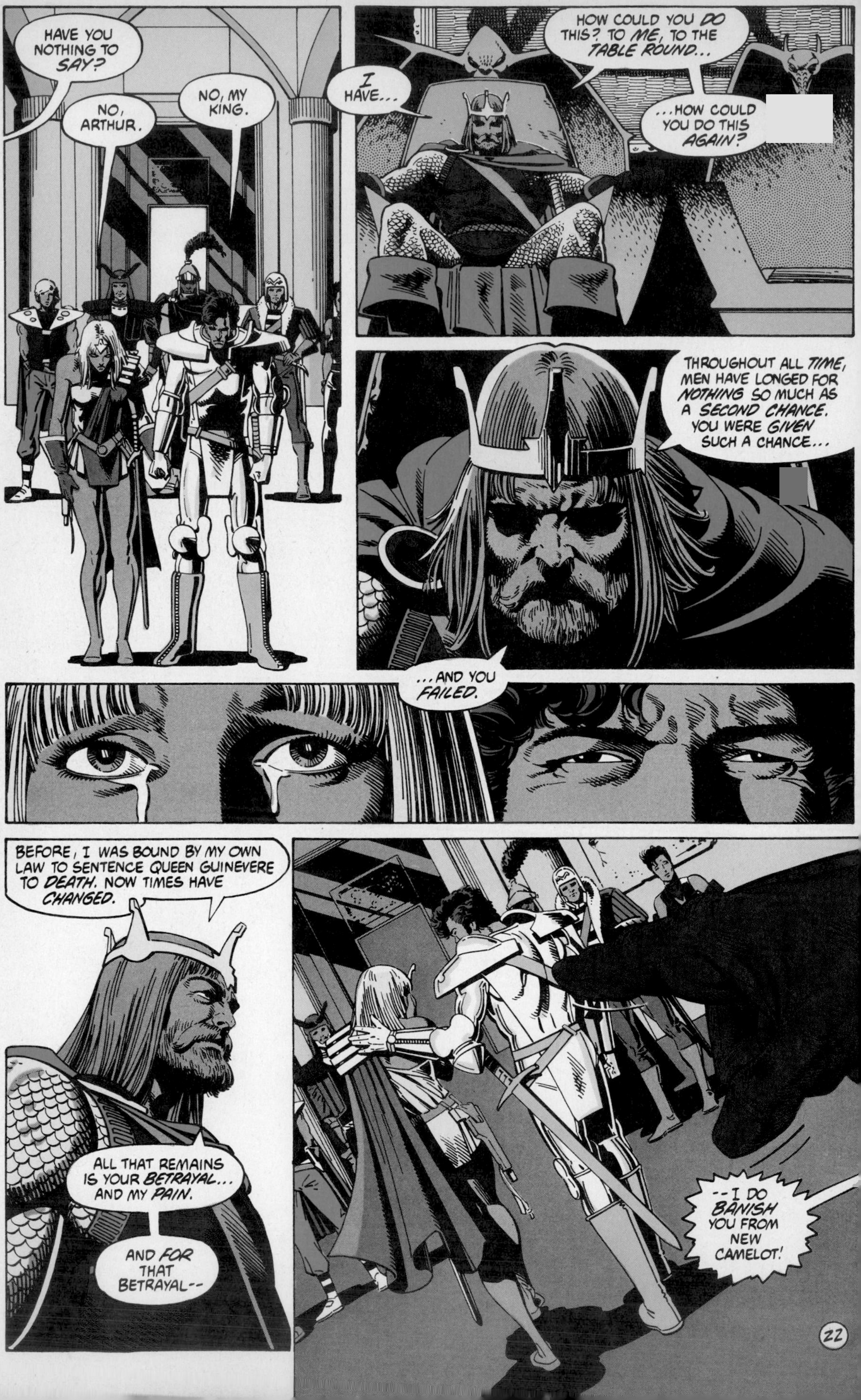
HAVE YOU NOTHING TO SAY?
NO, ARTHUR.
NO, MY KING.
I HAVE...
HOW COULD YOU DO THIS? TO ME, TO THE TABLE ROUND...
...HOW COULD YOU DO THIS AGAIN?
THROUGHOUT ALL TIME, MEN HAVE LONGED FOR NOTHING SO MUCH AS A SECOND CHANCE. YOU WERE GIVEN SUCH A CHANCE...
...AND YOU FAILED.
BEFORE, I WAS BOUND BY MY OWN LAW TO SENTENCE QUEEN GUINEVERE TO DEATH. NOW TIMES HAVE CHANGED.
ALL THAT REMAINS IS YOUR BETRAYAL... AND MY PAIN.
AND FOR THAT BETRAYAL--
--I DO BANISH YOU FROM NEW CAMELOT!

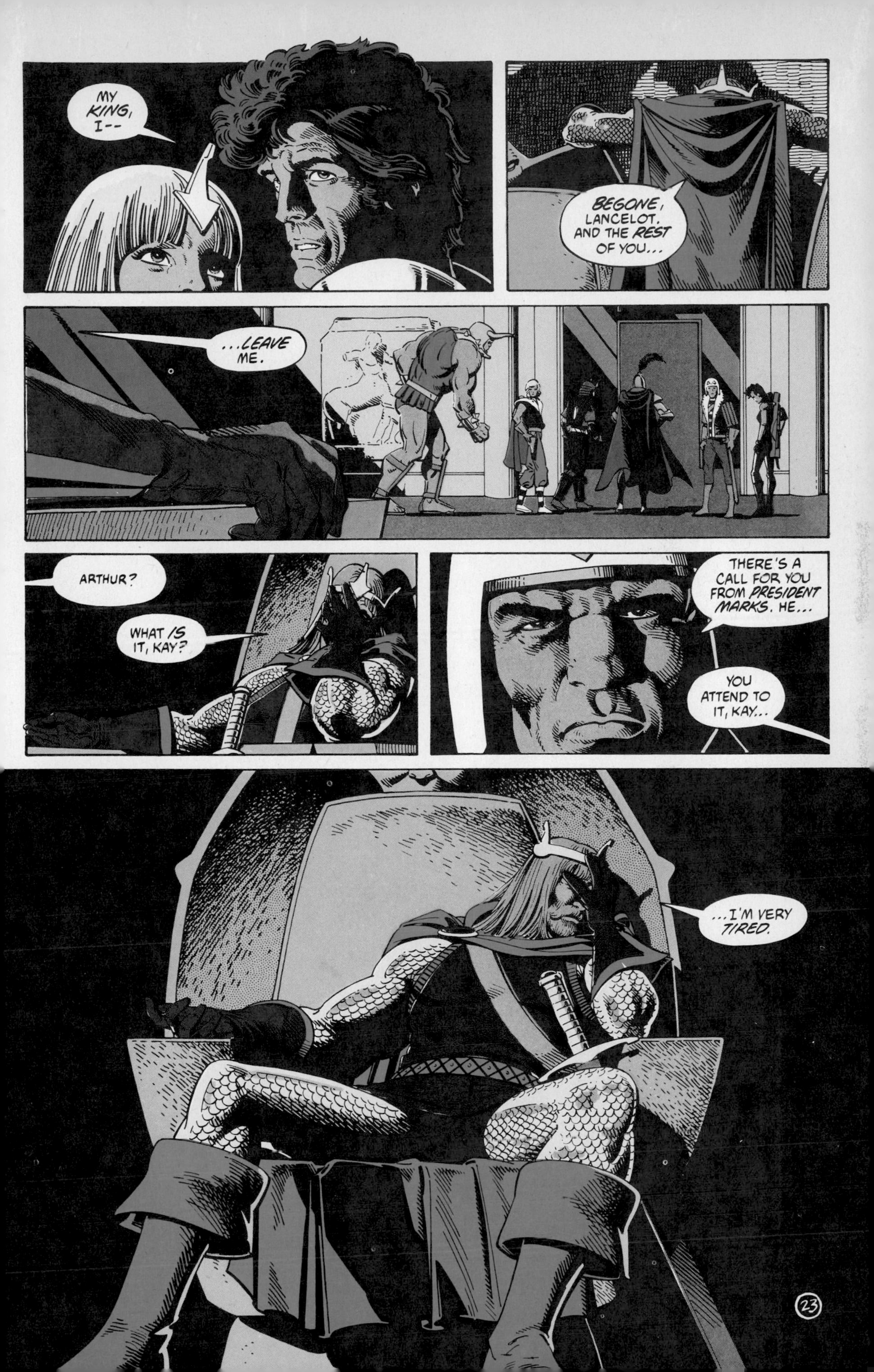
MY KING, I--
BEGONE, LANCELOT. AND THE REST OF YOU...
...LEAVE ME.
ARTHUR?
WHAT IS IT, KAY?
THERE'S A CALL FOR YOU FROM PRESIDENT MARKS. HE...
YOU ATTEND TO IT, KAY...
...I'M VERY TIRED.

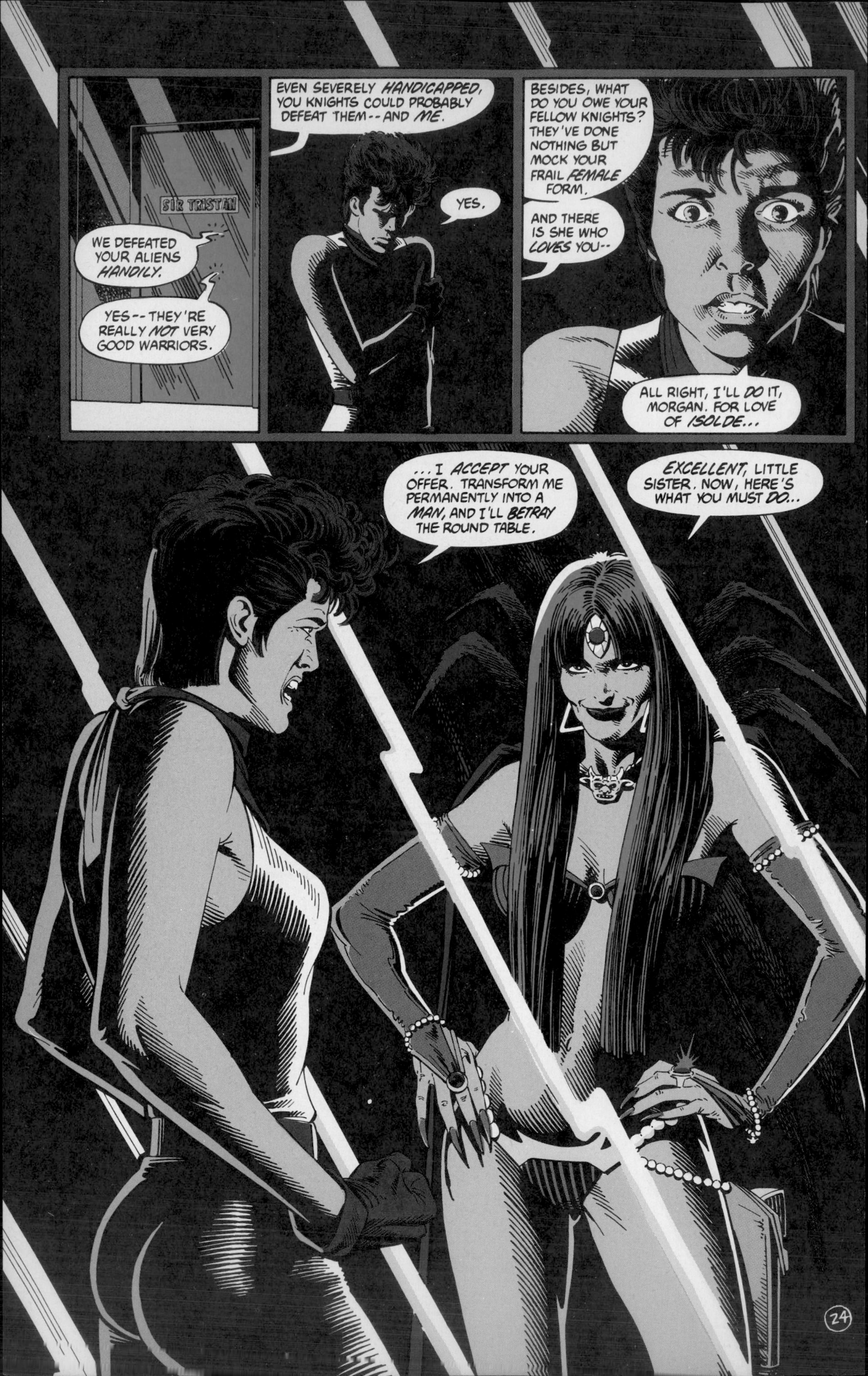
SIR TRISTAN
WE DEFEATED YOUR ALIENS HANDILY.
YES--THEY'RE REALLY NOT VERY GOOD WARRIORS.
EVEN SEVERELY HANDICAPPED, YOU KNIGHTS COULD PROBABLY DEFEAT THEM--AND ME.
YES.
BESIDES, WHAT DO YOU OWE YOUR FELLOW KNIGHTS? THEY'VE DONE NOTHING BUT MOCK YOUR FRAIL FEMALE FORM.
AND THERE IS SHE WHO LOVES YOU--
ALL RIGHT, I'LL DO IT, MORGAN. FOR LOVE OF ISOLDE...
...I ACCEPT YOUR OFFER. TRANSFORM ME PERMANENTLY INTO A MAN, AND I'LL BETRAY THE ROUND TABLE.
EXCELLENT, LITTLE SISTER. NOW, HERE'S WHAT YOU MUST DO...
24

chapter
8

Judas Knight

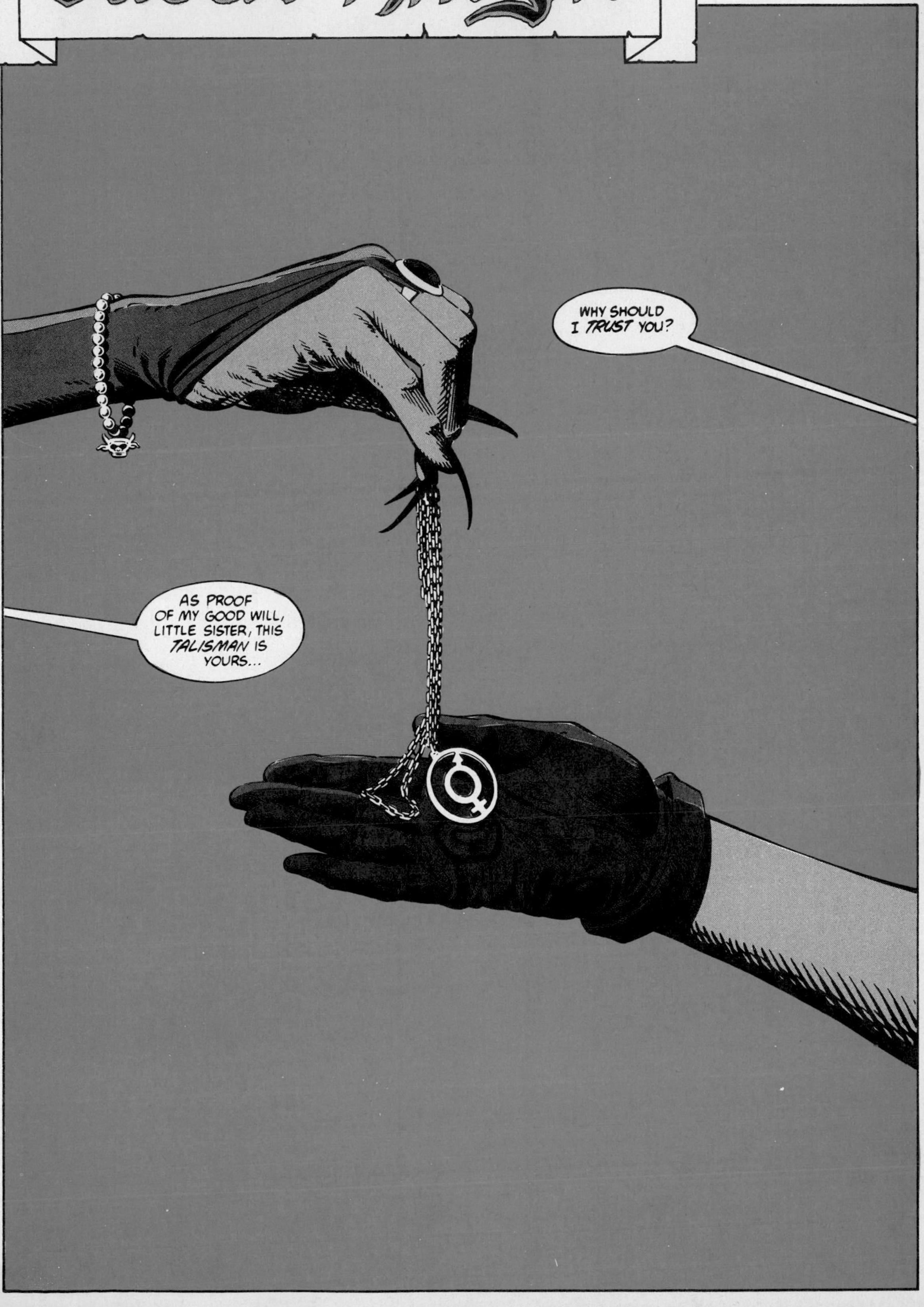
WHY SHOULD I *TRUST* YOU?
AS PROOF OF MY GOOD WILL, LITTLE SISTER, THIS *TALISMAN* IS YOURS...

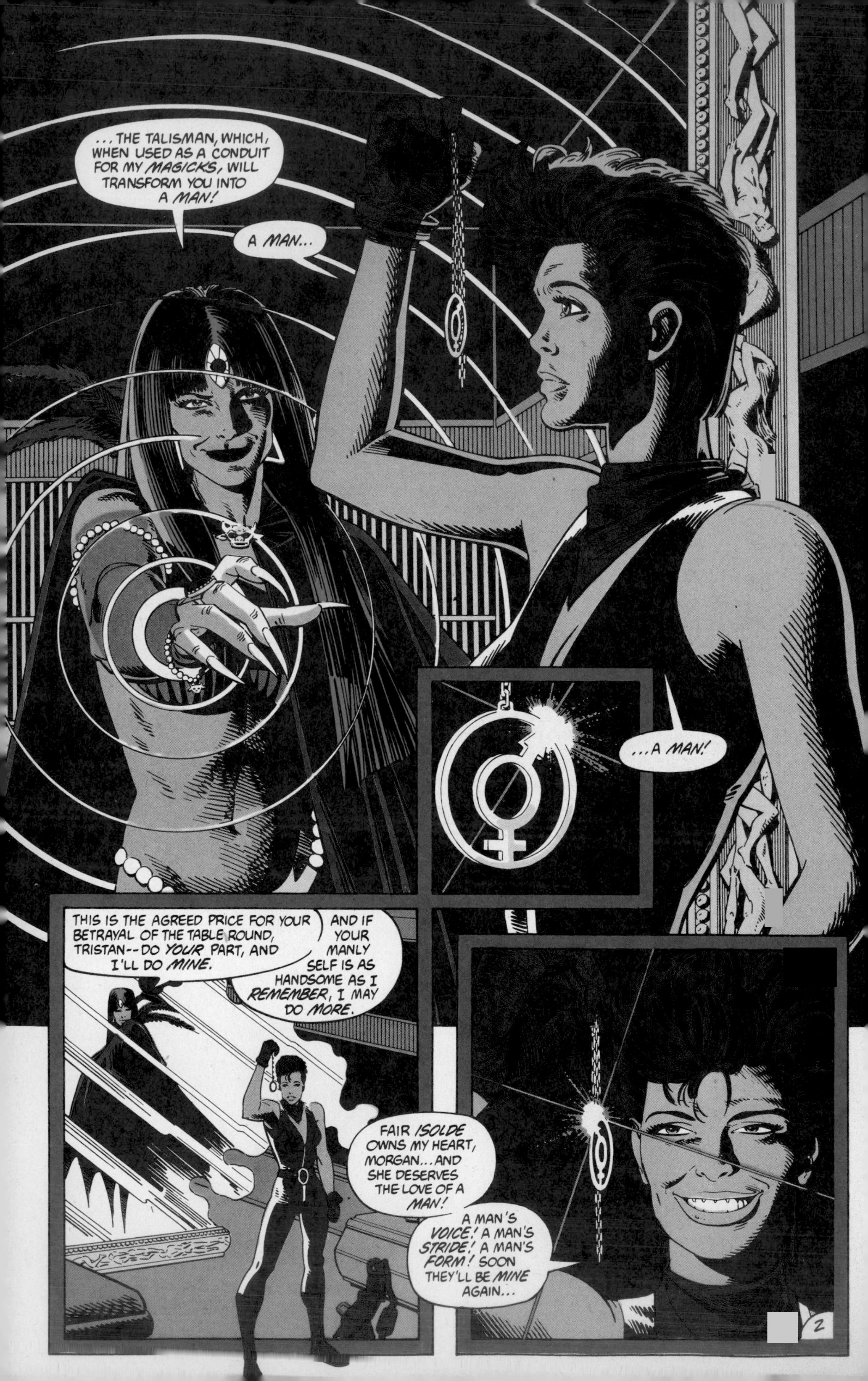

. . . THE TALISMAN, WHICH, WHEN USED AS A CONDUIT FOR MY MAGICKS, WILL TRANSFORM YOU INTO A MAN!
A MAN...
...A MAN!
THIS IS THE AGREED PRICE FOR YOUR BETRAYAL OF THE TABLE ROUND, TRISTAN--DO YOUR PART, AND I'LL DO MINE.
AND IF YOUR MANLY SELF IS AS HANDSOME AS I REMEMBER, I MAY DO MORE.
FAIR ISOLDE OWNS MY HEART, MORGAN... AND SHE DESERVES THE LOVE OF A MAN!
A MAN'S VOICE! A MAN'S STRIDE! A MAN'S FORM! SOON THEY'LL BE MINE AGAIN...

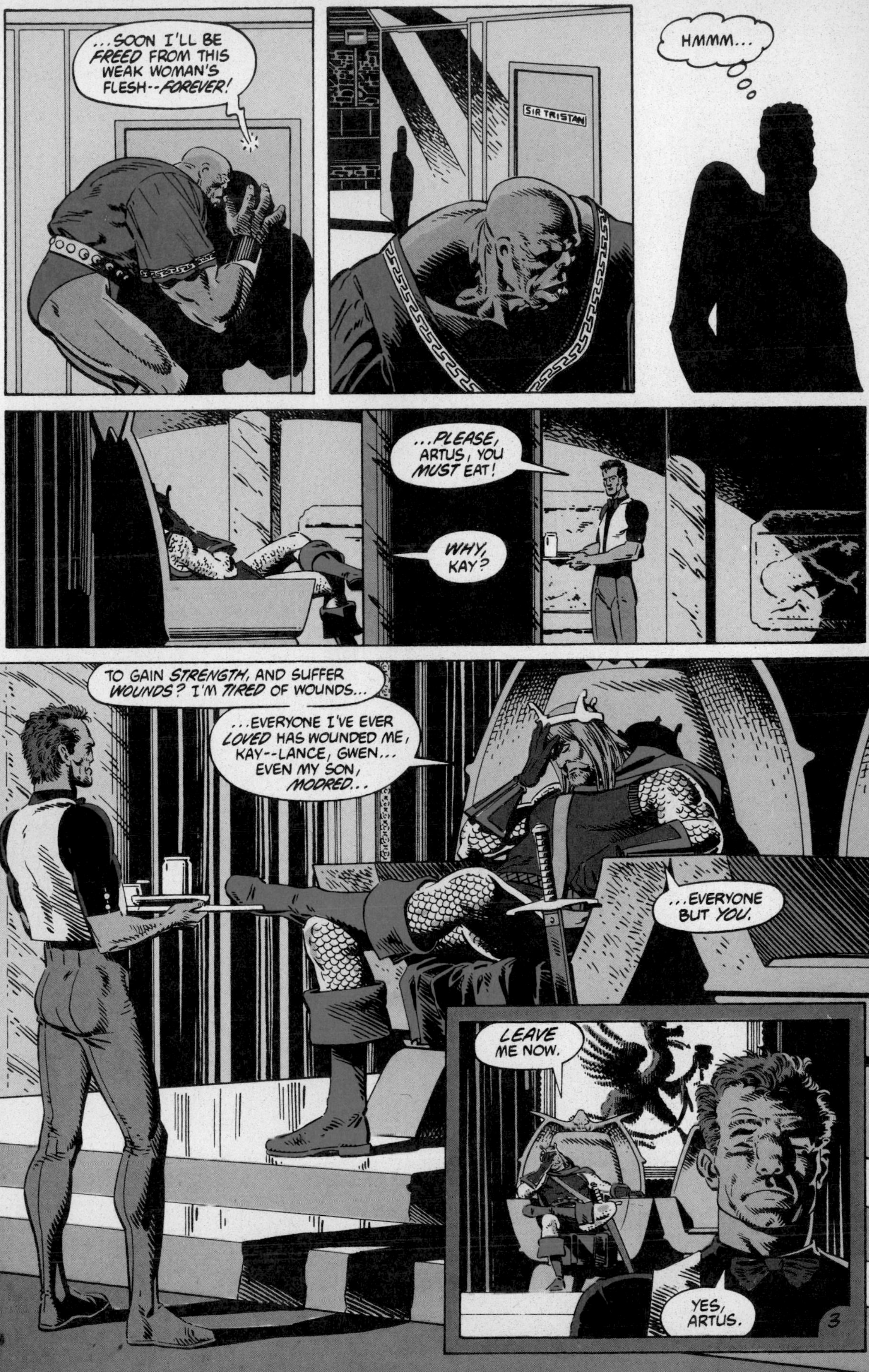

...SOON I'LL BE FREED FROM THIS WEAK WOMAN'S FLESH--FOREVER!
SIR TRISTAN
HMMM...
...PLEASE, ARTUS, YOU MUST EAT!
WHY, KAY?
TO GAIN STRENGTH, AND SUFFER WOUNDS? I'M TIRED OF WOUNDS...
...EVERYONE I'VE EVER LOVED HAS WOUNDED ME, KAY--LANCE, GWEN... EVEN MY SON, MODRED...
...EVERYONE BUT YOU.
LEAVE ME NOW.
YES, ARTUS.

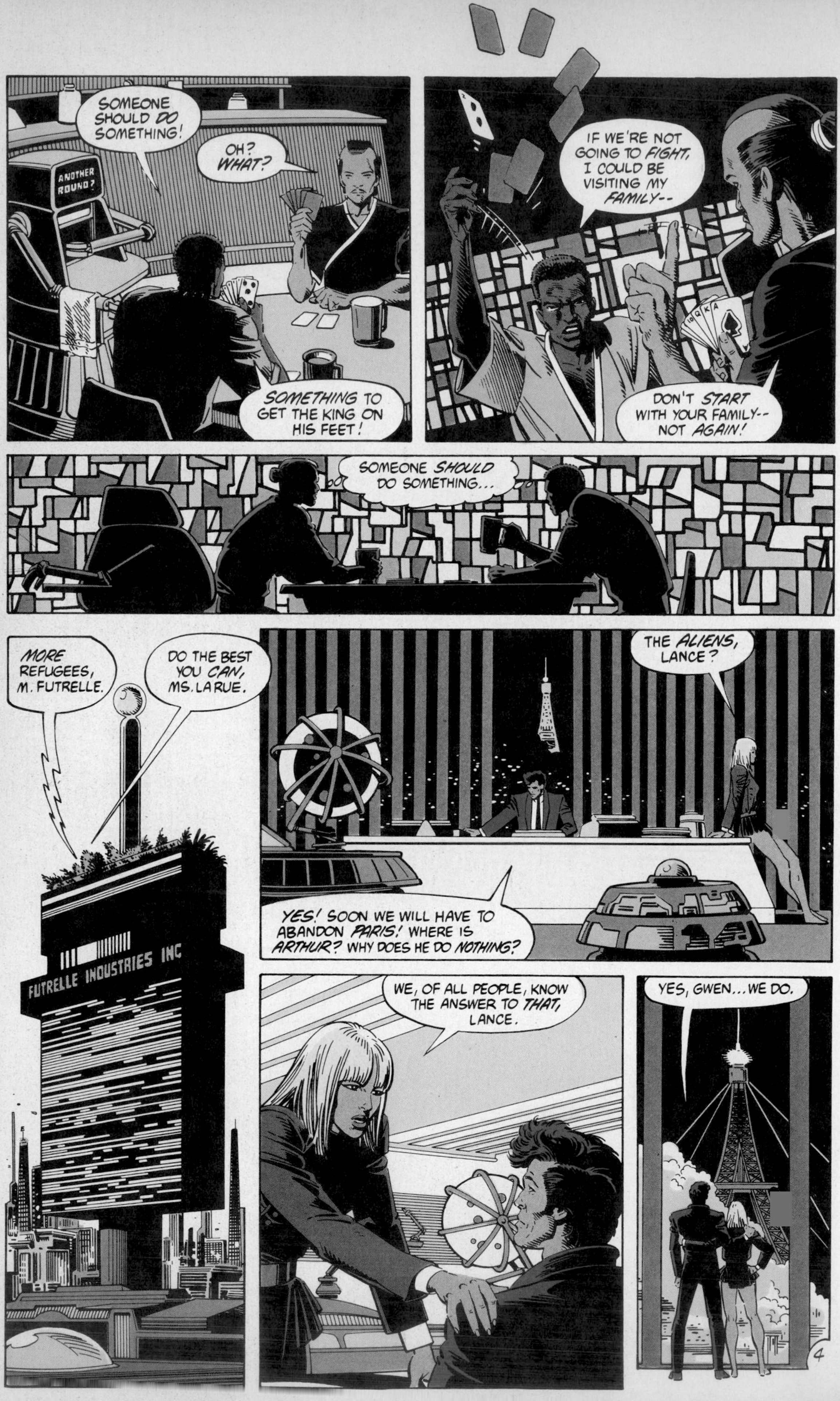
ANOTHER ROUND?
SOMEONE SHOULD DO SOMETHING!
OH? WHAT?
SOMETHING TO GET THE KING ON HIS FEET!
IF WE'RE NOT GOING TO FIGHT, I COULD BE VISITING MY FAMILY--
DON'T START WITH YOUR FAMILY-- NOT AGAIN!
SOMEONE SHOULD DO SOMETHING...
MORE REFUGEES, M. FUTRELLE.
DO THE BEST YOU CAN, MS. LARUE.
FUTRELLE INDUSTRIES INC
THE ALIENS, LANCE?
YES! SOON WE WILL HAVE TO ABANDON PARIS! WHERE IS ARTHUR? WHY DOES HE DO NOTHING?
WE, OF ALL PEOPLE, KNOW THE ANSWER TO THAT, LANCE.
YES, GWEN... WE DO.
4

BEGONE!

I WON'T TAKE THAT FOR AN *ANSWER*, MERLIN...

...I WANT TO KNOW WHY YOU'VE DONE NOTHING TO HELP *ARTHUR?* HASN'T HE FOUGHT YOUR *BATTLES* FOR YOU?

...DIDN'T HE *FREE* YOU FROM NYNEVE'S IMPRISONMENT BENEATH *STONEHENGE?*

HIS AILMENT IS OF THE HUMAN HEART, AND BEYOND MY *SKILL*...

...FOR IT IS BEYOND MY *EXPERIENCE.*

BUT HE IS YOUR PLANET'S ONLY *HOPE*, SO I WILL *TRY.*

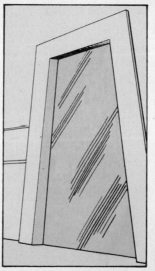

NOW *SWIFTLY*, MY *JUDAS KNIGHT*...

5

...ENTER THE LAIR OF THE DEVIL'S *SON*...

...AND SEIZE THE *CHARM!* HIS ENCHANTMENTS PREVENT ME FROM DESTROYING IT...FROM EVEN *APPROACHING* IT...

...BUT *YOU*-- YOU MAY BE SOMEWHAT LESS...*CIRCUMSPECT* IN YOUR ACTIONS!

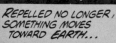

REPELLED NO LONGER, SOMETHING MOVES TOWARD EARTH...

...TOWARD NEW CAMELOT.

BEGONE, MERLIN. YOU COULD COAX ME OUT OF MY MELANCHOLIES WHEN I WAS A *BOY*...BUT I HAVE *GROWN*...

...AND MY *SORROWS* HAVE GROWN, AS WELL!

I CAN DO *NOTHING* FOR HIM...THOUGH HIS CONDITION IS MOST INTERESTING.

PLEASE, MERLIN! YOU MUST *TRY*--

OH, MERLIN...

...?

NO!

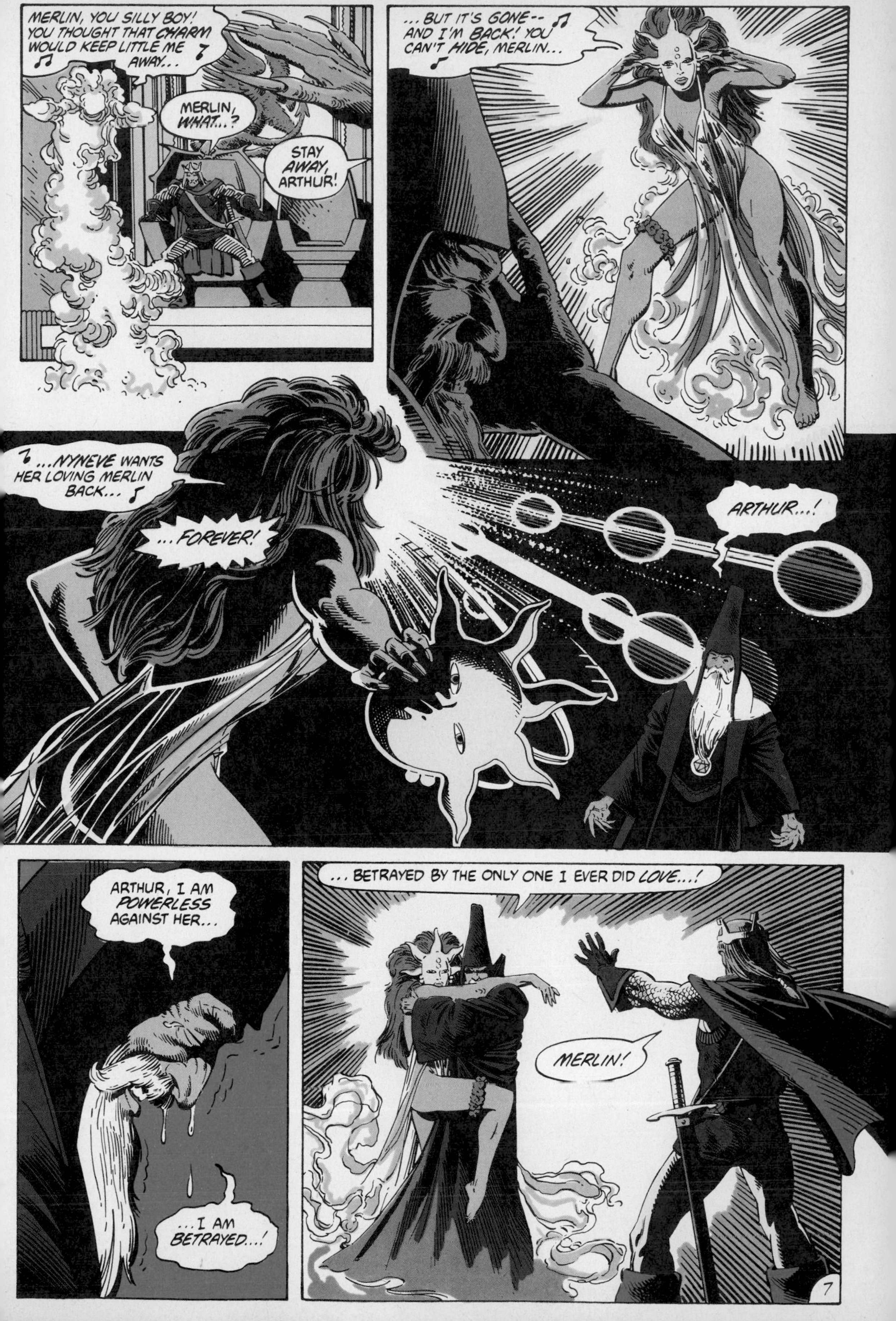
MERLIN, YOU SILLY BOY! YOU THOUGHT THAT CHARM WOULD KEEP LITTLE ME AWAY...
MERLIN, WHAT...?
STAY AWAY, ARTHUR!
...BUT IT'S GONE-- AND I'M BACK! YOU CAN'T HIDE, MERLIN...
...NYNEVE WANTS HER LOVING MERLIN BACK...
...FOREVER!
ARTHUR...!
ARTHUR, I AM POWERLESS AGAINST HER...
...I AM BETRAYED...!
...BETRAYED BY THE ONLY ONE I EVER DID LOVE...!
MERLIN!

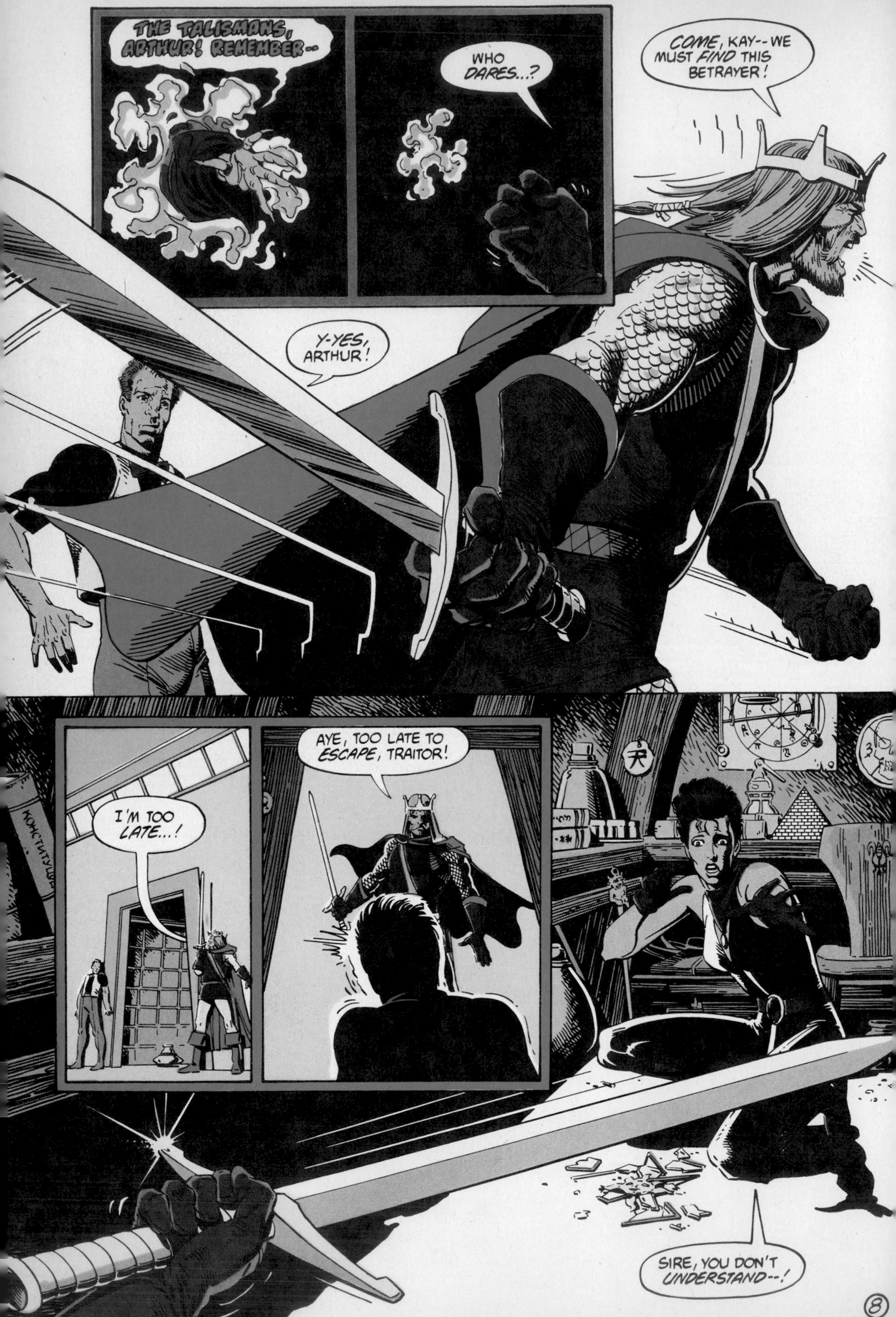
THE TALISMANS, ARTHUR! REMEMBER--
WHO DARES...?
COME, KAY--WE MUST FIND THIS BETRAYER!
Y-YES, ARTHUR!
I'M TOO LATE...!
AYE, TOO LATE TO ESCAPE, TRAITOR!
SIRE, YOU DON'T UNDERSTAND--!

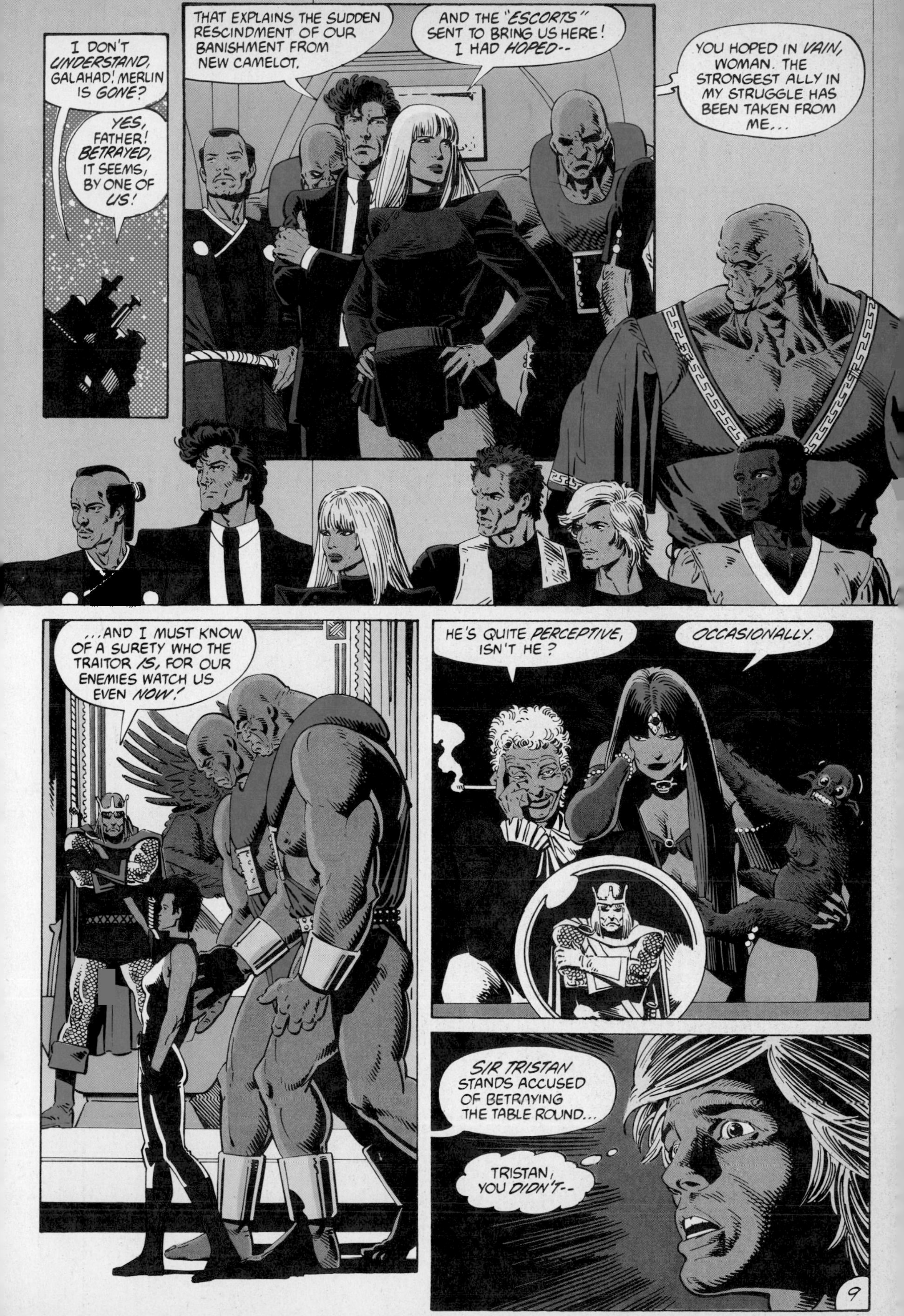
I DON'T UNDERSTAND, GALAHAD! MERLIN IS GONE?
YES, FATHER! BETRAYED, IT SEEMS, BY ONE OF US!
THAT EXPLAINS THE SUDDEN RESCINDMENT OF OUR BANISHMENT FROM NEW CAMELOT.
AND THE "ESCORTS" SENT TO BRING US HERE! I HAD HOPED--
YOU HOPED IN VAIN, WOMAN. THE STRONGEST ALLY IN MY STRUGGLE HAS BEEN TAKEN FROM ME...
...AND I MUST KNOW OF A SURETY WHO THE TRAITOR IS, FOR OUR ENEMIES WATCH US EVEN NOW!
HE'S QUITE PERCEPTIVE, ISN'T HE?
OCCASIONALLY.
SIR TRISTAN STANDS ACCUSED OF BETRAYING THE TABLE ROUND...
TRISTAN, YOU DIDN'T--

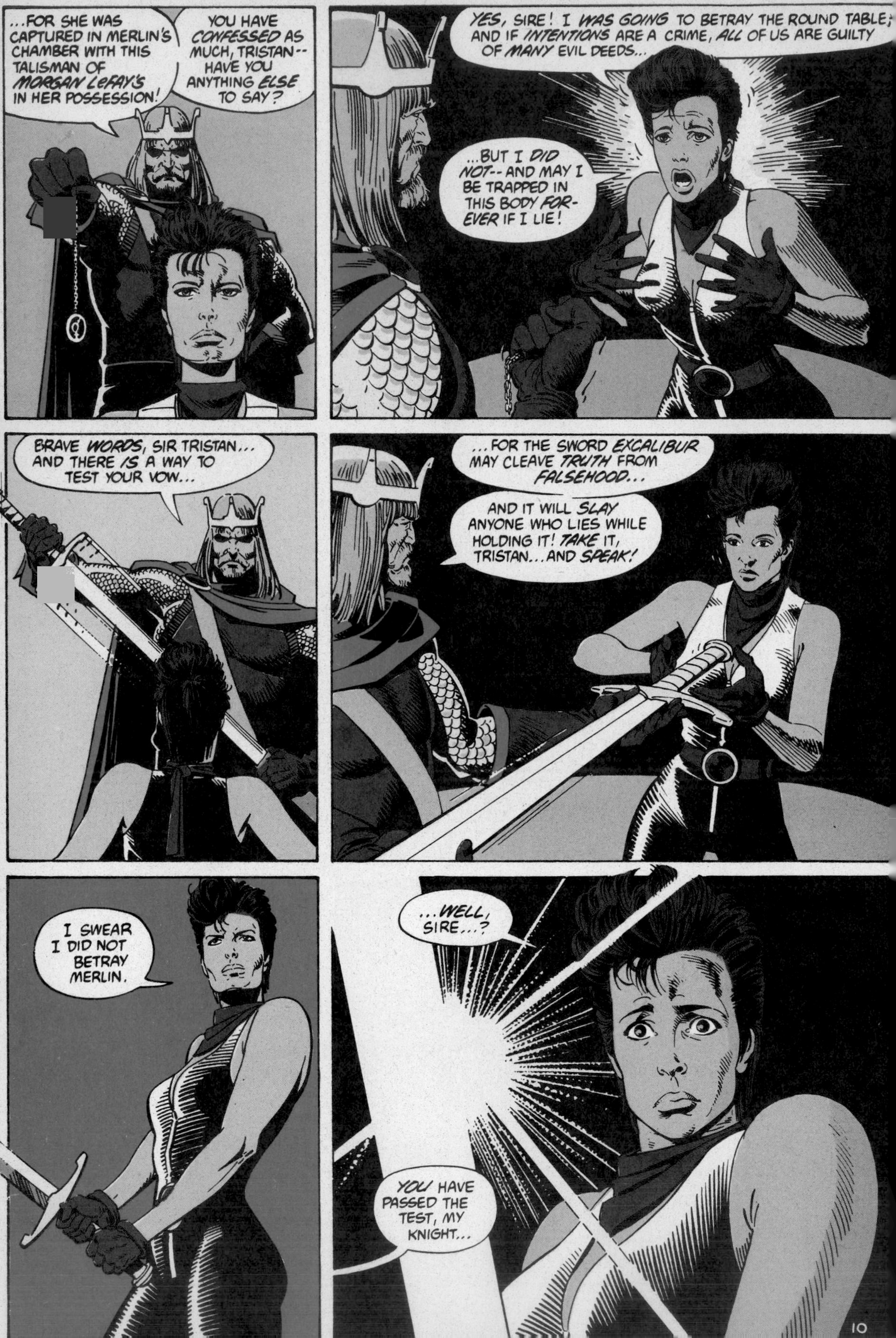
...FOR SHE WAS CAPTURED IN MERLIN'S CHAMBER WITH THIS TALISMAN OF MORGAN LeFAY'S IN HER POSSESSION!
YOU HAVE CONFESSED AS MUCH, TRISTAN-- HAVE YOU ANYTHING ELSE TO SAY?
YES, SIRE! I WAS GOING TO BETRAY THE ROUND TABLE; AND IF INTENTIONS ARE A CRIME, ALL OF US ARE GUILTY OF MANY EVIL DEEDS...
...BUT I DID NOT-- AND MAY I BE TRAPPED IN THIS BODY FOR-EVER IF I LIE!
BRAVE WORDS, SIR TRISTAN... AND THERE IS A WAY TO TEST YOUR VOW...
...FOR THE SWORD EXCALIBUR MAY CLEAVE TRUTH FROM FALSEHOOD...
AND IT WILL SLAY ANYONE WHO LIES WHILE HOLDING IT! TAKE IT, TRISTAN...AND SPEAK!
I SWEAR I DID NOT BETRAY MERLIN.
...WELL, SIRE...?
YOU HAVE PASSED THE TEST, MY KNIGHT...

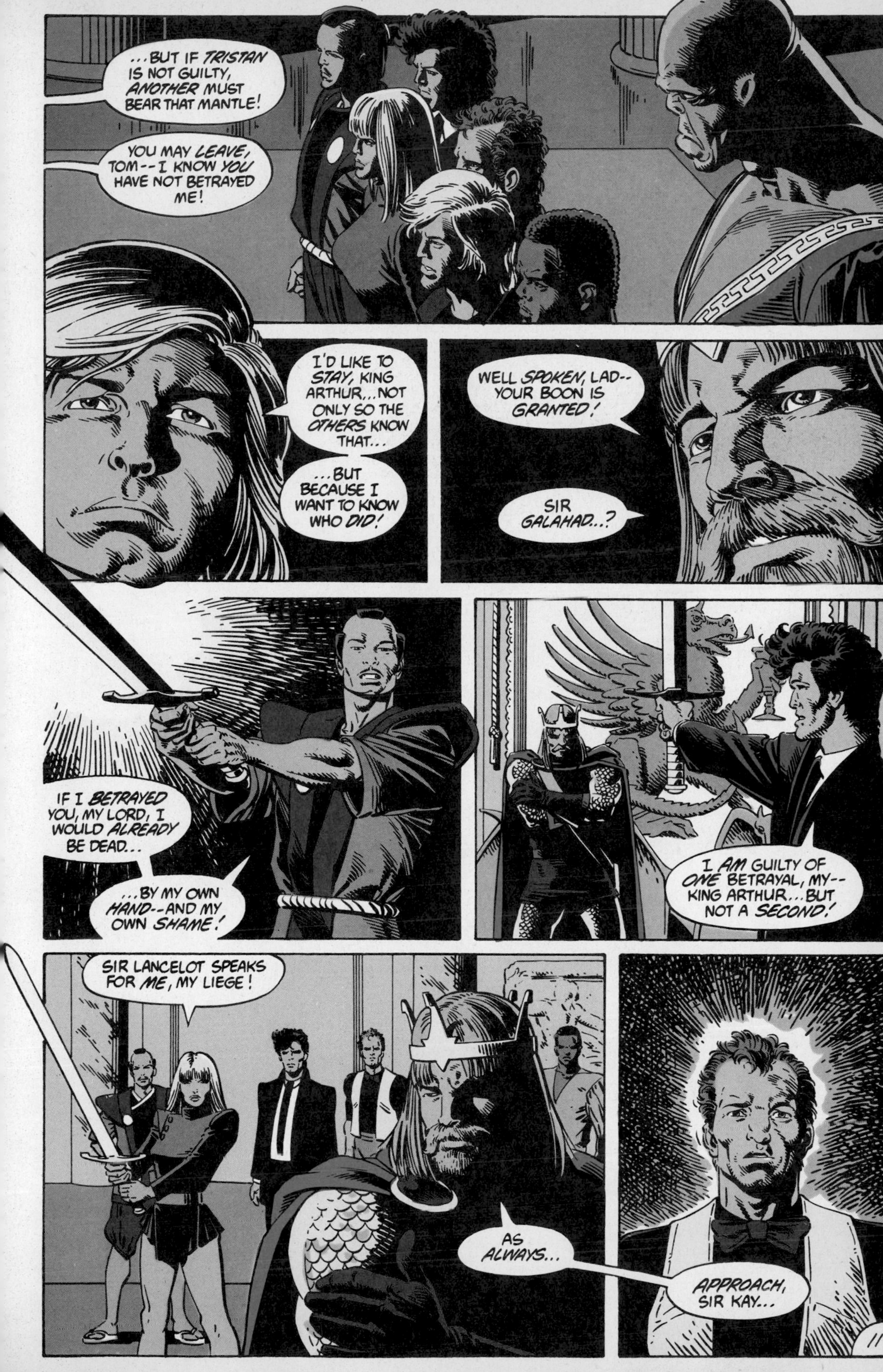
...BUT IF TRISTAN IS NOT GUILTY, ANOTHER MUST BEAR THAT MANTLE!
YOU MAY LEAVE, TOM--I KNOW YOU HAVE NOT BETRAYED ME!
I'D LIKE TO STAY, KING ARTHUR,..NOT ONLY SO THE OTHERS KNOW THAT...
...BUT BECAUSE I WANT TO KNOW WHO DID!
WELL SPOKEN, LAD--YOUR BOON IS GRANTED!
SIR GALAHAD...?
IF I BETRAYED YOU, MY LORD, I WOULD ALREADY BE DEAD...
...BY MY OWN HAND--AND MY OWN SHAME!
I AM GUILTY OF ONE BETRAYAL, MY--KING ARTHUR...BUT NOT A SECOND!
SIR LANCELOT SPEAKS FOR ME, MY LIEGE!
AS ALWAYS...
APPROACH, SIR KAY...

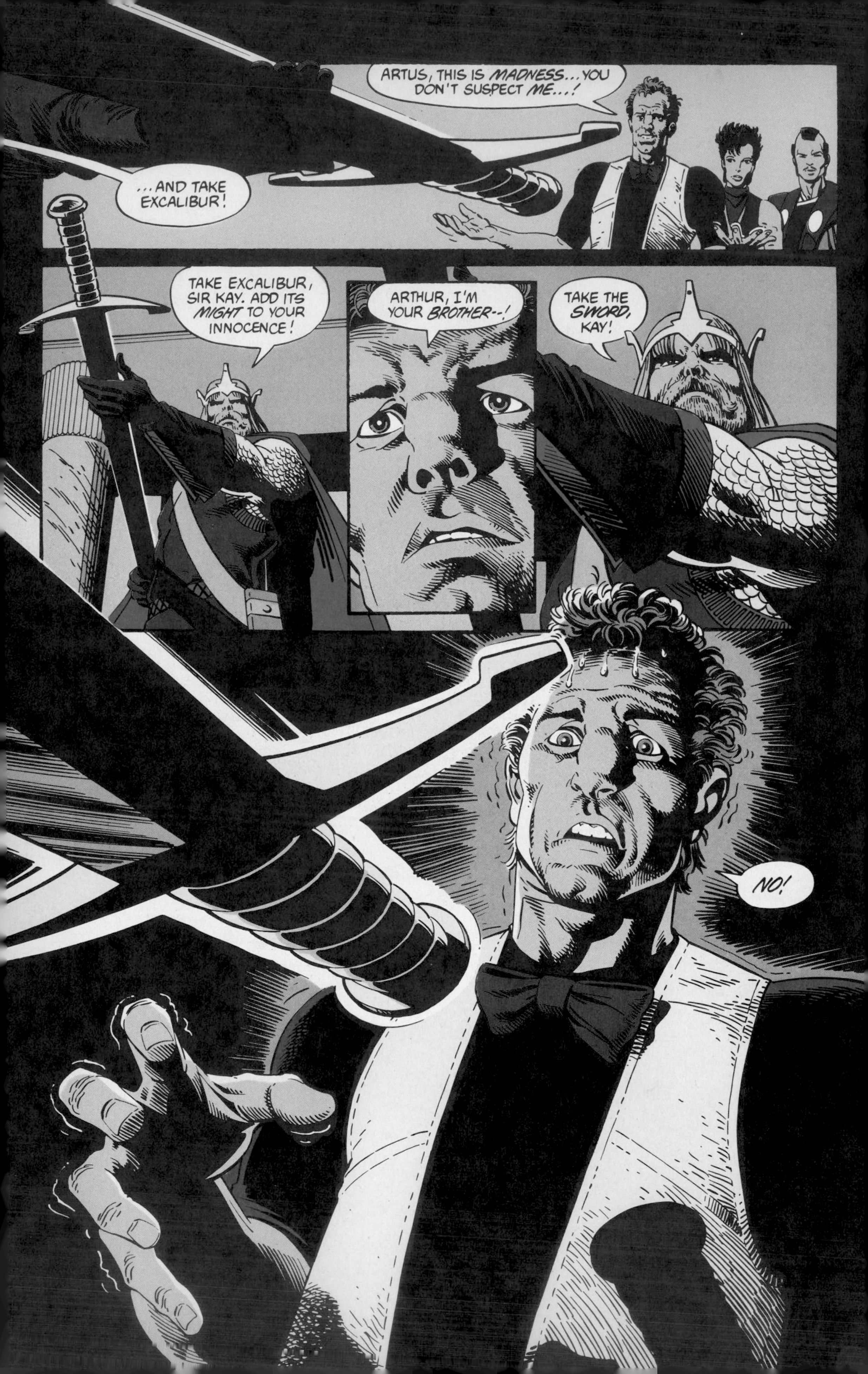
ARTUS, THIS IS MADNESS... YOU DON'T SUSPECT ME...!
...AND TAKE EXCALIBUR!
TAKE EXCALIBUR, SIR KAY. ADD ITS MIGHT TO YOUR INNOCENCE!
ARTHUR, I'M YOUR BROTHER--!
TAKE THE SWORD, KAY!
NO!

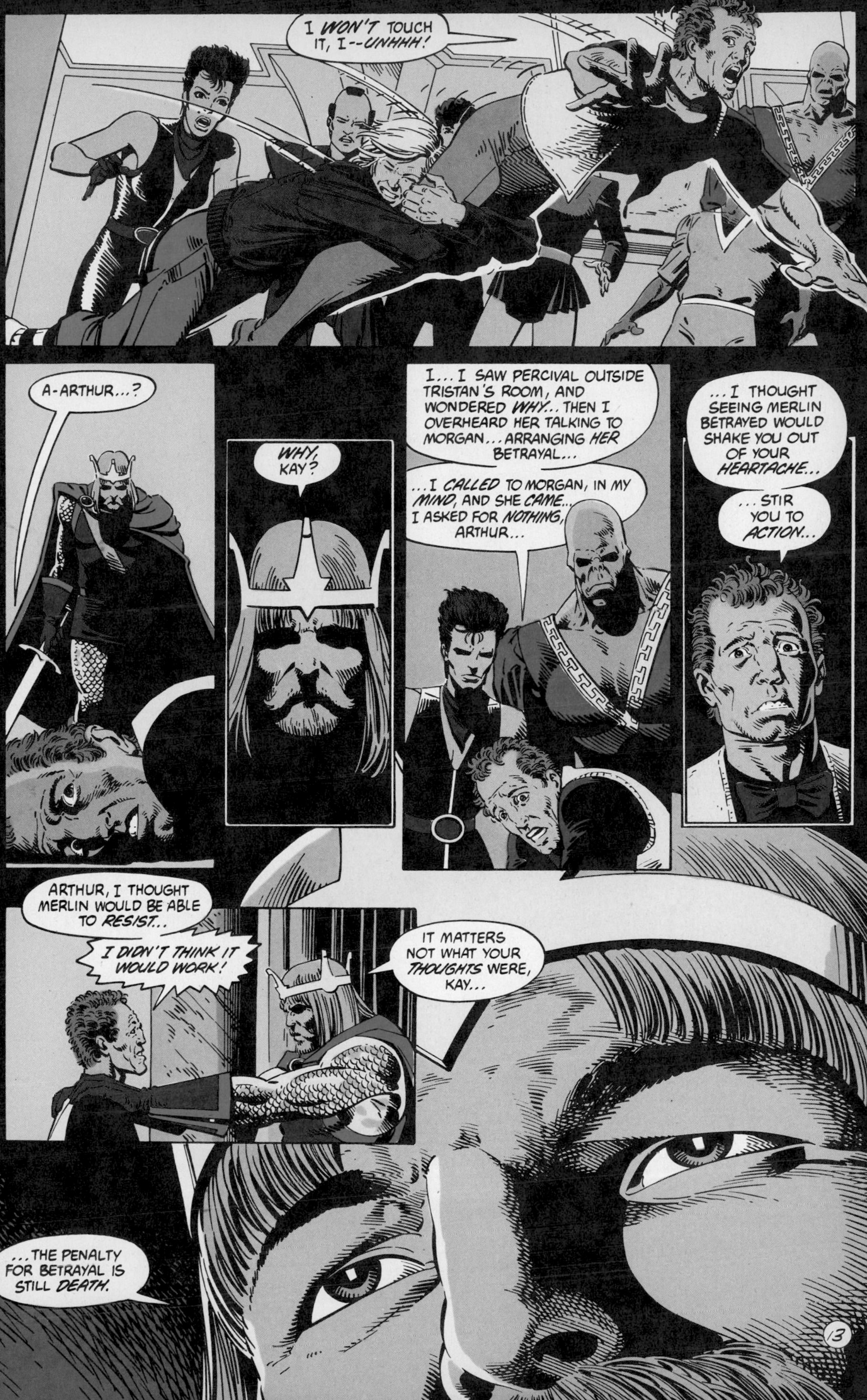

I WON'T TOUCH IT, I--UNHHH!
A-ARTHUR...?
WHY, KAY?
I... I SAW PERCIVAL OUTSIDE TRISTAN'S ROOM, AND WONDERED WHY... THEN I OVERHEARD HER TALKING TO MORGAN... ARRANGING HER BETRAYAL...
...I CALLED TO MORGAN, IN MY MIND, AND SHE CAME... I ASKED FOR NOTHING, ARTHUR...
...I THOUGHT SEEING MERLIN BETRAYED WOULD SHAKE YOU OUT OF YOUR HEARTACHE...
...STIR YOU TO ACTION...
ARTHUR, I THOUGHT MERLIN WOULD BE ABLE TO RESIST...
I DIDN'T THINK IT WOULD WORK!
IT MATTERS NOT WHAT YOUR THOUGHTS WERE, KAY...
...THE PENALTY FOR BETRAYAL IS STILL DEATH.

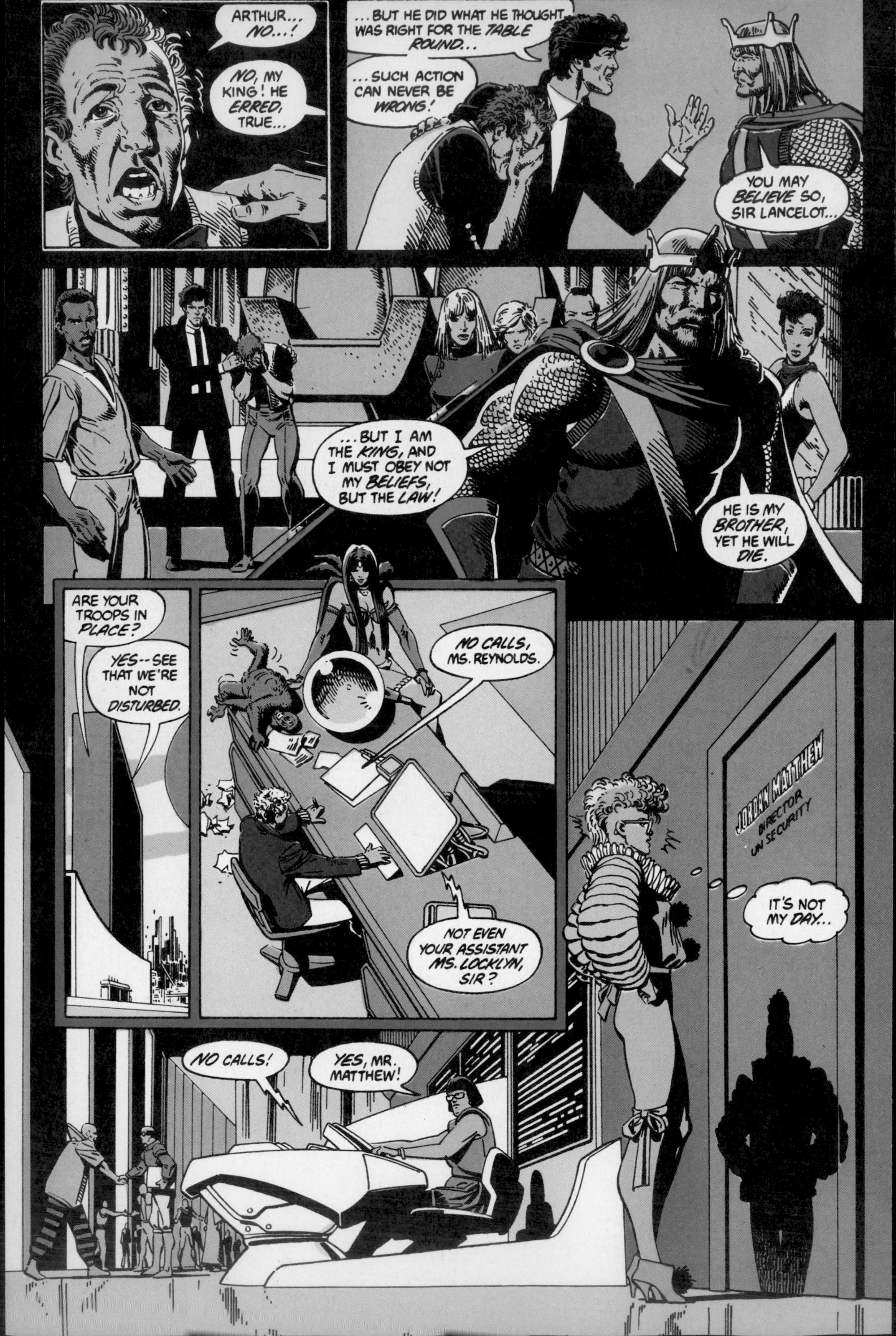
ARTHUR... NO...!
NO, MY KING! HE ERRED, TRUE...
...BUT HE DID WHAT HE THOUGHT WAS RIGHT FOR THE TABLE ROUND...
...SUCH ACTION CAN NEVER BE WRONG!
YOU MAY BELIEVE SO, SIR LANCELOT...
...BUT I AM THE KING, AND I MUST OBEY NOT MY BELIEFS, BUT THE LAW!
HE IS MY BROTHER, YET HE WILL DIE.
ARE YOUR TROOPS IN PLACE?
YES--SEE THAT WE'RE NOT DISTURBED.
NO CALLS, MS. REYNOLDS.
NOT EVEN YOUR ASSISTANT MS. LOCKLYN, SIR?
JORDAN MATTHEW
DIRECTOR
UN SECURITY
IT'S NOT MY DAY...
NO CALLS!
YES, MR. MATTHEW!

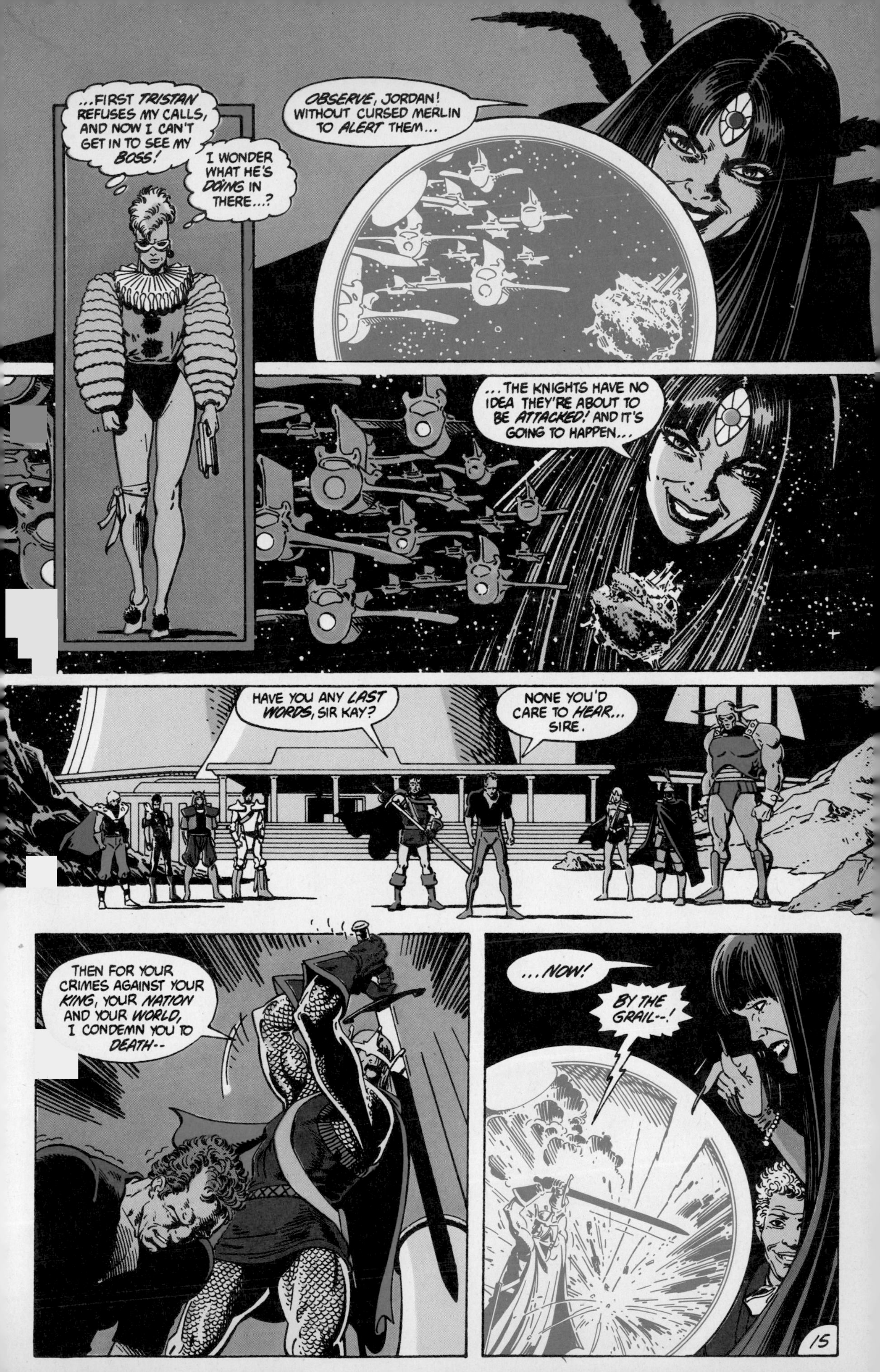

...FIRST TRISTAN REFUSES MY CALLS, AND NOW I CAN'T GET IN TO SEE MY BOSS!
I WONDER WHAT HE'S DOING IN THERE...?
OBSERVE, JORDAN! WITHOUT CURSED MERLIN TO ALERT THEM...
...THE KNIGHTS HAVE NO IDEA THEY'RE ABOUT TO BE ATTACKED! AND IT'S GOING TO HAPPEN...
HAVE YOU ANY LAST WORDS, SIR KAY?
NONE YOU'D CARE TO HEAR... SIRE.
THEN FOR YOUR CRIMES AGAINST YOUR KING, YOUR NATION AND YOUR WORLD, I CONDEMN YOU TO DEATH--
...NOW!
BY THE GRAIL--!

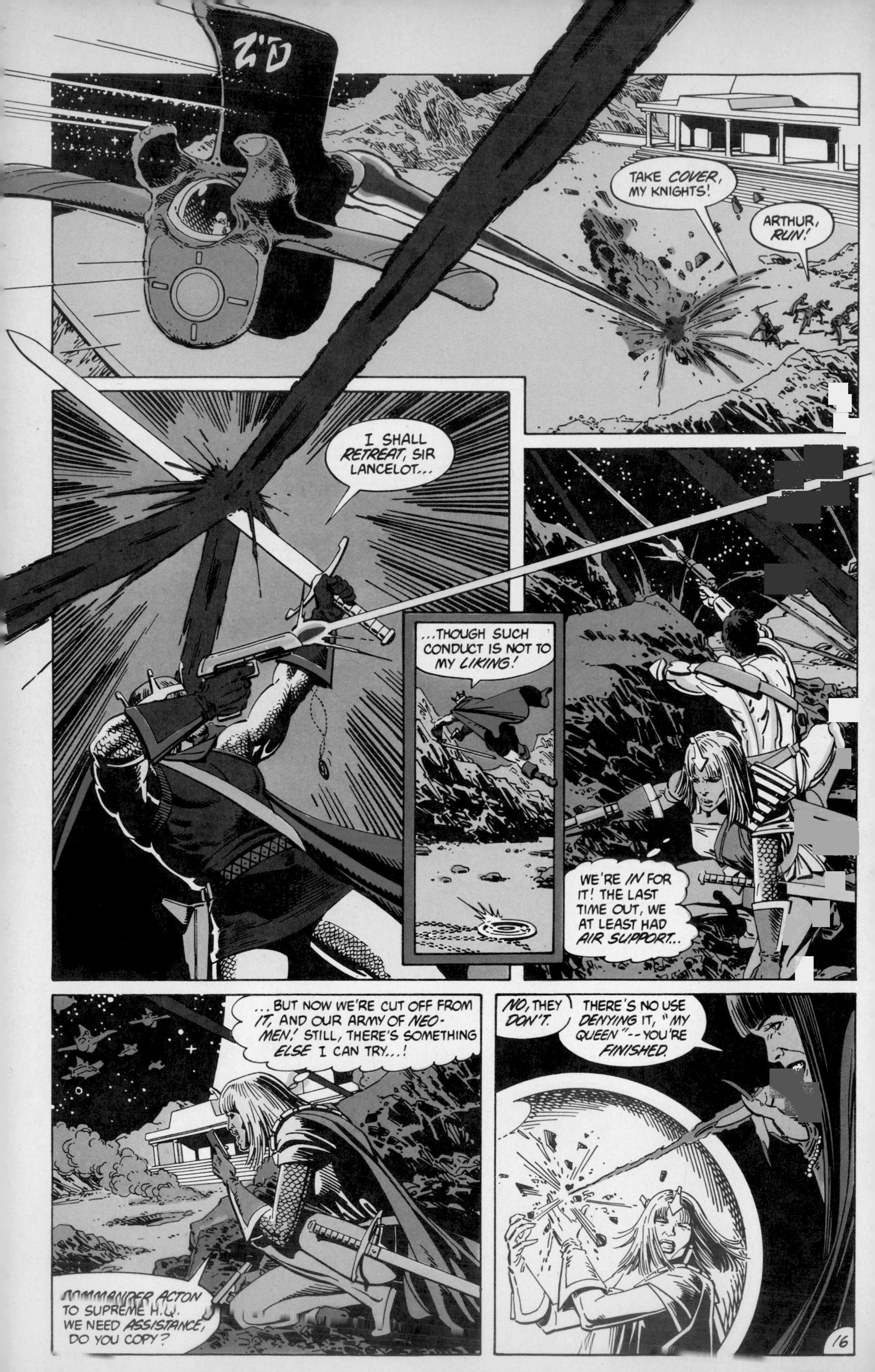
TAKE COVER, MY KNIGHTS!
ARTHUR, RUN!
I SHALL RETREAT, SIR LANCELOT...
...THOUGH SUCH CONDUCT IS NOT TO MY LIKING!
WE'RE IN FOR IT! THE LAST TIME OUT, WE AT LEAST HAD AIR SUPPORT...
...BUT NOW WE'RE CUT OFF FROM IT, AND OUR ARMY OF NEO-MEN! STILL, THERE'S SOMETHING ELSE I CAN TRY...!
COMMANDER ACTON TO SUPREME H.Q. WE NEED ASSISTANCE, DO YOU COPY?
NO, THEY DON'T.
THERE'S NO USE DENYING IT, "MY QUEEN"--YOU'RE FINISHED.

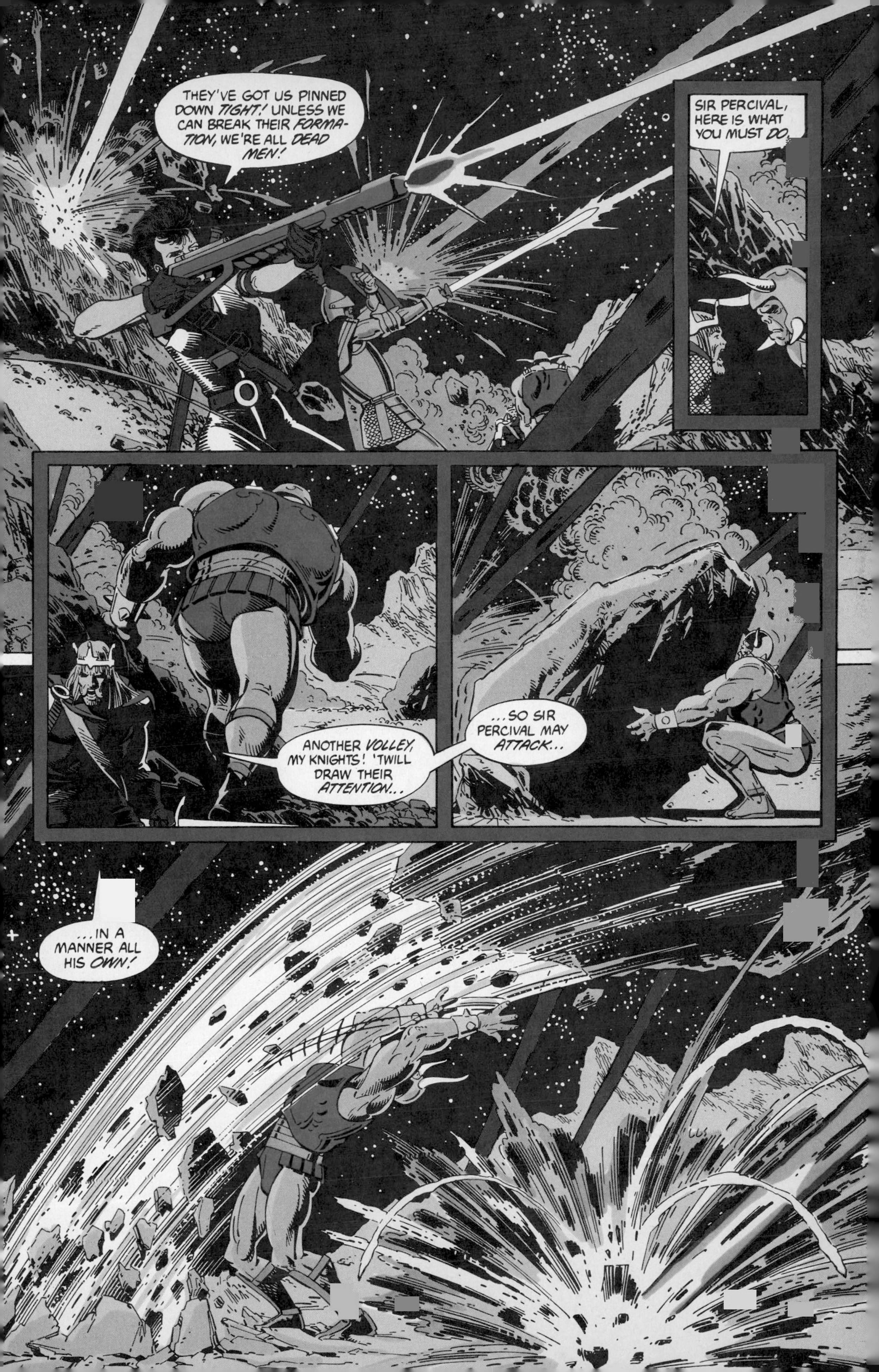
THEY'VE GOT US PINNED DOWN TIGHT! UNLESS WE CAN BREAK THEIR FORMATION, WE'RE ALL DEAD MEN!
SIR PERCIVAL, HERE IS WHAT YOU MUST DO.
ANOTHER VOLLEY, MY KNIGHTS! 'TWILL DRAW THEIR ATTENTION...
...SO SIR PERCIVAL MAY ATTACK...
...IN A MANNER ALL HIS OWN!

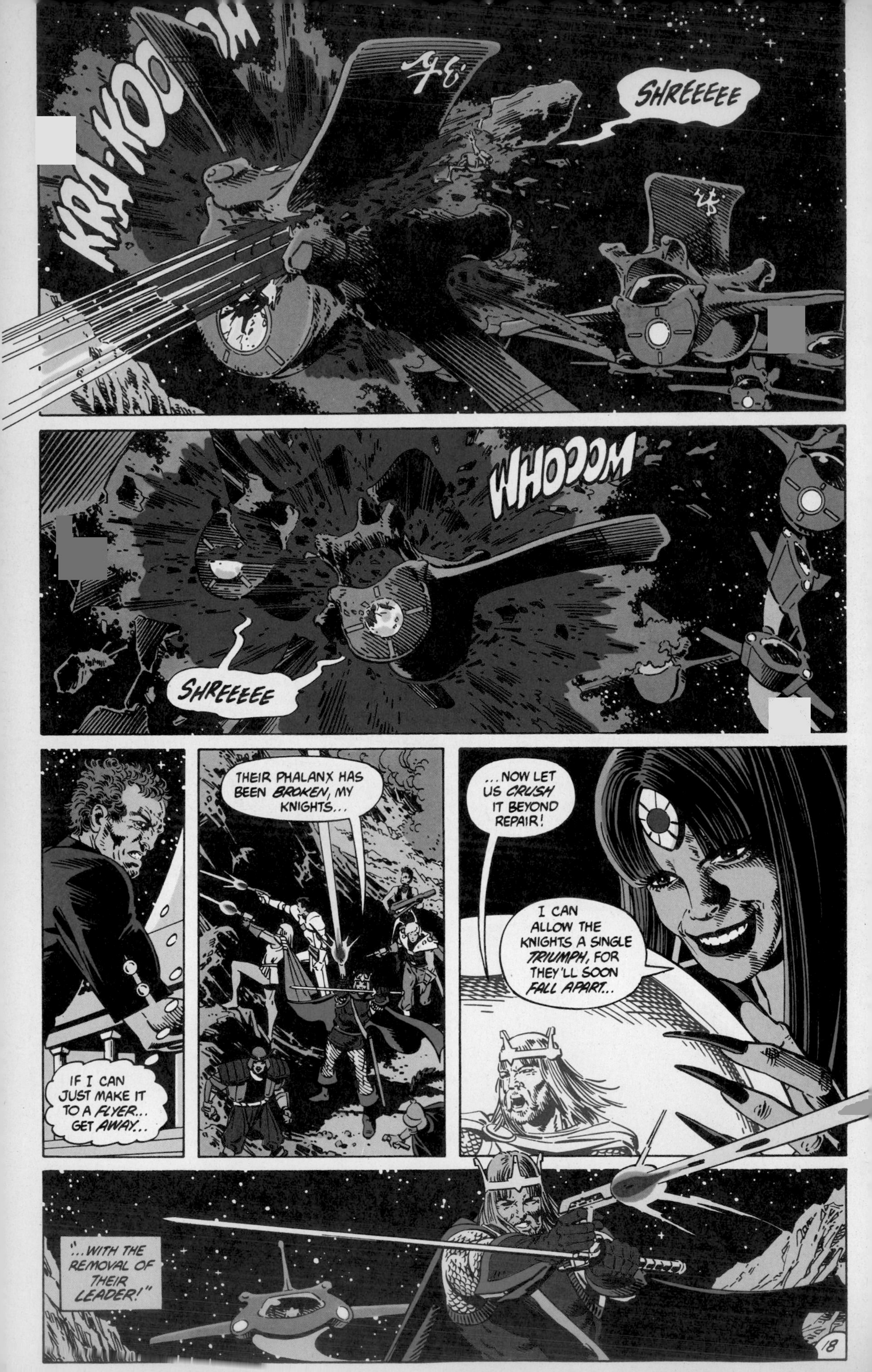
KRA-KOOOM
SHREEEEE
WHOOOM
SHREEEEE
IF I CAN JUST MAKE IT TO A FLYER... GET AWAY...
THEIR PHALANX HAS BEEN BROKEN, MY KNIGHTS...
...NOW LET US CRUSH IT BEYOND REPAIR!
I CAN ALLOW THE KNIGHTS A SINGLE TRIUMPH, FOR THEY'LL SOON FALL APART...
"...WITH THE REMOVAL OF THEIR LEADER!"

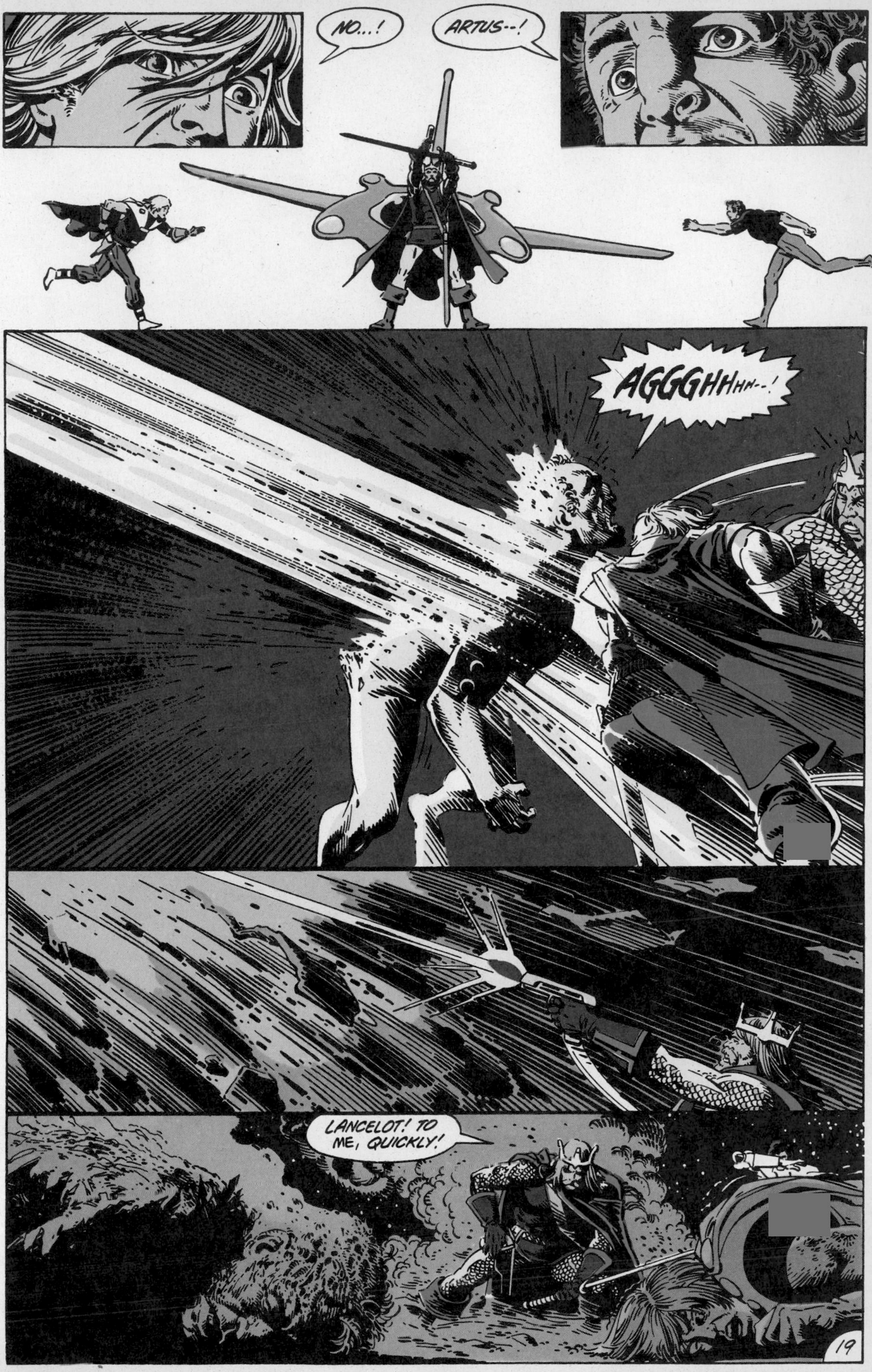
NO...!
ARTUS--!
AGGGHHhh--!
LANCELOT! TO ME, QUICKLY!

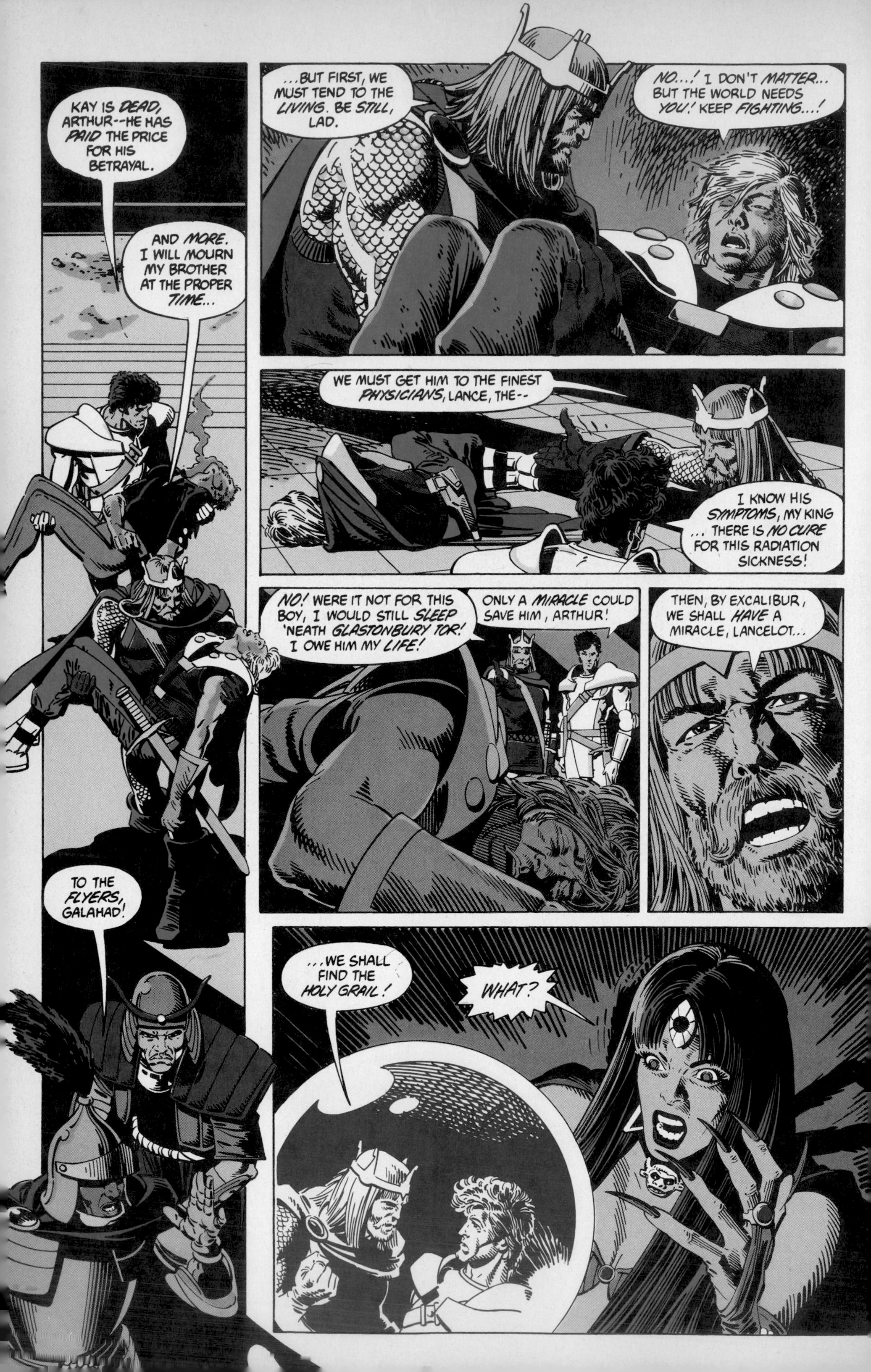
KAY IS DEAD, ARTHUR--HE HAS PAID THE PRICE FOR HIS BETRAYAL.
AND MORE. I WILL MOURN MY BROTHER AT THE PROPER TIME...
...BUT FIRST, WE MUST TEND TO THE LIVING. BE STILL, LAD.
NO...! I DON'T MATTER... BUT THE WORLD NEEDS YOU! KEEP FIGHTING...!
WE MUST GET HIM TO THE FINEST PHYSICIANS, LANCE, THE--
I KNOW HIS SYMPTOMS, MY KING ... THERE IS NO CURE FOR THIS RADIATION SICKNESS!
NO! WERE IT NOT FOR THIS BOY, I WOULD STILL SLEEP 'NEATH GLASTONBURY TOR! I OWE HIM MY LIFE!
ONLY A MIRACLE COULD SAVE HIM, ARTHUR!
THEN, BY EXCALIBUR, WE SHALL HAVE A MIRACLE, LANCELOT...
TO THE FLYERS, GALAHAD!
...WE SHALL FIND THE HOLY GRAIL!
WHAT?

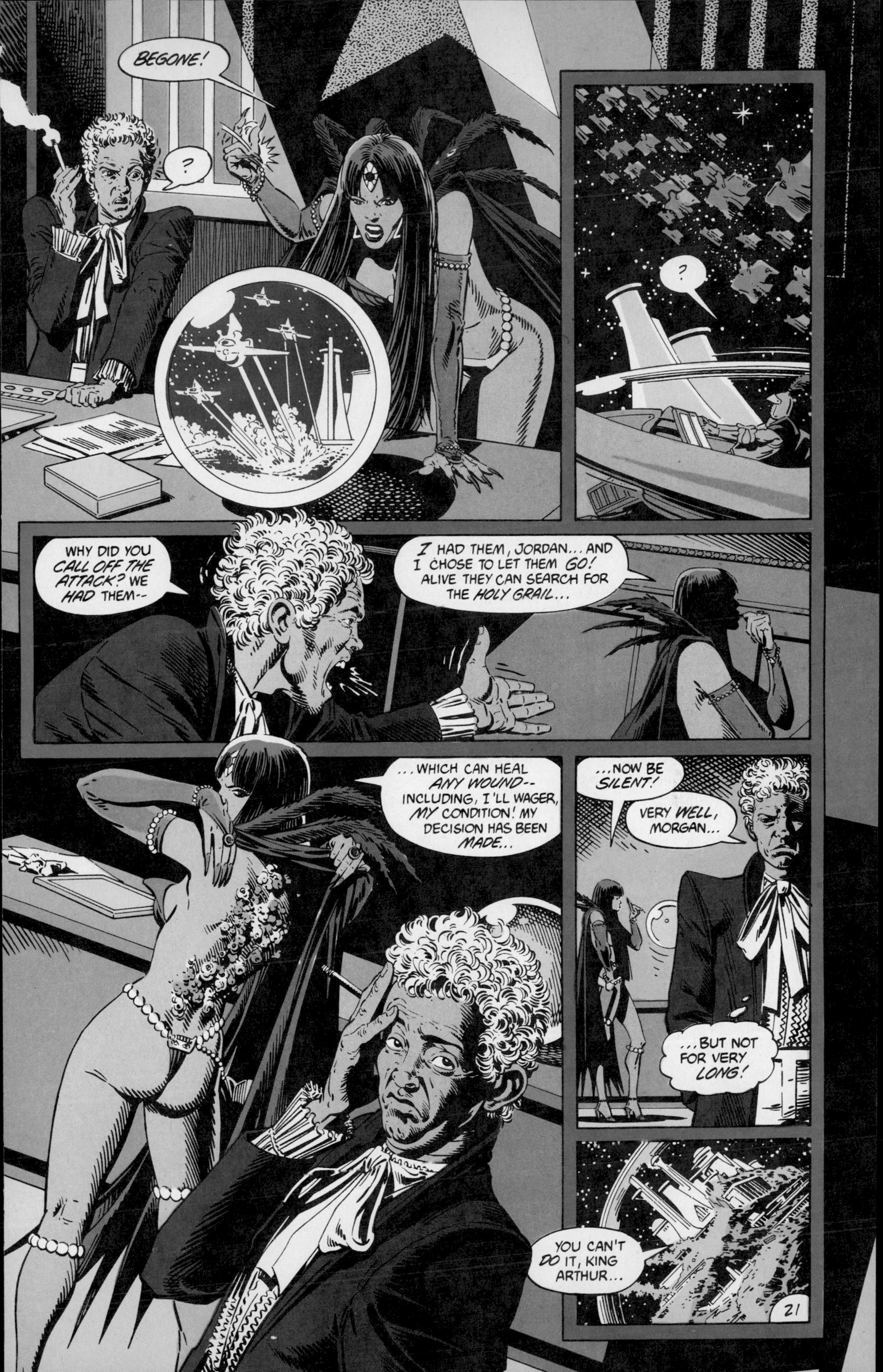
BEGONE!
?
?
WHY DID YOU CALL OFF THE ATTACK? WE HAD THEM--
I HAD THEM, JORDAN... AND I CHOSE TO LET THEM GO! ALIVE THEY CAN SEARCH FOR THE HOLY GRAIL...
...WHICH CAN HEAL ANY WOUND-- INCLUDING, I'LL WAGER, MY CONDITION! MY DECISION HAS BEEN MADE...
...NOW BE SILENT!
VERY WELL, MORGAN...
...BUT NOT FOR VERY LONG!
YOU CAN'T DO IT, KING ARTHUR...
21

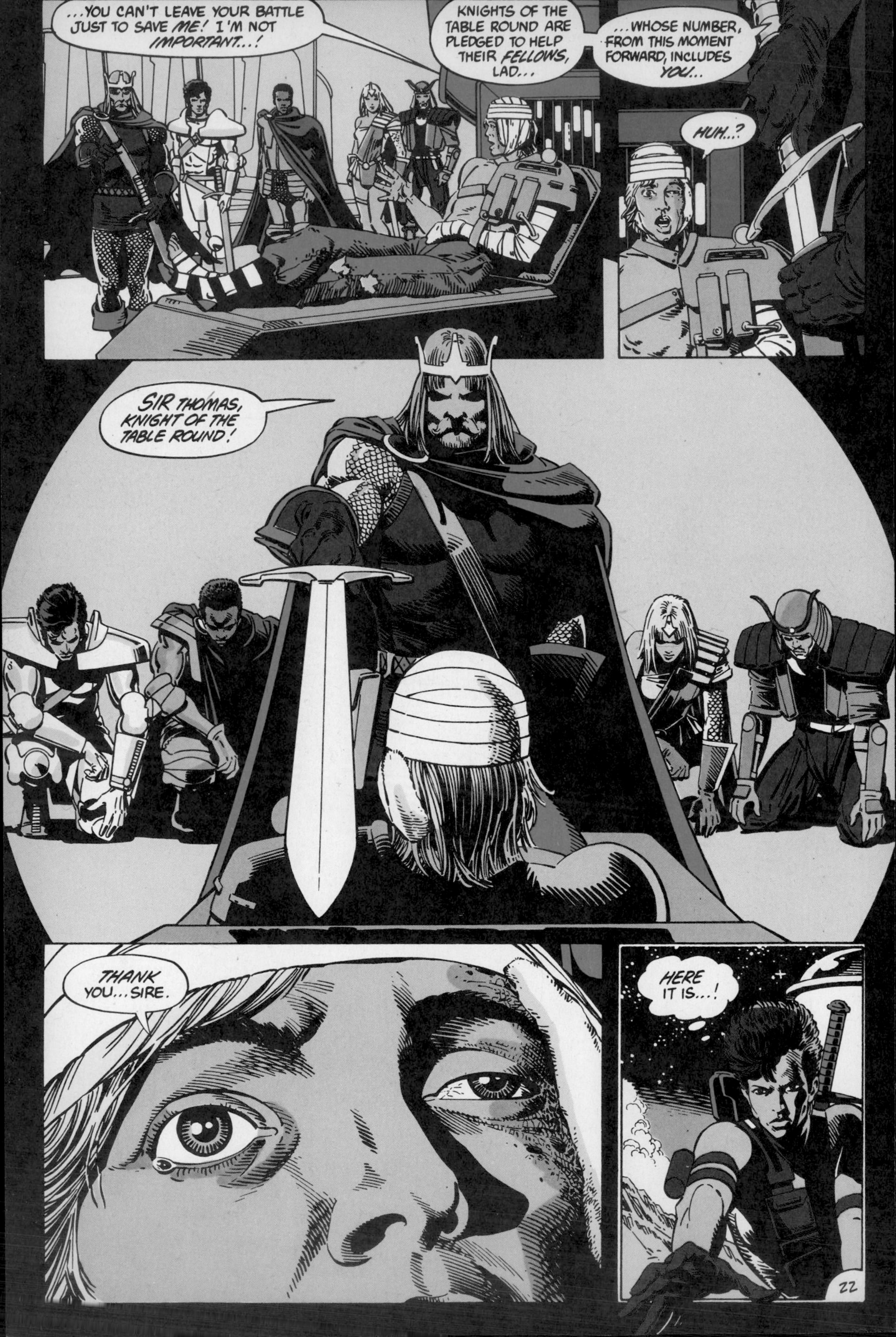
...YOU CAN'T LEAVE YOUR BATTLE JUST TO SAVE ME! I'M NOT IMPORTANT...!
KNIGHTS OF THE TABLE ROUND ARE PLEDGED TO HELP THEIR FELLOWS, LAD...
...WHOSE NUMBER, FROM THIS MOMENT FORWARD, INCLUDES YOU...
HUH...?
SIR THOMAS, KNIGHT OF THE TABLE ROUND!
THANK YOU... SIRE.
HERE IT IS...!
22

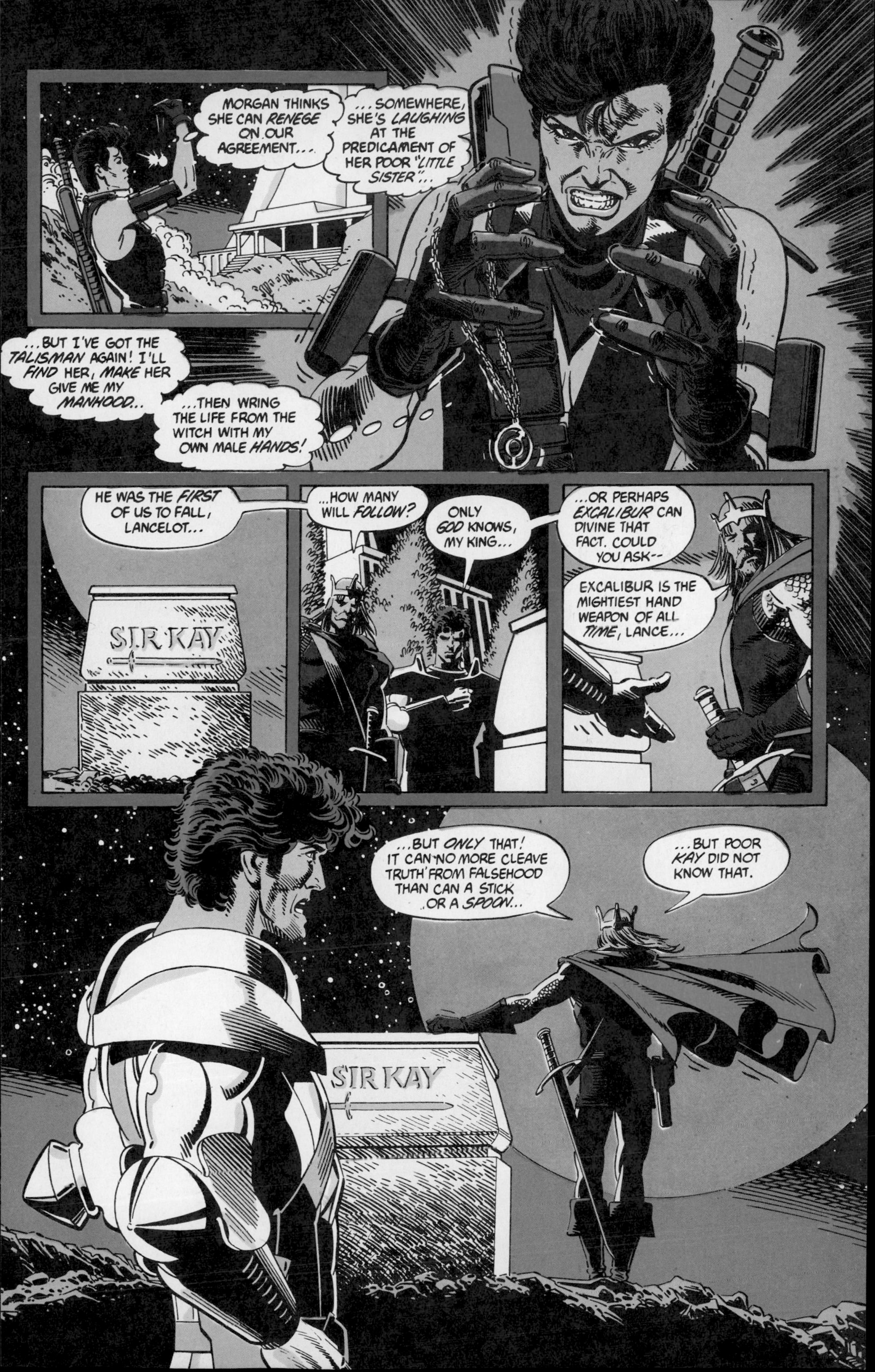

MORGAN THINKS SHE CAN RENEGE ON OUR AGREEMENT...
...SOMEWHERE, SHE'S LAUGHING AT THE PREDICAMENT OF HER POOR "LITTLE SISTER"...
...BUT I'VE GOT THE TALISMAN AGAIN! I'LL FIND HER, MAKE HER GIVE ME MY MANHOOD...
...THEN WRING THE LIFE FROM THE WITCH WITH MY OWN MALE HANDS!
HE WAS THE FIRST OF US TO FALL, LANCELOT...
SIR KAY
...HOW MANY WILL FOLLOW?
ONLY GOD KNOWS, MY KING...
...OR PERHAPS EXCALIBUR CAN DIVINE THAT FACT. COULD YOU ASK--
EXCALIBUR IS THE MIGHTIEST HAND WEAPON OF ALL TIME, LANCE...
...BUT ONLY THAT! IT CAN NO MORE CLEAVE TRUTH FROM FALSEHOOD THAN CAN A STICK OR A SPOON...
...BUT POOR KAY DID NOT KNOW THAT.
SIR KAY

chapter
9

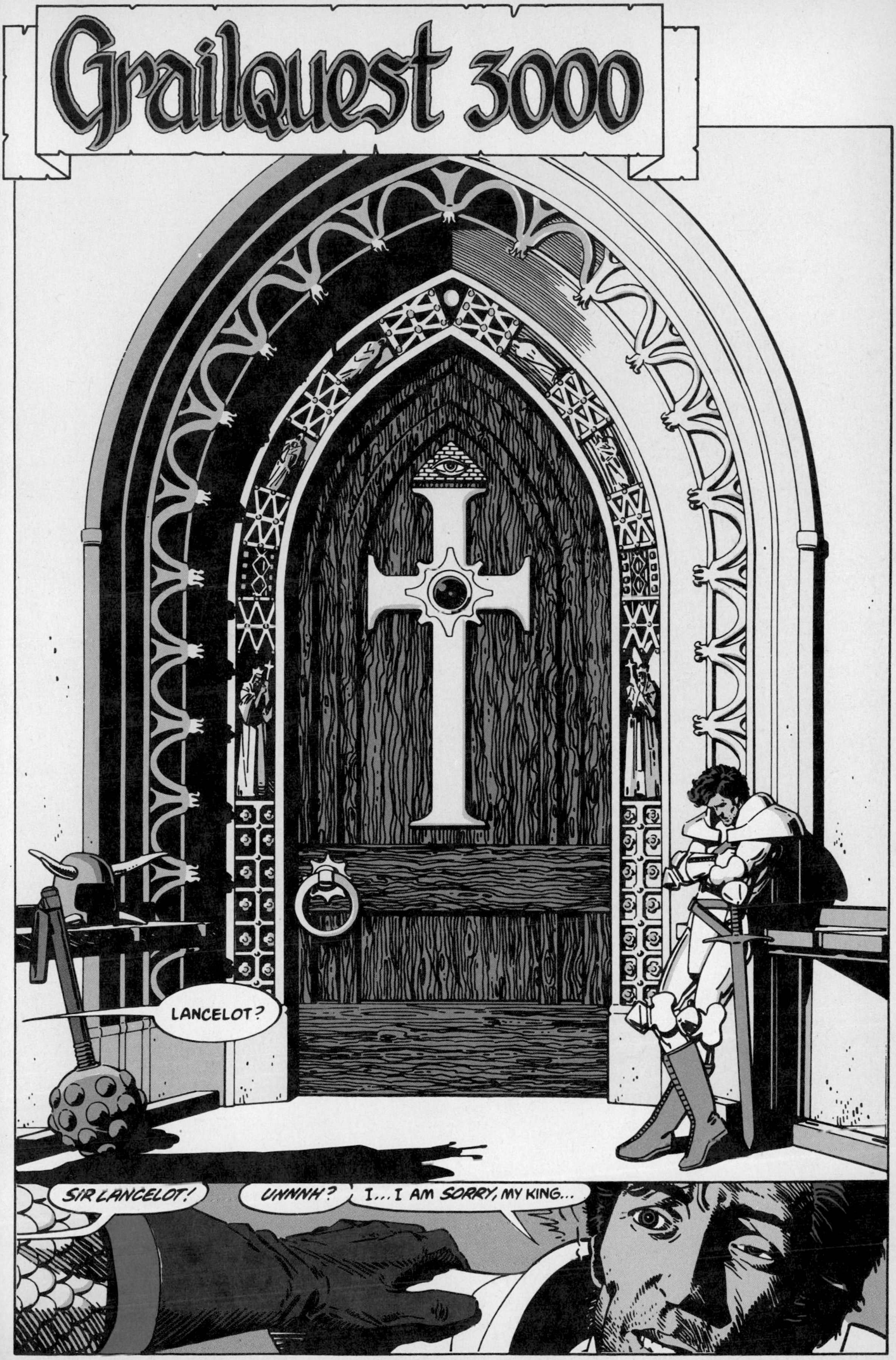
Grailquest 3000
LANCELOT?
SIR LANCELOT!
UNNNH?
I... I AM SORRY, MY KING...

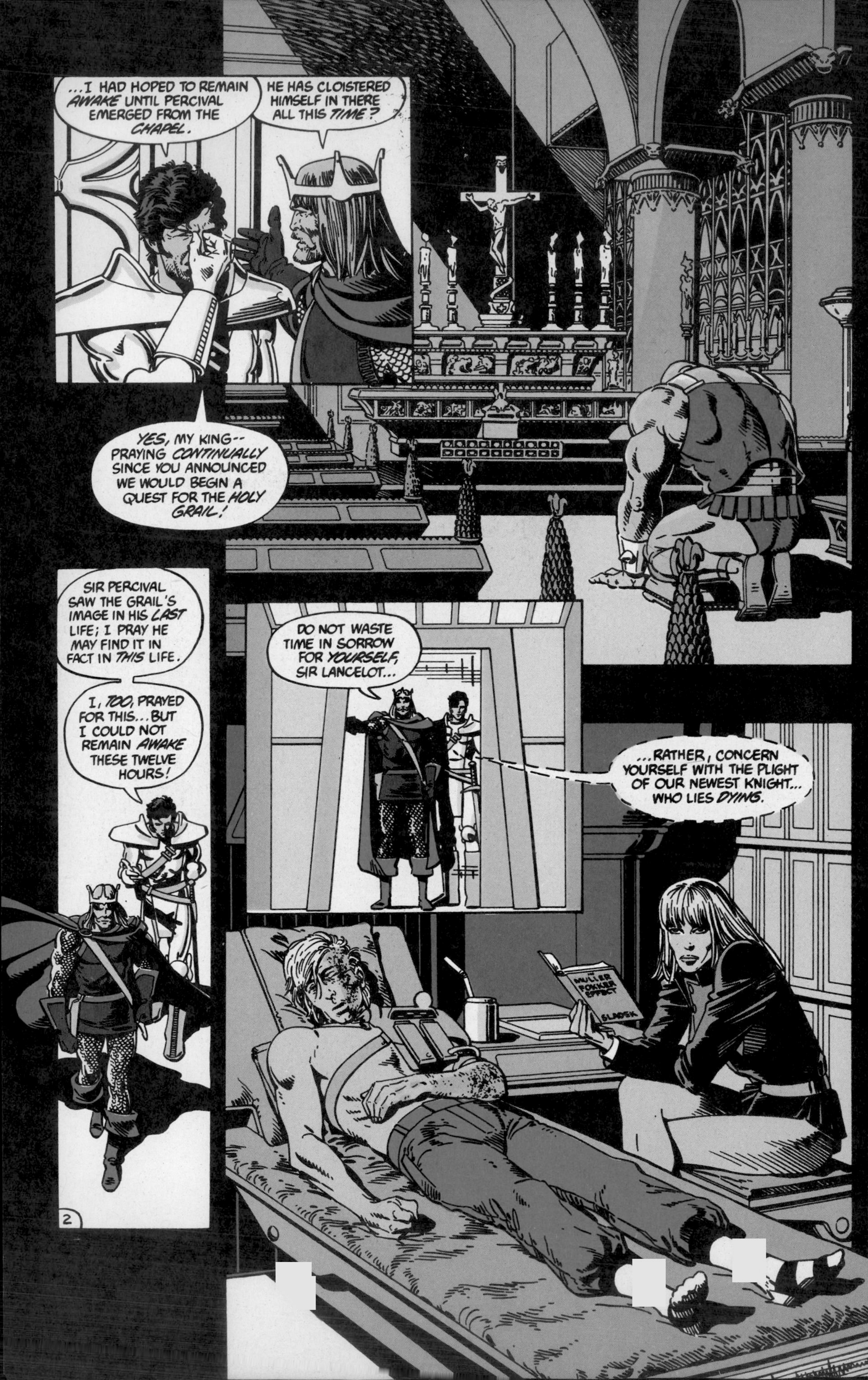
...I HAD HOPED TO REMAIN AWAKE UNTIL PERCIVAL EMERGED FROM THE CHAPEL.
HE HAS CLOISTERED HIMSELF IN THERE ALL THIS TIME?
YES, MY KING-- PRAYING CONTINUALLY SINCE YOU ANNOUNCED WE WOULD BEGIN A QUEST FOR THE HOLY GRAIL!
SIR PERCIVAL SAW THE GRAIL'S IMAGE IN HIS LAST LIFE; I PRAY HE MAY FIND IT IN FACT IN THIS LIFE.
I, TOO, PRAYED FOR THIS... BUT I COULD NOT REMAIN AWAKE THESE TWELVE HOURS!
DO NOT WASTE TIME IN SORROW FOR YOURSELF, SIR LANCELOT...
...RATHER, CONCERN YOURSELF WITH THE PLIGHT OF OUR NEWEST KNIGHT... WHO LIES DYING.
MULLER FOKKER EFFECT
SLADEK
2

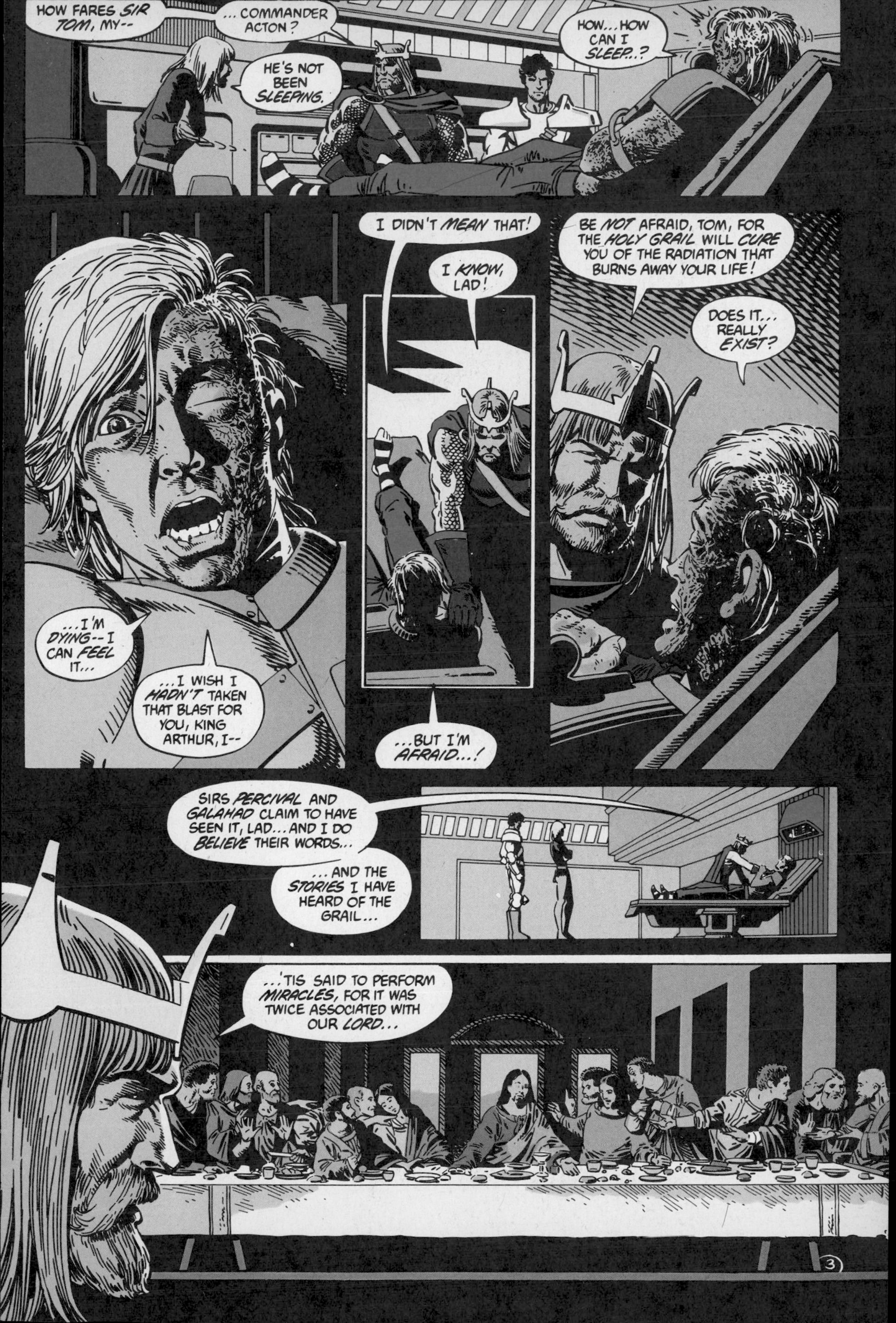

HOW FARES SIR TOM, MY--
...COMMANDER ACTON?
HE'S NOT BEEN SLEEPING.
HOW...HOW CAN I SLEEP...?
...I'M DYING--I CAN FEEL IT...
...I WISH I HADN'T TAKEN THAT BLAST FOR YOU, KING ARTHUR, I--
I DIDN'T MEAN THAT!
I KNOW, LAD!
...BUT I'M AFRAID...!
BE NOT AFRAID, TOM, FOR THE HOLY GRAIL WILL CURE YOU OF THE RADIATION THAT BURNS AWAY YOUR LIFE!
DOES IT... REALLY EXIST?
SIRS PERCIVAL AND GALAHAD CLAIM TO HAVE SEEN IT, LAD...AND I DO BELIEVE THEIR WORDS...
...AND THE STORIES I HAVE HEARD OF THE GRAIL...
...'TIS SAID TO PERFORM MIRACLES, FOR IT WAS TWICE ASSOCIATED WITH OUR LORD...
3

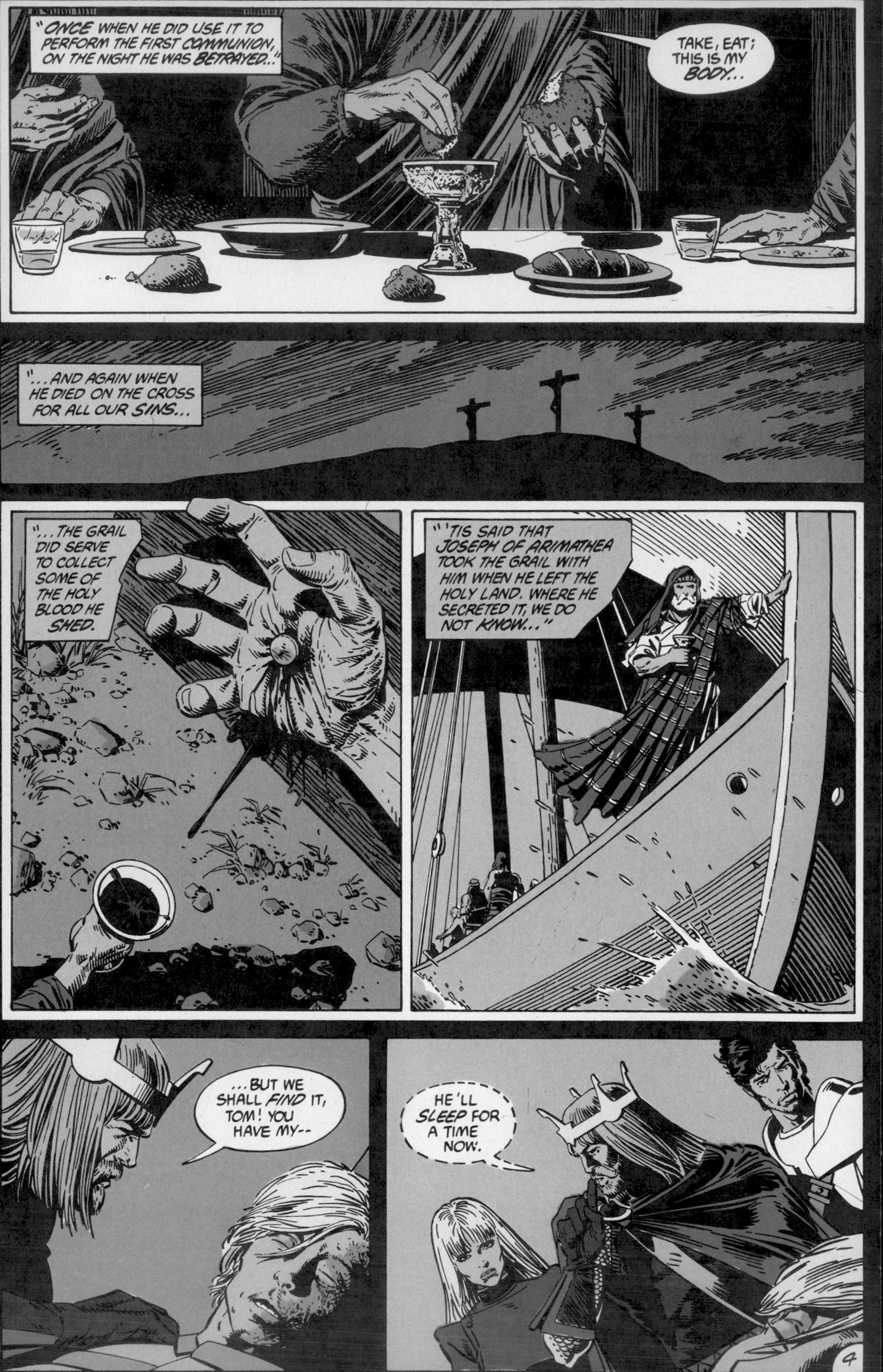
"ONCE WHEN HE DID USE IT TO PERFORM THE FIRST COMMUNION, ON THE NIGHT HE WAS BETRAYED..."
TAKE, EAT; THIS IS MY BODY...
"...AND AGAIN WHEN HE DIED ON THE CROSS FOR ALL OUR SINS...
"...THE GRAIL DID SERVE TO COLLECT SOME OF THE HOLY BLOOD HE SHED.
"'TIS SAID THAT JOSEPH OF ARIMATHEA TOOK THE GRAIL WITH HIM WHEN HE LEFT THE HOLY LAND. WHERE HE SECRETED IT, WE DO NOT KNOW..."
...BUT WE SHALL FIND IT, TOM! YOU HAVE MY--
HE'LL SLEEP FOR A TIME NOW.
4

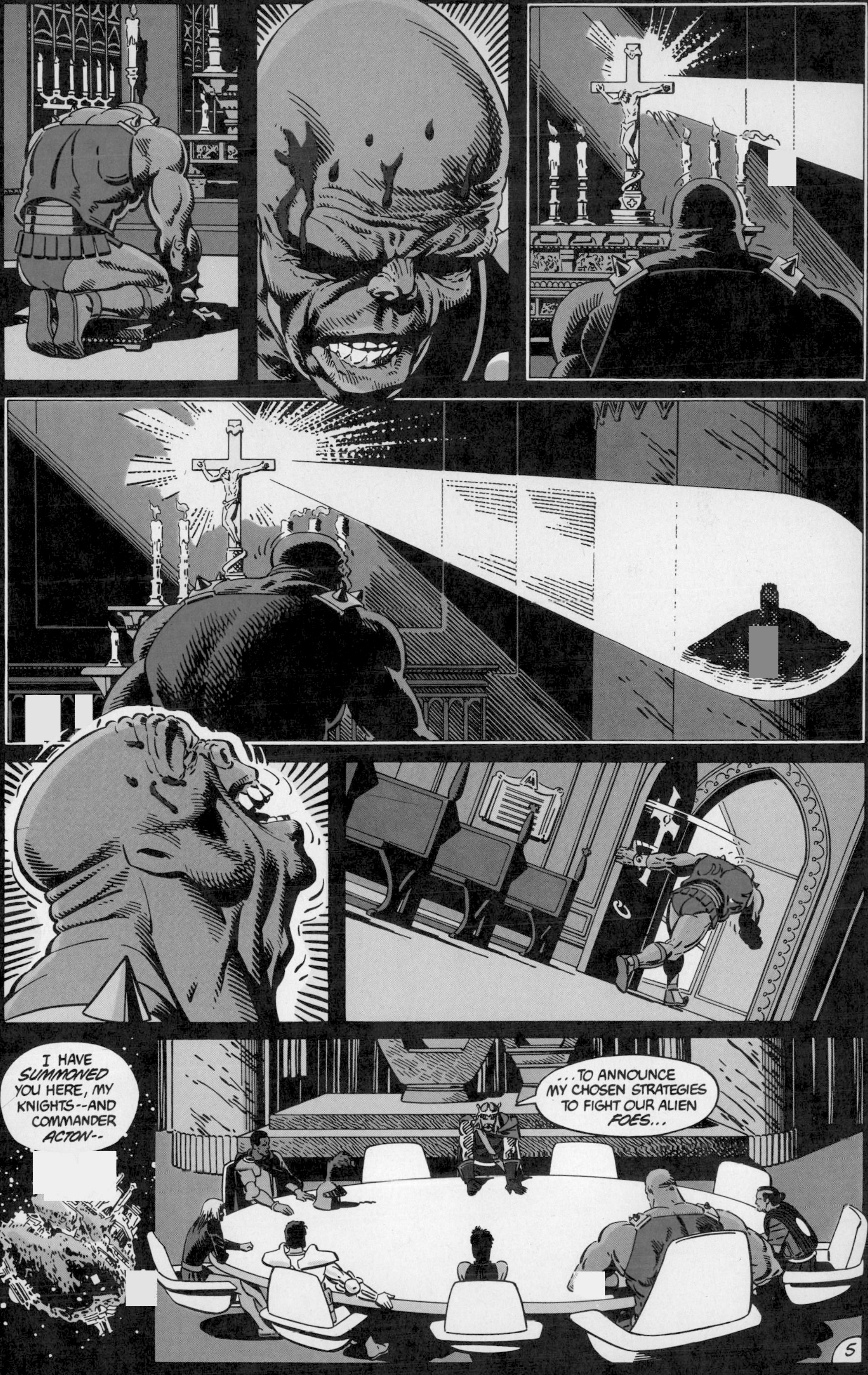
I HAVE SUMMONED YOU HERE, MY KNIGHTS--AND COMMANDER ACTON--
...TO ANNOUNCE MY CHOSEN STRATEGIES TO FIGHT OUR ALIEN FOES...

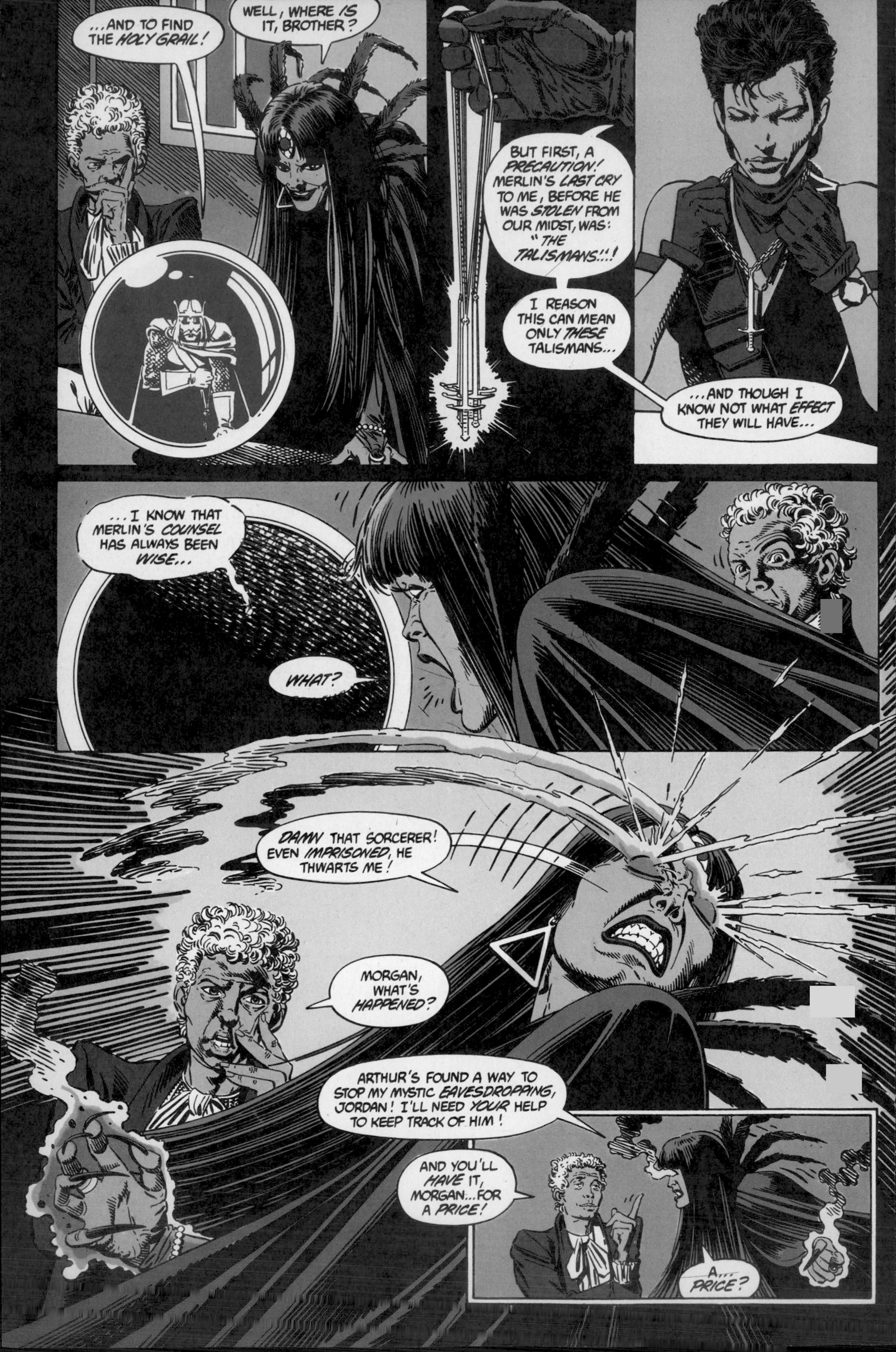
...AND TO FIND THE HOLY GRAIL!
WELL, WHERE IS IT, BROTHER?
BUT FIRST, A PRECAUTION! MERLIN'S LAST CRY TO ME, BEFORE HE WAS STOLEN FROM OUR MIDST, WAS: "THE TALISMANS!!!"
I REASON THIS CAN MEAN ONLY THESE TALISMANS...
...AND THOUGH I KNOW NOT WHAT EFFECT THEY WILL HAVE...
...I KNOW THAT MERLIN'S COUNSEL HAS ALWAYS BEEN WISE...
WHAT?
DAMN THAT SORCERER! EVEN IMPRISONED, HE THWARTS ME!
MORGAN, WHAT'S HAPPENED?
ARTHUR'S FOUND A WAY TO STOP MY MYSTIC EAVESDROPPING, JORDAN! I'LL NEED YOUR HELP TO KEEP TRACK OF HIM!
AND YOU'LL HAVE IT, MORGAN...FOR A PRICE!
A... PRICE?

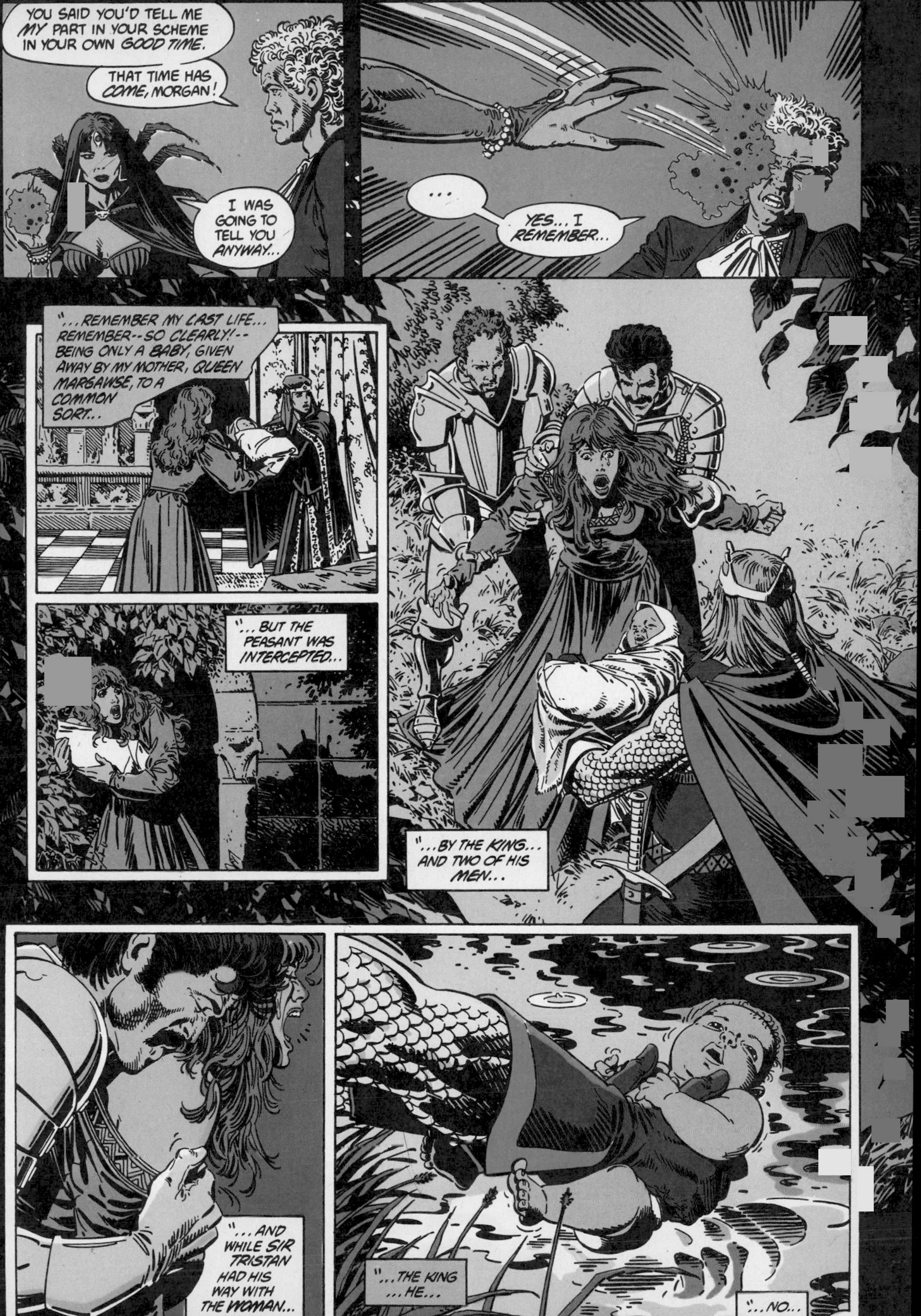

YOU SAID YOU'D TELL ME MY PART IN YOUR SCHEME IN YOUR OWN GOOD TIME.
THAT TIME HAS COME, MORGAN!
I WAS GOING TO TELL YOU ANYWAY...
...
YES... I REMEMBER...
"...REMEMBER MY LAST LIFE... REMEMBER--SO CLEARLY!--BEING ONLY A BABY, GIVEN AWAY BY MY MOTHER, QUEEN MARGAWSE, TO A COMMON SORT...
"...BUT THE PEASANT WAS INTERCEPTED...
"...BY THE KING... AND TWO OF HIS MEN...
"...AND WHILE SIR TRISTAN HAD HIS WAY WITH THE WOMAN...
"...THE KING ...HE...
"...NO...

"...NO..."

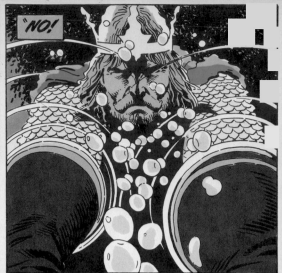
"NO!"

"...HE...HE THOUGHT ME DEAD...
AND LEFT ME TO BE BURIED,
WITH THE OTHER MALE
CHILDREN HE HAD KILLED...
BEFORE FINDING ME..."

"...BUT I WAS
NOT DEAD...
I LIVED..."

I REMEMBER...
HOW COULD I EVER
HAVE *FORGOTTEN*
MY NEAR-DEATH AT
THE HANDS OF
*ARTHUR
PENDRAGON*...

"...AND I WAS TAKEN AWAY
AFTER *ALL*...TO LIVE IN
SPITE OF GOOD
KING ARTHUR'S
WILL!"

8

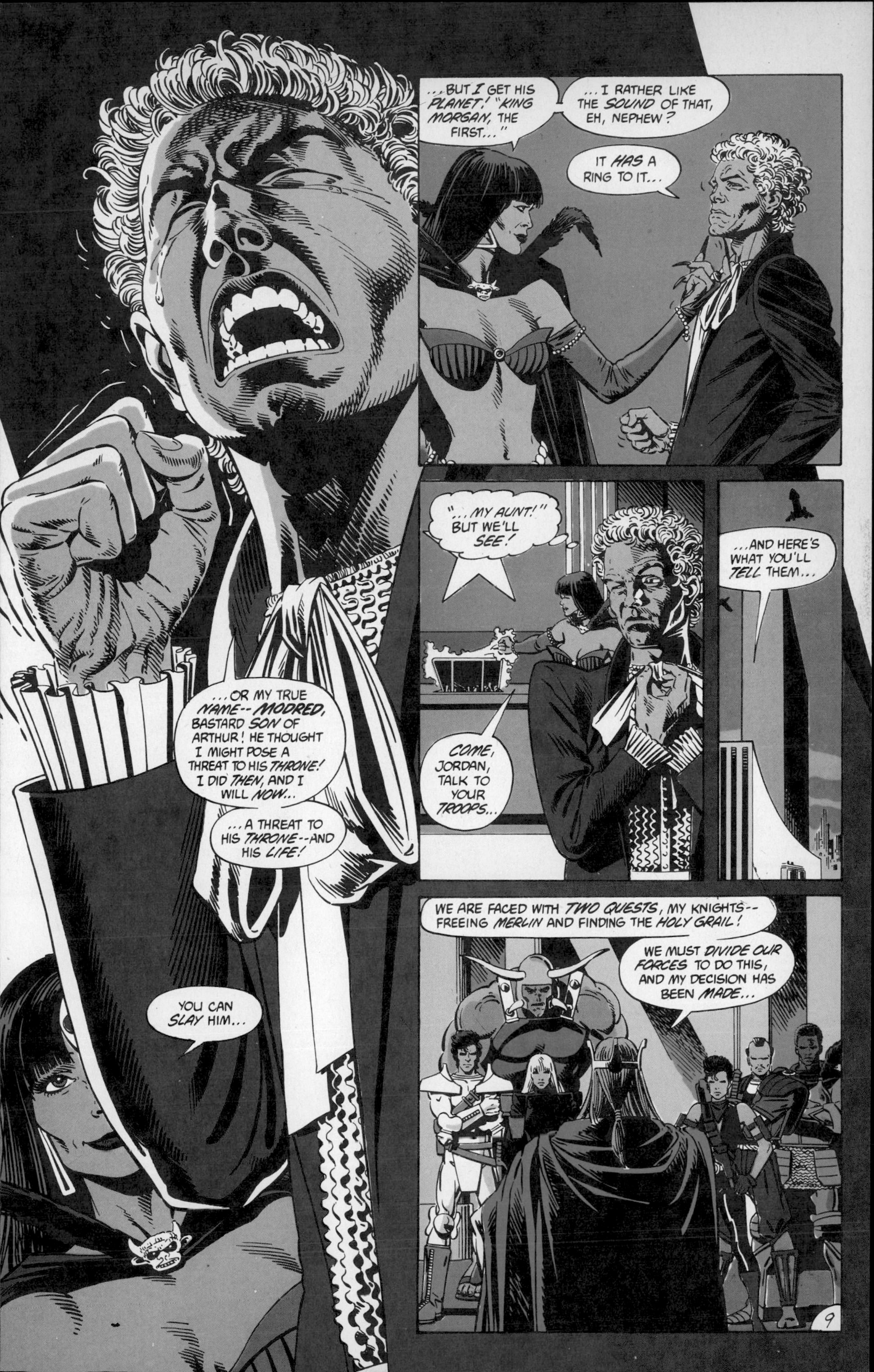

...BUT I GET HIS PLANET! "KING MORGAN, THE FIRST..."
...I RATHER LIKE THE SOUND OF THAT, EH, NEPHEW?
IT HAS A RING TO IT...
...OR MY TRUE NAME--MODRED, BASTARD SON OF ARTHUR! HE THOUGHT I MIGHT POSE A THREAT TO HIS THRONE! I DID THEN, AND I WILL NOW...
...A THREAT TO HIS THRONE--AND HIS LIFE!
YOU CAN SLAY HIM...
"...MY AUNT!" BUT WE'LL SEE!
COME, JORDAN, TALK TO YOUR TROOPS...
...AND HERE'S WHAT YOU'LL TELL THEM...
WE ARE FACED WITH TWO QUESTS, MY KNIGHTS--FREEING MERLIN AND FINDING THE HOLY GRAIL!
WE MUST DIVIDE OUR FORCES TO DO THIS, AND MY DECISION HAS BEEN MADE...
9

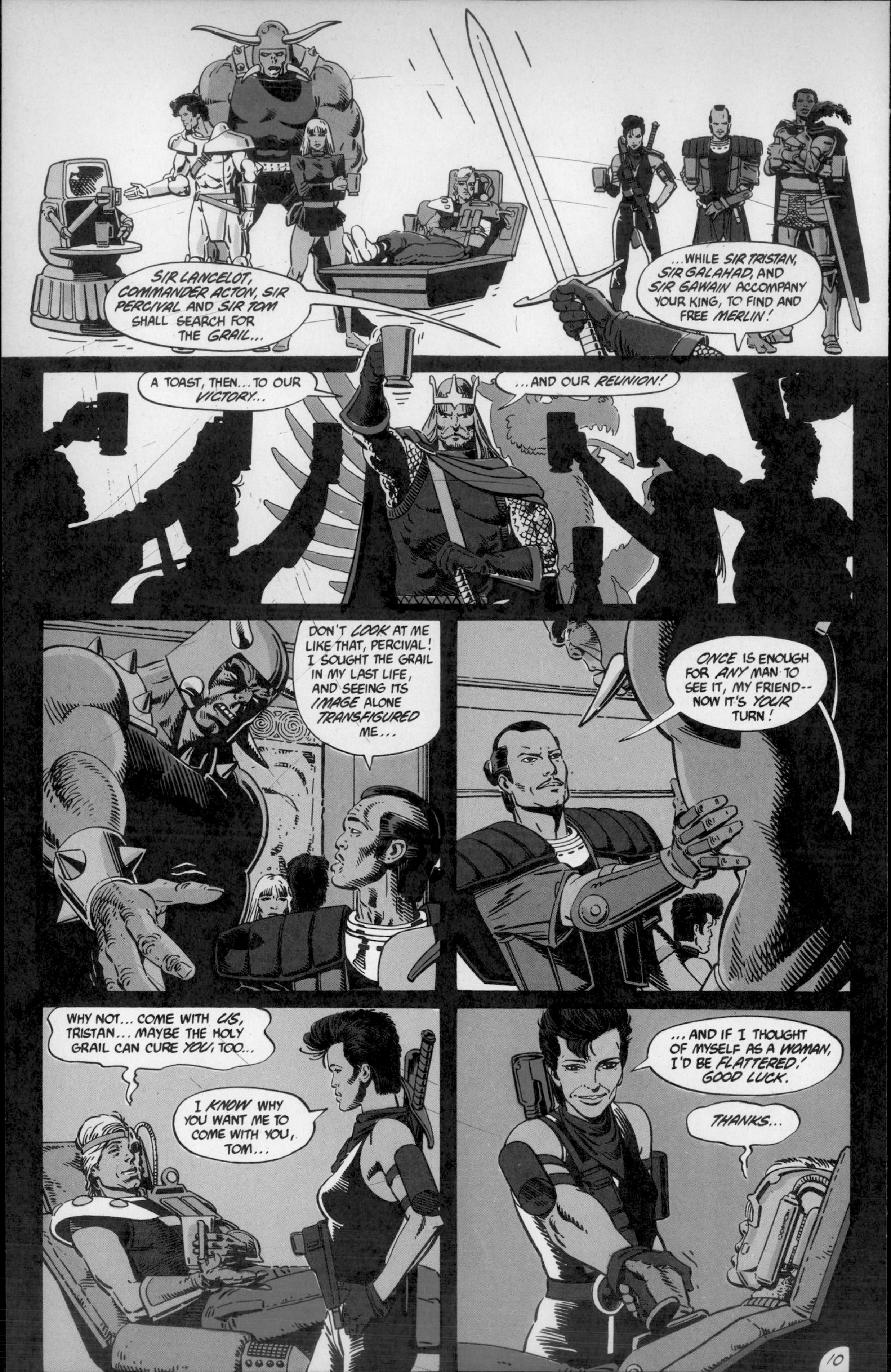
SIR LANCELOT, COMMANDER ACTON, SIR PERCIVAL AND SIR TOM SHALL SEARCH FOR THE GRAIL...
...WHILE SIR TRISTAN, SIR GALAHAD, AND SIR GAWAIN ACCOMPANY YOUR KING, TO FIND AND FREE MERLIN!
A TOAST, THEN... TO OUR VICTORY...
...AND OUR REUNION!
DON'T LOOK AT ME LIKE THAT, PERCIVAL! I SOUGHT THE GRAIL IN MY LAST LIFE, AND SEEING ITS IMAGE ALONE TRANSFIGURED ME...
ONCE IS ENOUGH FOR ANY MAN TO SEE IT, MY FRIEND-- NOW IT'S YOUR TURN!
WHY NOT... COME WITH US, TRISTAN... MAYBE THE HOLY GRAIL CAN CURE YOU, TOO...
I KNOW WHY YOU WANT ME TO COME WITH YOU, TOM...
...AND IF I THOUGHT OF MYSELF AS A WOMAN, I'D BE FLATTERED! GOOD LUCK.
THANKS...

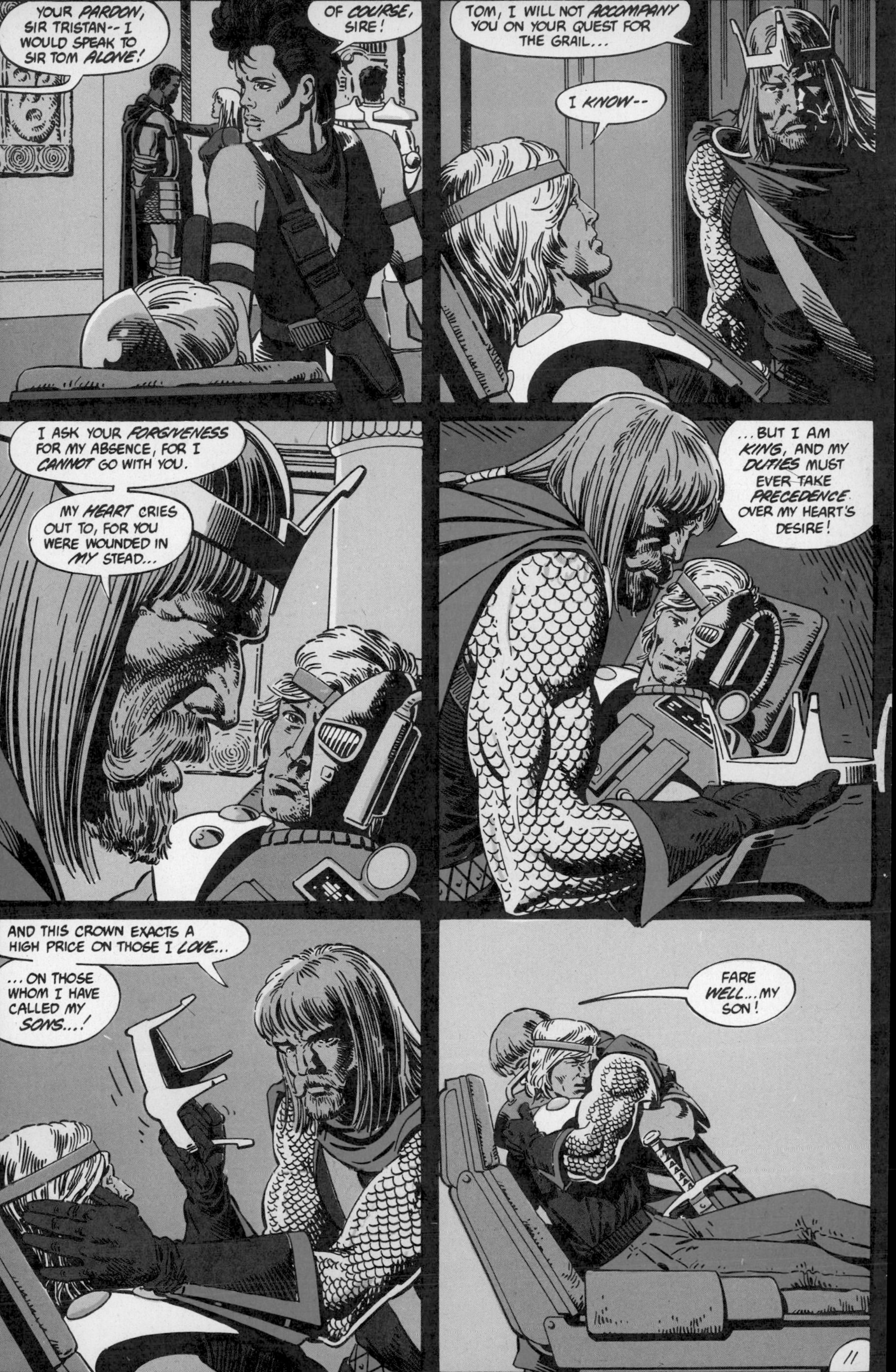
YOUR PARDON, SIR TRISTAN-- I WOULD SPEAK TO SIR TOM ALONE!
OF COURSE, SIRE!
TOM, I WILL NOT ACCOMPANY YOU ON YOUR QUEST FOR THE GRAIL...
I KNOW--
I ASK YOUR FORGIVENESS FOR MY ABSENCE, FOR I CANNOT GO WITH YOU.
MY HEART CRIES OUT TO, FOR YOU WERE WOUNDED IN MY STEAD...
...BUT I AM KING, AND MY DUTIES MUST EVER TAKE PRECEDENCE OVER MY HEART'S DESIRE!
AND THIS CROWN EXACTS A HIGH PRICE ON THOSE I LOVE...
...ON THOSE WHOM I HAVE CALLED MY SONS...!
FARE WELL... MY SON!

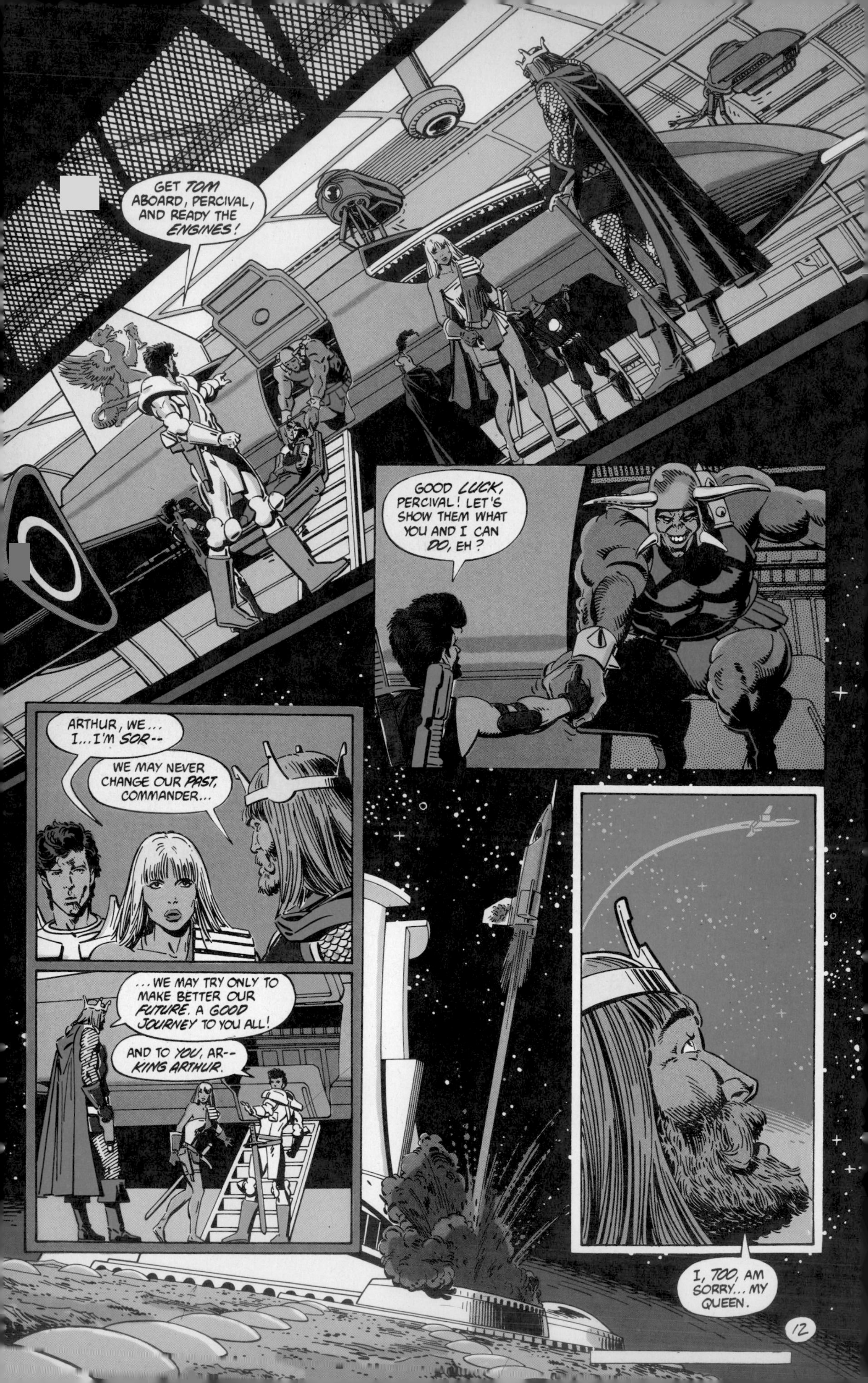
GET TOM ABOARD, PERCIVAL, AND READY THE ENGINES!
GOOD LUCK, PERCIVAL! LET'S SHOW THEM WHAT YOU AND I CAN DO, EH?
ARTHUR, WE... I...I'M SOR--
WE MAY NEVER CHANGE OUR PAST, COMMANDER...
...WE MAY TRY ONLY TO MAKE BETTER OUR FUTURE. A GOOD JOURNEY TO YOU ALL!
AND TO YOU, AR-- KING ARTHUR.
I, TOO, AM SORRY... MY QUEEN.
12

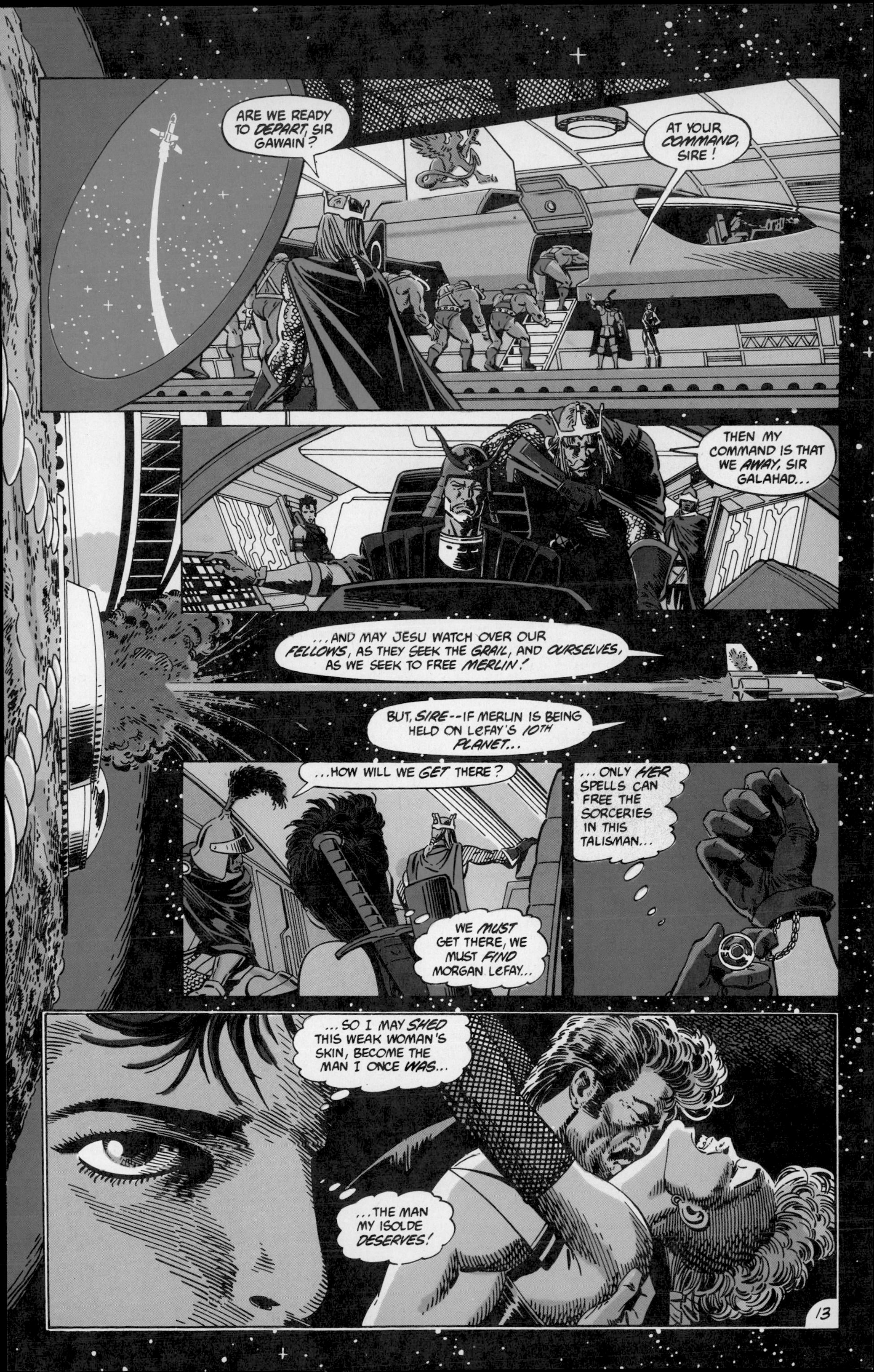

ARE WE READY TO DEPART, SIR GAWAIN?
AT YOUR COMMAND, SIRE!
THEN MY COMMAND IS THAT WE AWAY, SIR GALAHAD...
...AND MAY JESU WATCH OVER OUR FELLOWS, AS THEY SEEK THE GRAIL, AND OURSELVES, AS WE SEEK TO FREE MERLIN!
BUT, SIRE--IF MERLIN IS BEING HELD ON LeFAY'S 10TH PLANET...
...HOW WILL WE GET THERE?
...ONLY HER SPELLS CAN FREE THE SORCERIES IN THIS TALISMAN...
WE MUST GET THERE, WE MUST FIND MORGAN LeFAY...
...SO I MAY SHED THIS WEAK WOMAN'S SKIN, BECOME THE MAN I ONCE WAS...
...THE MAN MY ISOLDE DESERVES!

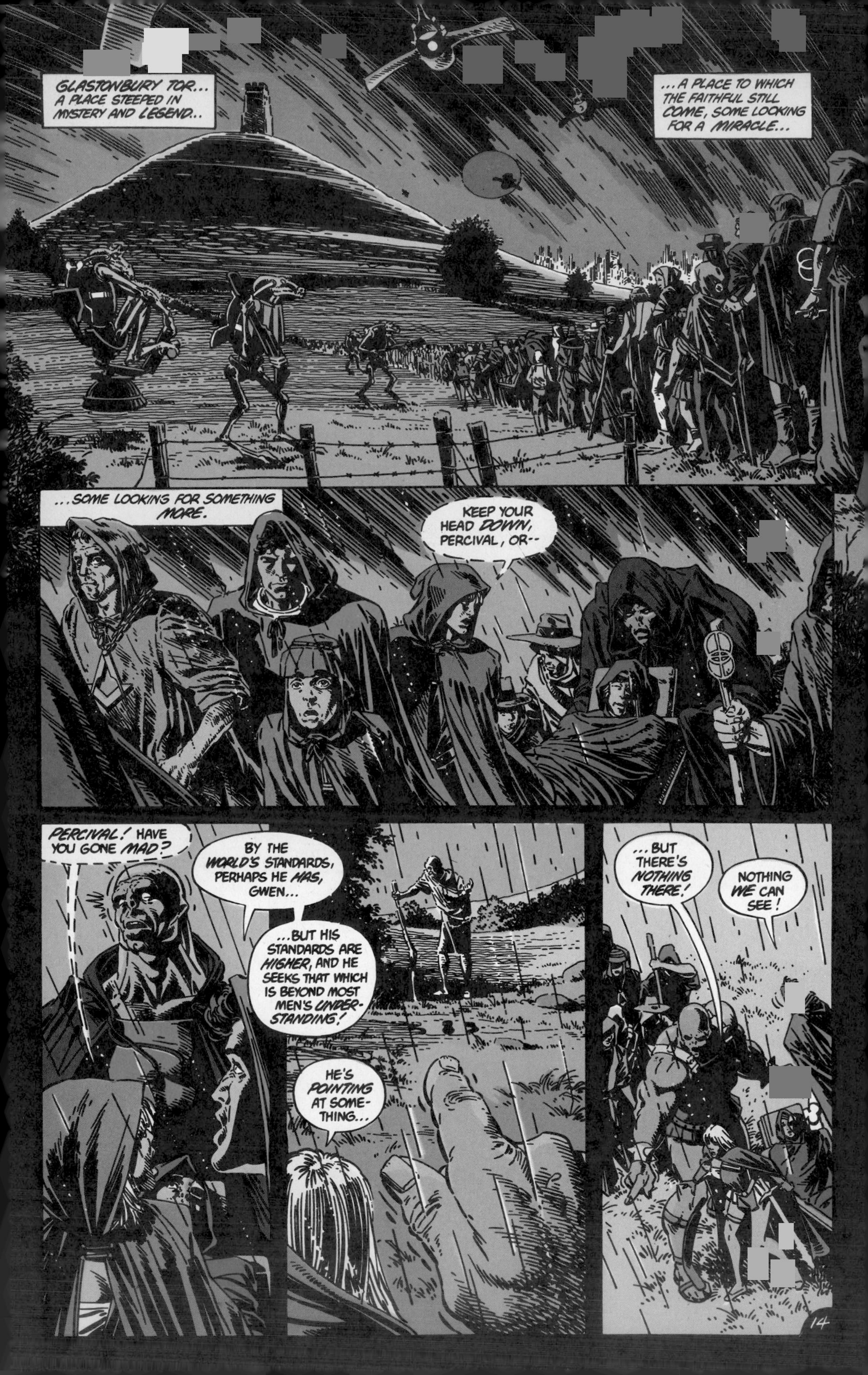
GLASTONBURY TOR... A PLACE STEEPED IN MYSTERY AND LEGEND...
...A PLACE TO WHICH THE FAITHFUL STILL COME, SOME LOOKING FOR A MIRACLE...
...SOME LOOKING FOR SOMETHING MORE.
KEEP YOUR HEAD DOWN, PERCIVAL, OR--
PERCIVAL! HAVE YOU GONE MAD?
BY THE WORLD'S STANDARDS, PERHAPS HE HAS, GWEN...
...BUT HIS STANDARDS ARE HIGHER, AND HE SEEKS THAT WHICH IS BEYOND MOST MEN'S UNDERSTANDING!
HE'S POINTING AT SOMETHING...
...BUT THERE'S NOTHING THERE!
NOTHING WE CAN SEE!
14

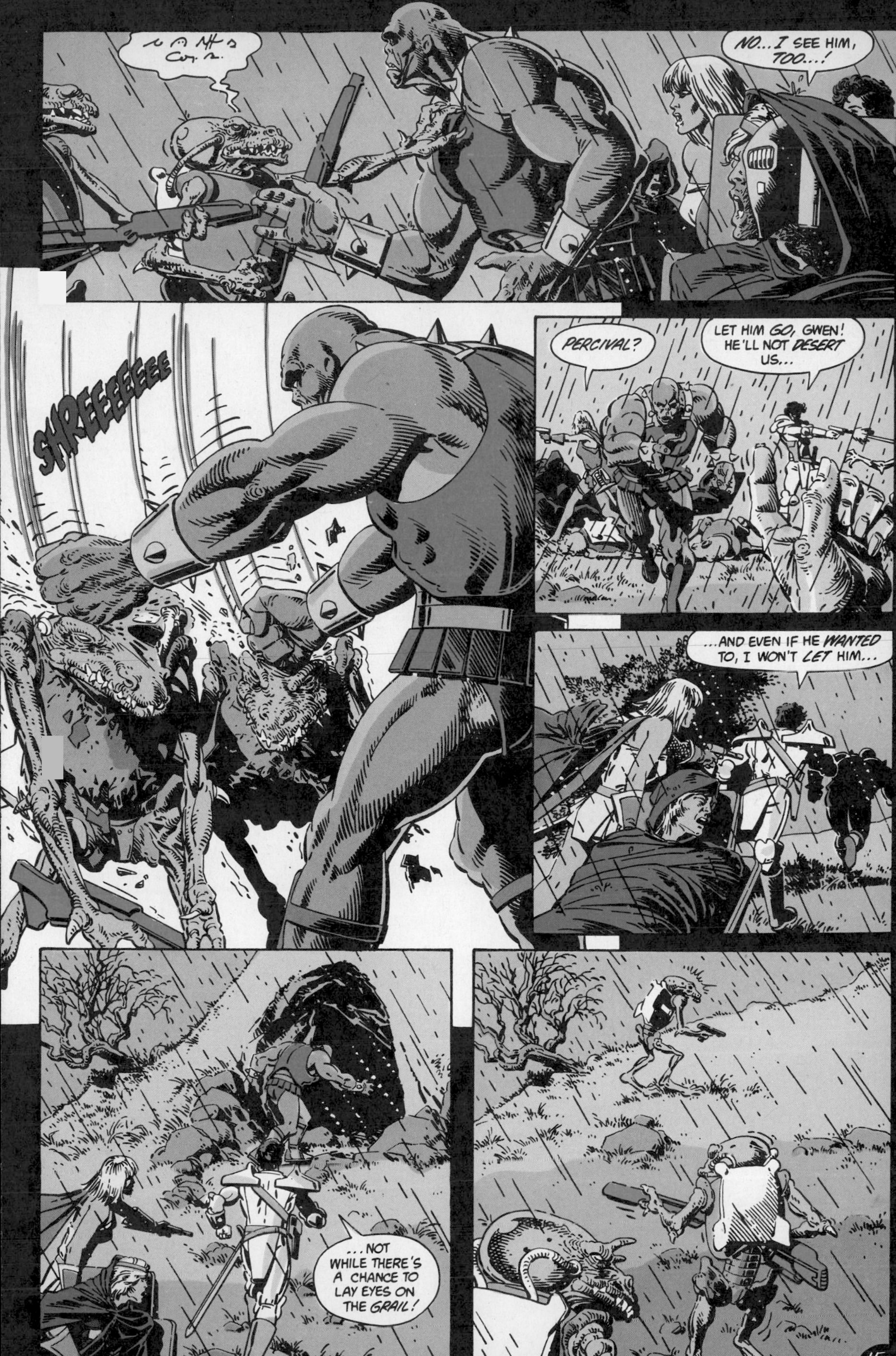
NO...I SEE HIM, TOO...!
SHREEEEEEEE
PERCIVAL?
LET HIM GO, GWEN! HE'LL NOT DESERT US...
...AND EVEN IF HE WANTED TO, I WON'T LET HIM...
...NOT WHILE THERE'S A CHANCE TO LAY EYES ON THE GRAIL!

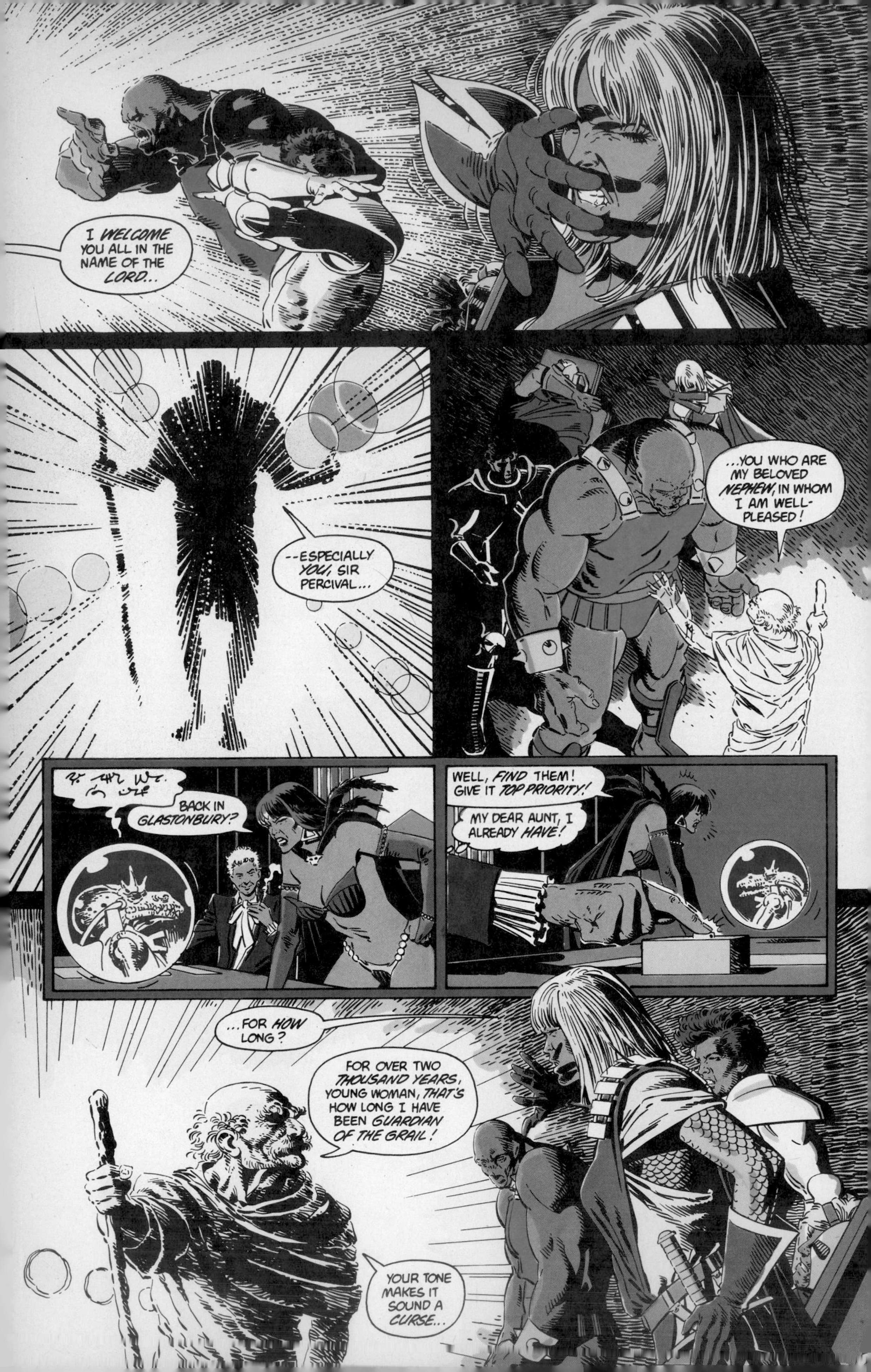

I WELCOME YOU ALL IN THE NAME OF THE LORD...
--ESPECIALLY YOU, SIR PERCIVAL...
...YOU WHO ARE MY BELOVED NEPHEW, IN WHOM I AM WELL-PLEASED!
BACK IN GLASTONBURY?
WELL, FIND THEM! GIVE IT TOP PRIORITY!
MY DEAR AUNT, I ALREADY HAVE!
...FOR HOW LONG?
FOR OVER TWO THOUSAND YEARS, YOUNG WOMAN, THAT'S HOW LONG I HAVE BEEN GUARDIAN OF THE GRAIL!
YOUR TONE MAKES IT SOUND A CURSE...

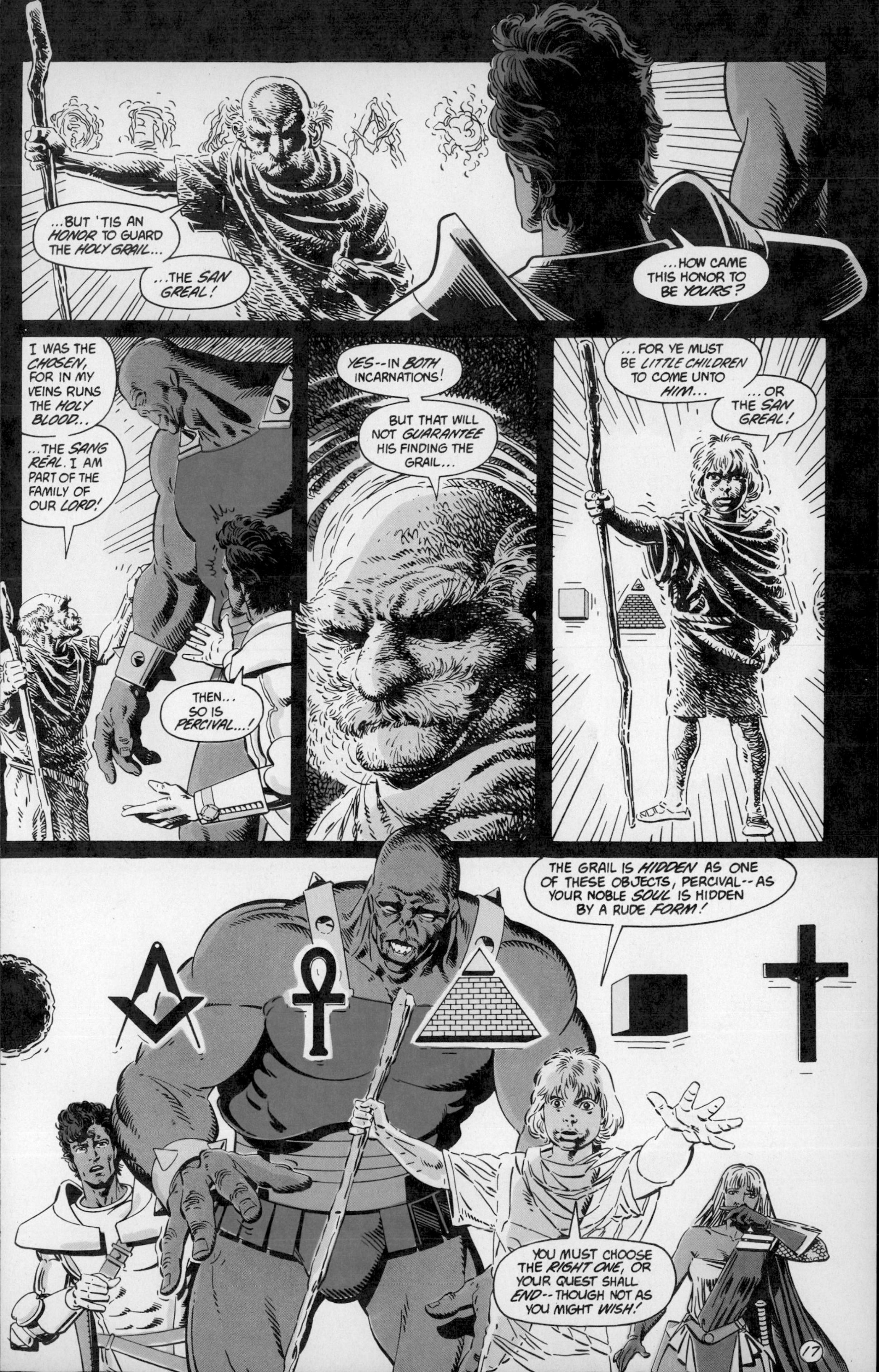
...BUT 'TIS AN HONOR TO GUARD THE HOLY GRAIL...
...THE SAN GREAL!
...HOW CAME THIS HONOR TO BE YOURS?
I WAS THE CHOSEN, FOR IN MY VEINS RUNS THE HOLY BLOOD...
...THE SANG RÉAL. I AM PART OF THE FAMILY OF OUR LORD!
THEN... SO IS PERCIVAL...!
YES--IN BOTH INCARNATIONS!
BUT THAT WILL NOT GUARANTEE HIS FINDING THE GRAIL...
...FOR YE MUST BE LITTLE CHILDREN TO COME UNTO HIM...
...OR THE SAN GREAL!
THE GRAIL IS HIDDEN AS ONE OF THESE OBJECTS, PERCIVAL--AS YOUR NOBLE SOUL IS HIDDEN BY A RUDE FORM!
YOU MUST CHOOSE THE RIGHT ONE, OR YOUR QUEST SHALL END--THOUGH NOT AS YOU MIGHT WISH!

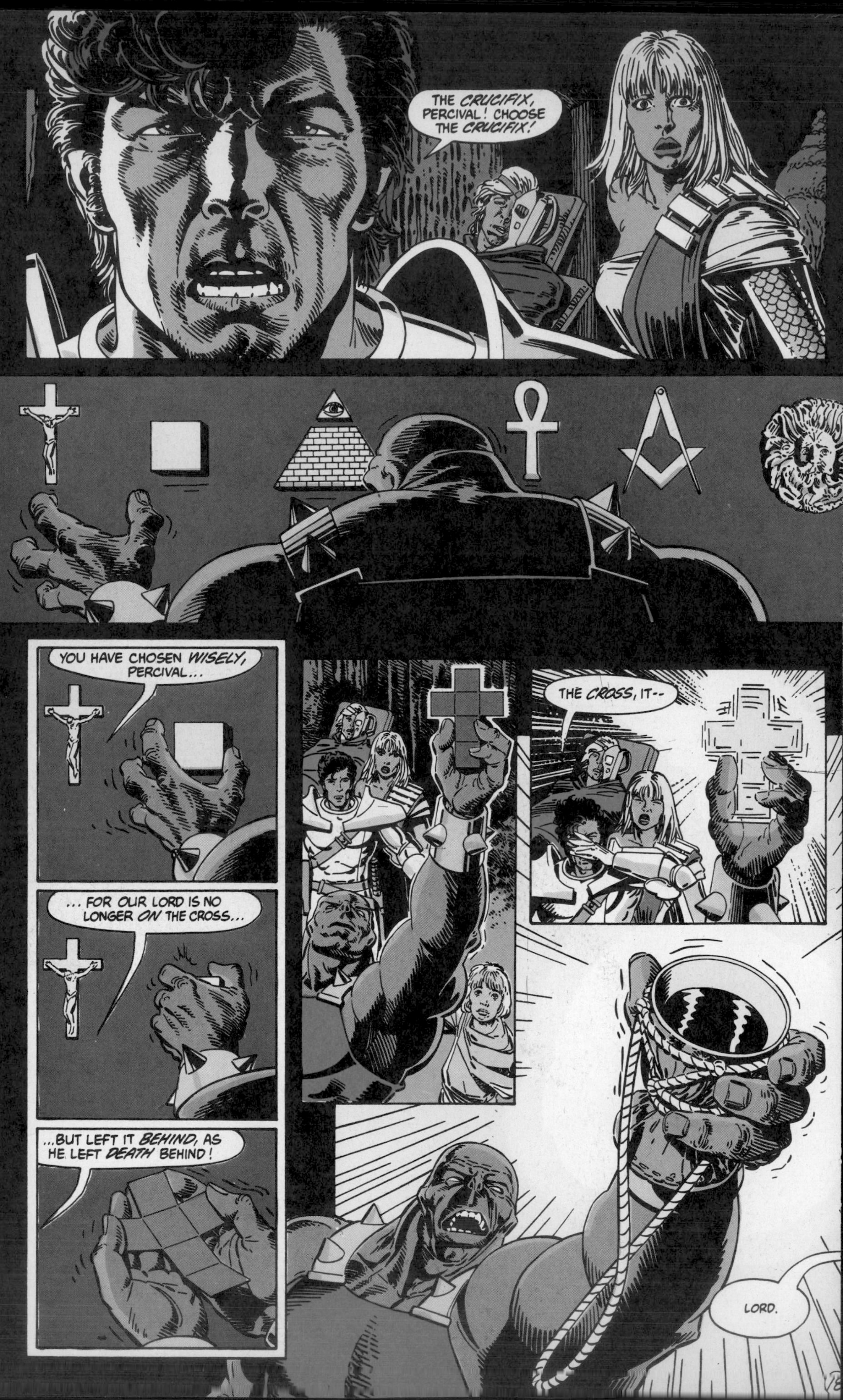
THE CRUCIFIX, PERCIVAL! CHOOSE THE CRUCIFIX!
YOU HAVE CHOSEN WISELY, PERCIVAL...
... FOR OUR LORD IS NO LONGER ON THE CROSS...
...BUT LEFT IT BEHIND, AS HE LEFT DEATH BEHIND!
THE CROSS, IT--
LORD.

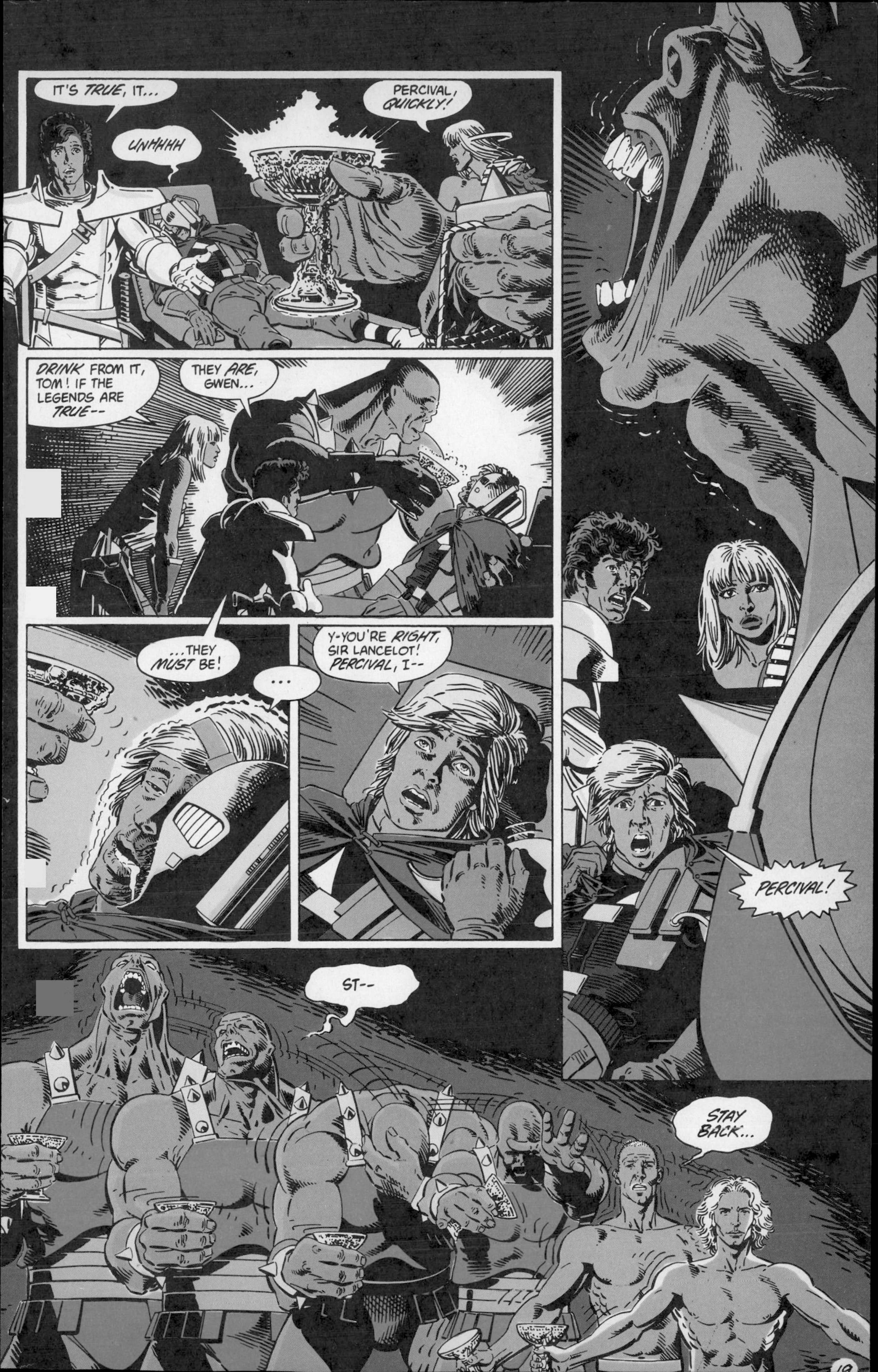
IT'S TRUE, IT...
UNHHHH
PERCIVAL, QUICKLY!
DRINK FROM IT, TOM! IF THE LEGENDS ARE TRUE--
THEY ARE, GWEN...
...THEY MUST BE!
...
Y-YOU'RE RIGHT, SIR LANCELOT! PERCIVAL, I--
PERCIVAL!
ST--
STAY BACK...

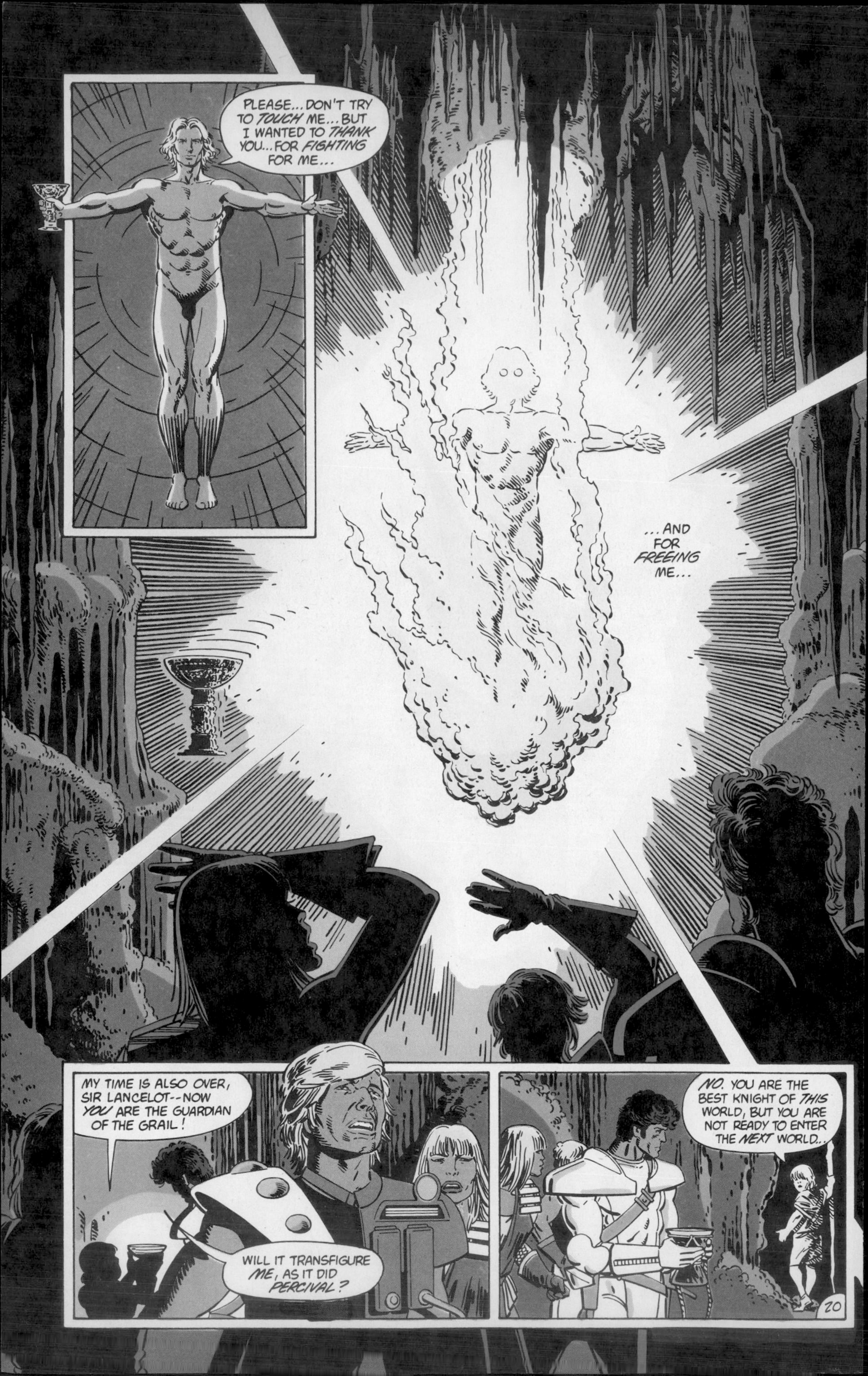

PLEASE... DON'T TRY TO TOUCH ME... BUT I WANTED TO THANK YOU... FOR FIGHTING FOR ME...
...AND FOR FREEING ME...
MY TIME IS ALSO OVER, SIR LANCELOT--NOW YOU ARE THE GUARDIAN OF THE GRAIL!
WILL IT TRANSFIGURE ME, AS IT DID PERCIVAL?
NO. YOU ARE THE BEST KNIGHT OF THIS WORLD, BUT YOU ARE NOT READY TO ENTER THE NEXT WORLD...
20

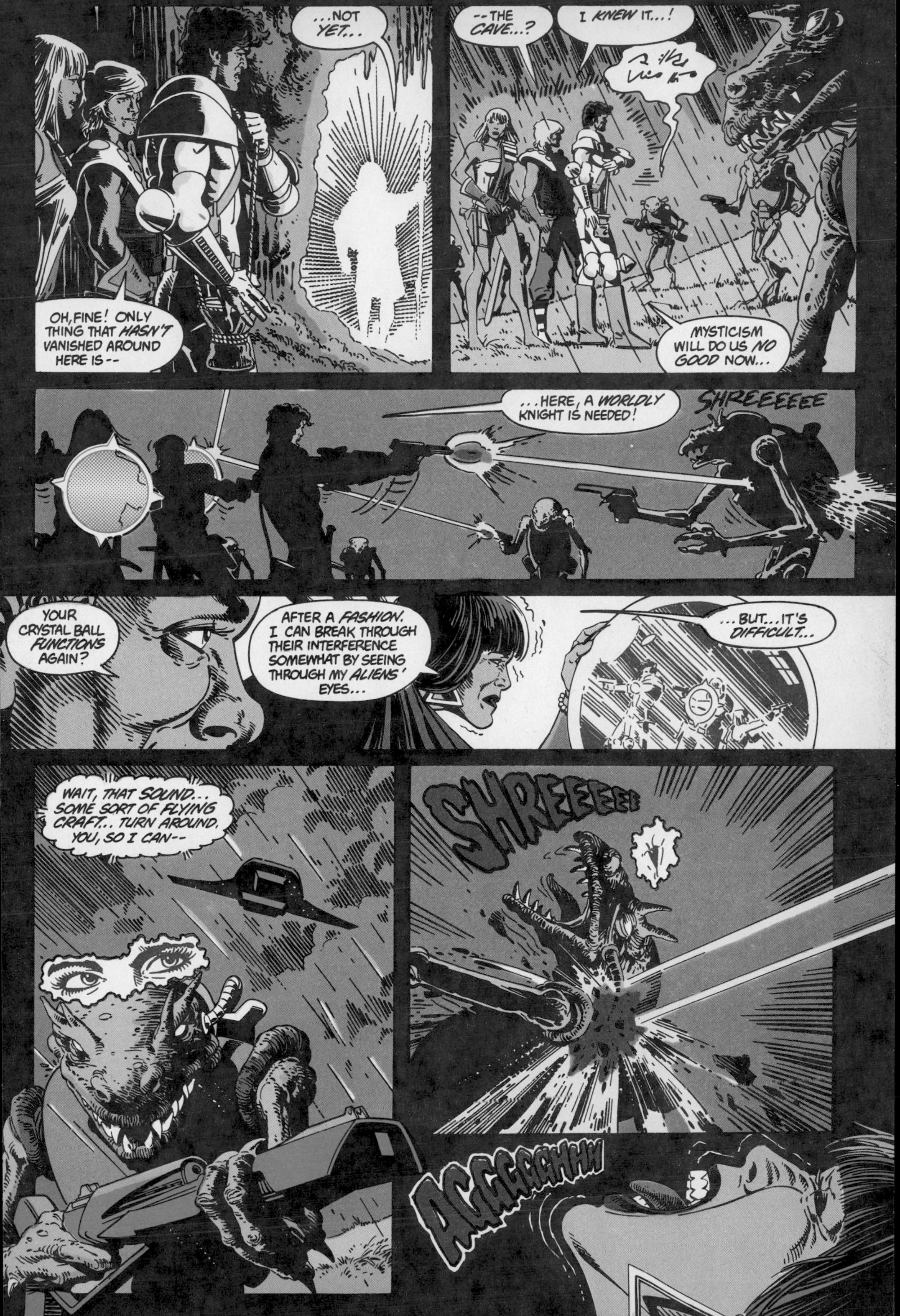
...NOT YET...
OH, FINE! ONLY THING THAT HASN'T VANISHED AROUND HERE IS--
--THE CAVE...?
I KNEW IT...!
MYSTICISM WILL DO US NO GOOD NOW...
...HERE, A WORLDLY KNIGHT IS NEEDED!
SHREEEEEE
YOUR CRYSTAL BALL FUNCTIONS AGAIN?
AFTER A FASHION. I CAN BREAK THROUGH THEIR INTERFERENCE SOMEWHAT BY SEEING THROUGH MY ALIENS' EYES...
...BUT...IT'S DIFFICULT...
WAIT, THAT SOUND... SOME SORT OF FLYING CRAFT... TURN AROUND, YOU, SO I CAN--
SHREEEEEE
AGGGGHHH

SHREEEE

UNGGGH!

GWEN?

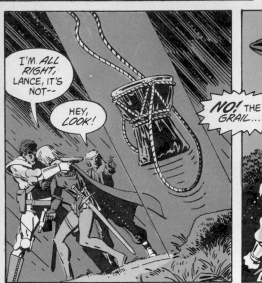

I'M ALL RIGHT, LANCE, IT'S NOT--

HEY, LOOK!

NO! THE GRAIL...!

GET DOWN, LANCE! I'LL GET US OUT OF HERE!

BZZZT

IT WASN'T YOUR FAULT, SIR LANCELOT, IT--

THE FIRST THING A ROUND TABLE KNIGHT LEARNS IS TO TELL THE TRUTH, LAD! AND THE TRUTH IS I WAS APPOINTED GUARDIAN OF THE GRAIL...

...AND I FAILED!

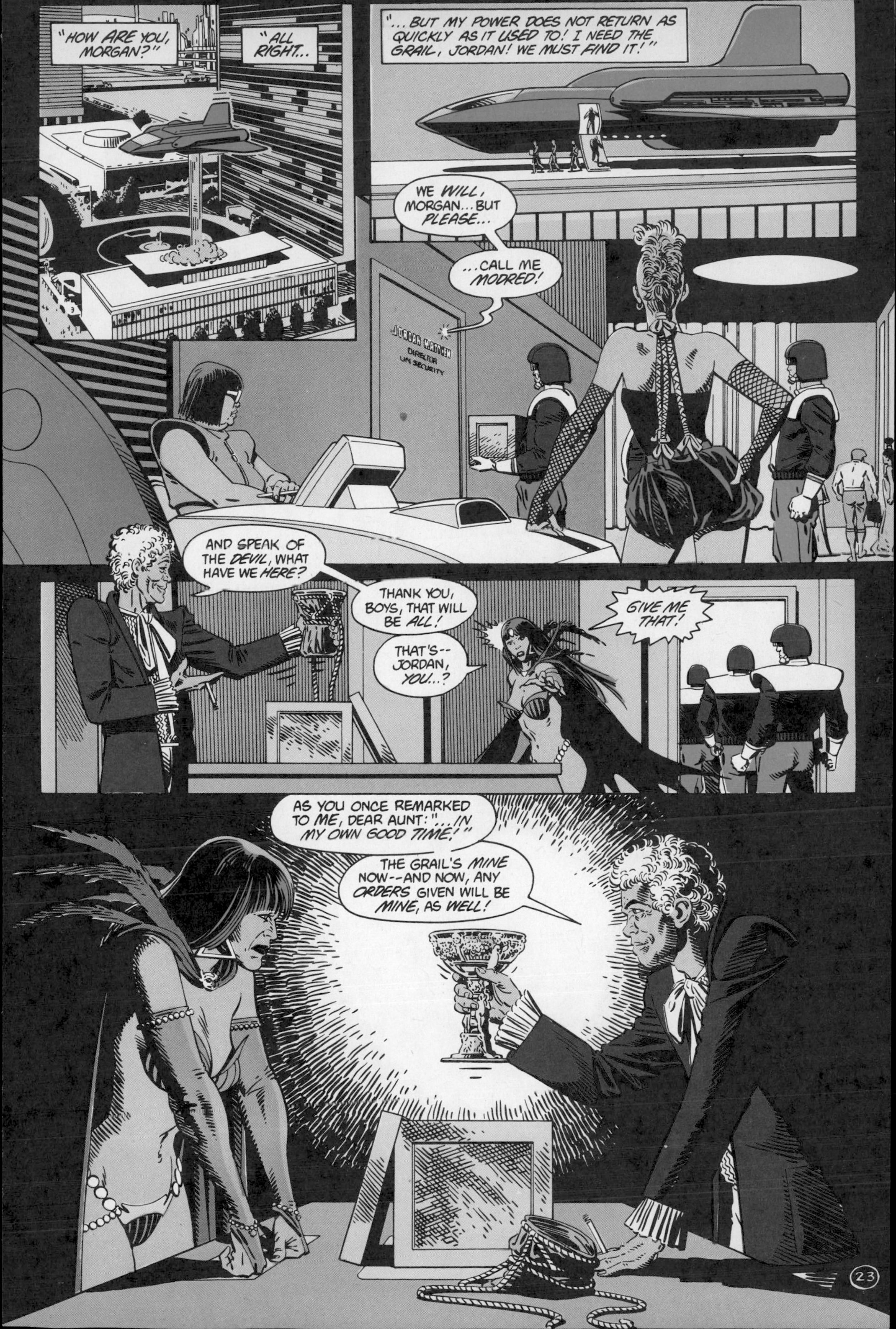
"HOW ARE YOU, MORGAN?"
"ALL RIGHT...
"...BUT MY POWER DOES NOT RETURN AS QUICKLY AS IT USED TO! I NEED THE GRAIL, JORDAN! WE MUST FIND IT!"
WE WILL, MORGAN... BUT PLEASE...
...CALL ME MODRED!
JORDAN MATHIEN DIRECTOR UN SECURITY
AND SPEAK OF THE DEVIL, WHAT HAVE WE HERE?
THANK YOU, BOYS, THAT WILL BE ALL!
THAT'S-- JORDAN, YOU...?
GIVE ME THAT!
AS YOU ONCE REMARKED TO ME, DEAR AUNT: "...IN MY OWN GOOD TIME!"
THE GRAIL'S MINE NOW--AND NOW, ANY ORDERS GIVEN WILL BE MINE, AS WELL!
23

chapter
10

Prelude To War!
YOUR FOUR-WAY CONNECTION IS READY, PRESIDENT MARKS!
THANK YOU, DARLIN'--TOP SECURITY SCRAMBLE, PLEASE!

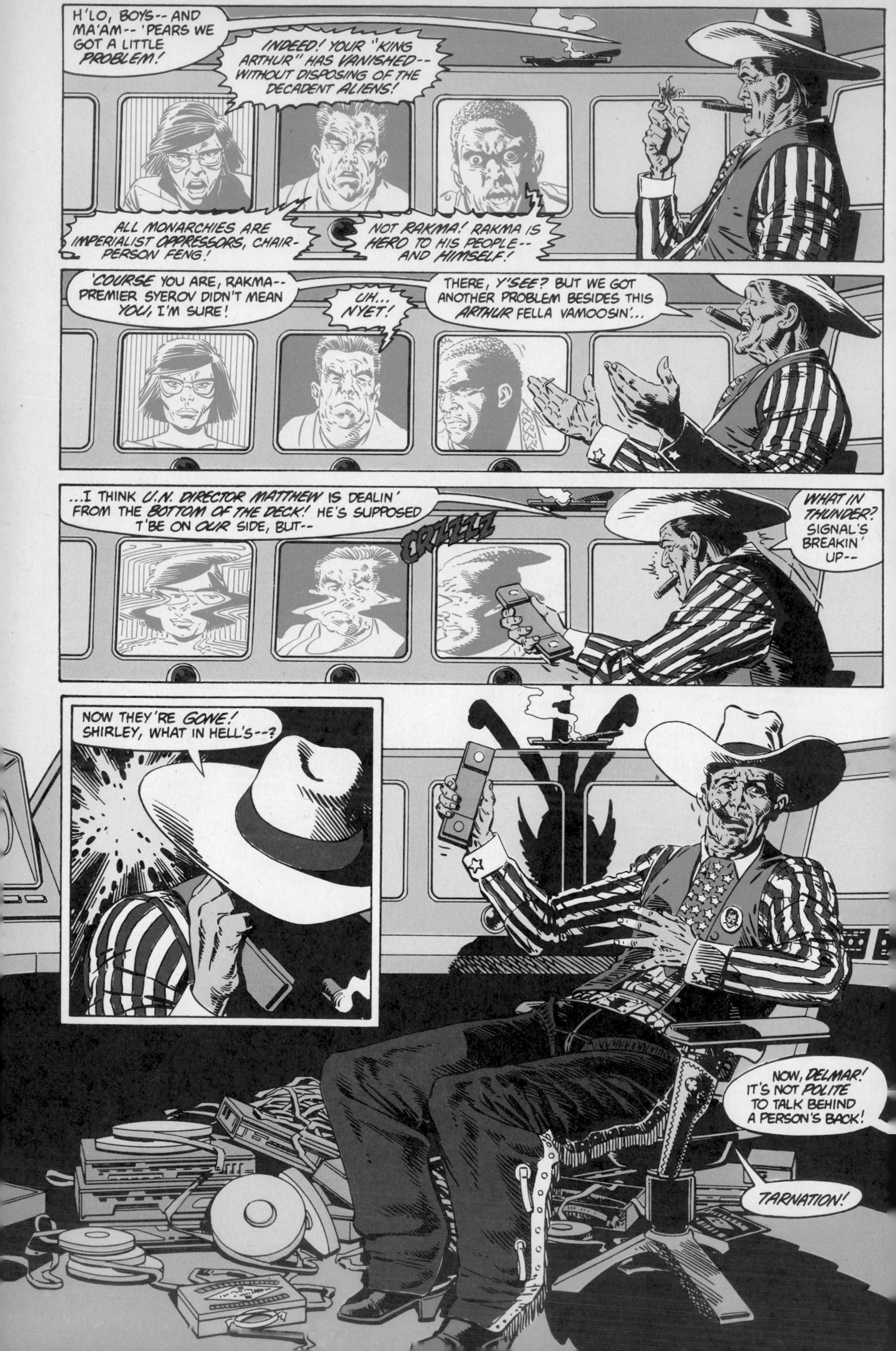
H'LO, BOYS-- AND MA'AM-- 'PEARS WE GOT A LITTLE PROBLEM!
INDEED! YOUR "KING ARTHUR" HAS VANISHED-- WITHOUT DISPOSING OF THE DECADENT ALIENS!
ALL MONARCHIES ARE IMPERIALIST OPPRESSORS, CHAIRPERSON FENG!
NOT RAKMA! RAKMA IS HERO TO HIS PEOPLE-- AND HIMSELF!
'COURSE YOU ARE, RAKMA-- PREMIER SYEROV DIDN'T MEAN YOU, I'M SURE!
UH... NYET!
THERE, Y'SEE? BUT WE GOT ANOTHER PROBLEM BESIDES THIS ARTHUR FELLA VAMOOSIN'...
...I THINK U.N. DIRECTOR MATTHEW IS DEALIN' FROM THE BOTTOM OF THE DECK! HE'S SUPPOSED T'BE ON OUR SIDE, BUT--
CRZZZZ
WHAT IN THUNDER? SIGNAL'S BREAKIN' UP--
NOW THEY'RE GONE! SHIRLEY, WHAT IN HELL'S--?
NOW, DELMAR! IT'S NOT POLITE TO TALK BEHIND A PERSON'S BACK!
TARNATION!

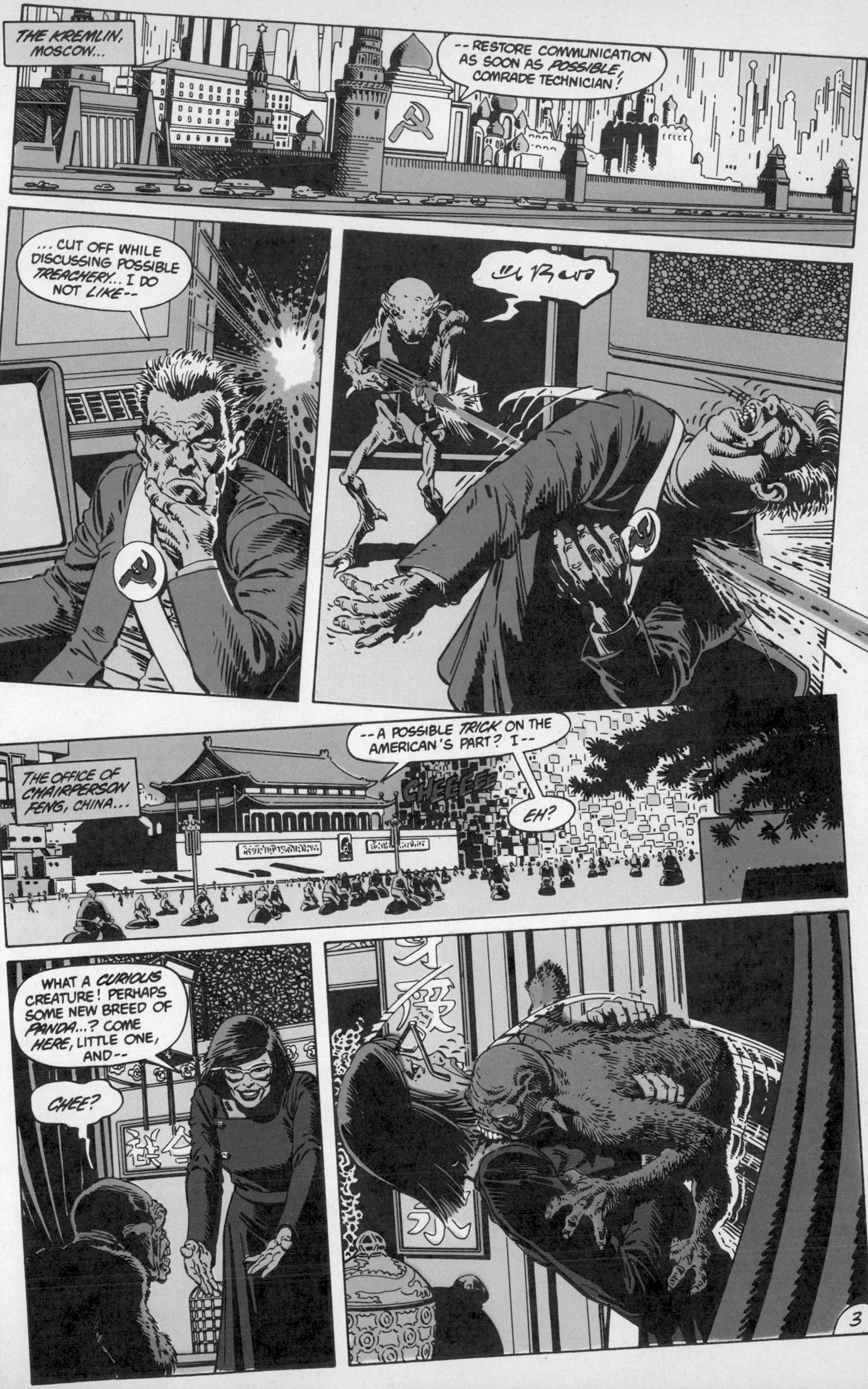
THE KREMLIN, MOSCOW...
--RESTORE COMMUNICATION AS SOON AS POSSIBLE, COMRADE TECHNICIAN!
...CUT OFF WHILE DISCUSSING POSSIBLE TREACHERY... I DO NOT LIKE--
THE OFFICE OF CHAIRPERSON FENG, CHINA...
--A POSSIBLE TRICK ON THE AMERICAN'S PART? I--
EH?
WHAT A CURIOUS CREATURE! PERHAPS SOME NEW BREED OF PANDA...? COME HERE, LITTLE ONE, AND--
CHEE?

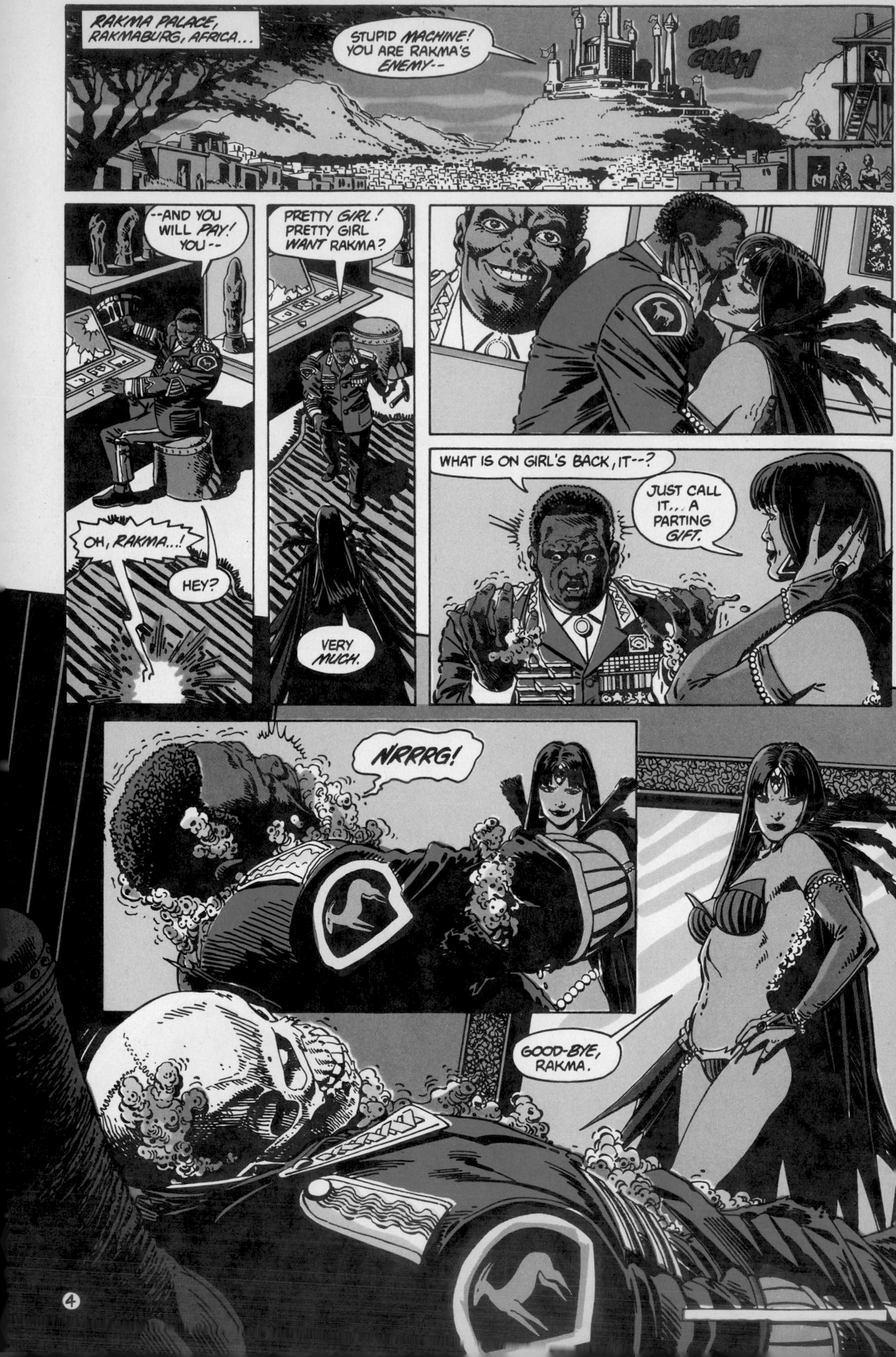
RAKMA PALACE, RAKMABURG, AFRICA...
STUPID MACHINE! YOU ARE RAKMA'S ENEMY--
BANG CRASH
--AND YOU WILL PAY! YOU--
OH, RAKMA...!
HEY?
PRETTY GIRL! PRETTY GIRL WANT RAKMA?
VERY MUCH.
WHAT IS ON GIRL'S BACK, IT--?
JUST CALL IT... A PARTING GIFT.
N'RRRG!
GOOD-BYE, RAKMA.

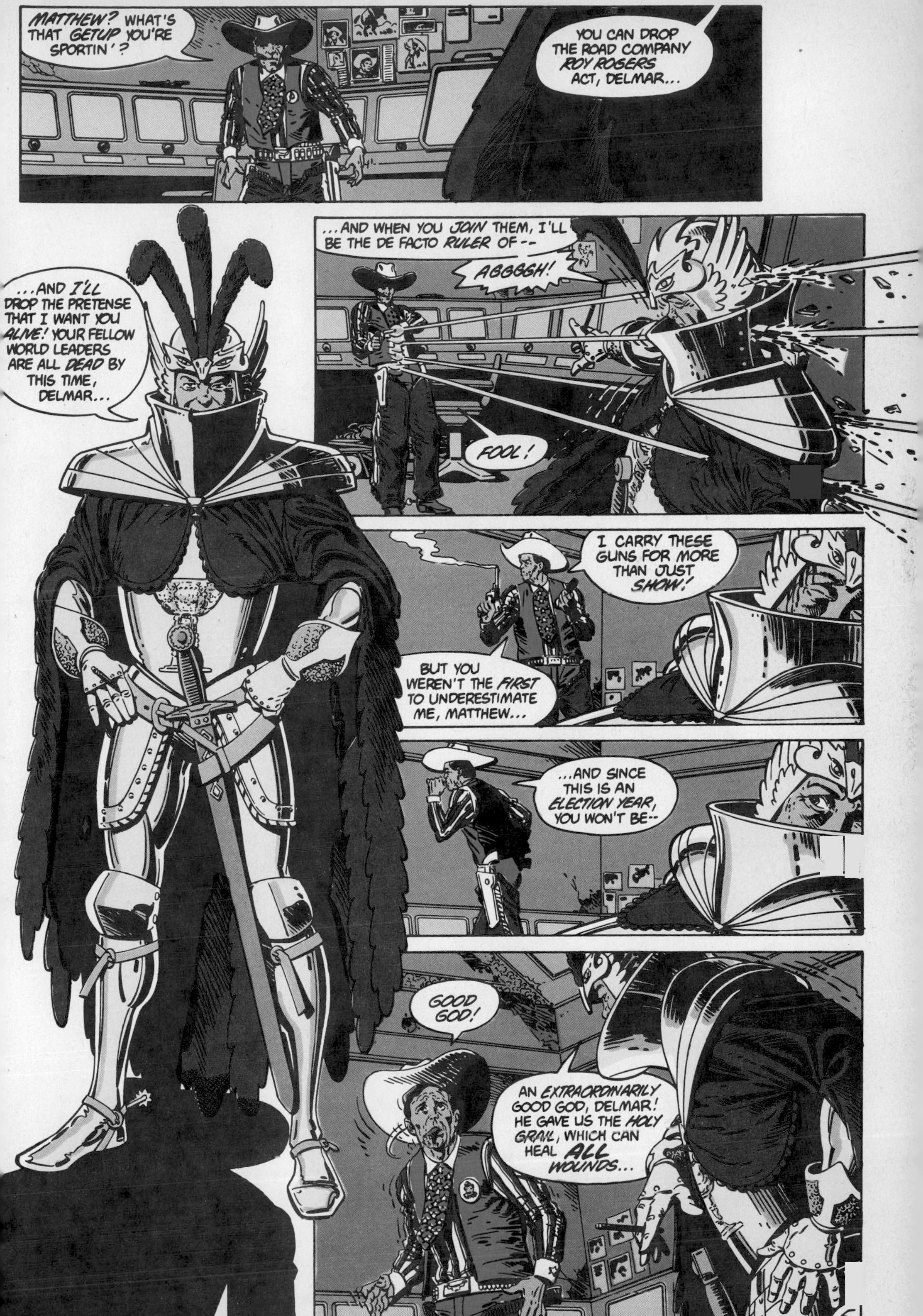
MATTHEW? WHAT'S THAT GETUP YOU'RE SPORTIN'?
YOU CAN DROP THE ROAD COMPANY ROY ROGERS ACT, DELMAR...
...AND I'LL DROP THE PRETENSE THAT I WANT YOU ALIVE! YOUR FELLOW WORLD LEADERS ARE ALL DEAD BY THIS TIME, DELMAR...
...AND WHEN YOU JOIN THEM, I'LL BE THE DE FACTO RULER OF--
ABGGGH!
FOOL!
I CARRY THESE GUNS FOR MORE THAN JUST SHOW!
BUT YOU WEREN'T THE FIRST TO UNDERESTIMATE ME, MATTHEW...
...AND SINCE THIS IS AN ELECTION YEAR, YOU WON'T BE--
GOOD GOD!
AN EXTRAORDINARILY GOOD GOD, DELMAR! HE GAVE US THE HOLY GRAIL, WHICH CAN HEAL ALL WOUNDS...
5

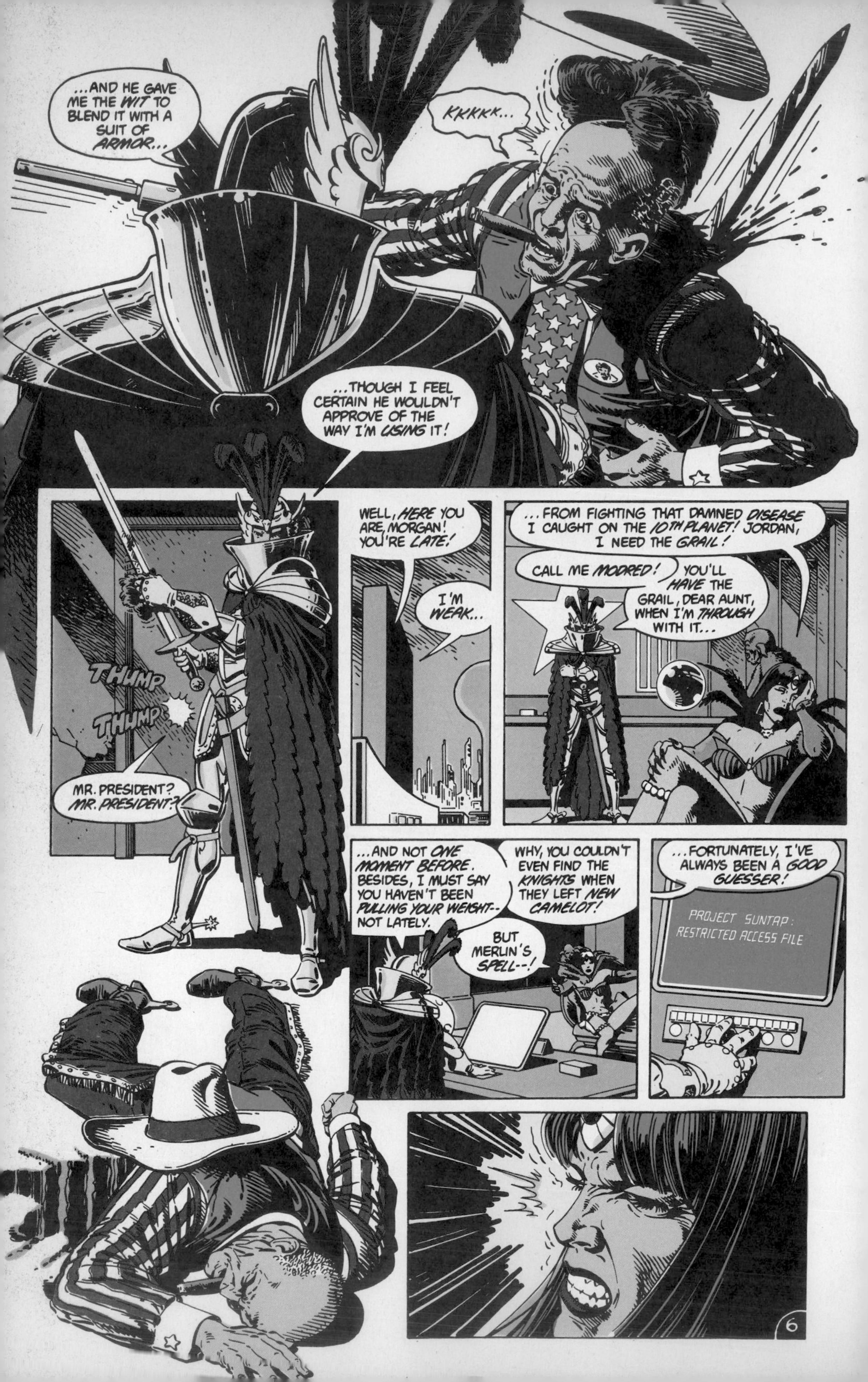
...AND HE GAVE ME THE WIT TO BLEND IT WITH A SUIT OF ARMOR...
KKKKK...
...THOUGH I FEEL CERTAIN HE WOULDN'T APPROVE OF THE WAY I'M USING IT!
THUMP
THUMP
MR. PRESIDENT? MR. PRESIDENT?
WELL, HERE YOU ARE, MORGAN! YOU'RE LATE!
I'M WEAK...
...FROM FIGHTING THAT DAMNED DISEASE I CAUGHT ON THE 10TH PLANET! JORDAN, I NEED THE GRAIL!
CALL ME MODRED!
YOU'LL HAVE THE GRAIL, DEAR AUNT, WHEN I'M THROUGH WITH IT...
...AND NOT ONE MOMENT BEFORE. BESIDES, I MUST SAY YOU HAVEN'T BEEN PULLING YOUR WEIGHT-- NOT LATELY.
WHY, YOU COULDN'T EVEN FIND THE KNIGHTS WHEN THEY LEFT NEW CAMELOT!
BUT MERLIN'S SPELL--!
...FORTUNATELY, I'VE ALWAYS BEEN A GOOD GUESSER!
PROJECT SUNTAP: RESTRICTED ACCESS FILE

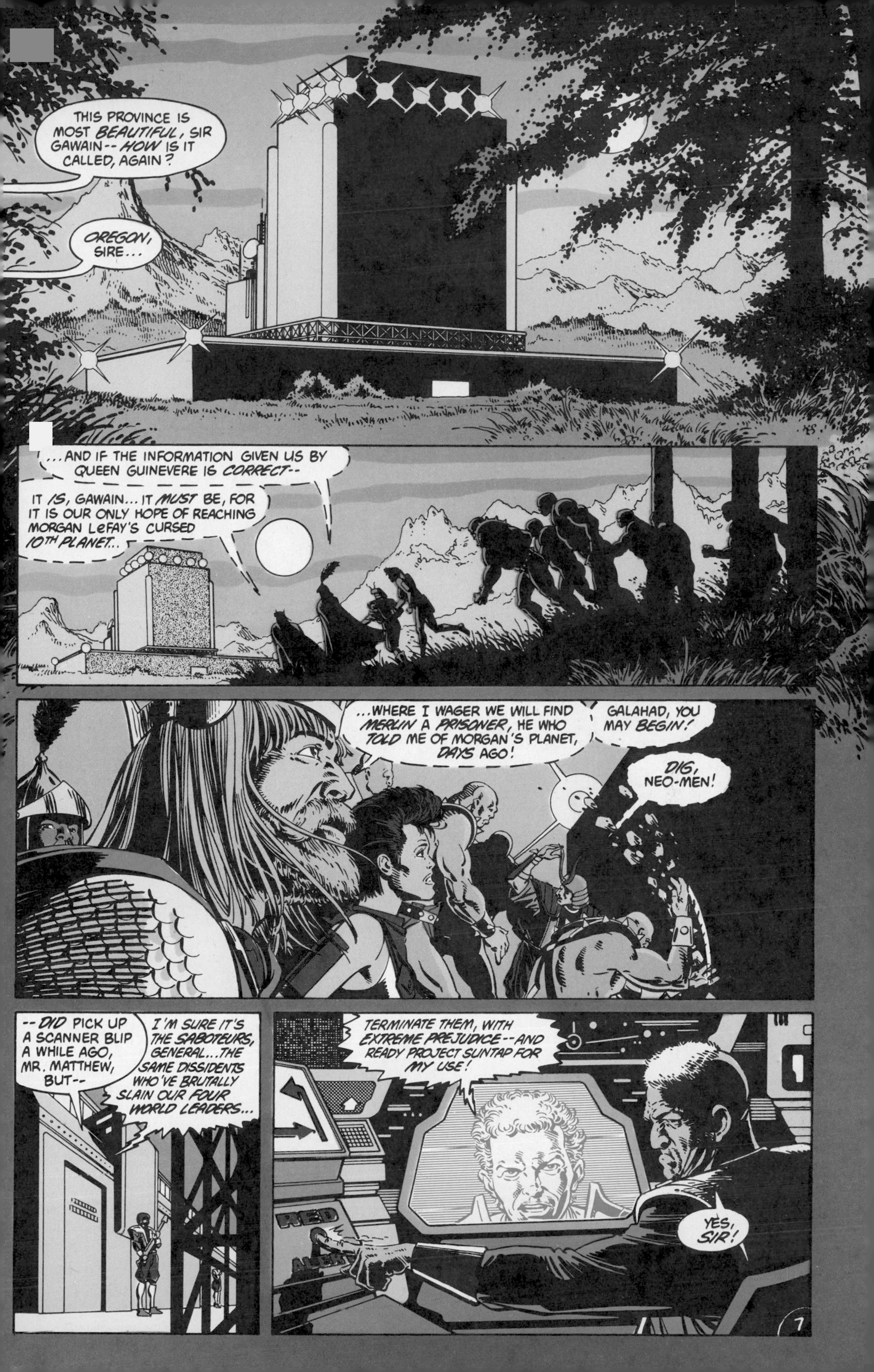

THIS PROVINCE IS MOST BEAUTIFUL, SIR GAWAIN--HOW IS IT CALLED, AGAIN?
OREGON, SIRE...
...AND IF THE INFORMATION GIVEN US BY QUEEN GUINEVERE IS CORRECT--
IT IS, GAWAIN... IT MUST BE, FOR IT IS OUR ONLY HOPE OF REACHING MORGAN LeFAY'S CURSED 10TH PLANET...
...WHERE I WAGER WE WILL FIND MERLIN A PRISONER, HE WHO TOLD ME OF MORGAN'S PLANET, DAYS AGO!
GALAHAD, YOU MAY BEGIN!
DIG, NEO-MEN!
--DID PICK UP A SCANNER BLIP A WHILE AGO, MR. MATTHEW, BUT--
I'M SURE IT'S THE SABOTEURS, GENERAL... THE SAME DISSIDENTS WHO'VE BRUTALLY SLAIN OUR FOUR WORLD LEADERS...
TERMINATE THEM, WITH EXTREME PREJUDICE--AND READY PROJECT SUNTAP FOR MY USE!
RED
ALERT
YES, SIR!

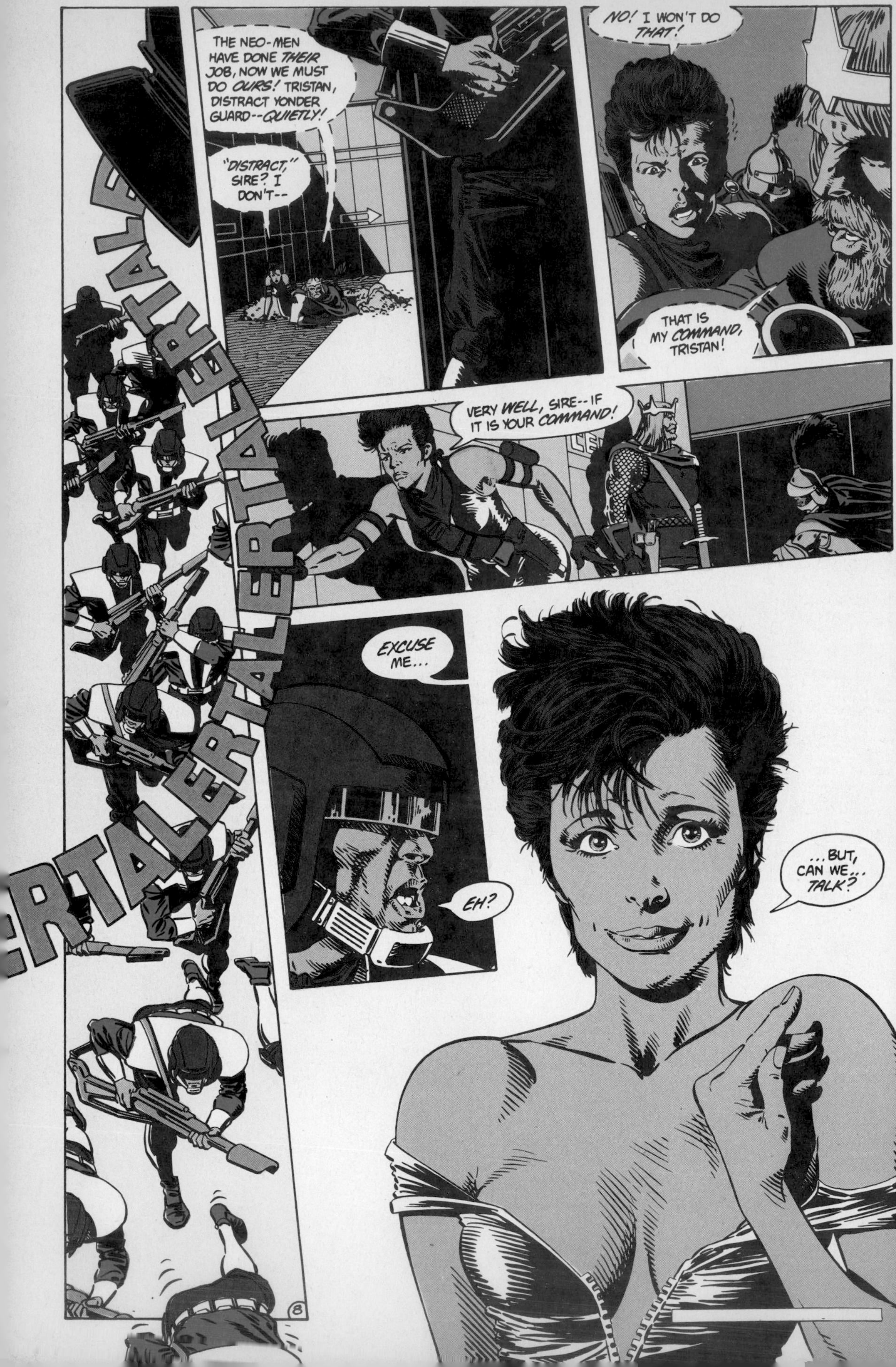
THE NEO-MEN HAVE DONE THEIR JOB, NOW WE MUST DO OURS! TRISTAN, DISTRACT YONDER GUARD--QUIETLY!
"DISTRACT," SIRE? I DON'T--
NO! I WON'T DO THAT!
THAT IS MY COMMAND, TRISTAN!
VERY WELL, SIRE--IF IT IS YOUR COMMAND!
ALERTALERTALERTALERTALERTALERT
EXCUSE ME...
EH?
...BUT, CAN WE... TALK?
8

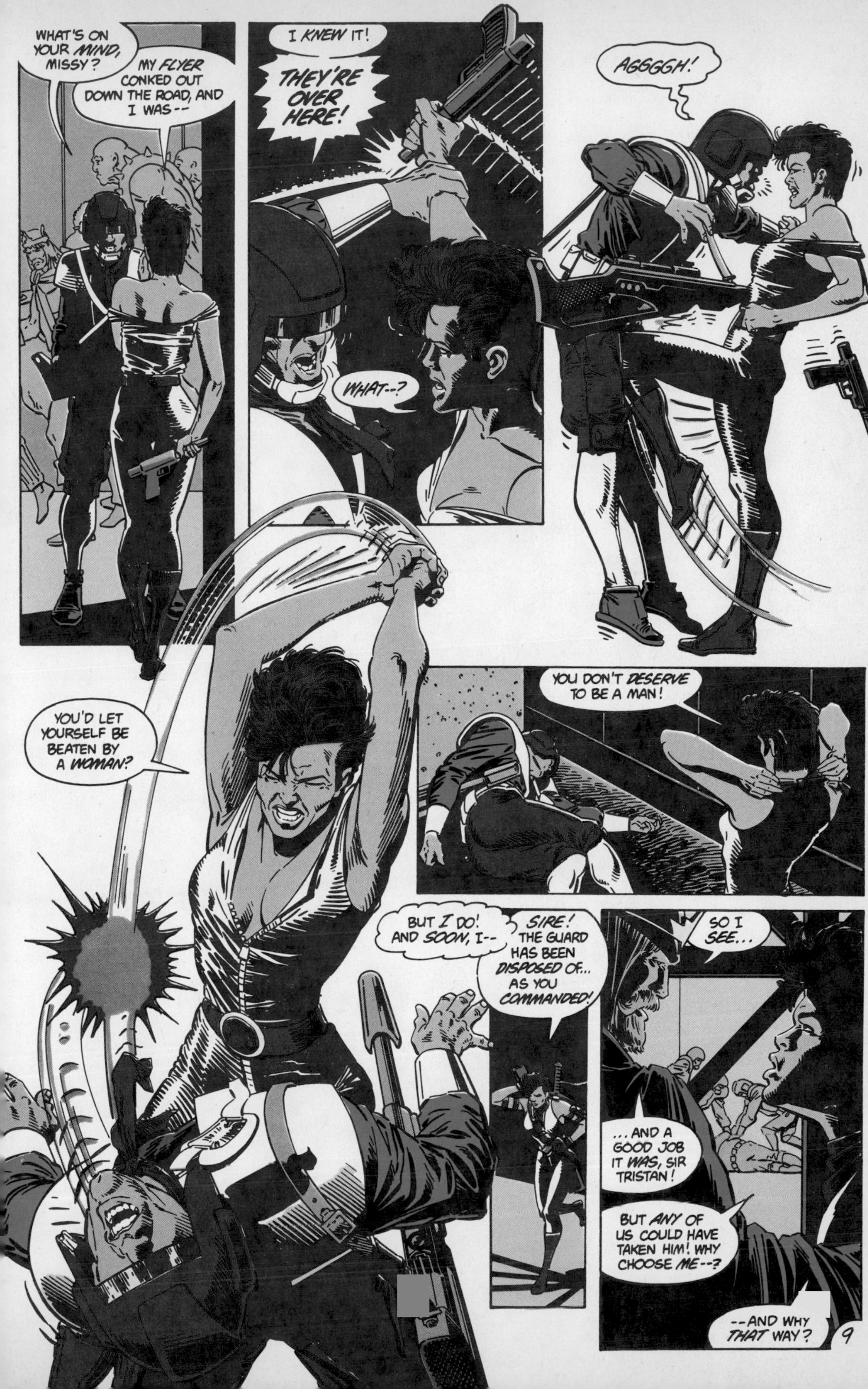
WHAT'S ON YOUR MIND, MISSY?
MY FLYER CONKED OUT DOWN THE ROAD, AND I WAS--
I KNEW IT!
THEY'RE OVER HERE!
WHAT--?
AGSGGH!
YOU'D LET YOURSELF BE BEATEN BY A WOMAN?
YOU DON'T DESERVE TO BE A MAN!
BUT I DO! AND SOON, I--
SIRE! THE GUARD HAS BEEN DISPOSED OF... AS YOU COMMANDED!
SO I SEE...
...AND A GOOD JOB IT WAS, SIR TRISTAN!
BUT ANY OF US COULD HAVE TAKEN HIM! WHY CHOOSE ME--?
--AND WHY THAT WAY?

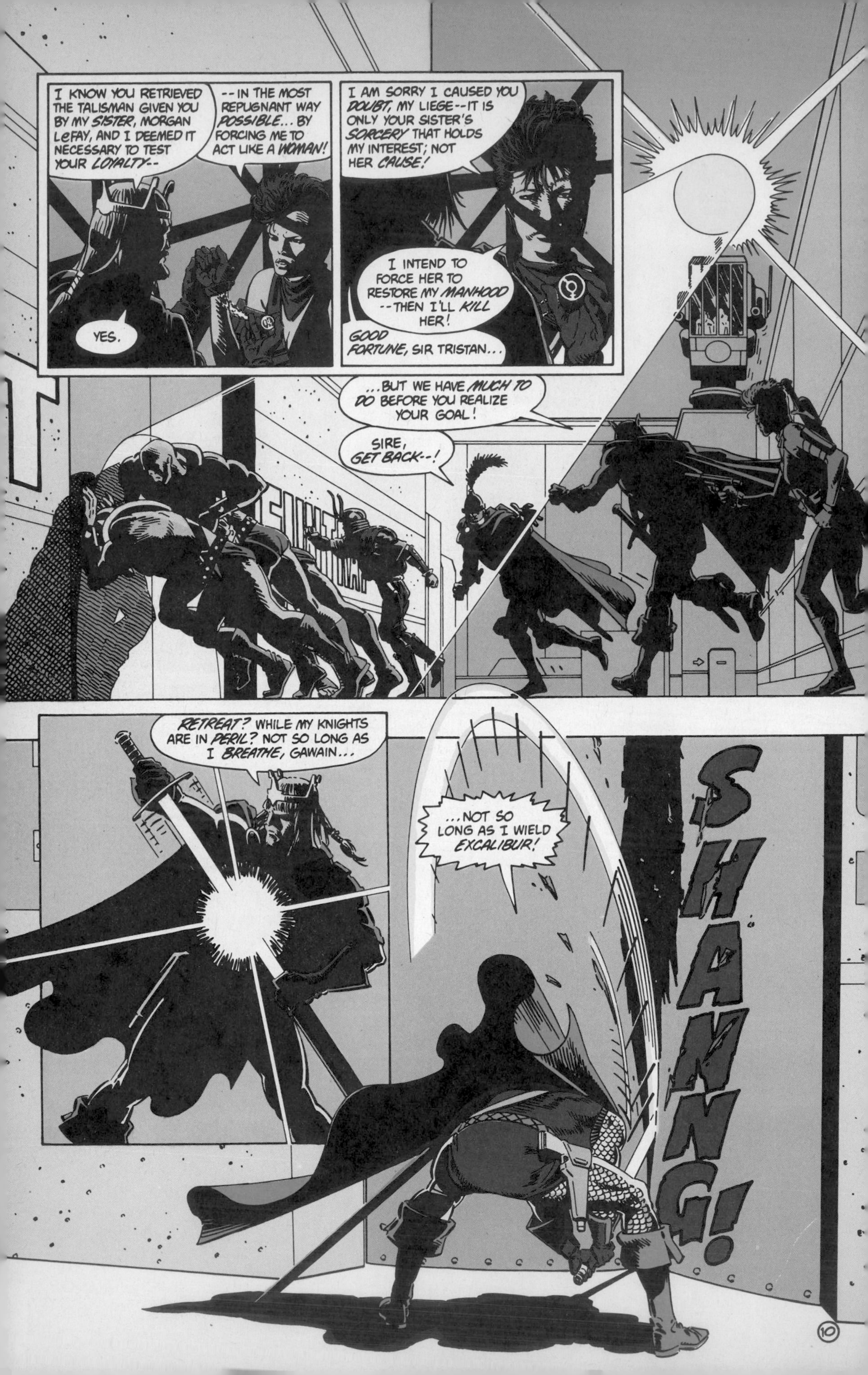
I KNOW YOU RETRIEVED THE TALISMAN GIVEN YOU BY MY SISTER, MORGAN LeFAY, AND I DEEMED IT NECESSARY TO TEST YOUR LOYALTY--
--IN THE MOST REPUGNANT WAY POSSIBLE... BY FORCING ME TO ACT LIKE A WOMAN!
YES.
I AM SORRY I CAUSED YOU DOUBT, MY LIEGE--IT IS ONLY YOUR SISTER'S SORCERY THAT HOLDS MY INTEREST; NOT HER CAUSE!
I INTEND TO FORCE HER TO RESTORE MY MANHOOD --THEN I'LL KILL HER!
GOOD FORTUNE, SIR TRISTAN...
...BUT WE HAVE MUCH TO DO BEFORE YOU REALIZE YOUR GOAL!
SIRE, GET BACK--!
RETREAT? WHILE MY KNIGHTS ARE IN PERIL? NOT SO LONG AS I BREATHE, GAWAIN...
...NOT SO LONG AS I WIELD EXCALIBUR!
SHANNG!
10

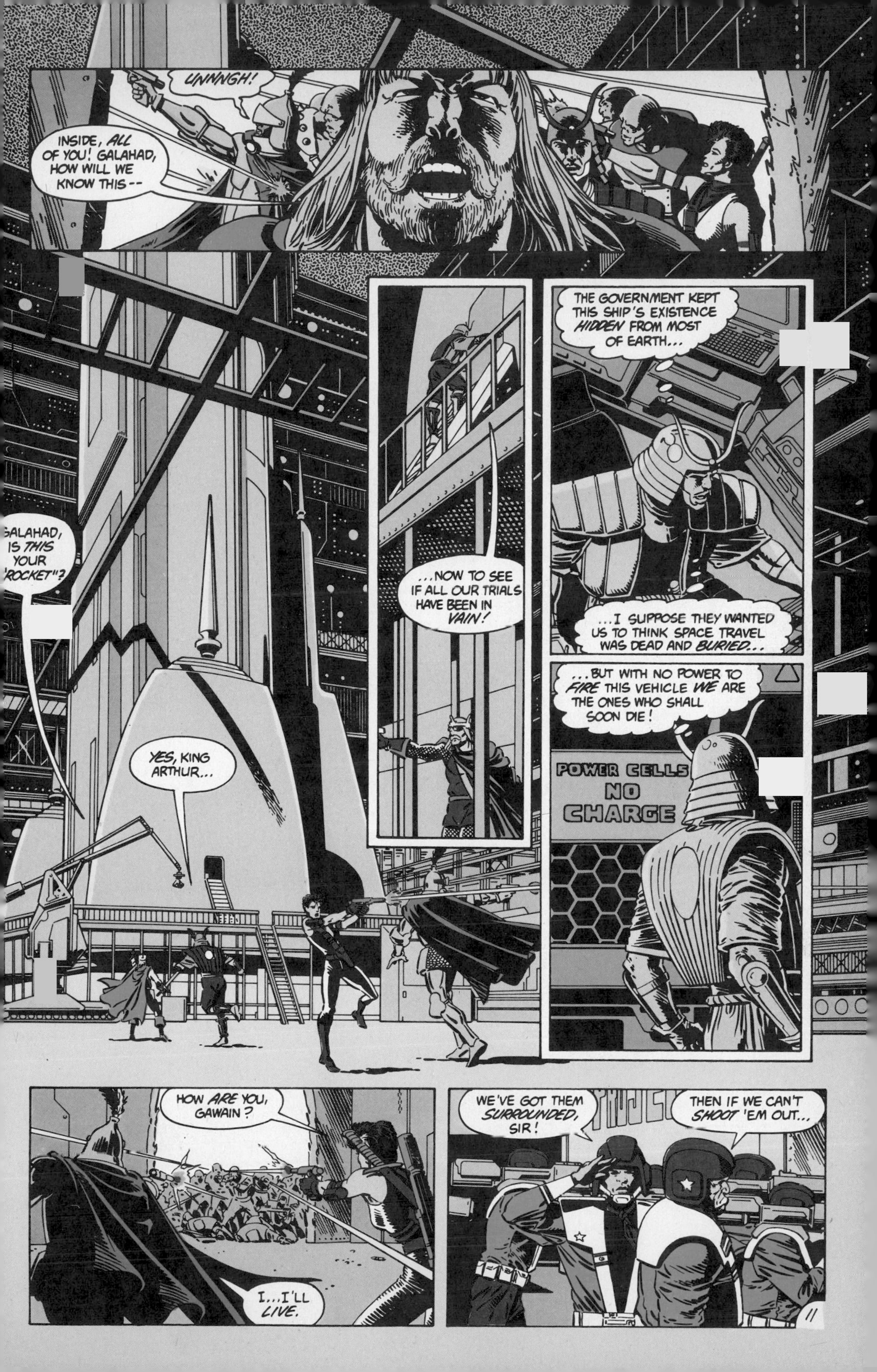
UNNNGH!
INSIDE, ALL OF YOU! GALAHAD, HOW WILL WE KNOW THIS --
GALAHAD, IS THIS YOUR "ROCKET"?
YES, KING ARTHUR...
...NOW TO SEE IF ALL OUR TRIALS HAVE BEEN IN VAIN!
THE GOVERNMENT KEPT THIS SHIP'S EXISTENCE HIDDEN FROM MOST OF EARTH...
...I SUPPOSE THEY WANTED US TO THINK SPACE TRAVEL WAS DEAD AND BURIED...
...BUT WITH NO POWER TO FIRE THIS VEHICLE WE ARE THE ONES WHO SHALL SOON DIE!
POWER CELLS
NO
CHARGE
HOW ARE YOU, GAWAIN?
I...I'LL LIVE.
WE'VE GOT THEM SURROUNDED, SIR!
THEN IF WE CAN'T SHOOT 'EM OUT...
11

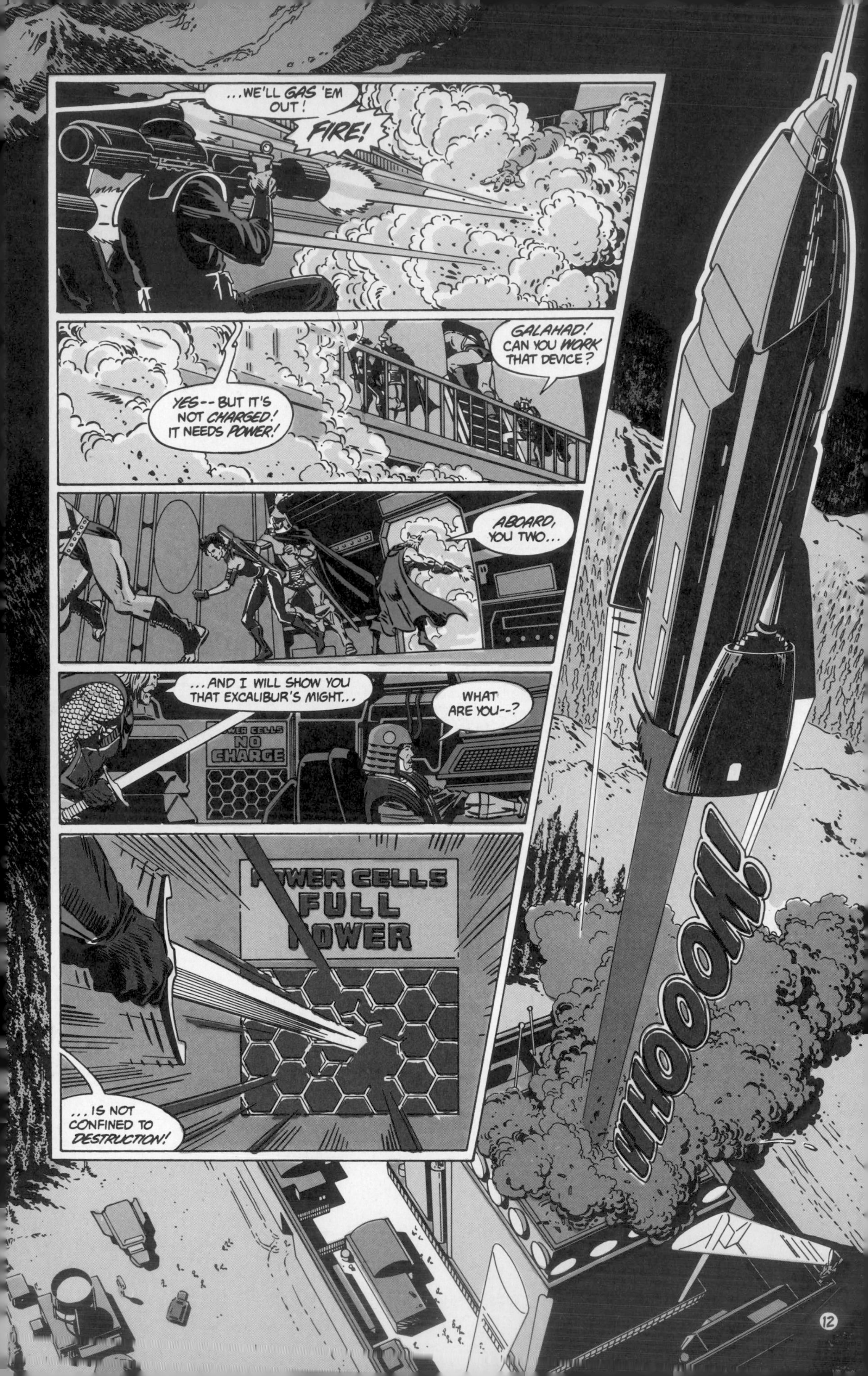
...WE'LL GAS 'EM OUT!
FIRE!
GALAHAD! CAN YOU WORK THAT DEVICE?
YES--BUT IT'S NOT CHARGED! IT NEEDS POWER!
ABOARD, YOU TWO...
...AND I WILL SHOW YOU THAT EXCALIBUR'S MIGHT...
WHAT ARE YOU--?
NO CHARGE
...IS NOT CONFINED TO DESTRUCTION!
FULL
WHOOOM!!

WE ARE NEARING *ESCAPE VELOCITY*, MY LIEGE, AND OUR WINDOW.

"WINDOW," SIR GALAHAD?

THE...UH...MOST OPPORTUNE SPOT TO LEAVE EARTH'S *ATMOSPHERE*, SIRE-- FOR OUR PURPOSES, IT IS LOCATED OVER *ENGLAND*.

ENGLAND?

ENGLAND. ARTHUR PENDRAGON KNOWS NOT THE PHRASES THAT THE POETS HAVE SCRIBED, PRAISING HIS NATIVE ISLE...

...HE KNOWS ONLY THAT HE LOVES IT MORE THAN WORDS CAN SAY...

ENGLAND.

...AND HE WONDERS IF HE WILL EVER SEE IT AGAIN.

ALL OF YOU, STATION YOURSELVES FOR A *JOLT*. THIS SHIP WAS DESIGNED TO TAP ENERGY FROM THE *SUN*, FOR USE ON *EARTH*...

ENGAGE SAILS

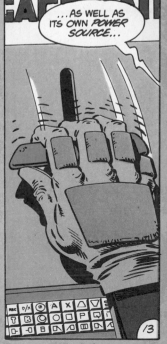

...AS WELL AS ITS OWN *POWER SOURCE*...

13

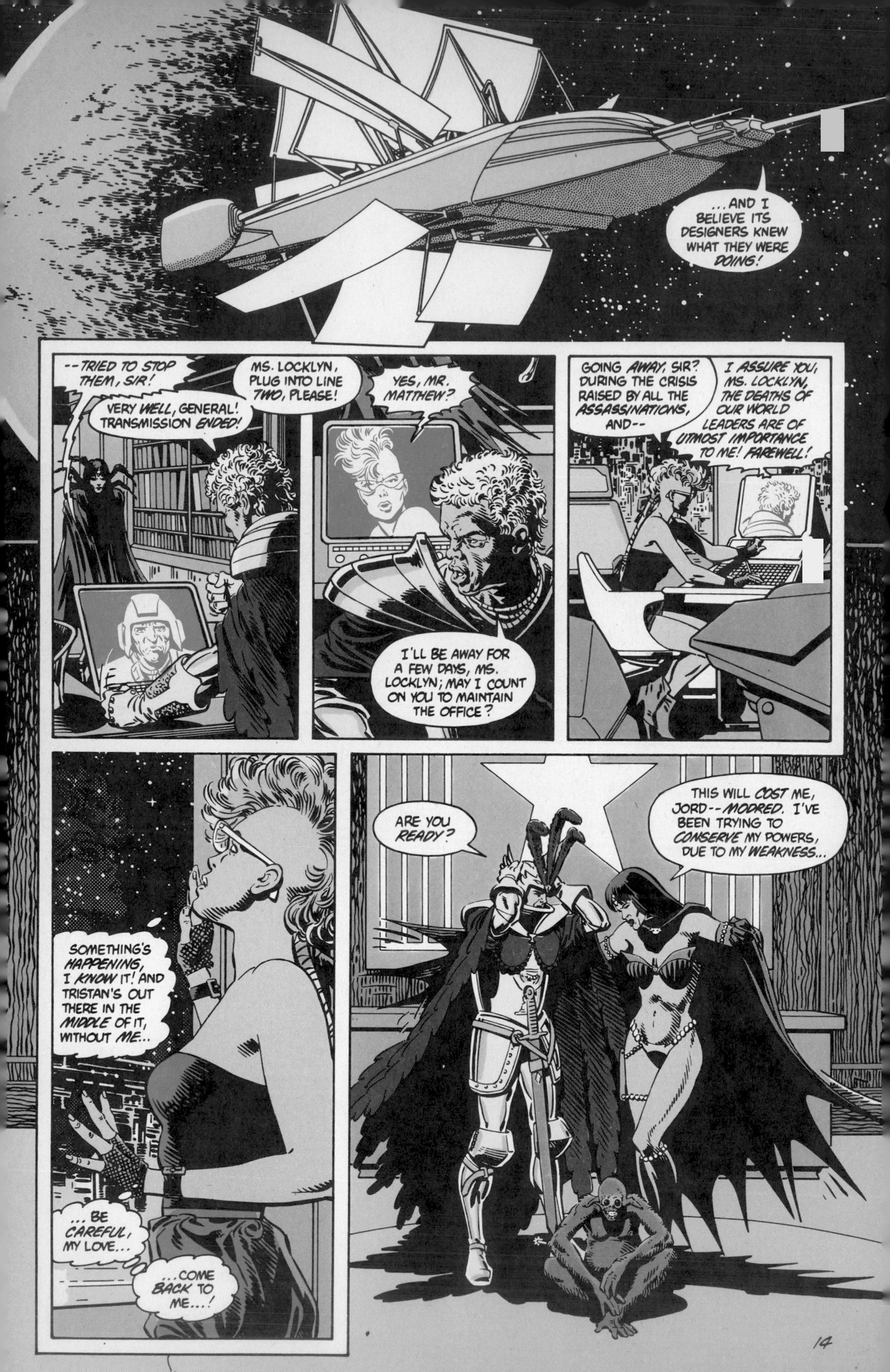
...AND I BELIEVE ITS DESIGNERS KNEW WHAT THEY WERE DOING!
--TRIED TO STOP THEM, SIR!
VERY WELL, GENERAL! TRANSMISSION ENDED!
MS. LOCKLYN, PLUG INTO LINE TWO, PLEASE!
YES, MR. MATTHEW?
I'LL BE AWAY FOR A FEW DAYS, MS. LOCKLYN; MAY I COUNT ON YOU TO MAINTAIN THE OFFICE?
GOING AWAY, SIR? DURING THE CRISIS RAISED BY ALL THE ASSASSINATIONS, AND--
I ASSURE YOU, MS. LOCKLYN, THE DEATHS OF OUR WORLD LEADERS ARE OF UTMOST IMPORTANCE TO ME! FAREWELL!
SOMETHING'S HAPPENING, I KNOW IT! AND TRISTAN'S OUT THERE IN THE MIDDLE OF IT, WITHOUT ME...
...BE CAREFUL, MY LOVE...
...COME BACK TO ME...!
ARE YOU READY?
THIS WILL COST ME, JORD--MODRED. I'VE BEEN TRYING TO CONSERVE MY POWERS, DUE TO MY WEAKNESS...

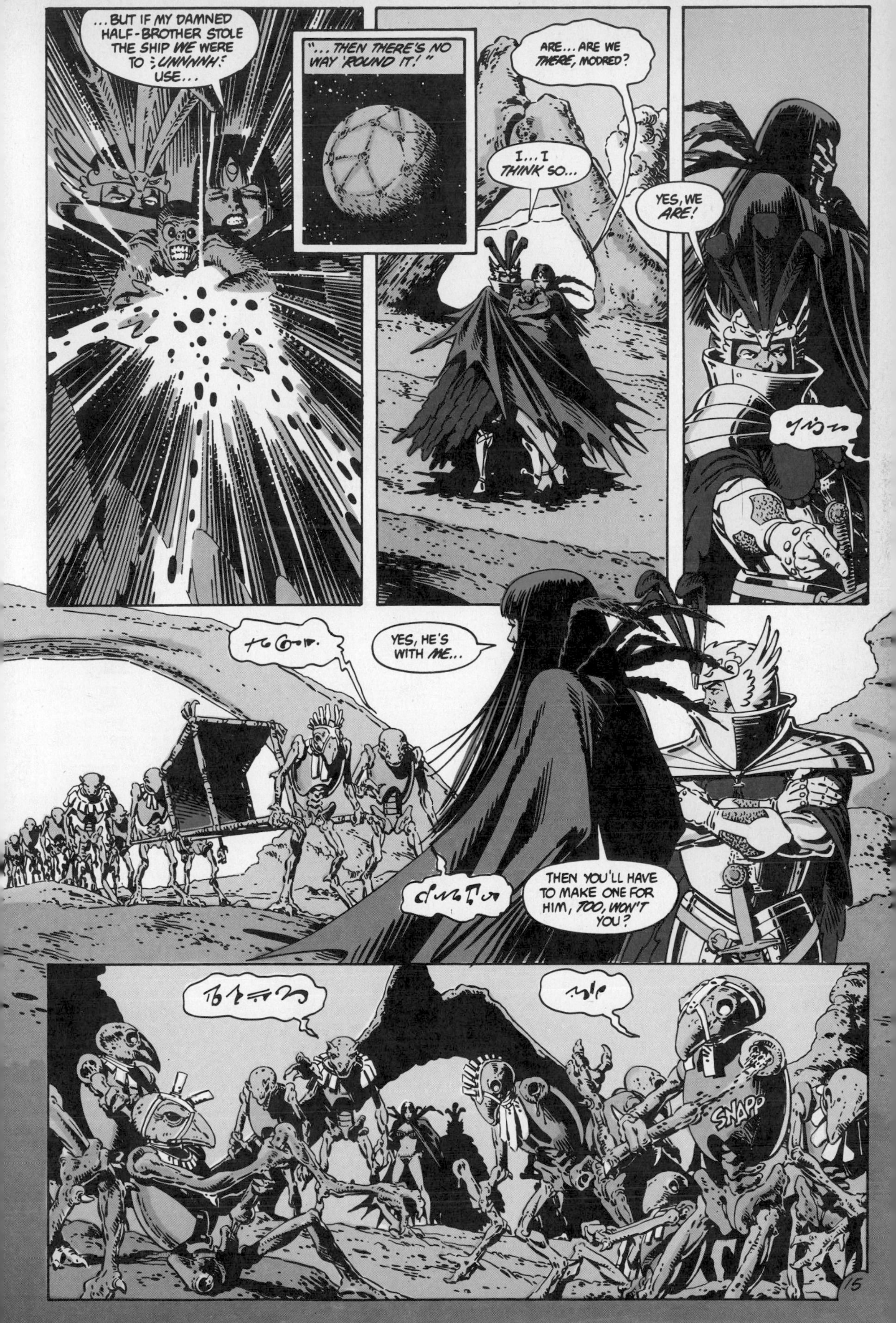
...BUT IF MY DAMNED HALF-BROTHER STOLE THE SHIP WE WERE TO ;UNNNNH; USE...
"...THEN THERE'S NO WAY 'ROUND IT!"
ARE... ARE WE THERE, MODRED?
I... I THINK SO...
YES, WE ARE!
YES, HE'S WITH ME...
THEN YOU'LL HAVE TO MAKE ONE FOR HIM, TOO, WON'T YOU?
SNAPP
15

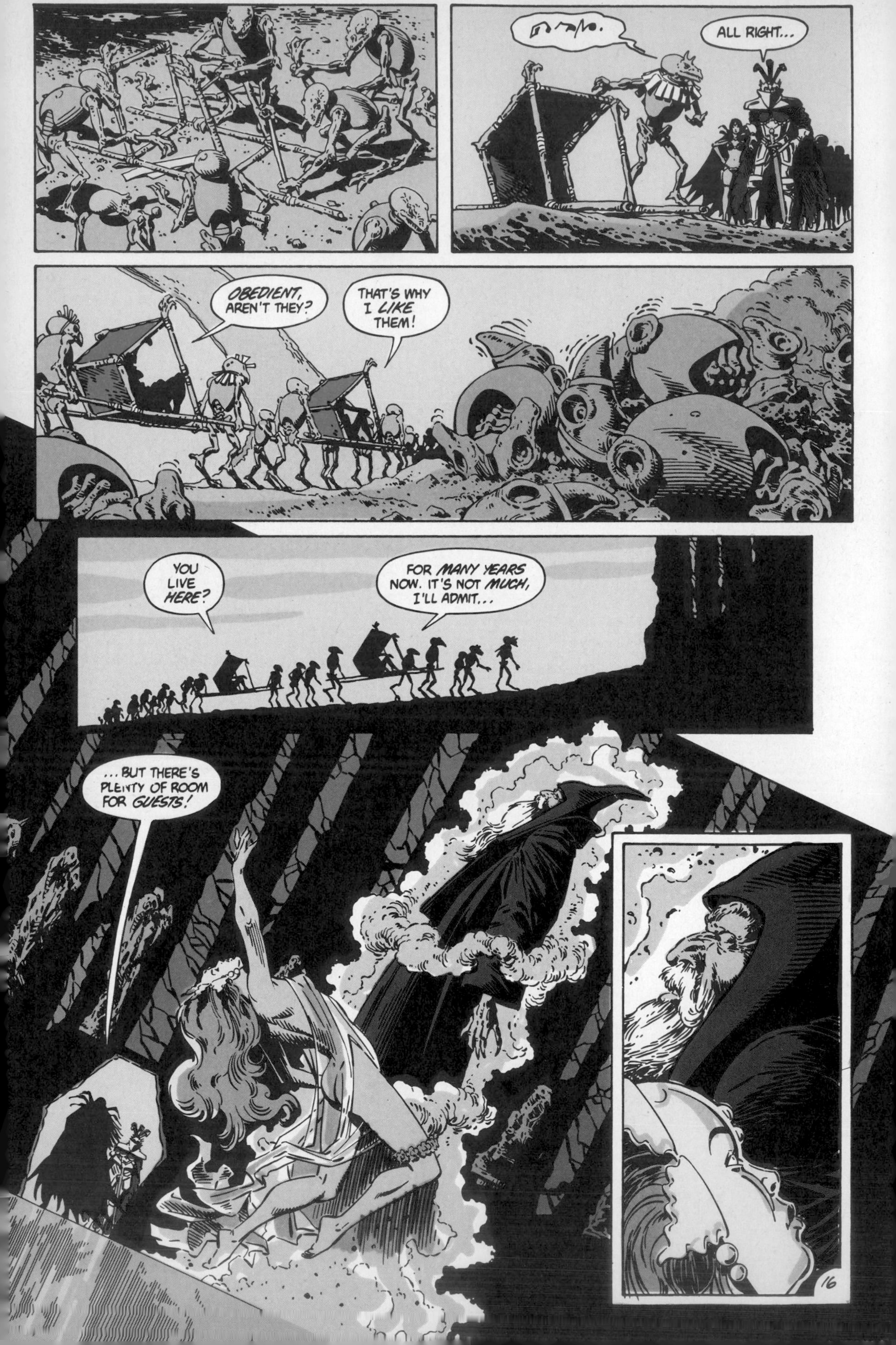
ALL RIGHT...
OBEDIENT, AREN'T THEY?
THAT'S WHY I LIKE THEM!
YOU LIVE HERE?
FOR MANY YEARS NOW. IT'S NOT MUCH, I'LL ADMIT...
...BUT THERE'S PLENTY OF ROOM FOR GUESTS!
16

SALISBURY DOWN NUCLEAR PLANT
B792
CYCLOTRON
ALARM
CYC

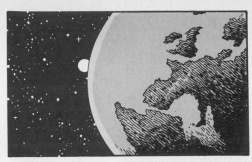

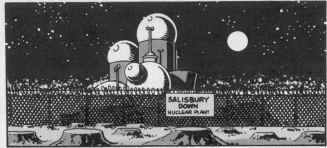

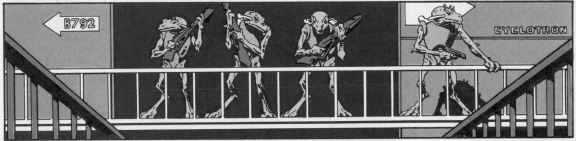

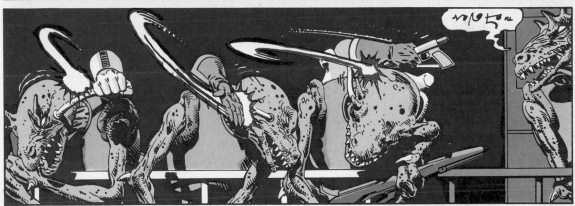

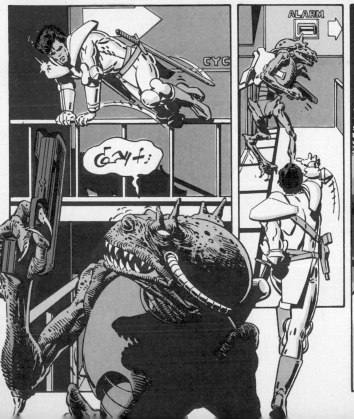

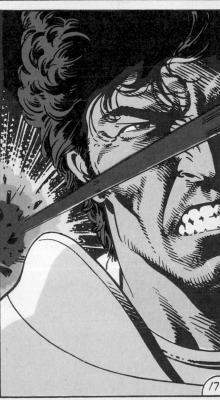

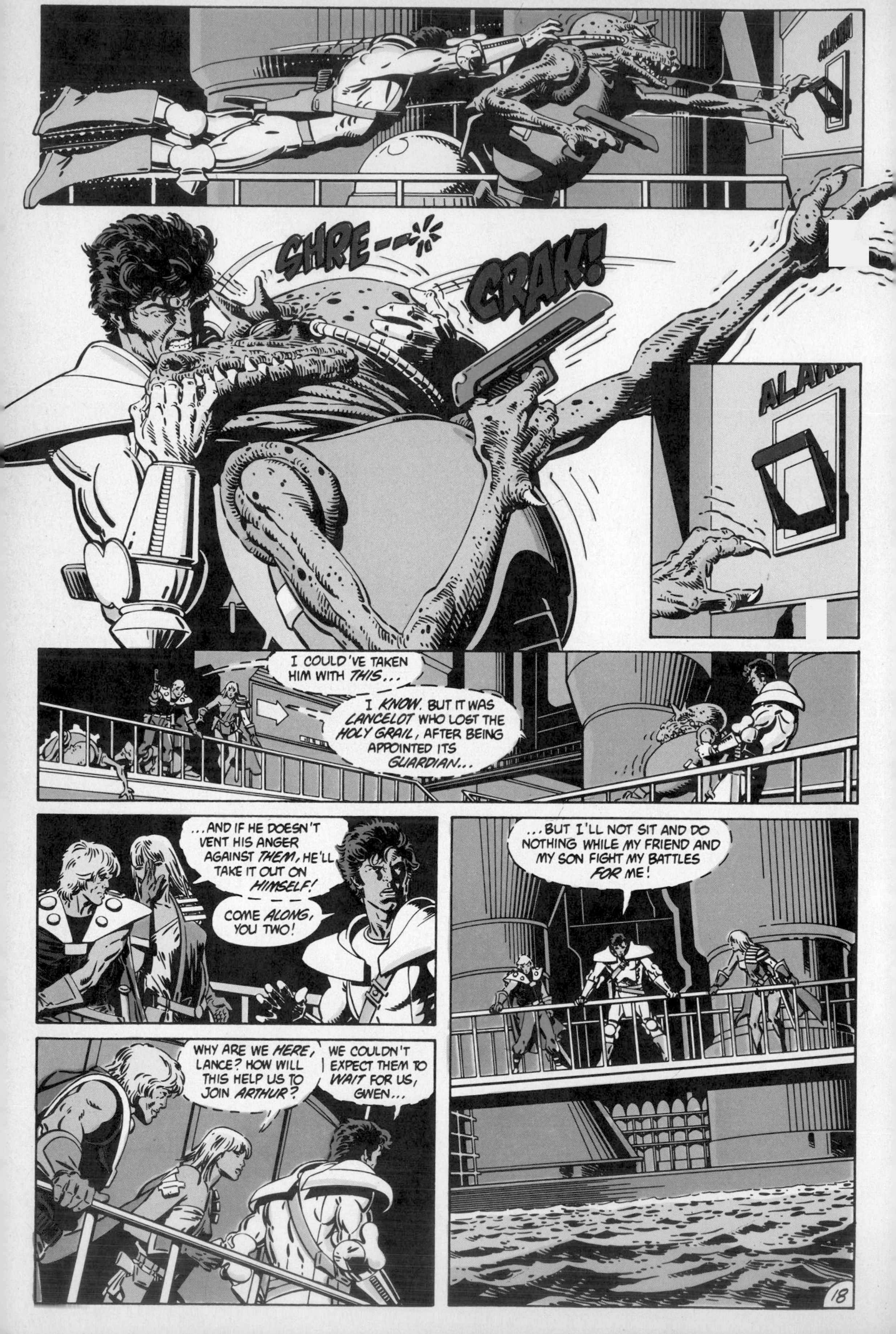
ALARM
SHRE--
CRAK!
ALAR
I COULD'VE TAKEN HIM WITH THIS...
I KNOW. BUT IT WAS LANCELOT WHO LOST THE HOLY GRAIL, AFTER BEING APPOINTED ITS GUARDIAN...
...AND IF HE DOESN'T VENT HIS ANGER AGAINST THEM, HE'LL TAKE IT OUT ON HIMSELF!
COME ALONG, YOU TWO!
...BUT I'LL NOT SIT AND DO NOTHING WHILE MY FRIEND AND MY SON FIGHT MY BATTLES FOR ME!
WHY ARE WE HERE, LANCE? HOW WILL THIS HELP US TO JOIN ARTHUR?
WE COULDN'T EXPECT THEM TO WAIT FOR US, GWEN...
18

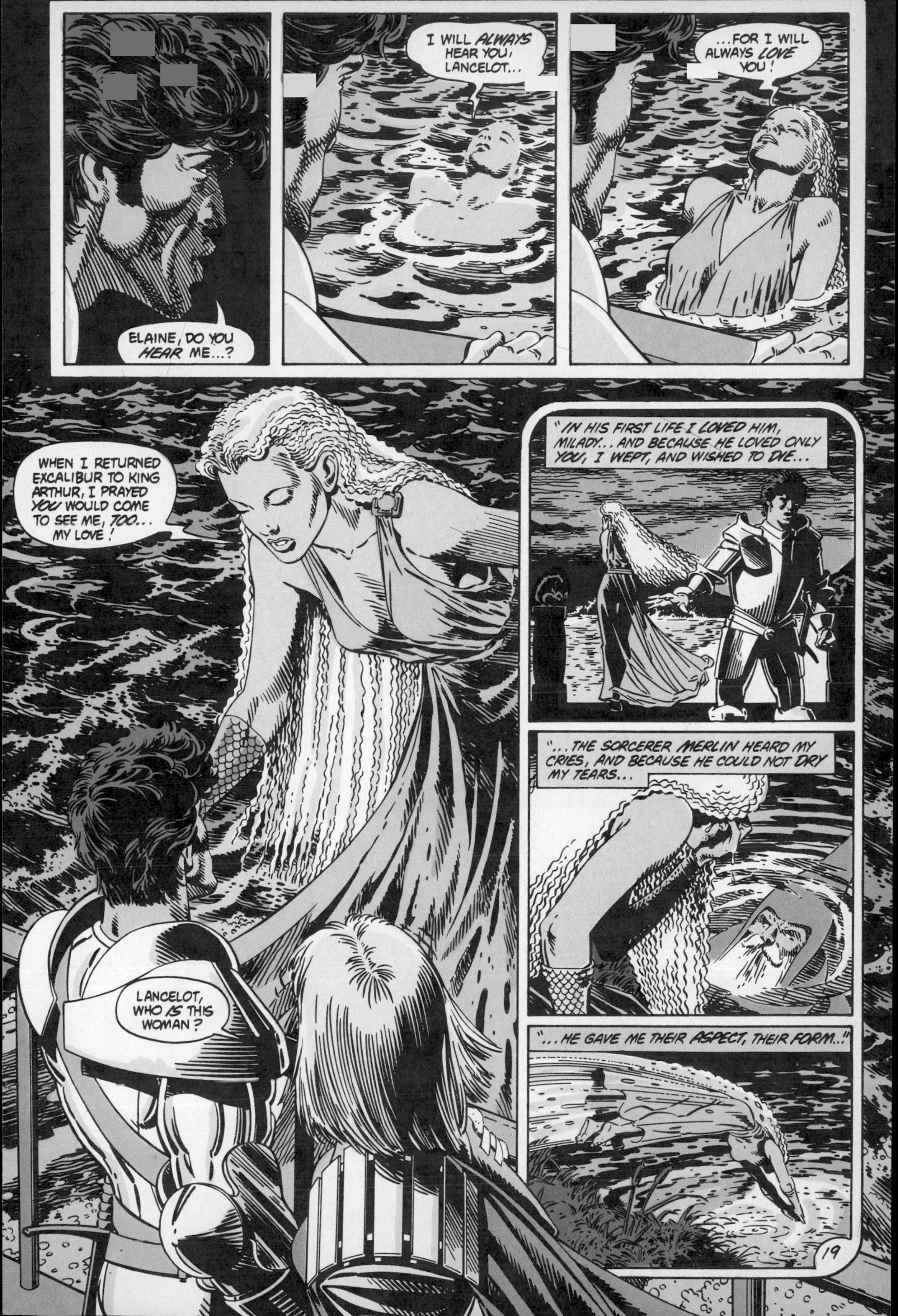
ELAINE, DO YOU HEAR ME...?
I WILL ALWAYS HEAR YOU, LANCELOT...
...FOR I WILL ALWAYS LOVE YOU!
WHEN I RETURNED EXCALIBUR TO KING ARTHUR, I PRAYED YOU WOULD COME TO SEE ME, TOO... MY LOVE!
"IN HIS FIRST LIFE I LOVED HIM, MILADY... AND BECAUSE HE LOVED ONLY YOU, I WEPT, AND WISHED TO DIE...
LANCELOT, WHO IS THIS WOMAN?
"...THE SORCERER MERLIN HEARD MY CRIES, AND BECAUSE HE COULD NOT DRY MY TEARS...
"...HE GAVE ME THEIR ASPECT, THEIR FORM..."

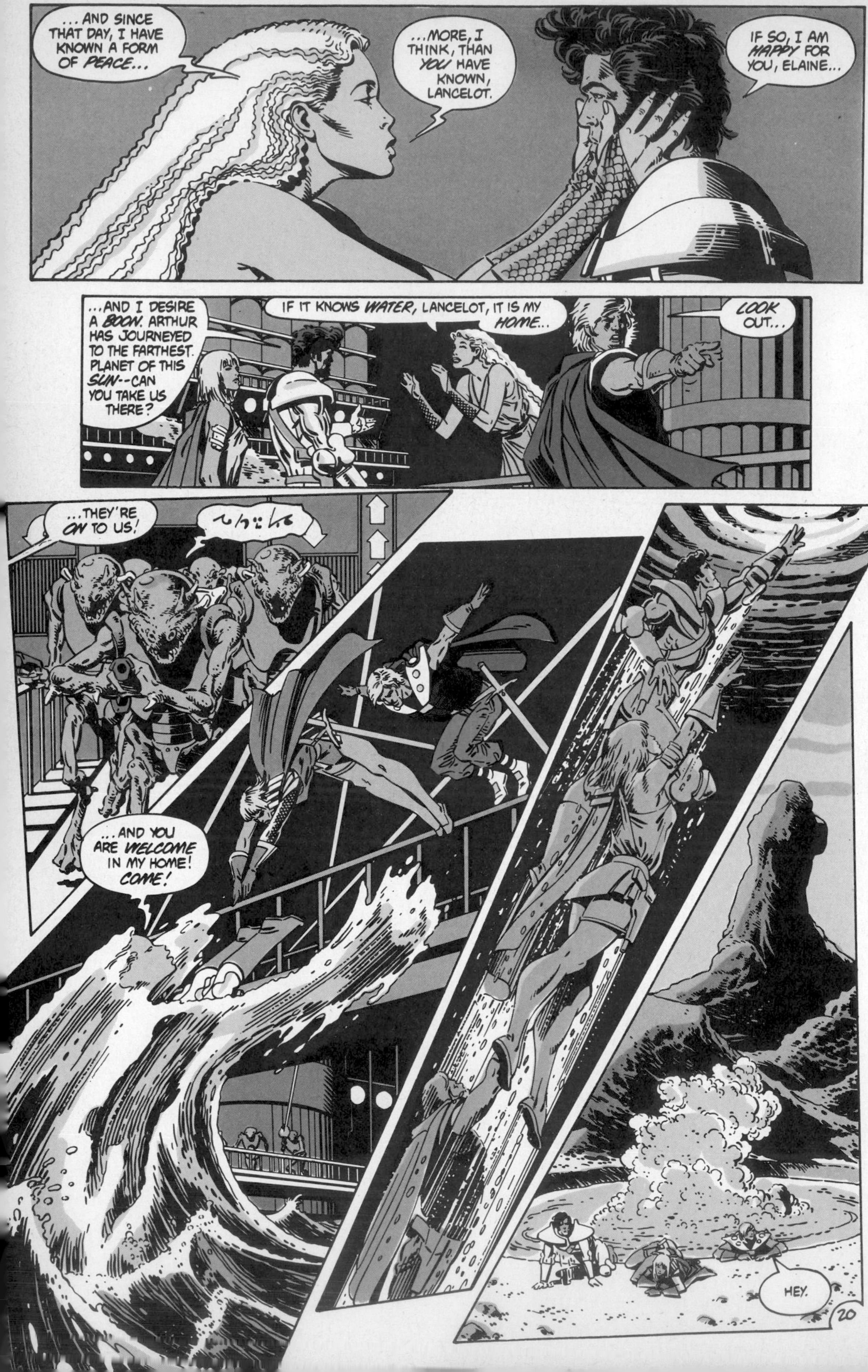
...AND SINCE THAT DAY, I HAVE KNOWN A FORM OF PEACE...
...MORE, I THINK, THAN YOU HAVE KNOWN, LANCELOT.
IF SO, I AM HAPPY FOR YOU, ELAINE...
...AND I DESIRE A BOON. ARTHUR HAS JOURNEYED TO THE FARTHEST PLANET OF THIS SUN--CAN YOU TAKE US THERE?
IF IT KNOWS WATER, LANCELOT, IT IS MY HOME...
LOOK OUT...
...THEY'RE ON TO US!
...AND YOU ARE WELCOME IN MY HOME! COME!
HEY.

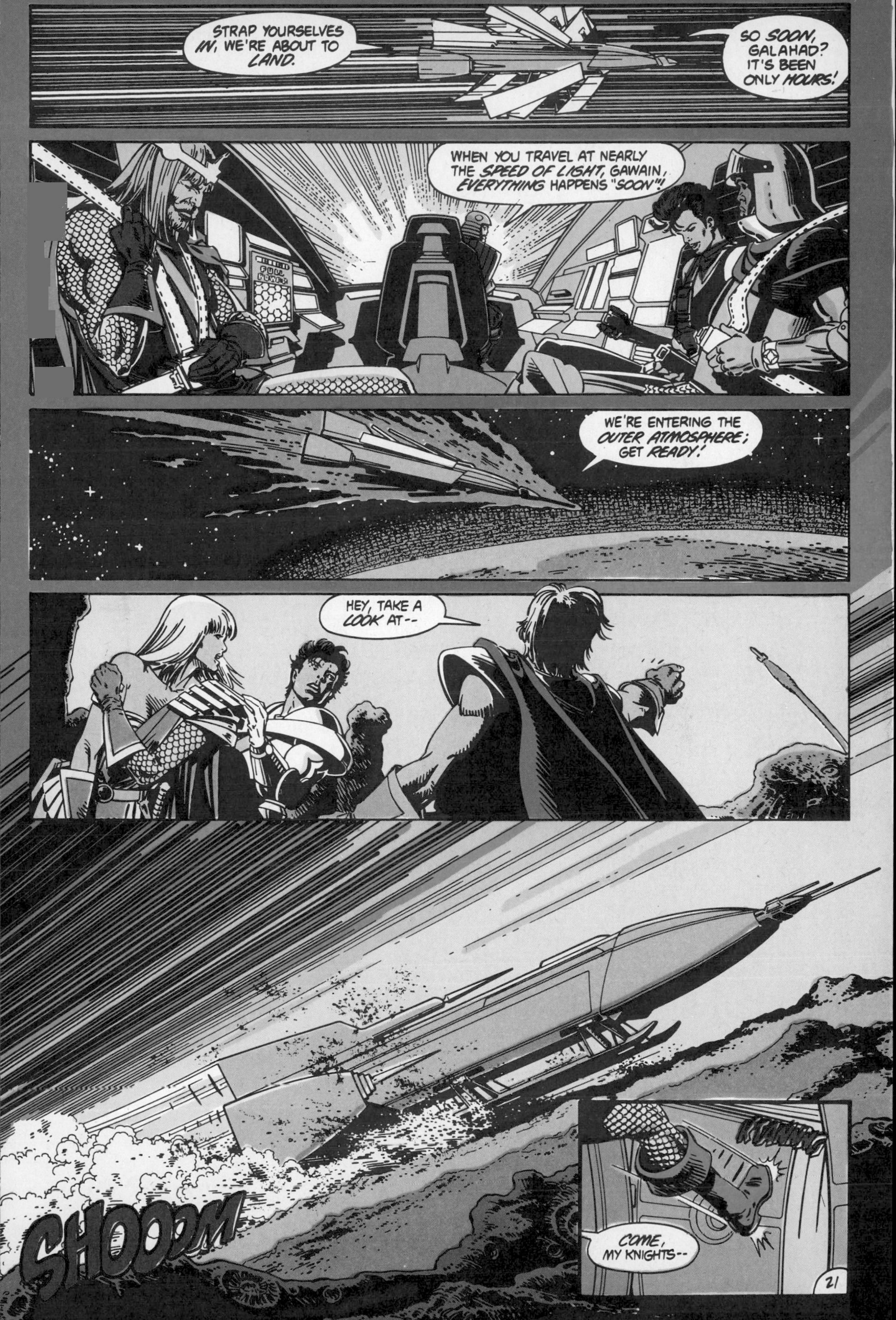
STRAP YOURSELVES IN, WE'RE ABOUT TO LAND.
SO SOON, GALAHAD? IT'S BEEN ONLY HOURS!
WHEN YOU TRAVEL AT NEARLY THE SPEED OF LIGHT, GAWAIN, EVERYTHING HAPPENS "SOON"!
WE'RE ENTERING THE OUTER ATMOSPHERE; GET READY!
HEY, TAKE A LOOK AT--
SHOOOM
KRANNNG
COME, MY KNIGHTS--

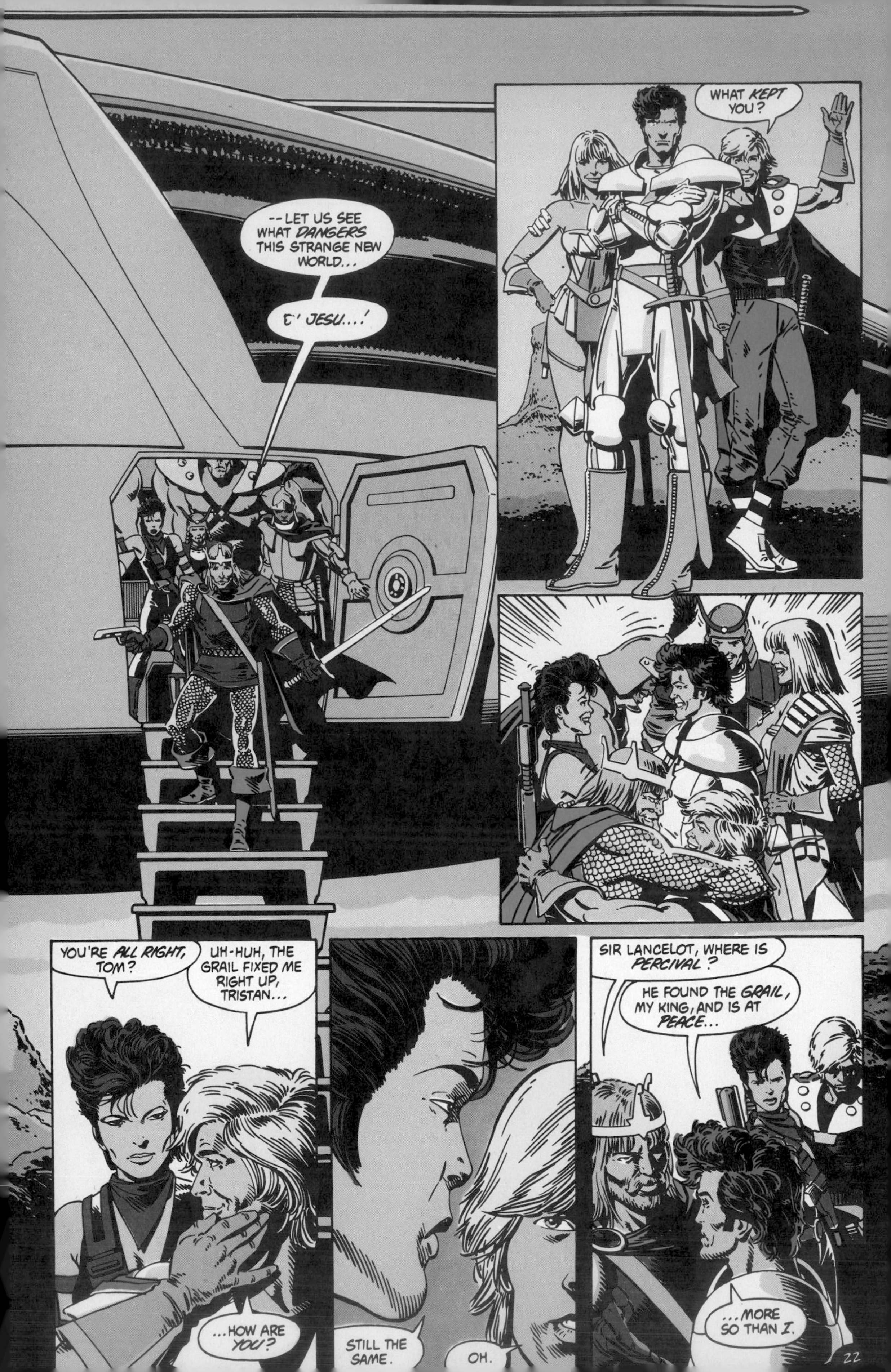
--LET US SEE WHAT *DANGERS* THIS STRANGE NEW WORLD...
E' JESU...!
WHAT *KEPT* YOU?
YOU'RE *ALL RIGHT,* TOM?
UH-HUH, THE GRAIL FIXED ME RIGHT UP, TRISTAN...
...HOW ARE *YOU*?
STILL THE SAME.
OH.
SIR LANCELOT, WHERE IS *PERCIVAL*?
HE FOUND THE *GRAIL*, MY KING, AND IS AT *PEACE*...
...MORE SO THAN *I*.

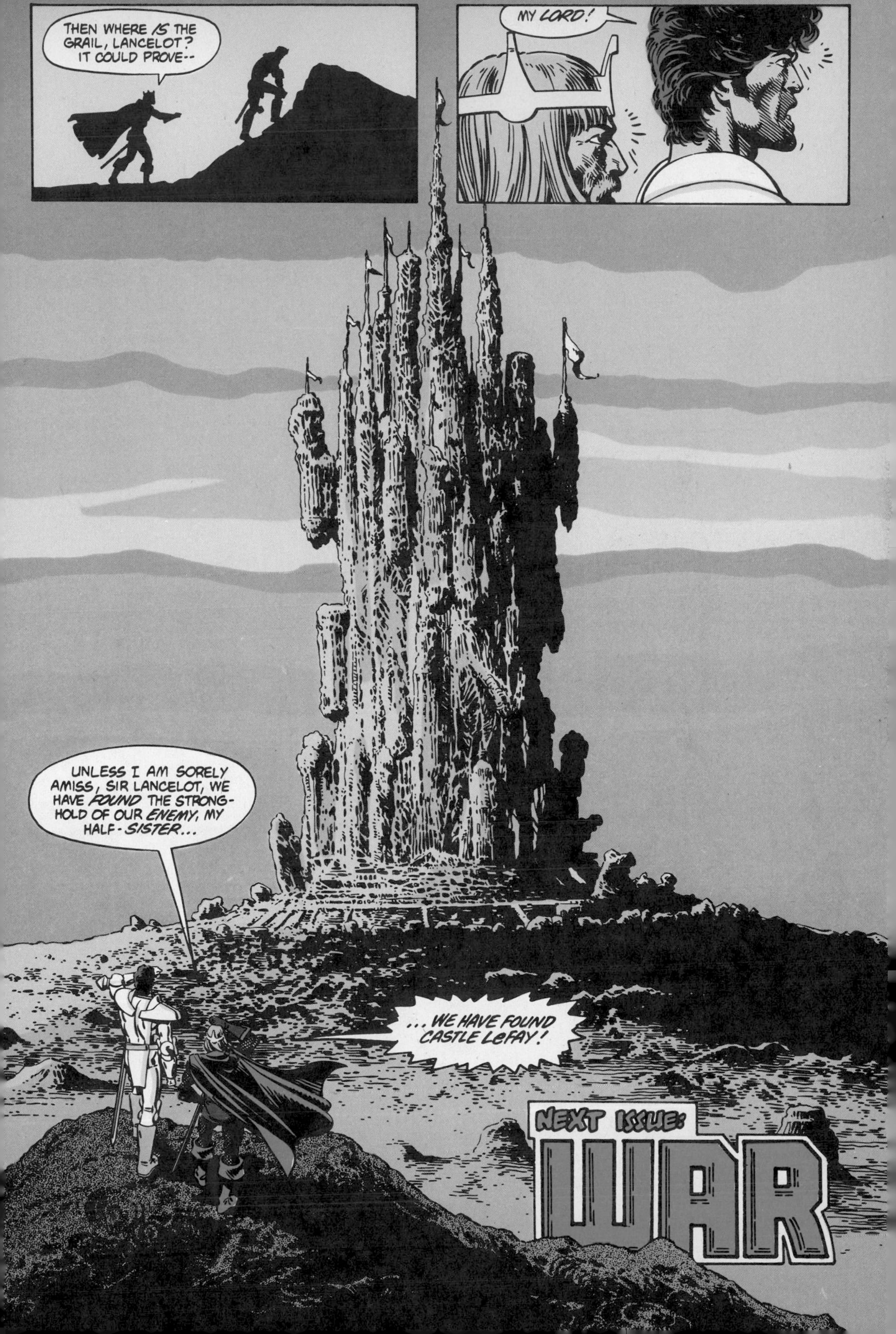

THEN WHERE IS THE GRAIL, LANCELOT? IT COULD PROVE--
MY LORD!
UNLESS I AM SORELY AMISS, SIR LANCELOT, WE HAVE FOUND THE STRONG-HOLD OF OUR ENEMY, MY HALF-SISTER...
...WE HAVE FOUND CASTLE LeFAY!
NEXT ISSUE:
WAR

Chapter
11

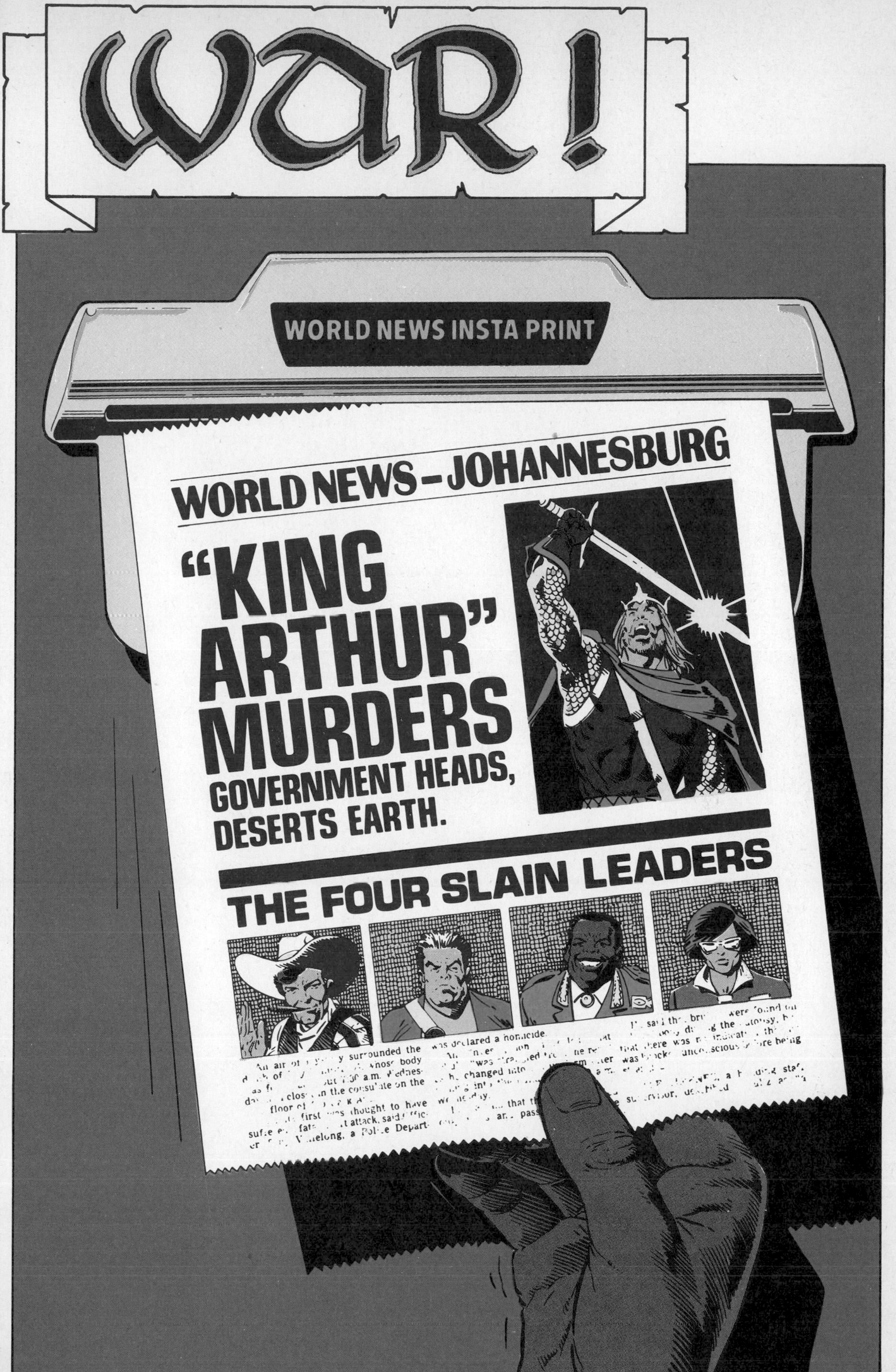
WAR!
WORLD NEWS INSTA PRINT
WORLD NEWS – JOHANNESBURG
"KING ARTHUR" MURDERS GOVERNMENT HEADS, DESERTS EARTH.
THE FOUR SLAIN LEADERS

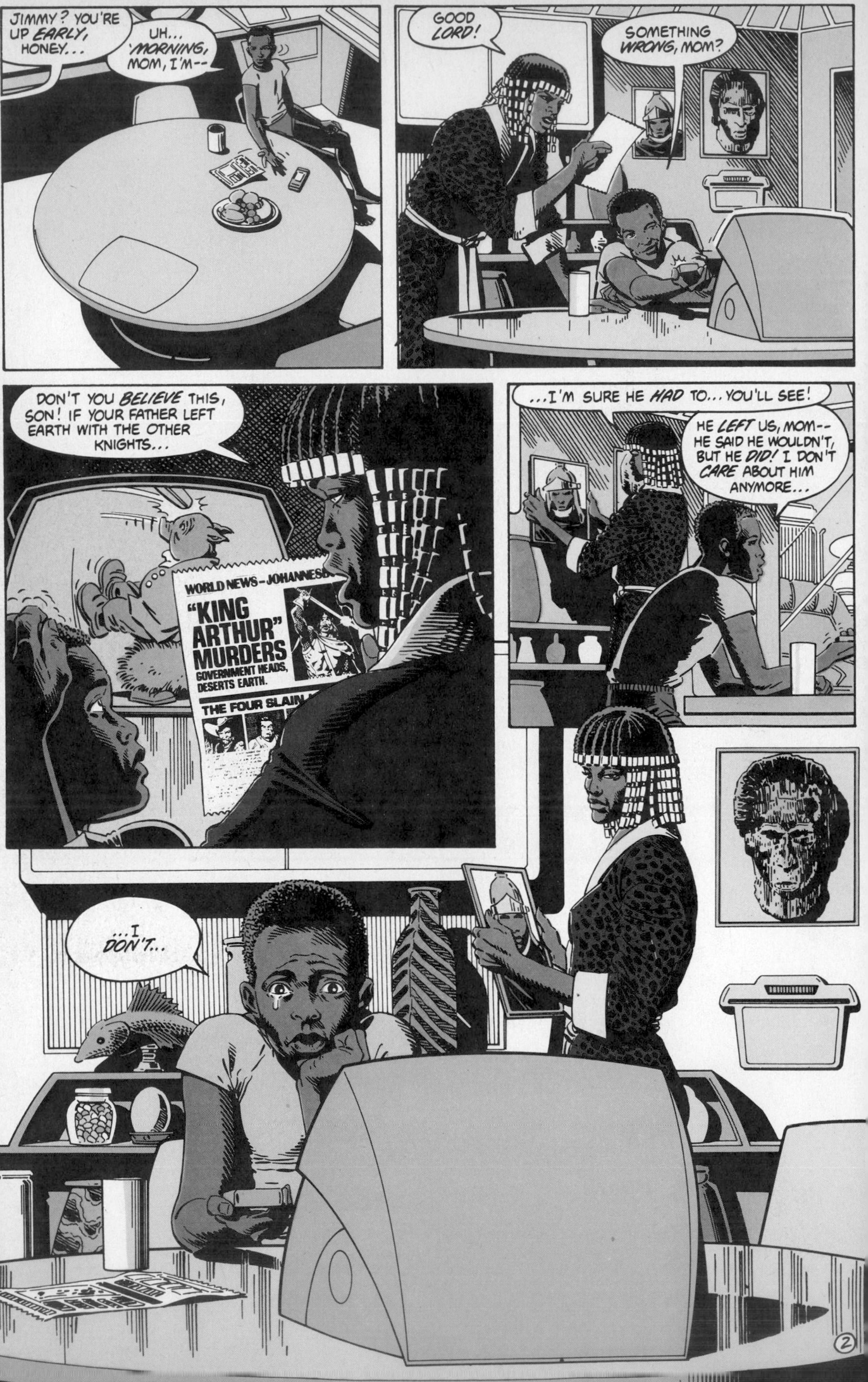

JIMMY? YOU'RE UP EARLY, HONEY...
UH... 'MORNING, MOM, I'M--
GOOD LORD!
SOMETHING WRONG, MOM?
DON'T YOU BELIEVE THIS, SON! IF YOUR FATHER LEFT EARTH WITH THE OTHER KNIGHTS...
WORLD NEWS--JOHANNES
"KING ARTHUR" MURDERS GOVERNMENT HEADS, DESERTS EARTH.
THE FOUR SLAIN
...I'M SURE HE HAD TO... YOU'LL SEE!
HE LEFT US, MOM-- HE SAID HE WOULDN'T, BUT HE DID! I DON'T CARE ABOUT HIM ANYMORE...
...I DON'T...
2

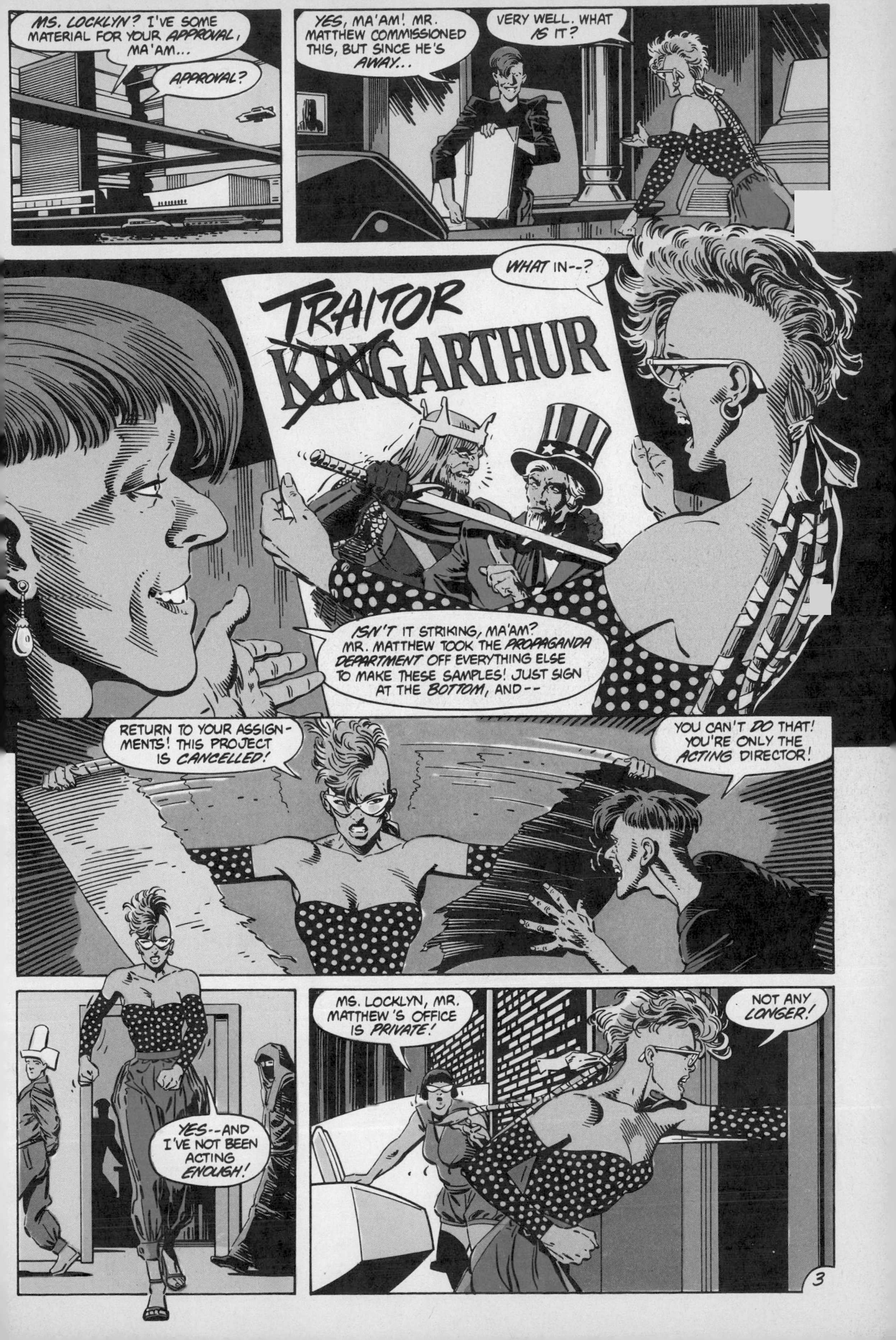
MS. LOCKLYN? I'VE SOME MATERIAL FOR YOUR APPROVAL, MA'AM...
APPROVAL?
YES, MA'AM! MR. MATTHEW COMMISSIONED THIS, BUT SINCE HE'S AWAY...
VERY WELL. WHAT IS IT?
WHAT IN--?
TRAITOR
KING ARTHUR
ISN'T IT STRIKING, MA'AM? MR. MATTHEW TOOK THE PROPAGANDA DEPARTMENT OFF EVERYTHING ELSE TO MAKE THESE SAMPLES! JUST SIGN AT THE BOTTOM, AND--
RETURN TO YOUR ASSIGNMENTS! THIS PROJECT IS CANCELLED!
YOU CAN'T DO THAT! YOU'RE ONLY THE ACTING DIRECTOR!
YES--AND I'VE NOT BEEN ACTING ENOUGH!
MS. LOCKLYN, MR. MATTHEW'S OFFICE IS PRIVATE!
NOT ANY LONGER!

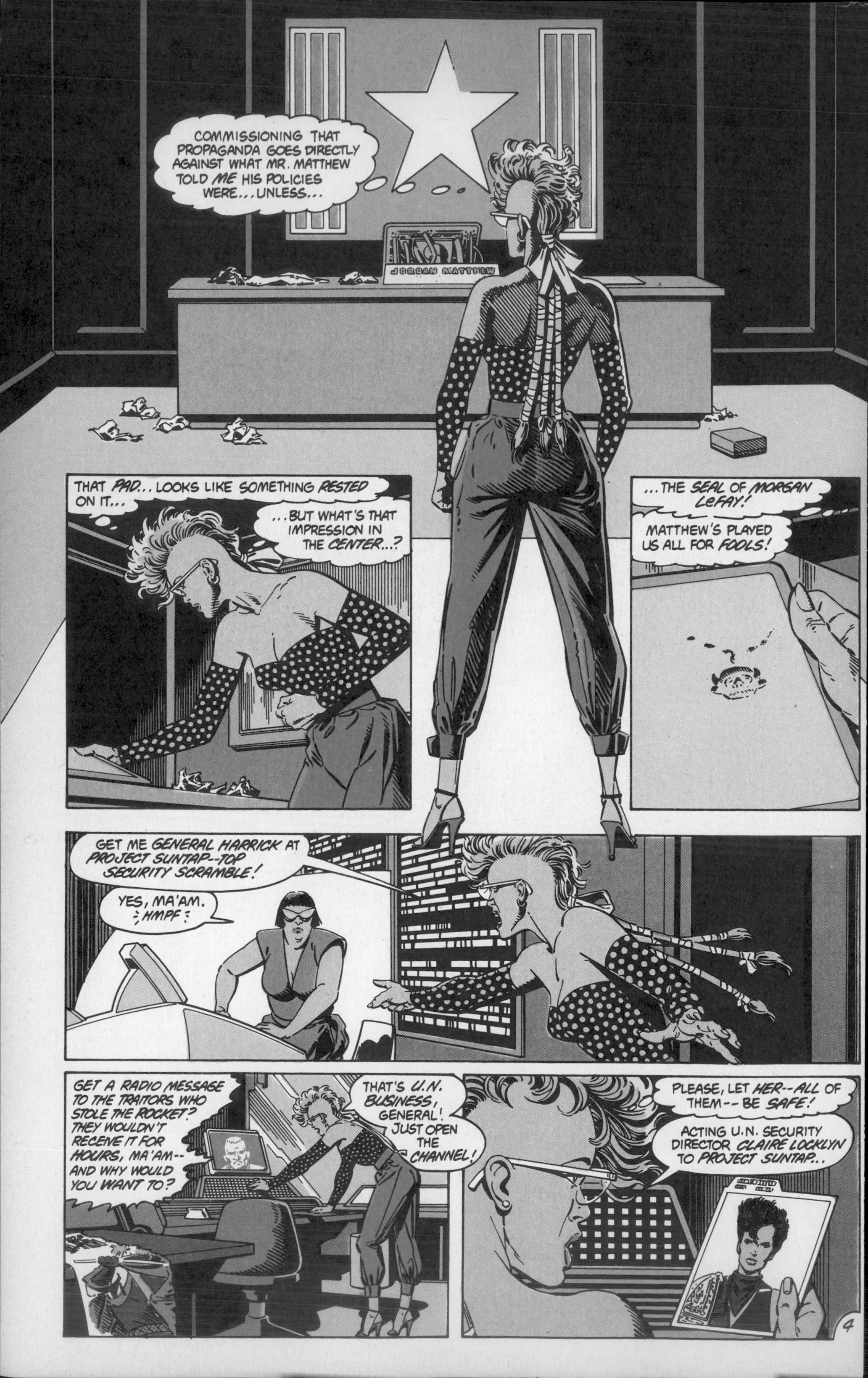
COMMISSIONING THAT PROPAGANDA GOES DIRECTLY AGAINST WHAT MR. MATTHEW TOLD ME HIS POLICIES WERE... UNLESS...
JORDAN MATTHEW
THAT PAD... LOOKS LIKE SOMETHING RESTED ON IT...
...BUT WHAT'S THAT IMPRESSION IN THE CENTER...?
...THE SEAL OF MORGAN LeFAY!
MATTHEW'S PLAYED US ALL FOR FOOLS!
GET ME GENERAL HARRICK AT PROJECT SUNTAP--TOP SECURITY SCRAMBLE!
YES, MA'AM. :HMPF:
GET A RADIO MESSAGE TO THE TRAITORS WHO STOLE THE ROCKET? THEY WOULDN'T RECEIVE IT FOR HOURS, MA'AM-- AND WHY WOULD YOU WANT TO?
THAT'S U.N. BUSINESS, GENERAL! JUST OPEN THE CHANNEL!
PLEASE, LET HER--ALL OF THEM--BE SAFE!
ACTING U.N. SECURITY DIRECTOR CLAIRE LOCKLYN TO PROJECT SUNTAP...
4

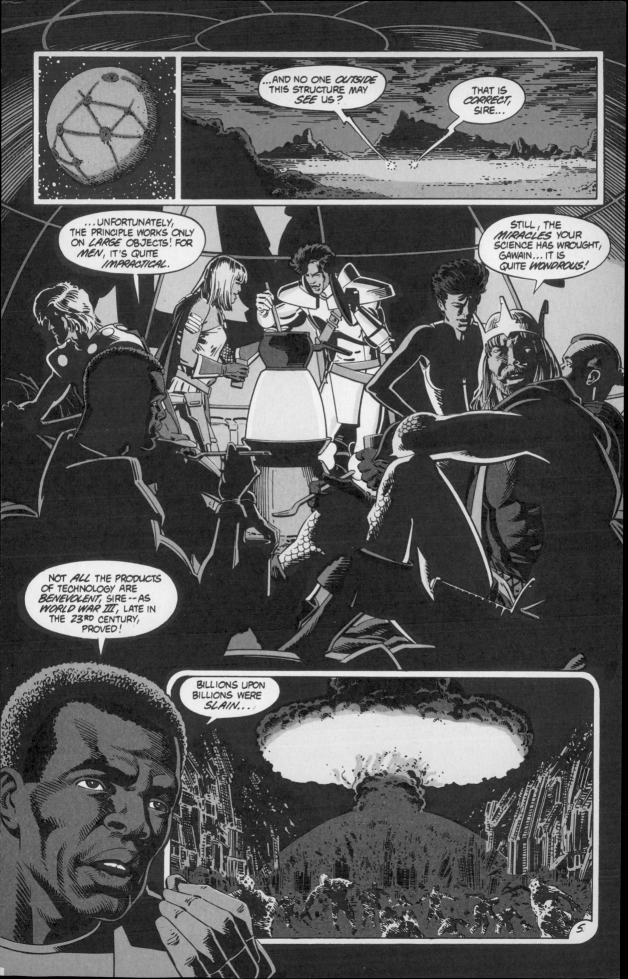

...AND NO ONE *OUTSIDE* THIS STRUCTURE MAY *SEE US?*

THAT IS *CORRECT,* SIRE...

...UNFORTUNATELY, THE PRINCIPLE WORKS ONLY ON *LARGE OBJECTS!* FOR *MEN,* IT'S QUITE *IMPRACTICAL.*

STILL, THE *MIRACLES* YOUR SCIENCE HAS WROUGHT, GAWAIN... IT IS QUITE *WONDROUS!*

NOT *ALL* THE PRODUCTS OF TECHNOLOGY ARE *BENEVOLENT,* SIRE -- AS *WORLD WAR III,* LATE IN THE 23RD CENTURY, PROVED!

BILLIONS UPON BILLIONS WERE *SLAIN...*

5

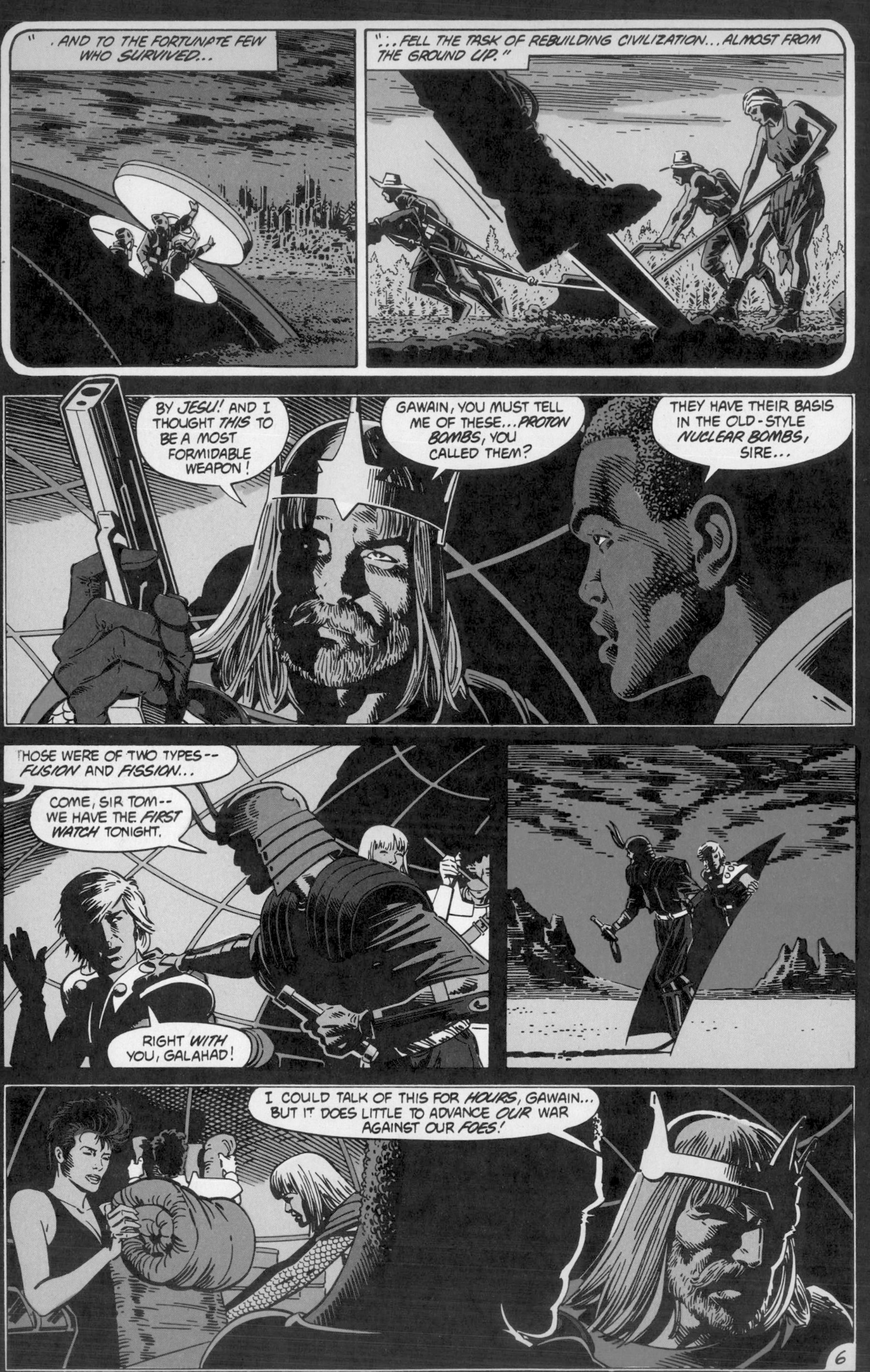
". . . AND TO THE FORTUNATE FEW WHO SURVIVED...
"...FELL THE TASK OF REBUILDING CIVILIZATION... ALMOST FROM THE GROUND UP."
BY JESU! AND I THOUGHT THIS TO BE A MOST FORMIDABLE WEAPON!
GAWAIN, YOU MUST TELL ME OF THESE... PROTON BOMBS, YOU CALLED THEM?
THEY HAVE THEIR BASIS IN THE OLD-STYLE NUCLEAR BOMBS, SIRE...
THOSE WERE OF TWO TYPES-- FUSION AND FISSION...
COME, SIR TOM-- WE HAVE THE FIRST WATCH TONIGHT.
RIGHT WITH YOU, GALAHAD!
I COULD TALK OF THIS FOR HOURS, GAWAIN... BUT IT DOES LITTLE TO ADVANCE OUR WAR AGAINST OUR FOES!
6

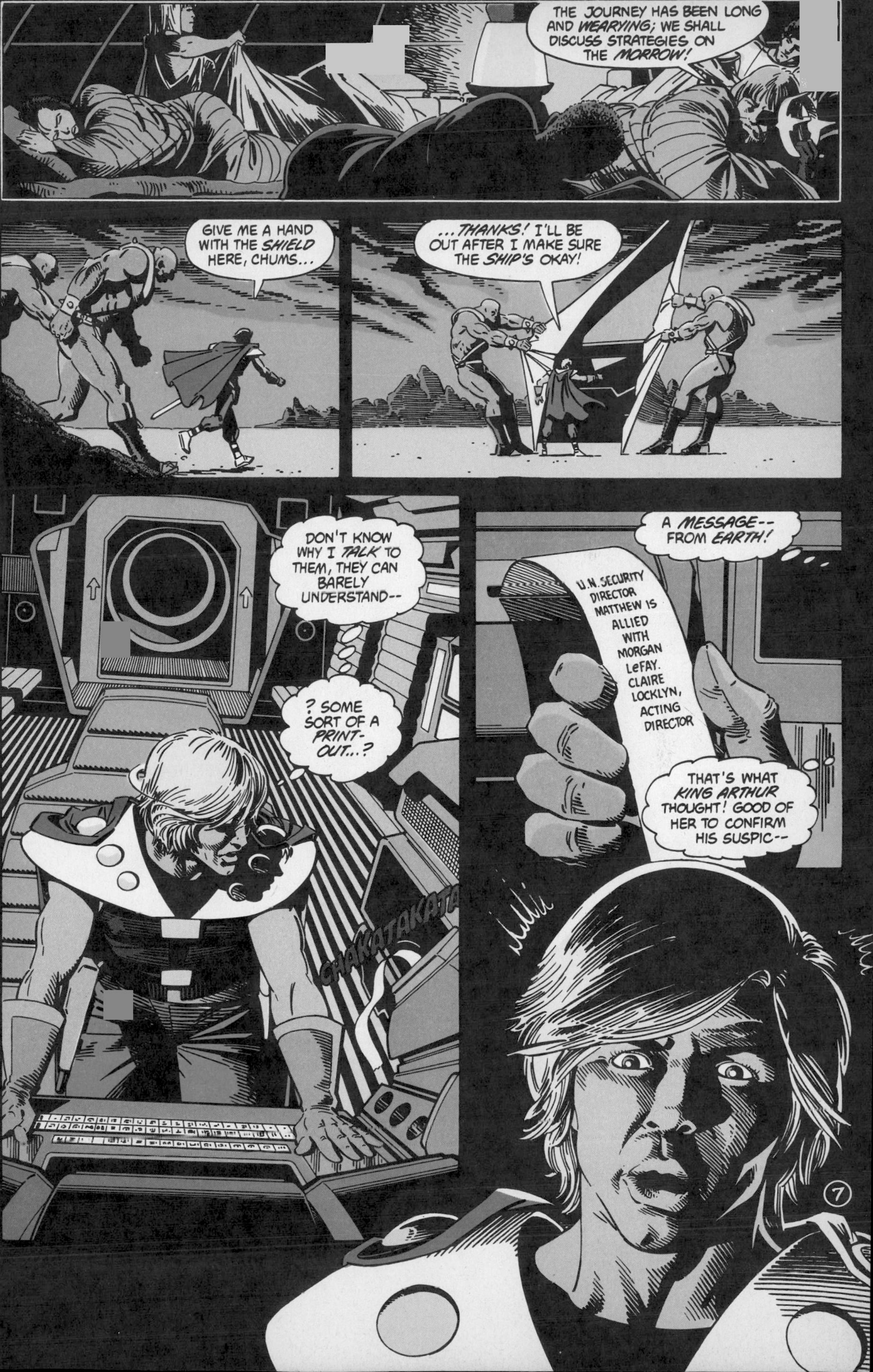
THE JOURNEY HAS BEEN LONG AND WEARYING; WE SHALL DISCUSS STRATEGIES ON THE MORROW!
GIVE ME A HAND WITH THE SHIELD HERE, CHUMS...
...THANKS! I'LL BE OUT AFTER I MAKE SURE THE SHIP'S OKAY!
DON'T KNOW WHY I TALK TO THEM, THEY CAN BARELY UNDERSTAND--
? SOME SORT OF A PRINT-OUT...?
CHAKATAKATA
A MESSAGE-- FROM EARTH!
U.N. SECURITY DIRECTOR MATTHEW IS ALLIED WITH MORGAN LeFAY. CLAIRE LOCKLYN, ACTING DIRECTOR
THAT'S WHAT KING ARTHUR THOUGHT! GOOD OF HER TO CONFIRM HIS SUSPIC--
7

MY LOVE TO TRISTAN.

ISOLDE

END TRANSMISSION

DAMN!

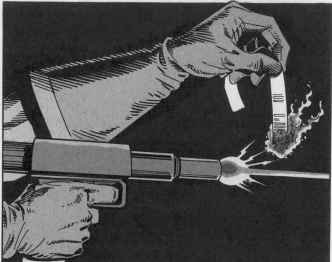

TRISTAN, DO YOU *HEAR* IT?

YES, MY QUEEN... A KIND OF *HUMMING*...

...BUT WHY DO ONLY *WE* HEAR IT?

OBVIOUSLY BECAUSE WE'RE BOTH *WOMEN!*

8

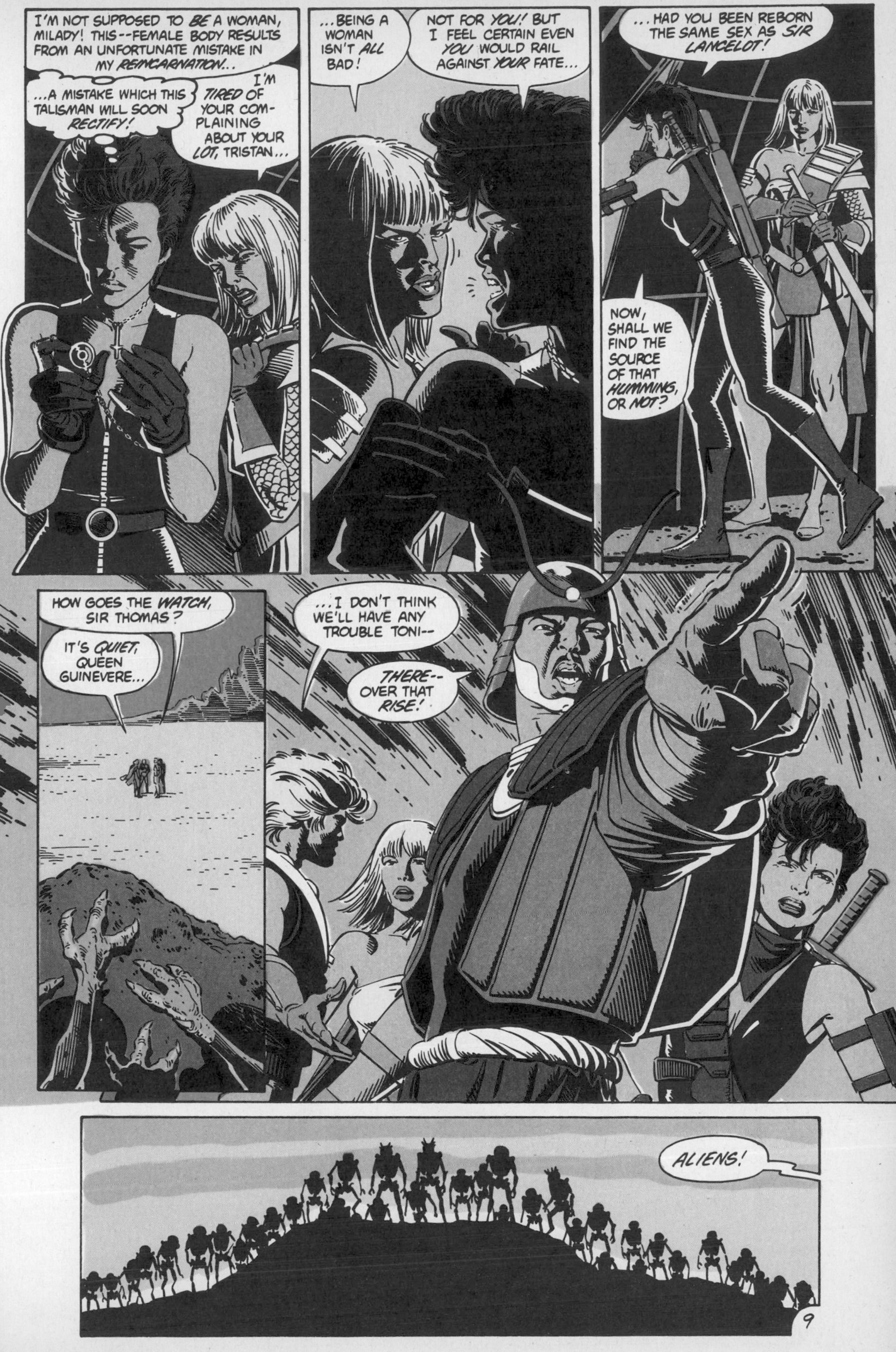
I'M NOT SUPPOSED TO BE A WOMAN, MILADY! THIS--FEMALE BODY RESULTS FROM AN UNFORTUNATE MISTAKE IN MY REINCARNATION..
...A MISTAKE WHICH THIS TALISMAN WILL SOON RECTIFY!
I'M TIRED OF YOUR COMPLAINING ABOUT YOUR LOT, TRISTAN...
...BEING A WOMAN ISN'T ALL BAD!
NOT FOR YOU! BUT I FEEL CERTAIN EVEN YOU WOULD RAIL AGAINST YOUR FATE...
...HAD YOU BEEN REBORN THE SAME SEX AS SIR LANCELOT!
NOW, SHALL WE FIND THE SOURCE OF THAT HUMMING, OR NOT?
HOW GOES THE WATCH, SIR THOMAS?
IT'S QUIET, QUEEN GUINEVERE...
...I DON'T THINK WE'LL HAVE ANY TROUBLE TONI--
THERE-- OVER THAT RISE!
ALIENS!

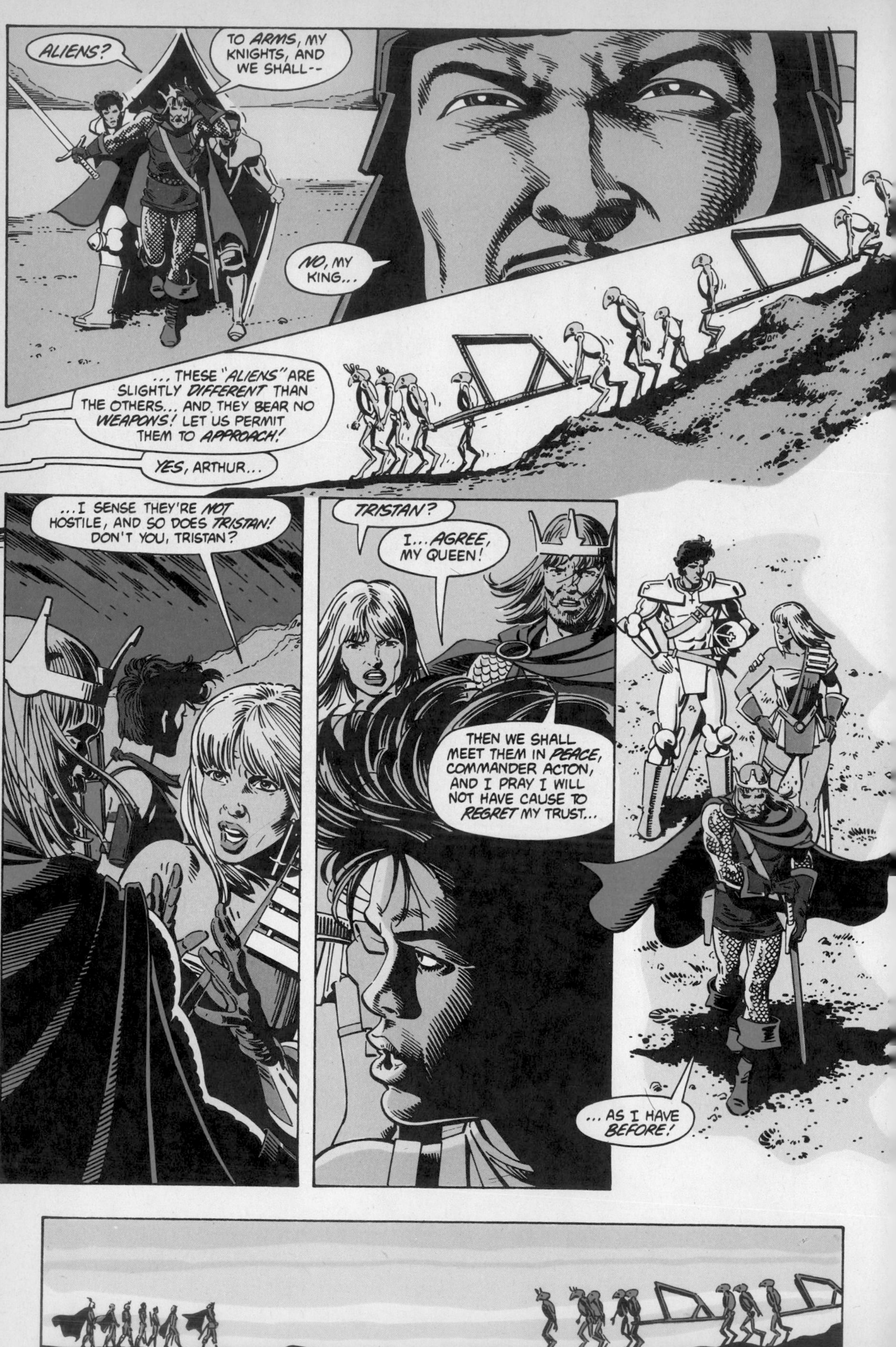
ALIENS?
TO ARMS, MY KNIGHTS, AND WE SHALL--
NO, MY KING...
...THESE "ALIENS" ARE SLIGHTLY DIFFERENT THAN THE OTHERS... AND THEY BEAR NO WEAPONS! LET US PERMIT THEM TO APPROACH!
YES, ARTHUR...
...I SENSE THEY'RE NOT HOSTILE, AND SO DOES TRISTAN! DON'T YOU, TRISTAN?
TRISTAN?
I...AGREE, MY QUEEN!
THEN WE SHALL MEET THEM IN PEACE, COMMANDER ACTON, AND I PRAY I WILL NOT HAVE CAUSE TO REGRET MY TRUST...
...AS I HAVE BEFORE!

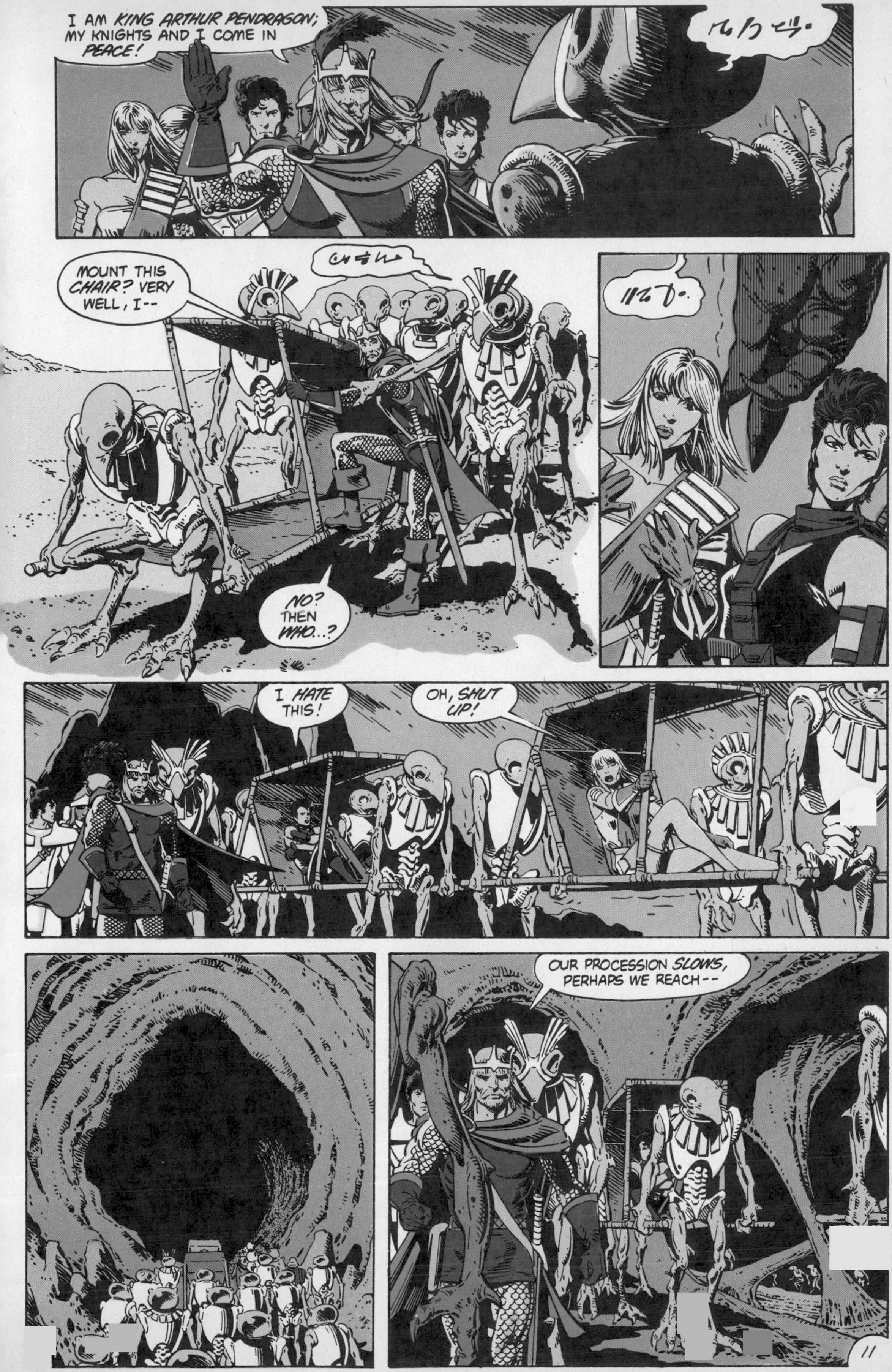
I AM KING ARTHUR PENDRAGON; MY KNIGHTS AND I COME IN PEACE!
MOUNT THIS CHAIR? VERY WELL, I--
NO? THEN WHO...?
I HATE THIS!
OH, SHUT UP!
OUR PROCESSION SLOWS, PERHAPS WE REACH--

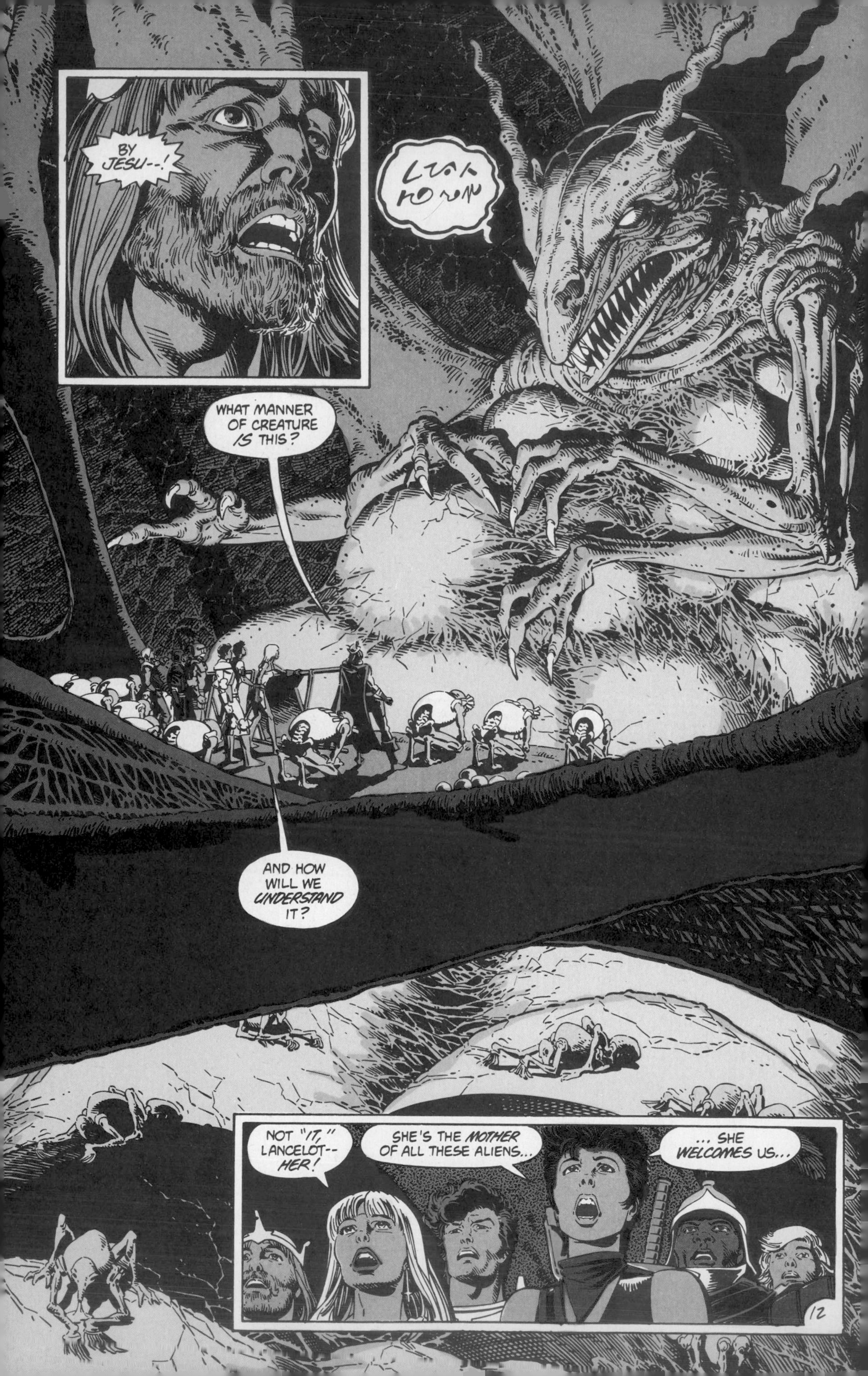
BY JESU--!
WHAT MANNER OF CREATURE *IS* THIS?
AND HOW WILL WE *UNDERSTAND* IT?
NOT "*IT*," LANCELOT-- *HER*!
SHE'S THE *MOTHER* OF ALL THESE ALIENS...
... SHE *WELCOMES* US...
12

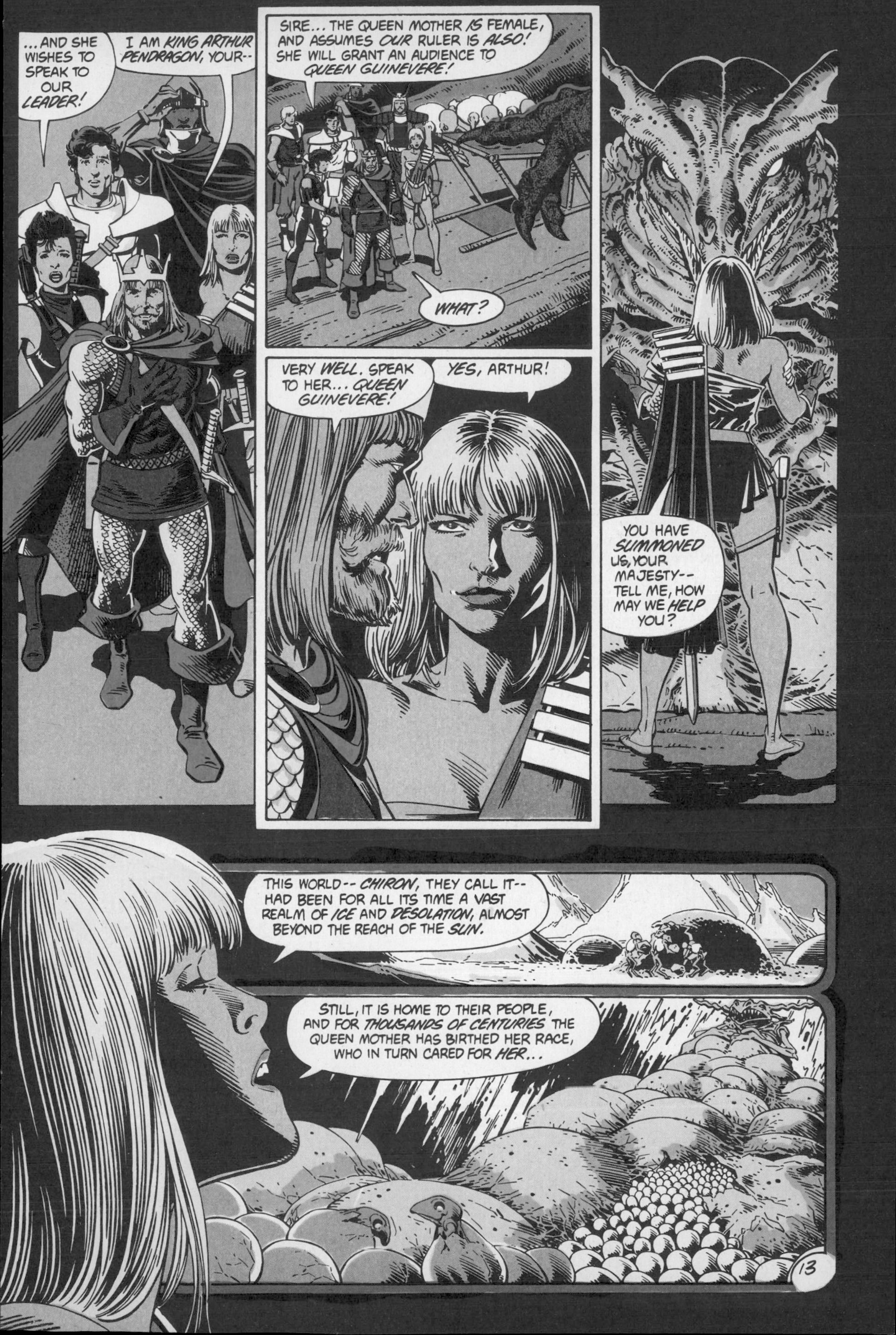

...AND SHE WISHES TO SPEAK TO OUR LEADER!
I AM KING ARTHUR PENDRAGON, YOUR--
SIRE... THE QUEEN MOTHER IS FEMALE, AND ASSUMES OUR RULER IS ALSO! SHE WILL GRANT AN AUDIENCE TO QUEEN GUINEVERE!
WHAT?
VERY WELL. SPEAK TO HER... QUEEN GUINEVERE!
YES, ARTHUR!
YOU HAVE SUMMONED US, YOUR MAJESTY-- TELL ME, HOW MAY WE HELP YOU?
THIS WORLD-- CHIRON, THEY CALL IT-- HAD BEEN FOR ALL ITS TIME A VAST REALM OF ICE AND DESOLATION, ALMOST BEYOND THE REACH OF THE SUN.
STILL, IT IS HOME TO THEIR PEOPLE, AND FOR THOUSANDS OF CENTURIES THE QUEEN MOTHER HAS BIRTHED HER RACE, WHO IN TURN CARED FOR HER...

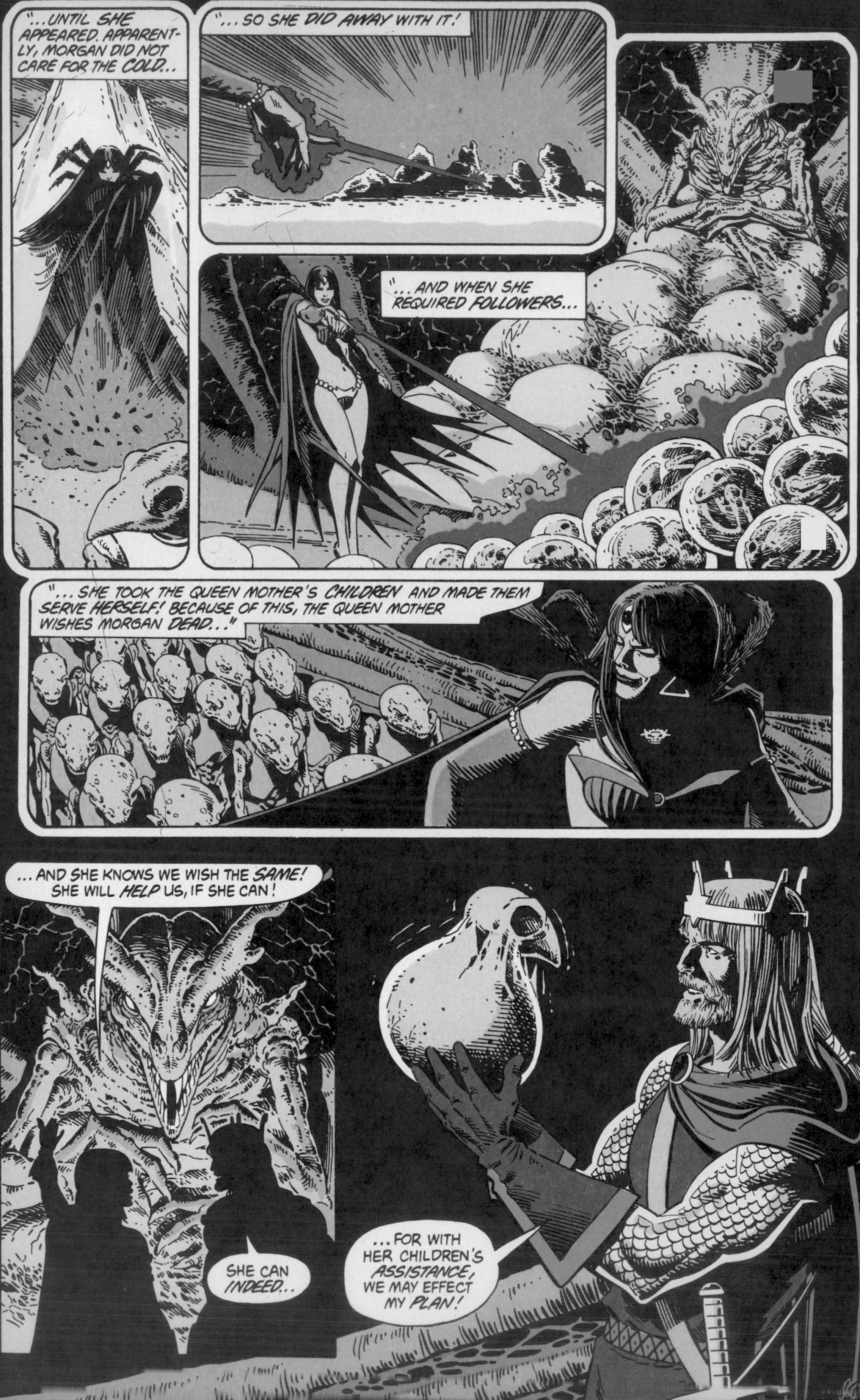
"...UNTIL SHE APPEARED. APPARENTLY, MORGAN DID NOT CARE FOR THE COLD...
"...SO SHE DID AWAY WITH IT!
"...AND WHEN SHE REQUIRED FOLLOWERS...
"...SHE TOOK THE QUEEN MOTHER'S CHILDREN AND MADE THEM SERVE HERSELF! BECAUSE OF THIS, THE QUEEN MOTHER WISHES MORGAN DEAD..."
...AND SHE KNOWS WE WISH THE SAME! SHE WILL HELP US, IF SHE CAN!
SHE CAN INDEED...
...FOR WITH HER CHILDREN'S ASSISTANCE, WE MAY EFFECT MY PLAN!

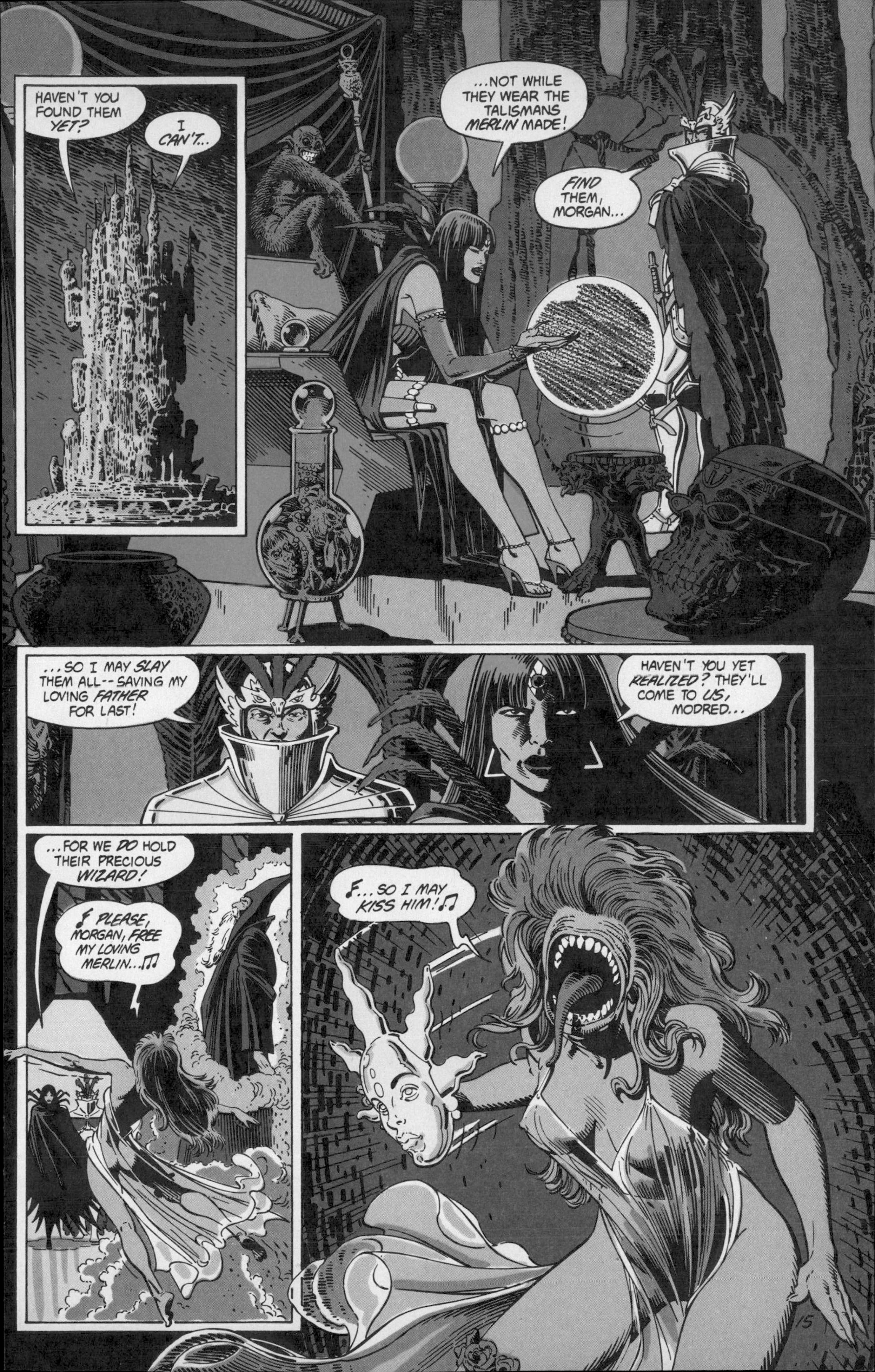

HAVEN'T YOU FOUND THEM YET?
I CAN'T...
...NOT WHILE THEY WEAR THE TALISMANS MERLIN MADE!
FIND THEM, MORGAN...
...SO I MAY SLAY THEM ALL--SAVING MY LOVING FATHER FOR LAST!
HAVEN'T YOU YET REALIZED? THEY'LL COME TO US, MODRED...
...FOR WE DO HOLD THEIR PRECIOUS WIZARD!
♪ PLEASE, MORGAN, FREE MY LOVING MERLIN...♫
♪...SO I MAY KISS HIM!♫

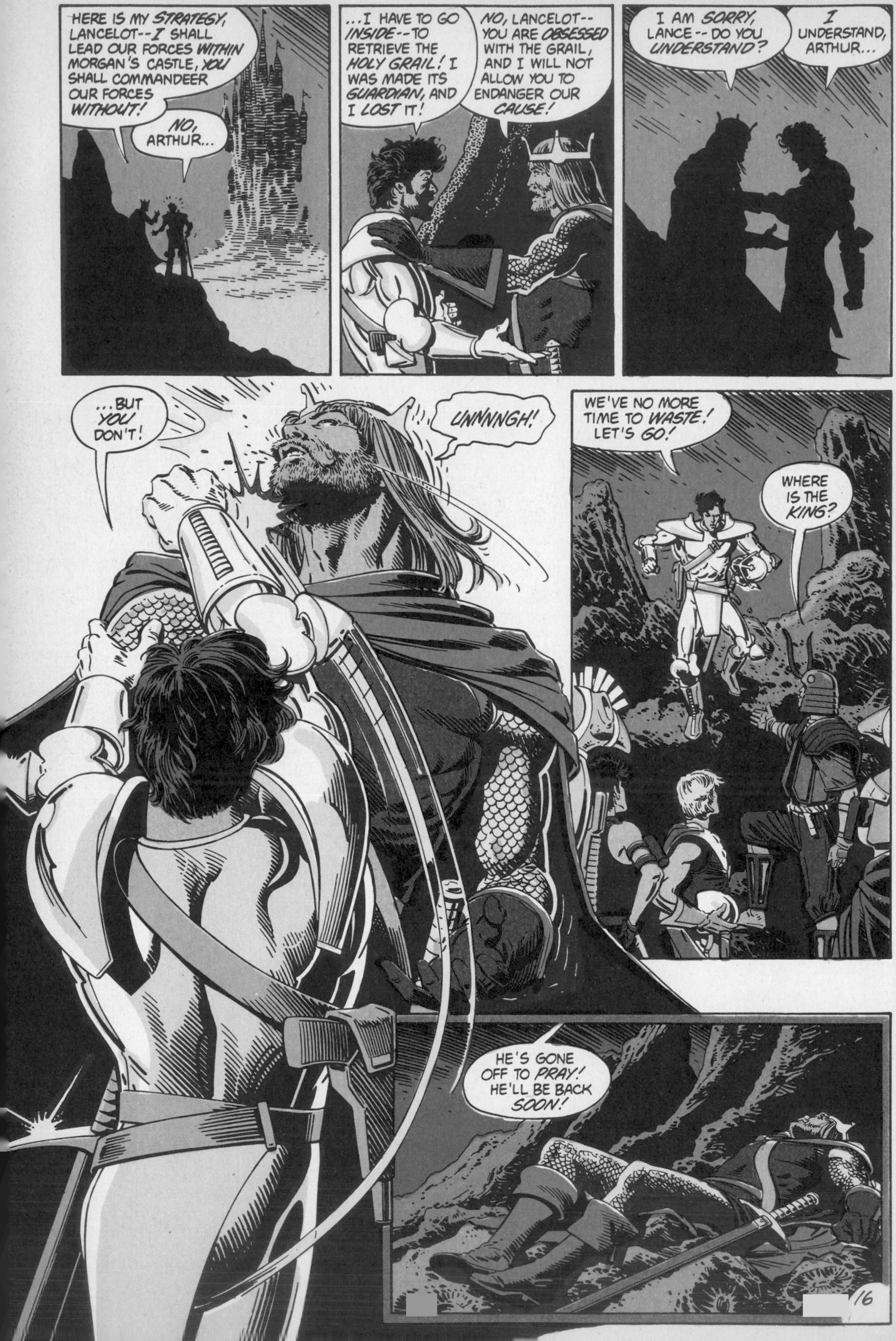
HERE IS MY STRATEGY, LANCELOT--I SHALL LEAD OUR FORCES WITHIN MORGAN'S CASTLE, YOU SHALL COMMANDEER OUR FORCES WITHOUT!
NO, ARTHUR...
...I HAVE TO GO INSIDE--TO RETRIEVE THE HOLY GRAIL! I WAS MADE ITS GUARDIAN, AND I LOST IT!
NO, LANCELOT--YOU ARE OBSESSED WITH THE GRAIL, AND I WILL NOT ALLOW YOU TO ENDANGER OUR CAUSE!
I AM SORRY, LANCE--DO YOU UNDERSTAND?
I UNDERSTAND, ARTHUR...
...BUT YOU DON'T!
UNNNNGH!
WE'VE NO MORE TIME TO WASTE! LET'S GO!
WHERE IS THE KING?
HE'S GONE OFF TO PRAY! HE'LL BE BACK SOON!

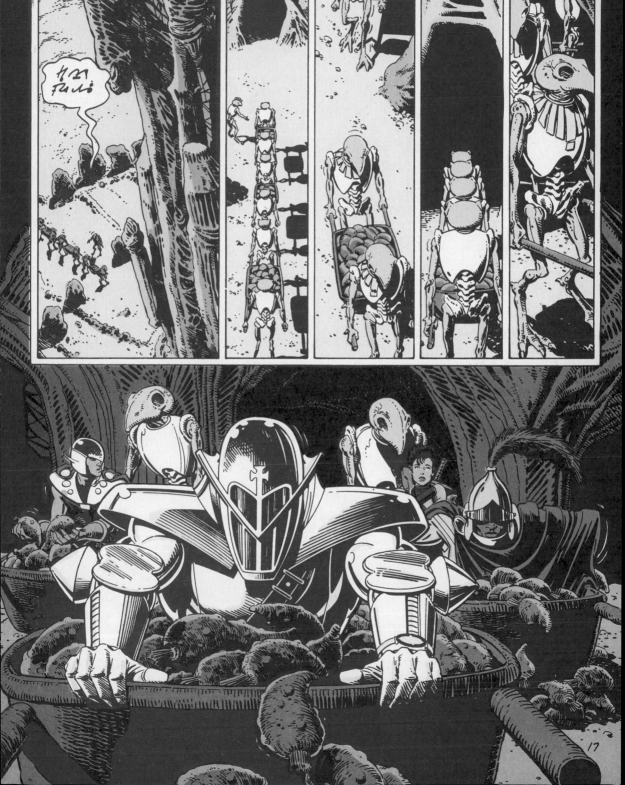

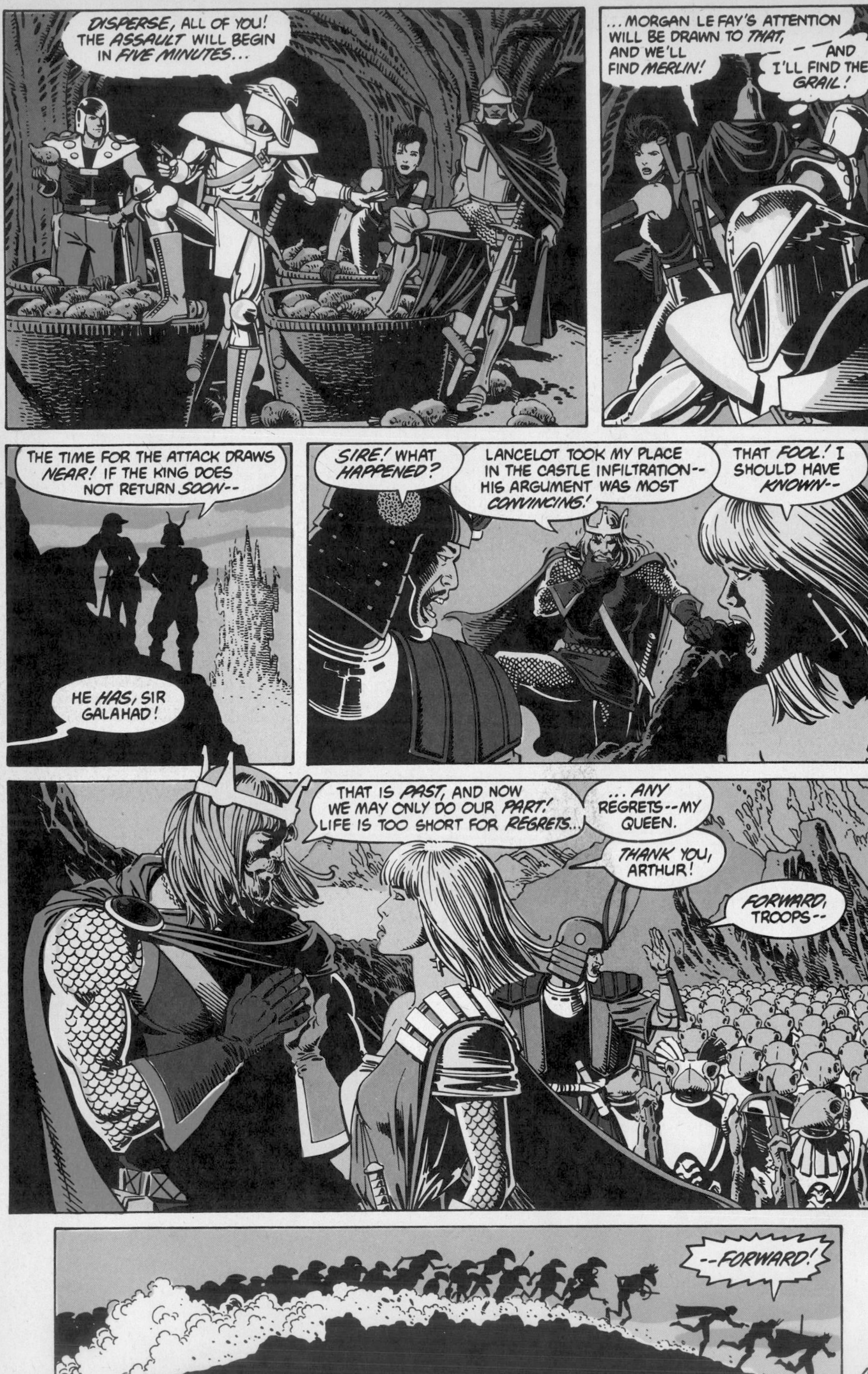
DISPERSE, ALL OF YOU! THE ASSAULT WILL BEGIN IN FIVE MINUTES...
...MORGAN LE FAY'S ATTENTION WILL BE DRAWN TO THAT, AND WE'LL FIND MERLIN!
AND I'LL FIND THE GRAIL!
THE TIME FOR THE ATTACK DRAWS NEAR! IF THE KING DOES NOT RETURN SOON--
HE HAS, SIR GALAHAD!
SIRE! WHAT HAPPENED?
LANCELOT TOOK MY PLACE IN THE CASTLE INFILTRATION--HIS ARGUMENT WAS MOST CONVINCING!
THAT FOOL! I SHOULD HAVE KNOWN--
THAT IS PAST, AND NOW WE MAY ONLY DO OUR PART! LIFE IS TOO SHORT FOR REGRETS...
...ANY REGRETS--MY QUEEN.
THANK YOU, ARTHUR!
FORWARD, TROOPS--
--FORWARD!

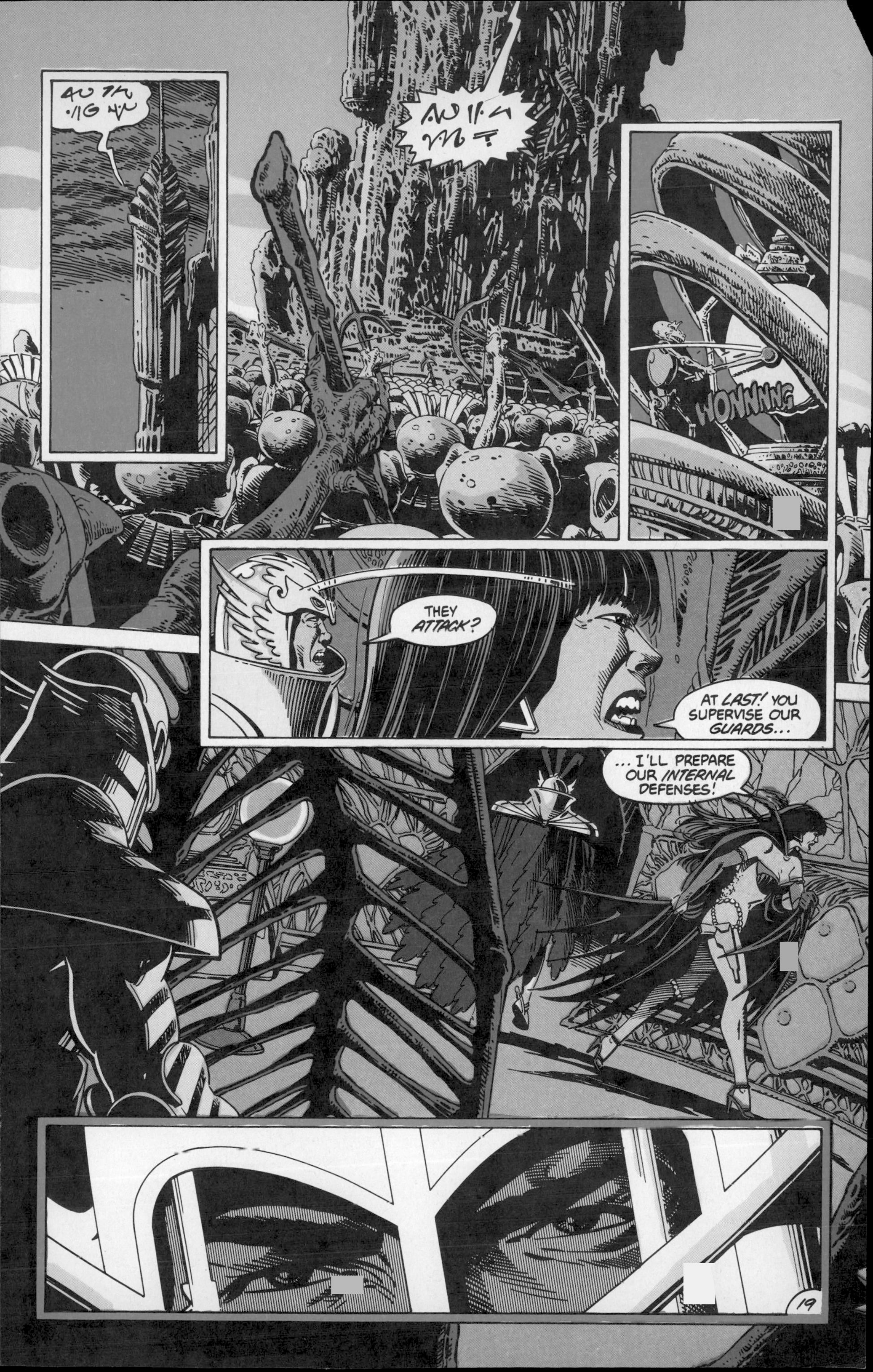
WONNNNG
THEY ATTACK?
AT LAST! YOU SUPERVISE OUR GUARDS...
...I'LL PREPARE OUR INTERNAL DEFENSES!

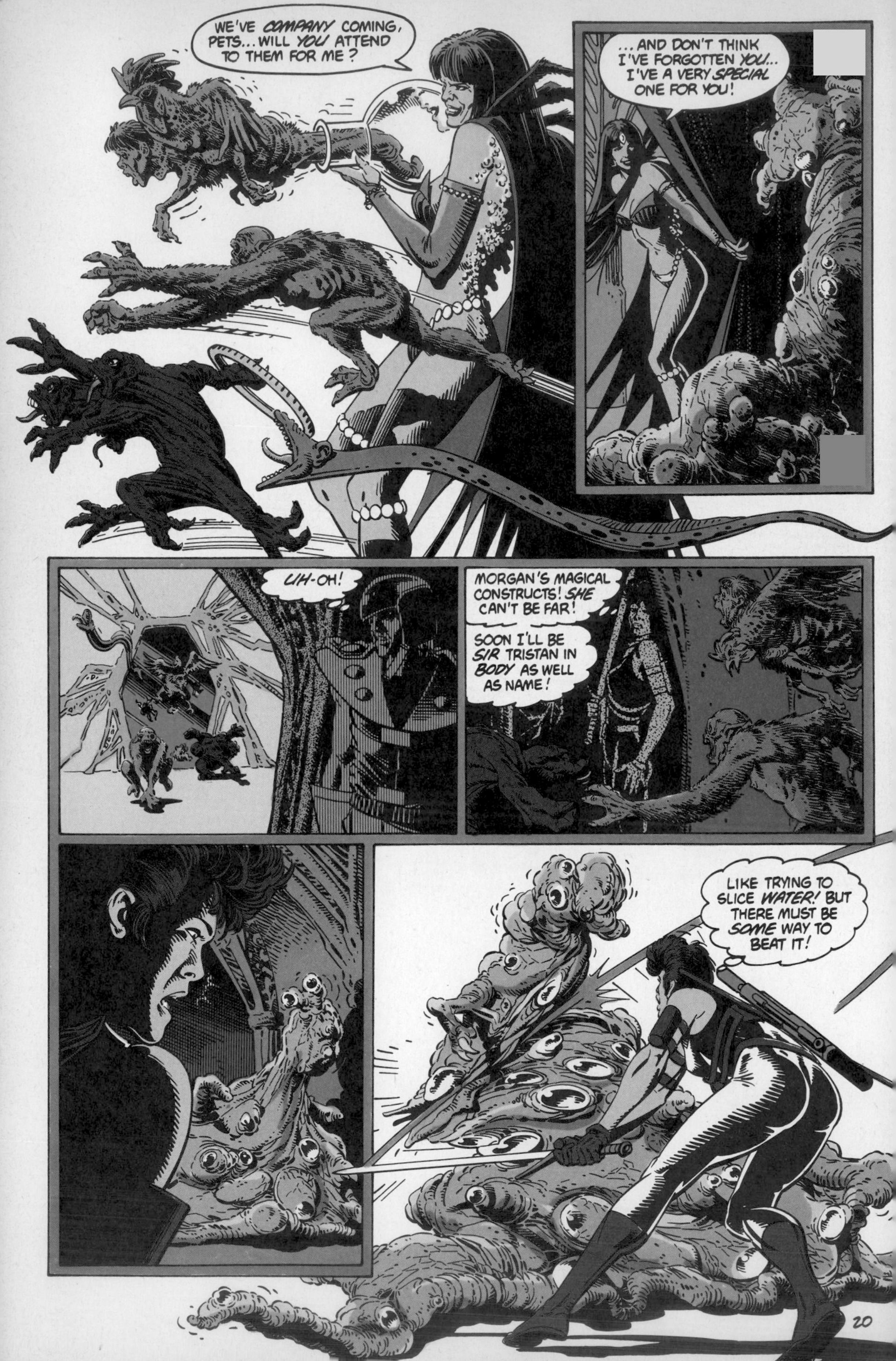
WE'VE COMPANY COMING, PETS... WILL YOU ATTEND TO THEM FOR ME?
...AND DON'T THINK I'VE FORGOTTEN YOU... I'VE A VERY SPECIAL ONE FOR YOU!
UH-OH!
MORGAN'S MAGICAL CONSTRUCTS! SHE CAN'T BE FAR!
SOON I'LL BE SIR TRISTAN IN BODY AS WELL AS NAME!
LIKE TRYING TO SLICE WATER! BUT THERE MUST BE SOME WAY TO BEAT IT!

MATTHEW!

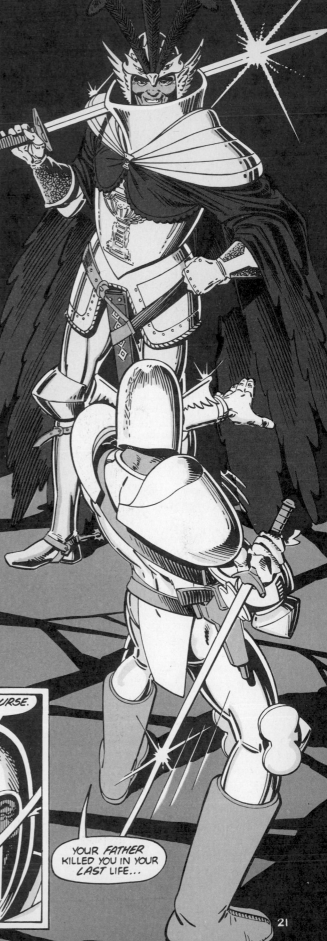

YOU? THERE IS NO END TO YOUR RESOURCE-FULNESS!

OR YOUR EVIL! IT IS NOT ENOUGH FOR YOU TO MERELY STEAL THE HOLY GRAIL...

...YOU FURTHER DEFILE IT BY FUSING IT WITH A SUIT OF ARMOR! DOES YOUR BLASPHEMY KNOW NO BOUNDS, MATTHEW?

YOU MIGHT AS WELL CALL ME BY MY TRUE NAME...

...SIR MOORED!

MOD--?

OF COURSE.

YOUR FATHER KILLED YOU IN YOUR LAST LIFE...

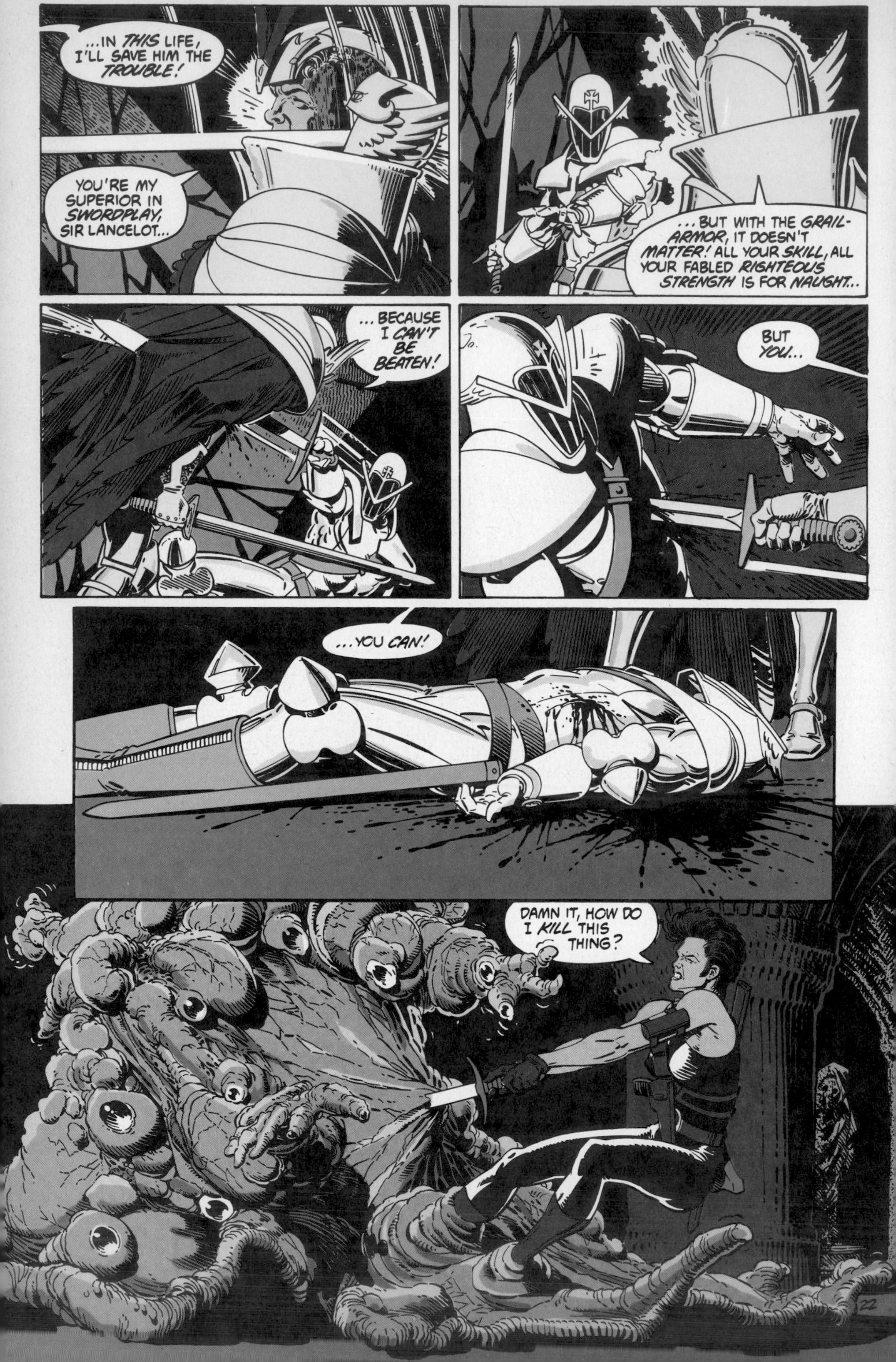

...IN THIS LIFE, I'LL SAVE HIM THE TROUBLE!
YOU'RE MY SUPERIOR IN SWORDPLAY, SIR LANCELOT...
...BUT WITH THE GRAIL-ARMOR, IT DOESN'T MATTER! ALL YOUR SKILL, ALL YOUR FABLED RIGHTEOUS STRENGTH IS FOR NAUGHT...
...BECAUSE I CAN'T BE BEATEN!
BUT YOU...
...YOU CAN!
DAMN IT, HOW DO I KILL THIS THING?

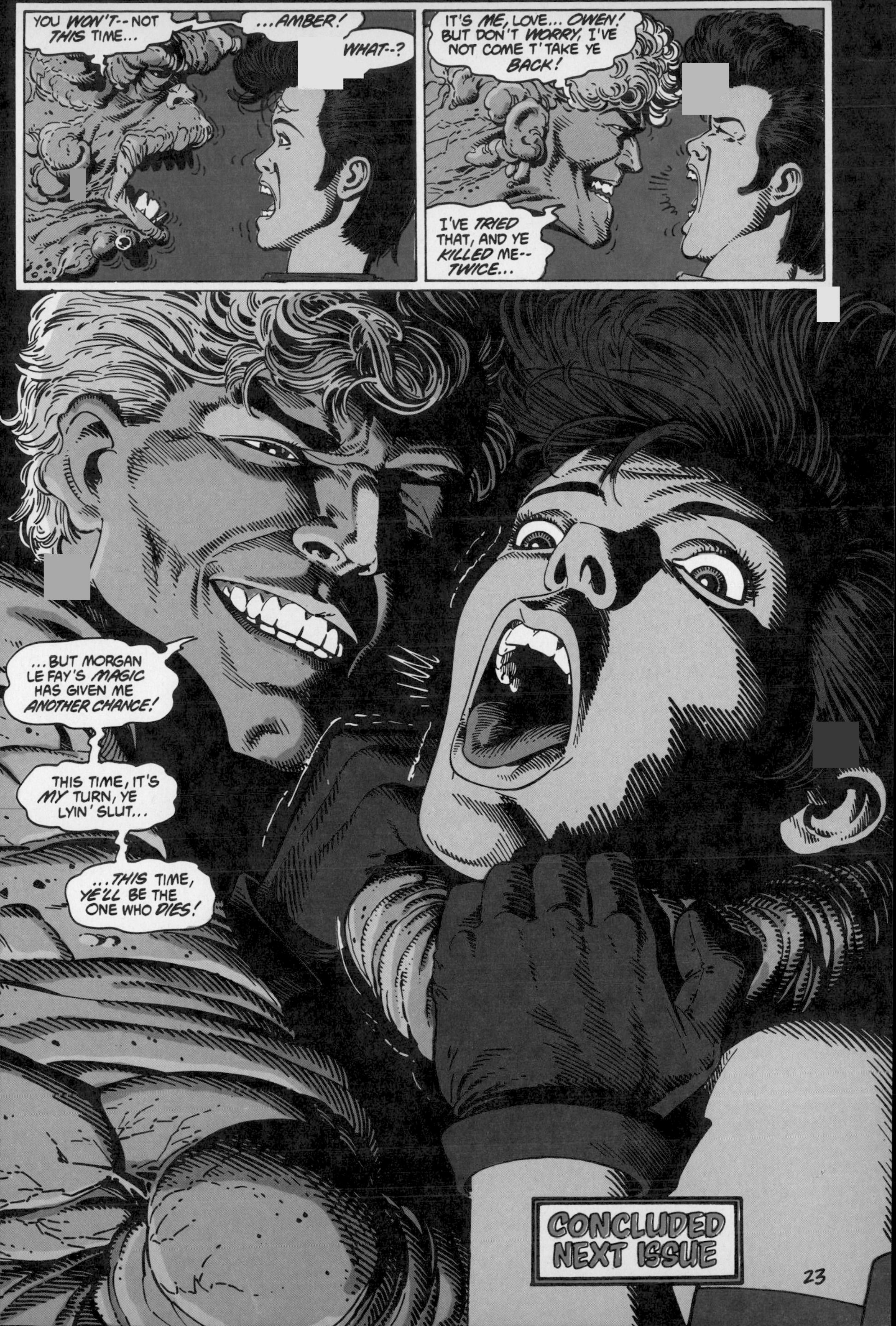
YOU WON'T--NOT THIS TIME...
...AMBER!
WHAT--?
IT'S ME, LOVE... OWEN! BUT DON'T WORRY, I'VE NOT COME T' TAKE YE BACK!
I'VE TRIED THAT, AND YE KILLED ME--TWICE...
...BUT MORGAN LE FAY'S MAGIC HAS GIVEN ME ANOTHER CHANCE!
THIS TIME, IT'S MY TURN, YE LYIN' SLUT...
...THIS TIME, YE'LL BE THE ONE WHO DIES!
CONCLUDED NEXT ISSUE

chapter
12

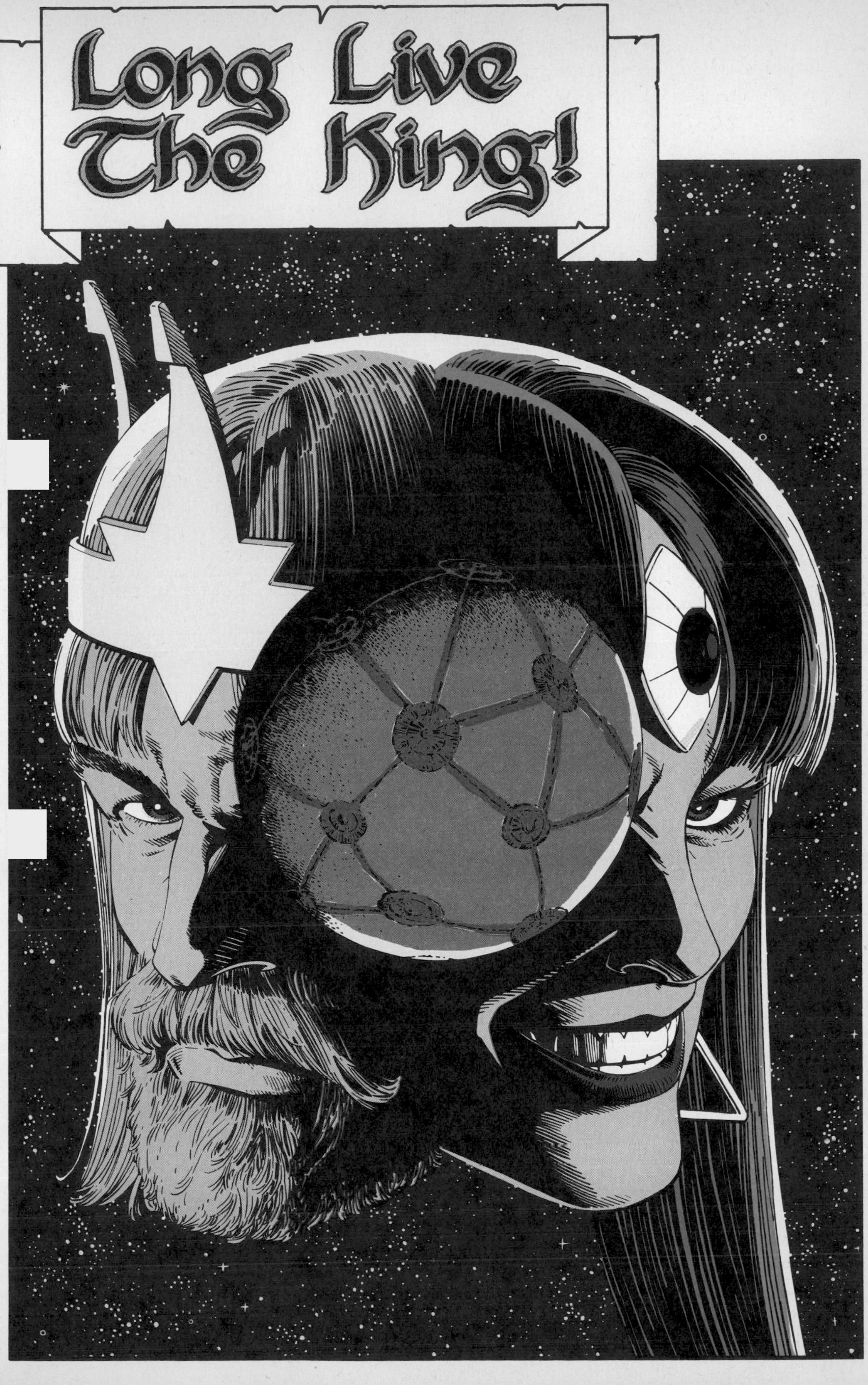
Long Live The King!

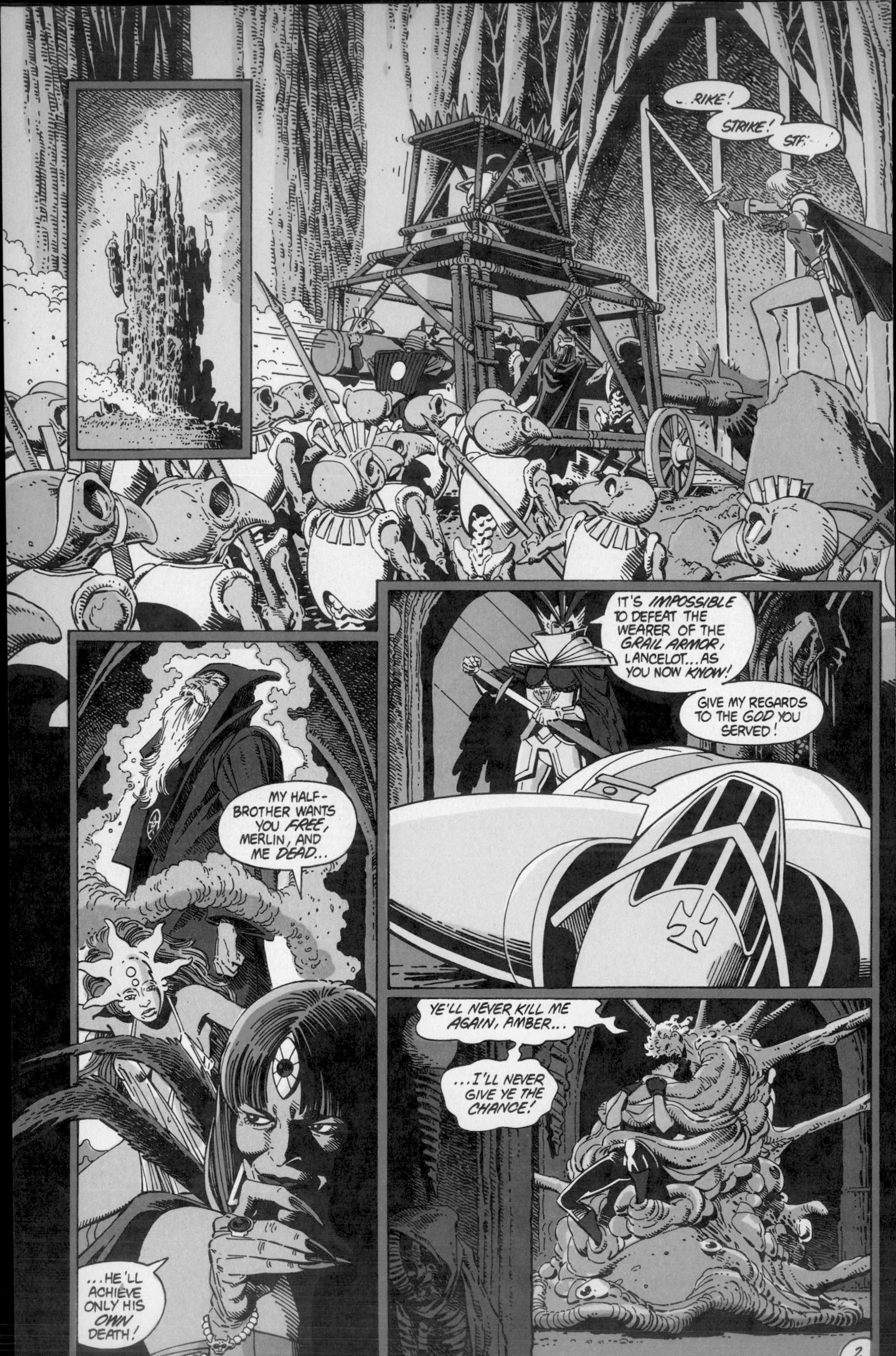
..RIKE!
STRIKE!
STF.
IT'S IMPOSSIBLE TO DEFEAT THE WEARER OF THE GRAIL ARMOR, LANCELOT...AS YOU NOW KNOW!
GIVE MY REGARDS TO THE GOD YOU SERVED!
MY HALF-BROTHER WANTS YOU FREE, MERLIN, AND ME DEAD..
...HE'LL ACHIEVE ONLY HIS OWN DEATH!
YE'LL NEVER KILL ME AGAIN, AMBER...
...I'LL NEVER GIVE YE THE CHANCE!

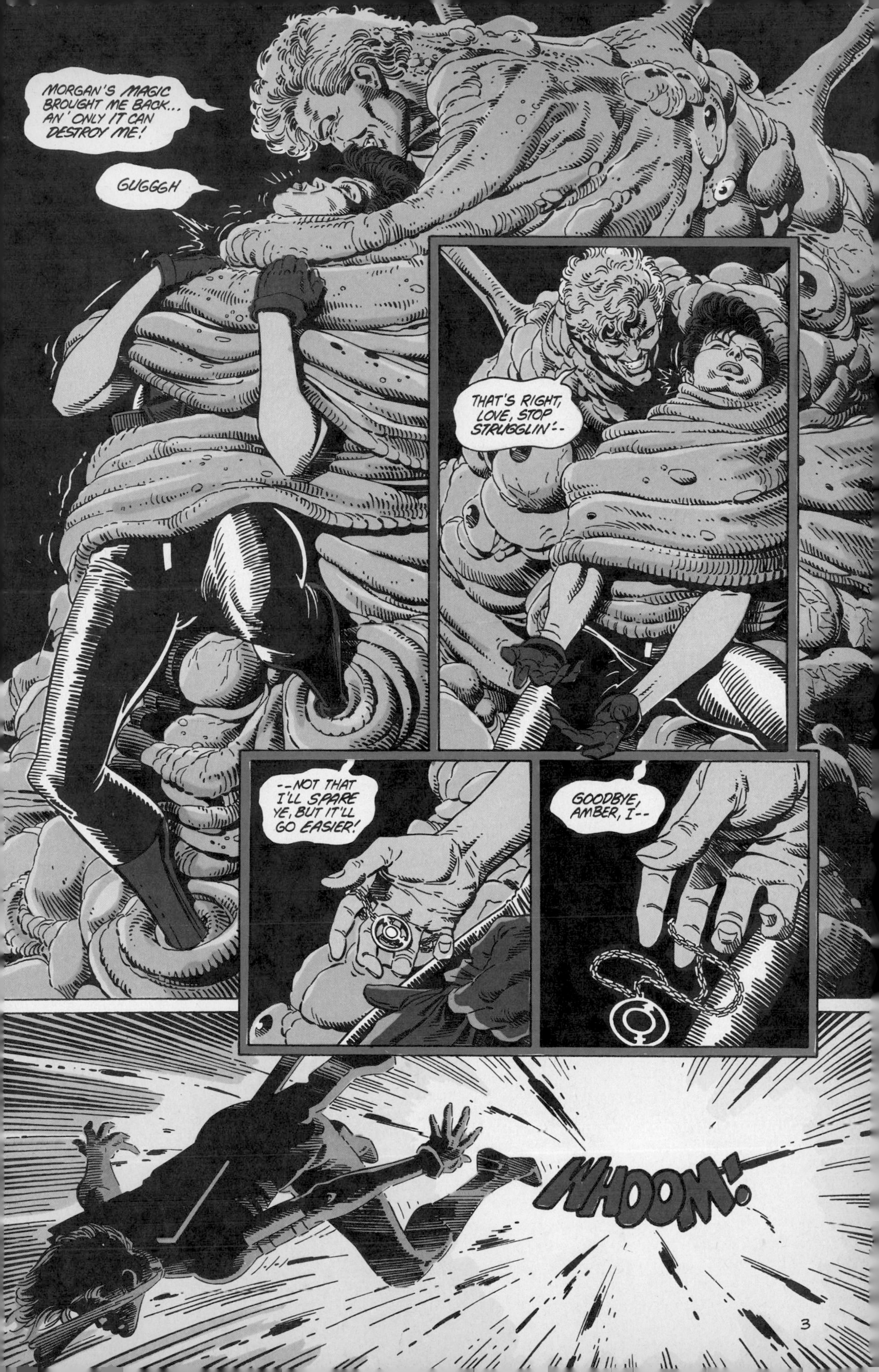
MORGAN'S MAGIC BROUGHT ME BACK... AN' ONLY IT CAN DESTROY ME!
GUGGGH
THAT'S RIGHT, LOVE, STOP STRUGGLIN'--
--NOT THAT I'LL SPARE YE, BUT IT'LL GO EASIER!
GOODBYE, AMBER, I--
WHOOM!

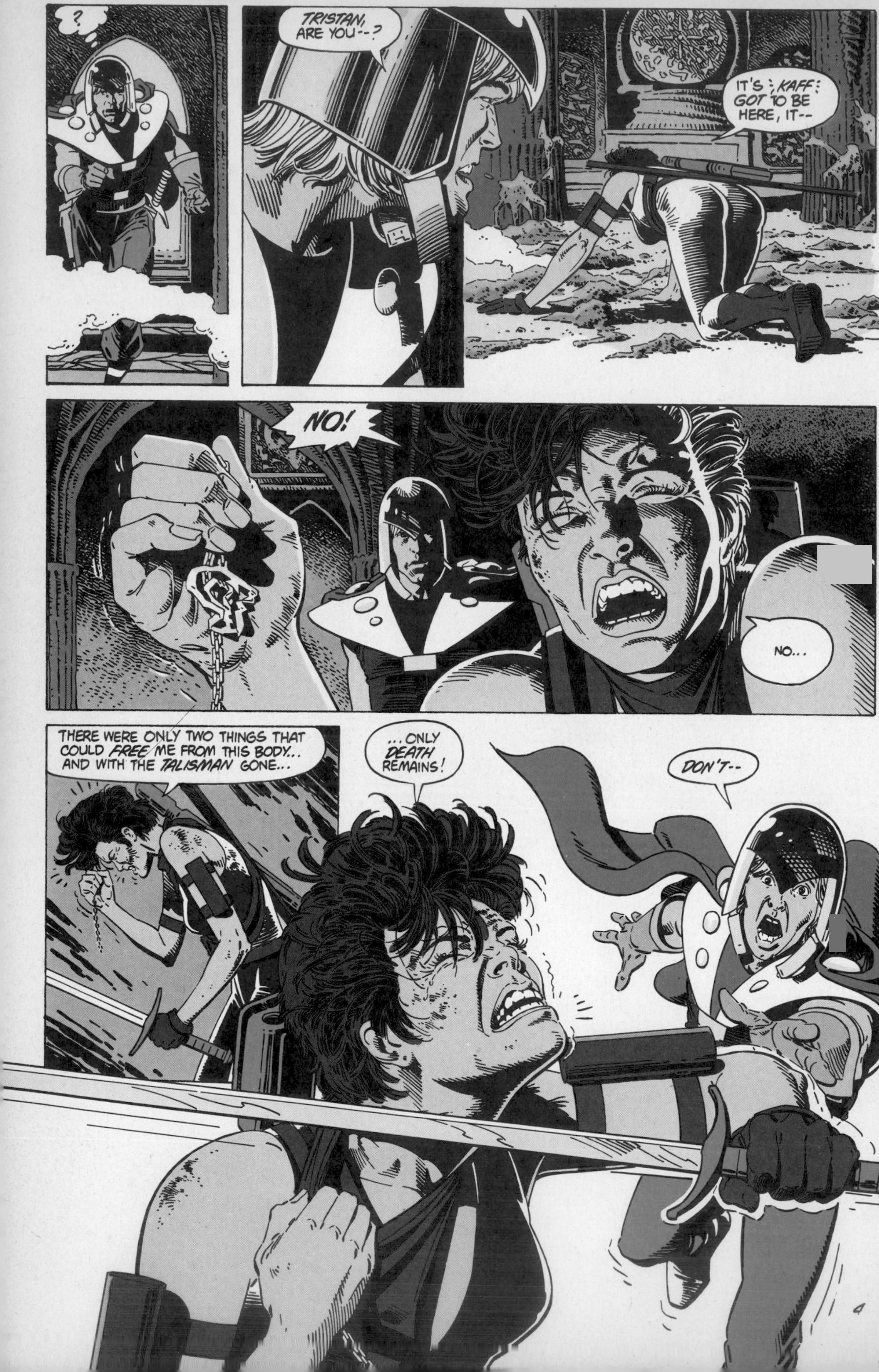
?
TRISTAN, ARE YOU--?
IT'S KAFF GOT TO BE HERE, IT--
NO!
NO...
THERE WERE ONLY TWO THINGS THAT COULD FREE ME FROM THIS BODY... AND WITH THE TALISMAN GONE...
...ONLY DEATH REMAINS!
DON'T--

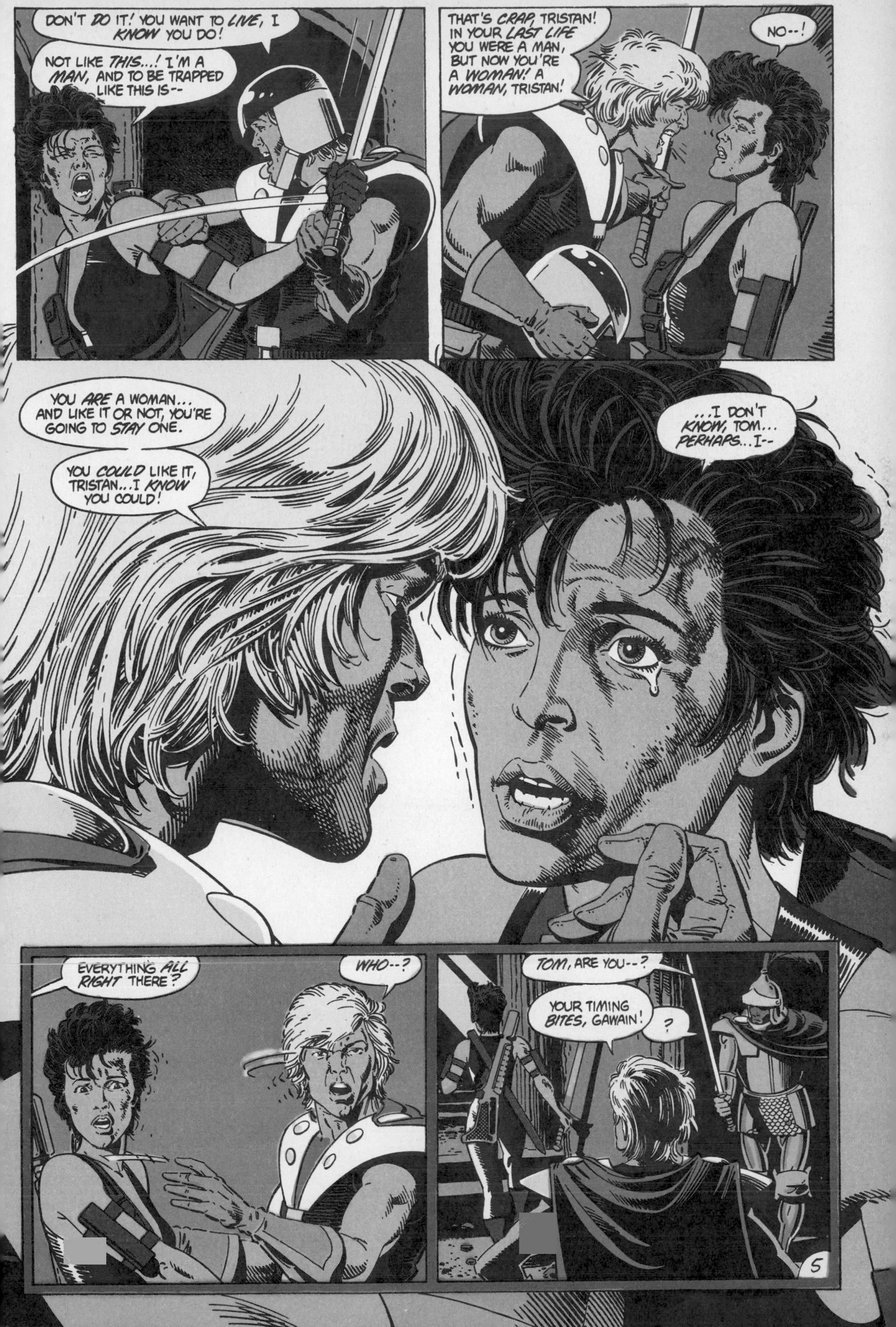
DON'T DO IT! YOU WANT TO LIVE, I KNOW YOU DO!
NOT LIKE THIS...! I'M A MAN, AND TO BE TRAPPED LIKE THIS IS--
THAT'S CRAP, TRISTAN! IN YOUR LAST LIFE YOU WERE A MAN, BUT NOW YOU'RE A WOMAN! A WOMAN, TRISTAN!
NO--!
YOU ARE A WOMAN... AND LIKE IT OR NOT, YOU'RE GOING TO STAY ONE.
YOU COULD LIKE IT, TRISTAN...I KNOW YOU COULD!
...I DON'T KNOW, TOM... PERHAPS...I--
EVERYTHING ALL RIGHT THERE?
WHO--?
TOM, ARE YOU--?
YOUR TIMING BITES, GAWAIN!
?

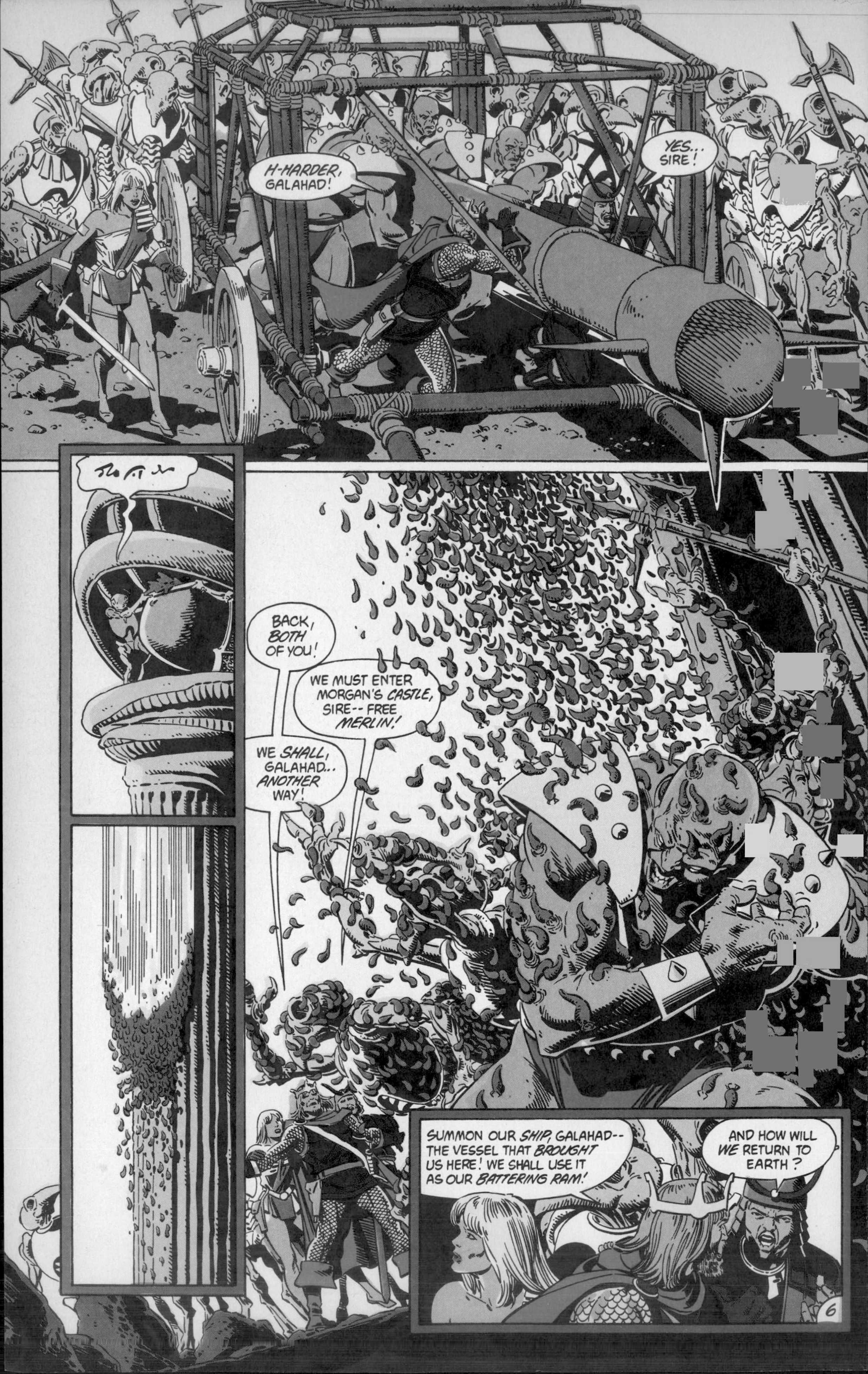
H-HARDER, GALAHAD!
YES... SIRE!
BACK, BOTH OF YOU!
WE MUST ENTER MORGAN'S CASTLE, SIRE-- FREE MERLIN!
WE SHALL, GALAHAD... ANOTHER WAY!
SUMMON OUR SHIP, GALAHAD-- THE VESSEL THAT BROUGHT US HERE! WE SHALL USE IT AS OUR BATTERING RAM!
AND HOW WILL WE RETURN TO EARTH?

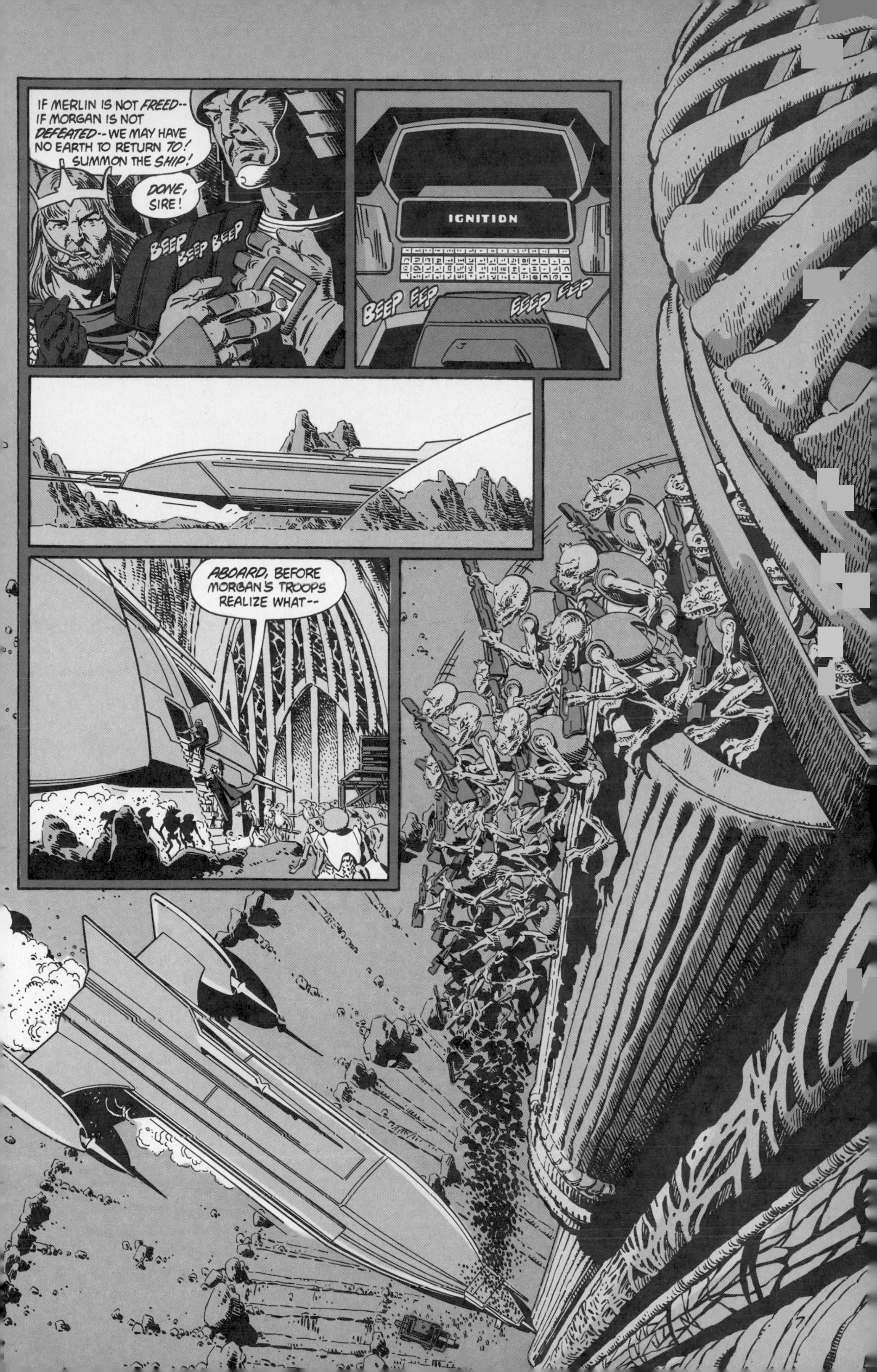
IF MERLIN IS NOT FREED-- IF MORGAN IS NOT DEFEATED-- WE MAY HAVE NO EARTH TO RETURN TO! SUMMON THE SHIP!
DONE, SIRE!
BEEP BEEP BEEP
IGNITION
BEEP EEP
BEEP EEP
ABOARD, BEFORE MORGAN'S TROOPS REALIZE WHAT--

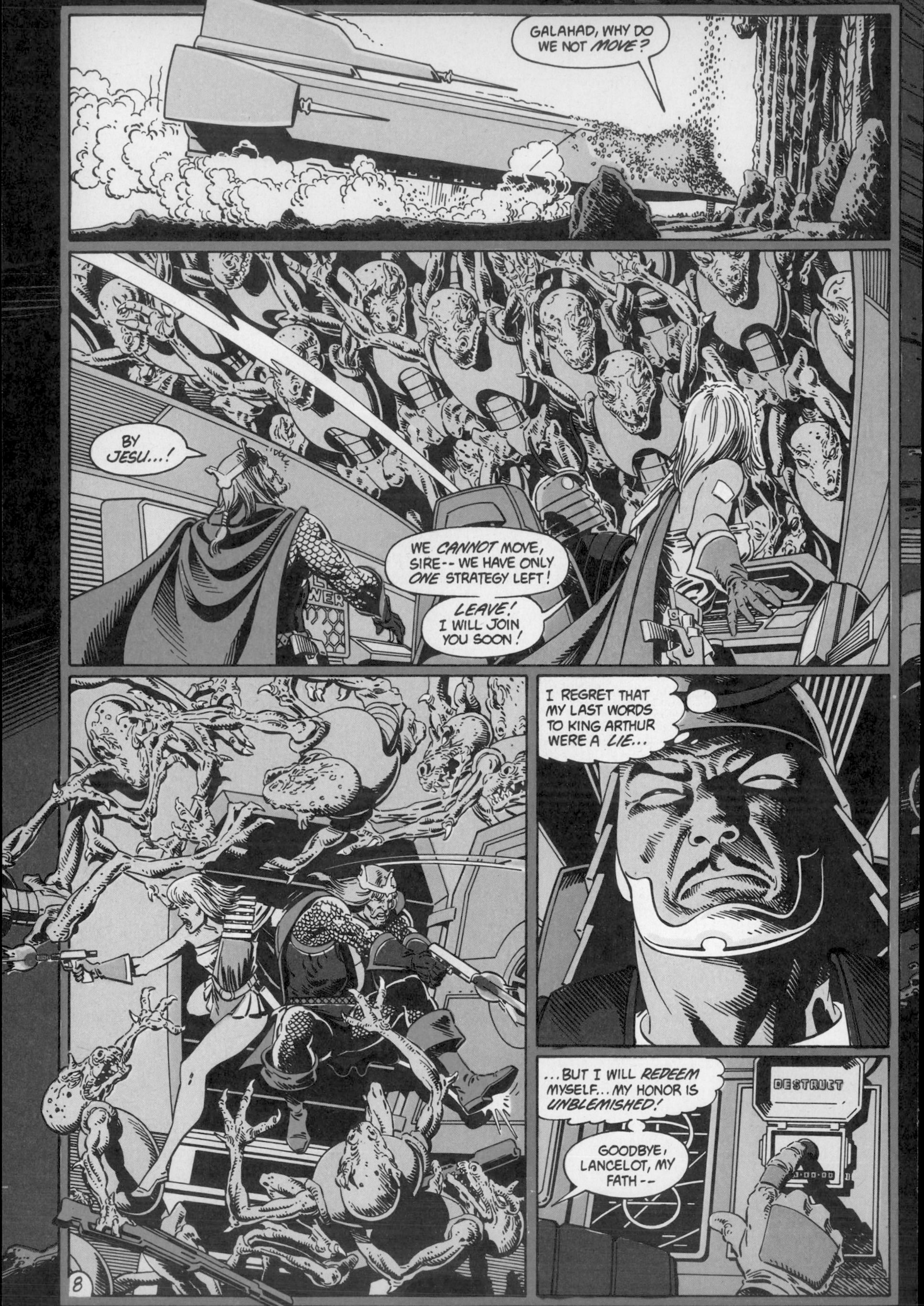

GALAHAD, WHY DO WE NOT *MOVE*?
BY JESU...!
WE *CANNOT* MOVE, SIRE-- WE HAVE ONLY *ONE* STRATEGY LEFT!
LEAVE! I WILL JOIN YOU SOON!
I REGRET THAT MY LAST WORDS TO KING ARTHUR WERE A *LIE*...
...BUT I WILL *REDEEM* MYSELF... MY HONOR IS *UNBLEMISHED!*
DESTRUCT
GOODBYE, LANCELOT, MY FATH--

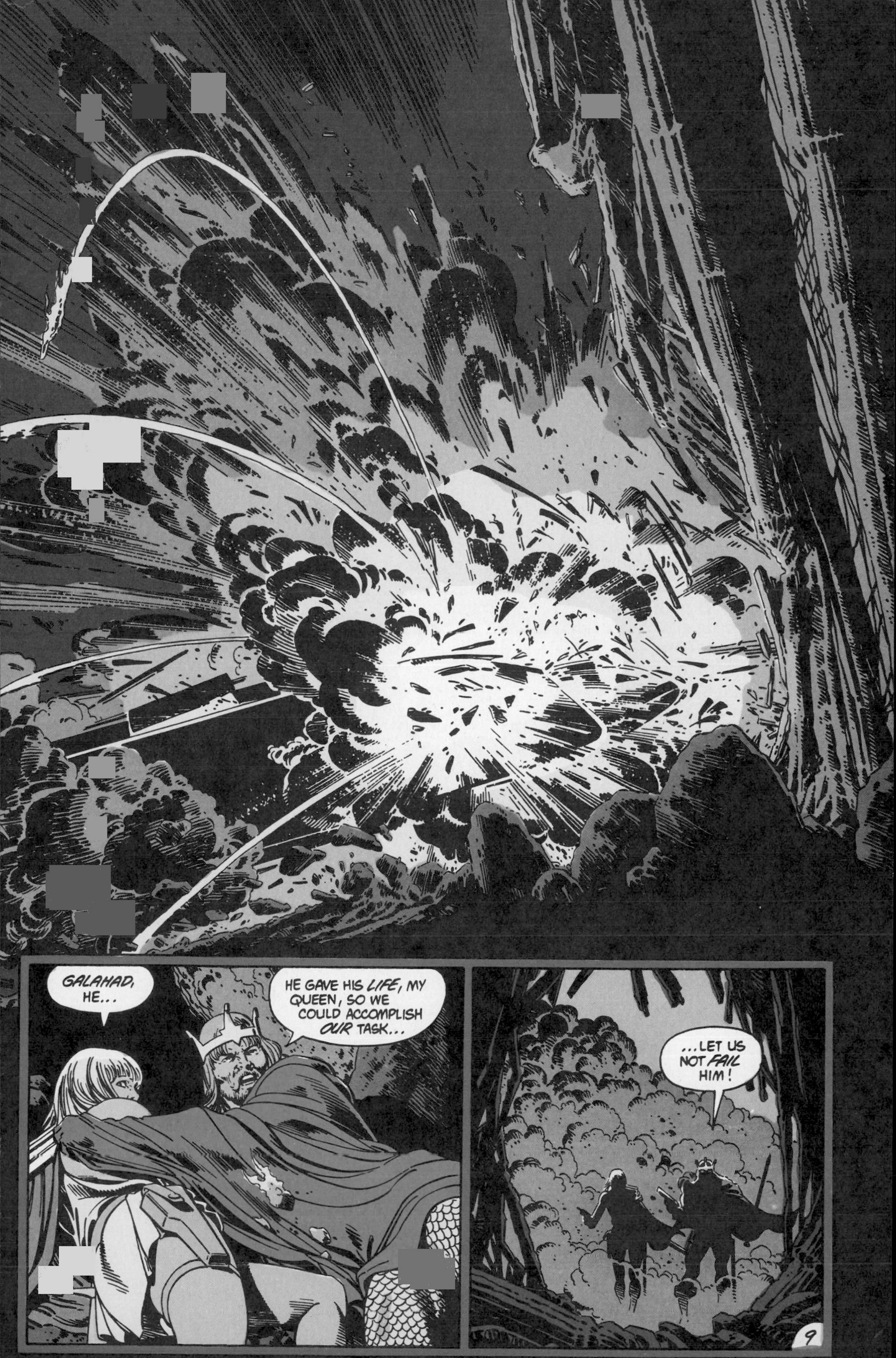
GALAHAD, HE...
HE GAVE HIS LIFE, MY QUEEN, SO WE COULD ACCOMPLISH OUR TASK...
...LET US NOT FAIL HIM!

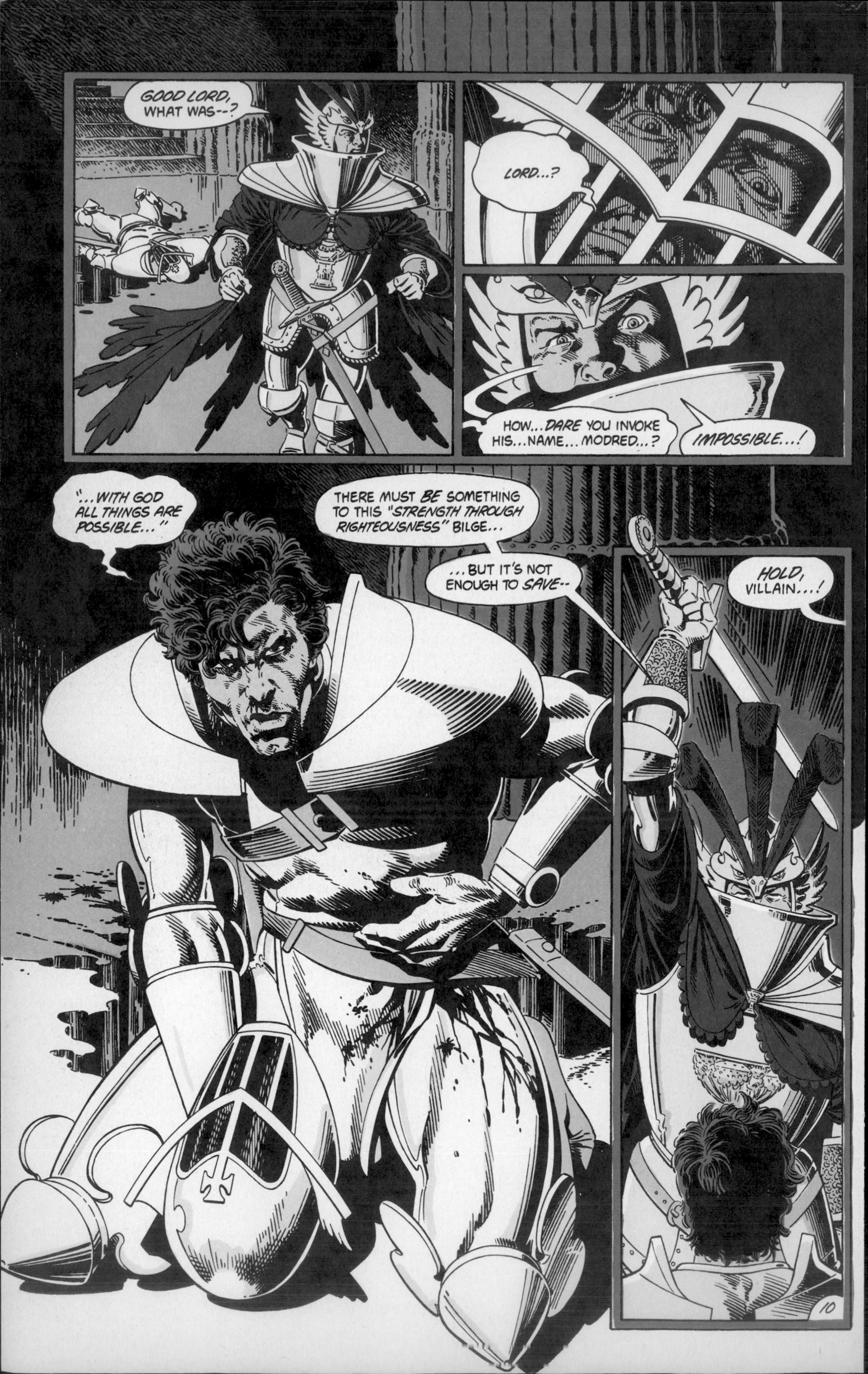
GOOD LORD, WHAT WAS--?
LORD...?
HOW... DARE YOU INVOKE HIS... NAME... MODRED...?
IMPOSSIBLE...!
"...WITH GOD ALL THINGS ARE POSSIBLE..."
THERE MUST BE SOMETHING TO THIS "STRENGTH THROUGH RIGHTEOUSNESS" BILGE...
...BUT IT'S NOT ENOUGH TO SAVE--
HOLD, VILLAIN...!
10

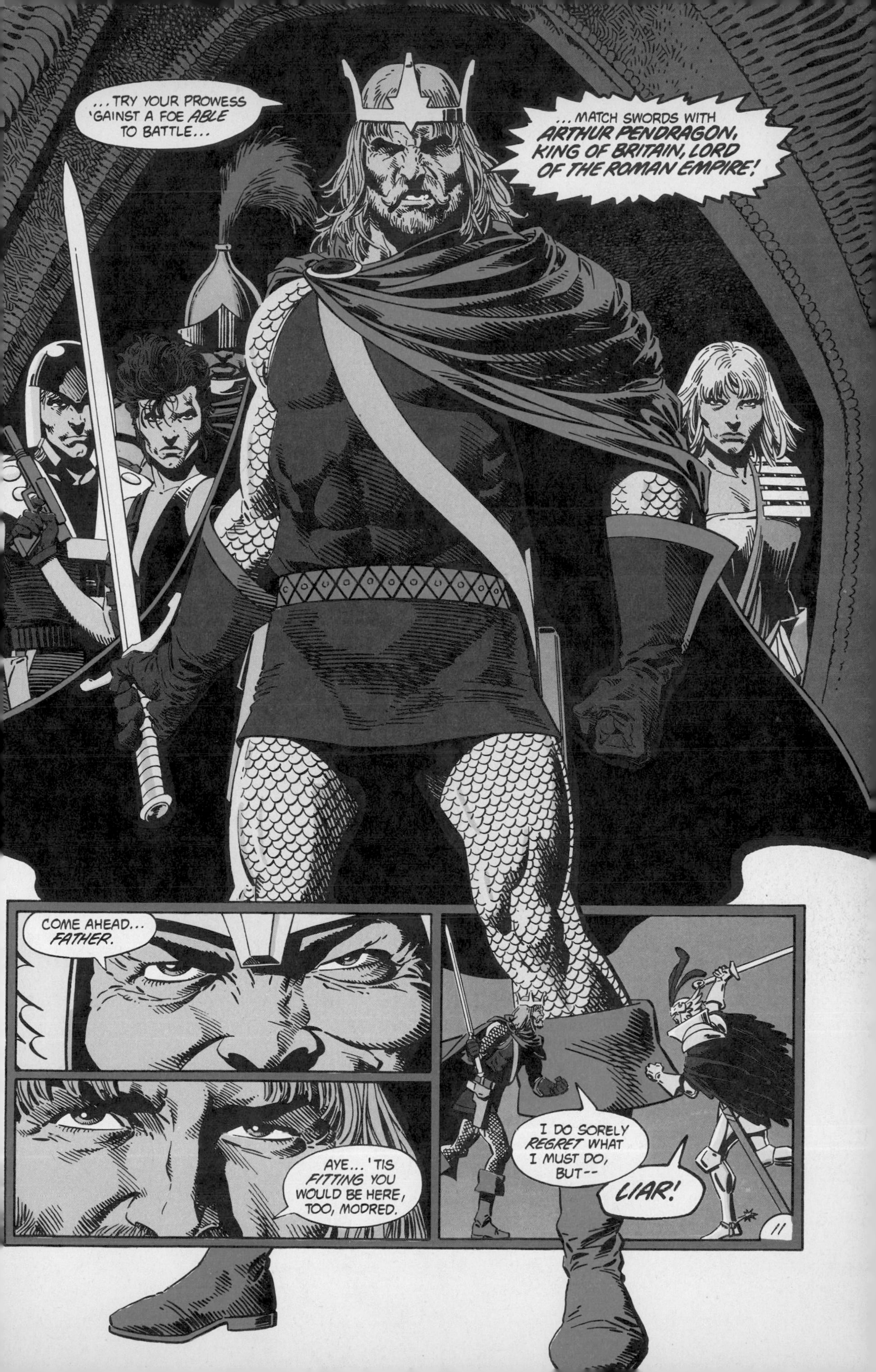
...TRY YOUR PROWESS 'GAINST A FOE ABLE TO BATTLE...
...MATCH SWORDS WITH ARTHUR PENDRAGON, KING OF BRITAIN, LORD OF THE ROMAN EMPIRE!
COME AHEAD... FATHER.
AYE... 'TIS FITTING YOU WOULD BE HERE, TOO, MODRED.
I DO SORELY REGRET WHAT I MUST DO, BUT--
LIAR!
11

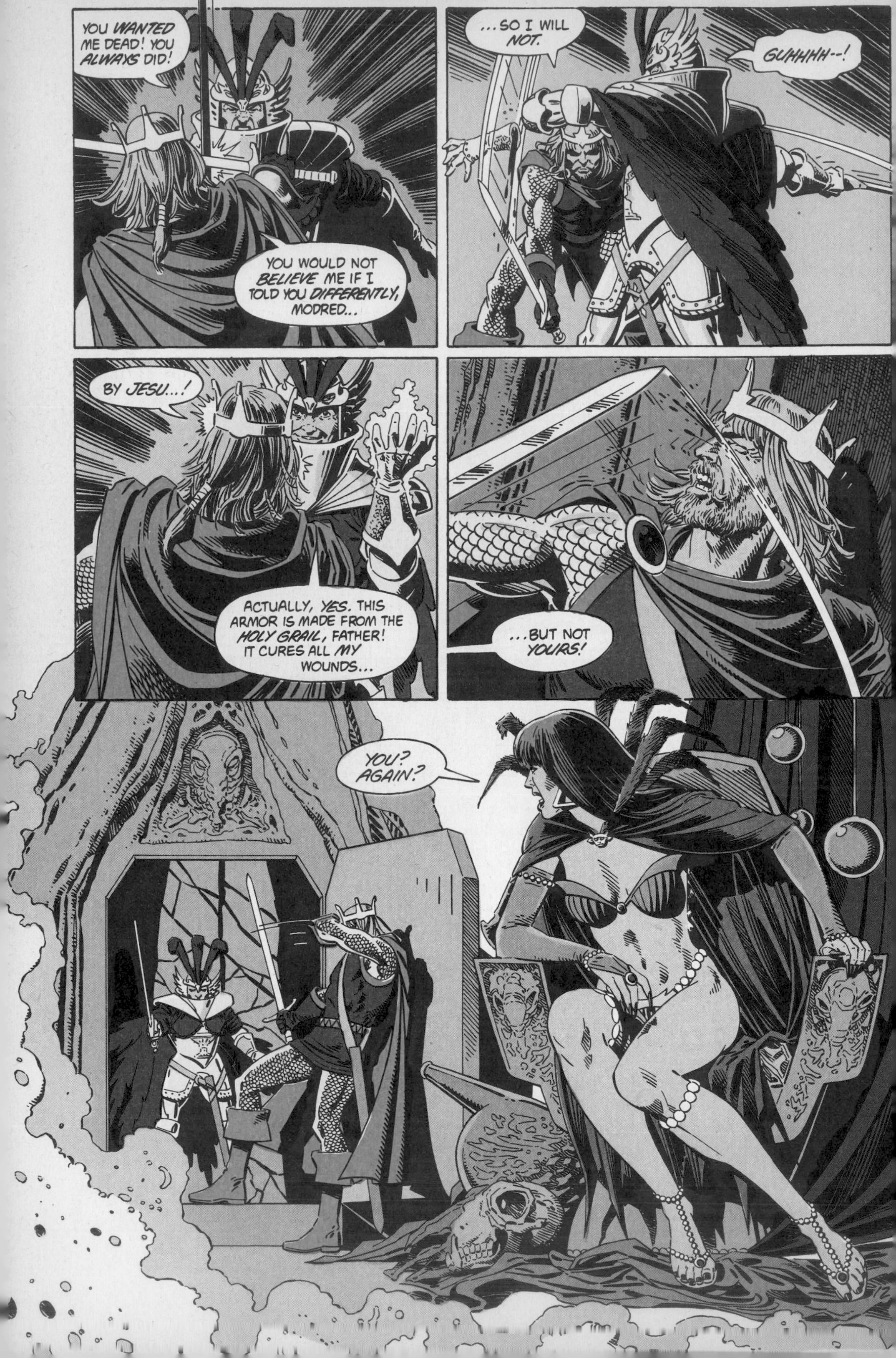
YOU WANTED ME DEAD! YOU ALWAYS DID!
YOU WOULD NOT BELIEVE ME IF I TOLD YOU DIFFERENTLY, MODRED...
...SO I WILL NOT.
GUHHHH--!
BY JESU...!
ACTUALLY, YES. THIS ARMOR IS MADE FROM THE HOLY GRAIL, FATHER! IT CURES ALL MY WOUNDS...
...BUT NOT YOURS!
YOU? AGAIN?

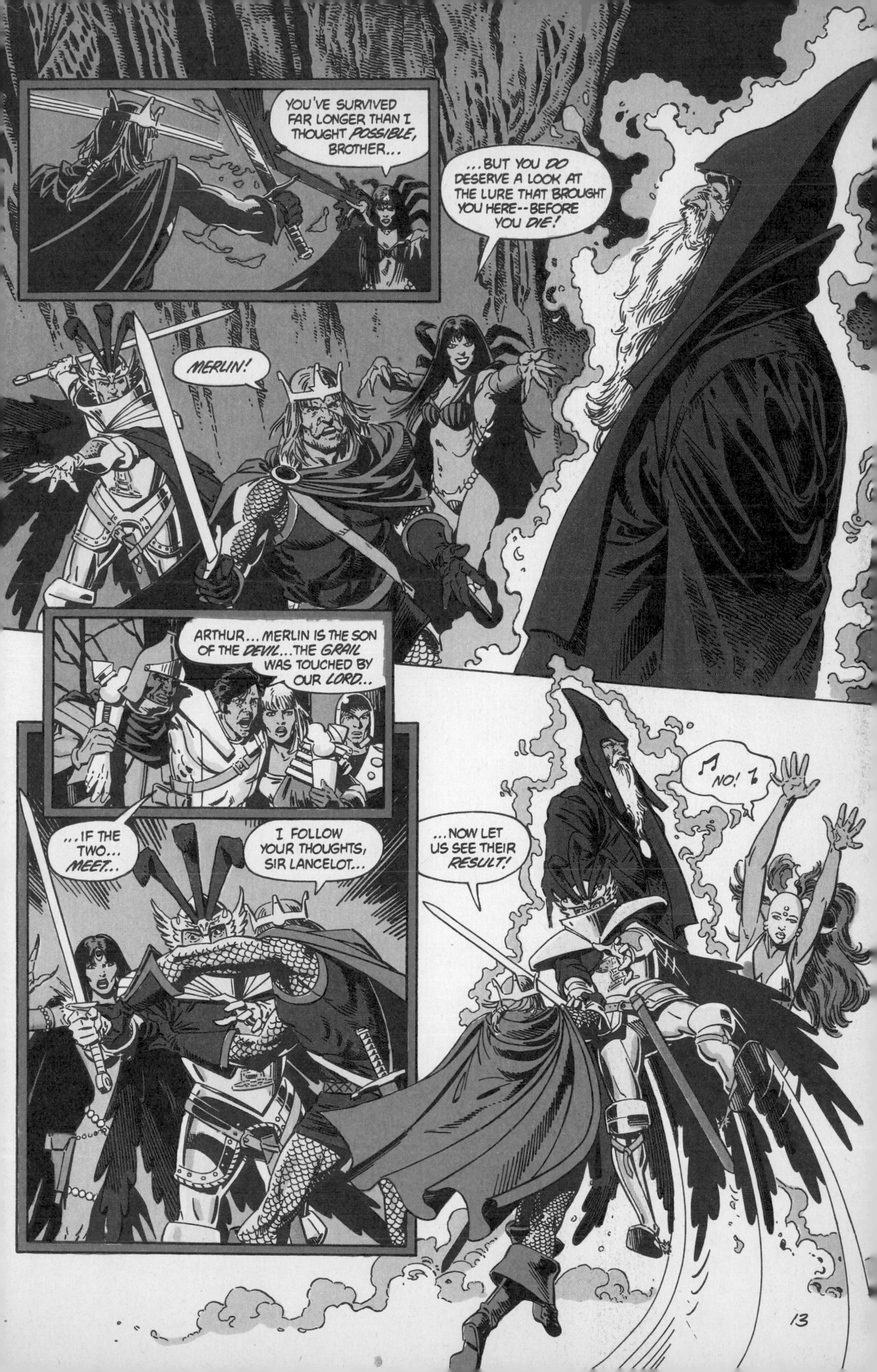
YOU'VE SURVIVED FAR LONGER THAN I THOUGHT POSSIBLE, BROTHER...
...BUT YOU DO DESERVE A LOOK AT THE LURE THAT BROUGHT YOU HERE--BEFORE YOU DIE!
MERLIN!
ARTHUR... MERLIN IS THE SON OF THE DEVIL... THE GRAIL WAS TOUCHED BY OUR LORD...
...IF THE TWO... MEET...
I FOLLOW YOUR THOUGHTS, SIR LANCELOT...
...NOW LET US SEE THEIR RESULT!
♪ NO! ♪

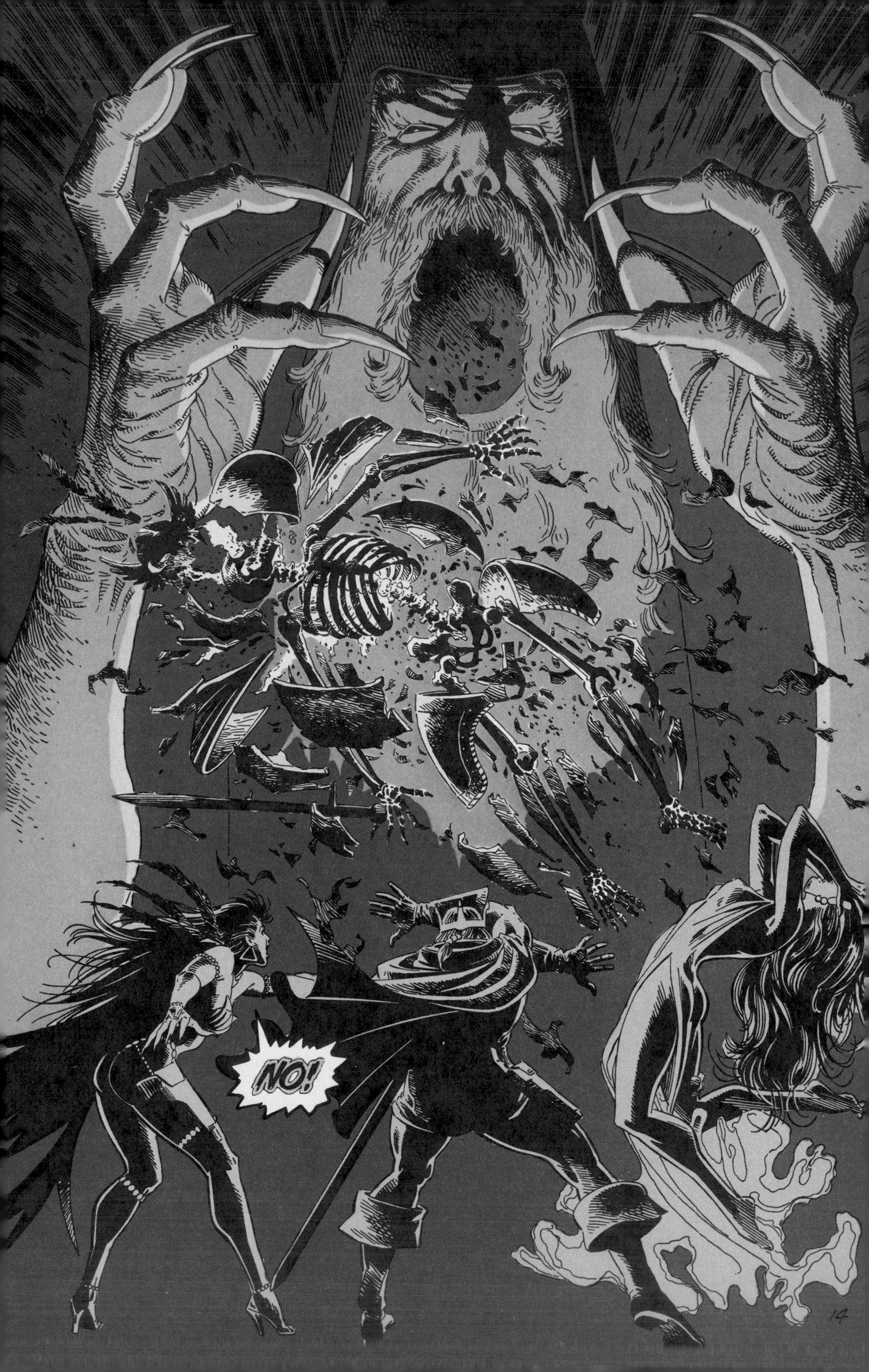
NO!

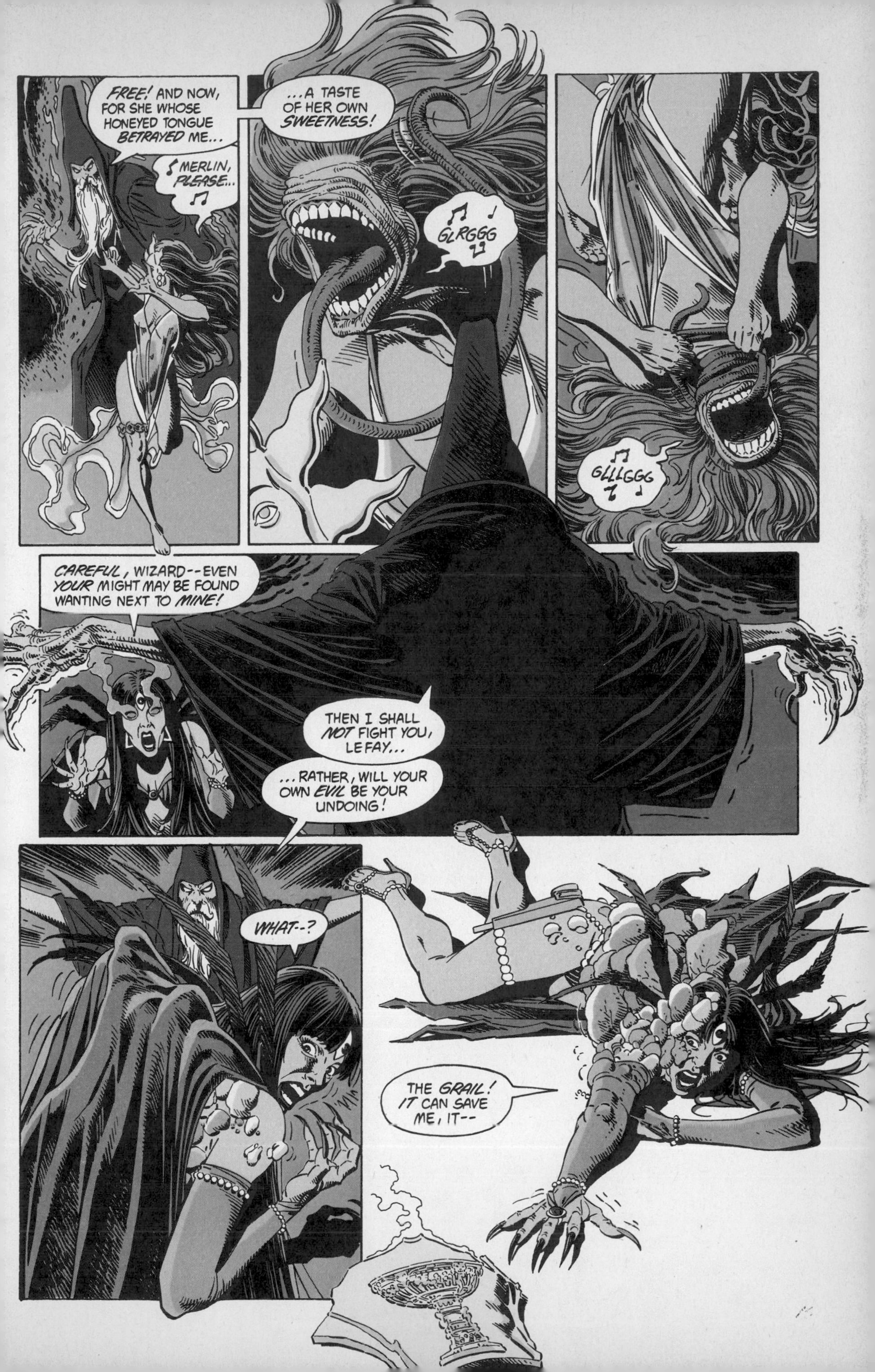
FREE! AND NOW, FOR SHE WHOSE HONEYED TONGUE BETRAYED ME...
...A TASTE OF HER OWN SWEETNESS!
MERLIN, PLEASE...
GLRGGG
GLLLGGG
CAREFUL, WIZARD--EVEN YOUR MIGHT MAY BE FOUND WANTING NEXT TO MINE!
THEN I SHALL NOT FIGHT YOU, LEFAY...
...RATHER, WILL YOUR OWN EVIL BE YOUR UNDOING!
WHAT--?
THE GRAIL! IT CAN SAVE ME, IT--

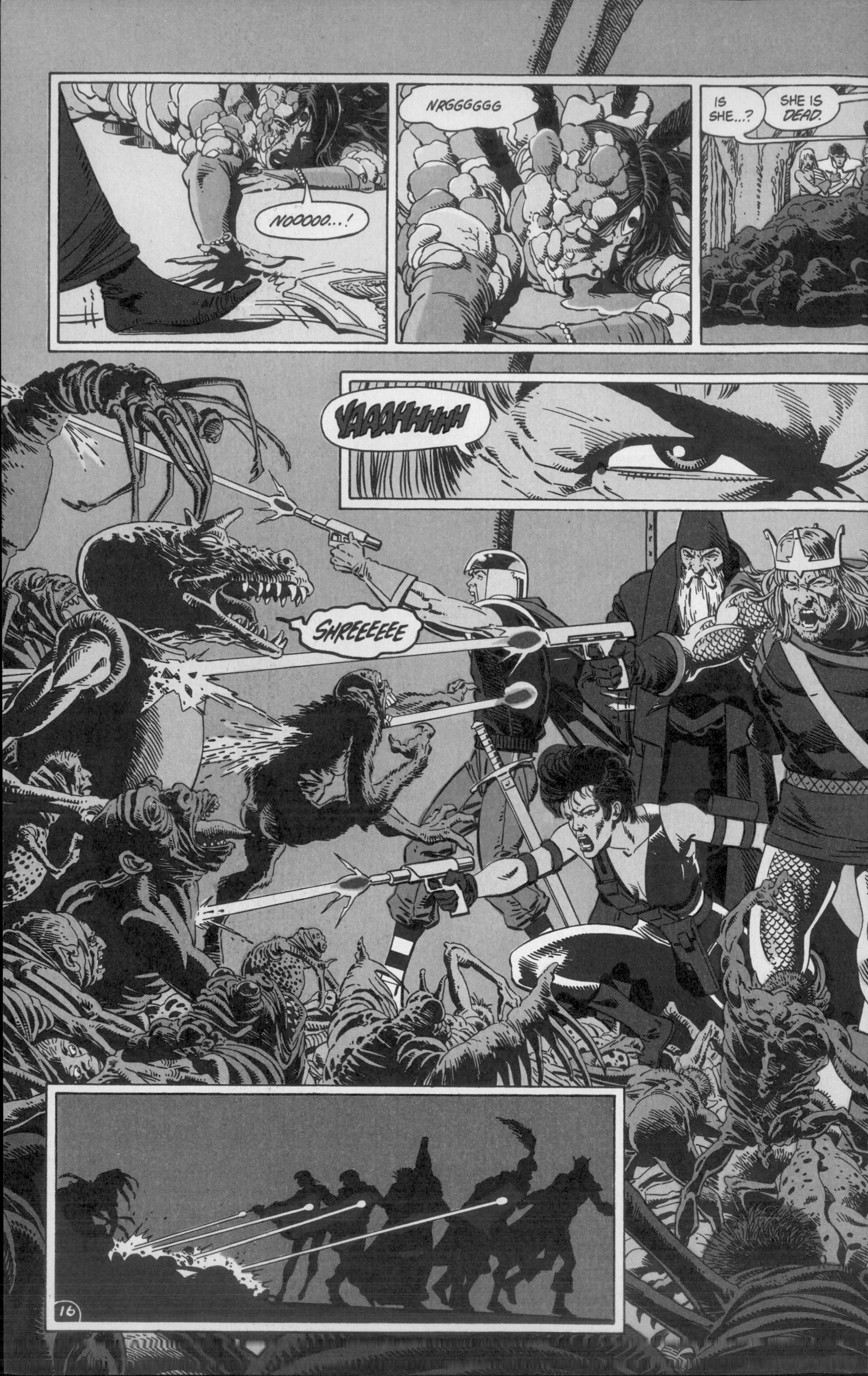
NOOOOO...!
NRGGGGGG
IS SHE...?
SHE IS DEAD.
YAAAHHHHH
SHREEEEEE

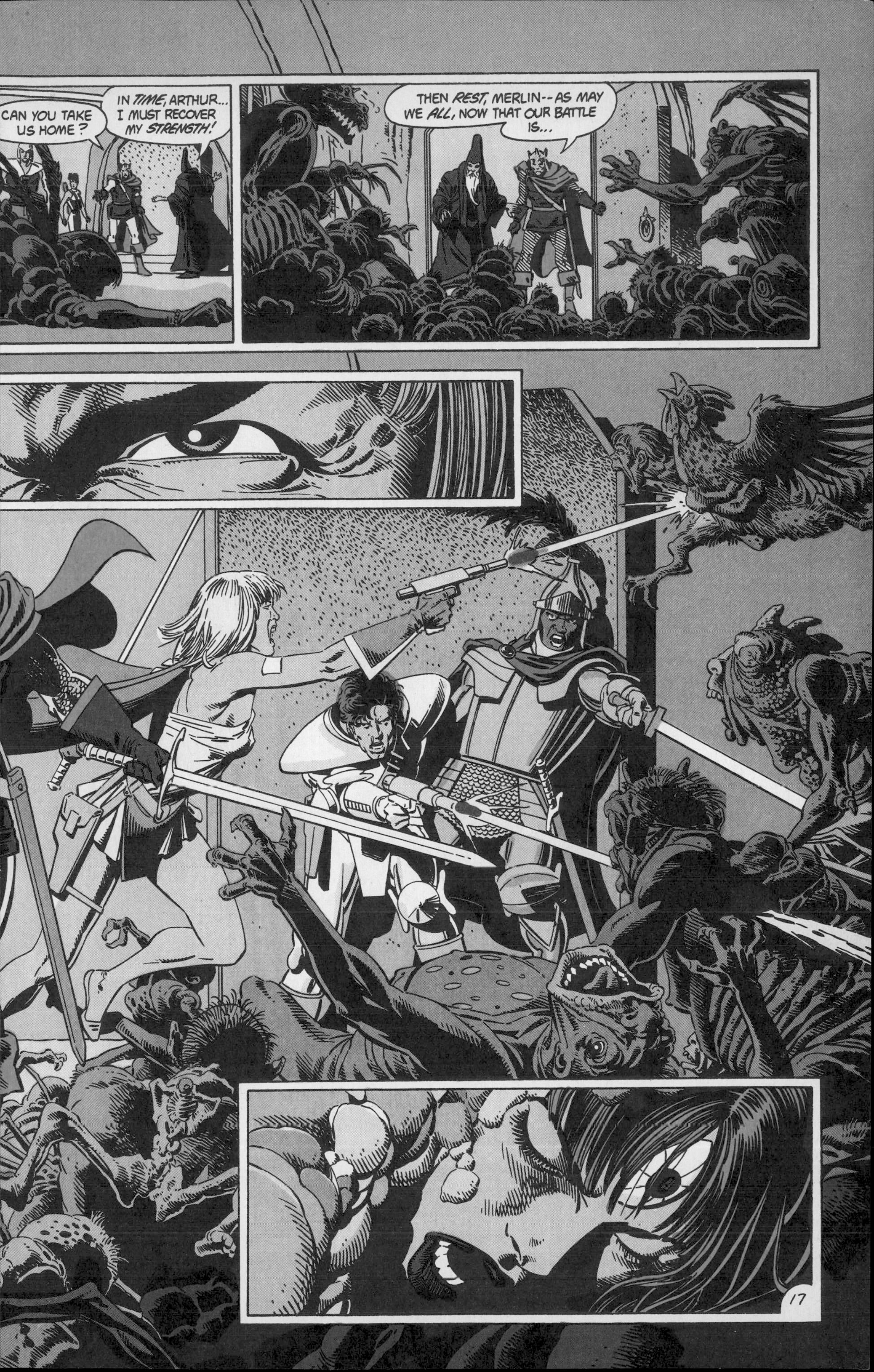
CAN YOU TAKE US HOME?
IN TIME, ARTHUR... I MUST RECOVER MY STRENGTH!
THEN REST, MERLIN--AS MAY WE ALL, NOW THAT OUR BATTLE IS...
17

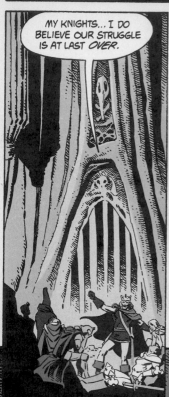

MY KNIGHTS... I DO BELIEVE OUR STRUGGLE IS AT LAST *OVER*.

IT'S *OVER*...NOW I CAN RETURN TO MY *FAMILY*.

WE CAN GO *HOME*, TRISTAN--PICK UP OUR *LIVES* AGAIN!

I CAN'T.

YOU *CAN*... IF YOU *WANT* TO.

NOT... OVER *YET*... BROTHER...

...NOT WHILE I *LIVE*... NOT WHILE MY *MAGICKS* ARE MINE...

18

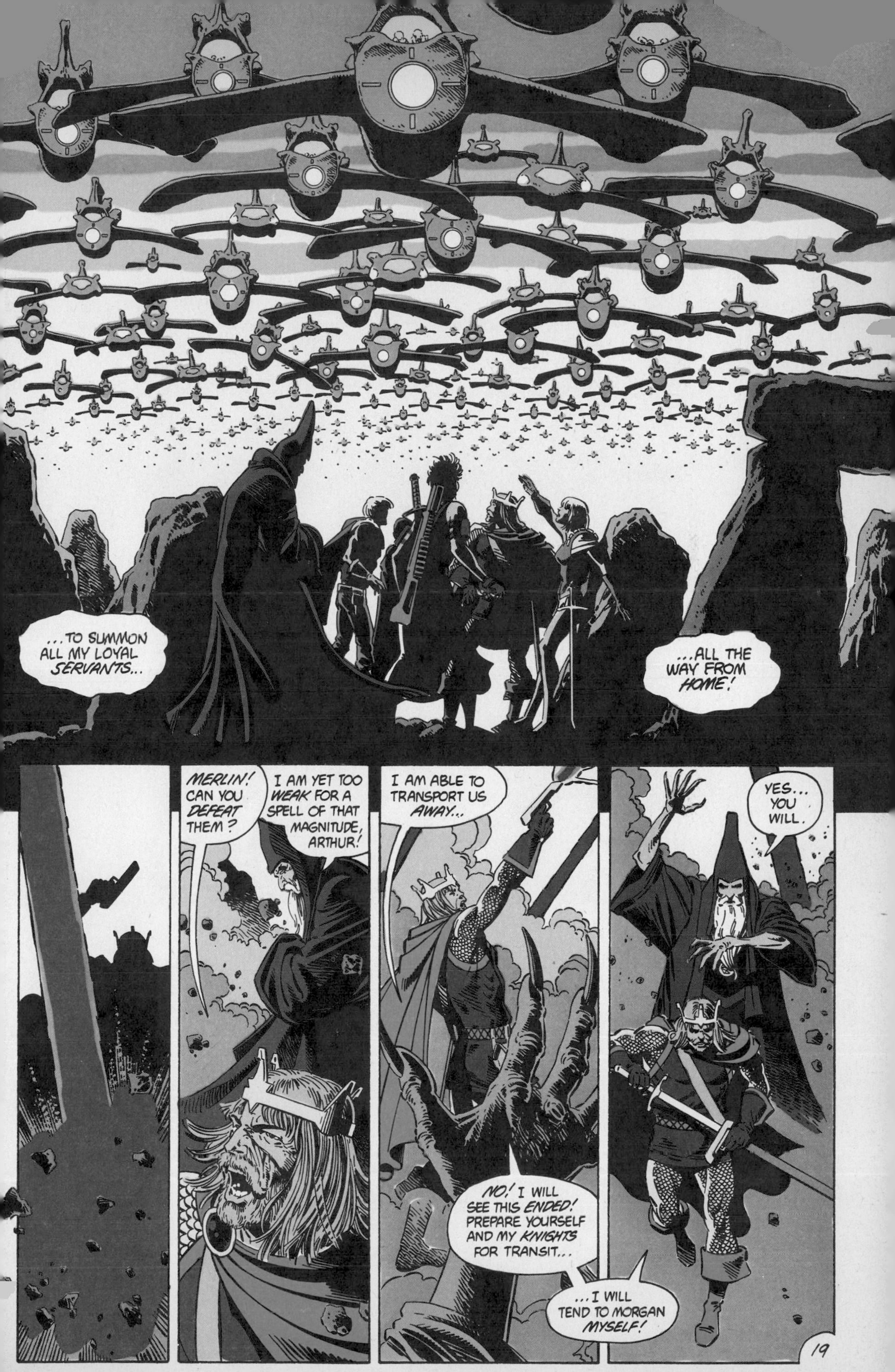
...TO SUMMON ALL MY LOYAL SERVANTS...
...ALL THE WAY FROM HOME!
MERLIN! CAN YOU DEFEAT THEM?
I AM YET TOO WEAK FOR A SPELL OF THAT MAGNITUDE, ARTHUR!
I AM ABLE TO TRANSPORT US AWAY...
NO! I WILL SEE THIS ENDED! PREPARE YOURSELF AND MY KNIGHTS FOR TRANSIT...
...I WILL TEND TO MORGAN MYSELF!
YES... YOU WILL.

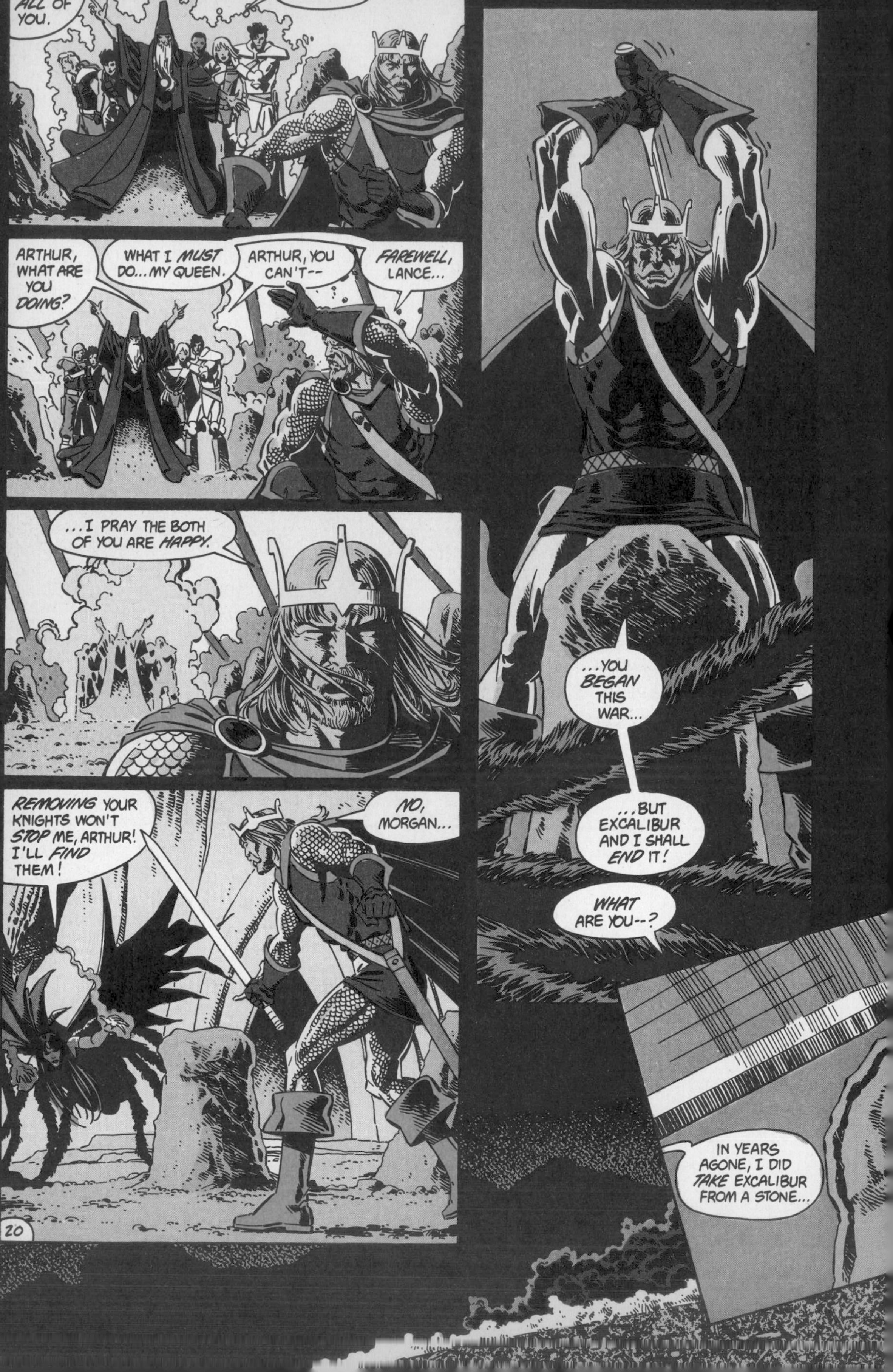
COME, ALL OF YOU.
ARTHUR?
ARTHUR, WHAT ARE YOU DOING?
WHAT I MUST DO... MY QUEEN.
ARTHUR, YOU CAN'T--
FAREWELL, LANCE...
...I PRAY THE BOTH OF YOU ARE HAPPY.
REMOVING YOUR KNIGHTS WON'T STOP ME, ARTHUR! I'LL FIND THEM!
NO, MORGAN...
...YOU BEGAN THIS WAR...
...BUT EXCALIBUR AND I SHALL END IT!
WHAT ARE YOU--?
IN YEARS AGONE, I DID TAKE EXCALIBUR FROM A STONE...

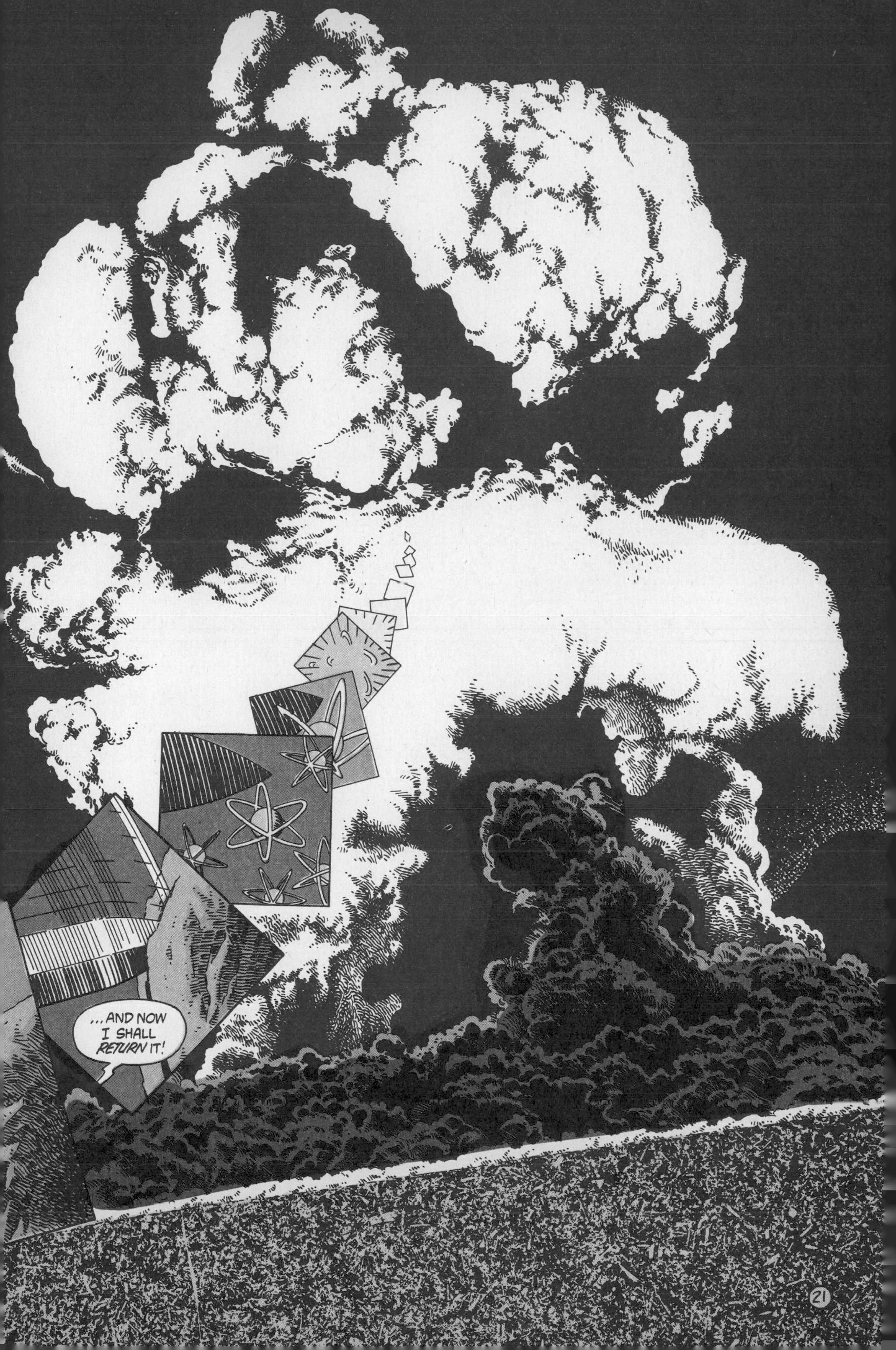
...AND NOW I SHALL RETURN IT!

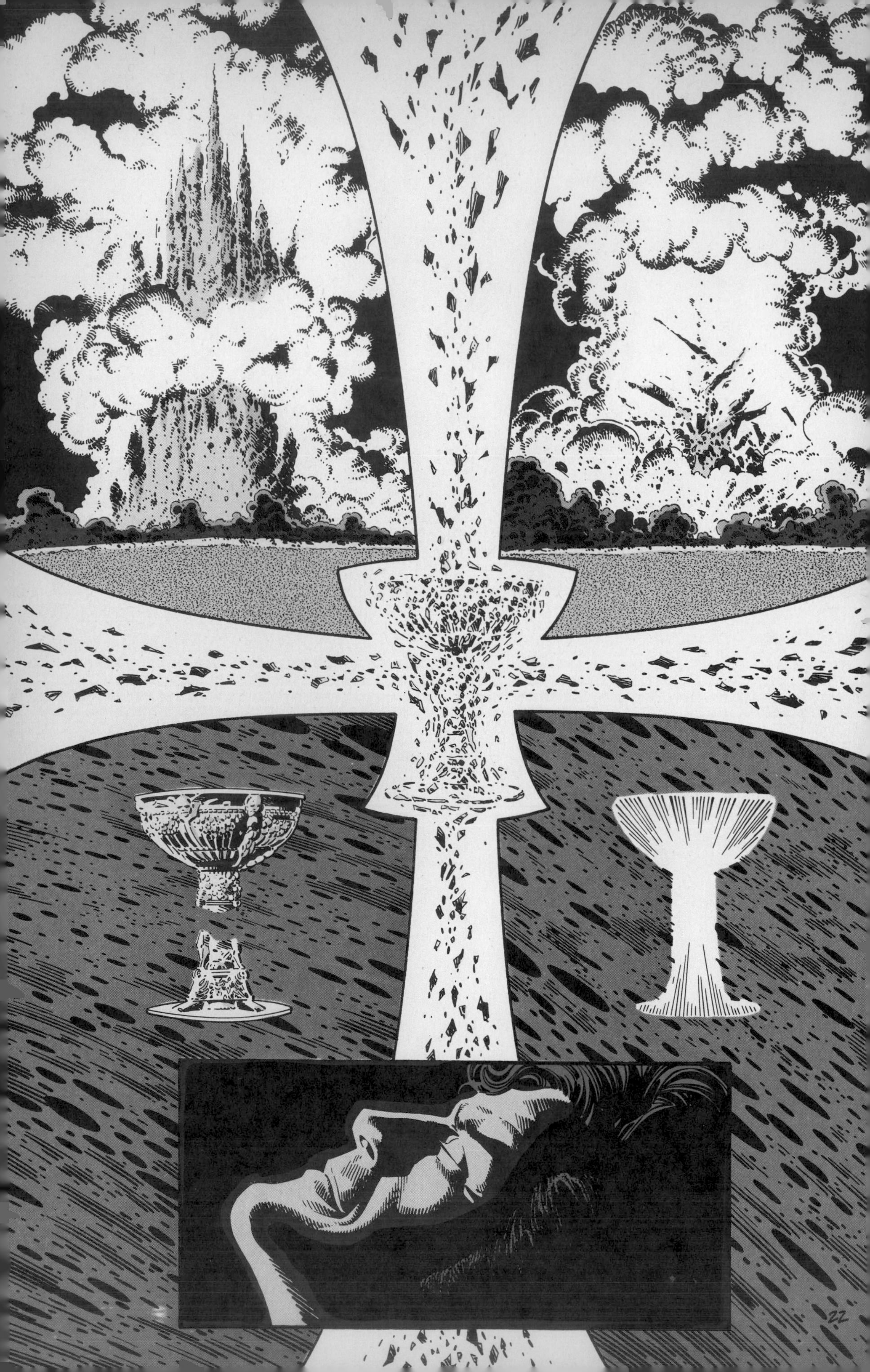

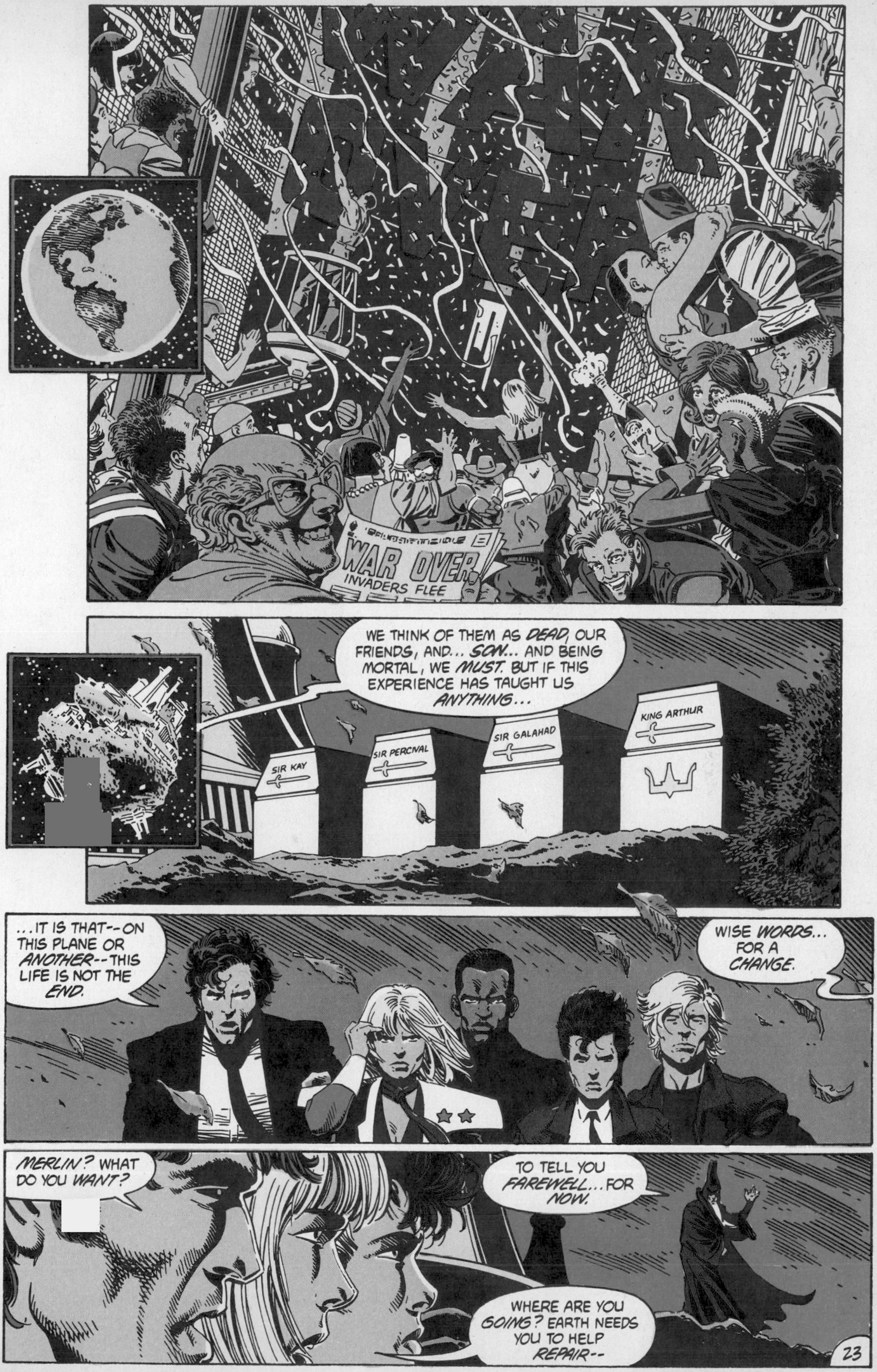
WAR OVER
INVADERS FLEE
WE THINK OF THEM AS DEAD, OUR FRIENDS, AND... SON... AND BEING MORTAL, WE MUST. BUT IF THIS EXPERIENCE HAS TAUGHT US ANYTHING...
SIR KAY
SIR PERCIVAL
SIR GALAHAD
KING ARTHUR
...IT IS THAT--ON THIS PLANE OR ANOTHER--THIS LIFE IS NOT THE END.
WISE WORDS... FOR A CHANGE.
MERLIN? WHAT DO YOU WANT?
TO TELL YOU FAREWELL... FOR NOW.
WHERE ARE YOU GOING? EARTH NEEDS YOU TO HELP REPAIR--

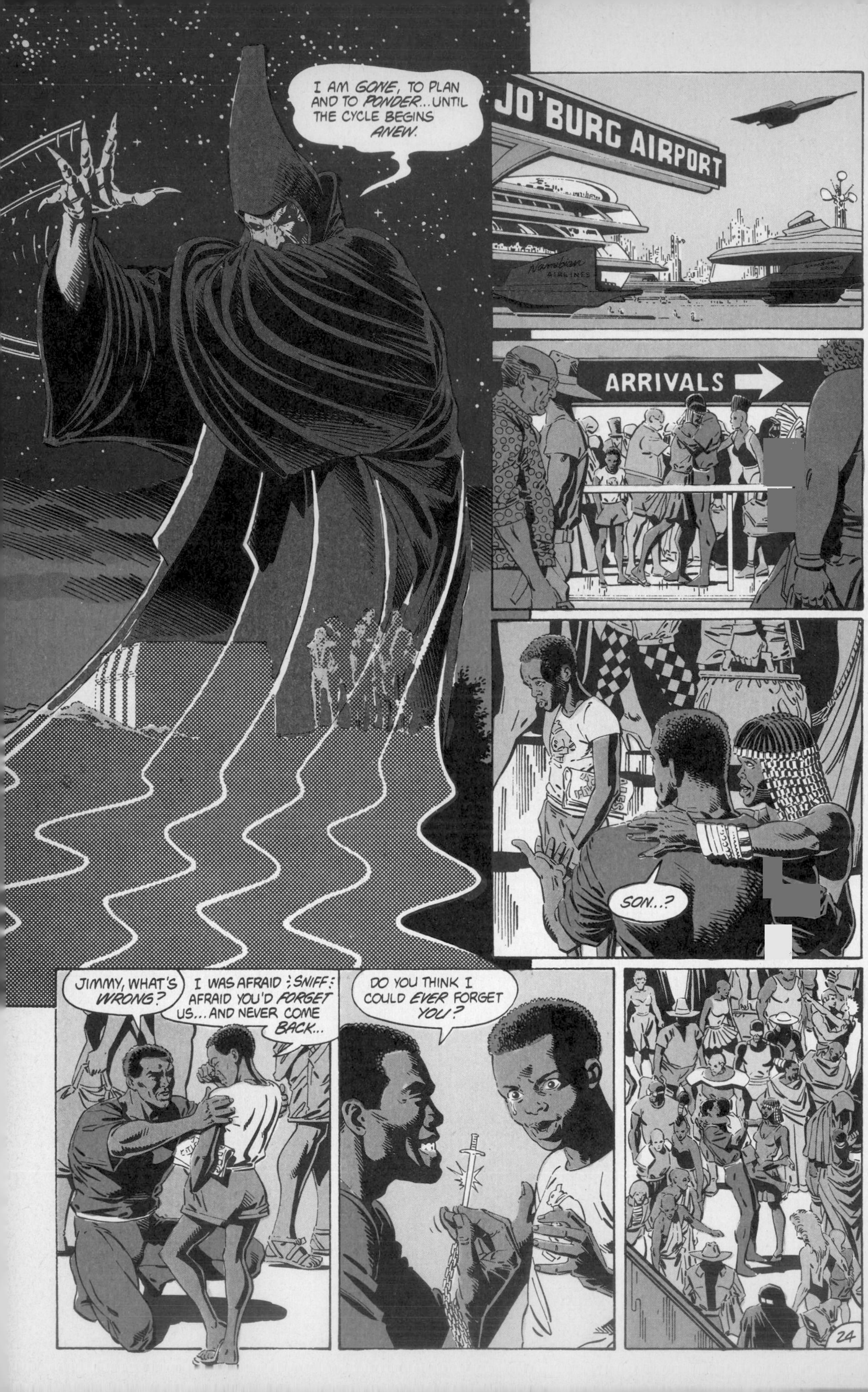
I AM GONE, TO PLAN AND TO PONDER...UNTIL THE CYCLE BEGINS ANEW.
JO'BURG AIRPORT
ARRIVALS
SON...?
JIMMY, WHAT'S WRONG?
I WAS AFRAID :SNIFF: AFRAID YOU'D FORGET US...AND NEVER COME BACK...
DO YOU THINK I COULD EVER FORGET YOU?
24

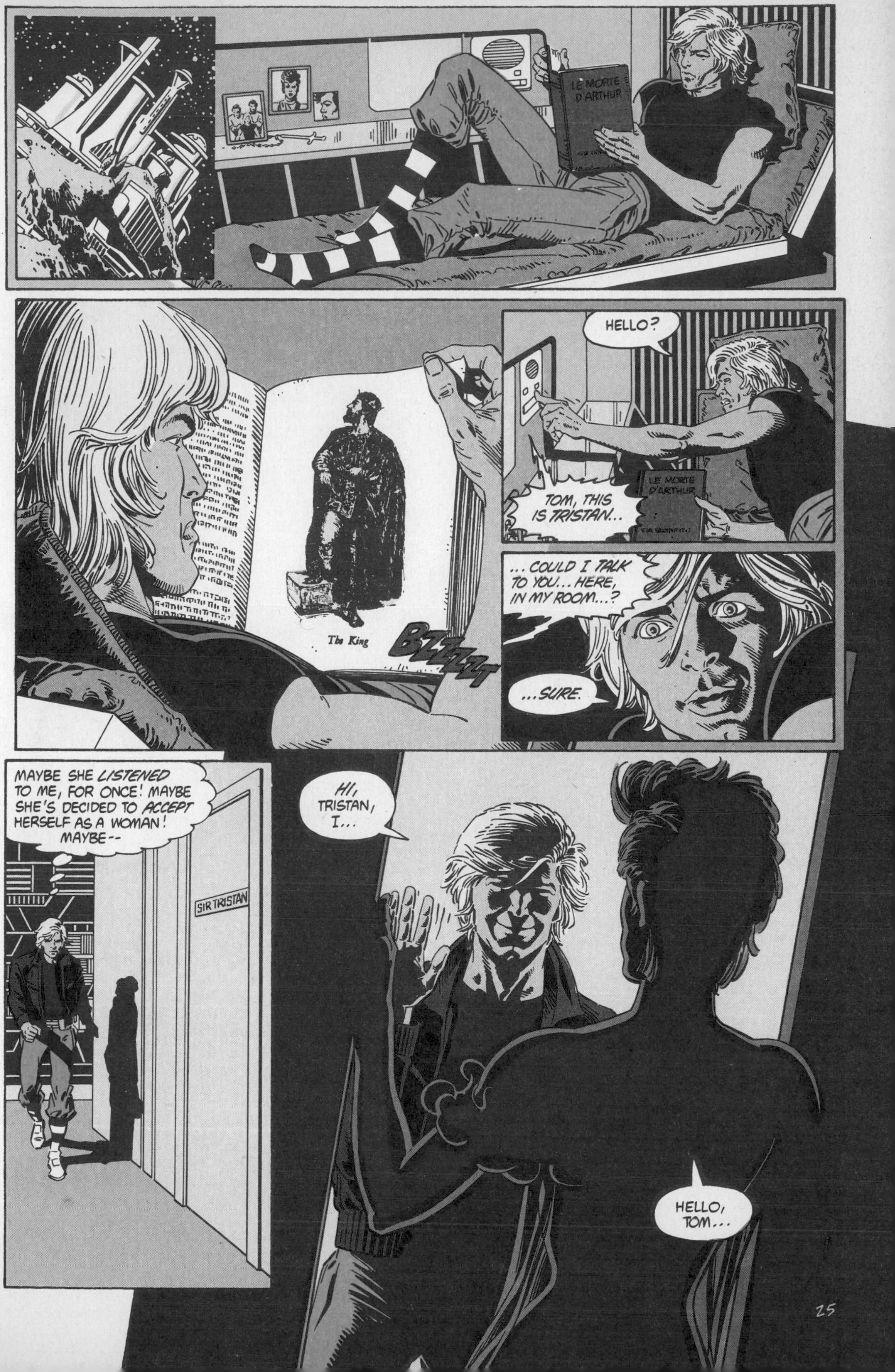

LE MORTE D'ARTHUR
The King
BZZZZT
HELLO?
TOM, THIS IS TRISTAN...
LE MORTE D'ARTHUR
...COULD I TALK TO YOU...HERE, IN MY ROOM...?
...SURE.
MAYBE SHE LISTENED TO ME, FOR ONCE! MAYBE SHE'S DECIDED TO ACCEPT HERSELF AS A WOMAN! MAYBE--
SIR TRISTAN
HI, TRISTAN, I...
HELLO, TOM...

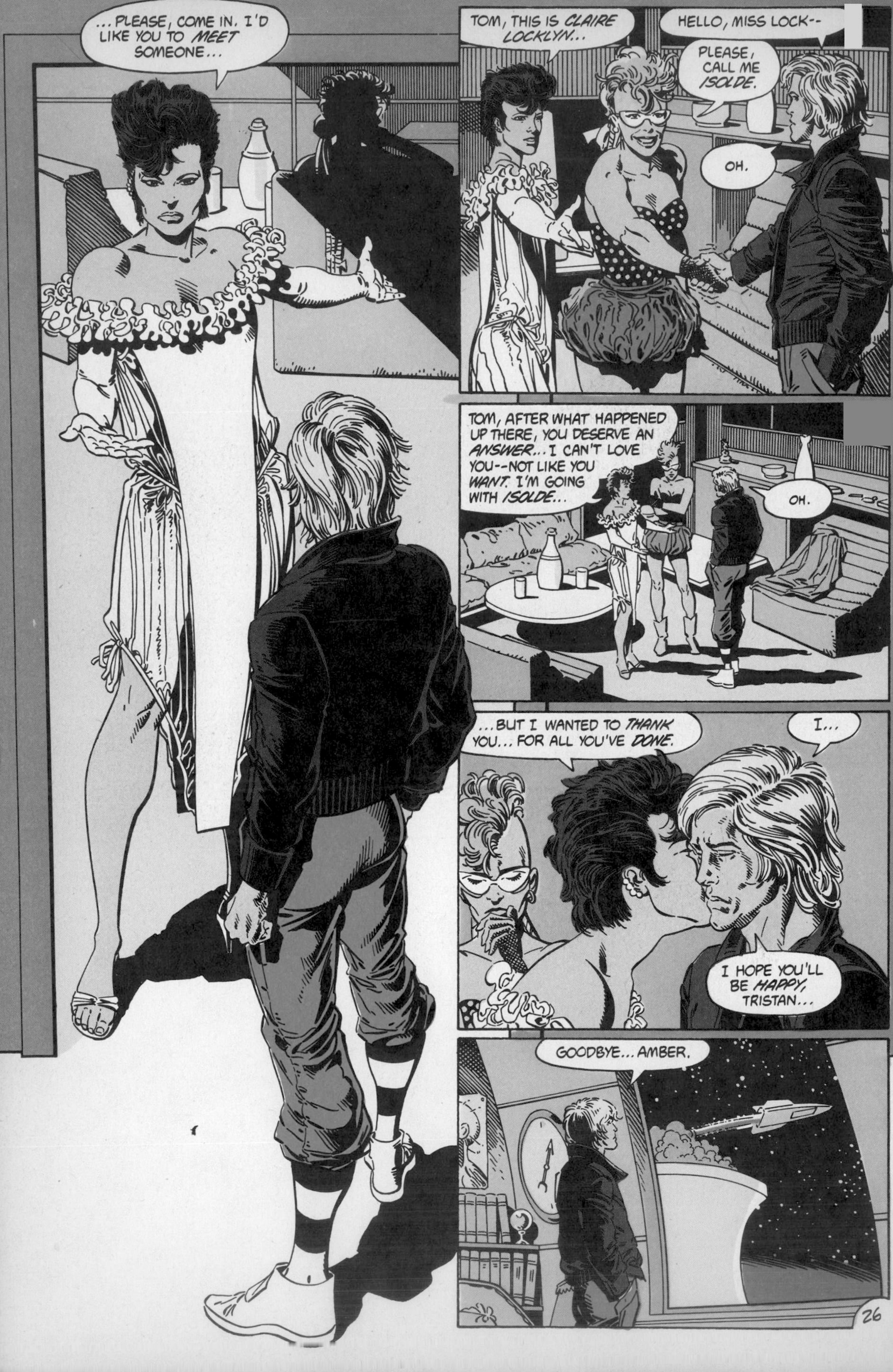
...PLEASE, COME IN. I'D LIKE YOU TO MEET SOMEONE...
TOM, THIS IS CLAIRE LOCKLYN...
HELLO, MISS LOCK--
PLEASE, CALL ME ISOLDE.
OH.
TOM, AFTER WHAT HAPPENED UP THERE, YOU DESERVE AN ANSWER... I CAN'T LOVE YOU--NOT LIKE YOU WANT. I'M GOING WITH ISOLDE...
OH.
...BUT I WANTED TO THANK YOU... FOR ALL YOU'VE DONE.
I...
I HOPE YOU'LL BE HAPPY, TRISTAN...
GOODBYE... AMBER.

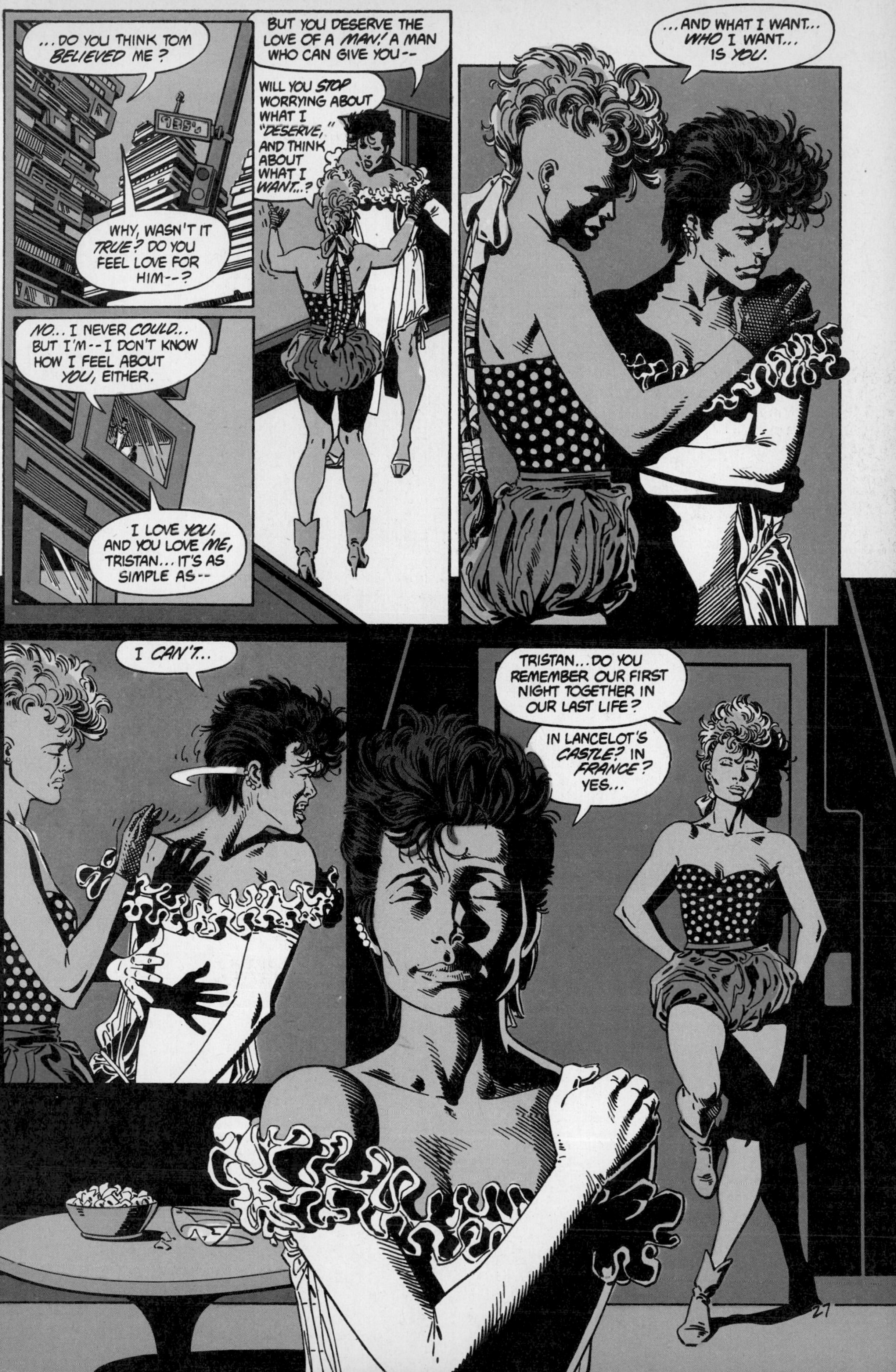
...DO YOU THINK TOM BELIEVED ME?
WHY, WASN'T IT TRUE? DO YOU FEEL LOVE FOR HIM--?
BUT YOU DESERVE THE LOVE OF A MAN! A MAN WHO CAN GIVE YOU--
WILL YOU STOP WORRYING ABOUT WHAT I "DESERVE," AND THINK ABOUT WHAT I WANT...?
NO... I NEVER COULD... BUT I'M--I DON'T KNOW HOW I FEEL ABOUT YOU, EITHER.
I LOVE YOU, AND YOU LOVE ME, TRISTAN... IT'S AS SIMPLE AS--
...AND WHAT I WANT... WHO I WANT... IS YOU.
I CAN'T...
TRISTAN...DO YOU REMEMBER OUR FIRST NIGHT TOGETHER IN OUR LAST LIFE?
IN LANCELOT'S CASTLE? IN FRANCE? YES...

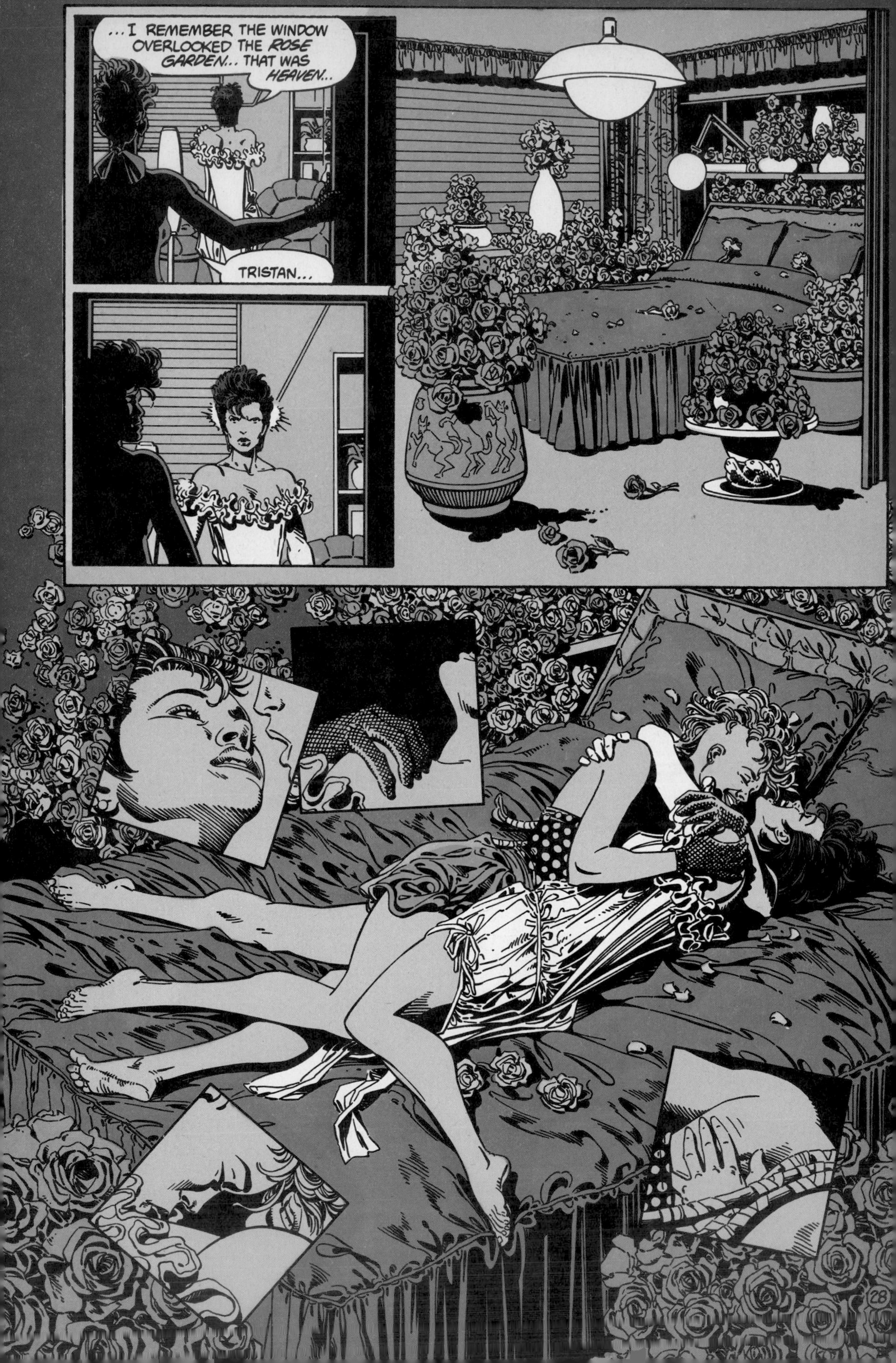
...I REMEMBER THE WINDOW OVERLOOKED THE ROSE GARDEN... THAT WAS HEAVEN...
TRISTAN...

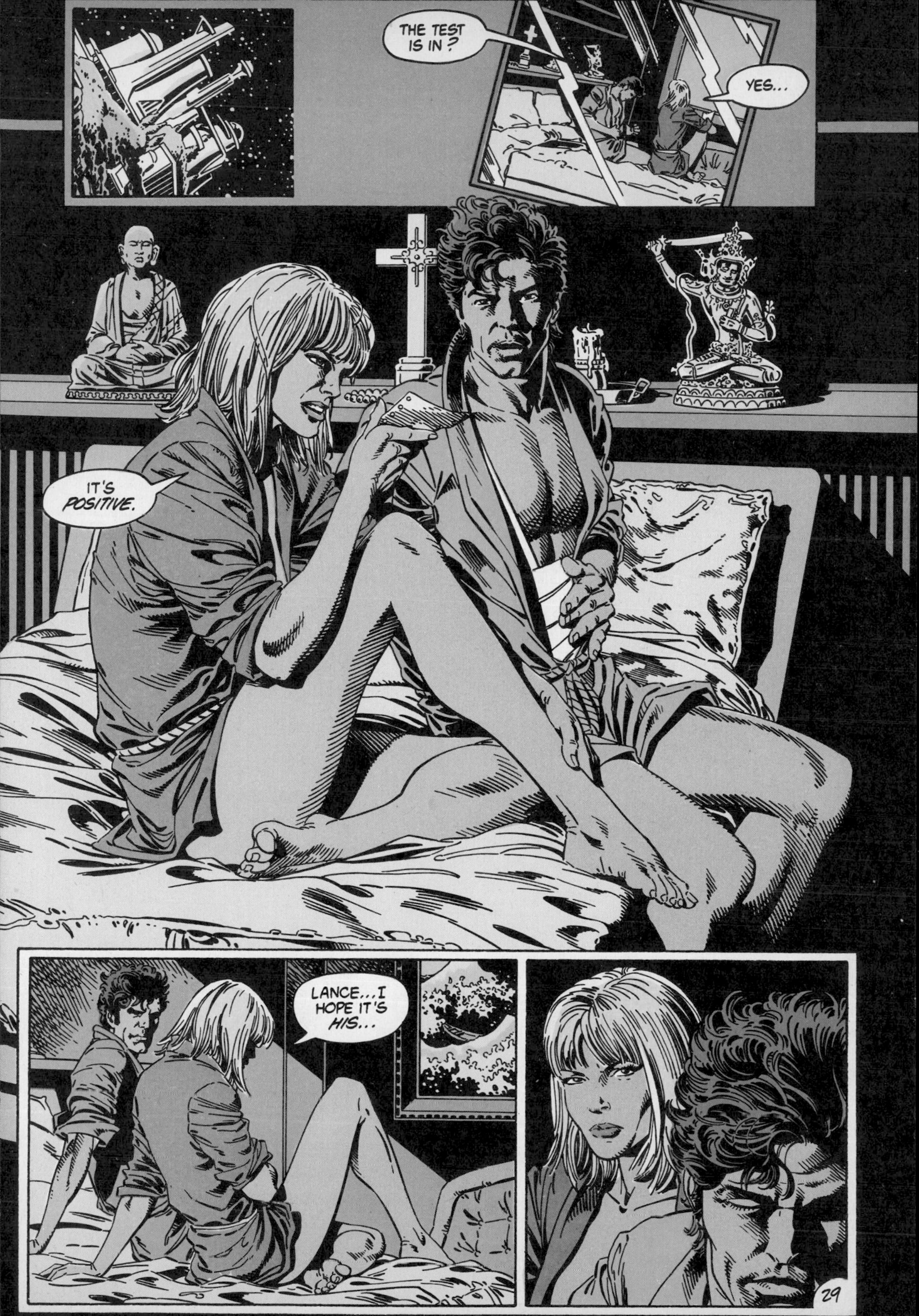

THE TEST IS IN?
YES...
IT'S *POSITIVE.*
LANCE... I HOPE IT'S *HIS...*

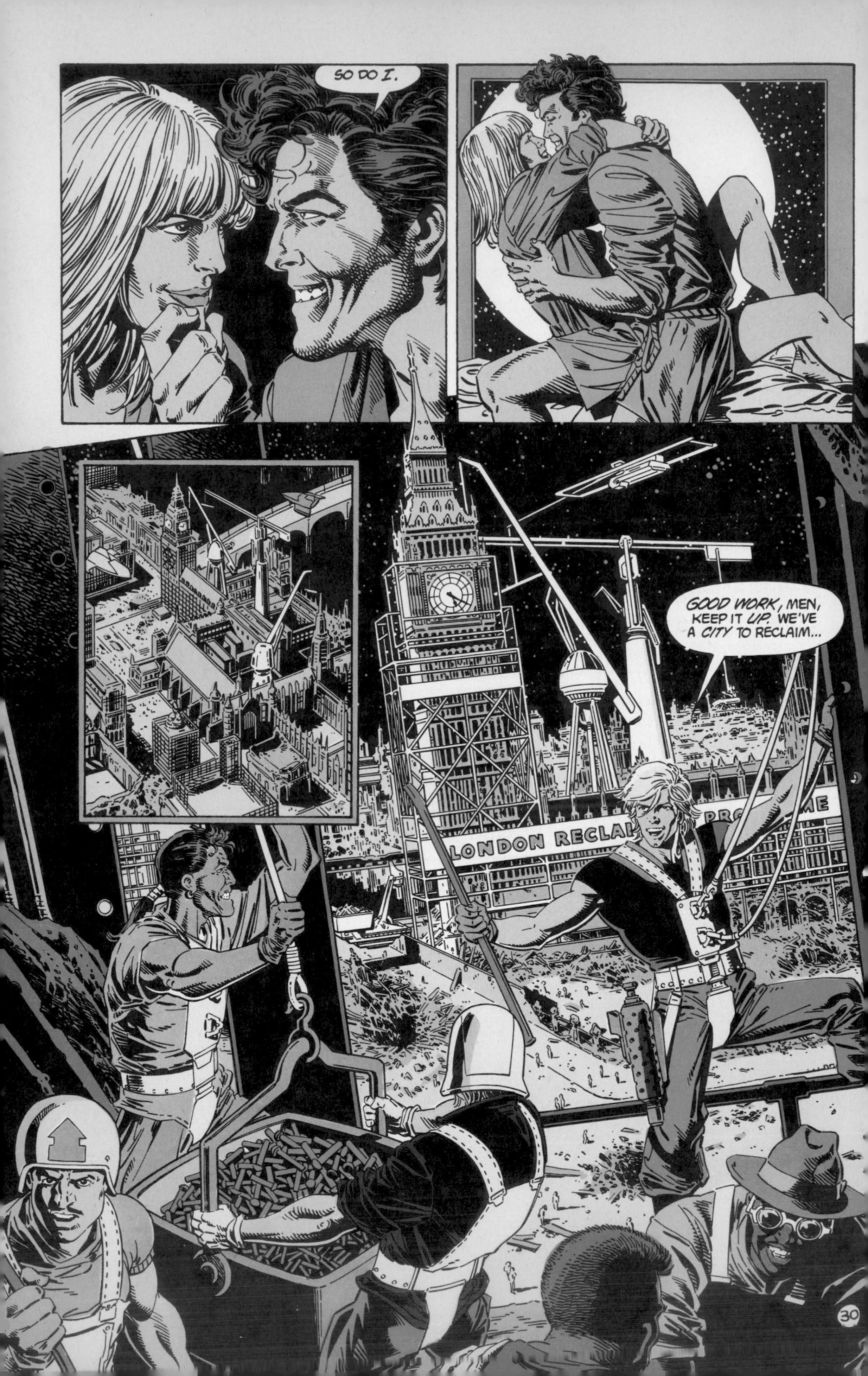
SO DO I.
GOOD WORK, MEN, KEEP IT UP. WE'VE A CITY TO RECLAIM...
LONDON RECLA
PRO ME
30

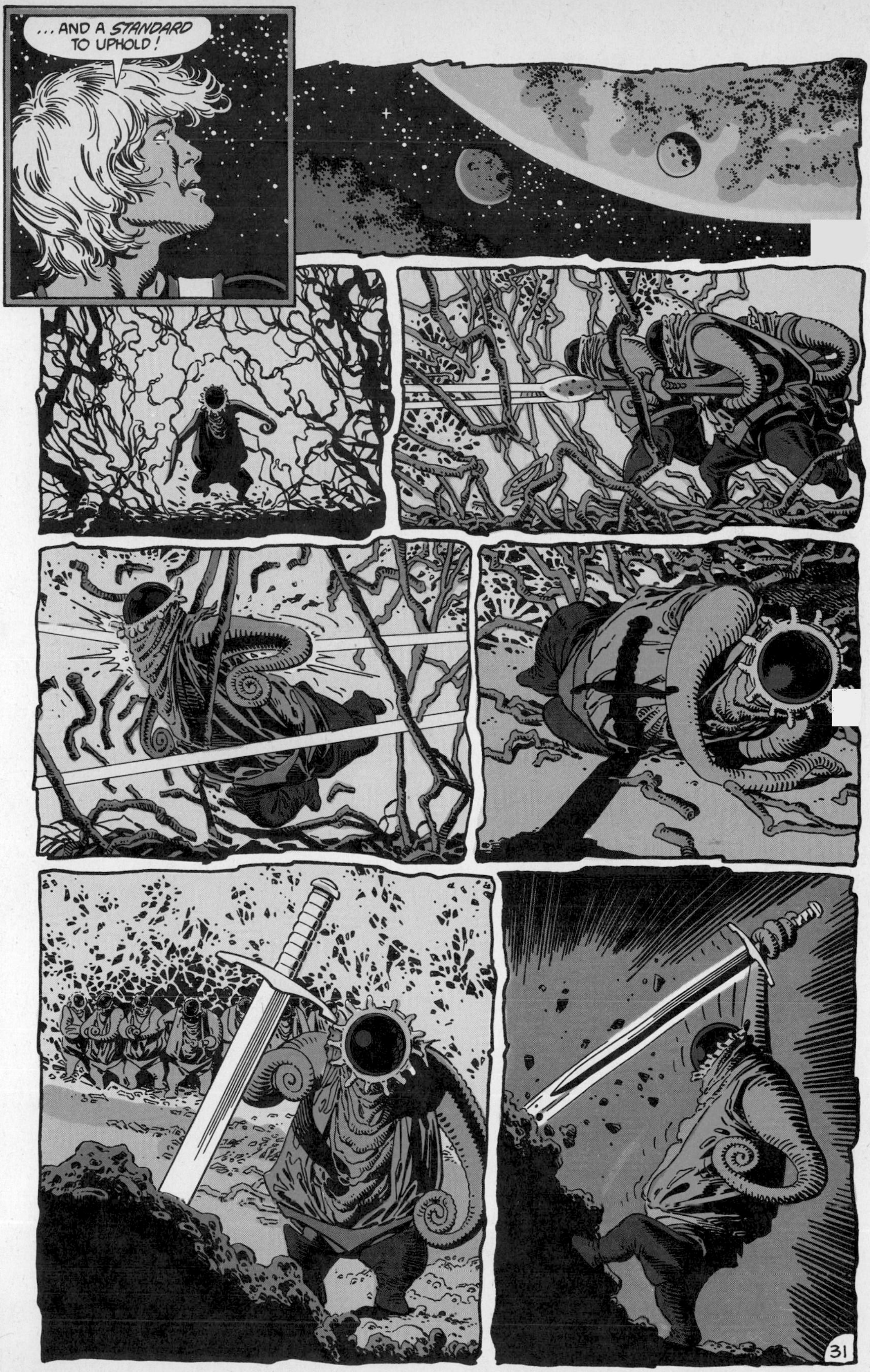

... AND A STANDARD TO UPHOLD!
31

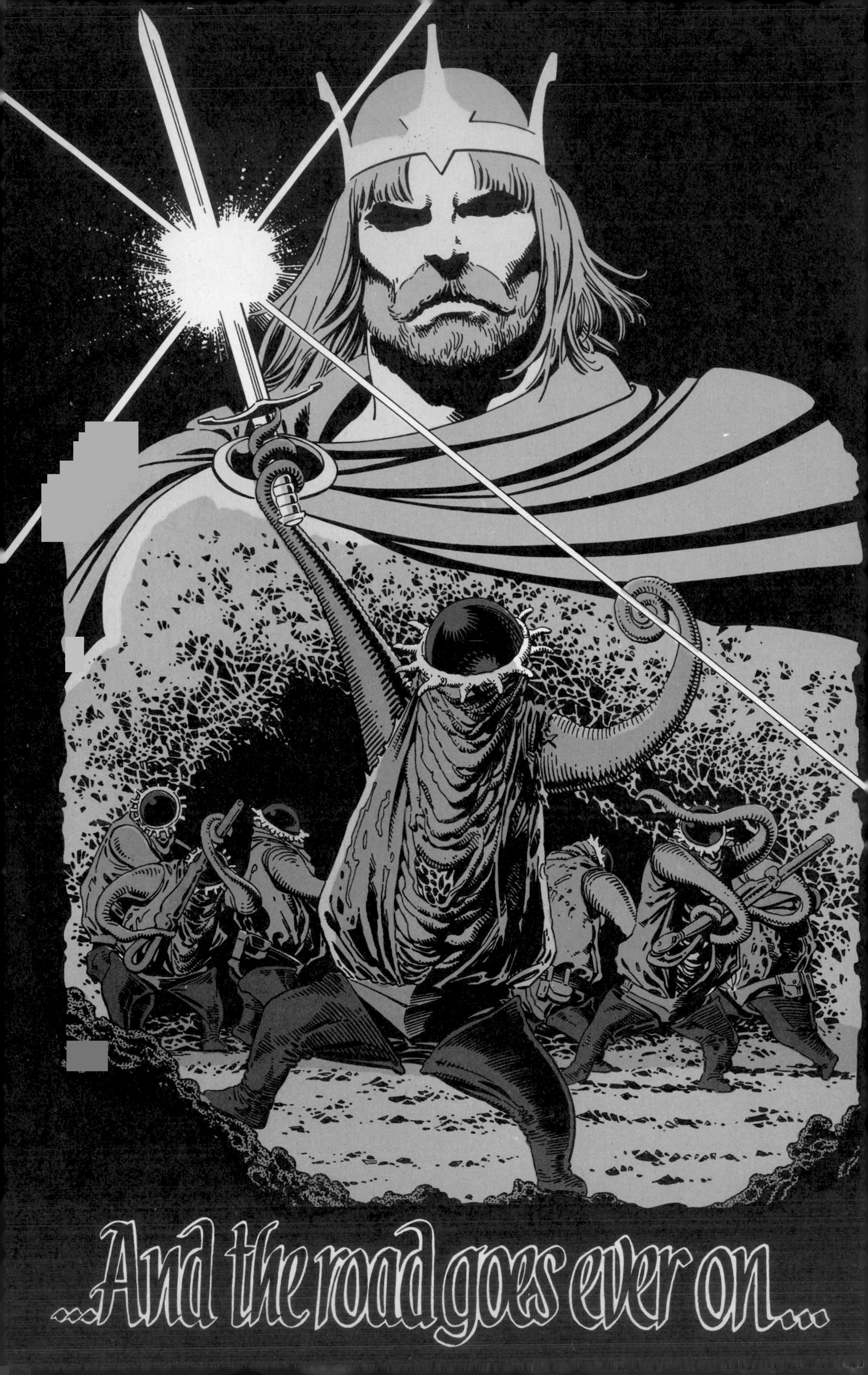
...And the road goes ever on...

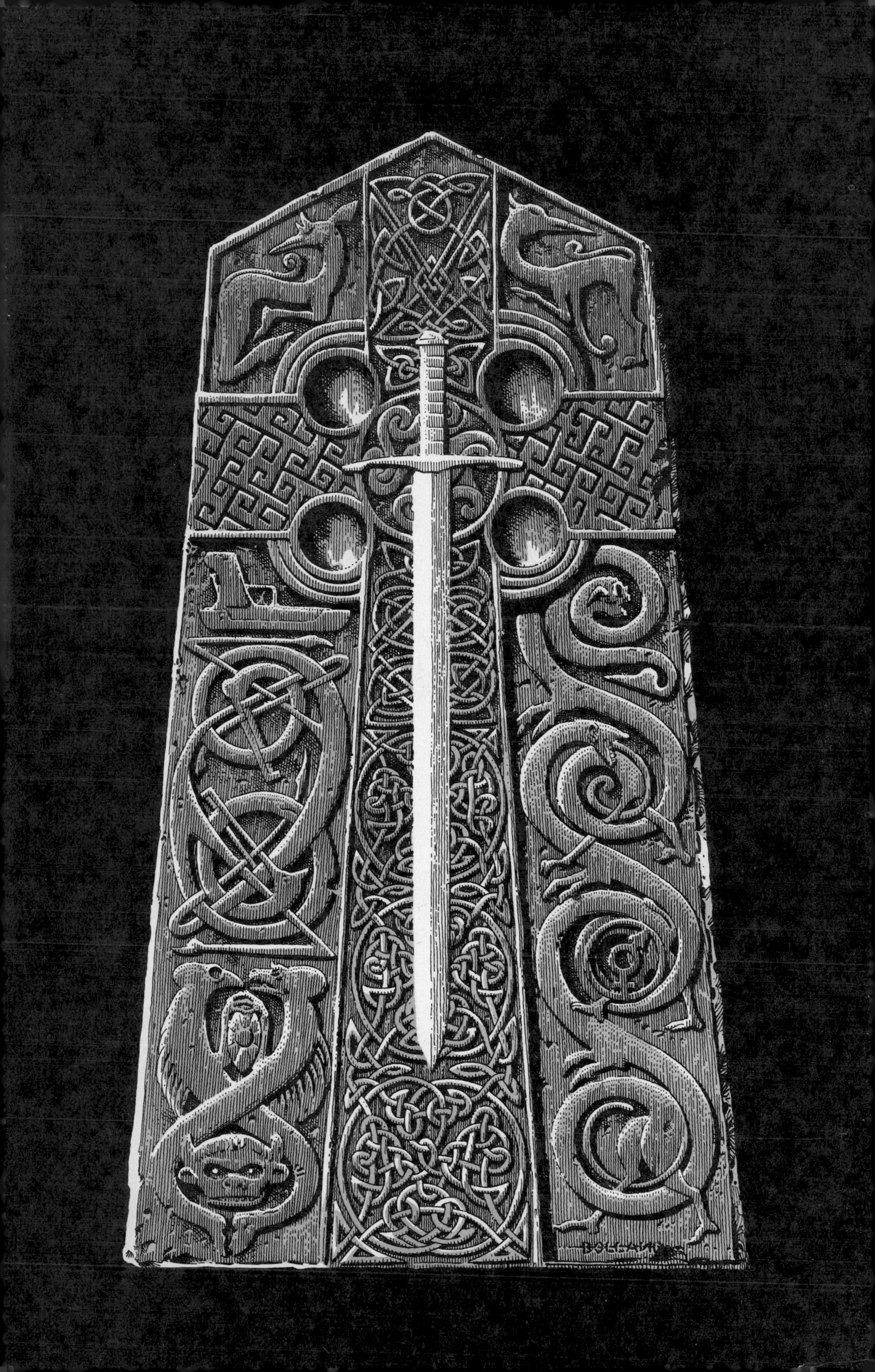

ABOUT THE CREATORS

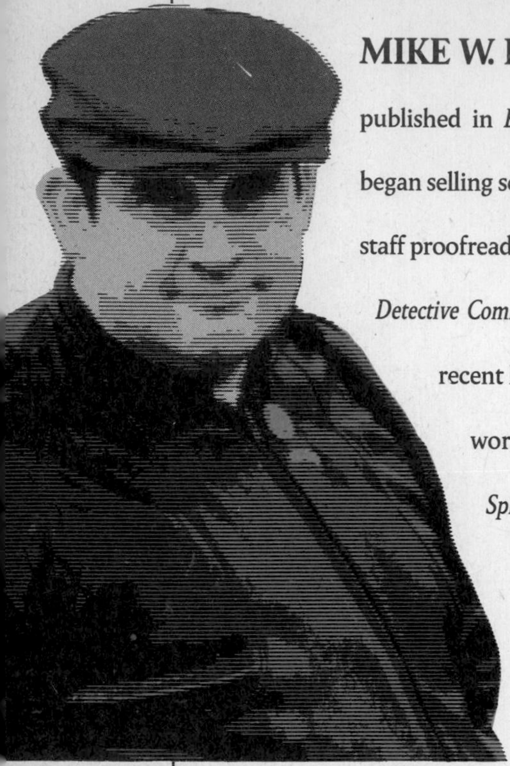

MIKE W. BARR Mike W. Barr's first professional fiction was published in *Ellery Queen's Mystery Magazine* in 1973. In 1974, he began selling scripts to DC Comics, where he subsequently served as staff proofreader and editor. His other work for DC has appeared in *Detective Comics*, *The Outsiders*, *Green Lantern*, *Green Arrow*, and the recent hardcover graphic novel *Batman: Son of the Demon*. His work for other publishers includes *Captain America*, *Spider-Man*, *E-Man*, *Real War Stories*, and his most recent creation, a detective series entitled *The MAZE Agency*.

BRIAN BOLLAND British-born Brian Bolland has been a leading comic book illustrator for a number of years and has produced work for nearly every major comics publisher on both sides of the Atlantic. He began his career drawing "unmentionable underground comics," eventually graduating to *2000 A.D.*'s Judge Dredd. A brief list of his credits includes *Green Lantern*, *Superman*, *Batman*, *Warrior*'s Zirk, *Powerman* for Nigeria, and "a French portfolio in questionable taste." He is currently completing a Batman graphic novel, *The Killing Joke*, for DC.

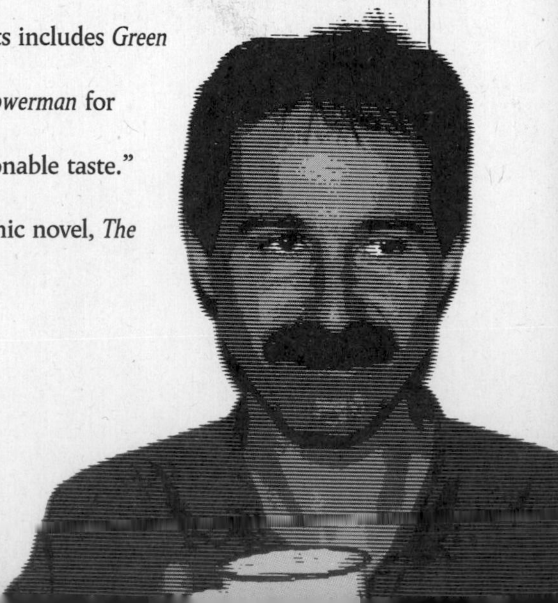